Horoscopes of the USA and Canada

Second Edition

Marc H. Penfield

Copyright 1996 by Marc Penfield
All rights reserved.

No part of this book may be reproduced or transmitted in any form or by any means, electronic or mechanical, including photocopying or recording, or by any information storage and retrieval system, without written permission from the author and publisher. Requests and inquiries may be mailed to: American Federation of Astrologers, Inc., 6535 S. Rural Road, Tempe, AZ 85284-2040.

ISBN: 0-86690-465-4

First Printing: 1996
Second Edition: 2005

Cover Design: Jack Cipolla

Published by:
American Federation of Astrologers, Inc.
6535 S. Rural Road
Tempe, AZ 85285-2040

Printed in the United States of America

Dedication

This book is dedicated to my parents,

Dr. and Mrs. Walter R. Hess

of

Sun City, Arizona

who gave me the opportunity as a young

man to travel these great lands

and who through the years have given

me constant support and understanding

in my chosen field of endeavor

Contents

Author's Notes	ix
Acknowledgements	x
Introduction	1
Planets	3
Houses	3
Aspects	3
The Relationship Between These Horoscopes and You	4
The American People	5
Declaration of Independence	10
Revolutionary War Ends	13
Signing of the Constitution	14
The Bill of Rights	14
Louisiana Purchase	15
The Embargo Act	15
The War of 1812	16
Spain Cedes Florida	16
The Monroe Doctrine	17
Erie Canal Opens	17
Indian Removal Act	18
Nullification Proclamation	18
Fall of the Alamo	19
The Panic of 1837	19
Mexican War	20
Gold Discovered in California	20
Compromise of 1850	21
The Gadsden Purchase	21
Dred Scott Decision	22
The Civil War	22
Slavery Abolished	23
Purchase of Alaska	23
Transcontinental Railroad	24
The Panic of 1873	24
Custer's Last Stand	25
The Pendleton Act	25
The Panic of 1893	26
Spanish-American War	26
Panama Canal Treaty	27
Income Tax	27
World War I	28
Prohibition	28
Stock Market Crash	29
The New Deal	29
Social Security Act	30
Wages and Hours Act	30
World War II	31
Atomic Bomb Test	31
The Marshall Plan	32
The Korean War	32
Civil Rights Movement	33
Interstate Highway System	33
Space Program Begins	34
Cuban Missile Crisis	34
President Kennedy Assassinated	35
Vietnam War	35
Medicare Act	36
The Moon Landing	36
Resignation of Nixon	37
Iranian Hostage Crisis	37
Stock Market Crash	38
Savings and Loan Crisis	38
The Gulf War	39
NAFTA	39
Financial Collapse	40
Terrorist Attacks	40
Invasion of Iraq	41
The U.S. Constitution	42
The Beginning of the Federal Government in the U.S.	43
Alabama	45
Birmingham	46
Huntsville	46
Mobile	47
Montgomery	47
Tuscaloosa	48
Alaska	49
Anchorage	50
Fairbanks	50
Juneau	51
Sitka	51
Arizona	52
Flagstaff	53
Phoenix	53
Prescott	54
Tucson	54
Yuma	55
Arkansas	56
Fayetteville	57
Fort Smith	57
Hot Springs	58
Little Rock	58
Pine Bluff	59
California	60
Anaheim	61
Bakersfield	61
Berkeley	62
Beverly Hills	62
Burbank	63
Carmel	63
Fresno	64
Long Beach	64
Los Angeles	65
Hollywood	66
San Fernando Valley	66
Monterey	68
Oakland	68
Palm Springs	69
Pasadena	69
Sacramento	70
Salinas	70

San Diego	71
San Francisco	71
San Jose	72
San Luis Obispo	73
Santa Barbara	73
Santa Cruz	74
Santa Monica	74
Stockton	75
Ventura	75
Colorado	76
Aspen	77
Boulder	77
Colorado Springs	78
Denver	78
Estes Park	79
Fort Collins	79
Greeley	80
Leadville	80
Pueblo	81
Connecticut	82
Bridgeport	83
Hartford	83
New Haven	84
New London	84
Waterbury	85
Delaware	86
Dover	87
Wilmington	87
Florida	88
Daytona Beach	89
Fort Lauderdale	89
Gainesville	90
Jacksonville	90
Key West	91
Miami	91
Miami Beach	92
Orlando	92
Pensacola	93
St. Augustine	93
St. Petersburg	94
Tallahasssee	94
Tampa	95
West Palm Beach	95
Georgia	96
Athens	97
Atlanta	97
Augusta	98
Columbus	98
Macon	99
Savannah	99
Hawaii	100
Hilo	101
Honolulu	101
Idaho	102
Boise	103
Idaho Falls	103
Lewiston	104
Pocatello	104
Illinois	105
Chicago	106
Decatur	107
Evanston	108
Peoria	108
Rockford	109
Springfield	109
Urbana	110
Indiana	111
Bloomington	112
Evansville	112
Fort Wayne	113
Gary	113
Indianapolis	114
South Bend	114
Terre Haute	115
Iowa	116
Cedar Rapids	117
Davenport	117
Des Moines	118
Iowa City	118
Sioux City	119
Waterloo	119
Kansas	120
Dodge City	121
Kansas City	121
Topeka	122
Wichita	122
Kentucky	123
Frankfort	124
Lexington	124
Louisville	125
Owensboro	125
Paducah	126
Louisiana	127
Baton Rouge	128
Lake Charles	128
Monroe	129
New Orleans	129
Shreveport	130
Maine	131
Augusta	132
Bangor	132
Lewiston	133
Portland	133
Maryland	134
Annapolis	135
Baltimore	135
Cumberland	136
Hagerstown	136
Massachusetts	137
Boston	138
Cambridge	139
Concord	139
Fall River	140
Lawrence	140
Lowell	141
Nantucket	141
New Bedford	142
Pittsfield	142
Plymouth	143
Provincetown	143

Salem	144	Newark	184
Springfield	144	Paterson	184
Worcester	145	Trenton	185
Michigan	146	New Mexico	186
Ann Arbor	147	Albuquerque	187
Detroit	147	Las Cruces	187
Flint	148	Roswell	188
Grand Rapids	148	Santa Fe	188
Kalamazoo	149	New York	189
Lansing	149	Albany	190
Muskegon	150	Binghamton	190
Saginaw	150	Buffalo	191
Minnesota	151	Elmira	191
Duluth	152	New York City	192
Minneapolis	152	Bronx	193
Rochester	153	Brooklyn	194
Saint Cloud	153	Queens	194
Saint Paul	154	Richmond	194
Mississippi	155	Niagara Falls	194
Biloxi	156	Rochester	195
Gulfport	156	Schenectady	195
Jackson	157	Syracuse	196
Meridian	157	Troy	196
Natchez	158	Utica	197
Oxford	158	North Carolina	198
Vicksburg	159	Asheville	199
Missouri	160	Chapel Hill	199
Columbia	161	Charlotte	200
Jefferson City	161	Durham	200
Joplin	162	Greensboro	201
Kansas City	162	Raleigh	201
Saint Joseph	163	Winston-Salem	202
Saint Louis	164	North Dakota	203
Springfield	165	Bismarck	204
Montana	166	Fargo	204
Billings	167	Grand Forks	205
Butte	167	Minot	205
Great Falls	168	Ohio	206
Helena	168	Akron	207
Missoula	169	Canton	207
Nebraska	170	Cincinnati	208
Grand Island	171	Cleveland	208
Lincoln	171	Columbus	209
North Platte	172	Dayton	210
Omaha	172	Springfield	210
Nevada	174	Toledo	211
Carson City	175	Youngstown	211
Las Vegas	175	Oklahoma	212
Reno	176	Lawton	213
Virginia City	176	Muskogee	213
New Hampshire	178	Oklahoma City	214
Concord	179	Tulsa	214
Manchester	179	Oregon	215
Nashua	180	Eugene	216
Portsmouth	180	Medford	216
New Jersey	181	Portland	217
Atlantic City	182	Salem	218
Camden	182	Pennsylvania	219
Elizabeth	183	Allentown	220
Jersey City	183	Altoona	220

Bethlehem	221	Newport News	258
Erie	221	Norfolk	259
Harrisburg	222	Portsmouth	259
Johnstown	222	Richmond	260
Lancaster	223	Roanoke	260
Philadelphia	223	Virginia Beach	261
Pittsburgh	224	Williamsburg	261
Reading	225	Washington	262
Scranton	226	Olympia	263
Wilkes-Barre	226	Seattle	263
Rhode Island	227	Spokane	264
Newport	228	Tacoma	265
Providence	228	Yakima	265
South Carolina	229	West Virginia	266
Charleston	230	Charleston	267
Columbia	230	Huntington	267
Greenville	231	Parkersburg	268
Spartanburg	231	Wheeling	268
South Dakota	232	Wisconsin	269
Aberdeen	233	Appleton	270
Pierre	233	Green Bay	270
Rapid City	234	Kenosha	271
Sioux Falls	234	La Crosse	271
Tennessee	235	Madison	272
Chattanooga	236	Milwaukee	272
Knoxville	236	Oshkosh	273
Memphis	237	Racine	273
Nashville	237	Wyoming	274
Texas	239	Casper	275
Abilene	240	Cheyenne	275
Amarillo	240	Laramie	276
Austin	241	Rock Springs	276
Beauumont	241	Sheridan	277
Corpus Christi	242	Washington DC	278
Dallas	242	Puerto Rico	282
El Paso	243	Ponce	283
Fort Worth	243	San Juan	283
Galveston	244	Virgin Islands	284
Houston	244	Charlotte Amalie	284
Laredo	245		
Lubbock	246	**Canada**	
San Antonio	246	Canada	285
Waco	247	Alberta	290
Wichita Falls	247	Calgary	291
Utah	248	Edmonton	291
Logan	249	British Columbia	292
Ogden	249	Vancouver	293
Provo	250	Victoria	293
Salt Lake City	250	Manitoba	294
Vermont	252	Brandon	295
Bennington	253	Winnipeg	295
Burlington	253	New Brunswick	296
Montpelier	254	Fredericton	297
Rutland	254	Saint John	297
Virginia	255	Newfoundland	298
Alexandria	256	Saint John's	299
Arlington	256	Nova Scotia	300
Charlottesville	257	Halifax	301
Hampton	257	Ontario	302
Lynchburg	258	Hamilton	303

London	303	Saskatchewan	311
Ottawa	304	Regina	312
Sudbury	304	Saskatoon	312
Toronto	305	Northwest Territories	313
Prince Edward Island	306	Nunavut	314
Charlottetown	307	Yukon Territory	315
Quebec	308	Dawson	316
Montreal	309	Whitehorse	316
Quebec City	310		

Author's Notes

Since the publication of *America: An Astrological Portrait of Its Cities and States* in 1976, many additional pieces of information have surfaced, changing either the date or time of many earlier charts.

The following have different birthdates:
Denver, Colorado
Indianapolis, Indiana
Duluth, Minnesota
Lincoln, Nebraska
Albany, New York
Portland, Oregon
Sioux Falls, South Dakota
Fort Worth, Texas
Milwaukee, Wisconsin
Washington, D.C.

The following have slightly different birthtimes:
Minneapolis, Minnesota
Atlantic City, New Jersey
Newark, New Jersey
Memphis, Tennessee
Dallas, Texas
West Virginia
Ottawa, Ontario

Because I did not have the founding date for the following cities, I had to use the incorporation or charter date in my original book. These cities now have accurate founding dates:

Montgomery, Alabama
Miami, Florida
Saint Petersburg, Florida
Tallahassee, Florida
Tampa, Florida
Honolulu, Hawaii
Baton Rouge, Louisiana
Grand Rapids, Michigan
Kansas City, Missouri
Portsmouth, New Hampshire
Trenton, New Jersey
Asheville, North Carolina
Charlotte, North Carolina
Toledo, Ohio
Chattanooga, Tennessee
Olympia, Washington
Saint John, Newfoundland

The chart for Newfoundland has been changed from April 1, 1949 to March 31, 1949 and its capital city now has as its chart the incorporation date of January 1, 1902, as the earlier one (1497) proved to be inaccurate.

Marc H. Penfield

Acknowledgements

A million thanks to all the historians, librarians and researchers who so willingly complied with my continual queries for accurate data. They are to be commended for their assiduous efforts in enabling each and every city in this book to be as accurate as is humanly possible.

Special thanks must go to Ralph Shelton, of Seattle, for his unusual insight into the deeper meanings of each chart. He has worked with degree symbolism as it relates to the charts of the fifty states, and many of the horoscopes in this book have been slightly corrected due to his valuable research. However, Ralph does not relocate the charts of the states as I do, so his interpretations are based on the time in Washington when the president signed the Bill of Admission.

Thanks must also be given to Ms. Carolyn Dodson, of Nashville, for her book which gave many hard-to-find bits of data on American cities. While she used noontime throughout most of the book, the original data was extremely valuable.

Special thanks must go to Dr. W.R. Van Courtland of Hollywood, California for his many long hours assisting me in the rectification of each and every chart. A typical Aquarian, his flashes of genius are second to none. Without his guidance and insights into world history, many of the charts could not have been completed.

Introduction

For as long as I can remember, wanderlust has required me to investigate the four corners of this globe. From my first trip to Florida at age six, to the trip I will plan for one of my clients, foreign places have always intrigued me. When I was in high school, I would get lost in the corner bookstore browsing through the travel section, and when I went to Chicago, I always managed to return home with a newspaper from some city I'd never seen. Whenever possible, I would also buy a map of that locale and duly memorize it: an uncanny ability I possess which has come in quite handy in my many years as a travel agent. During those years, I compiled a notebook listing all the historical, cultural and commercial establishments of all cities in the United States over 250,000 in population. I often wondered what happened to those notes.

But in all my years of travel, I was too busy noticing the exterior of those places I visited or moved to, rather than investigating the ``personality'' of the community. Not until I became acquainted with astrology in 1964 was the avenue paved for a better understanding of the people in those places I wished to see. After reading hundreds of books on the ``cosmic sciences,'' I reasoned that if astrology had any validity whatsoever, that it would work for larger entities as well. Louis MacNeice's book was the first one I read which illustrated the charts of nations, and others by Carter, etc., gave additional information. Most of the time, however, they talked about eclipse and event charts, and seldom talked about the birth horoscope of the place involved in their discussion. I figured it was about time to investigate this for myself, seeing as how no one else was going to do it for me.

Also about this time, I met Mary Vohryzek of San Francisco, who introduced me not only to Johndro's concept of geodetic equivalents, but to Ebertin's theory of cosmobiology. Suddenly, the light went on in my head, and I was no longer quite so perplexed. Shortly after I moved to Los Angeles, my boss asked me to catalogue the books on American history that lined the shelves of the bookshop I worked for. Within a month or so, I began to notice that many of the tomes were actually biographies of cities and states: most of them giving founding dates, but no times. In the wink of an eye, I composed a form letter and mailed it to 1,000 public libraries, universities and historical societies asking them for additional information. The response was absolutely fantastic: ninety-five percent replied to my inquiry. Many sent photocopies of material unavailable in book form, while others sent an entire pamphlet or book. When two or more sources differed as to their concept of the true founding date, I sent a further inquiry to the mayor of that locale, and let him or her take the responsibility for seeing that I got the correct information.

After viewing horoscopes of some of the larger United States cities, I began to notice a strange correlation between the natal Ascendant of the city, and the position of transiting Pluto when that locale decided to incorporate. Pluto was always in ``hard'' aspect to the rising degree, give or take a few on either side. What Ebertin termed as the three midpoints indicating fame were also tenanted in hard aspect to the Ascendant. These midpoints are Sun/Jupiter, Sun/Pluto, and Jupiter/Pluto.

But now you ask, exactly what did I use for the founding date for the cities listed in this book? There is no hard and fast rule-of-thumb, and the variety seems to be endless. Here are some examples:

1. Discovery by Europeans — Honolulu
2. Land grant — Dallas
3. Dedication — Philadelphia
4. Fort established — Chicago
5. Mission dedicated — St. Paul
6. Formally named — Boston
7. Legislative act — Madison
8. First sale of lots — Las Vegas
9. First survey of plat filed — Akron
10. Town company formed — Denver
11. First settled by Europeans — Los Angeles

When all else failed, I was forced to use the incorporation date as no accurate date of first settlement could be found.

In a few instances, I was given only the month of settlement, and I thus had to rectify the chart from scratch (Portland, Oregon). In one case, the year was even in question (Santa Fe, New Mexico), so the chart you see for that city is based on years of historical research.

Please note that unless indicated, all charts in this book have been rectified, as practically all sources could not supply me with the time of day their community was founded.

The states in the United States were founded in divergent ways as well. The first thirteen colonies were required to ratify the Constitution before they could be admitted to the Union. All states admitted since 1790, with the exception of Ohio, Vermont, and West Virginia, were ``born'' when the incumbent president signed the Bill of Admission. Vermont's bill was signed by Washington one month before it became effective in March 1791, Jefferson forgot to sign Ohio's bill, and West Virginia's admission bill ws signed by Lincoln in April 1863.

Birthtimes for the original thirteen states were relatively easy to find even though many sources simply stated ``mid-afternoon,'' etc. Every state admitted since 1889 had its time recorded in the Los Angeles Times. All others have been rectified, and are so noted.

Please note that all state charts are erected for the capital at the time that state was admitted into the Union; they are not drawn up for Washington where the bill was signed. If your state has moved its legislative offices since the date it entered the Union, you could erect another chart for the current state capital if you desire.

When erecting the state horoscopes, I noticed that the Sun on the date when that region became a territory, and the Midheaven in Washington when that territory became a state, were often in hard aspect. For example, when Kansas was created a territory in 1854, the Sun was ten degrees Pisces. When Buchanan signed its admission bill in 1861, the Midheaven in Washington was ten degrees Pisces. Since the thirteen colonies were never territories, I've chosen the date when they were granted their first charter by the British crown, in lieu of a territory date. The results are identical. For the states of Vermont, Texas and California, which were neither royal colonies or territories, I've used the date when they declared their independence; again, the same correlation existed.

Another interesting insight occurred when I progressed the charts of those southern states that seceded from the Union in the early days of the Civil War. The progressed Midheaven was usually in hard aspect to Uranus, the planet of separation. Coincidence?

The assumption that the first settlement in an area should define the characteristics of the inhabitants in that region prompted me to delineate the St. Augustine chart as representative of the American people. I believe the U.S.'s nature is more clearly defined through this chart than the Declaration of Independence chart.

It is my personal opinion after years and years of research, that the correct horoscope for the Untied States must have Scorpio rising. I won't go into detail about the other charts floating around; all that I will say is that none of them are based on historical truth. If you will investigate the workings of Congress that July day, you will find that the document got out of committee shortly after 2:00 p.m., and was then sent to John Hancock for his signature. Only he, and his secretary, signed it that day. Congress adjourned about 4:00 p.m. and went home to dinner.

For your interest, I have also included the charts for the signing of the Constitution, as well as when that document became effective in 1789. I think either one of these could describe the workings of the U.S. national government quite well, but to date I've had little success with them.

Now, I think it's about time we talk about the various methods and systems used in this book.

DATES: New Style dates are used throughout, with the exception for events occurring prior to 1583. With respect to all British settlements, I had to erect two charts for each locale, as authors didn't specify which calendar they were referring to.

TIMES: Standard time zones are used continuously. I find it much easier to calculate the horoscope when using standard times, not to mention finding the adjusted calculation date (ACD) when I'm doing progressions. For some strange reason, incorporation charts work very well when you remember to use standard time. For example, using the July 1, 1856 chart for San Francisco's charter as a county (12:01 a.m. PST); if you did not use PST, you would be three years off in predicting the calamity that befell that city in 1906.

HOUSE SYSTEM: I prefer the Porphyry house system, as it equally trisects all quadrants; it is a system of space, not of time. The Ascendant and Midheaven are identical to Placidus and Koch, however.

LONGITUDE AND LATITUDE: The Times Atlas of the World was used for all localities not mentioned in books by either Neil Michelsen or the American Federation of Astrologers.

PROGRESSIONS: In the first paragraph or so pertaining to the cities, the aspects in parentheses refer to progressed aspects, not to natal positions. My method of progression is the standard. I find the solar arc for the event indicated, add it to the natal Midheaven and look up the corresponding Ascendant in the tables of houses. I do not use solar arc progressions to the Ascendant, although you may care to.

DESCRIPTIONS: In the second paragraph or so, you will find planetary positions, either by house or sign. This refers to the natal positions in the horoscope only. In a few cases, I will refer to transits, but not often.

Please keep the above in mind as you read this book.

STATISTICAL DATA: Population figures are from the U.S. Census Bureau, elevation is from the Encyclopedia Britannica, while area is from the Encyclopedia of American Cities.

Last, I apologize to all whose hometowns are not listed in this book. I sought to illustrate only those places with sufficient population, and usually chose the four largest communities in each state. The state capital was always chosen, but suburbs were usually eliminated. In a few instances, I have put in resorts such as Aspen and Palm Springs.

I don't claim to know the inherent individuality and unique personality of each city in this book. True, I have visited most of them, and for those cities not fully described, it is because my unfamiliarly with that location prompted me not to write about something I know nothing about. If you find some unusual quirk about your town which I failed to mention, by all means, forward it to my publisher.

Marc Penfield
Hollywood, California
July 6, 1996

The Planets in Mundane Astrology

THE SUN: Governs the will of the people. Their inherent characteristics (along with the Ascendant) are shown by this planet. The Sun rules all political activities and persons in power and authority.

THE MOON: Rules the common people, their personality and desire for change. It governs the basic necessities of life: food, clothing and shelter.

MERCURY: Rules the people's ability to communicate and gather diverse pieces of information. It also shows their literary interest and desire for movement.

VENUS: Represents the people's desire to make their community more attractive. It governs high society and the arts as well as all forms of culture, traditional or modern.

MARS: Represents the energy of the people. It has dominion over all manufacturing and industrial concerns, especially the steel industry. It rules the police and the military.

JUPITER: Governs the religious and moral principles of the people, and their capacity for law and order. Jupiter will show the people's desire to elevate themselves, be it physical, financial or spiritual.

SATURN: Rules conservatism, and all right-wing elements. It shows the people's desire to accomplish a desired goal and their degree of ambition. Saturn also shows the most restrictive elements which must be dealt with lest ruin and disgrace tarnish the reputation of the community.

URANUS: Governs the radical and progressive elements, and thus all left-wing activities. It rules riots, rebellions, and all actions which upset the equilibrium of the community.

NEPTUNE: Governs the ideals of the people. It also shows their desire to communicate with outsiders, for it rules the mass media, all chain stores and places of franchisement.

PLUTO: Represents the group effort and the degree of cooperation that is to be expected to accomplish a desired goal. It governs all transformations, such as urban renewal, political mergers, foreign alliances and treaties.

The Houses in Mundane Astrology

THE FIRST HOUSE: Represents the people and the first impression one perceives when viewing a particular city or state. The disposition and personality of the people residing there as well as their interests are shown through this house, which acts as a lens through which the rest of the horoscope is filtered.

THE SECOND HOUSE: Represents the people's attitude towards material possessions and their sense of values. It will show their potential wealth and assets. It rules all places where earnings are deposited.

THE THIRD HOUSE: Represents the people's ability and desire to communicate. It rules the postal services, the mass media and all forms of transportation and literary communication.

THE FOURTH HOUSE: represents the people's desire for security, especially through the ownership of real estate. It governs homes, apartment houses and all places of residence, permanent or transient. It rules agriculture, farmers, miners and all those who deal with the land.

THE FIFTH HOUSE: represents the ability of the people to amuse themselves. It governs the theater, the cinema, gambling and prostitution. This house also rules another form of speculation: the stock market. It also rules children and all forms of their education.

THE SIXTH HOUSE: Represents the workers of the country, especially those in the employ for the government. All civil service workers, the police, and the military come under jurisdiction of this house. This house, along with the Ascendant, denote the ability to combat the relationship between general health indications and the people's ability and desire to work.

THE SEVENTH HOUSE: Represents the people's ability to relate to outsiders. It shows their desire to form alliances and treaties. Failure to adjust and balance these relations may lead to conflict, for this house is the house of war.

THE EIGHTH HOUSE: Represents the people's debts and taxes. Whereas the second house will show their income, the eighth house shows what they must give to the city or state. All forms of payment, be it insurance or credit cards, are shown by this house. The eighth house also will show which area or areas of life must be regenerated and transformed in order for the entire organism to function at maximum efficiency.

THE NINTH HOUSE: Represents the people's desire for law and order. It governs the courts and the church. The attitude towards all higher forms of education will be shown by this house. All international concerns and commercial interests come under its rule.

THE TENTH HOUSE: Represents the leader of the people, be it their mayor, governor, or president. It also shows the community's attitude toward those in authority and the consequent reputation of that community. Transits and progressions to this house (as well as to the Ascendant) are extremely important in predicting the outcome of elections.

THE ELEVENTH HOUSE: Represents the friends of the people; their congressmen, state or national; and their city representatives. This house also rules outright philanthropy and all forms of betterment of the community.

THE TWELFTH HOUSE: Represents the hidden ills of the community. The hospitals, asylums, jails and prisons come under its dominion, as well as those who work in those institutions, such as doctors, nurses and the people who combat crime. All people who benefit from welfare and the unemployed are shown by this house.

Aspects in Mundane Astrology

Modern astrologers list aspects according to their impact: soft and hard. Older and more traditional practitioners of astrology prefer to designate aspects as being either good or bad, positive or negative. It all depends upon the outlook of the individual involved. I prefer to think of aspects as either stating particular conditions (such as soft aspects) or clarifying possible obstacles with which one must learn to cope (such as hard aspects).

The soft aspects are:

THE SEXTILE (60 DEGREES): It indicates opportunities presented to an individual along with many social contacts.

THE TRINE (120 DEGREES): It indicates a harmonious interaction between one sphere of life and another.

The hard aspects are:

THE SEMISQUARE (45 DEGREES) AND THE SESQUARE (135 DEGREES): They indicate minor frustrations and annoyances.

THE SQUARE (90 DEGREES): It indicates obstacles which must be overcome and areas for greatest improvement.

THE OPPOSITION (180 DEGREES): It indicates opposition and reorientation to the wishes of the community.

THE INCONJUNCT OR QUINCUNX (150 DEGREES): It indicates an adjustment which must be made. It is a health aspect.

THE CONJUNCTION cannot be termed "soft" or "hard" for it depends solely upon the planets conjoined. The conjunction blends varying qualities into one unit, often with an effect of mutation.

The Relationship Between These Horoscopes and You

Many students are interested not only in the horoscopes of various cities and states and how they function, but also with the relationship to their individual horoscopes. With this in mind, I will give you a few things to look for when comparing charts. First, chart the number of aspects between your chart and the chart of the city or state in question. If the soft aspects outweigh the hard aspects, life in that particular locality will be more beneficial for you than if it were the other way around. The more conjunctions between your chart and the chart of the locale, the more attracted you are to that place and the more affinity you will have. Sextiles and trines are beneficial, but you also need a few squares and oppositions to get the show on the road. Allow a maximum orb of only three degrees, applying and separating.

Second, look at the position of your Sun and the house it occupies in the horoscope of the city or state. If the Sun is in either the first or the tenth house, you will be noticed and receive honors in that community, and the affinity between you and the city/state will be strong. For those who desire to hold office of a political nature, I would recommend choosing a city which has your Sun in its tenth house. If the Sun is placed in either of the two remaining angular houses, there is less chance of being known for individual actions, more for the associations you join and the company you keep. For those desiring peace and quiet, choose the fourth house, for it will often make you somewhat of a hermit.

If the Sun is in the seventh house, expect opposition and conflict, along with many chances to form partnerships, etc.

If the Sun is placed in a succedent house, you will be forced to share your actions with others, either financially (if the Sun is in the second or the eighth) or socially and creatively (if the Sun is in the fifth or the eleventh house). The fifth house will make your creative juices flow more freely, while the eleventh house will bring you into many beneficial associations. With the Sun in either the second or eighth house, expect a flux of finances.

When the Sun falls into the city or state's sixth or twelfth house, your health (physical, emotional, or mental) will be tested. Sometimes if Jupiter also falls into one of these two houses, your health might improve if you move to this locale. But the Sun, especially in the twelfth house, will confine you and make many of your efforts go unnoticed and unrewarded. If the Sun falls into either the third or the ninth house, these locales will prove beneficial for study and communication, but the feeling will be very transient and your desire to move on to another locale will, more than not, be always present.

Third, look at the aspects again between your chart and the city or state in question. If your Sun and Mars are in good aspect, energy and creativity will be in the forefront. If either the Moon or Venus are more prominent, expect an active social life and much popularity. When Mercury is the most heavily aspected planet, there will be much coming and going, but little stability. When Jupiter dominates, the locale involved will be extremely fortunate for you, often to excess. If your Saturn is well aspected, you can expect a good business career; if the contrary is true, unemployment and frustration will ensue. When the outer planets (Uranus, Neptune, and Pluto) dominate, you will be a vanguard for those in your community, showing them the way to break down existing conditions, often with unusual and radical methods. Uranus will incline you to be rather nervous in the locale while Neptune will put you in tune with the populace, often with media involvement. When Pluto dominates, expect radical transformations, especially where your health is concerned. Conditions will continually crop up which will test your courage and survival, especially where finances are concerned.

With all this in mind, I hope that you have the opportunity to relocate and experience the best that the community you have chosen has to offer. For those of you who are already situated in a fortunate community, my blessings. You are among the rare few.

The American People

The First Permanent Settlement in America

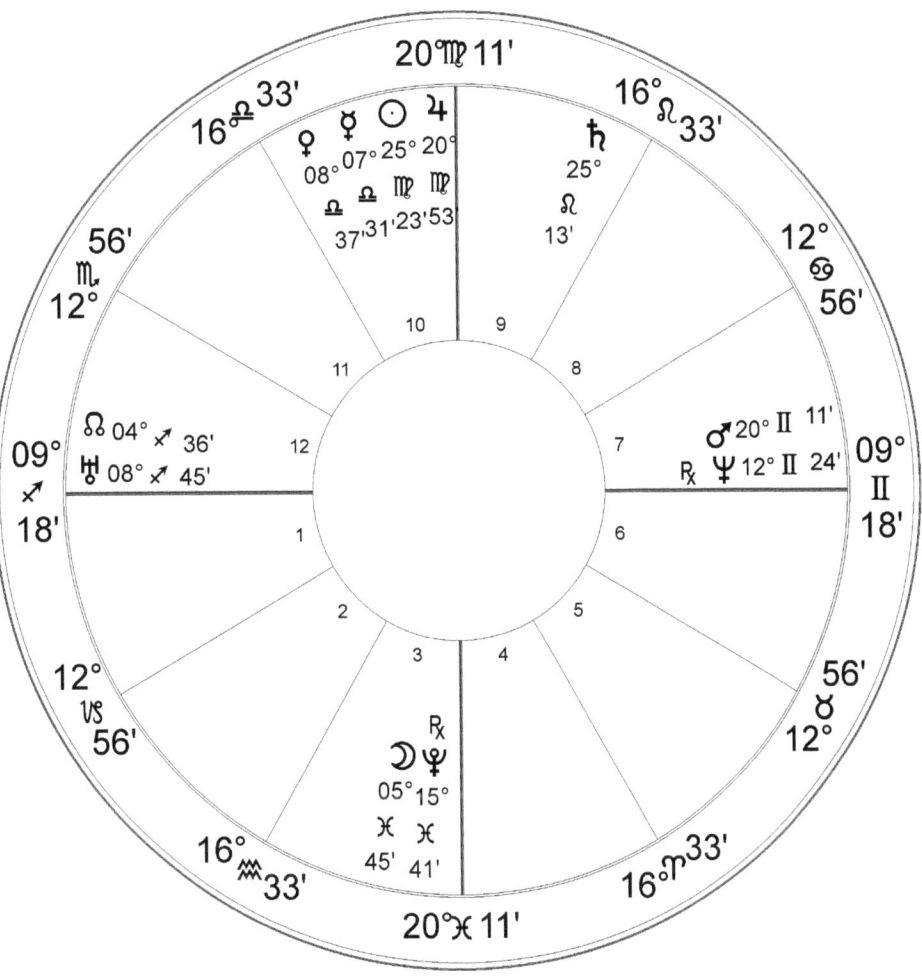

September 18, 1565
St. Augustine, Florida
29N54, 81W19
Noon EST
Source: American Federation of Astrologers

It is my opinion that the characteristics of the American people and their destiny may be ascertained from the St. Augustine chart which I spoke of earlier in this book. As it is the oldest permanent European settlement in the country, I use it on the same premise that I would use the founding chart for a city.

Looking at the chart, we note that five planets are in angles, and three others are within two degrees. Seven planets are in mutable signs and four planets in air signs. This equates to mutable air = Gemini. The composite of the American people is definitely Geminian, for they love novelty, movement and communication. Their adaptability and love of experimentation has given the English language many new words. Hardly is there a person in America who knows, much less speaks, the King's English. There are two political parties and two houses of congress. Many Americans own two cars and two houses. They love things in pairs. Even the bitterest war this country has ever fought was fought between two geographical divisions, the North and the South. Some are convinced that the fighting is still going on.

Americans are high strung, strong willed and impulsive. Their love of independence and freedom can be traced to Uranus rising on the Ascendant. The country has torn down the conventions of the Old World, creating a lively and original environment that many foreigners find hard to take. Americans love speed, whether in the home, on the highways or in the air. They are always in a hurry to get somewhere, and the highway death toll is ample proof of this characteristic. They worship and adore science and technology and all the new-fangled benefits such have given them. Americans are gadget-happy, and its no wonder that more energy is used in a single day than most other countries do in a single month.

The forefathers came to this country for religious or political freedom. They fought their way across uncharted and uninhabited regions to forge this great nation. Uranus rules exploration, and since they can no longer pioneer (except in Alaska), domain of the universe is sought. Uranus in Sagittarius aspires to exalted heights and the good life we have known for over two centuries. Even with the current shortages of food and energy, the good life will no doubt continue, for Americans are a people who seek to change the status quo and consequently adapt quite easily. Somehow, being never satisfied, Americans yearn for the greener pastures and constantly expand their influence to many other lands.

The position of the Moon and Pluto in the third house gives the desire to explore realms of communication unheard of a hundred years ago. Methods of transportation have been transformed through the invention of the automobile and millions have been given the chance to hear voices across thousands of miles through the telephone. Radio, television and motion pictures have transcended both time and distance to bring the world closer together. Pisces seeks to internationalize and integrate all people into a common unit. The vast array of people in this country is representative of a United Nations, and while most live in harmony, many prejudices relating to race, color, creed or national origin are just now being erased. Americans are a charitable people, loving the underdog. Their system of welfare and Social Security takes care of those who are either too ill equipped or too old to fend for themselves. Their international policy extends throughout the world, giving those less fortunate the chance for a better life.

With the Sun and Jupiter at the Midheaven, America will always occupy a position of prominence among the nations of the world. Americans have a great desire for achievement and success, and most rise above their original station in life. Being an ambitious people with strong egos, Americans are more interested in foreign relations than in domestic relations. This is because six signs are in fire and air, the masculine and extrovertive signs. They stretch their hands (and their budgets), giving Americans the reputation of a universal Santa Claus. The American obsession with health and cleanliness may be traced to the Sun and Jupiter in Virgo. Advances made in medicine in the past century towards combating epidemics and illnesses that earlier had checked population growth have been great. The methods of production (the assembly line, for example) have transformed the industrial world. Since Virgo is a mutable sign, the variety of occupations available to Americans is incalculable. If a job doesn't exist at present, wait a while and someone probably will invent it. Many workers are unionized and big business will always play an integral part in American lives.

With Mercury in the tenth house, most Americans have the ability to be well trained for their occupations. Being a nation of multi-talented people, few hold down just one job as did their grandfathers. Many even have part-time jobs. They are always seeking better jobs and this requires education. The educational system is probably the best in the world, even if many do not partake of it. Americans aspire to do many things occupationally and usually succeed. With Venus also in the tenth house, they aspire to "keep up with the Joneses," whoever they are. They seek to rise socially and many marry above their station in life, tackling projects that may be socially acceptable but which they are not yet able to handle. Venus in Libra causes them to see both sides of the question and to try and avert a conflict. They have founded, and entered into, many international organizations, and will no doubt continue to do so in the future. America is not a nation of intellects or profound thinkers, but American are well versed on many divergent subjects and their curiosity and level of comprehension are above average.

Mars in the seventh house points to the aggressive attitude Americans have taken toward foreign nations. While America has never openly provoked a war, it has stepped in when it was felt that the rights of others were in danger. America's superior technology and forceful nature usually won the battle in half the time. The exception to this rule was the Vietnam conflict, but with the transits of Uranus and Pluto square Mars, the reasons for entering this war may be obscured for many years, for obvious reasons. The danger in foreign alliances arises when America tries to dominate others, for it does not easily give in and compromise. Americans are a highly independent people, preferring to go their own way instead of listening to the lessons of history. Possibly the high divorce rate in recent years may be attributed to this position of Mars. Americans are finally, not without difficulty however, eradicating the Victorian concepts of morality, and while many still practice the double standard, the feminist movement has given birth to the idea of mutual sharing of responsibilities. Gemini on the seventh prefers independence and often lacks responsibility and a mature attitude toward marriage. With Mars in Gemini, the Sun in Virgo, and Sagittarius rising, America should be a nation of bachelors. Many young people have discovered that marriage isn't all it's been cracked up to be and many have found alternative means of union. With regard to foreign affairs, America should learn to mind its own business and let the rest of the world take care of itself, like it was in the beginning.

Neptune in the seventh house causes Americans to view foreigners with rose colored glasses. Conceding the fact that they love the underdog, it's from a distance. When the reality of poverty among America's neighbors gets too close to home, they tend to ignore and subjugate. Many were the people (like the Irish and the Polish) who had to surmount this attitude of indifference and sectarianism. But due to the trines of Mercury and Venus in the tenth house, most immigrants rose quickly and contributed heavily to the might of this nation.

Saturn in the ninth house points to the inherent love of law and order in all Americans. Fortunately, they are not as anarchistic as the French, as politically erratic as the Italians or as smug as the English. The Puritanical way of life demanded a structure that adhered to the concept that all that was not functional or utilitarian must be eliminated. Saturn in Leo has not made America a nation of playboys or possessing the "joie de vivre" so characteristic of many Europeans. It is a nation of workers, often believing that material goods are the highest attainment. Laws that have been on the books for years continue to be enforced even though they have outlived their usefulness. The legal system is fair and impartial (as many say) but the structure of the law is unbending (Saturn in a fixed sign) and often takes more time than is necessary to create reforms. It is a nation of people who have strong religious opinions. Even the atheists like Madelyn Murray O'Hair are adamant in their beliefs. The people have strong opinions on everything from soup to nuts and unfortunately are given to unwarranted criticism in realms of philosophy. If ever there was a typically American motto, probably Theodore Roosevelt said it when he spoke "work hard, play hard." America must learn to be more tolerant of the opinions of others and not let bigotry and prejudice influence viewpoints. This is one aspect of American life where the people do adhere to the past with tenacity. While this attitude has served them well in the past, they are living in a changing world and the laws and morality must be changed if they are to survive. Unfortunately, much of their philosophy is not only outmoded but extremely dangerous and harmful to future generations.

Americans sure have the ability to make money. The square of Mars to Jupiter is known as the "millionaires' aspect." America is the wealthiest country in the world and with their compulsive worship of the dollar, the people will continue to rake in the dough, no doubt, in future generations. They energetically expand their lives through taking chances and the benefits that have accrued from this are great. Even the size of this country is great. Do you realize that all of Europe west of Russia could be placed east of the Mississippi River? Alaska is larger than France, Spain, West Germany and England combined. The sheer immensity of anything American astounds most foreigners, for Americans never do anything in a small way. The American virtues, as well as their vices, are great.

One can lay the horoscope over a map of the United States and arrive at some startling coincidences. Place the center of the wheel in the middle of Illinois (the current center of population for the forty-eight states) and notice which areas of the country are ruled by each sign.

Sagittarius rules Virginia, the Tidewater, and the area around the nation's capital. This region is famous for its spirit of independence, as well as the potential it offers to sportsmen in the form of hunting, sailing, or horseback riding. With Uranus rising, it would be reasonable to assume that this part of the country would be the first to be explored as well as the part of the country where independence would be declared. Capricorn rules the populous northeast, New York, New Jersey, and New England. This is the land of big business and industry. New York is not only the most powerful city in the country, but in the world. Politically, economically, and financially, this sector of the country has contributed more to our way of life than any other part. It was in this section that the laws were formed and where the first national capital was located. Even the soil of New England is typically Capricornian. It's too rocky for much agriculture, so industry was the natural alternative.

Aquarius rules upper New York State, which contains both the Erie Canal and the St. Lawrence Seaway, both avenues of interstate or international commerce. The rather friendly attitude of upstate New Yorkers contrasts sharply to the cold and businesslike residents of New York City. In this sector, the Oneida Community was founded along with the Mormon faith.

Pisces rules the part of the country which contains the Great Lakes. As Pisces also rules pollution, it comes as no surprise that the most polluted lake (Erie) and river (Cuyahoga) are located in this sector. Many missions were established by the French in the 17th and 18th centuries and the people of the Great Lakes possess what many feel are the typical American virtues of understanding and strong religious feeling.

Aries rules the Great Plains and the beginning of the West. As Aries falls on the western side of the chart, it is natural that Americans have, for more than two centuries, followed the advice of Horace Greeley when he said, "Go west, young man, go west." As Aries also rules physical energy and violence, the West naturally would be the scene of bitter battles, either between the Indians and the White Man or between his own kind. Marshals and gunfighters are both folk heroes to a sector that relied upon the gun for means of survival.

Taurus rules the great Midwest, the heartland of the country. The main industries are grain crops and the breeding of cattle. Products of the earth have made these people the most earthy of all Americans and definitely the most stable and dependable. An area of few great cities, it prefers the small town and open spaces, for the residents of this part of the country are very close to nature.

Gemini governs northern California, a polyglot region that inspired so many Americans to emigrate after the discovery of gold. And if New York can be said to be the melting pot of Europe, then California can certainly ascribe to the reputation for being the melting pot of the United States. No other state in the country has so varied a climate. With Neptune in this sector, California was often a land that was too good to be true, the proverbial "El

Dorado," the land of milk and honey. With Mars in Gemini, it's no wonder that California has the most extensive educational system of any state and the most vast system of freeways in the land.

Cancer rules the end of life and the southern part of California, Arizona and New Mexico. Many persons have chosen this sector of the country in which to retire, due to its beneficial climate.

Leo rules the great Southwest, including Texas. Leo brags a lot, and what person hasn't heard tales about Texas and its fantastic accomplishments? As Leo is a barren and arid sign, some of the most magnificent scenery in the world is to be found in this region, including the Grand Canyon of the Colorado.

Virgo rules the Deep South, where discrimination and segregation were once so prominent. This part of the country was the first to feel the weight of the Civil Rights Act of the mid-sixties due to the position of Jupiter. As Virgo is an earth sign, most of the south is agricultural, and its people simple, basic, and down-to-earth.

Libra rules Georgia and South Carolina, symbols of the old South, elegant in the extreme. Most of Florida is in this section, and possibly no other state in the union has transformed a wasteland into one of the most beautiful paradises on earth. The relaxed ambience of this state is so characteristic of Libra, which no doubt appeals to the many retired persons in the state.

Scorpio rules North Carolina and Appalachia. Probably no other area in the country retains the language and the characteristics of their forefathers as do the people in this region. Many times have tales been told of people living in the backwoods who are out of touch with the modern world. Scorpio desires to possess and adhere to that which it deems fitful, and will brook all opposition toward intrusion.

Let us now examine the transits of the outer planets and see how they have affected the American lives in the past two centuries.

Uranus passed over the Descendant in 1776 when the Declaration of Independence was signed. It crossed the Midheaven in 1799 when conflict became imminent with France, and all treaties with that country were voided. In 1816, it crossed the Ascendant. The War of 1812 was over and America gained a new sense of freedom and independence. When Uranus crossed the Nadir in 1841, the western migration began and before long the Gold Rush would accelerate the movement. In 1860, the Civil War was imminent and eleven southern states voted to secede from the Union when Uranus crossed the Descendant. Upon crossing the Midheaven in 1882, labor unions began to take shape and before long, the worker would have a new sense of freedom from deplorable conditions. With the crossing of the Ascendant in 1902, Uranus signaled a new birth for the United States. Roosevelt sent the U.S. Navy around the world, showing other nations that America was now a power to be reckoned with. When Uranus crossed the Nadir again in 1925, America was living life to the hilt. The Roaring Twenties were in full swing and women began to feel freer as they cut their hair and shortened their dresses. World War II was more than two years old when Uranus crossed the Descendant in 1944. The allied landing on Normandy signaled the end of the bloodiest and costliest war in the history of mankind. America finally became the world's greatest power and foreign alliances became an American way of life. When Uranus crossed the U.S. Midheaven again in 1966, American was in the space race and actions were taken to assist several minority groups—namely, the blacks, through the passage of the Civil Rights Act, and the aged, who began to partake of Medicare benefits.

Now, let us look at Neptune. When the Declaration of Independence was signed in 1776, Neptune was crossing the Midheaven. Abraham Lincoln had just been born when Neptune crossed the Ascendant in 1811, and as Neptune rules slavery, I think this is quite a coincidence. The War of 1812 was fought soon after due to the impressment (kidnaping) of American seamen. When Neptune crossed the Nadir in 1857, the Dred Scott Decision was rendered, Lincoln and Douglas began their debates and the Republican Party was born. Crossing the Descendant in 1892, Neptune signaled the vast migration of southern Europeans to this country, creating squalid housing and overcrowding in the cities. The Battle of Wounded Knee was fought at this time. Hitler annexed Austria and the Sudetenland in 1938 when Neptune crossed America's Midheaven, creating a perplexing situation in the minds of many Americans. Foreign isolation was short lived, however, as America entered World War II three years later. Neptune crossed the Ascendant in 1975, signaling the time for all Americans to take off the rose colored glasses and view situations for what they really are. This was a time of food and energy shortages, as well as scandals involving Watergate and the CIA. Kidnapings and bombings, assassination attempts and increasing crime will be the order of the day unless the chaos and confusion (Neptune) is terminated and Americans stop acting like spoiled brats, feeling that so many of their liberties have been taken away. One should journey to other lands and see how others live and be thankful they have it so good in their country.

Finally, let us look at Pluto. In 1752, when Pluto crossed America's Ascendant, the Gregorian Calendar was adopted in this country. Shortly after, the French and Indian wars were fought to determine who had dominion over American soil. Had the British lost, very possibly, America would have become a possession of France instead of Britain. When it crossed the Nadir in 1814, the War of 1812 was over. While America had already purchased Louisiana from the French in 1803, most territorial acquisitions were made before Pluto left the sign of Aries. Upon crossing the Descendant in 1893, along with Neptune the previous year, America entered the Gay Nineties after experiencing the worst financial panic in American history. Inventions, such as the telephone, the automobile, the phonograph, and motion pictures were soon to become a reality. Pluto crossed the Midheaven in 1967 during the period of great unrest due to the Vietnam War. Young people broke away from their elders and formed a new society, while others sought to tear down the society by assassinating leaders such as Robert F. Kennedy and Martin Luther King. This was the period of race riots when cities burned and thousands left the country because they refused to fight in a war which they deemed immoral. The presidency underwent vast changes during Pluto's transit of the Midheaven, as was witnessed during the administration of Richard Nixon, the most corrupt period in the country history. Hopefully America will find new strength in the coming years through its leaders, even though the current fad is defamation of every public figure available.

America has come a long way in the past two centuries, changing the world's way of life more than it had changed in the past 2,000 years. With the adaptability and basic dissatisfaction of the American people for a better way, they hopefully will continue to exert a strong influence in international affairs in the future. But now is the time for them to see themselves for what they really are and to tend to their own domestic conditions, which need so desperately to be corrected. American ethics and attitudes will first have to be transformed in order for them to feel comfortable in the modern world. In many ways, they are thinking in Puritanical terms and performing in a space age manner. Good luck, America!

The Declaration of Independence

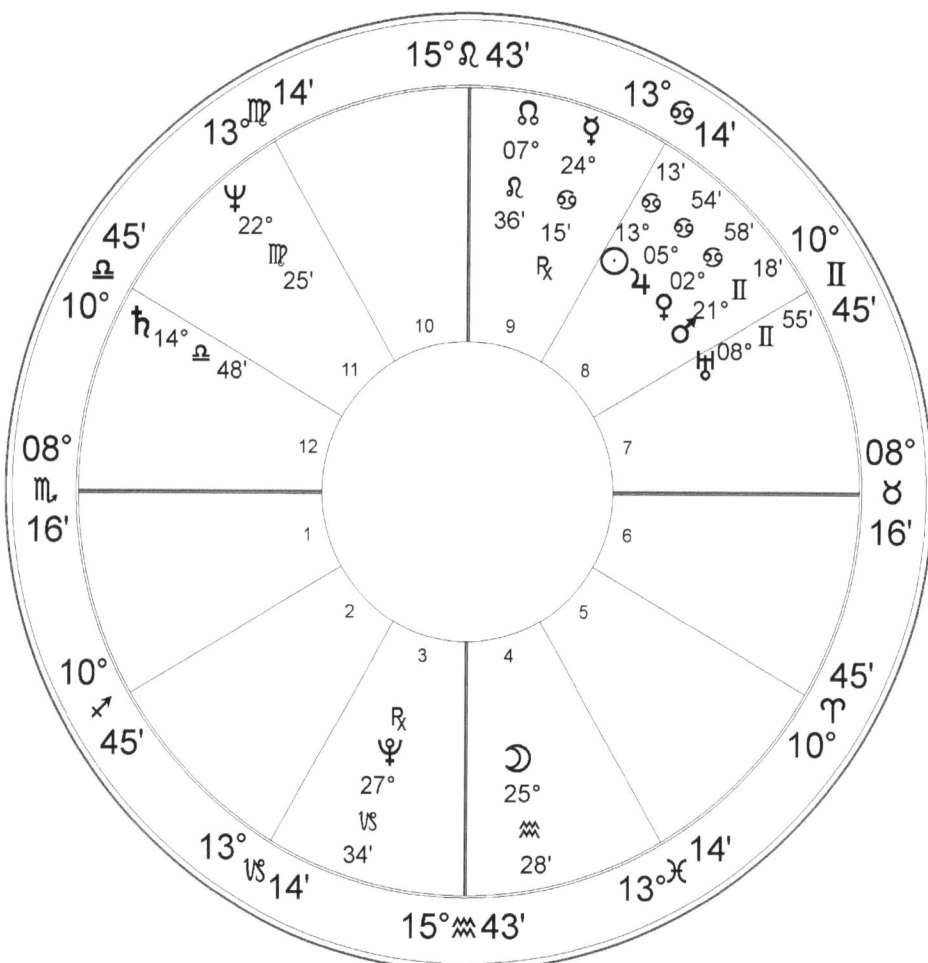

July 4, 1776
Philadelphia, Pennsylvania
39N57, 75W10
2:20 p.m. EST

Sources: Patriots in Purple by H.S. Allan; The Great Seal of the United States by Paul Foster Case; United States State Department; all suggest a time shortly after 2:00 p.m.

Signed in Philadelphia, Pennsylvania on July 4, 1776 at 2:20 p.m. EST.

In the spring of 1776, the American colonies were ready for complete independence from Britain with whom they had been fighting a war since April 19, 1775. In the ensuing months, both North Carolina and Rhode Island had issued their own respective "declarations of independence," but a united effort by all colonies was not forthcoming until June 7. At that time, Richard Henry Lee proposed that all colonies had the right to be free and to choose their own destinies. Four days later a committee composed of Jefferson, Adams, Sherman, Franklin and Livingston was nominated to draft a formal document. Jefferson did most of the writing, and his first draft was completed by June 28. Several items were deleted, such as reference to the King of England and condemnation of the slave trade. Finally, on July 2, all colonies except New York (which had not been given the authority to vote for independence) voted to adopt the resolution. That night, John Adams wrote to his wife that "this day will be the most memorable epoch in the history of America. I believe that it will be celebrated as the great anniversary."

Congress convened at 9:00 a.m. on July 4 and, according to Jefferson, it was a hot and muggy day. "Everyone was running around with their shirts off or open. A livery stable next door caused horseflies to come in and bite people. I'm convinced that those flies helped to launch this nation, for nobody paid much attention to what they were signing." Page 228 of the book entitled Patriot in Purple by Herbert S. Allan, states that "for three days impassioned oratory, pro and con, echoed through the government chamber At last, about two o'clock in the afternoon of the fourth, the great white paper was reported out of committee to the House with a recommendation for approval, and was immediately ratified. Hancock and his secretary, Charles Thomson, were then ordered to authenticate it with their signatures in the customary manner of handling all Congressional measures. They were also directed to have copies printed for dispatching to the colonial assemblies and to the army. The printing was done by next morning." Congress then adjourned at 4:00 p.m., and the document was sent to John Dunlap, who was ordered to print it on broadsides.

The first public reading of the Declaration took place on the steps of Independence Hall at high noon on July 8, 1776, by John Nixon. On the nineteenth, Congress resolved that the document should be placed on parchment. Finally, on August 2, delegates from all the colonies began to sign. Many who affixed their signatures that day were not present the previous July 4 when independence was voted upon, for they had been replaced by their respective colonial assemblies. The final signature, that of Thomas McKean, wasn't affixed until 1781.

Because of a $2,500 reward offered by Britain to learn the names of the signers, formal publication was withheld until January 1777. You see, all those present that July day were traitors, and the British punishment for treason was hanging.

In his book, *The Great Seal of the United States of America*, Paul Foster Case also uses a time of "shortly after 2 p.m.," Scorpio being representative of the seal of the country. Case used thirteen degrees of Scorpio rising, however, which makes the Ascendant trine the Sun. Case also pointed out that many who signed the Declaration were Masons, members of a very high-minded and philosophical organization who held their meetings in secret. Many also were practicing Rosicrucians, like Franklin. The sign of Scorpio on the eastern horizon seems to fit nicely with the birth of America, doesn't it? The U.S. State Department also vouches for the 2:00 p.m. time, as illustrated on July 4, 1976 when President Ford was instructed to ring the Liberty Bell at that precise moment.

Other horoscopes "floating around" of the USA are obviously inaccurate. Let me illustrate. A chart with Virgo rising (for about 9:00 a.m.) was for the moment Congress convened, and too early for the final vote. Likewise for the Libra rising chart (about 12:15 p.m.) with Saturn rising. The vote hadn't yet taken place. And the Sagittarius rising chart is too late, as Congress had already adjourned. In recent years, this chart, however, had been given some measure of credibility due to a notation found in one of Sibley's notebooks. Sibley was an English astrologer of the late 18th century, but he gives the time as 10:15 p.m., London time. Why he chose to use a chart with five hours' difference is anybody's guess. This is the chart Dane Rudhyar used in his book, *The Astrology of America's Destiny*.

The Gemini rising chart (about 2:13 a.m.) is so obviously false that one wonders where it came from. Seems that some early 20th century astrologer started using it, and soon after it became quite popular. To my knowledge, the only chart ever used in the 19th century (after viewing hundreds of old magazines, etc.) was the Sagittarius chart. This Gemini chart is a fabrication, pure and simple, and even the Library of Congress is at a loss to explain how it might have happened. If you are in the habit of using the time when an event is proclaimed, then you will have to use July 8, 1776, at noon. This is the chart that possibly got confused with the earlier Libra rising chart for July 4, but remember that on July 8 the Moon (ruler of the Midheaven) had moved into Aries and was placed in the seventh house.

One of the best ways, I believe, to approximate a birthtime is to use the progressed Moon. Secondary placements are shown in the illustrations, but the radix (solar arc) positions are somewhat less familiar. In order of major events, the radix Moon is as follows.

1787—4 Pisces 02—U.S. Constitution
Approaching trine to Jupiter (law and justice), which became exact after Washington's inauguration.

1803—21 Pisces 36—Louisiana Purchase
Separating square from Mars (Napoleon sold it to America on threat of war with Spain) and an approaching opposition to Neptune (Barbary pirates threatened the seas).

1812—29 Pisces 43—War of 1812
Approaching sesquare to the Midheaven and semisquare to the Nadir. Within two years, both the Capitol Building (Midheaven) and the White House (Nadir) were burned.

1823—10 Aries 46—Monroe Doctrine
Semisquare her own position. Moon rules the ninth house. European powers had aggravated America enough that the foreign powers were told to stay out of the Western Hemisphere.

1846—2 Taurus 33—Mexican War
Sextile Venus, ruler of the seventh house of war. We easily grabbed much of Mexico's territory.

1848—4 Taurus 10—Gold Discovered
Sextile Jupiter/Venus midpoint, sextile Jupiter exactly when the '49ers trekked to California.

1861—17 Taurus 07—Civil War
Approaching semisquare to Venus, ruler of the seventh house of war, and the twelfth house, which rules slavery.

1898—23 Gemini 55—Spanish-American War
Semisquare and sesquare the Nodes (which are in the third/ninth houses), as well as the Ascendant/Descendant axis.

1917—13 Cancer 03—World War I
Almost conjunct natal Sun in the ninth house. Was approaching a square to Saturn when the Armistice was signed.

1929—25 Cancer 47—Stock Market Crash
Inconjunct its own position as it would be in any horo-

scope used.

1941—8 Leo 07—Pearl Harbor

Just past the conjunction of the North Node in the ninth house and approaching square to the Ascendant. Eight months earlier, the Moon had semisquared Neptune, ruler of the dependencies fifth house.

1950—16 Leo 49—Korean War

About one degree past a conjunction of the Midheaven, within the year, it would semisquare natal Venus, ruler of the seventh house of war.

1963—0 Virgo 30—Kennedy Assassination

Semisquare Saturn (ruler of the third house which includes Cuba (and traditional ruler of the chief executive).

1969—6 Virgo 16—Moon Landing

Just past a sextile to Jupiter (ruler of long journeys).

1974—11 Virgo 24—Nixon Resignation

Two years prior, when Watergate took place, the Moon was semisquare Mercury, in the ninth house.

1979—16 Virgo 44—American Hostages in Iran

Solstice point to the natal Sun, which is in the ninth house.

Another interesting fact is to note when the Midheaven and Ascendant change from one sign to another. This clearly marks the ending of one manner of acting/reacting, and the beginning of another. It also helps to explain the divergent epochs in America's history.

Midheaven

1776-1791 (Leo)

Tug of war between the Hamiltonians, who desired a strong central government (Leo Midheaven), and the Jeffersonians, who wanted limited government control and individual states' rights (Aquarius Nadir). During this period, all the original thirteen colonies were admitted to the Union.

1791-1822 (Virgo)

Conflicts with foreigners (square Sagittarius) involving impressment of seamen and piracy (opposition Pisces).

1822-1853 (Libra)

Desire to maintain peace (Monroe Doctrine) and the time of the Missouri Compromise of 1821 and 1850.

1853-1884 (Scorpio)

Necessity to take a stand and to fight, if needed. After the Civil War, a period called Reconstruction took place in the South. Great fortunes in steel, mining, and banking were made.

1884-1913 (Sagittarius)

Periods of labor unrest (square Virgo) and massive foreign immigration (opposition Gemini). This was the time of empire building, when Roosevelt sent the U.S. Navy around the world.

1913-1943 (Capricorn)

Period of awakening and great activity. Also, a period of depressions, both after the Great War and during the 1930s. Social programs instituted, and the government begins to take on a larger role in daily life.

1943-1972 (Aquarius)

Entering into many international organizations such as NATO, SEATO, ANZUS, OAS, etc., formed the United Nations and started to meddle in the foreign affairs of other countries. Also the period of the Civil Rights Movement, Vietnam, and the Space Race. A great period of scientific advancement and individual alienation from society.

1972-2001 (Pisces)

Started with Watergate and the resignation of Nixon. Arab oil embargoes caused havoc for a while, and American embassies became targets for terrorists. Return to religion and spiritualism, plus increased aggravation over illegal aliens (square Sagittarius). Minorities began to come out of the closet and feminism increased.

Ascendant

1776-1805 (Scorpio)

A time of survival against nature and a time of building a strong and united country. Americans just wanted to be left alone to enjoy their new found freedom.

1805-1846 (Sagittarius)

Started with the explorations of Lewis and Clark. Before long, the Santa Fe and Oregon trails were sending settlers west. A time of increased interest in foreign affairs (Monroe Doctrine) and religions persecution (Mormons).

1846-1876 (Capricorn)

A time of strife and turmoil, beginning with the Mexican War, continuing through the Civil War and ending with Reconstruction. The country became stronger during this period and many fortunes increased, while the Southern aristocracy passed away.

1876-1897 (Aquarius)

Begins with the nation's centennial, which introduced many new inventions to the world. During this period Edison was making a name, giving Americans the electric light, phonograph, motion picture camera, plus Bell's new gadget, the telephone. This was the period of the Gay '90s, rife with extravagance (opposition Leo) and excesses (square Scorpio).

1897-1913 (Pisces)

Began by taking responsibility for the former Spanish colonies seized during the war. The period of the Belle Epoque, or the Edwardian Era, a time when glamour reigned. It ended with the sinking of the Titanic (Ascendant conjunct malefic fixed star Scheat at twenty-eight degrees Pisces); America's world would never again be so safe and secure. American naivete and ignorance were soon ended.

1913-1929 (Aries)

America started to take its rightful place in the world arena by entering World War I. The Roaring '20s followed and women were "emancipated" at long last by being given the vote. This violent, but exciting, era ended with the Stock Market Crash.

1929-1950 (Taurus)

Money, or the lack of it, was uppermost in the minds of all Americans during this period. During the Depression, steps were taken not only to employ millions of workers, but to guarantee their security during old age. World War II increased the economy, but another depression followed.

1950-1979 (Gemini)

During this epoch, Americans were on the move. Millions moved from farm to city and from state to state; even the heavens could not contain them. The Vietnam War caused thousands to burn their draft cards (opposition Sagittarius) and drugs soon became a major problem for the nation's youth (square Pisces). Many simply left the rat race behind and returned to the simple life (square Virgo) and began to grow their own food, free of chemicals and pollutants.

1979-2019 (Cancer)

Having just begun, we can already see the signs of a return to family life and patriotism. Children will again become welcome additions as Americans learn to become more socially oriented. Emotions will become more open (some violence, too) and the destiny of the country will occupy center stage. Foreign alliances will be tested (square Libra) and limitation of government will be sought (opposition Capricorn). The only danger I see is that a major war will erupt during this period (square Aries) just like the first time America had a cardinal sign on the Ascendant (Civil War). We might see the end of the single family home and a dwindling of the food supply, as erratic weather patterns play havoc with the crops. Clearly, food, clothing and shelter will be the keywords for the remainder of the century.

I've chosen the most important events in American history to illustrate the workings of the Declaration of Independence chart.

Please note: All of the following charts in this section are progressions from the Declaration of Independence chart shown earlier.

Revolutionary War Ends

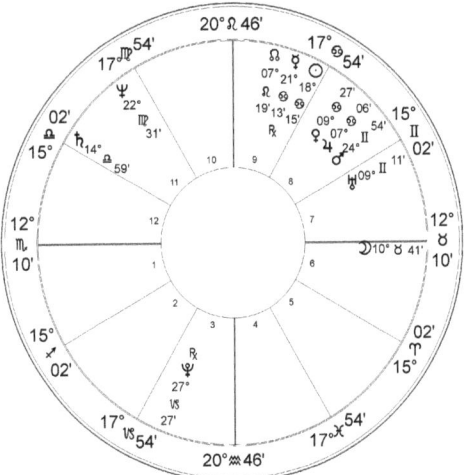

October 19, 1781

Americans had been fighting the British to win their independence ever since the first shot was fired at Lexington and Concord six and a half years earlier. With the aid of the French under the Marquis de Lafayette, the head of the British army, Lord Cornwallis, was trapped at Yorktown, Virginia and forced to surrender to General George Washington. Freedom for the United States is shown by Venus and Jupiter trining the natal Ascendant along with the Midheaven sextiling natal Mars. Two years later, with the signing of the Treaty of Paris, the American Revolution was officially over as the Ascendant trined the U.S. natal Sun, ruler of the national Midheaven.

Signing of the Constitution

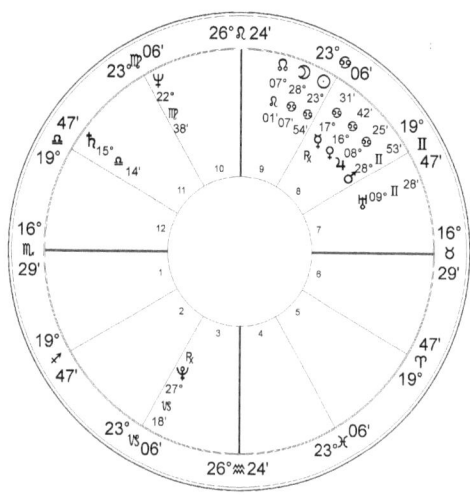

September 17, 1787

A convention was held in Philadelphia in May 1787 under a progressed new Moon to frame a Constitution for the new nation. The old Articles of Confederation had become outdated and gave too much autonomy to the individual colonies. Opposition arose between the Jeffersonians, who desired limited government, and the Hamiltonians, who wished for a strong central authority. After four months of heated debate, the document was finally agreed upon and signed as the Moon opposed natal Pluto and the Sun was sitting on top of natal Mercury. Many wondered if the states would ratify this document, but when New Hampshire fixed its seal of approval in June 1788, the Constitution was the law of the land. Jupiter was about to trine the natal Ascendant and the progressed Ascendant was trining progressed Venus, ruler of the seventh house of agreements.

The Bill of Rights

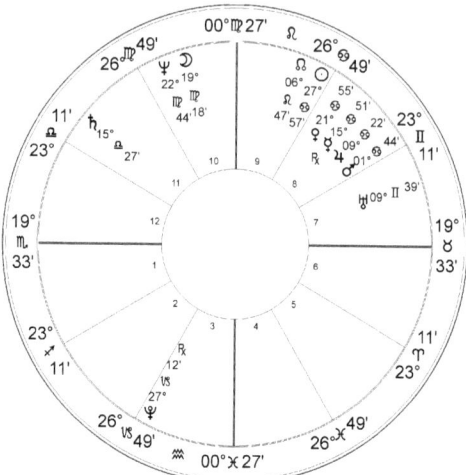

December 15, 1791

In the months after the Constitution was signed, most delegates expressed concern that a Bill of Rights should be inserted to protect the liberties of all Americans. Most who signed the Constitution did so only on the proviso that a Bill of Rights would be forthcoming. The first ten amendments to the oldest continuous body of law in the world came into force as the Sun opposed Pluto and the Moon sextiled the progressed Ascendant. This Bill of Rights would insure protection against undue governmental interference as shown by the Midheaven semisquaring Saturn, ruler of all things relating to authority.

Louisiana Purchase

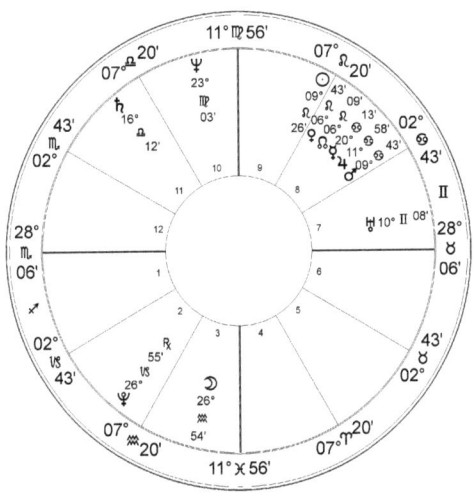

December 20, 1803

To expand his empire in Europe, Napoleon needed cash to finance his armies. When President Jefferson heard of Napoleon's dilemma, he sent emissaries to buy New Orleans, but when Napoleon threw in the entire region of Louisiana, America agreed to the opportunity to double the size of the fledgling nation. America paid $15 million for the region which stretched from the Mississippi to the Rockies, about three cents an acre. The ruler of the natal fourth house, which governs territorial acquisitions (Uranus), was being sextiled by the Sun, ruler of the Midheaven. Saturn, ruler of the third house, was sextile the natal Midheaven and the Sun was squaring the natal Ascendant. The Moon had returned to its own place in the natal fourth house and the Ascendant was sextile Pluto, natally in the third house, which governs neighboring territories or countries.

The Embargo Act

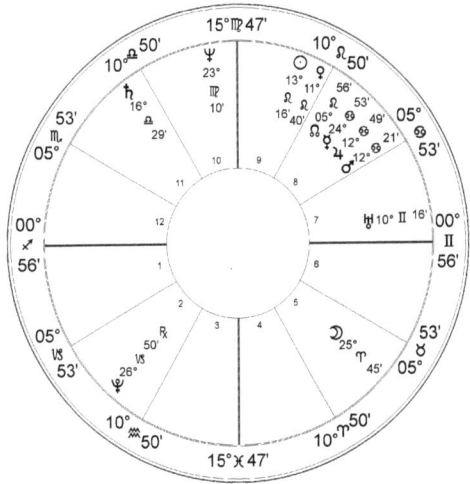

December 22, 1807

Due to Britain's continuing conflict with France, American seamen were being kidnaped to man English frigates. To put pressure on European countries, America cut off trade with all foreign nations and no American ship was allowed to unload its cargo in a foreign port. The law was disastrous for Americans as dock workers, sailors and merchants went broke. During the fourteen month embargo, America lost $16 million in customs revenues. The Moon was squaring Mercury in the natal ninth house, indicating the impact on trade and commerce, doubly so as the Moon also squared Pluto, ruler of the natal Ascendant. The Ascendant was semisquare Saturn, which governs restrictions. American determination to stop piracy on the high seas also was shown by Mars and Jupiter about to cross the natal Sun, but tensions between the U.S. and Great Britain remained strained.

The War of 1812

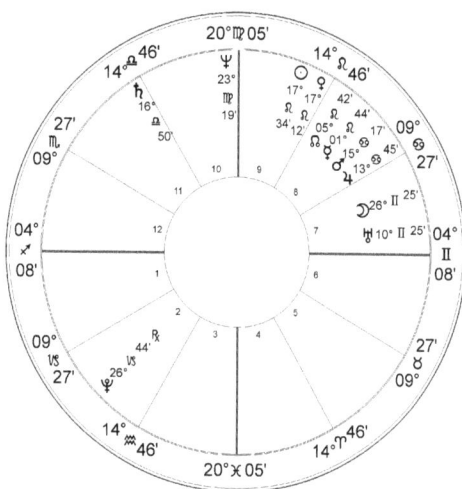

June 16, 1812

As Britain continued to ignore American demands to stop hijacking American ships and kidnaping seamen, conflict again erupted with the "mother country." Britain also was arming Indian tribes on the western frontier. Madison's first objective was to take Canada and Americans did fight in that country but failed to gain a foothold. The British retaliated by burning many public buildings in Washington, D.C. and then marched north to capture Fort McHenry in Baltimore harbor. Witnessing the fight was a lawyer named Francis Scott Key, who wrote the words to the Star Spangled Banner, which in 1931 became the U.S. national anthem. When the ``Second American Revolution'' began, the Moon was trine its natal position at the same time that Venus, ruler of the seventh house of war, was crossing the natal Midheaven. The U.S. won this war as Jupiter was crossing the natal Sun at the same time that the Midheaven was squaring natal Mars, traditional ruler of conflict.

Spain Cedes Florida

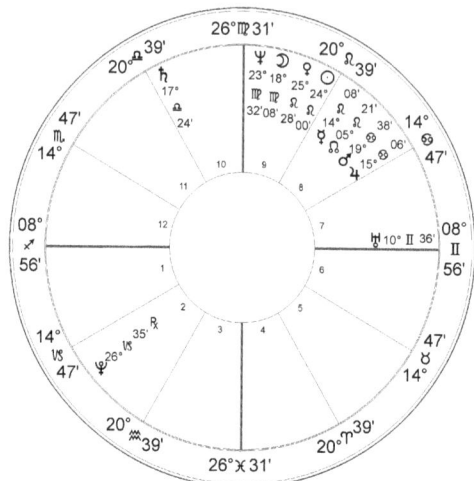

February 22, 1819

The only region east of the Mississippi that didn't belong to the United States was called East and West Florida, which stretched along the Gulf of Mexico from New Orleans to the Atlantic coast. Spain finally decided to sell this region for $15 million as the Ascendant opposed natal Uranus, ruler of the natal fourth house of territory. No money, however, was ever paid directly to Spain as American lawmakers thought it wiser to reimburse the settlers instead. The Midheaven was trining Pluto and Venus was opposing the natal Moon, aspects involving rulers of the natal Ascendant, Descendant and ninth house. Before long, settlement escalated in Florida despite continued skirmishes from Indian tribes.

Shortly afterward, America experienced its first major financial crisis, which was caused when the Bank of the United States tightened credit and demanded repayment of loans made to state banks to be made in specie (gold or silver) instead of paper money which was being overprinted, thus threatening massive inflation and national bankruptcy. Note: Ascendant opposition Uranus (natally in eighth house of debt and credit).

The Monroe Doctrine

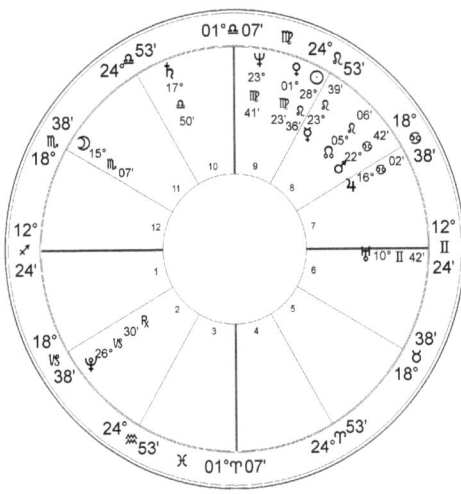

December 2, 1823

President Monroe was concerned that Spain might attempt to recapture its former colonies in Latin America and that Russia also might extend its claims from Alaska to include the Oregon Territory. The Monroe Doctrine warned all European powers against intervening in the western hemisphere—the Americas were not to be considered as regions for future colonization. This foreign policy would endure for another century. The Sun at this time was semisquare its natal position and the Moon was squaring the natal Midheaven, two obvious points of aggravation and irritation. The doctrine, however, was a message of peace as shown by the Moon trine natal Sun and Venus sextile its own place. The desire to avoid conflict was shown by Mercury, ruler of the eleventh house of objectives and ambitions, sextile Mars at the same time that Neptune, natally in the eleventh house, was sextiling natal Mercury, ruler of that house.

Erie Canal Opens

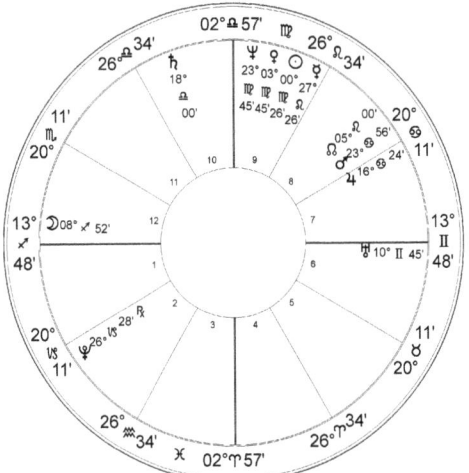

October 26, 1825

For generations, Americans had dreamed of a waterway connecting the eastern seaboard to the Great Lakes. In 1817, New York State agreed to finance a canal as progressed Venus sextiled its own position. Eight years later and $7 million in debt, the canal was finally completed. New York realized a hefty profit of $115 million in tolls over the years and the Erie Canal gave impetus to westward expansion into the Midwest, shown by Mars about to conjunct natal Mercury, the planet which rules trade and commerce. The Moon also was opposing natal Uranus, ruler of the fourth house of territorial expansion.

Indian Removal Act

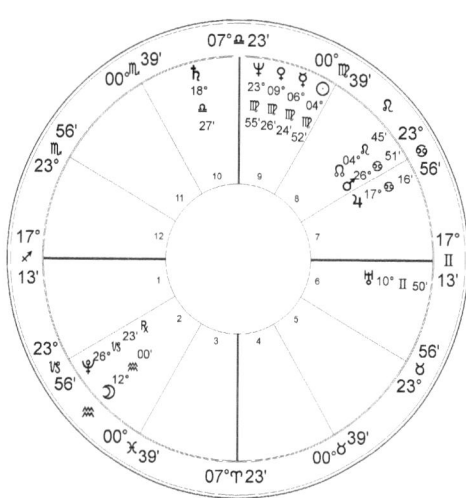

May 28, 1830

To insure more free land for white settlement east of the Mississippi, all Indian tribes were ordered removed to the Great Plains. This highly unjust elimination of native tribes from their homeland was accomplished under Mars opposing natal Pluto. Mars also was inconjunct the natal Moon in the fourth house. The migration didn't really begin in earnest until the late 1830s when gold was discovered in Georgia. More than 15,000 Cherokees were moved out of Georgia alone and twenty-five percent died before they reached their new home. Most tribes lived out their lives in abject poverty, shown by the Ascendant sextiling progressed Saturn, natally in the U.S. twelfth house of self-undoing. I'm sure this hideous action seemed like a good idea at the time as Mercury was sextile natal Jupiter and the Midheaven was trine natal Uranus.

Nullification Proclamation

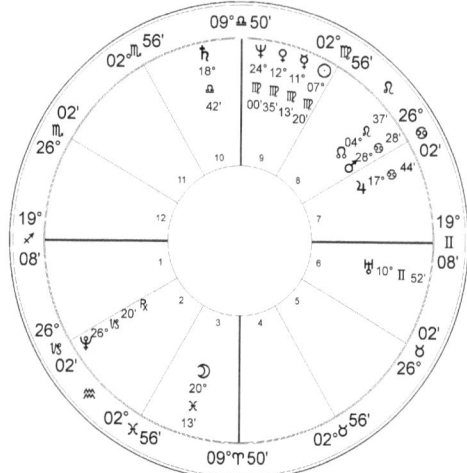

December 10, 1832

Many southern states believed they had the right to protest any law passed by Congress in Washington, so when the abominable tariffs of 1828 and 1832 were enacted, some states threatened secession. John Calhoun of South Carolina warned that any attempt by the federal government to force his state to abide by those tariffs would result in violence as Mars opposed natal Pluto. President Jackson's edict involving the tariffs put an end to talk of secession as the Sun sextiled the natal Ascendant, thus preserving the Union for another twenty-eight years. The unpopularity of the tariffs is shown by the Moon squaring the progressed Ascendant, but rebellion was averted as the Midheaven trined Uranus.

Fall of the Alamo

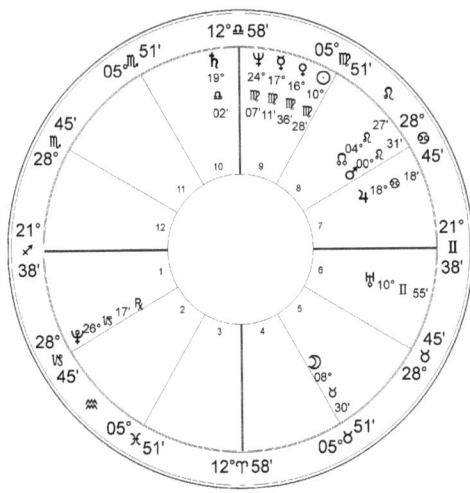

March 6, 1836

In the winter of 1836, Texans became disgruntled with their Mexican overlords and desired complete and total freedom. To quell the impending crisis, Mexico sent General Santa Anna to San Antonio to put down a possible uprising with 5,000 soldiers. After a twelve day siege, all 150 men inside the Alamo were killed, including Davy Crockett, Jim Bowie and Colonel Travis. The Midheaven at this time was squaring the U.S. natal Sun and the Ascendant was opposing natal Mars. The Moon had just crossed the U.S. Descendant and six weeks later, Sam Houston met Santa Anna on a battlefield outside present day Houston and secured the independence of Texas. Before long, Texans applied for U.S. statehood, but northerners opposed the annexation as it would add another slave state to the Union.

The Panic of 1837

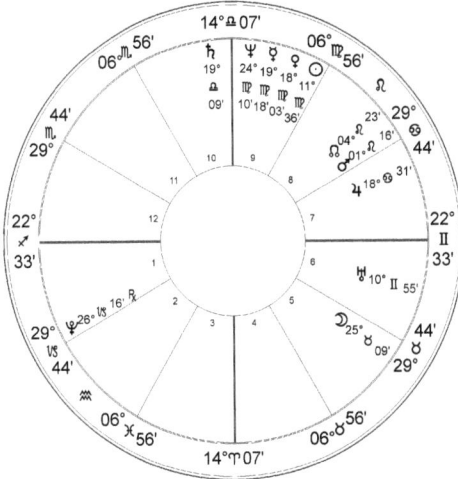

May 10, 1837

The second major financial panic in the nation's history (the first was in 1819) occurred after years of Americans speculating in public lands. Banks suspended converting paper money into gold and silver as the Moon trined Pluto, ruler of the natal Ascendant, and Neptune, ruler of the fifth house of speculation and gambling. The crisis lasted for six years, shown by the Midheaven approaching natal and progressed Saturn, which governs depressions and slowdowns.

Mexican War

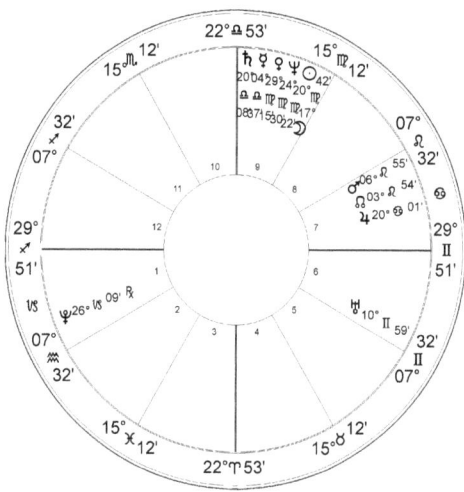

May 13, 1846

Six months after Texas became a state, a border dispute erupted between the Mexicans, who stated the boundary was at the Neuces River, and the Americans, who felt the Rio Grande was the boundary. To grab even more land for the U.S., President Polk sent in Generals Zachary Taylor and Winfield Scott to push back the Mexicans. About the same time, Fremont captured several forts in California from the Mexicans. It was the era of "Manifest Destiny," which held that America had the right to rule everything from the Atlantic to the Pacific. Note that Venus, ruler of the seventh house of war, was semisquaring the natal Midheaven and Mars was approaching a square to the natal Ascendant. Both aspects became exact by the time the Treaty of Guadelupe Hidalgo was signed in February 1848 ceding all lands west of the Louisiana Purchase and south of the forty-second parallel to the United States. The Midheaven was sesquare natal Uranus, ruler of the natal fourth house of territorial acquisitions, and the U.S. paid Mexico $15 million for its lost territory. Ironically, one month after the Mexican War began under nefarious aspects of the Sun conjunct natal Neptune and square Mars, the Oregon boundary question also was settled in America's favor.

Gold Discovered in California

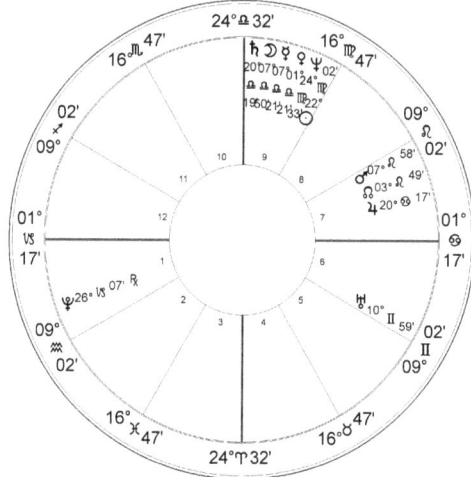

January 24, 1848

When gold was discovered by an employee of John Sutter on land in the foothills of the Sierra Nevada outside Sacramento, the greatest migration the country had known up to that time ensued as thousands pulled up stakes and headed for the promised land to seek their fortune. Mars sitting on top of the natal North Node in Leo (gold) and the Sun (gold) squaring natal Mars brought the '49ers across the plains, mountains, and deserts. The Sun also was conjunct natal Neptune, the ruler of the U.S. natal fifth house of speculation, prospecting and gambling. The Moon conjunct Mercury and trine natal Uranus brought so many settlers to the west coast that California was admitted as a state only two years later. Few found their fortune, but most decided to remain in California, beguiled as they were by its beauty and potential agricultural abundance.

Compromise of 1850

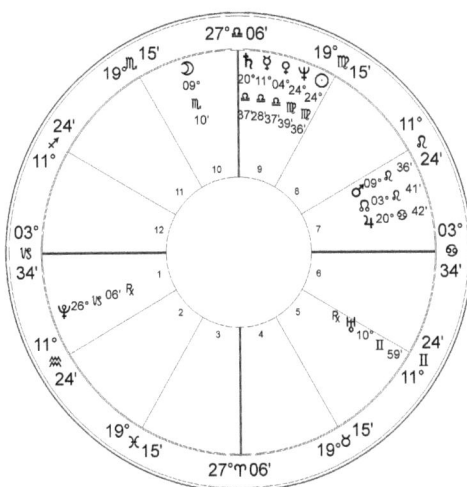

September 9, 1850

This act was Henry Clay's final attempt to resolve the issue of slavery. The compromise admitted California as a free state (even though a good portion lay below the dividing line of thirty-six and a half degrees north) and created the Utah and New Mexico territories without deciding the issue of slavery within their boundaries. This act also included the Fugitive Slave Act, which required the federal government to take an active role in returning runaway slaves to their masters, shown by the Sun conjunct progressed Neptune, the planet that has traditionally ruled slavery. Most states chose to ignore this part of the compromise as they passed liberty laws to protect slaves within their borders. Fugitives also were denied the right to a trial or to defend themselves at a hearing. The Midheaven about to square natal Pluto signified this coercion and force by those in Washington. The Ascendant was opposing natal Venus, ruler of the natal U.S. seventh and twelfth houses. Another seed was sown which would one day erupt in a civil war as Mars was squaring the natal Ascendant over which the Moon had just crossed.

The Gadsden Purchase

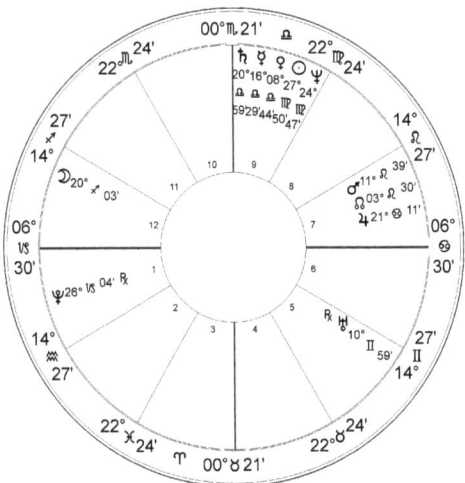

December 30, 1853

After the Mexican War, the northern boundary of that country was in dispute. Engineers desired to build a railroad through the region south of the Gila River in Arizona, so the U.S. purchased this narrow strip of land for $10 million from Mexico as the Sun trined natal Pluto in the third house of neighboring countries. The Ascendant also was opposing natal Jupiter, which governs expansion.

Six months later, the Kansas-Nebraska Act repealed the Missouri Compromise and permitted settlers in that region to decide for themselves whether they wanted to permit slavery or not. This gave birth to "Bleeding Kansas" and the Republican Party two years later.

Dred Scott Decision

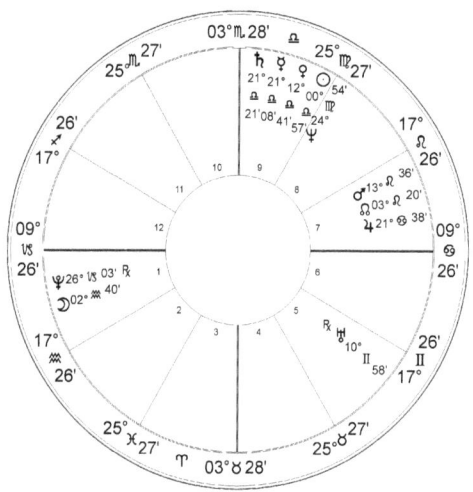

March 6, 1857

Dred Scott was a slave who had sued for his freedom and won, but the decision was later reversed by a higher court. The Supreme Court, under Justice Roger Taney, refused to hear the case, stating that since Scott was a slave, he could not sue as he was not a citizen of either Missouri or the United States. This decision declared the Missouri Compromise unconstitutional, thus making slavery legal in any state that wished to adopt it. The U.S. Sun was semisquare the natal Midheaven and the Ascendant was approaching a semisquare to the natal Moon, ruler of the ninth house of law.

Six months later, on September 15, 1857, the third financial crisis in the nation's history occurred. It was called the Panic of 1857 and was caused by rapid overexpansion of the railroads, flimsy banking laws and a drop in the price of gold, which caused a run on banks. The Moon at 10 Aquarius was trine progressed Uranus, ruler of the progressed second house of finance and banks.

The Civil War

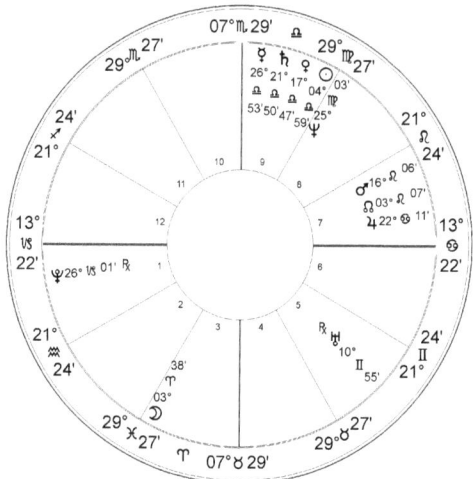

April 12, 1861

South Carolina seceded from the Union on December 20, 1860 and six weeks later, the Confederacy was born in Montgomery, Alabama. At the moment federal troops fired on Fort Sumter in Charleston harbor, the Moon was square natal Venus, ruler of the seventh house of war, and the Sun was square Jupiter, ruler of the second house of economic interests and assets, which included slaves. Mars was crossing the natal Midheaven at the same time transiting Pluto was crossing the natal Descendant. The Ascendant was in opposition to the natal Sun, which threatened our national survival and before long it would square natal Saturn, ruler of governmental authority. One should also note that the Midheaven was about to cross the same degree as the natal Ascendant, which also squares the Nodes, indicating this fated and karmic conflict due to the issue of slavery which had festered in the U.S. for two and a half centuries. The Civil War was the bloodiest conflict the nation has ever endured: more than 365,000 Union soldiers were killed and 282,000 were wounded. No tally has ever been made on the Confederate side. The South would remain under military rule for twelve years after the Civil War during a period called Reconstruction, an apt term for a period in U.S. history when Scorpio was on the progressed Midheaven.

Slavery Abolished

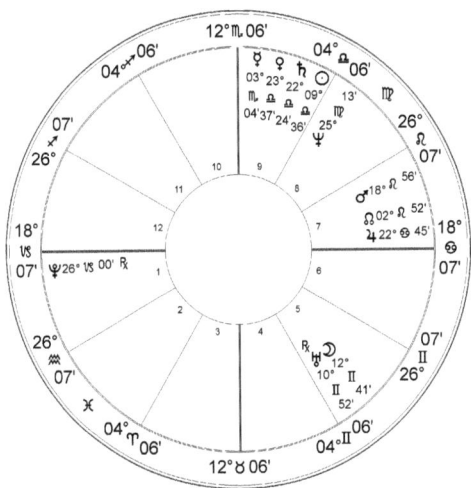

December 18, 1865

When President Lincoln freed the slaves by signing the Emancipation Proclamation in 1863, he freed only those slaves in regions rebelling against the United States. Slaves living in border states like Delaware, Maryland, Kentucky and Missouri had to wait until the Thirteenth Amendment to the Constitution became law eight months after the Civil War ended and Lincoln was assassinated. Slavery was abolished under the Moon inconjunct the Midheaven at the same time it sesquared natal Pluto. Theoretically, Negroes had the same rights and liberties as their white brethren, but within a year, many secret organizations, like the Ku Klux Klan, emerged to stem advances made by Negroes, shown by the Ascendant inconjunct progressed Mars.

Purchase of Alaska

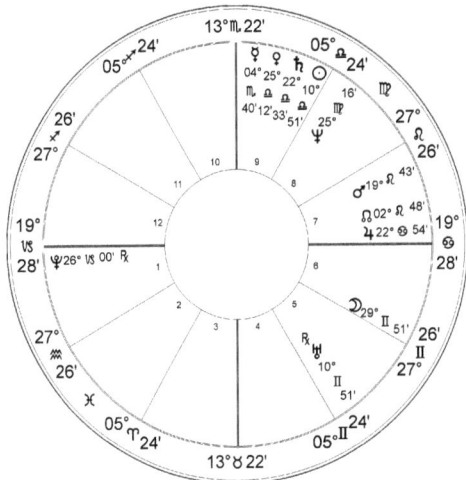

March 30, 1867

With the fur trade no longer vitally important to the Russians, emissaries of the Czar decided to sell Alaska to recuperate losses incurred during the Crimean War. America bought the region for $7.2 million, about two cents an acre, as the Midheaven trined the natal Sun and Venus squared natal Mercury and progressed Pluto. Despite the bargain, many felt Alaska was a frozen wasteland and called it ``Seward's Folly'' after the man who negotiated the deal. Residents of Alaska were given three years to decide whether to remain in the territory as Americans or to return to Russia and retain their original citizenship.

Transcontinental Railroad

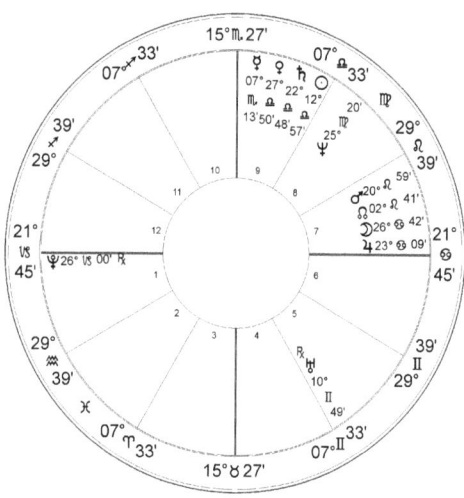

May 10, 1869

In 1863, President Lincoln signed a bill creating the Union Pacific Railroad, which would merge with the already established Central Pacific Railroad, thus creating the world's first transcontinental rail system. Construction began simultaneously in Omaha and Oakland, each crew working frantically to outdo the other. At a place called Promontory Point in Utah, the two railroads met and the "golden spike" was driven, thus uniting the country from coast to coast as the Ascendant was trining natal Neptune at the same time it was inconjunct natal Mars, ruler of steel. The Moon opposing Pluto laid the groundwork for increased Indian troubles as settlers demanded more and more land for ranching and farming.

The Panic of 1873

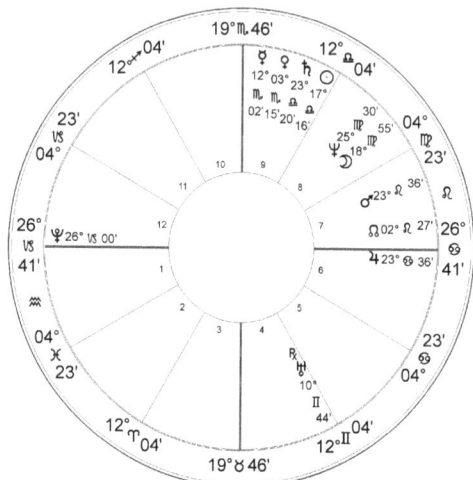

September 19, 1873

Due to rapid business expansion during Reconstruction, which produced massive inflation and the enormous debt incurred during the Civil War, the financial picture at the beginning of Grant's second term looked ominous. Adding insult to injury, the Chicago fire two years earlier severely depressed the insurance industry, so when Jay Cooke's banking empire failed, it precipitated a depression that lasted for five years, causing five million to become unemployed and business failures totaling more than $500 million. The Ascendant conjunct Pluto, ruler of wealth, occurred at the same time Saturn was squaring natal Mercury, ruler of trade and commerce. Jupiter also was beginning a long conjunction to natal Mercury. The government wanted to print more currency, but Grant refused to sign the bill as Venus trined its natal position.

Custer's Last Stand

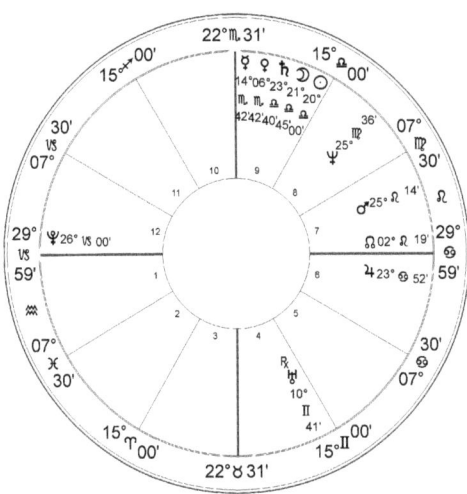

June 25, 1876

Nine days before America was to celebrate its centennial, the largest massing of Indian tribes in history took place on the plains of eastern Montana at a site called Little Bighorn. General Custer seriously misjudged the strength of Sitting Bull and his allies who wiped out the entire regiment as Venus, ruler of the natal seventh house of war, squared the natal Nodes. Venus, one must remember, also is ruler of the U.S. twelfth house of self-undoing, and when connected to the Nodes, the event is karmic, due to the repeated bad treatment of the Indians. The Moon trine natal Mars made the West safer for white settlement, especially in the Black Hills where gold had recently been discovered. Clearly, the Indians had reached the end of their rope, shown by the last degree of Capricorn on the Ascendant. That degree also sesquares the Mars/Uranus midpoint in the U.S. chart.

The Pendleton Act

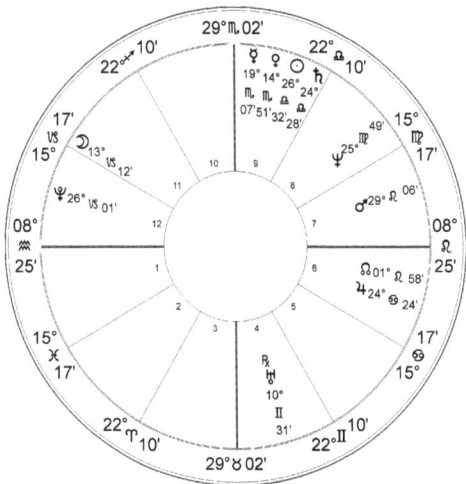

January 16, 1883

When President Garfield was assassinated in late 1881 by a disgruntled office seeker, the Midheaven was sextile Pluto and the Ascendant sesquare natal Mars, ruler of the sixth house of government employees. The time was ripe for reforming the civil service, which was still run on lines set up under Jackson's administration, called the Spoils System. No longer would appointments be made according to party affiliation; future applicants would be judged solely on their abilities. The Sun trine natal Moon and the Moon opposing natal Sun changed the federal workforce forever.

Panic of 1893

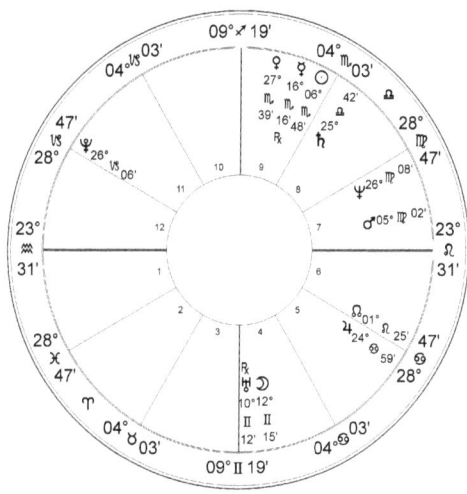

May 4, 1893

The fifth major financial crisis in U.S. history was touched off by the failure of the Philadelphia & Reading Railroad three months earlier and also by the Silver Purchase Act which forced the government to purchase that metal at market prices, thus seriously undermining the prevailing gold standard. When the bottom fell out of the market, more than four million workers became unemployed. Europe also was caught in this slump. The Moon, which rules silver, was sesquare natal Pluto, having just crossed Uranus. Saturn was squaring Jupiter and Pluto, one ruler of the natal Ascendant, the other ruling the U.S. second house of wealth. More than 15,000 businesses failed, including one-fourth of the nation's railroads. The ensuing four year depression put a serious damper on the supposedly Gay Nineties.

Spanish-American War

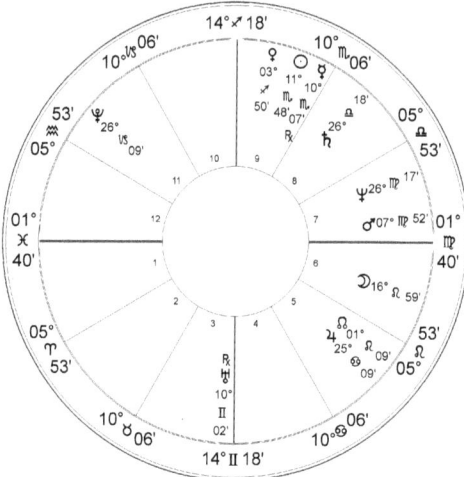

April 24, 1898

Americans were sympathetic towards Cubans seeking independence from Spain. After the U.S. battleship Maine was mysteriously blown up in Havana harbor in February, William Randolph Hearst whipped up the flames for war. The Moon was conjunct the natal Midheaven and Mars was sextile the natal Ascendant, indicative of the short duration of this conflict. Within a few months, Dewey had captured the Philippines and Roosevelt had ousted the Spanish from Cuba. The Ascendant approaching a trine to natal Venus, ruler of the seventh house of war, made it that much easier to grab the Philippines and Cuba along with Guam and Puerto Rico. Cuba remained under U.S. military occupation until 1902 when it was granted independence and the Philippines got their freedom in 1946. Puerto Rico remains a U.S. Commonwealth, while Guam is a self-governing territory.

Panama Canal Treaty

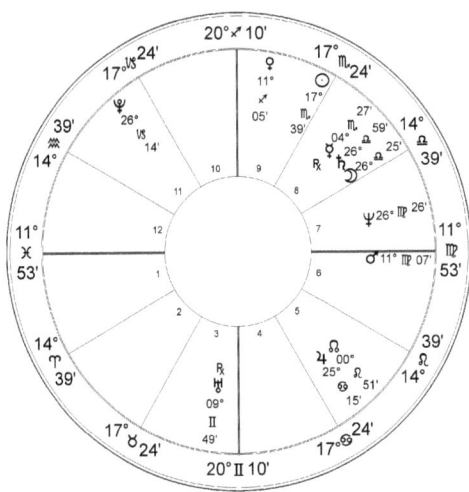

February 23, 1904

Ever since Balboa discovered the Pacific Ocean, men had dreamed of a canal connecting the Atlantic and Pacific Oceans. Several concessions were granted by Colombia over the years, but all attempts failed. The U.S. originally desired a sea level canal through Nicaragua, but when geological studies deemed this unwise, America set its sights on Panama. With American aid and approval, Panama declared its independence from Colombia in November 1903 under Jupiter conjuncting natal Mercury, which also opposed Pluto. To compensate Colombia, the U.S. agreed to pay $10 million as the Moon was conjunct Saturn and square Jupiter and Pluto. But before the canal could be constructed, yellow fever and malaria had to be wiped out, shown by Mars, ruler of the natal sixth house, sesquare Pluto. The Ascendant was sesquare natal Pluto as well. The Panama Canal was the largest engineering project ever undertaken and was completed in 1914 at a cost of $380 million. Amid considerable controversy, the Panama Canal Zone was returned to Panama in 1979 when the U.S. Midheaven was squaring Uranus, ruler of the natal fourth house.

Income Tax

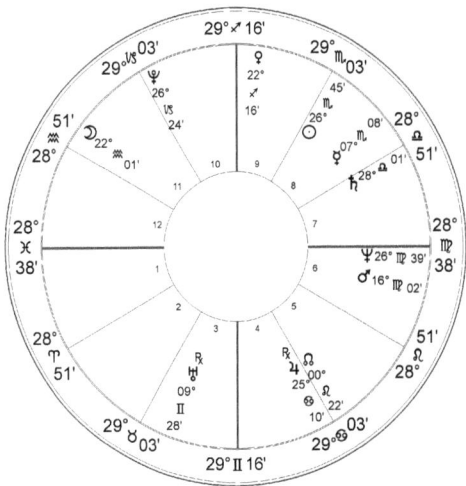

March 1, 1913

According to the Constitution, taxes could be levied only in proportion to the population, not the aggregate income. The Sixteenth Amendment changed that forever as the Ascendant sextiled natal Pluto, nominal ruler of all eighth house matters like taxes. The Ascendant also was inconjunct Saturn on the cusp of that house. Even though the first tax was only one percent of wages, it was extremely unpopular and some tried to avoid it altogether—shown by Venus opposing natal Mars, which occupied the natal eighth house.

In December 1913, the Federal Reserve system was established whereby twelve regional banks were set up by the government to act as regional centers so the "Fed" could control credit as well as the money supply, which determined the interest rate. The Sun sextile natal Pluto enabled the government to supposedly eliminate the wild business fluctuations of the past.

World War I

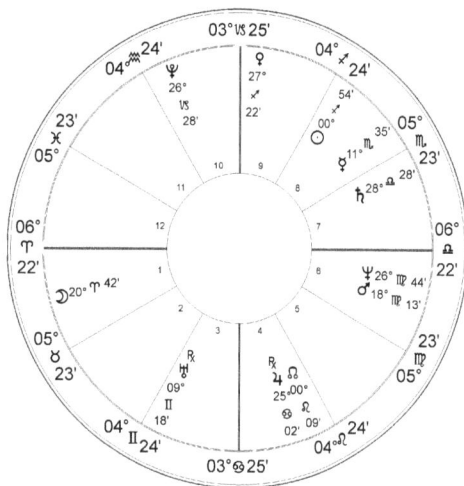

April 6, 1917

Prohibition

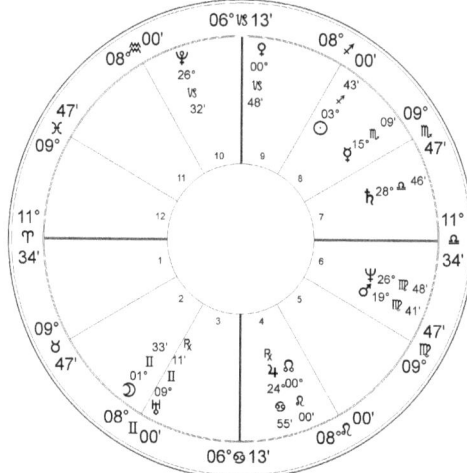

January 16, 1920

For years, Germany had designs on expanding its empire, so when the Austrian Archduke Franz Ferdinand was assassinated in Sarajevo in late June 1914, Germany entered the fray. This precipitated the largest worldwide conflict in history. Despite horrible losses on the battlefields of Europe, America was determined to stay neutral, even after German subs sank the Lusitania in May 1915. But as America now had Aries on the Ascendant, it could no longer remain isolated and sit on the sidelines while Germany laid waste to much of Europe. President Wilson declared war as Venus, ruler of the seventh house of warfare, passed a sextile to natal Moon and was approaching a sextile to Saturn. The Midheaven was opposing natal Venus, as well. American doughboys were sent into battle with all banners flying high—shown by the Ascendant squaring natal Jupiter, the planet of optimism. Most thought the war would be over by Christmas, but reality soon set in and thousands lay dead in the trenches. The armistice was signed on November 11, 1918 and two months later, President Wilson journeyed to Paris to sign the Treaty of Versailles. The League of Nations was founded to arbitrate any future international conflicts, but he U.S. Senate refused to ratify, thus taking America back into self-imposed isolation, so typical of a nation with natal Scorpio on the Ascendant.

For decades, organizations such as the WCTU and the Anti-Saloon League had attempted to ban the sale and manufacture of alcoholic substances. But after World War I, thirty-one states were dry, so a movement to make the entire country dry was enacted. The amendment, known as the Volstead Act, came into force in January 1920 and ushered in one of the most crime ridden periods in U.S. history. With the Ascendant sextiling Uranus and the Midheaven opposing natal Jupiter, it sounded like a good idea at the time. The law was largely ignored in big cities where speakeasies sprang up and gangsters stepped in to fill the supply and demand for booze. Rum running from Canada and the Caribbean became commonplace as Mercury, ruler of trade and commerce, squared the natal Midheaven.

In August 1920, another amendment to the Constitution gave women the right to vote—shown by Venus sesquare the natal Midheaven and the Sun inconjunct natal Venus.

Stock Market Crash

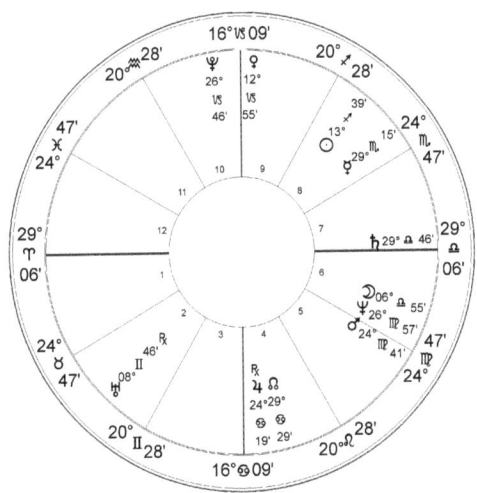

October 29, 1929

Beginning in late 1928, business began to slow down as did consumer spending. Americans had been living it up during the Roaring '20s far beyond their means; stocks were purchased on margin, so the prosperity Americans felt was an illusion. With the final degree of Aries on the Ascendant opposing Saturn, the New York Stock Market crashed and more than 16 million shares went down the drain. The Dow Jones average, which had peaked at 381 shortly before the Depression, began a three year slide to bottom out at forty-one shortly before Roosevelt took office. The Sun, which governs all forms of speculation and gambling, was inconjunct its own position, indicating a major adjustment and alteration had to be made with concomitant sacrifices. The Moon was squaring natal Jupiter, ruling the U.S. natal second house of wealth at the same time that Venus, ruler of finance in general, was opposing natal Sun. Before long, the entire planet was engulfed in the worst economic depression in history. The Ascendant opposing Saturn indicated a time of depression, sadness and suicide. The bottom was reached in mid-1933 when more than twelve million were unemployed, about twenty-five percent of the population. A quarter of the banks failed and farm prices fell more than thirty percent during the first two years of the Depression. Adding insult to injury, severe weather disturbances, such as dust storms and severe flooding, ravaged a large portion of the country as well.

The New Deal

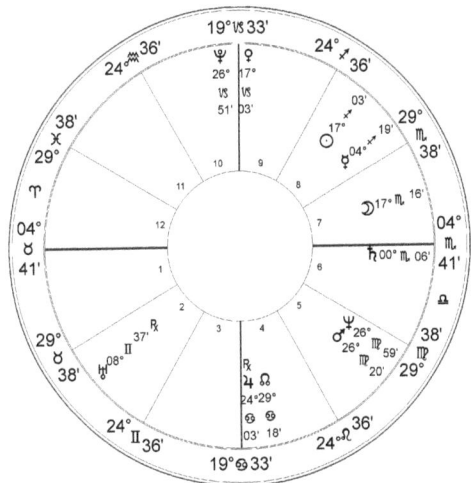

March 4, 1933

In the midst of the worst time in U.S. history, America began to see light at the end of the tunnel when Franklin D. Roosevelt was elected to the presidency. In his first 100 days in office, more legislation was passed than at any time in U.S. history as Mars trined natal Pluto; thus, the ruler of the U.S. natal sixth house was in good aspect to the ruler of the natal Ascendant. Roosevelt was extremely popular as shown by the Sun just past a trine to natal Midheaven; in many ways, it was a marriage made in heaven. One of Roosevelt's first acts was to declare a bank holiday as accountants were sent in to audit the books. FDR then founded the FDIC and called in all outstanding gold, taking the country off the gold standard. America began to pull itself up as Venus was inconjunct the natal Midheaven and the Ascendant sextiled that same planet. One also should note that the Ascendant was about to sextile natal Jupiter, ruler of the second house, for confirmation of the economic resurgence at this time. Roosevelt founded the CCC, which hired more than three million people to build roads, plant trees and work on conservation projects. The TVA was founded to harness waters of the Tennessee River and supply electricity to impoverished regions of the South. The SEC was formed to correct abuses which led to the stock market crash, and the NHA aided the housing industry and the WPA built everything from public buildings to highways and bridges. The NRA created the WPA to provide grants to states for construction projects.

Social Security Act	Wages and Hours Act
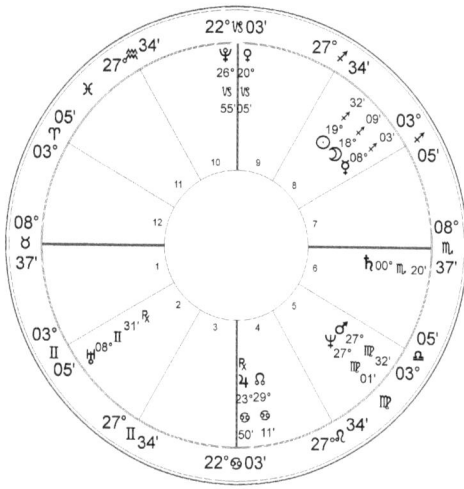	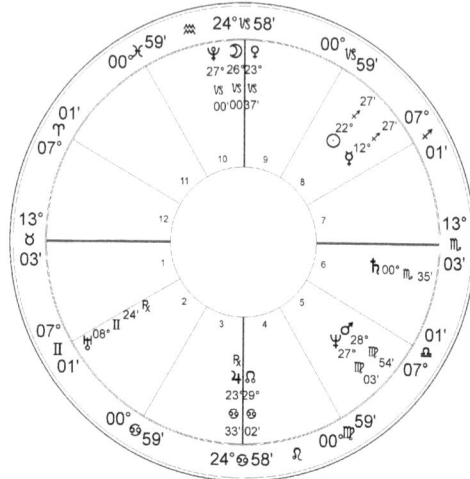
August 14, 1935	**June 25, 1938**

This legislation insured an income for retired individuals as well as unemployment compensation for those out of work. The largesse of this act is shown by Mars conjunct Neptune, the planets which rule the natal sixth house and the nominal twelfth house. Mars, natally in the eighth house of debts, and Neptune were trine Pluto and the Midheaven. Most American workers are forced to take Social Security (FICA) as a payroll deduction, the worker's contribution being matched by the employer. Mercury opposing natal Uranus indicated the largely humanitarian bent of this legislation, while the Ascendant opposing its natal degree indicated the flip-flop in lifestyle. Many felt the U.S. was becoming a welfare state, fostering a system which would one day bankrupt the country.

This law finally granted workers a minimum wage and protected them against long hours without overtime pay. The Midheaven opposing natal Mercury, ruler of employment, and the Moon conjunct Pluto illustrated how this act created America's middle class. The Ascendant sextile natal Sun again pointed to the government's role in shaping the lives of Americans. Yet the minimum wage has failed to keep pace with the cost of living. When this law was first enacted, the set wage was fifty cents per hour; the current rate is $4.25 per hour. But the cost of living has gone up twenty-fold while the minimum wage has increased only tenfold. In order for this inequity to be resolved, the minimum wage would have to increased to $10 per hour in order for current workers to enjoy the same benefits and advantages held by their forefathers.

World War II

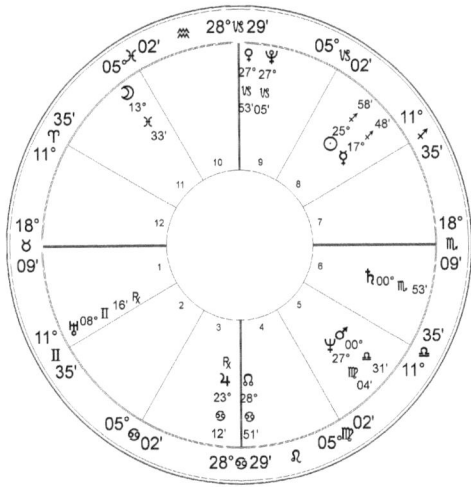

December 7, 1941

Atomic Bomb Test

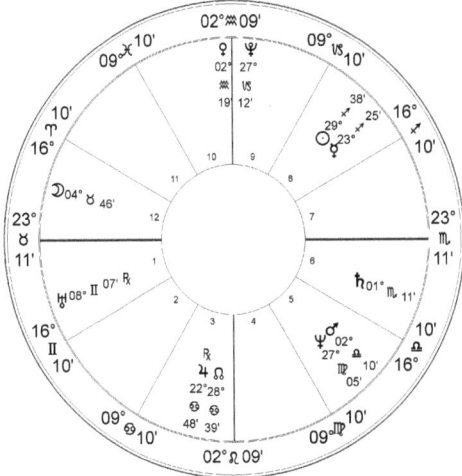

July 16, 1945

When Hitler invaded Poland in late 1939, the progressed Midheaven was within orb to Pluto. At first, America tried to stay out of the conflict, just as it had initially done in World War I. But with Britain reeling under Nazi air raids and its shipping lanes blockaded, Roosevelt agreed to a Lend-Lease program which cost $50 billion. Roosevelt wanted to create an incident whereby America could enter the war and that event occurred when the Japanese bombed Pearl Harbor on the island of Oahu in Hawaii in December 1941. The Sun was sextile the natal Moon at the same time the Moon was trine the U.S. natal Sun. Venus, ruler of the seventh house of war, was conjunct natal Pluto, ruler of the natal Ascendant. America went to war on two fronts—one in Europe and the other in the Far East. During the early years of the war, transiting Pluto was squaring the natal Ascendant, indicating the enormous loss of life for Americans. The first battles were fought in the Pacific but the U.S. did not assault the Nazis until troops landed in North Africa in November 1942. By January 1944, U.S. troops had landed in southern Italy and by June, the massive D-Day invasion began to drive the Germans back to their homeland. Germany finally surrendered in May 1945, a week after Hitler committed suicide.

In late 1942 two years after the progressed Midheaven conjuncted natal Pluto, the first atomic chain reaction took place in Chicago. Research for an atomic bomb was conducted in Los Alamos, New Mexico under strict secrecy as the Germans also were trying to develop a similar weapon. The first detonation took place two months after the war in Europe ended in mid-July 1945 and three weeks later, "Fat Man" and "Little Boy" (as the bombs were called) were dropped on Hiroshima and Nagasaki, Japan. Mars trine the Midheaven and Venus conjunct the Midheaven brought an end to the bloodiest conflict the world has ever known. The Moon sextile natal Jupiter brought victory and the Ascendant sextile Neptune made the U.S. a charter member of the United Nations. Remember that Neptune sits in the U.S. natal eleventh house. World War II had cost 292,000 Americans their lives and 672,000 others were on the casualty list.

The Marshall Plan

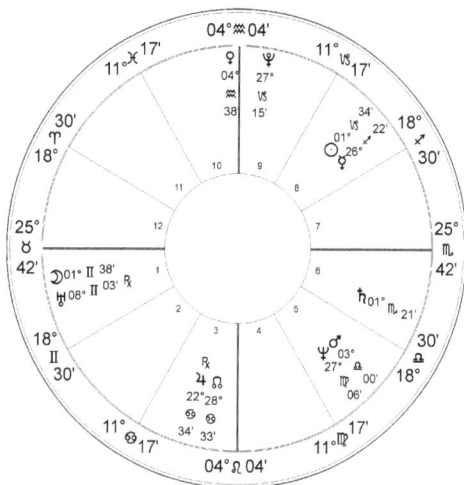

June 5, 1947

As America's Sun entered Capricorn, we assumed responsibility for cleaning up the mess caused by six years of war in Europe. Relief was sent in the form of food, machinery and technology to rebuild the war torn continent as Jupiter trined natal Neptune, the planet of relief operations. Mercury also was sextile the U.S. natal Moon, one ruling the ninth house and the other occupying that house in the natal chart. Venus conjunct the Midheaven at the same time the Midheaven was inconjunct that same planet indicated the openhandedness with which the U.S. helped others, even Germany which the U.S. had defeated two years earlier. What other nation in the world would treat its former enemy in this manner? Venus, ruler of the seventh house of enemies or allies, is conjunct Jupiter in the U.S. chart, and Jupiter governs the second house of finance. The Marshall Plan cost the U.S. $13 billion and for decades America was the protector of Europe, shown by the Sun sextile Saturn. Mars squaring natal Venus, however, pointed to this time being the beginning of the Cold War, which lasted another forty-two years until the Berlin Wall came down. The Truman Doctrine later in the year granted appropriations for Greece and Turkey in their fight against Communist guerrillas.

The Korean War

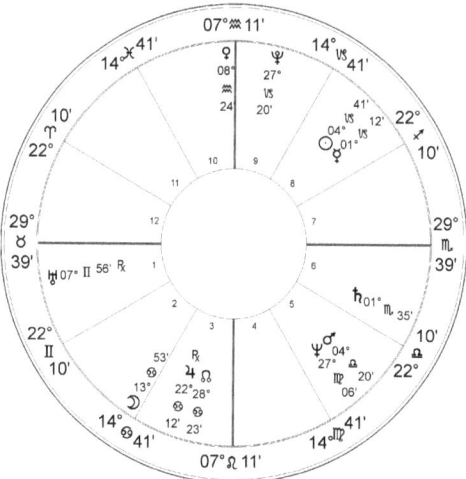

June 27, 1950

After World War II, the Korean peninsula was divided between the south, which was democratic, and the north, which was under Communist rule. When the north invaded the south in late June 1950, the United Nations sent in a police force as the U.S. Sun was opposing natal Jupiter and the Moon was sitting on natal Sun. The Moon also was squaring natal Saturn, pointing to this war being one of containment and limitations. The Midheaven sitting on the natal south Node and sesquare natal Mars indicated the somewhat fated nature of this conflict. Mars square natal Jupiter illustrated the conflict between President Truman and General MacArthur, who wanted to drive the Communists completely out of Korea. Truman said no and MacArthur was fired. More than 34,000 Americans lost their lives in this war and 115,000 were placed on the casualty list.

Civil Rights Movement

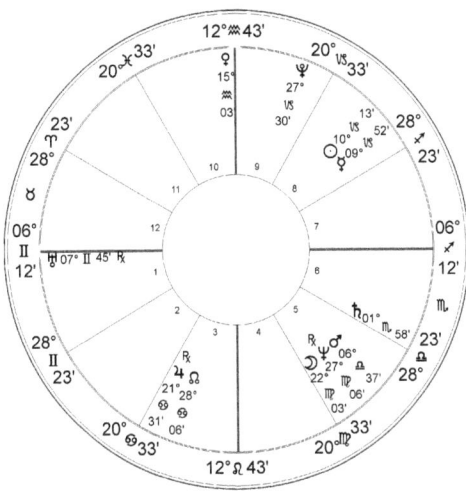

December 1, 1955

When Rosa Parks refused to give up her seat and move to the back of the bus, as was customary in those days for a Black person in the South, a boycott of the entire bus system in Montgomery, Alabama began; it lasted one year. The movement of Negroes to gain full equality under the law as promised in the Constitution was begun under Mars square natal Jupiter; the Ascendant was about to trine progressed Mars, as well. Before long, boycotts and sit-in demonstrations were commonplace throughout the South, most of them peaceful and non-violent as Saturn was trine natal Venus and Venus was trine natal Saturn. The leader of this movement of non-violence was Martin Luther King, a preacher from Atlanta with his Sun in Capricorn and Taurus rising. Some Southern governors, such as Faubus in Arkansas and Wallace in Alabama, refused to obey orders from the Supreme Court to integrate the schools and federal troops had to be sent in to keep the peace—shown by the Midheaven inconjunct natal Sun. The Moon was conjunct natal Neptune, which rules all minority groups, and had just passed a sextile to Jupiter, the planet of law.

Interstate Highway System

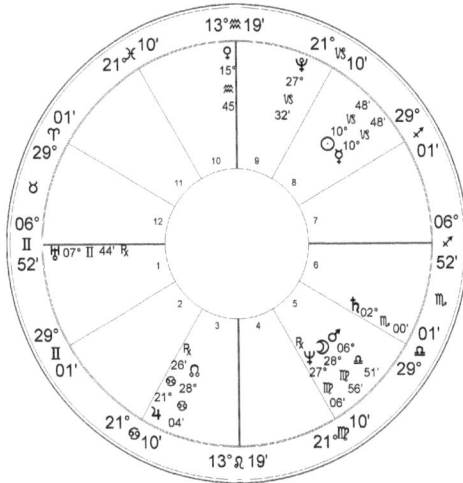

June 29, 1956

Congress authorized construction of a 42,000 mile highway system which was to be completed within four decades. The original cost was placed at $27 billion, but the final tally would be more than five times that much. During World War I, General Pershing first envisioned a national highway grid which could be used to evacuate Americans in case of attack. This act completely redesigned cities and vast stretches of land were appropriated in the name of urban renewal as the Ascendant semisquared Jupiter. Many neighborhoods were split in half and the middle class escaped to the suburbs as Mercury and the Sun semisquared the U.S. natal Moon in the natal fourth house. The Moon also was trine natal Pluto, located in the third house of transportation and long distance journeys.

Space Program Begins

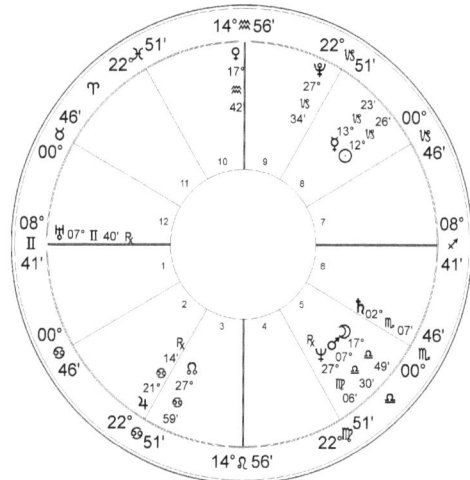

January 31, 1958

When the Russians sent up their first space satellite, Sputnik, in October 1957, it caught America totally off guard, as shown by the Ascendant conjunct Uranus, the planet of space exploration. Within months America's first space capsule, Explorer I, was sent into orbit as Mars trined Uranus and the Midheaven trined natal Saturn, ruler of the U.S. third house.

Cuban Missile Crisis

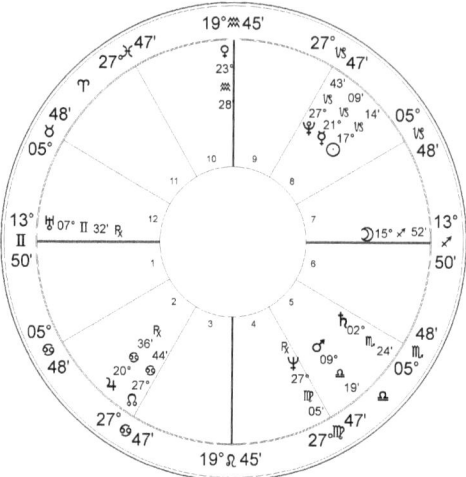

October 22, 19621

When Castro took over Cuba in 1959, he did it to oust Bautista, not to install Communism. But because American interests were expropriated, the U.S. slapped an embargo on Cuba in January 1961, after which Castro sought aid from whomever he could. Tensions between Cuba and the U.S. escalated after President Kennedy entered office. In April 1961, CIA trained Cuban exiles landed at the Bay of Pigs to try to oust Castro, but failed miserably. By late 1962, intelligence sources had learned that the Soviet Union was constructing missile launching sites on Cuba and Kennedy ordered a quarantine of the island. Kennedy ordered Khrushchev to dismantle the bases or face the inevitability of nuclear confrontation. The U.S. Midheaven was sesquare natal Jupiter and inconjunct that planet's progressed position. Open warfare was avoided as the Ascendant was trine natal Saturn at the same time the U.S. Moon was trine the natal Midheaven. The Russians backed down and dismantled the missile sites on the proviso the U.S. not invade Cuba. Mercury had moved to inconjunct natal Mars and Venus was inconjunct natal Mercury, both indications of a tactful solution to a period in U.S. history when, for a few days, the world was on the brink of nuclear war.

President Kennedy Assassinated

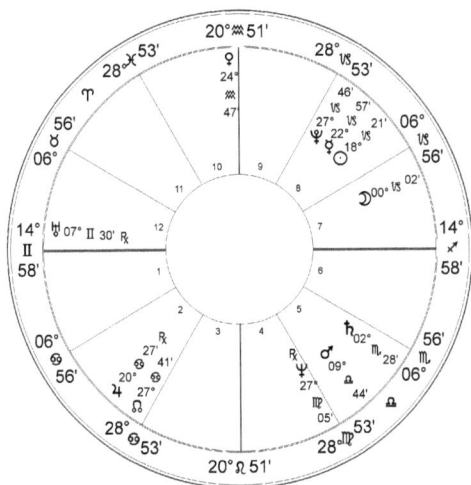

November 22, 1963

The most nebulous event in recent American history occurred in Dallas, Texas when President Kennedy was shot in a motorcade by Lee Harvey Oswald, according to the conclusions of the Warren Commission. Venus, ruler of the U.S. natal seventh and twelfth houses, was conjunct natal Moon. As the Moon rules the U.S. natal ninth house, possible foreign countries were responsible, most notably Cuba, in retaliation for the Bay of Pigs. Saturn, natally in the twelfth house of secrets, was about to trine natal Venus, ruler of the twelfth house, while the Midheaven was about to trine natal Mars. Kennedy's assassination occurred under the long term Neptune trine to natal Pluto, an aspect which also brought the U.S. deeper and deeper into the Vietnam conflict.

Vietnam War

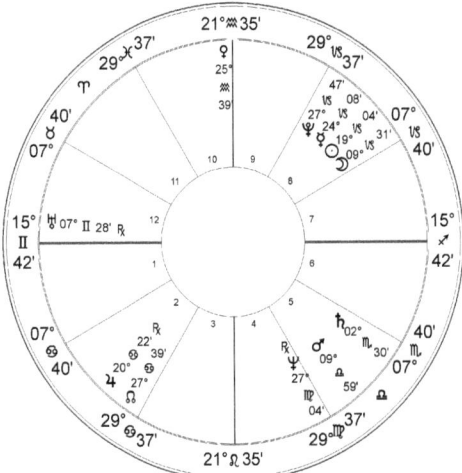

August 7, 1964

In 1950, President Truman sent an advisory committee to aid the French, who were fighting to maintain their authority in Vietnam. Four years later, the French were defeated at Dienbienphu and after the Geneva accords, the country was divided in two. Military personnel were sent under Eisenhower's administration to train South Vietnamese troops and during Kennedy's brief time in office, military advisors rose from 2,000 to 15,000. In August 1964, North Vietnamese torpedo boats attacked U.S. destroyers in the Gulf of Tonkin; five days later, Congress authorized President Johnson to take necessary steps to maintain peace. It was the beginning of the most controversial war America had ever fought. The Midheaven trine natal Mars seemed to indicate U.S. military superiority, but America seriously misjudged the Viet Cong, whose guerrilla tactics kept throwing American troops into a quandary, as shown by the Midheaven also sesquare natal Jupiter, planet of good judgment, self-righteousness and optimism. Somehow, the U.S. got sucked into this conflict as indicated by the South Node conjunct Pluto. Many young people, especially on college campuses, protested the war, as shown by Mercury opposing its natal position. At the height of the war, more than 525,000 American soldiers were stationed in Vietnam. Combat troops were scaled back after 1969 but air strikes continued for another three years. Peace finally came in late January 1973 after 58,000 American soldiers had lost their lives in this undeclared war.

Medicare Act

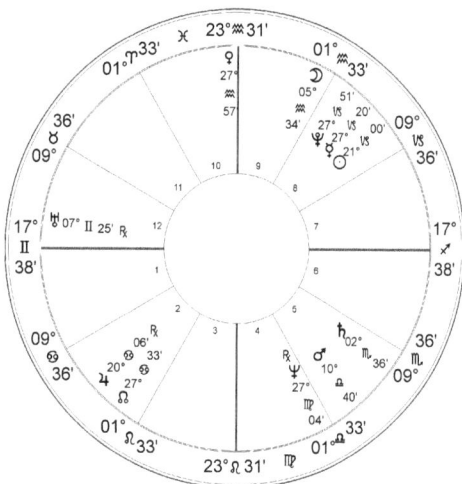

July 1, 1966

Government financing of medical care for those sixty-five years of age and older finally began many years after European countries had similar plans. State sponsored Medicaid also was put into force to ease increasing hospital costs and doctor bills as the Midheaven was inconjunct Neptune, the planet of hospitalization. Complete medical coverage, however, was avoided for those under retirement age, as shown by the Moon inconjunct Jupiter, ruler of the U.S. second house (America couldn't afford it) and Mercury conjunct Pluto and the South Node. Mars, which rules physicians, fought socialized medicine, preferring increased profit and professional independence, as shown by Mars sesquare natal Moon. Medicare was funded through the Social Security system and provided hospital insurance for a low monthly premium while Medicaid provided benefits for the poor, regardless of age.

The Moon Landing

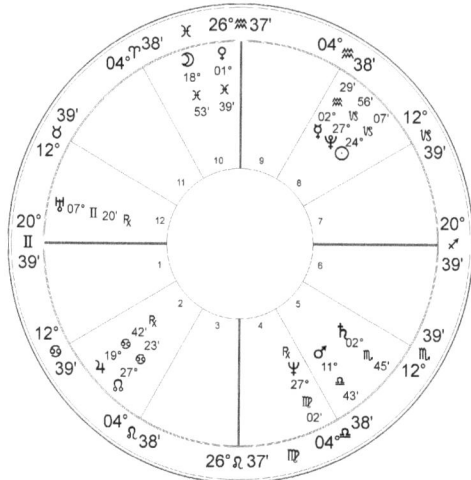

July 20, 1969

The most stupendous scientific achievement of the 20th century took place as the Midheaven was conjunct the U.S. natal Moon, ruler of the ninth house of long distance journeys. Venus was trine its own position and Saturn trined that planet as well. The Ascendant was approaching a conjunction to natal Mars, ruler of the sixth house of technology. Moon landings were abandoned after 1972.

Resignation of Nixon

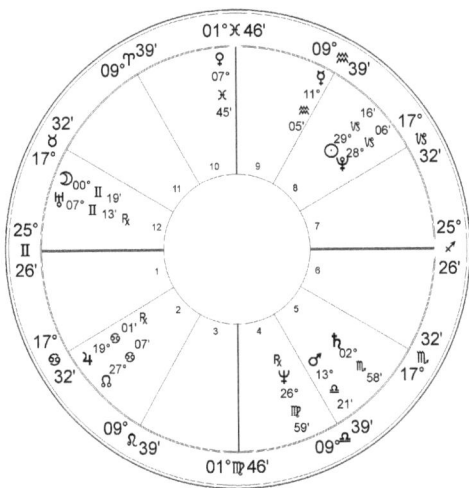

August 9, 1974

Iranian Hostage Crisis

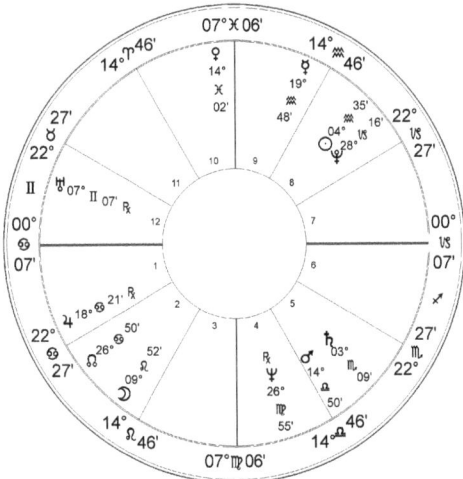

November 4, 1979

The darkest moment in American presidential history occurred when Mars squared the U.S. natal Sun, ruler of the tenth house of power and authority. This aspect clearly indicated the animosity and controversy surrounding Nixon, and Mars was about to conjunct natal Saturn, traditional ruler of the Midheaven. Saturn rules the U.S. third house, which governs communication of all kinds, including tapes. However, Saturn was trine natal Venus, so America allowed Nixon to resign before his probable impeachment. This also was shown by the Midheaven trine natal Venus, ruler of the twelfth house of forgiveness and pardons.

When the Shah of Iran fled into exile at the beginning of 1979, revolutionary forces under the Ayatollah Kohmeini took over the country. Ten months later, Iranian militants took sixty hostages from the American embassy in Teheran as the Moon squared the U.S. natal Ascendant. The suddenness of this incident is shown by the Midheaven square natal Uranus, the planet of surprises and shocks. In exchange for the safe return of the hostages, the terrorists demanded the Shah be returned to Iran to stand trial for crimes against the Iranian people. After initially releasing eight hostages, the remaining fifty-two were held captive for another fourteen months. Venus, ruler of the natal seventh house of war, was trine natal Sun so the U.S. didn't go to war over this incident. Mars had progressed to an exact conjunction with natal Saturn, illustrating why the U.S. government literally froze at the hands of the terrorists. This progression also was in force during the two energy crises which turned the country upside down. The hostages were finally released on the day President Reagan was inaugurated in exchange for unfreezing Iranian assets within the U.S.

Stock Market Crash

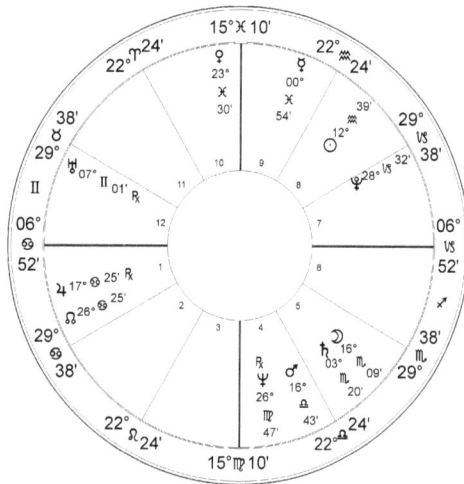

October 19, 1987

The Dow Jones soared to new heights during the summer of 1987, but after August, a slide began which culminated in a 508 point drop and the prosperity of recent years came to a crashing halt. Americans had been on a roll as shown by the Ascendant conjunct natal Jupiter. The federal deficit rose alarmingly, consumers were spending more and saving less, as shown by the Midheaven inconjunct natal Saturn. Inconjuncts demand adjustment. The Sun was inconjunct its natal place, just as it was in 1929 when the previous market crash occurred. The drop also was shown by Mercury, which rules trading, sesquare natal Saturn. Many stocks were inflated in proportion to their true worth, illustrated by Venus opposing natal Neptune, ruler of the natal fifth house of speculation. Americans for too long had gambled on Reaganomics, the trickle down theory that if tax cuts were given to the wealthy, benefits would eventually flow down to the rest of the people. Progressed Mars square progressed Jupiter indicated this theory just didn't hold water, for during Reagan's administration America went from the world's largest creditor nation to the world's greatest debtor nation, all within the span of eight years. The national debt was $1 trillion in 1980; eight years later it had doubled. The square from the planet which rules the U.S. natal sixth house of employment to the planet which governs our second house of wealth pointed to a crisis between keeping workers and making a profit. Many companies began to downsize or lay off employees, or in extreme cases simply moved their operations overseas.

Savings and Loan Crisis

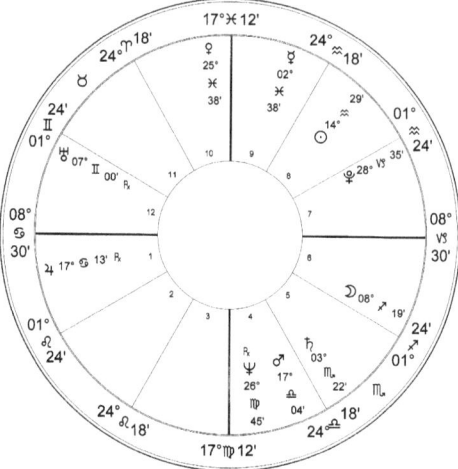

August 9, 1989

Ten months after the stock market crash, President Bush signed a bill to bail out hundreds of insolvent savings and loan institutions which had failed due to mismanagement of stock portfolios, bad investments and a depressed real estate market. When the banking industry was deregulated, corruption surfaced and many Americans were taken for a financial ride and millions were taken to the cleaners. The Midheaven trine Jupiter, ruler of the natal second house of banks, also was inconjunct Mars, which natally sits in the eighth house of debts. The outcome was inevitable, as shown by the Sun trine natal Saturn, but the cost of more than $300 billion over a thirty year period will be a severe burden for all Americans to shoulder. The Moon opposing natal Uranus in the natal eighth house pointed to the shock many Americans felt when they found their portfolios practically worthless. Massive foreclosures ensued and real estate prices, which had been overinflated for years, began a long downward slide which continues to this day.

The Gulf War

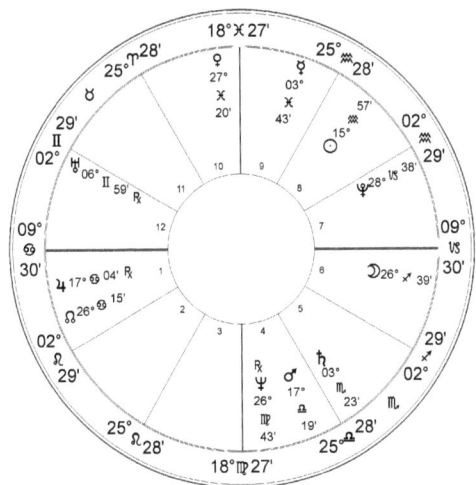

January 16, 1991

When Saddam Hussein of Iraq invaded Kuwait in August 1990, the U.S. began Operation Desert Shield along with an economic embargo which was supposed to contain Iraqi ambitions against other Persian Gulf countries. The Sun was crossing the fourth house cusp at this time, indicating a low point in U.S. history. When Operation Desert Storm began under guidelines from the United Nations, the U.S. sent more than 530,000 troops to the region which were joined by forces from other stations within the U.N. Warplanes bombed Baghdad and Iraq retaliated by sending missiles to Tel Aviv and setting 732 fires in the oil fields of Kuwait, which burned off six million barrels per day. The war was over in six weeks due to Venus, ruler of the seventh house of war, being sextile natal Pluto and the South Node. Venus also was opposing Neptune, indicating the chemical warfare used by the Iraqis, as well as the numerous oil fires.

NAFTA

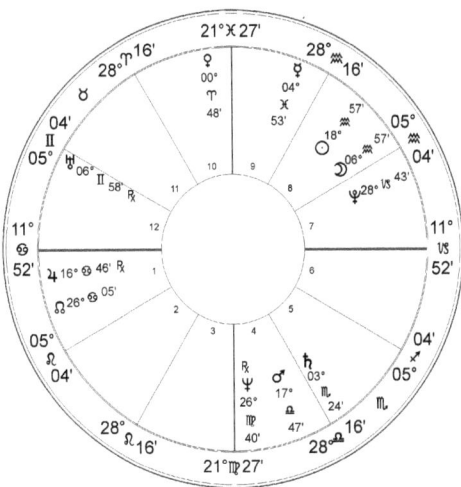

January 1, 1994

With Europe now a Common Market area, talks began between the United States, Canada and Mexico in the spring of 1991 to form a similar trading block. The presidents of all three countries signed the North American Free Trade Agreements in December 1992, but their respective legislatures still had to ratify the agreement. Opposition arose in the U.S. because many believed this document would send more and more jobs south of the border and that Mexico might not be vigilant enough to enforce strict environmental guidelines enacted in the U.S. during the previous two decades. The Midheaven squaring natal Mars, ruler of the sixth house of work and employment, also opposing natal Neptune, ruler of pollution and poisons, illustrated this hesitancy. The U.S. Senate ratified NAFTA in November 1993 just as the Moon trined natal Uranus. Trade barriers could now be lifted and goods moved across borders with few controls, shown by Mercury, the planet of trade and commerce, trine natal Jupiter, ruler of the second house of income. The Sun sesquare Venus, however, gave concern that the U.S. might be selling its autonomy and integrity down the drain, as shown by the fact that while Venus rules the U.S. seventh house of partnerships and agreements, it also rules the natal twelfth house of secret enmity and self-undoing. The Midheaven adversely aspecting the natal Nodes in the third and ninth houses also shows this potential for disaster.

Financial Collapse

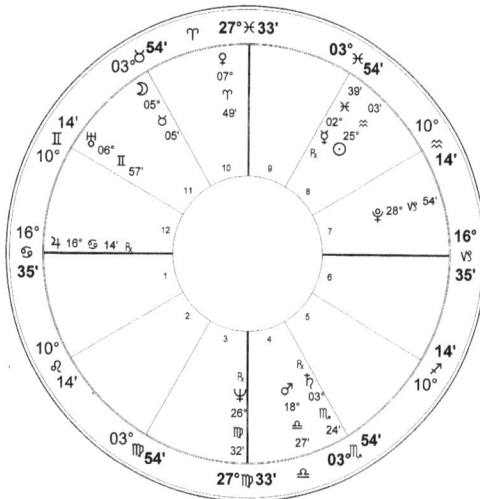

January 14, 2000

In the closing years of the 20th century, Americans were living high on the hog due to an orgy of speculation on the stock markets. Dot.com firms were proliferating at breakneck speed and their perceived value was escalating higher and higher. By 1999, NASDAQ's index stood at 2000; one year later it peaked over 5000. The Down Jones index peaked at 11, 722 in early 2000, as did the S&P 500, which hit 1527. Then the bottom fell out and companies went bust in record numbers. Over the next two years, the Dow Jones lost 38 percent, NASDAQ plummeted to 72 percent of its former peak and the S&P 500 lost 35 percent. Securities lost 62, percent and mergers were off by more than 40 percent. Consumer confidence plummeted and corporate scandals (i.e., Enron) seemed to be the norm. Consumer debt climbed to an all-time high even though the Fed's prime interest rate was lowered numerous times to avoid even more drastic measures. The only item which escalated seemed to be housing costs. Coincidentally, this was a repeat of what the Japanese Nikkei index went through during the '90s, when it lost 76 percent of its assets. Interestingly, when the Stock Market crashed in late 1929, the U.S. progressed Midheaven stood at 16 Capricorn; in early 2000, this was exactly opposite the U.S. progressed Ascendant.

The progressed Midheaven at 27 Pisces was sextile the U.S. natal Pluto, ruler of the Ascendant and the governor or riches and now ruler of the nation's progressed fifth house of speculation. But the progressed Midheaven was also in opposition to progressed Neptune, ruler of the natal fifth house--hence the bubble bursting and taking a massive nosedive. Note also that Jupiter, which governs speculation, was conjunct the progressed Ascendant, and Jupiter rules the country's natal second house. Americans were going on a binge of another kind: their weight and waistlines also were expanding at an alarming rate. Illnesses such as heart disease and diabetes, once seen mainly in older Americans, were now afflicting children. America was gorging itself on junk food, and the progressed Sun conjunct natal Moon might indicate this negative trend. It was time for Americans to go on a diet, both physically and financially.

Terrorist Attacks

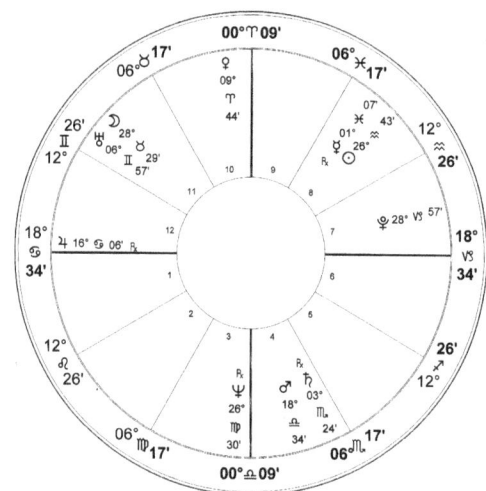

September 11, 2001

American problems with the Middle East began to escalate in late 1979, when the Iranian hostage crisis took place a short time before the Soviets invaded neighboring Afghanistan. Many felt that with the "selection" of George W. Bush by the Supreme Court to be the 43rd president, the chickens would come home to roost due to the Bush family's involvement in the region's petroleum. Bush lost the popular vote to Al Gore, but his camp tried to stop several recounts and succeeded in part through the help of his brother, the governor or Florida.

Shortly after Bush's inauguration, messages began to arrive at the white House of a possible terrorist attack. As they were neither date nor place specific, nothing much was done. On September 11, 2001, four airplanes took off from east coast cities that were shortly hijacked by Moslem fanatics who had a major grudge against the western world, especially the U.S. Two planes hit the World Trade Center in New York City, which eventually toppled both towers, killing nearly 3,000. Another plane broadsided the Pentagon outside Washington, DC and the fourth plane was brought down in western Pennsylvania, possibly also headed for the nation's capital.

A terrorist group called Al Qaeda under the command of Osama Bin Laden, a Saudi national once employed by the CIA in Afghanistan, claimed credit for the attacks. All air traffic was suspended and the financial institutions in lower Manhattan were shuttered for nearly a week. One month later, U.S. troops were sent to Afghanistan to rid that country of the Taliban, which was giving support to Bin Laden, who vowed to destroy the American way of life.

The progressed Midheaven at 29 Pisces indicated the end of our old way of life. Ancient astrologers saw this degree as one of drowning because it conjuncts the fixed star Scheat. The final degrees of any sign on the angles usually involve a high degree of zealousness, fanaticism and recklessness because there's nothing left to lose. Note also the progressed Ascendant square progressed Mars, the god of war, in the fourth house of U.S. homeland and security--hence the rapid formation of the Department of Homeland Security. America was in attack mode and many civil liberties also were threatened.

Note that the Moon and Pluto sextile the progressed Midheaven, thus cosmobiologically the equation becomes Moon/Pluto = MC. Ebertin says this midpoint indicates fanaticism and jealousy and taking offense at perceived insults and injustices. The Moslem world takes offense at American support of Israel, which is deemed an interloper into the Arab-dominated Middle East. U.S. dependency on petroleum, most of which comes from the Middle East, is definitely a sore point. The Moon/Pluto midpoint clearly states that the Western/Arab world has a relationship of "can't live with 'em, can't live without them either." The progressed Sun inconjunct progressed Neptune might also point to this dilemma, whose only solution seems to be compromise and adjustment, something the American president with Pluto on the Ascendant was unwilling to consider.

Invasion of Iraq

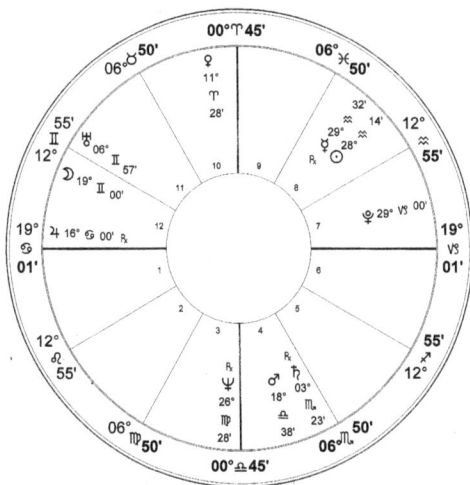

March 15, 2003

The War on Terror bogged down in Afghanistan and Osama Bin Laden continued to elude capture. The U.S. did manage to oust the Taliban, and a democratic government was formed in Afghanistan. The conflict then expanded to demand the ouster of Saddam Hussein, leader of Iraq since 1979, whom the U.S. thought to be harboring "weapons of mass destruction." The real reason was probably to get rid of Hussein so the West could run a pipeline through Iraq to the Persian Gulf. The U.S. State Department also felt Hussein was harboring Al Qaeda terrorists and was partly responsible for the 9/11 terrorist attacks. United Nations weapons inspectors found no "weapons of mass destruction" and it was later found Hussein had no direct connection to Al Qaeda. They were all lies put forth by the U.S. to justify the invasion of Iraq.

Coalition troops began to bomb Baghdad in March 2003, and Hussein was captured by the end of the year and awaits trial by his own people for crimes against humanity. The bloodshed in Iraq, both of civilians and soldiers, continues unabated two years later, even after a new government was formed in June 2004.

The progressed Moon was about to trine the U.S. natal Mars when the invasion began. Coincidentally, it also was trine progressed Mars, which is about to go retrograde, indicating more troop losses down the road, whether in the Middle East or elsewhere as the U.S. probably will rethink its military objectives. The progressed Sun was sesquare its natal position; the last time this occurred was in 1914, when the U.S. invaded neighboring Mexico during that country's revolution. This aspect often points to an individual overstepping boundaries and bullying the opposition into submission. Depending upon your viewpoint, either Bush or Hussein is that person.

Progressed Mercury sesquare natal Sun and Saturn points to the false information or "intelligence" that justified the U.S. invasion; it was a rush to judgment without all the facts being known or even accurate. Progressed Venus, ruler of the natal U.S. seventh house of conflict, was semisquare natal Moon, ruler of the ninth house of foreign countries. With the progressed Midheaven now in Aries (a position it will occupy for the next three decades), this could indicate that America might well become more of an aggressor nation that tries to set the world right to its own advantage for the sake of "democracy," which is subservient to American interests. Only time will tell.

The U.S. Constitution

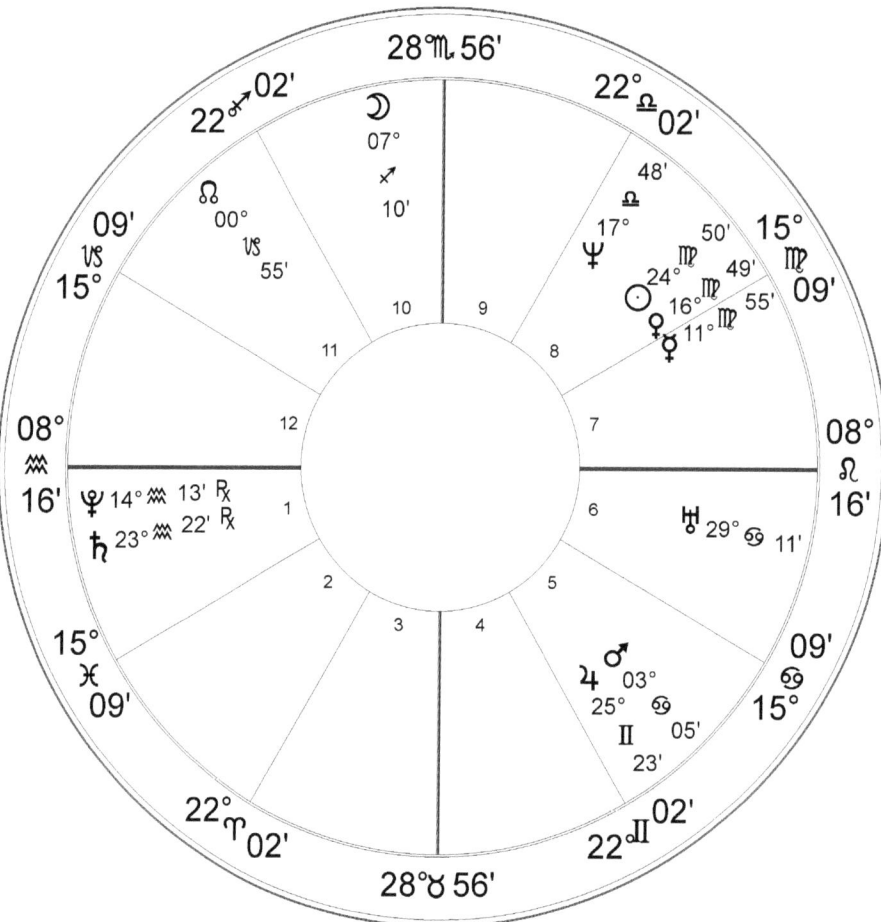

September 17, 1787, Philadelphia, Pennsylvania, 39N57, 75W10, 4:00 p.m. LMT
Source: Diary of James Madison states the Constitution signing was completed about 4:00 p.m.

Delegates began to assemble in Philadelphia during the summer to frame a Constitution for the new country. Prior attempts, such as the Confederation, had failed because each state had acted independently and the central government had little, if any, power. Still, many states did not want a central government, as their rights, they believed, would be forfeited.

Finally, the Constitution was signed about 4:00 p.m. on September 17, 1787. The entire proceedings had been conducted behind closed doors and few outsiders knew exactly what had taken place during the months prior to the signing. But the Constitution had still not passed the final test. Would the individual state governments accept it? Delaware cast all doubts aside when it became the first state to ratify on December 7, 1787, and by the following June, the ninth state (New Hampshire) had ratified and the Constitution became effective. The date of March 4, 1789 was chosen to be the beginning of the federal government in the land, and this was the official inauguration day for all presidents until 1941.

Note the sign of Scorpio. Like the Declaration of Independence, this sign is placed on an angle, this time at the Midheaven. The Sun is in Virgo (the same degree as the St. Augustine chart) and the Moon is opposite the Ascendant of the St. Augustine chart. This is no mere coincidence, for all charts blend into a unique harmony, even thought each chart has a distinct and separate meaning.

For example, the St. Augustine chart shows the inherent characteristics and temperament of the American people, whether they act as individuals or as a unit. It shows the destiny and the method and manner in which Americans project themselves both at home and abroad.

The Declaration of Independence chart, however, is the true chart for the United States, even though formal government didn't take place until nearly thirteen years later. From this chart, one can plot the course of the country's history, as has been shown.

The chart for the signing of the Constitution shows none of these qualities. It only clarifies and intensifies those qualities mentioned in the two previous charts. For unlike the St. Augustine chart or the Declaration chart, the signing of the Constitution in essence meant little, for it still had to pass the ratification of the individual states.

The Beginning of the Federal Government in the U.S.

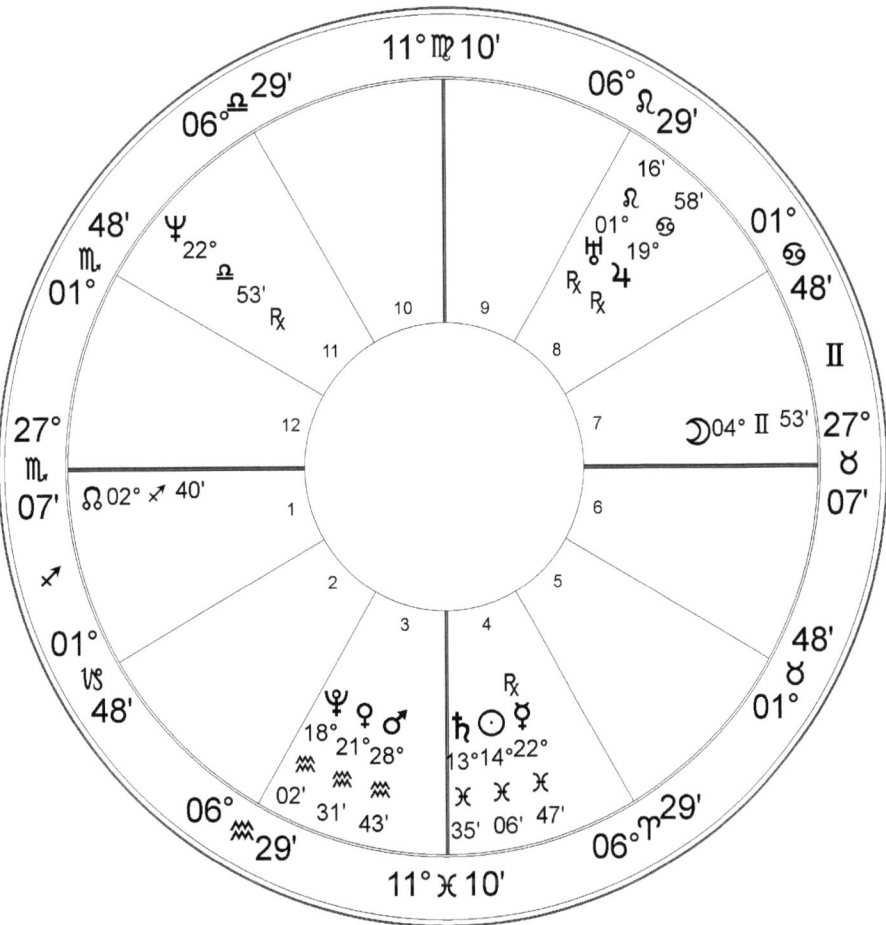

The sign Scorpio is rising again, just like it was when the Declaration of Independence was signed. Virgo figures prominently, again, this time being the sign on the Midheaven, while the Moon is approaching an opposition to the Ascendant of the St. Augustine chart. I find it rather difficult to delineate incorporation charts which have their birthtime at midnight. The true nature of the government, according to this chart and all other charts of incorporation, should be concentrated in domestic areas, and we all know this is not the case with America. Maybe some noted researcher or astrologer will enlighten me as to the intrinsic meaning of all these charts, for I fail to see the full meaning behind them. But as the facts stand, many cities in the U.S., especially those in the original thirteen colonies, were incorporated at this time.

Please Note

Information contained inside the parentheses that begins with Midheaven or MC, as well as Ascendant or ASC, refers to the progressed Midheaven or Ascendant at the time of a specific event. For example, on page 51, under Juneau, Alaska, it says "it became the capital of Alaska in 1900"; (Midheaven sextile Venus) refers to the progressed Midheaven in 1900, not the fact that the Midheaven was sextile Venus in the natal chart.

On page 53, under the city of Phoenix, the last words of the final paragraph where it says (Moon in Virgo) refers to the natal chart, which has Moon in Virgo. The same holds true on page 230, when at the bottom of the section on Charleston, South Carolina, I mention (Leo rising) and (both luminaries in Aries) that again relate to the natal chart.

Alabama

December 14, 1819
Huntsville
86W35, 34N44
2:00 p.m. CST

Source: Alabama State Historical Society says "early afternoon;" time rectified.

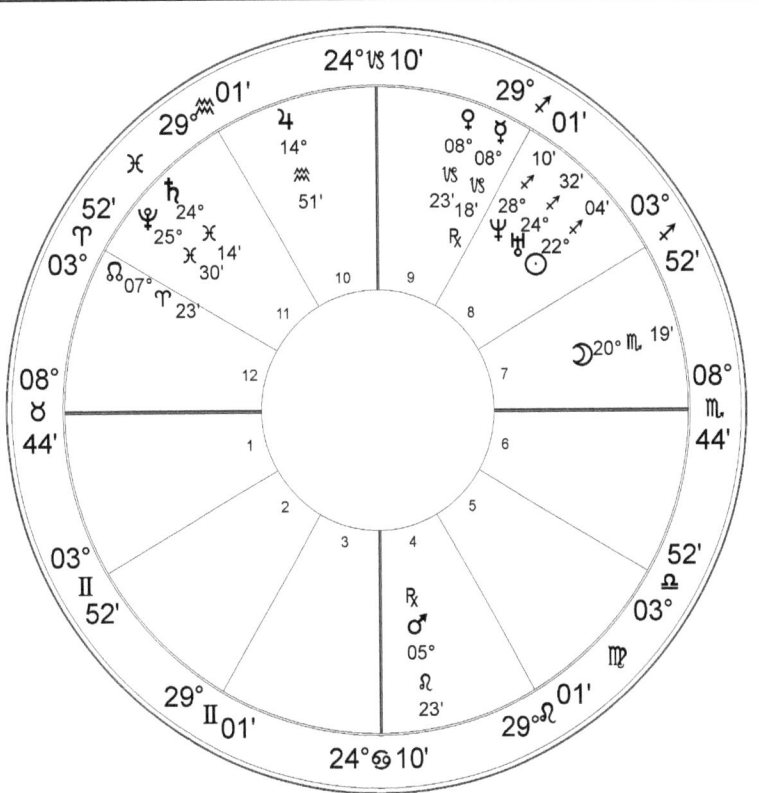

First settled by Americans at Mobile in 1702, it passed into British hands in 1763 and to Spain twenty years later. In 1795, the U.S. acquired all of the state with the exception of the area around Mobile, which remained in Spanish hands until 1810 when the U.S. annexed west Florida. In 1814 Andrew Jackson defeated the Creek Indians and opened up the interior of Alabama for settlement. On March 3, 1817, the Territory of Alabama was created; two years later, it entered the Union. On January 11, 1861, Alabama seceded from the Union, and one month later, the Confederate States of America was founded in Montgomery on February 9, 1861. Readmitted to the Union on June 25, 1868, it became a steel producer by 1880 when the first blast furnace opened. With the establishment of the Space Research Center at Huntsville in 1950, Alabama became, along with Florida and Texas, one of the chief centers for space exploration. The first spark of the civil rights movement began in Alabama in 1955 when a bus boycott was started in Montgomery; during the next decade, many marches and demonstrations, many of them against Governor George Wallace, took place.

Lying in the Cotton Belt of the South, Alabama is a leader in iron and steel production. It ranks second in bauxite, has large resources of coal and timber, and ranks second in pulp and third in paper. Cotton is no longer king, for soybeans now rank as the chief crop. Alabama is fourth in pecans, second in peanuts, and fourth in chickens.

Area: 51,609 square miles

Birmingham

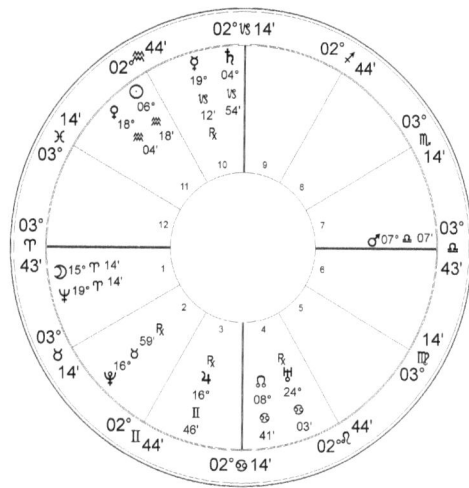

January 26, 1871
86W48, 33N31
9:35 a.m. CST

Birmingham's sole purpose for being is its proximity to the three ingredients needed to produce steel: limestone, coal and iron ore. First settled in 1813, the railroad arrived in 1870 and prompted the Elyton Land Company to purchase the site on January 26, 1871. Lots were offered for sale on June 1 and the city was incorporated in December.

Two years later, Birmingham suffered a double calamity: a cholera epidemic and nationwide financial panic drove thousands from the city (Ascendant opposition Mars). In 1880, the first blast furnace opened, and by 1907 the city became the "Pittsburgh of the South" when US Steel decided to locate its southern headquarters there (Aries rising rules steel).

Birmingham was one of the focal points of the civil rights movement, and has seen much racial strife and turmoil in its short history. In 1963 a bomb went off in a church killing four black girls, and in July 1967 a race riot erupted (Midheaven square Mars).

Incorporated: December 19, 1871
Elevation 382 feet
Area: 90 square miles
Source: Birmingham Public Library

Huntsville

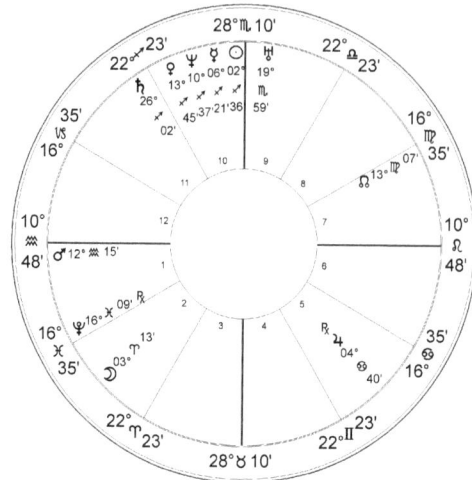

November 25, 1811
86W35, 34N44
11:15 a.m. CST

Founded originally as Twickenham by John Hunt in 1805, it became the capital of Alabama from 1819 until 1826 (Midheaven conjunct Mercury). Burned by federal troops in April 1862 (Ascendant inconjunct Sun), it remained a sleepy southern town until the arrival of the space industry in 1950. By 1958, NASA's Space Vehicle Center was established (Midheaven trine Saturn) and Huntsville today is one of the leaders in the exploration of the universe (Aquarius rising).

Incorporated: 1860
Elevation: 610 feet
Area: 113 square miles
Source: Huntsville Public Library

Mobile

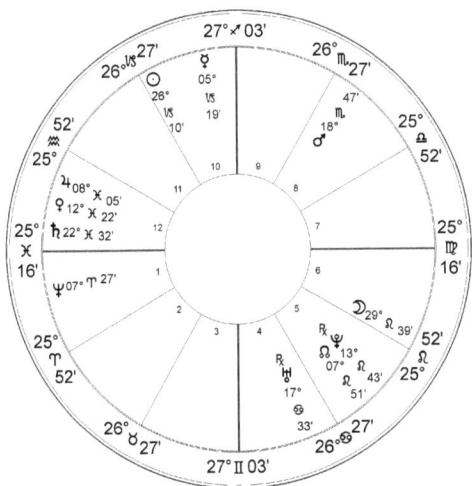

January 16, 1702
88W03, 30N41
9:57 a.m. CST

Founded by Le Moyne in 1702 about twenty-seven miles upstream from its present location, it was moved to its present site in 1710 after a hurricane wiped out the original settlement (Ascendant conjunct Neptune). The hurricanes of 1733 (Ascendant square Pluto) and September 1979 (Midheaven semisquare Pluto) also caused extensive damage. Mobile has also endured epidemics of yellow fever in 1853 (Sun quincunx Sun) and 1897 (Midheaven square Neptune).

Burned by the British in 1779 (Ascendant semisquare Pluto), it became one of the chief ports of the South prior to the Civil War, which caused it to be blockaded by Union forces (Midheaven semisquare Uranus). After the Civil War, the city approached financial collapse, and in 1879 declared bankruptcy (Midheaven square Saturn). It wasn't reincorporated until 1887. Hurricane Gilbert tore through the city in September 1988, causing extensive damage and a loss of 260 lives in its wake (Midheaven opposite Neptune, Ascendant square Saturn).

Considerably more cosmopolitan than other cities in Alabama, Mobile hosted the first Mardi Gras in 1704. Along with the Azalea Festival, Mobile comes alive in the spring. The city is famous for its huge oak trees and lush tropical foliage.

Pisces rising makes the citizens of Mobile relaxed, for they take life pretty much as it comes. They possess a blithe acceptance of the weather and resignation towards fate.

Incorporated: December 17, 1819
Elevation: 8 feet
Area: 142 square miles
Source: *The Founding of Mobile* by Peter Hamilton

Montgomery

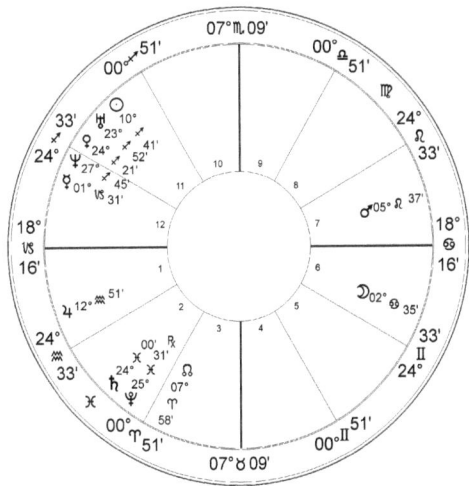

December 3, 1819
86W19, 32N23
9:18 a.m. CST

Founded as two villages called Philadelphia Town and Alabama Town in August 1817, they merged to form the City of Montgomery in 1819. It became the capital of the state in 1847 (Midheaven trine Mars).

For a brief period between February and May 1861, Montgomery was the capital of the Confederate States of America. Jefferson Davis was sworn in as its first and only chief executive on the steps of the state capitol. It suffered heavily at the hands of the Union armies during the Civil War, and in April 1865 was burned by its own citizens (Midheaven square Saturn/Pluto, conjunct Uranus).

Montgomery can rightly be called the birthplace of the civil rights movement. In 1955, Rosa Parks refused to give up her seat on a bus and move to the back, as was the custom in those days. Boycotts led by Martin Luther King resulted in the Voting Rights Act of 1965.

Incorporated: 1837
Elevation: 160 feet
Area: 50 square miles
Source: *American Guide Series*

Tuscaloosa

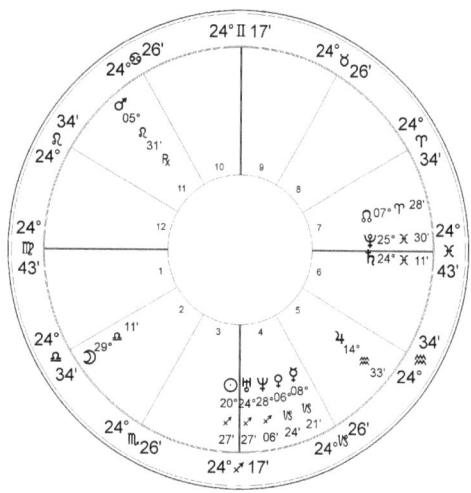

December 13, 1819
87W34, 33N12
12:01 a.m. CST

First settled in 1809, four years later an Indian revolt caused the community to be burned to the ground. Resettled in 1815, it was the capital of Alabama from 1826 until 1847. The University of Alabama was founded here in 1831, and during the Civil War it was captured by Union armies in April 1865.

Incorporated: March 12, 1873
Elevation: 113 feet
Source: Tuscaloosa Public Library

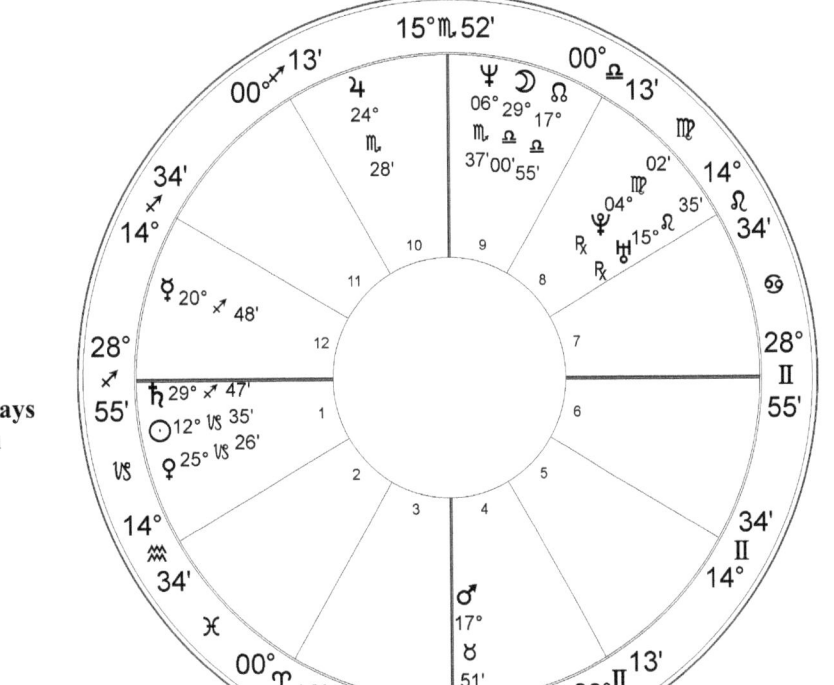

Alaska

January 3, 1959
Juneau
134W25, 58N18
9:01 a.m. PST
Source: Los Angeles Times says
12:01 p.m. in Washington

Alaska was discovered by Vitus Bering, exploring for Russia, in 1741. The first settlement was established at Kodiak in 1784, and fifteen years later, the City of Sitka was founded. Fur trading was the chief reason for Russia's interest in this "icebox," but with the sum of $7.2 million handed to the Russians on October 18, 1867, it passed into American hands at the cost of about two cents an acre. Many thought it was nothing more than snow and ice and labeled it "Seward's Folly." With the discovery of gold in 1896 they soon changed their minds and prospectors, called "Sourdoughs," came by the droves to both Nome and the Klondike in neighboring Yukon. On August 24, 1912, the Territory of Alaska was organized. In 1942 Japanese planes attacked the Aleutians and occupied Attu, Kiska and Agattu Islands. American troops retook the islands the following year and shortly afterward the DEW Line was established. Alaska finally became a state in 1959; five years later the most severe earthquake ever to hit the North American continent rocked most of the southern part of the state. Damage was widespread and 131 were killed. Oil was discovered at Prudhoe Bay on the north coast in 1968, and was believed to be the largest reserve in the world. In 1977 the pipeline was completed at a cost of $7.7 billion, and oil now flows a distance of 800 miles to the port city of Valdez at a rate of more than one million barrels a day.

The largest state in area, Alaska has more than 6,640 of coastline on the mainland; if you count its numerous islands, the total goes up to 33,900 miles. The westernmost part of Alaska, Little Diomede Island, is a scant two and a half miles from Russia, across the Bering Strait. The Aleutian Islands stretch for 1,200 miles like the claw of a lobster.

Alaska ranks number one in fish. Oil is the primary mineral resource. Forest products and furs are also large contributors to the economy.

Area: 586,412 square miles

Anchorage

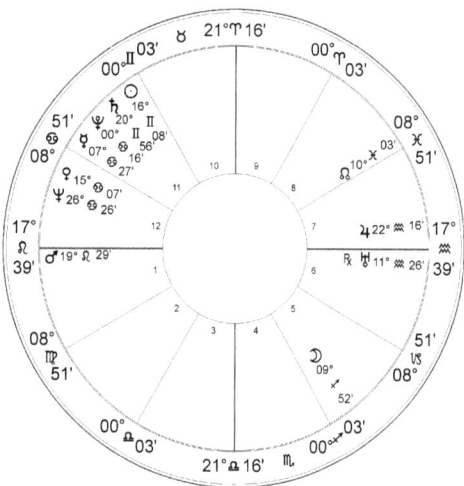

June 7, 1914
149W54, 61N13
8:17 a.m. CAT

The largest and most northern city on the American continent was founded in 1914 by railroad crews. The first sale of lots was held July 10, 1915. The largest earthquake ever to hit North America occurred on Good Friday, March 27, 1964 (Ascendant square Sun). Several portions of the city fell into the Cook Inlet, while others sank several feet. Due to its location, the city is important to the defense of the country, and its airport handles numerous daily flights to the Orient.

Incorporated: November 11, 1920
Elevation: 118 Feet
Area: 1,900 square miles
Source: Anchorage Public Library

Fairbanks

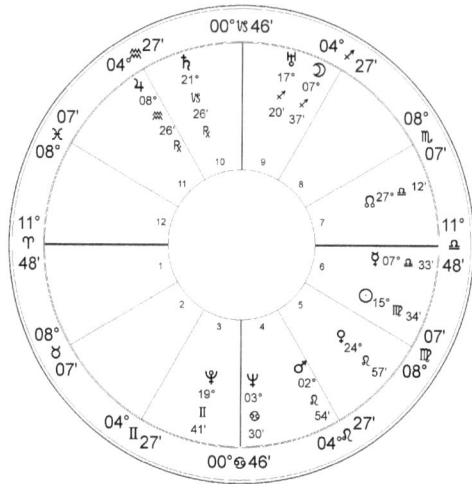

September 8, 1902
147W43, 64N51
6:45 p.m. CAT

Founded in 1902 by prospectors during a town meeting, the University of Alaska was founded in 1917 in nearby College, Alaska (Midheaven trine Sun). In 1967 the Chena River overflowed, causing considerable damage (Midheaven trine Neptune). Fairbanks was the focal point of the Alaska Pipeline during its construction from November 1973 to June 1977. During these years the city had all the trappings of a boom town, including high prices and an increasing crime wave.

Lying only 130 miles south of the Arctic circle, Fairbanks gets icebound in winter, but the summers can be quite hot, by Alaskan standards. The coldest temperature ever recorded there was sixty-six degrees below zero; the highest was ninety-six degrees above zero.

Incorporated: November 10, 1903
Source: *A Guide to Alaska* by Merle Colby

Juneau

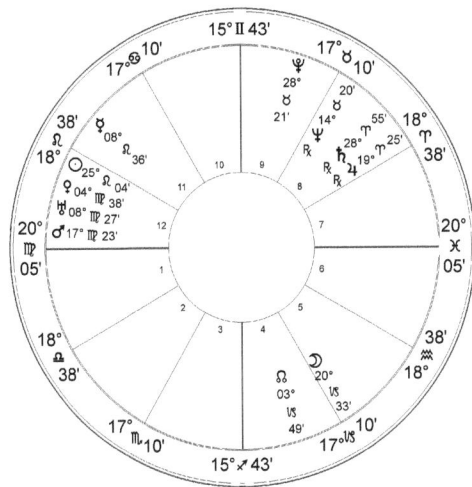

August 17, 1880
134W25, 58N18
7:10 a.m. YST

Founded by Joe Juneau in 1880 when he was panning for gold, it became the capital of Alaska in 1900 (Midheaven sextile Venus). In 1970 it merged with neighboring Douglas to form the second largest city in the world in area. Since 1974, the future of Juneau has been in doubt, for Alaskans voted to relocate the capital to a more central location (Midheaven conjunct Mars).

Juneau is the only capital city in our country that cannot be reached by either railroad or automobile. Situated on a narrow strip of land between the Gastineau Channel and the mountains, its only contact with the outside world is by ferryboat or airplane. Nearby is the impressive Mendenhall Glacier.

Incorporated: June 27, 1900
Elevation: 50 feet
Area: 3,068 square miles
Source: Juneau Public Library

Sitka

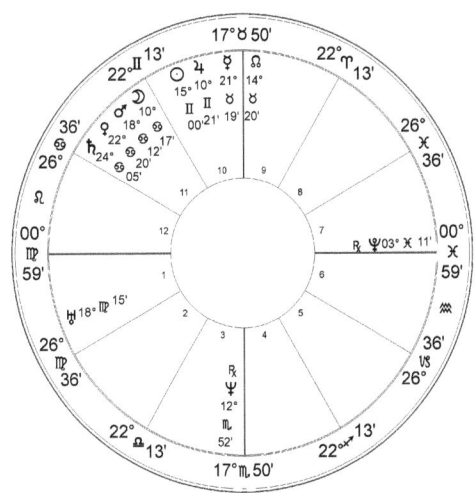

June 5, 1799
135W20, 57N03
10:06 a.m. YST

Founded by Lord Baranof in 1799, the settlement was attacked by Indians in 1801 (Ascendant opposition Pluto), who massacred the men and took the women and children as prisoners. Russians bombarded the encampment in 1804 (Ascendant semisquare Mars) and a new city was begun. On October 18, 1867, the Russians transferred Alaska to the United States (Midheaven conjunct Venus, Ascendant trine Sun) and Sitka became the capital of Alaska until 1900.

Incorporated: 1920
Source: *History of Alaska* by H.H. Bancroft; *Story of Sitka* by C.L. Andrew says July 18, 1799.

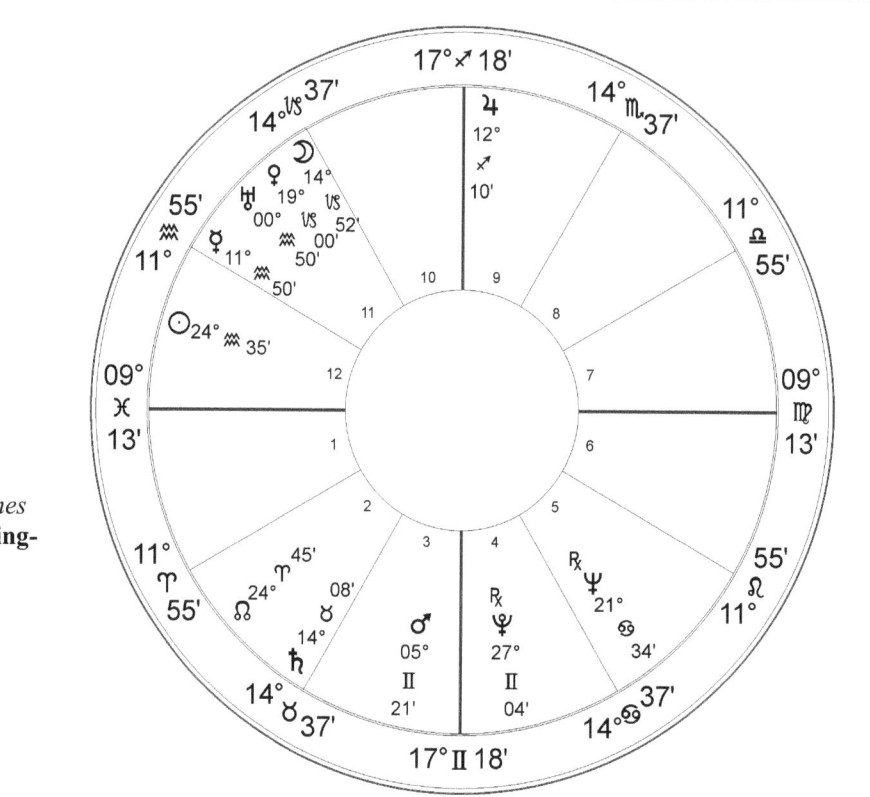

Arizona

**February 14, 1912
Phoenix
112W04, 33N27
8:00 a.m. MST
Source:** *Los Angeles Times* **says 10:00 a.m. in Washington**

During the 1540s this colorful land was first explored by Spain, among them Coronado looking for Cibola, the fabled city of gold. Catholic missions were founded in the late 17th century, but the first real European settlement was made at Tucson in 1775. The U.S. acquired the region after the Mexican War, except for a small portion along the Mexican border called the Gadsden Strip, which was purchased in 1853. On February 24, 1863, the Territory of Arizona was created. Later that year Kit Carson subdued the Navajos at Canyon de Chelly, but settlement was sparse due to the frequent Apache uprisings between 1871 and 1886. With the capture of Geronimo, the Apaches were no longer a threat and the region was opened for safe settlement. Arizona became the forty-eighth state in 1912, but it wasn't until 1948 that the Indians got the right to vote. Arizona is the fastest growing state in the Union due to the healthful climate which attracts many retired persons.

Arizona ranks number one in copper (fifty percent of the U.S. total) and produces one-sixth of its silver. Cotton is the chief agricultural crop and Arizona is ranked fourth in U.S. output. Arizona is ranked tenth in sheep and is a large producer of citrus.

Area: 113,909 square miles

Flagstaff

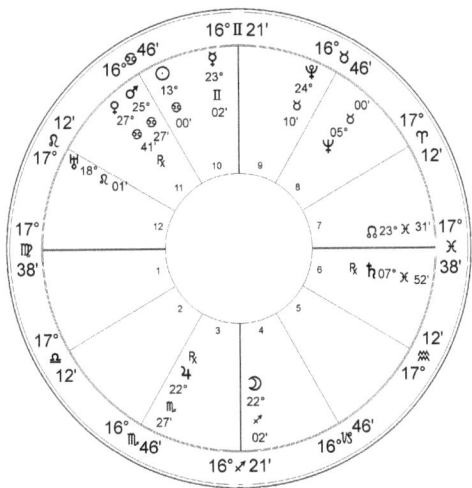

July 4, 1876
111W39, 35N12
10:35 a.m. MST

Flagstaff was founded when a group of pioneers stripped a pine tree, tied a flag to it and hoisted the emblem on the 100th anniversary of the Declaration of Independence. In 1894 the Lowell Observatory was founded (Midheaven semisquare Uranus). Flagstaff is gateway to the Grand Canyon and hosts an annual Indian powwow each July.

Incorporated: 1928
Elevation: 6,907 feet
Source: *American Guide Series*

Phoenix

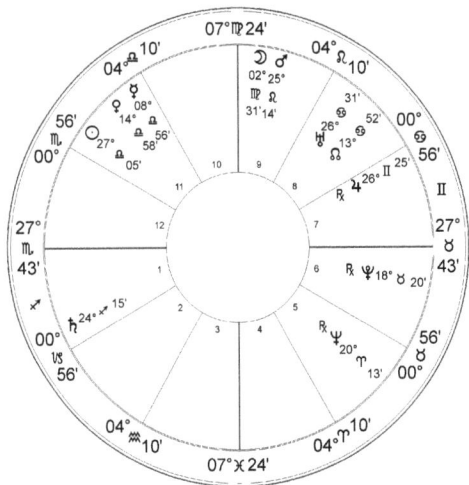

October 20, 1870
112W04, 33N27
9:09 a.m. MST

The first settlers were the Hohokam Indians who left the region about 1450. When Jack Swilling went there in 1867, he noticed the numerous canals in the region left over from their civilization and named the site after the mythical bird that rose from its ashes (the Phoenix is one of the symbols of Scorpio). The town site was formally platted in 1870, and Phoenix became the territorial capital in 1889 (Midheaven square Jupiter sextile Uranus). The Salt River overflowed in 1891, but with the completion of the Roosevelt Dam in 1911, future inundations have been largely curbed. In 1926 the railroad finally connected the city to the East (Midheaven sextile Moon). Since 1950 the population has increased eight-fold, no doubt due to the large influx of retirees escaping from colder climes.

Phoenix is ringed by mountains and lies in the Valley of the Sun. It's a typical middle class city, but increasing in sophistication and culture. Despite the thermal conditions during summer it is a dynamic and vibrant place. With irrigation, Phoenix is becoming a large agricultural center (Moon in Virgo).

Incorporated: February 25, 1881
Elevation: 1,080 feet
Area: 325 square miles
Source: *Story of Arizona* by Will Robinson. The AFA uses a chart with Saturn conjunct the Ascendant in late Sagittarius.

Prescott

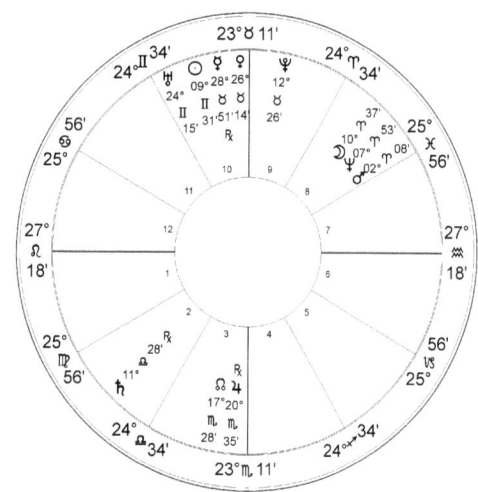

May 30, 1864
112W28, 34N33
11:19 a.m. MST

Founded in 1864 and named for the famous historian, it was the capital of Arizona until 1889. The first public rodeo in America was held here on July 4, 1888.

Incorporated: 1881
Elevation: 5,347 feet
Source: *Founding a Wilderness* by Pauline Henson

Tucson

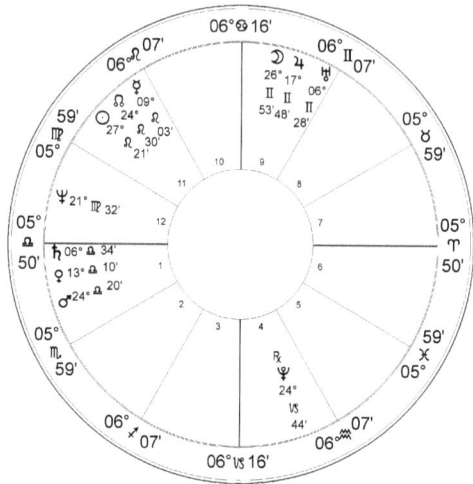

August 20, 1775
110W58, 32N13
8:56 a.m. MST

Padre Kino founded a mission just south of the city in 1700 and called it San Xavier del Bac. The military founded a presidio in 1775, and until 1854 (Midheaven trine Pluto) Tucson was the only walled city in the U.S. (Saturn in the first house). The capital of Arizona from 1867 to 1877, it was a rough, tough and bawdy town. It battled not only with the settlers, but with the Indians. In 1887 it became home to the University of Arizona (Midheaven sextile Sun). In recent years it has grown considerably due to the influx of retired persons.

Incorporated: February 7, 1877
Elevation: 2,390 feet
Area: 92 square miles
Source: Tucson Public Library

Yuma

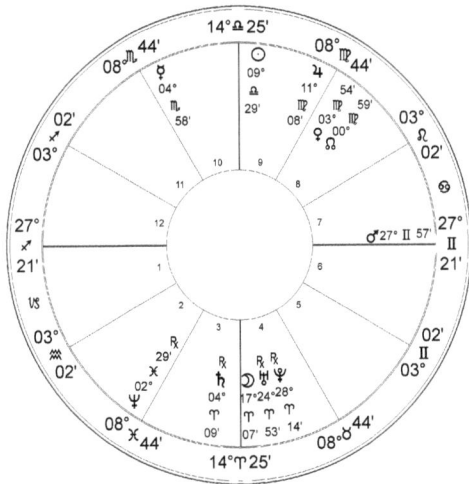

October 2, 1849
114W38, 32N43
11:46 a.m. PST

In 1779 Padre Garces founded Mission del la Purisima Concepcion on the west bank of the Colorado River; two years later all were killed by Indians. Not until 1849 when Fort Calhoun was founded was the region again settled. A military post, Fort Yuma, was founded on February 22, 1852. Colorado City was founded in July 1854 and later called Arizona City; its name was changed to Yuma in 1873. A gold rush in 1858 (Midheaven opposition Uranus) brought many settlers to the region via the Butterfield Stage.

Yuma receives more sunshine annually than any other city in the country. Strangely enough, the name Yuma means "smoke," a more apt description for Los Angeles.

Incorporated: April 7, 1914
Elevation: 137 feet
Source: Yuma Public Library

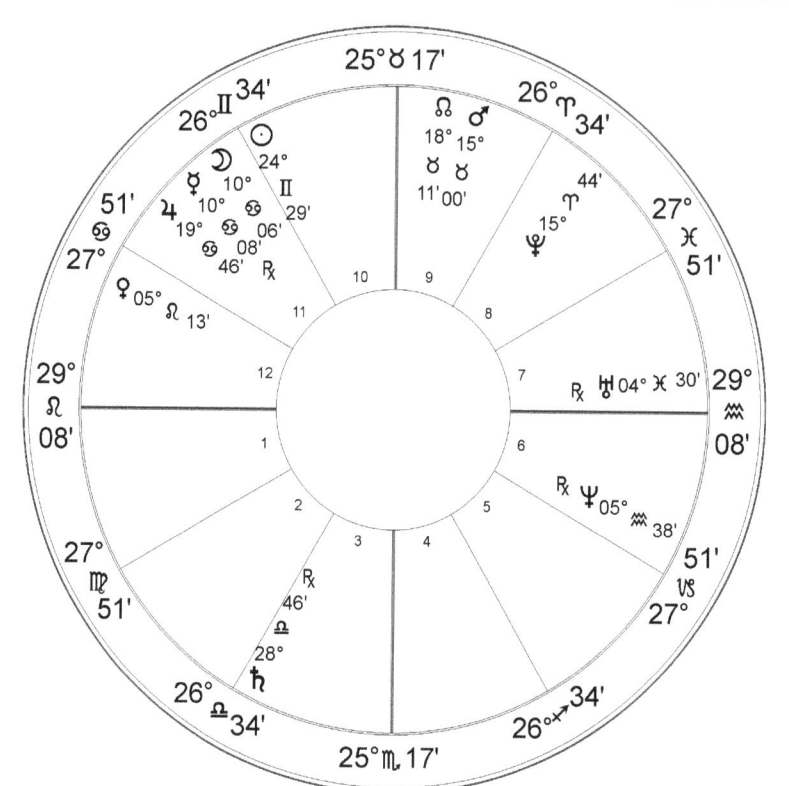

Arkansas

June 15, 1836
Little Rock
92W17, 34N45
10:05 a.m. CST
Source: Rectified

The region was first explored (for Spain) in 1541 by De Soto, who also discovered the Mississippi River. Henri de Tonti established the first trading post in 1686 at Arkansas Post, and the region was acquired in the Louisiana Purchase of 1803. The Territory of Arkansas was created on March 2, 1819; seventeen years later, Arkansas entered the Union. The state seceded May 6, 1861, and was readmitted June 22, 1868. The only diamond mine in the U.S. was discovered near Murfreesboro in 1906 and in 1921 oil production began at El Dorado. Arkansas was the scene of a bitter conflict between the U.S. National Guard and Governor Faubus in 1957 when President Eisenhower sent in troops so schools could be integrated. In 1970 the Arkansas River was finally made navigable.

Half of the farm income comes from cotton and the state ranks fifth in U.S. production. It ranks first in rice, third in chickens and fourth in turkeys. Arkansas produces more bauxite than any other state, and ranks number one in bromine and vanadium. Oil is the chief mineral resource.

Area: 53,104 square miles

Fayetteville

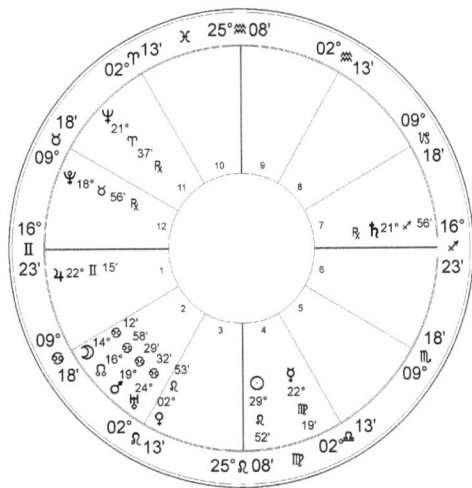

August 23, 1870
94W10, 36N04
12:01 a.m. CST

Fayetteville was founded in 1828 when the fist sale of lots was held. Made a county seat the following year, it was burned by Union troops in 1862. The University of Arkansas was founded in 1871.

Incorporated: August 23, 1870
Elevation: 1,427 feet
Source: Fayetteville City Hall

Fort Smith

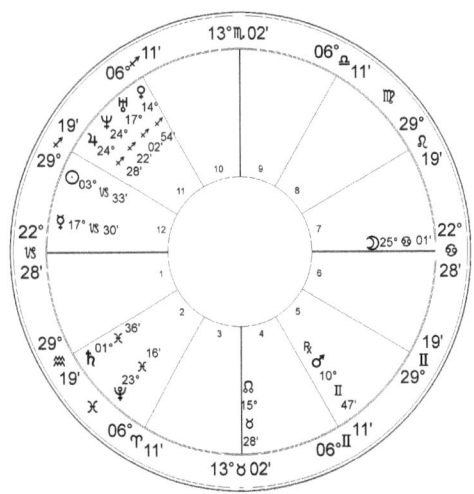

December 25, 1817
94W25, 35N23
8:45 a.m. CST

Stephen Long founded this garrison town on Christmas Day 1817 to quell the uprisings of the Osage and Cherokee tribes. The present town was founded five years later (Midheaven sextile Mercury). It was the headquarters of the infamous hanging Judge Parker, who reigned supreme over the Indian Territory from 1875 until 1896.

Incorporated: 1851
Elevation: 450 feet
Source: Fort Smith Public Library

Hot Springs

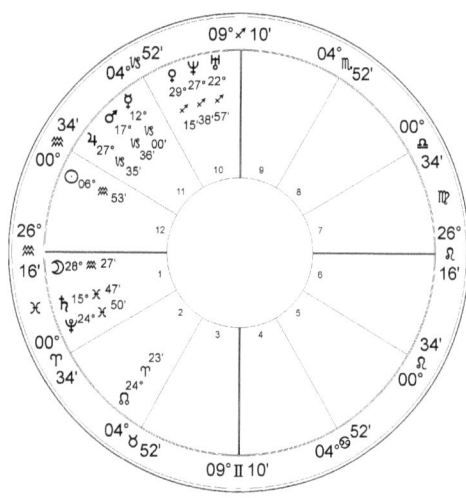

January 27, 1819
93W03, 34N30
8:18 a.m. CST

First settled in 1807, a patent was applied for in 1819 to survey the region, which was done the following year. The first hotel opened in 1820, and the first bathhouse in 1830. On April 20, 1832, the federal government established a reservation (Midheaven conjunct Uranus). Briefly the capital of Arkansas in 1862, it was burned the following year (Ascendant sesquare Uranus). The city was separated from the U.S. Reservation on February 14, 1876, and the present city was laid out. In 1913 a fire leveled fifty city blocks (Ascendant square Venus) and on March 4, 1921, the reservation became a national park.

Like Lourdes, Hot Springs is a natural spa which has given countless thousands relief from a variety of ailments. Located in the Ouachita Mountains, it is unquestionably the most cosmopolitan community in the state. Within the borders of the national park are forty-seven springs which bubble forth a steady stream of 143 degree mineral water.

Incorporated: January 18, 1879
Elevation: 599 feet
Source: Archives of the county historian

Little Rock

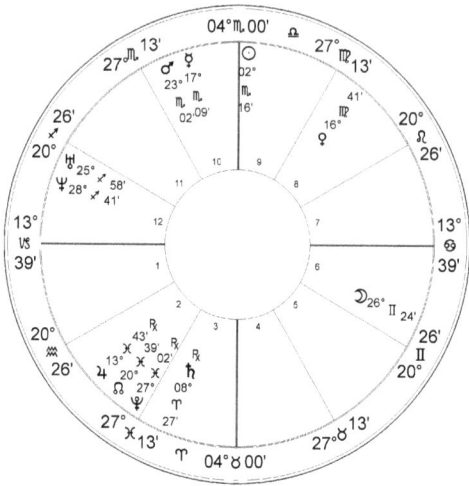

October 25, 1820
92W17, 34N45
Noon CST

The region was named in 1722 by Le Harpe, who noticed an outcropping of rock, La Petite Roche. First settled in 1812, it was chosen to be the capital of the Arkansas Territory in 1820 due to its central location. Occupied by Union forces in September 1863 (Midheaven square Venus), it survived the Civil War practically intact. During the Civil Rights movement of the 1950s, Governor Faubus caused quite a stir when he called out his troops to prevent integration at the nation's largest high school. Eisenhower counteracted when he called out the National Guard (Midheaven conjunct Pluto square Moon). Faubus then closed the entire school system for one year.

Resembling a city of much larger size, Little Rock has some of the cleanest air in the nation due to the plethora of natural gas. Hardly a hillbilly city, it is busy and progressive. It's the only capital city in the country that can boast of three capitol buildings, all of them still standing.

Incorporated: November 2, 1835
Elevation: 291 feet
Area: 57 square miles
Source: *Arkansas* by John Fletcher. *Historic Towns of the Southern States* by Lyman Powell says October 24, 1820

Pine Bluff

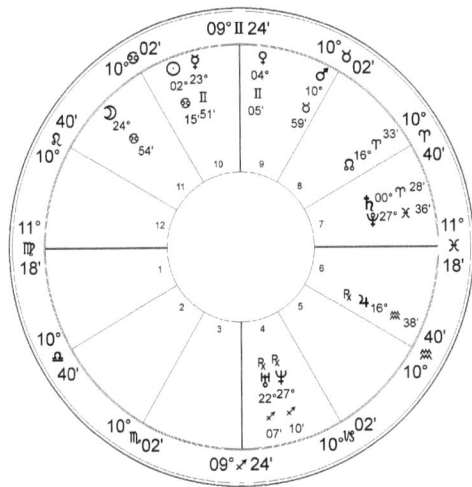

**June 24, 1819
92W01, 34N13
10:31 a.m. CST**

First settled as Mount Marie in June 1819, it was renamed in 1832 (Midheaven conjunct Mercury). Federal boats were stopped here in April 1861 (Midheaven inconjunct Uranus) and in October 1863 the Confederates attempted to take the town (Ascendant sextile Uranus). A massive flood in 1908 caused extensive damage (Ascendant trine Pluto).

Incorporated: 1839
Elevation: 221 feet
Source: Rectified, exact date unknown

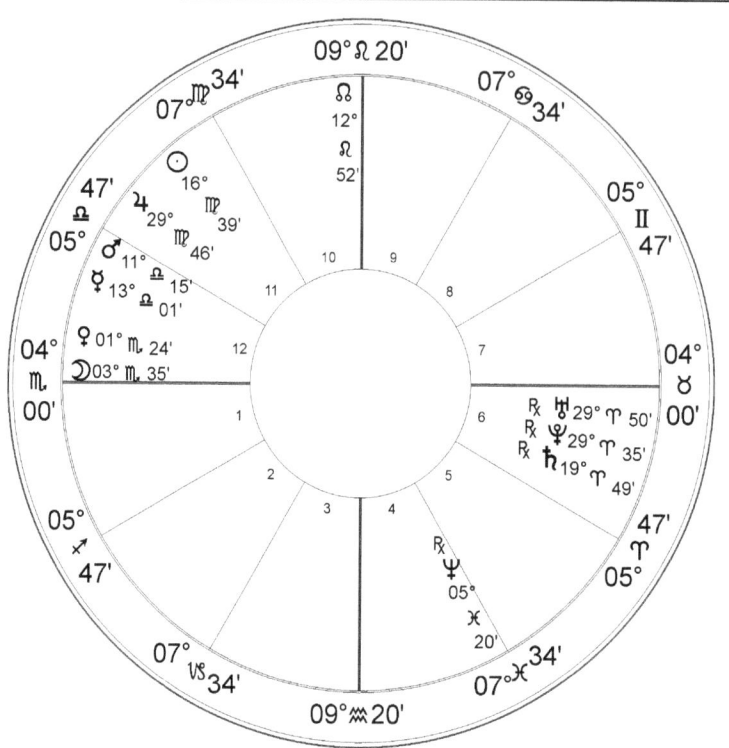

California

September 9, 1850
San Jose
121W53, 37N20
9:41 a.m. PST
Source: Rectified from sources which stated the president signed the Bill of Admission shortly before he went to lunch.

The coastline was first explored by Cabrillo in 1542, but it wasn't until 1769, with the founding of the mission by Father Junipero Serra, that any permanent settlement was attempted. Named after a mythical queen in a Spanish novel by Montalvo, it was originally thought to be an island. A chain of missions was founded along the El Camino Real all the way up to Sonoma by the Spanish. Americans took possession of the state when the Bear Flag was raised at Sonoma on June 14, 1846. Three weeks later Fremont declared the territory independent of Mexico. Gold was discovered at Sutter's Mill two years later, and the '49ers came by the thousands. Admitted to the Union in 1850, it soon became the richest mining state in the nation with the discovery of silver in neighboring Nevada. The Comstock Lode made San Francisco the largest, most cosmopolitan and sophisticated city in the West. Real estate developers created a land boom in the 1880s in southern California and towns blossomed forth by the hundreds. Many who were lured to this land of milk and honey by the advertisers soon found that it was indeed an Eden, and many decided to stay. Even with the collapse of land prices, Los Angeles emerged from a sleepy, frontier town into a booming metropolis by the turn of the century. Earthquakes have always been a part of California's history and in this century five have caused much damage: the 1906 quake almost leveled San Francisco; the 1933 shake wrecked Long Beach; the 1952 tremor in Bakersfield uprooted a feeling of security in residents of that valley town; and the 1971 and 1994 quakes in Los Angeles reminded Californians that they live on very shaky ground. Other big quakes, like the 1857 Tejon Pass quake and the 1872 Owens Valley earthquake caused little damage, but intensity were quite strong. As the region was sparsely settled at the time, no lives were lost.

California stretches all the way from the pine forest and snow capped volcanic peaks of Lassen and Shasta in the north to the infernos of the Mojave and Colorado deserts of the south. Dividing the state are two long mountain ranges, the Coast Range and the Sierra Nevada. Between them lie the rich Sacramento and San Joaquin Valleys, the fruit and vegetable market of the U.S. The coastline north of San Francisco is dotted with redwoods, the oldest trees on earth, while south of the Golden Gate is the picturesque Monterey Peninsula and the Big Sur country. The shoreline from Santa Barbara to the Mexican border is Mediterranean in appearance as well as climate. No other state in the nation has so varied extremes in climate as does California. If you're bored with the beach, you can often go to the mountains and ski within a few hours.

California is the eighth largest economy in the world, and without it much of the nation would suffer. California ranks number one in chickens, third in turkeys and sheep, and seventh in cattle. It produces the most avocados, grapes, raisins, peaches, plums, prunes, lemons, nectarines, olives, dates, almonds, walnuts and sugar beets. It was second in oranges, grapefruit and cotton, and third in rice; its fishing industry is the second largest after Alaska and it's third in oil and timber. Aircraft and aerospace industries, along with tourism, also are important.

California is the second largest industrial state and the nation's first agricultural region. It's clearly a giant in many fields. And don't forget the motion picture, television and record industries that are located there.
Area: 158,693 square miles

Anaheim

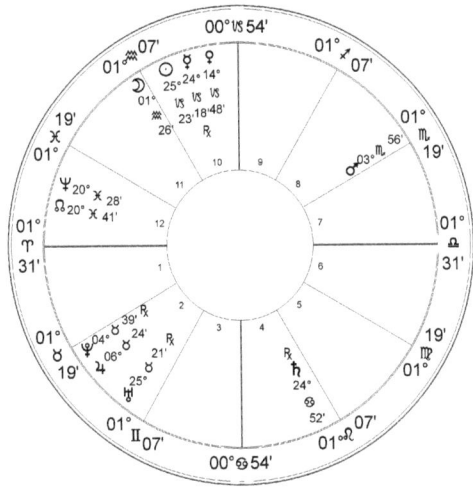

January 15, 1858
117W55, 33N50
10:16 a.m. PST

Founded by German immigrants as a farm cooperative in the fall of 1857, the first land was developed the following January. Only three decades ago, orange groves dotted the countryside, but with the establishment of Disneyland in 1955 (Ascendant trine Neptune), Anaheim mushroomed into the biggest attraction in the world. Even Russian Premier Khrushchev insisted on visiting the Magic Kingdom. Nearby attractions such as Knott's Berry Farm and the Movieland Wax Museum help make Anaheim a major convention site. In the vicinity is the heaviest concentration of hotels, motels and restaurants in southern California. In April 1982 a fire burned 525 apartments in a four block region, causing the city council to ban wood shingled roofs (Midheaven opposition Mars).

Incorporated: 1915
Elevation: 160 feet
Area: 40 square miles
Source: California Place Names

Bakersfield

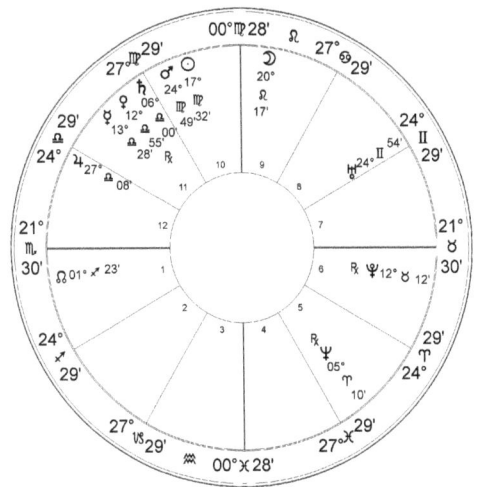

September 10, 1863
119W01, 35N23
10:49 a.m. PST

Founded in 1863, it became a county seat eleven years later. A fire destroyed most of the city in 1899 (Midheaven opposition Neptune) and an earthquake on July 21, 1952 (Ascendant square Pluto) leveled much of this valley town.

Bakersfield is located in the San Joaquin Valley, the nation's richest and most productive agricultural region. Kern County, of which Bakersfield is the seat, is also the largest oil producing region in the country.

Incorporated: 1873
Elevation: 406 feet
Source: W.W. Robinson, historian

Berkeley

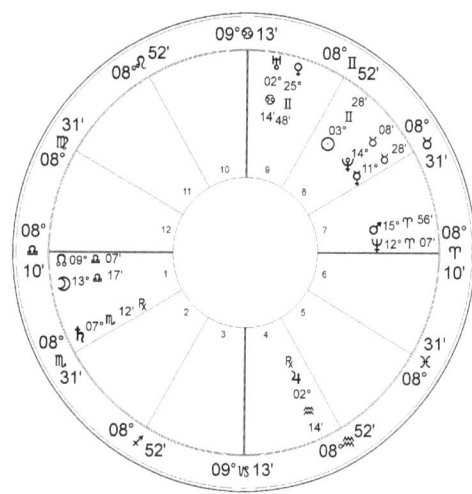

**May 24, 1866
122W16, 37N52
2:40 p.m. PST**

In 1820 this region was granted to Peralta, and in 1853 several San Francisco businessmen purchased the tract and called it Ocean View. Named Berkeley in 1866, the University of California opened its doors in 1873 (Ascendant conjunct Moon). The earthquake which caused so much havoc in San Francisco on April 18, 1906 also caused extensive damage on this side of the bay (Midheaven square Mercury/Saturn). A fire in September 1923 burned more than 600 buildings (Midheaven square Sun).

During the 1960s and the Vietnam War era, Berkeley was the scene of numerous demonstrations. It's a typical college town (ruler of the Ascendant in the ninth house) and it has drawn much attention over the years (Moon in the first house).

Incorporated: 1909
Elevation: 10 feet
Area: 11 square miles
Source: Archives of the University of California say May 24, 1866 at 3:00 p.m.; rectified

Beverly Hills

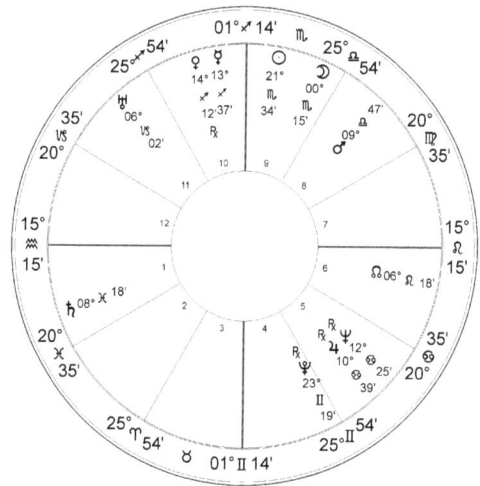

**November 14, 1906
118W25, 34N04
12:18 p.m. PST**

Originally known as El Rancho de las Aguas during colonial times, the city was founded as a housing tract in 1906. Beverly Hills fought hard not to become a part of Los Angeles, efforts due largely to the many movie stars living within its borders.

Called "The Golden Ghetto" because of its high concentration of wealth, it's an enclave of serenity and beauty completely surrounded by Los Angeles. Some of the most expensive real estate in the world is to be found there, and Rodeo Drive can boast of having the highest rentals of any street in the world per square foot.

Incorporated: 1914
Elevation: 200 feet
Area: 6 square miles
Source: Beverly Hills Public Library

Burbank

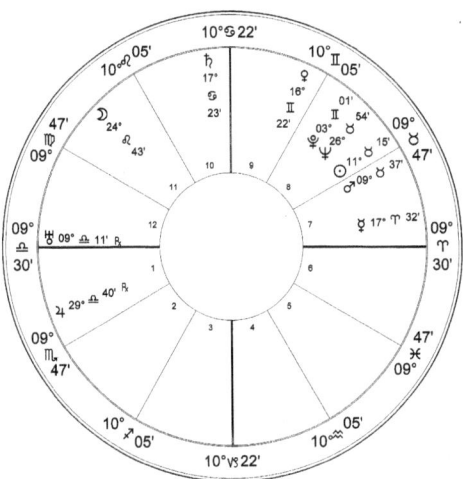

May 1, 1887
118W18, 34N10
4:00 p.m. PST

In 1867, local rancher David Burbank bought two old Spanish land grants and merged them into the Rancho de la Providencia. Two decades later a townsite was platted and named for him during the land boom created by the railroads. Burbank had southern California's first big airport (now Bob Hope) in May 1929 (Midheaven trine Mercury sextile Venus in ninth house), and during World War II, more than 100,000 were employed at the massive Lockheed aviation plant (Midheaven square Pluto, Ascendant square Moon).

Burbank is home to many motion picture studios like Warner Bros. and Disney. It's also home base for west coast operations of NBC and ABC. Johnny Carson once joked about "beautiful downtown Burbank," a true oxymoron as there wasn't much there. Burbank began reinventing itself in the 1980s, and for the first time began to renovate its downtown area. Previously, residents had to go over the city line to Los Angeles or Glendale to see movies made in their own home town (Uranus retrograde rising as ruler of the fifth house?). Now there are more than 30 cinemas in town.

Incorporated: September 11, 1911
Elevation: 560 feet
Source: W.W. Robinson, historian

Carmel

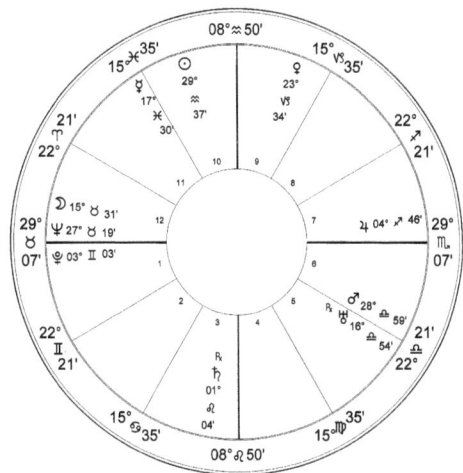

February 18, 1888
121W53, 36N32
11:00 a.m. PST

Father Junipero Serra moved the Mission San Carlos Borromeo from Monterey to Carmel in August 1771 to protect local residents (mostly women) from undue attentions of the male soldiers at its Presidio. Modern Carmel wasn't born until February 1888, when a Catholic retreat was established. Carmel was a quiet resort for decades until Clint Eastwood, the movie star, became mayor in 1986 (Midheaven conjunct Moon), and the place hasn't been the same since.

Carmel is extremely environmentally-conscious (Taurus rising) and has a love-hate relationship with tourists who descend on this rural village, especially in the summer (Pluto rising opposition Jupiter). Carmel has a love affair with its trees, which arcade its narrow streets. In many ways Carmel has shunned modern conveniences: there are no house numbers and no street lighting, no parking meters (they stripe your car instead) and no mail deliveries. Carmel is home to numerous artists and writers who dwell in this fairy-tale village just north of Big Sur and bordering Pebble Beach.

Incorporated: February 18, 1888
Elevation:
Source: Carmel City Hall

Fresno

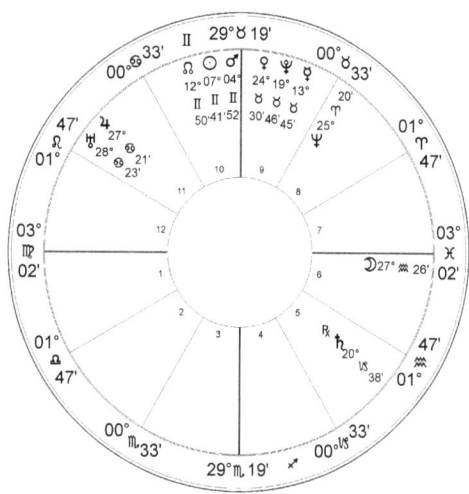

May 28, 1872
119W47, 36N44
11:21 a.m. PST

Founded as a railroad station in 1872, it was platted on September 25, 1874. The Smyrna fig was developed there, and thanks to irrigation, the region within 100 miles of Fresno produces much of the fruit and vegetables that line the counters in grocery stores (Virgo rising).

Incorporated: September 29, 1885
Elevation: 292 feet
Area: 58 squares miles
Source: *California Place Names*

Long Beach

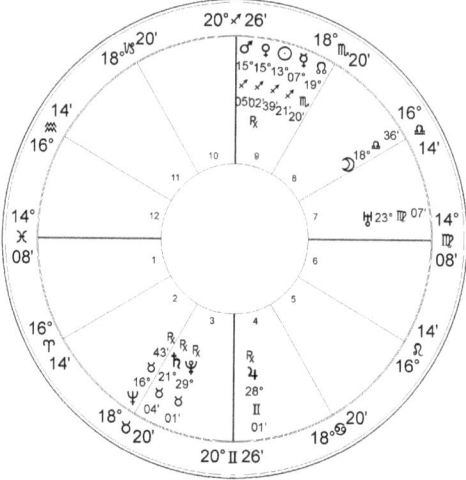

December 5, 1882
118W11, 33N47
12:13 p.m. PST

Founded originally as Wilmore City in 1882, it was refounded on July 30, 1887 and named Long Beach, for obvious reasons. The port was completed in 1914 (Midheaven trine Uranus) and oil was discovered at Signal Hill in 1923 (Ascendant conjunct Neptune). The earthquake of March 10, 1933 caused thousands of buildings to collapse. The death count was 115 and had the quake occurred a few hours earlier when children were in school, the toll would have been considerably higher. The city bought the liner Queen Mary in 1967, tore out its bowels and opened it to the public as a museum.

Once known as "Iowa West" because of its high concentration of Midwesterners, Long Beach often displays an inferiority complex (Sun square Pisces Ascendant) because of its titanic neighbor to the north, Los Angeles. It's a pleasant seaside community that takes life pretty much as it comes. Along with neighboring San Pedro, it has the largest harbor on the Pacific, and is home to many aircraft companies (stellium in Sagittarius in the ninth house).

Incorporated: 1888 and 1897
Elevation: 35 feet
Area: 50 square miles
Source: *Long Beach* by W.W. Robinson

Los Angeles

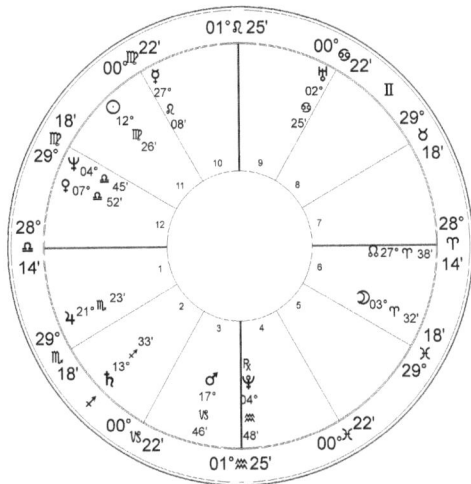

September 4, 1781
118W15, 34N03
9:11 a.m. PST

On August 1, 1769, Portola named the place La Pueblo de la Reina de los Angeles de Porciuncula. Twelve years later, De Neve and forty-four settlers from nearby Mission San Gabriel founded the city. Capital of the California Republic in 1835, it was chartered by the Mexicans that same year, and by the Americans in 1850. During the 1850s, Los Angeles was the most lawless city in the land. By 1871, anti-Chinese sentiments erupted in the lynching of nineteen Orientals. With the arrival of the railroad in 1876, settlers poured in by the thousands. Price wars erupted on the railroad, and a land boom sent prices soaring. The boom collapsed in 1887 (Ascendant semisquare Saturn) but many stayed on to enjoy this land of eternal sunshine. With its limited natural resources, largely due to a lack of water, Los Angeles in 1900 could conceivably grow no bigger. But Mulholland brought water from Owens Valley and by 1913 (Midheaven conjunct Saturn), Los Angeles had more wet stuff than it could ever use. During the early 20th century the movie industry was founded in Hollywood in 1911 and the port completed in San Pedro. Los Angeles doubled its size the following year when it annexed the vast San Fernando Valley. This made Los Angeles the largest city in area in the world (Jupiter in the first house).

During the Depression, immigrants from Arkansas and Oklahoma trekked across the plains expecting a better life. In 1932, Los Angeles hosted the Olympics, and the following year, an earthquake destroyed many schools and offices (Midheaven square Moon opposition Uranus). During World War II thousands of servicemen came through the city on their way to the Orient, and after the war many decided to return. In 1957 the former building height limit of 150 feet (necessitated due to earthquakes) was repealed and now Los Angeles boasts the tallest building west of the Mississippi.

The 1960s weren't kind to Los Angeles. The decade opened with the Bel Air fire in November 1961, which burned many expensive homes in that plush neighborhood; two years later the Baldwin Hills Dam burst. But the most terrifying event of the 1960s occurred during August 1965 when the neighborhood of Watts erupted in flames (Midheaven conjunct Pluto). Torrential rains during the winter of 1968-69 caused many homes to slide down hills, and with the opening of the 1970s, Los Angeles experienced another earthquake. On the morning of February 9, 1971, citizens were awakened to violent shaking that eventually caused the collapse of hospitals in the San Fernando Valley. Parts of that valley were evacuated when a dam threatened to break. More than 65 were killed, and many overpasses on the freeway system were in ruins (Ascendant square Mercury).

During the remainder of the 1970s Los Angeles experienced a culture shock. No longer was it a city of white middle class people, for the arrival of Mexicans, many of them entering illegally, made Los Angeles the second largest Mexican city in the world. After the Vietnam War, boatloads of refugees settled in the area, and now Los Angeles is on its way to becoming our country's first third-world city, as more than half of its citizens are those of minority groups. One thing this influx created was more variety in the cuisine offered, for prior to their arrival, Los Angeles was known as the land of fast food franchises (Moon in Aries in the sixth house).

In recent years the region around Los Angeles has been the scene of much media attention. The Whittier quake of October 1987 (Midheaven opposite Mercury, Ascendant inconjunct Mars) and the Sierra Madre tremor of March 1991 caused nerves to rattle in the San Gabriel Valley east of the city. The videotaped beating of a black motorist, Rodney King, by the police escalated into the most costly urban riot in American history in April 1992 when the officers responsible for the beating were acquitted. Three days of looting followed with many parts of the city going up in flames. When it was over, fifty-two people were dead and more than $10 billion in damages was logged (Midheaven trine Uranus semisquare Mars, Ascendant inconjunct Jupiter sesquare progressed Pluto). Then, just as Los Angeles was beginning to recover from a recession, the Northridge earthquake leveled numerous apartment complexes and businesses in January 1994 (Midheaven inconjunct Neptune). More than fifty-eight people were killed and the loss to property and businesses will run close to $100 billion before the final tally. In early 2005, the City of Angels was deluged with more than two and a half times its normal rainfall, causing scores of homes to slide down hillsides. Many canyon roads were impassable, causing longer than normal delays on roads that were still serviceable (Ascendant conjunct Uranus square Moon and Neptune inconjunct Pluto).

Los Angeles is a huge city in area (Jupiter in the first house) so it's hard to make generalizations about a place as complex and diverse. One of the most materialistic cities in the country (Sun trine Mars in Capricorn), it's not all that laid back (Libra rising) and just as competitive as New York or Washington. The deception arises because the ruler of the Ascendant is in the twelfth house conjunct Neptune.

Los Angeles is a clean city, full of people who love the outdoors. They take care of their bodies (Sun in Virgo) and explore new and unusual means of higher spiritual thought (Uranus in the ninth house). Angelenos drive fast, but cautiously (Mars in Capricorn), to get to their single family homes (Uranus in Cancer) and along the way they might stop off at a fast food joint (Moon in the sixth house).

The Angeleno lives in an area prone to earthquakes (Pluto in the fourth house) and floods during the torrential winter rains. He digs his solitude (ruler of the Ascendant in the twelfth house) and is not unafraid to explore new and sometimes kinky means of sexual awareness (Venus conjunct Neptune).

The Sun square Saturn has given Los Angeles the drive and ambition to become the largest port on the Pacific, the financial heart of the West, and home of the entertainment industry. The only negative things are the smog and lack of rapid transit. Both have been a sore spot ever since the city tore down its electrified railroad in 1951.

Incorporated: April 4, 1850
Elevation: 340 feet
Area: 465 square miles
Source: *American Guide Series* for date; American Federation of Astrologers for time

Hollywood

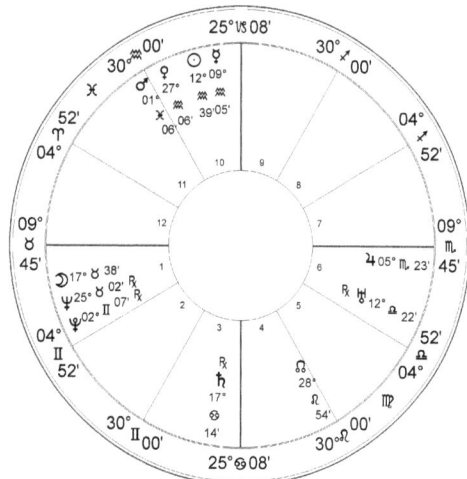

February 1, 1887
118W20, 34N06
10:55 a.m. PST

Founded by Mrs. Wilcox in 1887, it was named after her summer home in Illinois. Incorporated as an independent city on November 14, 1903, it surrendered its independence in 1910 and joined Los Angeles due to a lack of adequate water. The first movie studio opened in 1911 and the famed Hollywood Bowl saw its first outdoor concert in 1919.

Today, Hollywood is just another large neighborhood of the City of Los Angeles, fraught with the same problems that plague any city with the reputation of Hollywood. Drug addiction, prostitution, teenage runaways and a housing shortage seem a far cry from what most perceive this community to be. Once the glamour capital of the world, due to the numerous movie and television studios located nearby, the only real tourist attractions left are the Chinese Theatre and the Walk of Fame, where the names of stars are imbedded into the sidewalk.

Incorporated: 1903
Elevation: 286 feet
Area: 10 square miles
Source: *The First 100 Years* by Bruce Torrence

San Fernando Valley

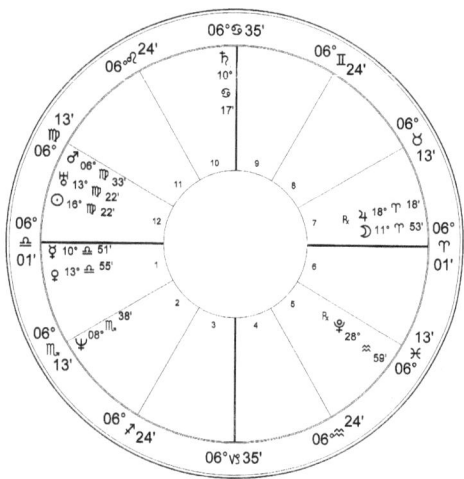

September 8, 1797
118W29, 34N18
7:05 AM PST

The Valley was founded in September 1797, when the Mission San Fernando Rey de Espana was founded 24 miles north of El Pueblo de los Angeles. The Spanish surrendered to General Fremont in January 1847 (Midheaven semisquare Saturn, Ascendant inconjunct Jupiter) and three years later California entered the Union. The first town was platted in 1874, the same year the railroad arrived (Ascendant trine Moon sextile Mercury). Over the next few years other small towns sprang up, including the civic heart of the Valley, Van Nuys, which was born on February 22, 1911 at 1:00 p.m. (Midheaven trine Pluto).

In November 1913, the L.A. Aqueduct was completed, but its lifesaving contents couldn't be touched by the Valley unless the region agreed to become part of the bigger city (Midheaven semisquare Sun, Ascendant square Moon and Mercury). To insure its survival the Valley capitulated and merged with Los Angeles in May 1915 (Ascendant trine Sun semisquare Pluto). The first airfield opened in December 1928 (Midheaven sextile Sun) six months before Burbank airport further east. The Valley had always been prone to flooding and the torrents of March 1938 killed 96 residents (Midheaven sesquare Moon, Ascendant square Neptune). The Sepulveda Flood Control Basin, completed in 1940, controlled future inundations along with encasing the Los Angeles River in concrete all the way to the ocean (Midheaven square Pluto).

The population doubled despite the Depression, and by the time of the attack on Pearl Harbor the region had 112,000 residents. Thousands were hired to work in the aircraft and defense plants and, after the war, hordes flocked to this formerly rural region and the population quadrupled. A decade later the population doubled again. The region's first university, Cal State Northridge, opened in 1960 (Midheaven trine Jupiter, Ascendant trine Saturn), the same year the color barrier was breached, allowing blacks to move out of their ghetto. Proposition 13, which limited property taxes, was largely propelled by Valley residents in 1978 (Midheaven trine Mars, Ascendant square Saturn), and school busing arrived later that year (Ascendant opposition Mercury). Thousands moved away or put their kids in private schools.

The Valley, like all of southern California, is prone to earthquakes. The quakes of December 1812 damaged the Mission (Midheaven semisquare Mars, Ascendant opposition Jupiter), but the Mission suffered no damage during the Ft. Tejon quake of January 1857 (Midheaven conjunct Mars, Ascendant semisquare Mercury sesquare Saturn). Schools were the major casualty during the Long Beach tremor of March 1933 (Ascendant sesquare Sun), as they were in the rest of the city.

The Sylmar quake killed 65 in February 1971. Two major medical facilities were destroyed and thousands were evacuated below the Van Norman Dam as it threatened to collapse (Midheaven sextile Pluto). Damage was more than $500 million. The most costly disaster, however, occurred in January 1994, when a rift opened up beneath the Valley in Northridge. Thousands of homes and apartments were ruined, freeways and shopping centers collapsed and the damage ran upwards of $40 billion. Only 57 people were killed because most residents were at home in bed (Midheaven sesquare Mars, Ascendant trine Mars opposition Neptune). Six year later, after innumerable delays, the last leg of the subway arrived in North Hollywood (Ascendant trine Uranus).

The Valley is the personification of the American dream: single-story houses with backyard patios and swimming pools and plenty of fences or shrubbery to insulate residents from their neighbors (Sun and Uranus in twelfth). Due to the lack of public transportation, a car was a necessity and before long drive-in movies, restaurants, cleaners and even churches sprung up. Then came the huge malls and ubiquitous mini-malls and, yes, smog. Residents still want to preserve their small-town environment (Venus, Ascendant ruler, square Saturn, fourth house ruler). The Moon conjunct Jupiter demands elbow room, but their square to Saturn and opposition to Mercury necessitate very long commutes on the few freeways that traverse the region. The Valley has reached "middle age" and has the same problems that afflict the rest of the city. Often feeling they've been short-changed by City Hall, a secession movement in 2002 put the issue on the ballot. The measure failed but the feeling remains due to Saturn in the tenth square Venus, ruler of the Ascendant.

One of the Valley's main industries is entertainment. The first movie studio (Universal) opened in March 1915, and hundreds of TV shows are shot in the region, either on set or on location. The Valley also holds the dubious distinction of being the "porn capital" of the world. Could that be because Neptune sits in the second house in Scorpio, no less, and squares Pluto, the ruler of Scorpio in the fifth house of fun and pleasure?

Even though Valley residents may prefer to think they're different from the rest of Los Angeles due to that Sun and Uranus in the twelfth house, the truth belies that fact. Los Angeles and the Valley both have their Suns in Virgo, the Moon in Aries, Venus in Libra, Mars in earth signs and their Jupiter in Mars-ruled signs. Their Ascendants are also in Libra. But Valleyites are a stubborn lot and stick to their unique and individual communities, such as Tarzana, Encino, Studio City and North Hollywood. Los Angeles is on the other side of the hills, denser, more crowded and congested. If this seems strange, residents of Queens in New York City do the same.

Incorporated: May 22, 1915
Population: 1,350,000
Area: 222 square miles
Source: *San Fernando Valley* by Kevin Roderick and *American Guide Series*

Monterey

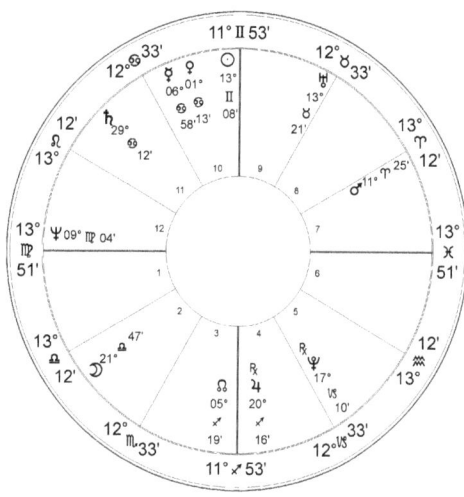

June 3, 1770
121W55, 36N37
Noon PST

Founded jointly by the clergy and the military, Monterey remained the capital of California until 1849. Attacked by pirates in 1818 (Midheaven conjunct Saturn), it was captured by Alvarado in 1836 after the firing of only one shot (Midheaven square Uranus).

Situated on the picturesque Monterey Peninsula, one of the most gorgeous spots on the Pacific Coast, the seventeen-mile drive takes you past Pebble Beach, the golf capital of the world, and ends up in Carmel, which has laws that protect that tiny community from modern development. If you want to know more about this region, read the novels of John Steinbeck. The city has many historic sights, and in nearby Carmel is the mission where Padre Junipero Serra, the founder of California, lies buried.

Incorporated: March 16, 1889
Elevation: 25 feet
Source: *Forts of the West* by Robert Frazer

Oakland

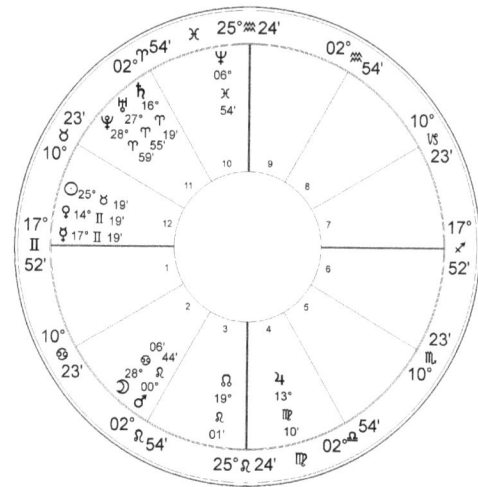

May 16, 1850
122W16, 37N49
6:24 a.m. PST

Founded during the halcyon days of the California Gold Rush in 1850, Oakland became the western terminus of the Union Pacific in 1869 (Midheaven opposition Jupiter). After the earthquake that leveled San Francisco on April 18, 1906, thousands made their homes in Oakland (Ascendant conjunct Mars). Nearby Alameda was the chief embarkation point for servicemen leaving for the Orient. When San Francisco refused to containerize its waterfront in the 1960s, Oakland became the chief port of the Bay area. The Loma Prieta earthquake of October 1989 caused massive damage to the waterfront and downtown areas. A portion of the Cypress Freeway pancaked and many historic buildings had to be closed (Ascendant inconjunct Neptune). A massive fire in the hills above the city burned more than 1,000 homes in August 1991 (Midheaven semisquare Sun).

If Long Beach is the stepchild of Los Angeles, then Oakland is the forgotten child of San Francisco. Its contributions have long been overlooked as people pass through this city on their way to the more glamorous city across the bay. Largely a working class city with a heavy concentration of poor people, downtown Oakland is quite attractive, being astride Lake Merritt. Oakland today is the transportation hub of the Bay region and is connected to San Francisco via Bay Area Rapid Transit (BART) and the Bay Bridge.

Incorporated: March 25, 1854
Elevation: 25 feet
Area: 53 square miles
Source: *The Beginnings of Oakland* by Peter Conmy

Palm Springs

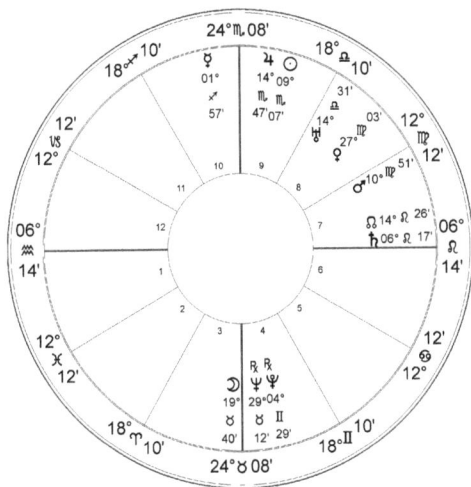

November 1, 1887
116W33, 33N50
12:30 p.m. PST

In 1884 the towns of Palm Valley and Agua Caliente were founded, and in 1887 the region was formally opened for settlement. The first sanatorium opened in 1909 when the community had only one store and one roadside inn. During the 1930s, Palm Springs was discovered by movie stars and today many of them call this their home. Palm Springs, along with Pebble Beach, calls itself the "golf capital of the world" and it has more swimming pools per capita than any city in the country. Summertime is like Dante's Inferno, with the winter being more temperate.

Incorporated: 1938
Elevation: 430 feet
Source: Palm Springs Public Library says November 1, 1887 at 12:30 p.m.

Pasadena

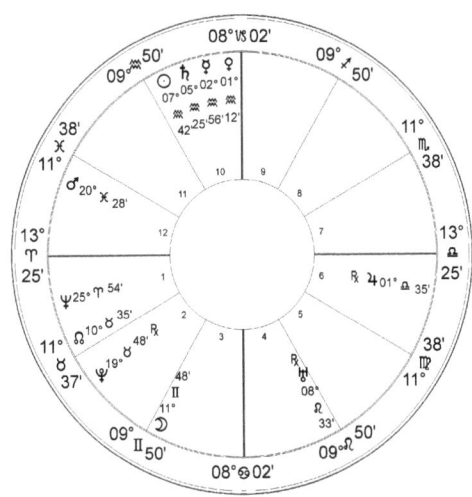

January 27, 1874
118W06, 34N09
10:00 a.m. PST

Originally known as Rancho San Pasqual in 1826, it was founded from lands owned by the Mission San Gabriel. Settled as Indiana Colony in 1873, it was formally founded during a picnic the following January. Its name was changed in 1875, and the first Tournament of Roses Parade took place on New Year's Day 1890 (Ascendant square Sun).

Pasadena is also home to Cal Tech (where seismic readings are done on earthquakes) and the Jet Propulsion Laboratory, which plays a large role in our space program. Santa Anita racetrack is in nearby Sierra Madre and the world famous Huntington Gardens are just east of the city in posh San Marino.

Incorporated: June 19, 1886
Elevation: 864 feet
Area: 36 square miles
Source: Pasadena Public Library says January 27, 1874 at 10:00 a.m.

Sacramento

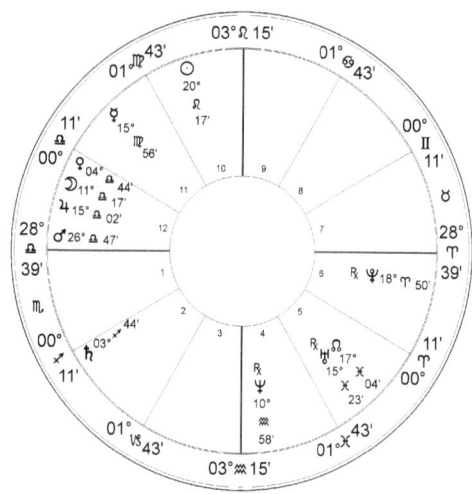

August 13, 1839
121W29, 38N35
11:02 a.m. PST

Captain John Sutter founded New Helvetia in 1839 and nine years later gold was discovered nearby in Coloma. The Gold Rush brought prosperity but an end to the peaceful way of life (Midheaven opposition Neptune sextile Moon). From 1849 to 1853, three floods almost wiped the town off the map and fires were a constant threat. Made capital of California in 1854 (Midheaven trine Pluto), it became the western terminus of the Pony Express in 1860. Linked to San Francisco Bay via canals in 1911, it became an oceangoing port (Midheaven conjunct Jupiter). The Port District was established in 1953.

Sacramento's chief business is government, for it is the capital of the most populous state in the nation. Recent renovations on the capitol building have made it practically earthquake proof. Sacramento is also famous for its camellias and its numerous trees (Libra rising).

Incorporated: February 27, 1850
Elevation: 30 feet
Area: 94 square miles
Source: *Sutter's Own Story* by Erwin Gudde

Salinas

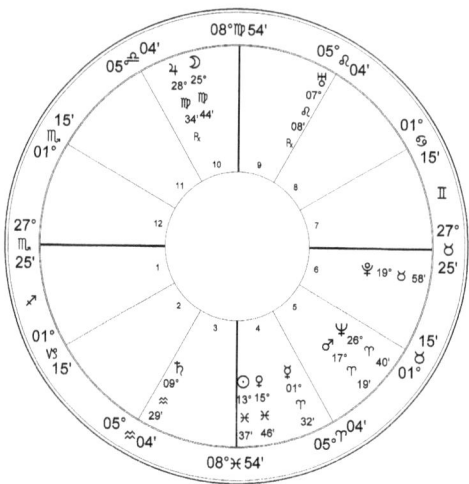

March 4, 1874
121W39, 36N40
12:01 AM PST

Salinas, which means salt marsh, was laid out in 1868 on the former Rancho El Sausal Nacional. Three gentlemen who founded the town wanted to give a right of way to the Southern Pacific Railroad, which arrived on November 7, 1872. Being close to the San Andreas fault, earthquakes are always a potential for disaster. The great San Francisco quake of April 1906 caused extensive damage to Salinas, as did the Loma Prieta quake of October 1989, especially to neighboring Watsonville, which was shaken off its foundations.

Salinas lies at the top of a valley of the same name which stretches more than 75 miles to the south. This is the "salad bowl of America," which produces most of America's lettuce, broccoli and artichokes. Salinas is also the birthplace of one of America's great novelists, John Steinbeck. His books, East of Eden and The Grapes of Wrath, intimately portray life in this region to the point that when I saw East of Eden and then read the book, I wanted to move there. By the late 1980s, I lived on the Monterey Peninsula just a few miles to the west.

In recent years Salinas has become a commuter suburb of the extremely expensive Silicon Valley to the north near San Jose because housing prices in Salinas are a bit cheaper . . . but, then, there's that long commute.

Incorporated: March 4, 1874
Elevation: 267 feet
Area: 19 square miles
Source: Monterey County Historical Society

San Diego

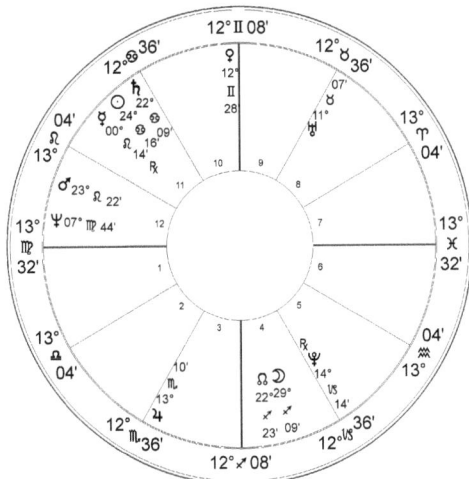

**July 16, 1769
117W09, 32N43
8:52 AM PST**

Cabrillo first discovered California at Point Loma in 1542, but until Padre Serra arrived in 1769, settlement wasn't attempted. The tiny community was moved six miles east in 1774, and in 1871 a new city was begun where the downtown area is currently situated. Two years after incorporation, in 1852, San Diego lost its charter due to lawlessness (Ascendant square Mars) and didn't regain it until 1872 (Midheaven sextile Saturn). During the 1880s, a land boom ensued until 1887 when the bottom fell out.

San Diego has been in the forefront of aviation ever since the first seaplane took off for the Orient in 1911 (Ascendant sextile Jupiter). In 1915 the city hosted the Panama-California Exposition in Balboa Park; many of those structures were left standing after the fair and contribute much to this urban oasis. The first military base was established in 1917 (Midheaven sextile Neptune) and by World War II San Diego was the prime naval base of the Pacific.

San Diego has the most equable climate of any mainland U.S. city. Actually composed of many communities like La Jolla, Mission Beach, Ocean Beach and Sunset Cliffs, it resembles a small town more than the second largest city in the state (Virgo rising). Many residents are retired military people and a number of its temporary citizens are in the navy (Moon in the fourth house). Some of its residents argue that the city is getting too large while others think the place is dull and unexciting. Well, if you're bored with going to the finest zoo in the country, which is located in the finest city park in the land, or with Sea World or the Wild Animal Park, maybe this city which loves nature and wildlife (Virgo rising) isn't your cup of tea. If nightlife is what you're after, you can always journey fifteen miles south to Tijuana, Mexico, which swings all hours of the day and night. San Diego, you see, is basically a strict and conventional city (Sun conjunct Saturn), its residents are peaceful, unhurried and casual—sort of like Los Angeles with lower blood pressure. It's a clean, sunny and self-satisfied town (Venus at the Midheaven) that has fortunately had no natural disasters in its history.

Incorporated: March 27, 1850
Elevation: 20 feet
Area: 320 square miles
Source: *American Guide Series;* chart by Ralph Kraum

San Francisco

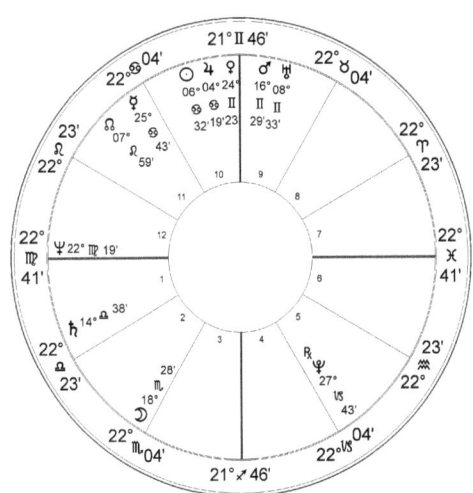

**June 27, 1776
122W25, 37N47
11:08 AM PST**

Founded one week before the Declaration of Independence was signed, the Presidio and Mission Dolores were dedicated within three months. The settlement was called Yerba Buena until the arrival of the Americans in 1846 who took possession of the city (Ascendant sextile Neptune, Midheaven sextile Jupiter). Three years later gold was discovered and San Francisco became the chief port of entry. Almost overnight the population swelled to 50,000 and the crime wave was on. Vigilante communities were formed which took the law into their own hands (Midheaven square Uranus). Because the city could no longer control the violence, it was decided to let the sheriff handle the problem; thus, San Francisco merged with its own county in 1856 (Ascendant square Uranus).

During those early years, scores of fires swept through the wooden community; earthquakes were another cause for alarm. The tremors of October 8, 1865 (Midheaven square Mars) and October 21, 1868 were particularly severe. The famed cable cars began running up Nob Hill in 1873 (Ascendant sextile Mercury) and by the turn of the century San Francisco was the wealthiest, most sophisticated and cosmopolitan city west of Chicago. All that changed on the morning of April 18, 1906.

At 5:13 a.m., the ground rumbled and soon the city was shaking. Fires that erupted soon consumed more than four square miles of the city, including 28,000 buildings and the loss of 450 lives. Almost 250,000 were homeless, and tents were set up in Golden Gate Park (Midheaven square Pluto, Ascendant opposition Sun/Jupiter). By 1915, things were rebuilt and San Francisco hosted the Panama-Pacific Exposition (Midheaven trine Sun).

With the completion of the Bay Bridge in 1936 (Midheaven sextile Pluto) and the Golden Gate Bridge the following year (Ascendant trine Uranus), the ferryboats went into decline. In 1939 the Golden Gate Expo was held, and at the end of World War II, the United Nations was founded (Midheaven opposition Uranus). The rapid transit system (BART) was finally completed in 1974 (Ascendant opposition Saturn). The mayor of San Francisco, George Moscone, and a supervisor (alderman), who happened to be homosexual, were both shot in November 1979 (Sun conjunct Pluto). The gay population rioted the following May when the assassin was given a light sentence.

The Loma Prieta earthquake of October 1989 caused the Marina district to erupt in flames as gas lines broke and homes buckled and pancaked into the soft subsoil (Midheaven trine Neptune, Ascendant sextile Sun). The quake also made the Embarcadero Freeway unsafe, so eventually this detested eyesore was torn down to the cheers of San Franciscans who had for years complained that the structure blocked their view of the bay.

Ask any foreigner what their favorite city in our country is, and San Francisco is often at the top of the list. Known for its incomparable views and fine restaurants (Sun in Cancer), it's a city that cherishes its past. Old Victorian houses are restored and painted in wild colors. Being a tight and compact city (Saturn rising), in order to really see the place, you'll have to get out and walk. Because of the Golden Gate, it's America's only air conditioned city, and the fog which creeps in each night keeps the lid on high temperatures (Neptune rising). San Francisco also is possessed of a narcissistic civic pride (Venus at Midheaven). It's a liberal community which has withstood the onslaught of the '49ers, the bohemians, hippies (Mars and Uranus in the ninth house) and now the emergence of the large gay community. It has a habit of absorbing them all (Neptune rising) and won't bat an eyelash if you happen to be weird or outrageous. San Francisco has the largest Chinese community outside the Orient, a large portion in Chinatown, the most densely populated area in the country.

San Francisco is a city for the senses (Sun in Cancer, Moon in Scorpio) for it will tantalize and lure you to experience things you never dreamed possible. Sometimes the promise is not as great as expected, so people drink or take drugs. This city has the highest alcoholism and suicide rate of any American city (Neptune rising square Venus and Midheaven). Pluto in the fifth house points to the number of unusual pleasures that can be found in this "Baghdad by the Bay."

Incorporated: April 15, 1850
Elevation: 65 feet
Area: 47 square miles
Source: *American Guide Series*. Diary of the priest who was one of the original settlers gives the founding time of 11:00 a.m.

San Jose

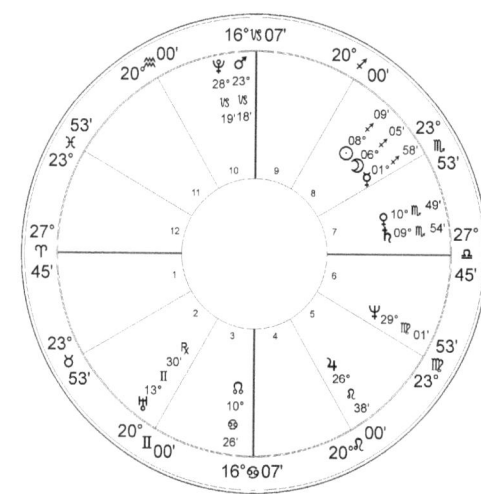

November 29, 1777
121W53, 37N20
2:41 PM PST

San Jose was founded as the first pueblo (town) in California, independent of either the clergy or the military. It was capital of California from 1849 until 1852 (Midheaven sextile Pluto). The real estate boom of the 1880s went bust in 1887 (Midheaven square Sun/Moon). During the 1906 earthquake, San Jose suffered considerable damage, but recovered quickly (Midheaven square Jupiter). With the advent of the electronic age and the space industry, San Jose has taken its place among those cities which prefer clean industries. Many aviation plants are located there (Uranus in the second house).

Incorporated: March 27, 1850
Elevation: 90 feet
Area: 152 square miles
Source: *American Guide Series*

San Luis Obispo

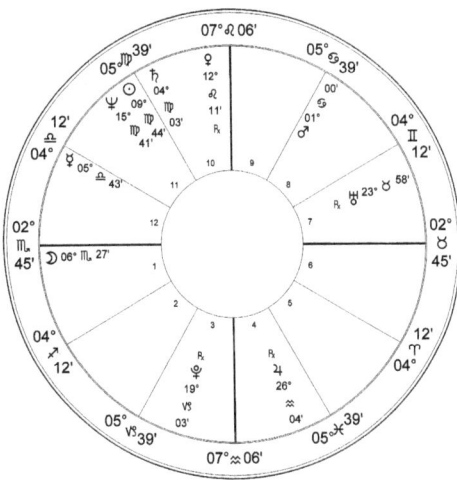

**September 1, 1772
120W40, 35N17
9:55 AM PST**

Father Junipero Serra founded the Mission San Luis Obispo de Tolosa in 1772, naming it after a French saint of the Middle Ages. Obispo means "bishop," and "Tolosa" is Spanish for the French city of Toulouse. The community remained quiet and isolated until 1894, when the railroad arrived (Midheaven square sun, Ascendant conjunct Jupiter). In 1901, California Polytechnic State University (Cal Poly) was founded (Midheaven square Neptune, Ascendant trine Moon).

Due to its location a bit inland from the Pacific Ocean, San Luis Obispo is considerably warmer than the neighboring seaside towns of Morro Bay and Pismo Beach, famous for its clams. At the southern entrance to the city is the world-famous Madonna Inn, where no two rooms are designed or decorated exactly the same. It's a sight to behold, especially at night.

Incorporated: 1856
Elevation: 238 feet
Source: *American Guide Series*

Santa Barbara

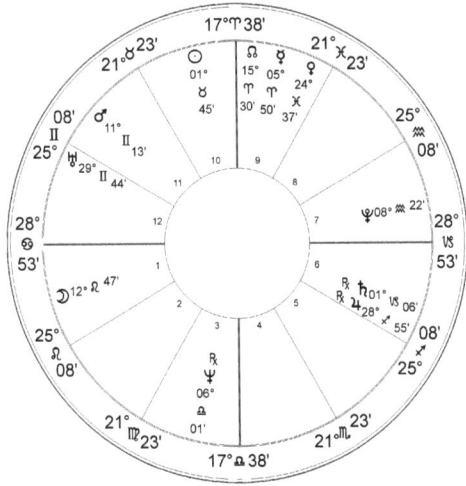

**April 21, 1782
119W42, 34N25
11:04 AM PST**

Founded by the military in 1782, the mission was erected four years later (Ascendant square Sun). The earthquake of December 1812 caused much of the city to crumble, but the quake of June 29, 1925 really messed up the town. Most of the downtown area was in ruins, and the mission tower fell down (Ascendant trine Venus). Since that time, efforts have been made to insure the architectural uniformity of all buildings in the downtown area. In 1864, a prolonged drought caused the cattle industry to die off (Ascendant conjunct Neptune). The famous oil spill of January 1969 brought the problem of pollution to the people of the world (Ascendant conjunct Jupiter opposition Uranus), and the damage to the wildlife and the beaches was incalculable.

Santa Barbara is probably the only city in California which cherishes its past (Sun in Taurus, Cancer rising) and has taken steps to prohibit future growth and to control modern buildings.

Incorporated: April 9, 1850
Elevation: 37 feet
Source: *American Guide Series*

Santa Cruz

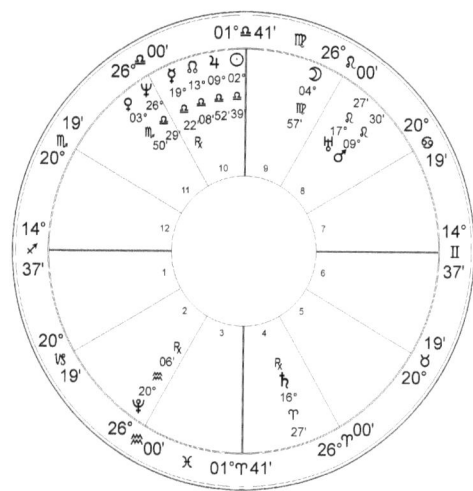

September 25, 1791
122W01, 36N58
11:52 AM PST

The site for the future mission of Santa Cruz was selected in 1791 and the cornerstone laid the following February. The civilian town of Branciforte was established in 1797, which later became the present city. On January 9, 1857, a severe earthquake caused extensive damage all around Monterey Bay (Ascendant conjunct Pluto). A branch of the University of California was established here in 1967. The Loma Prieta earthquake of October 1989 leveled numerous buildings in the downtown area (Midheaven opposite Mercury sextile Neptune, Ascendant sextile Sun).

Incorporated: 1866
Elevation: 15 feet
Source: California Historical Monuments

Santa Monica

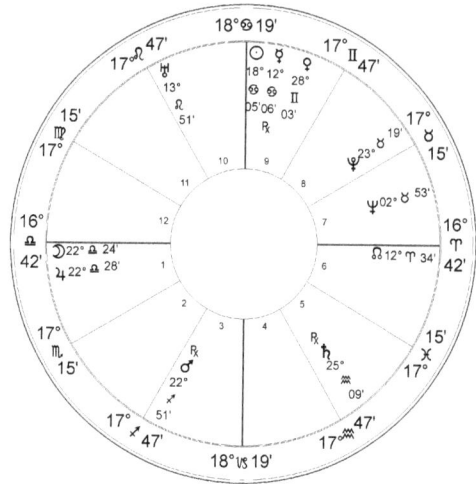

July 10, 1875
118W29, 34N01
Noon PST

Founded as a resort in 1875, it is the premier beach resort of Los Angeles County. Sitting atop a palisade overlooking the Pacific, the city has one of the stiffest rent control laws in the nation because of the number of retired people who live there.

Incorporated: 1886
Elevation: 100 feet
Area: 8 square miles
Source: Santa Monica Public Library

Stockton

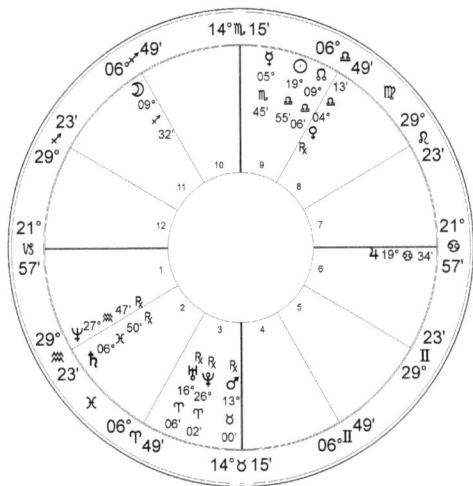

October 13, 1847
121W17, 37N58
1:25 PM PST

In 1845, Charles Weer purchased Rancho del Camp de las Franceses, and by the time the U.S. military occupation began in November 1846, this region was known as Tuleberg. Weber moved here in October 1847, one year before the army pulled out (Midheaven inconjunct Pluto). Weber renamed his settlement in 1849 to honor his friend Commodore Robert Stockton (Ascendant semisquare Moon). A fire in 1851 destroyed most of the original structures (Midheaven semisquare Venus) and the railroad arrived in 1869, creating abundant commercial opportunities for this farming community (Ascendant trine Sun inconjunct Jupiter). In 1871, the College of the Pacific opened its doors (Midheaven conjunct Moon).

Situated at the head of tidewater on the San Joaquin River, Stockton is a major port for the agricultural abundance of the San Joaquin Valley, the richest and most productive farming region in America. In 1928, engineers began constructing a deep water channel to connect Stockton to San Francisco Bay, thus enabling ocean going vessels to dock and unload their foreign cargo (Midheaven square Mercury, Ascendant square Neptune). Stockton is also a major producer of farm machinery such as harvesters and tractors. Caterpillar Tractor was founded here and its design was instrumental in development of the military tank.

Incorporated: July 23, 1850
Elevation: 23 feet
Area: 53 square miles
Source: *California Place Names* by Erwin Gudde

Ventura

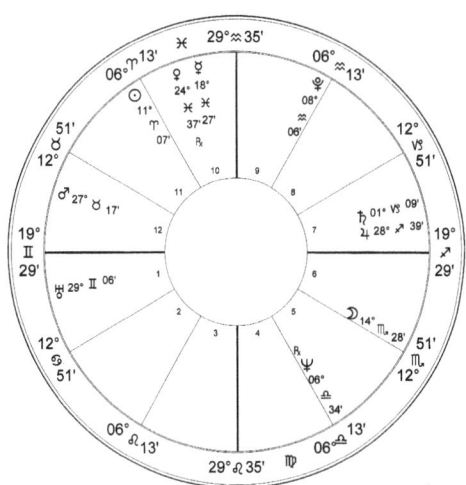

March 31, 1782
119W18, 34N17
9:30 AM PST

Mission San Buenaventura was the last mission founded by the father of California, Junipero Serra. A fire in the mission in 1791 caused extensive damage (Ascendant opposition Jupiter), and an 1812 earthquake rocked the surrounding region (Midheaven square Jupiter and Uranus, Ascendant trine Moon).

Ventura is a pleasant seaside community on the shores of the Pacific Ocean some 60 miles west of Los Angeles. Much of the surrounding area is devoted to agriculture, but tourism is also beginning to increase. Ventura County has one of the highest costs of living in the country, but also the lowest overall crime rate in California. Just north of Ventura is the town of Ojai, home of artists and craftspeople and numerous summer weekend fairs.

Incorporated: March 10, 1866
Elevation: 48 feet
Source: *American Guide Series*

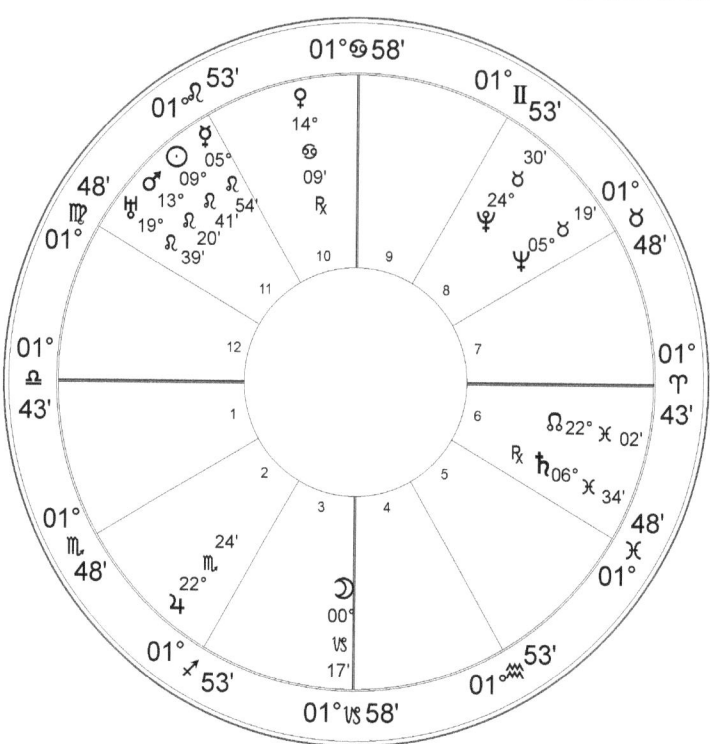

Colorado

**August 1, 1876
Denver
104W59, 39N45
9:26 AM MST
Source: Time rectified from sources which stated "around noon" in Washington.**

Colorado has been part of many nations. The eastern portion was part of the vast Louisiana Purchase of 1803, the central portion a part of Texas, and the western half part of the Mexican Cession of 1848. The state was first explored by Zebulon Pike in 1806, and the first American settlement was made in 1833 at Bent's Fort. The discovery of gold in 1858 brought thousands of fortune seekers, and three years later, on February 28, 1861, the Territory of Colorado was proclaimed. The chief obstacle to permanent settlement was the Indians, and in 1864 settlers killed hundreds of Cheyennes at the Sand Creek Massacre. Silver was found in 1875 and the following year Colorado became a state. Gold was discovered at Cripple Creek in 1891, which brought a new wave of settlers to this ore-rich state. Denver became the largest city between the Mississippi and the Pacific and was the center of a vast empire stretching from Canada to the Mexican border. Many farms were abandoned during the 1930s when the Dust Bowl ravaged the land. Recent discoveries of oil shale in the western part of the state have contributed to Denver becoming one of the energy capitals of our nation.

Colorado has the highest average elevation of any state in the nation, and 1,500 peaks tower more than 10,000 feet above sea level. The Rocky Mountains divide the eastern plains from the rugged and scenic western portion. Mesa Verde, the Garden of the Gods, Pike's Peak and Rocky Mountain National Park are all popular tourist areas, not to mention the winter ski resorts of Vail and Aspen.

Colorado ranks fourth in sugar beets and sheep, and eleventh in cattle. It has the world's largest supply of molybdenum and vast quantities of uranium, tin, vanadium, tungsten, lead and zinc, and large reserves of oil in shale deposits in the western part of the state.

Area: 104,247 square miles

Aspen

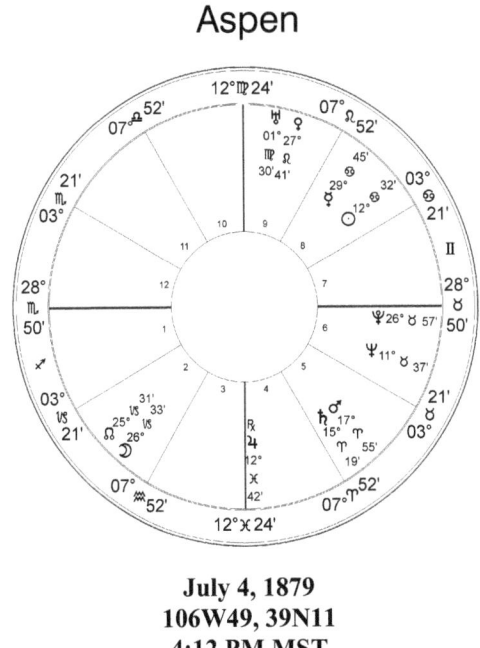

July 4, 1879
106W49, 39N11
4:12 PM MST

Founded by gold prospectors in 1879, it was almost abandoned that autumn when news of a prospective Indian uprising arrived. Originally called Ute City, it was christened Aspen in January 1880 because of the profusion of those colorful trees in the region. During its early years it was a long trip over Independence Pass to Leadville where the ore had to be shipped. With the arrival of the railroad in 1887, transportation was made considerably easier. By 1892, Aspen was mining $10 million a year and had a population of 11,000. In July of the following year the government created a depression when it repealed the Silver Purchase Act (Midheaven sesquare Neptune). By 1920, Aspen had only 700 residents and almost slid into oblivion. A New Yorker discovered the region in the mid-1930s and decided to create a ski resort. The first ski train arrived in 1937 and Aspen hasn't been the same since.

Incorporated: 1880
Elevation: 7,980 feet
Source: *Fabulous Aspen* by Caroline Bancroft

Boulder

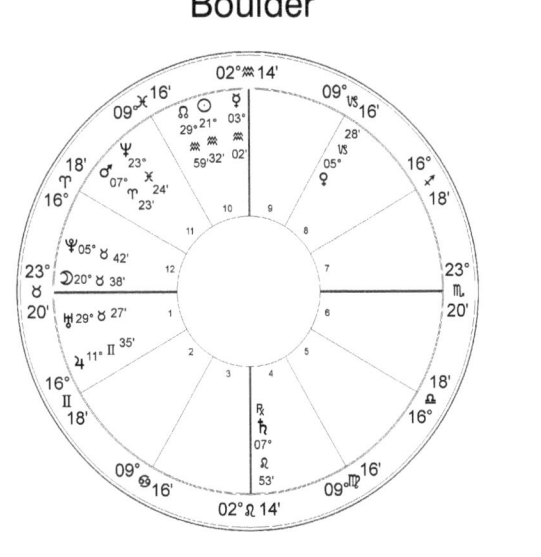

February 10, 1859
105W17, 40N01
10:58 AM MST

First settled in the fall of 1858, the Boulder Town Company was formed the following February. Indians scared off most of the settlers in 1865 (Midheaven opposition Saturn, Ascendant conjunct Uranus) and in 1871 the town was formally laid out (Ascendant sextile Mars and Saturn). The University of Colorado was founded in 1876 (Ascendant conjunct Jupiter). The National Bureau of Standards (which sets weights and measures) was founded in 1950 (Midheaven square Mercury).

Boulder is a center for scientific and environmental research (Sun in Aquarius, Uranus rising).

Incorporated: April 3, 1882
Elevation: 5,430 feet
Source: Boulder Public Library

Colorado Springs

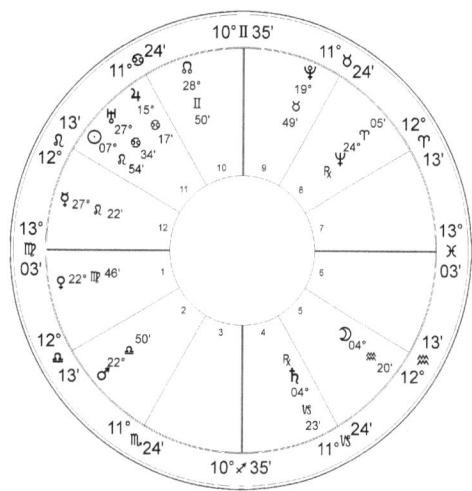

July 31, 1871
104W49, 38N50
8:00 AM MST

Gold seekers founded El Paso in 1859, changing its name to Colorado City seven years later. Fountain Colony was founded in 1871 as a resort for the wealthy. It soon became a health spa (Virgo rising, Mercury in the twelfth house). The U.S. Air Force Academy was founded near there in 1954.

The city lies at the edge of the Rockies, just east of Pike's Peak. Nearby are the Garden of the Gods, Cave of the Winds and the Will Rogers Shrine. Blessed with good scenery and a fine climate, the city has many wide streets lined with large trees and pretty flowers (Venus rising). Many military bases are located nearby: ENT AFB, home of NORAD and Fort Carson.

Incorporated: 1872
Elevation: 6,035 feet
Area: 85 square miles
Source: *Newport in the Rockies* by Marshall Sprague says 8:00 a.m.

Denver

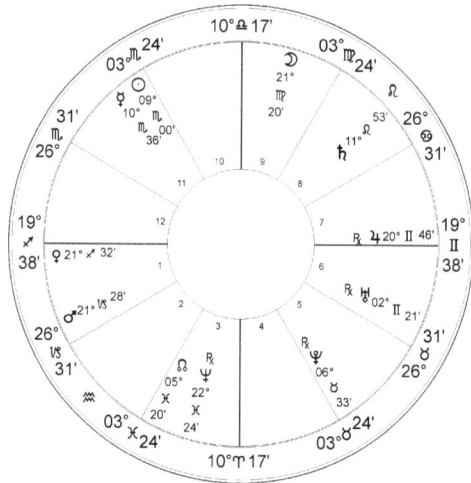

November 1, 1858
104W59, 39N45
9:55 AM MST

Founded by gold prospectors in July 1858, many decided to stay and form a community. The first attempt was only on paper, in September 1858, but Auraria was founded on November 1 and the Denver Town Company on November 22. All settlements merged in 1861 to form the present city (Ascendant conjunct Venus). Fire destroyed the city in 1863 and one year later Cherry Creek overflowed (Ascendant square Neptune). In 1867 Denver became the capital of the territory (Midheaven trine Jupiter). In 1886 an ordinance was passed limiting all future construction to masonry structures to prevent any future fires. The nationwide financial panic of 1893 brought business to a standstill (Ascendant conjunct Mars inconjunct Jupiter). In 1902 Denver merged with Denver County to form a metropolitan government (Ascendant trine Uranus) and the following year the vast system of mountain parks was begun. In 1962 the first of many mysterious earthquakes began, which was later traced to the dumping of poisonous gases. Denver's new, space age airport was finally opened in February 1995 after many delays due to its baggage system, which kept flubbing up matters (Ascendant square Neptune).

Denver is the largest metropolis between the Mississippi and the Pacific. Known as the "Queen City of the Plains," it's the heart of the vast Rocky Mountain empire which covers one-third of the U.S. Denver is a typical western town full of friendly, outgoing people (Sagittarius rising) who are quite conservative and middle class (Moon in Virgo). A bit insular, smug and square (Sun in Scorpio square Saturn), it's a financial, medical and retail center. In recent years, due to the energy boom in the Rockies, Denver has become home to many oil companies (Mars in the second house). But government remains the largest employer in this mile high city; more than 20,000 military personnel reside in the region and the combination of city, state and federal workers totals about 33,000. Denver also has a U.S. Mint and more government office buildings than any city outside Washington.

Denverites love the mountains and on weekends they head for the hills (Sagittarius rising). Within one hour you can be in pine forests and in two hours on the slopes skiing or mountain climbing.

Incorporated: November 7, 1861
Elevation: 5,280 feet
Area: 115 square miles
Source: *Denver* by William C. Jones; *American Guide Series* says November 22, 1858, while *The '59ers* by Stanley Zamonski says July 6, 1858.

Estes Park

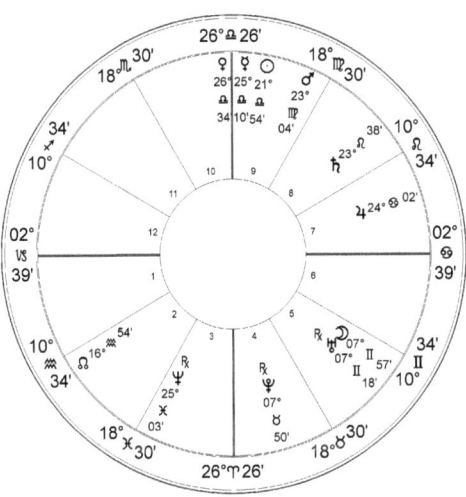

October 15, 1859
105W31, 40N23
12:05 PM MST

Long before the establishment of the Rocky Mountain National Park in 1915 (Midheaven sextile Sun), this picturesque community was famous as a summer resort. Situated in a pocket at the entrance to the park, mountains tower over the village, the highest being Long's Peak at 14,255 feet. In the park is the highest continuous automobile road in the country, Trail Ridge Road.

The day before Colorado's centennial (July 31, 1976), a torrential downpour dumped more than ten inches of rain in the Big Thompson Canyon east of Estes Park, thus sealing this community off from the outside world (Midheaven opposition Saturn). More than 140 drowned in the deluge and Highway 34 had to be completely rebuilt. On July 15, 1982, an earthen dam broke, sending torrents of water cascading through the center of town, burying homes and businesses alike in a morass of mud and debris (Ascendant square Mars and Neptune).

Incorporated: 1917
Elevation: 7,523 feet
Source: *Estes Park* by June Carothers

Fort Collins

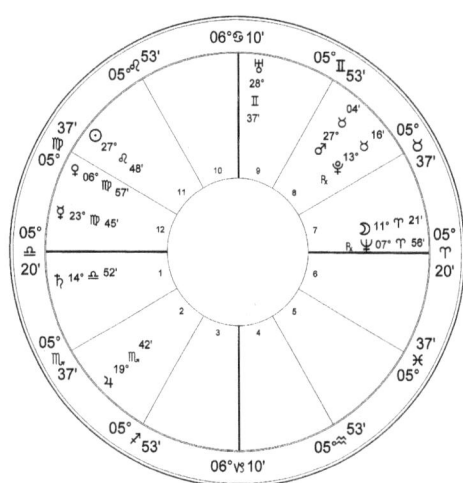

August 20, 1864
105W05, 40N35
8:30 AM MST

Camp Collins was founded at La Porte on the Cache La Poudre River in August 1862 by the Army to protect settlers going west on the Overland Trail. After a flood in June 1864 destroyed the camp, a special order was made in August 1864 to build a new fort. By March 1867, however, it was decided to abandon the fort altogether (Ascendant opposition Moon). In 1870, a teaching school was founded, now called Colorado State University (Midheaven square Sun sextile Pluto).

On January 6, 1873, a plat was filed and one month later, Fort Collins was incorporated (Midheaven square Saturn, Ascendant sesquare Mars). Agriculture was the mainstay of the economy for years. Recently, refugees from California have brought high tech to the region.

Incorporated: February 3, 1873
Elevation: 5,004 feet
Source: Wayne Sundberg, historian

Greeley

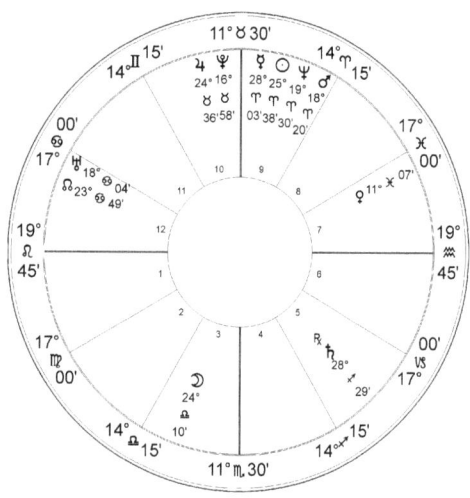

April 15, 1870
104W42, 40N25
1:00 PM MST

Founded as the Union Colony in New York at 3:00 PM on April 15, 1870, it was conceived as a utopian community. It was widely advertised (Leo rising) and forbade liquor in its early days. It was quite puritan in spirit. Today, Greeley is a college town, once the home of James Michener.

Incorporated: 1885
Elevation: 4,665 feet
Source: *History of Greeley* by David Boyd

Leadville

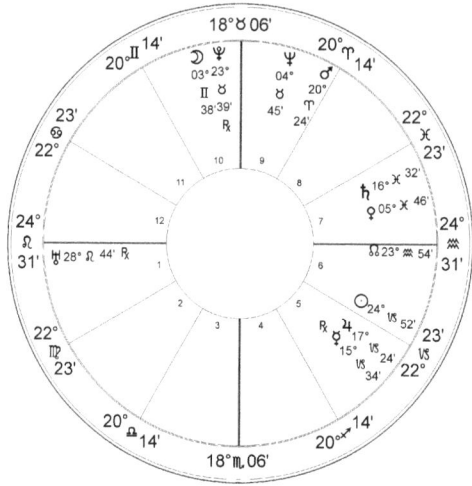

January 14, 1878
106W17, 39N15
7:30 PM MST

Gold was first discovered in Leadville in 1859, and with future strikes of lead and silver, this town became the largest mining community in the country when it was formally founded at a town meeting in 1878. Its population was 40,000 during the early 1880s, but with the repeal of the Silver Purchase Act in 1893 (which brought a nationwide financial panic), thousands left and Leadville became a ghost town. Leadville today is the highest incorporated city in the country and the center of Colorado's mining industry.

Incorporated: 1878
Elevation: 10,152 feet
Source: Leadville Public Library

Pueblo

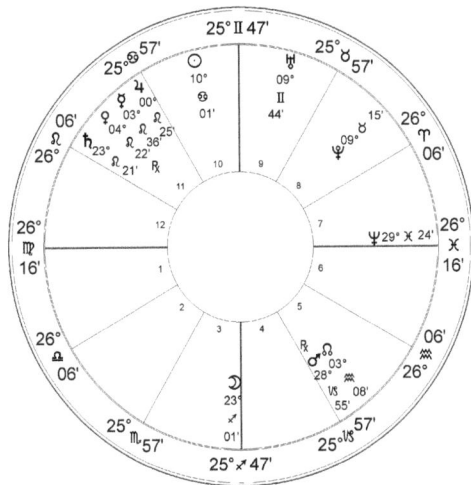

**July 1, 1860
104W36, 38N14
11:00 AM MST**

A trading post was founded here in 1842, and four years later the Mormons stopped on their way to Utah. Indians massacred what few settlers remained on Christmas Day 1854, which delayed permanent settlement until 1858 when Fountain City was founded. Platted in 1860 as the City of Pueblo, gold was discovered at Cripple Creek in 1893 (Midheaven opposition Mars). On July 3, 1921, the Arkansas River inundated the entire downtown area (Midheaven conjunct Saturn).

Pueblo is unlike most other large Colorado cities, for it's a steel town. The first mill opened in 1881, one of the first in the West.

Incorporated: 1873
Elevation: 4,690 feet
Source: Pueblo Public Library

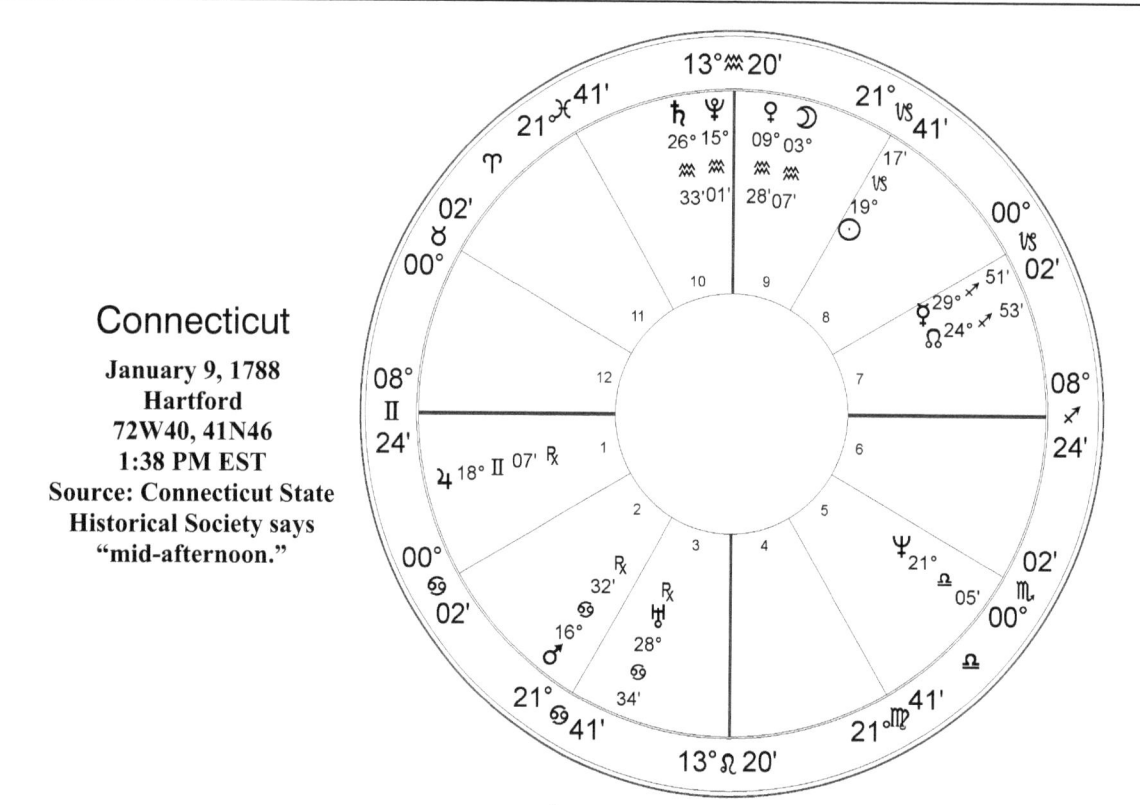

Connecticut

January 9, 1788
Hartford
72W40, 41N46
1:38 PM EST
Source: Connecticut State Historical Society says "mid-afternoon."

Connecticut was claimed by the Netherlands in 1614, and they established their first settlement at Hartford in 1633, the same year the English settled at Windsor. Three years later, along with the arrival of Thomas Hooker from Massachusetts, the Pequot War occurred and many Indians were slaughtered. On May 3, 1662, Connecticut was granted a Royal Charter and the colonists revolted in 1687 when Britain tried to take it away. Upon ratification of the Constitution in 1788, Connecticut became our fifth state. Manufacturing became the mainstay of the economy, especially with the invention of the cotton gin in 1793. County governments were abolished in 1960 and in 1974 Connecticut elected the first woman governor in the U.S., Ella Grasso.

Connecticut is the second smallest of the New England states, but the richest state per capita in the nation.

Connecticut is sharply divided between the heavily industrialized cities along the coast and rivers and the quiet, picturesque New England villages with their white churches and town greens. Manufacturing is the chief industry, and the state leads in production of jet engines, helicopters, nuclear subs, silverware and hardware. Hartford is one of the world's largest insurance centers and Stamford has many multinational corporations. Poultry and dairy products are the chief farm products.

Area: 5,009 square miles

Bridgeport

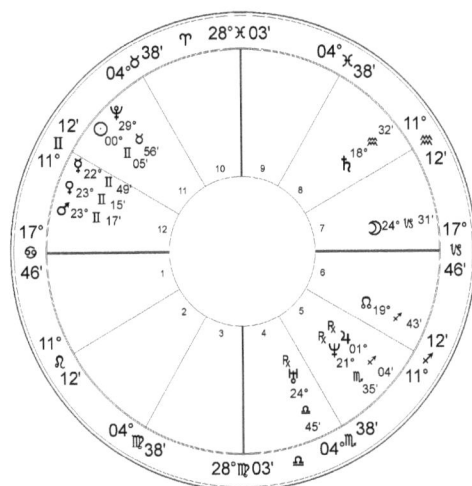

May 21, 1639
73W12, 41N11
7:50 AM EST

Founded as Fairfield in 1639, during the next century and a half it was known as Stratfield and Newfield (Neptune trine Ascendant). Its present name was adopted in 1800. With the arrival of the railroad in 1840, the whaling industry went into decline. The first "horseless carriage" was built there in 1894. From 1933 until 1957 Bridgeport had a Socialist mayor. Bridgeport is the largest and most industrialized city in the state and is a leading manufacturer of electrical and transportation equipment.

Incorporated: June 4, 1836
Elevation: 20 feet
Area: 18 square miles
Source: Bridgeport Public Library

Hartford

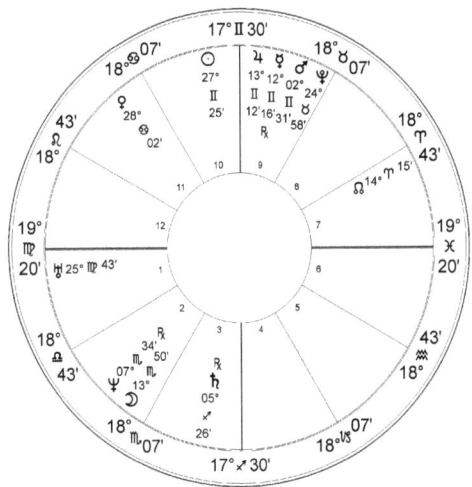

June 18, 1633
72W41, 41N46
11:08 AM EST

Founded as a Dutch trading post called New Hope in 1633, the present city was founded by Thomas Hooker, who arrived on June 30, 1636. The Fundamental Orders were adopted in 1639, which remained the basic code of ethics for many years. Hartford became capital of Connecticut in 1662 (Midheaven trine Moon) but the colony almost lost its charter in 1687 when Governor Andros tried to revoke it. Natives had hidden it in an oak tree (Midheaven square Neptune).

The insurance industry was founded here in 1794 and soon this city became the insurance capital of the nation. Hartford gave birth to the first revolver, machine made watch, bicycle, pay telephone and radar screen. Hartford is truly an inventive city (Uranus rising in Virgo).

Hartford suffered greatly during the 1938 hurricane (Ascendant square Neptune). The Charter Oak was destroyed and even the capitol building suffered damage.

Except for the skyscrapers surrounding the downtown area, Hartford looks pretty much like many other New England towns. Basically neat and tidy (Virgo rising), it's a pragmatic and businesslike community, very democratic and tolerant of other's viewpoints (Sun in Gemini and stellium in the ninth house). But there's still that strong reserve so typical of New Englanders. Insurance and tobacco are the largest industries in the city, along with government.

Incorporated: May 29, 1784
Elevation: 40 feet
Area: 17 square miles
Source: *History of Connecticut* by Samuel Peters; American Guide Series says June 6, 1633, while *History of Connecticut* by Marguerite Allis gives June 30, 1636.

New Haven

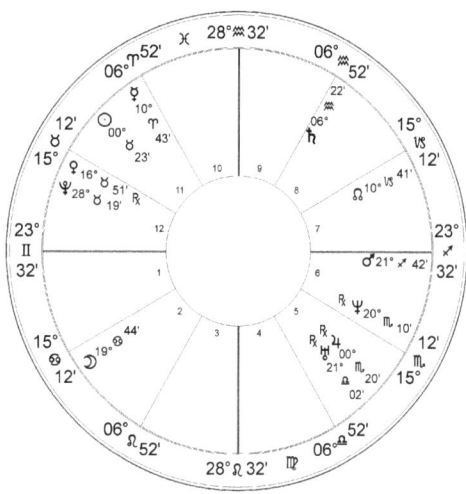

April 20, 1638
72W55, 41N18
8:00 AM EST

Founded as Quinnipiac in 1638, the church ruled the town from 1639 until 1662. Its early history was somber and puritanical. The first of many elm trees was planted in 1686, which made this city so famous in years prior to the disease which wiped out scores of trees. New Haven was made co-capital of the state in 1701 (Ascendant trine Mercury). Sacked by Governor Tryon in 1779 (Ascendant opposition Mercury) during the Revolution, it survived the war without too many scars. The first cotton gin was manufactured here in 1794 and the first telegraph in 1837. In 1875 it lost its status as one of the capitals of Connecticut (Midheaven conjunct Uranus square Moon). New Haven is, like Hartford, a city of many inventions (Uranus trine Ascendant and Midheaven). The first electric elevator, adding machine, sprinkler, stone crusher, corkscrew and submarine were manufactured here.

New Haven is a beautiful city with many sharp architectural contrasts. Many districts are quite handsome, while others are almost slums. It is a city of many cultures, the chief one being Yale University, which was founded in 1701 (Midheaven conjunct Sun opposition Jupiter). There is a conflict between the Elis (university students) and the townies (citizens of New Haven) for the university is tax exempt and could contribute more to the tax base of the city than it does. Along with Harvard and Columbia, it is the preeminent Ivy League school.

Incorporated: January 8, 1784
Elevation: 30 feet
Area: 18 square miles
Source: *American Guide Series*; New Haven Public Library says April 24, 1638.

New London

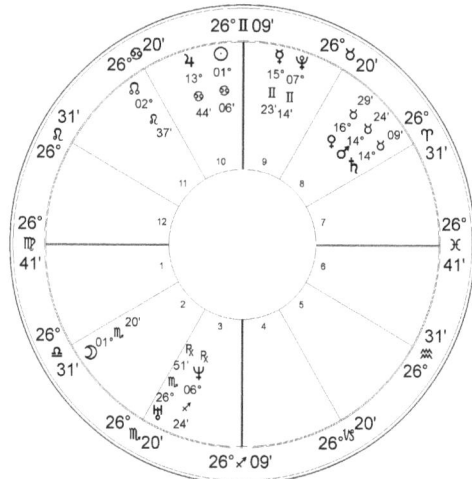

June 22, 1646
72W06, 41N22
11:28 AM EST

First settled by John Winthrop as Pequot in 1646, its name was changed twelve years later (Ascendant sextile Neptune). The first commission in the U.S. Marines was granted here on November 28, 1775 (Midheaven trine Sun) and six years later Benedict Arnold led the British in capturing and burning the city (Midheaven inconjunct Pluto). In 1784 the first whaling ship left the port of New London (Ascendant trine Mars and Saturn) and until the latter part of the following century that was the city's main industry.

New London is a city tied to the sea (Sun in Cancer, Moon in Scorpio). Since 1916 it has been a large submarine base (Ascendant conjunct Jupiter) and in 1932, the U.S. Coast Guard Academy opened its doors (Ascendant trine Uranus).

Incorporated: January 8, 1784
Elevation: 40 feet
Source: *History of New London* by Frances Caulkins

Waterbury

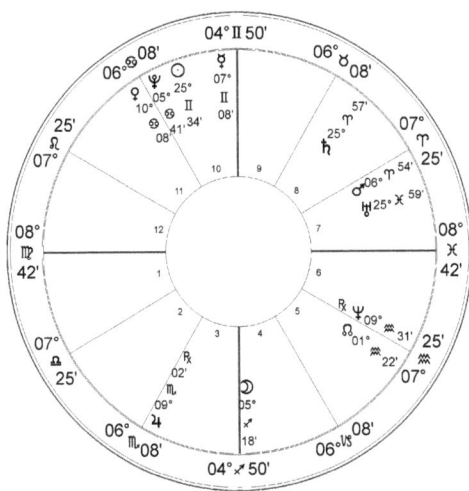

June 16, 1674
73W02, 41N33
10:23 AM EST

Settled by John Winthrop in 1651, the land was deeded by the Indians six years later and known as Mattatuck. Purchased in 1674 shortly before King Philip's War, it experienced a great flood in 1691 (Ascendant semisquare Jupiter sesquare Neptune) and an epidemic in 1712 caused most of the town to evacuate. Fire wiped out the downtown area in 1902 (Ascendant square Neptune opposition Jupiter) and in 1955 a hurricane caused more than $2 million in damages (Ascendant conjunct Pluto square Mars).

Waterbury is known as the "Brass Capital of the World" since the first such plant opened in 1800.

Incorporated: 1853
Elevation: 280 feet
Area: 28 square miles
Source: Carolyn Dodson for date; time rectified

Delaware

December 7, 1787
Dover
75W32, 39N10
2:17 PM EST
Source: Delaware Histori-
cal Society says 2:00 p.m

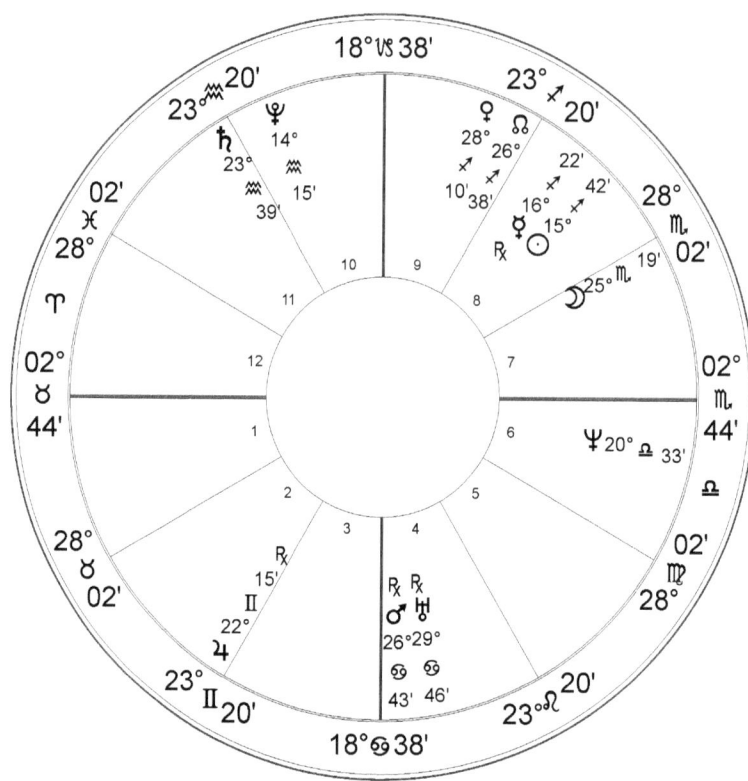

Discovered by Henry Hudson in 1609, the region was first settled in 1631 near Lewes. Peter Minuit founded Ft. Christiana (now Wilmington) seven years later for Sweden. Stuyvesant captured the state in 1655 and claimed the region for the Netherlands; nine years later England claimed the region as part of New York. It was made a part of Pennsylvania in 1682 and on April 2, 1683, William Penn received title to the state. His heirs ruled the state until 1776. Even though it was technically part of Pennsylvania, it fought as a separate state in the Revolution, as it had been semi-autonomous since 1704. Delaware became the first state to ratify the constitution in 1787, and the boundary dispute with Pennsylvania was finally settled by Mr. Mason and Mr. Dixon in the mid-19th century. Even though it was technically a slave state, being south of the Mason-Dixon line, it fought on the side of the Union during the Civil War. In 1951 the Delaware Memorial Bridge was completed, linking the state to New Jersey; twelve years later the turnpike was finished, thus completing the superhighway from Boston to Washington.

Occupying part of the Delmarva Peninsula, it is the second smallest state in the country: only ninety-six miles long and from nine to thirty-five miles wide. The large chemical plants around Wilmington, as well as the liberal and convenient corporation laws have made Delaware the third wealthiest state per capita in the country.

Area: 2,057 square miles

Dover

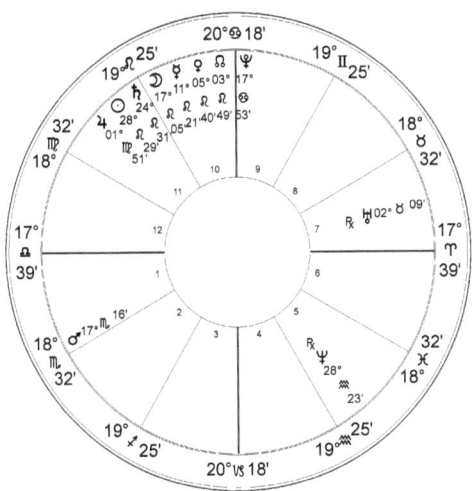

August 21, 1683
75W32, 39N10
9:30 AM EST

Founded on the orders of William Penn in 1683, the site wasn't formally laid out until 1717 (Midheaven conjunct Saturn). Dover became the capital of Delaware in 1777 (Midheaven sextile Saturn, Ascendant trine Jupiter) and ten years later was the first state to ratify the U.S. Constitution (Midheaven opposition Uranus).

Incorporated: 1929
Elevation: 55 feet
Source: Dover Public Library

Wilmington

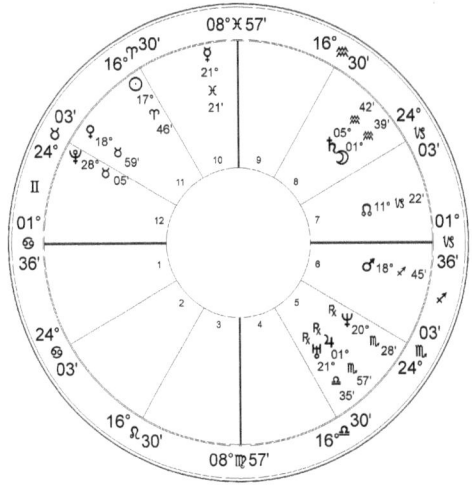

April 7, 1638
75W33, 39N45
9:41 AM EST

Founded by Peter Minuit as Fort Christiana in 1638, it was captured by the Dutch in 1655 (Midheaven sextile Pluto) and by the British nine years later (Ascendant square Uranus). It became Wilmington in 1739 when it was chartered as a borough. After the Battle of Brandywine in 1777, Wilmington was occupied by the British (Ascendant conjunct Uranus).

Wilmington is famous around the world for the vast chemical plants of E.I. du Pont de Nemours. Since 1802 when the first du Pont arrived from France and founded a gunpowder factory, it has been the chief employer in the state (Midheaven trine Mars square Venus).

Incorporated: January 25, 1832
Elevation: 135 feet
Source: *The Delaware Citizen; Swedes in America* by Adolph Benson says April 8, 1638

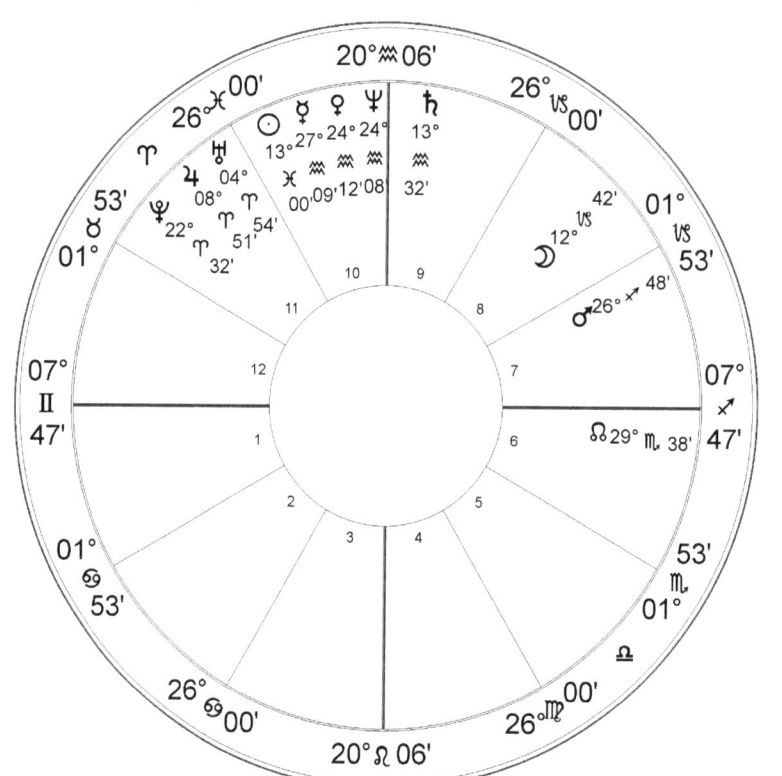

Florida

March 3, 1845
Tallahassee
84W17, 30N27
11:22 AM EST
Source: Florida State Historical Society says "about 10:00 to 11:00 a.m." Time rectified.

On Easter Sunday 1513, Ponce de Leon discovered the state and claimed it for Spain. He was looking for the Fountain of Youth and even though he didn't stick around very long, he would perpetuate a myth that would lure millions to this state in search of that very attraction. French Huguenots built a fort near Jacksonville in 1564, but it was destroyed by the Spanish who built St. Augustine the following year, the oldest permanent European settlement in the United States. Britain acquired the region in 1763 but lost it to Spain after the Revolution in 1783. The U.S. annexed west Florida in 1810, and four years later Pensacola was captured by Jackson. East Florida was also wrested from Spain by Jackson in 1818 during the first Seminole War. On March 30, 1822, the Territory of Florida was created. With the removal of the Seminoles during the second Seminole War (1835-1843), the region was safe for settlement and in 1845 Florida became a state. On January 10, 1861, it seceded from the Union and wasn't readmitted until June 25, 1868. With the construction of Flagler's railroad down the east coast of the state in the 1890s, thousands of tourists were drawn to this land of sunshine during the winter months. The first drainage of the Everglades took place in 1906, and in 1913 the most famous resort in the state, Miami Beach, was born. A massive hurricane in 1926 caused untold damage to the economy and the land boom of the 1920s collapsed. Cape Canaveral became the focal point for space exploration in the late 1950s and it was from here that Armstrong, Collins and Aldrin took off on their voyage to the Moon. Florida is currently experiencing a mass influx of refugees from Latin American countries like Cuba, Haiti and Colombia. Tensions are flaring as these newcomers take unskilled jobs away from the natives and the crime wave is accelerating at an unprecedented rate. Much of the problem stems from the relative ease with which drug smugglers can enter the state.

Florida, like Michigan and Alaska, lies on a peninsula. Most of the state lies just a few feet above the sea. In the interior is the lake region around Orlando, and this is cattle country. Florida produces eighty percent of the nation's citrus fruit, is second in vegetables but first in sugarcane. Florida also has the second largest fishing fleet in the U.S. Tourism is the mainstay of the economy, and while winter months are very popular, with the advent of air conditioning even the summers are bearable.

In the summer of 2004, four massive hurricanes ripped through Florida, creating untold havoc and billions of dollars in damage on both coasts.

Area: 58,560 square miles

Daytona Beach

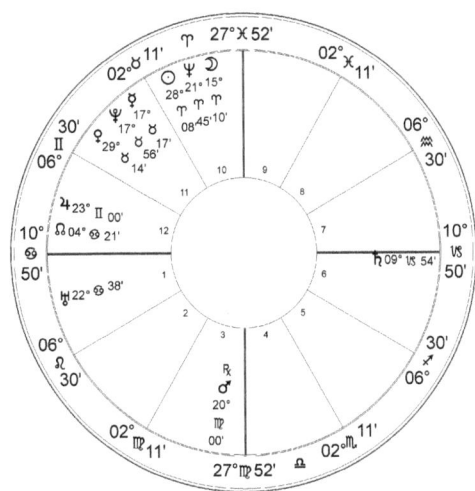

April 18, 1871
81W01, 29N13
10:31 AM EST

Given in a grant to Mathias Day in 1871, it boomed after Flagler brought his railroad through here in 1877. In 1903 the first auto race was held on the twenty-three miles of hard white sand (Midheaven conjunct Sun) for which this city is so famous.

Incorporated: August 4, 1876
Elevation: 7 feet
Source: Daytona Beach Public Library

Fort Lauderdale

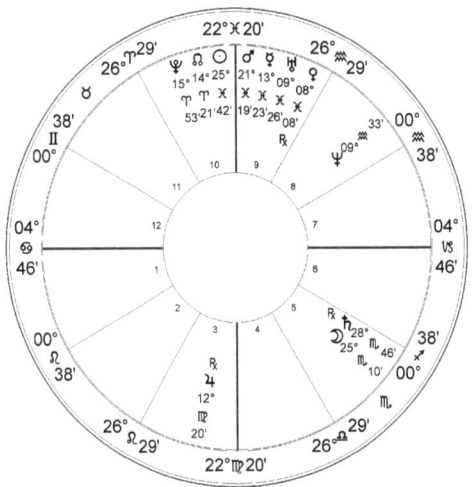

March 16, 1838
80W08, 26N07
12:17 PM EST

Founded in 1838, it was abandoned in 1842 (Midheaven conjunct Sun trine Moon). It wasn't resettled again until 1895. The economy went bust in 1926 after a hurricane devastated much beachfront property.

Fort Lauderdale was once famous for being "where the boys are" during the mass exodus of college students during spring break. Truly a city of the sea, Fort Lauderdale has more boats per capita than any city in the nation (Cancer rising).

Incorporated: 1917
Elevation: 10 feet
Area: 31 square miles
Source: *Checkered Sunshine* by Philip Weidling

Gainesville

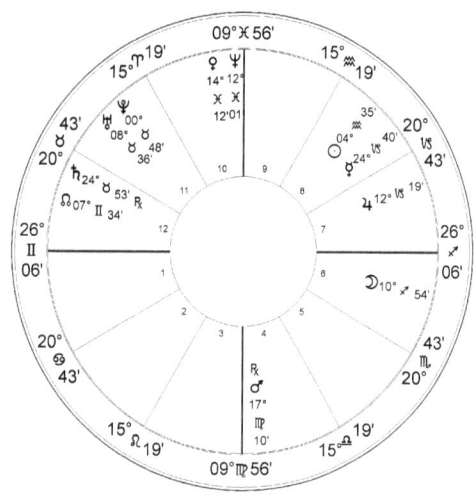

January 24, 1854
82W20, 29N40
3:00 PM EST

Founded in 1854 during a sale of lots, the county seat was moved here later that summer. The University of Florida moved here in 1905 (Midheaven conjunct Pluto).

Incorporated: 1907
Elevation: 185 feet
Source: *History of Gainesville* by C.H. Hildreth

Jacksonville

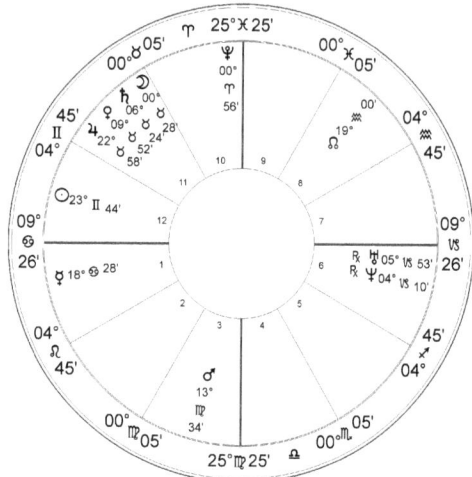

June 15, 1822
81W39, 30N20
6:37 AM EST

First settled in September 1816, the present city was founded in 1822. Jacksonville suffered considerably during the Seminole War of 1835 (Ascendant conjunct Mercury). The troubles lasted for fifteen years. Almost burned to the ground in 1854, it was occupied four times and burned twice during the Civil War (Ascendant square Venus). In 1888 it was the largest winter resort in the country until a yellow fever epidemic killed 427 people. A fire in May 1901 burned 2,300 buildings in the downtown area (Ascendant conjunct Mars). In 1968, Jacksonville merged with Duval County, thus becoming the largest city in area in the U.S.

Jacksonville is located on St. John's River, one of the few bodies of water that flows northward in the U.S. As Florida cities go, it doesn't cater much to tourists, for this is an insurance and finance center (Pluto in the tenth house, stellium in Taurus).

Incorporated: February 11, 1832
Elevation: 25 feet
Area: 850 square miles
Source: Jacksonville Public Library

Key West

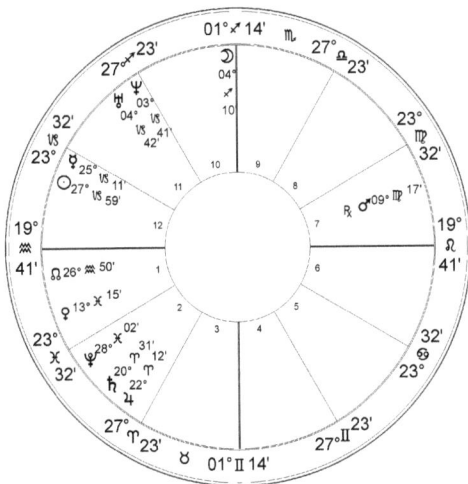

January 18, 1822
81W48, 24N33
8:34 AM EST

Founded as a naval depot in 1822, it became the wealthiest city per capita in the nation during the 1830s. The first cable to Cuba was laid in 1866 and four years later cigar manufacturing began. A fire in 1886 caused extensive damage to its historic quarter (Ascendant sesquare Neptune). Isolated from the mainland, it was connected by rail in 1912. By 1934 the city declared bankruptcy when eighty percent of its citizens were unemployed (Ascendant opposition Neptune). The following year, on Labor Day, a massive hurricane wiped out the railroad, again isolating the city (Ascendant opposition Uranus). The overseas highway was completed in 1938, one of the most beautiful in the country. In 1967 Key West became the first city in the country to get all its drinking water from the sea.

Key West is the southernmost city of the original forty-eight states, lying on an island at the end of the Florida Keys, a scant ninety miles from Havana. A gay and noisy city, it is a blend of both Africa and the Caribbean. Much of the old city has managed to retain its Spanish flavor even though many of the buildings are old and shabby. The newly arrived gay community has restored many of these structures in recent years.

Incorporated: January 12, 1828
Elevation: 7 feet
Area: 5 square miles
Source: *American Guide Series*

Miami

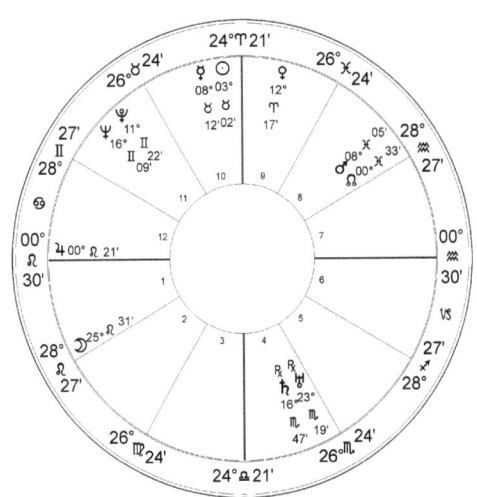

April 22, 1896
80W11, 25N47
11:46 AM EST

First settled by the Army during the Seminole War of 1835, it was known as Fort Dallas. Abandoned shortly afterward, the region remained largely uninhabited until Julia Tuttle managed to persuade Henry Flagler to extend his railroad south from Palm Beach, as south Florida managed to escape the disastrous freeze of 1895. The first train rolled into town on April 22, 1896; three months later, Miami was incorporated. During the Spanish-American War two years later (Midheaven semisquare Pluto), thousands of troops passed through the city, and soon the population began to swell. During the Roaring '20s, south Florida was the scene of the most spectacular land boom in American history. It crashed on September 16, 1926 when a devastating hurricane practically wiped Miami off the map (Midheaven opposition Uranus, Ascendant conjunct Moon). Miami didn't fully recover until after World War II with the advent of air conditioning.

In 1957 the City of Miami and Dade County decided to merge many of their duplicate functions into one municipal government (Midheaven semisquare Mercury); two years later, the first wave of Cuban immigrants began to arrive, thus transforming this city forever. Miami was fortunate in escaping the racial strife and turmoil that plagued most American cities during the 1960s. Due to the massive unemployment in the Black community, a riot erupted in Liberty City in May 1980, caused largely by the recent wave of Cuban and Haitian immigrants.

Miami in recent years has also been the scene of considerable drug smuggling from South America. The profits are so enormous that many traffickers have opened their own banks; more conservative banking institutions refused their business.

Miami is the heart of Florida's Gold Coast, gateway and financial capital of Latin America. Its airport handles more international flights than any other in the U.S. except New York and its port handles a great deal of cruise traffic. Until recently, Miami relied heavily on tourism for its survival, having little heavy industry except the garment business. Recently the tourist trade has been eclipsed by Atlantic City, Las Vegas and Caribbean countries where gambling is legal. Nevertheless, each winter thousands of frozen denizens of Brooklyn and the Northeast flock here to lie in the sun and bask in the salubrious ocean breezes. It's snowed only once in Miami's history (1977) so vacationers have little to worry about except the constant threat of hurricanes. Hurricane Andrew ravaged the southern part of the city in August 1992, becoming the most costly natural disaster in our nation's history up to that time (Midheaven semisquare Pluto).

Incorporated: July 28, 1896
Elevation: 10 feet
Area: 34 square miles
Sources: *USA Today*; *American Guide Series* gives the incorporation date, while *Miami USA* by Helen Muir states that on November 14, 1891 Julia Tuttle first envisioned the future city of Miami.

months and big name entertainers filled the showrooms of its huge hotels. Because of the thousands of rooms in its 350 hotels, it has hosted many conventions over the years.

Today, the south end of Miami Beach is undergoing a renovation that will restore many of its older apartment buildings, which are designed in the Art Deco style. Much of the area has been declared a historic enclave. Older poor people live there on fixed incomes, many of them Jewish, while to the north, condominiums line Collins Avenue up to Bal Harbour. This city has more elderly people per capita than any city in the country, but still attracts thousands of young people during spring break. Needless to say, tourism is the main industry of this city; in fact, it probably invented the word.

Incorporated: May 25, 1917
Elevation: 8 feet
Area: 8 square miles
Source: *Fabulous Hoosier* by Jane Fisher

Miami Beach

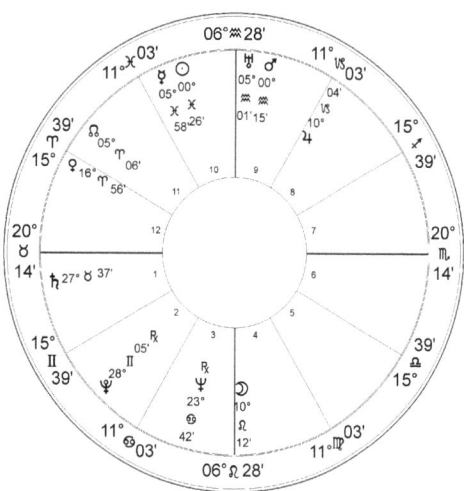

February 19, 1913
80W08, 25N47
11:00 AM EST

Founded on a mangrove swamp by Carl Fisher (of Fisher Body fame) from Detroit in 1913, it suffered the brunt of the disastrous September 16, 1926 hurricane that almost destroyed the future of this new-found community. The land boom collapsed and the city went into a depression (Ascendant square Sun/Mercury). During the decade before and after World War II, Miami Beach was the playground of the nation during the winter

Orlando

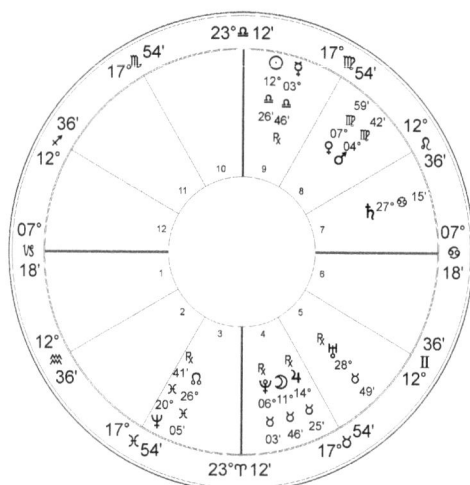

October 5, 1857
81W23, 28n33
12:54 PM EST

The first European settlement in the region was called Fort Gatlin, which was erected in 1837. Seven years later, settlement began outside the walls. The fort was abandoned in 1848, and in 1857, land was deeded for a city.

Until the arrival of Disney World in 1971 (Midheaven conjunct Neptune), Orlando was famous chiefly for being the hub of the vast citrus industry. Within the city are fifty-four lakes and forty-seven parks, for this is the heart of the lake region of central Florida. Within a radius of 100 miles are many cattle ranches and within an hour's drive, the Gulf of Mexico and the Atlantic Ocean.

Incorporated: 1875
Elevation: 111 feet
Area: 43 square miles
Source: *History of Orlando* by E.H. Gore

Pensacola

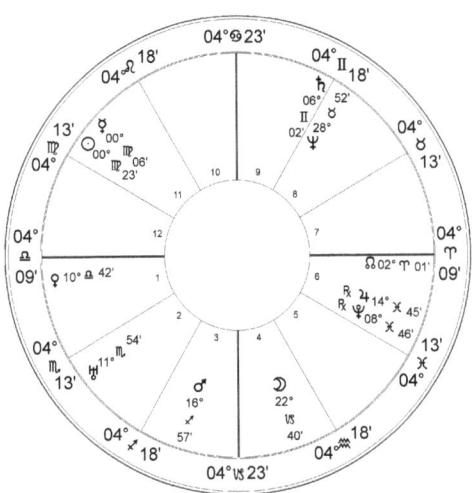

**August 14, 1559 (NS)
87W13, 30N25
8:00 AM CST**

First founded in 1559, it was abandoned two year later after a hurricane. Refounded in 1696 as Fort San Carlos (Midheaven sextile Moon), it was captured by the Frenchnin 1719 (Midheaven square Jupiter) and retaken by the Spanish four years later (Ascendant trine Uranus). The British took possession in 1763 (Ascendant opposition Uranus) until 1781. In 1818 Andrew Jackson took control (Ascendant square Pluto) but the next year the Spanish again recaptured the city (Ascendant trine Venus). Pensacola finally came into American hands in 1821 and was named capital of Florida. In 1822 a yellow fever epidemic killed many (Ascendant opposition Mars). During the Civil War the city surrendered in February 1862 (Midheaven sextile Venus) and a fire in 1880 caused many historic buildings to be gutted (Ascendant semisquare Venus). A Naval Air Station was established in 1913, and Pensacola remains largely a naval town to this day (Cancer Midheaven, Moon in the fourth house).

Incorporated: 1825
Elevation: 13 feet
Source: Carolyn Dodson for date; time rectified

Saint Augustine

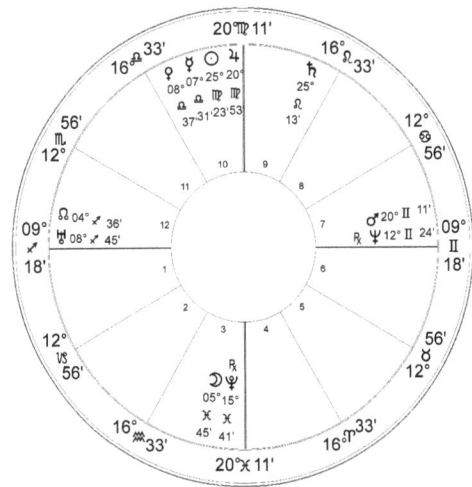

**September 18, 1565 (NS)
81W19, 29N54
Noon EST**

Near here, Ponce de Leon discovered Florida on Easter Sunday 1513. Founded in 1565 to counteract a French Huguenot settlement in the region, the city was attacked by Drake in 1586 (Midheaven trine Neptune), sacked by pirates in 1668 (Ascendant opposition Mercury/Venus), burned by the British in 1728 (Ascendant square Saturn) and attacked unsuccessfully by Oglethorpe in 1740. In 1821 the Spanish evacuated the city and the Americans took possession. The Dade Massacre of 1835 during the Seminole War caused many to wonder whether to remain (Midheaven conjunct Mars square Jupiter and Pluto). During the Civil War the city was blockaded and with the coming of the railroad in 1874, its status as a winter resort began to emerge (Ascendant sextile Saturn).

Besides Pensacola, St. Augustine can boast of being the only city in Florida which was founded by the Spanish instead of Americans. It's the oldest permanent European settlement in the U.S. and, thanks to preservation, many of its historic buildings remain. Take a leisurely stroll down its narrow streets overhung with balconies (a few are left) and forget that you're in America. It will be difficult, I can assure you.

Incorporated: December 28, 1824
Elevation: 15 feet
Source: American Federation of Astrologers

Saint Petersburg

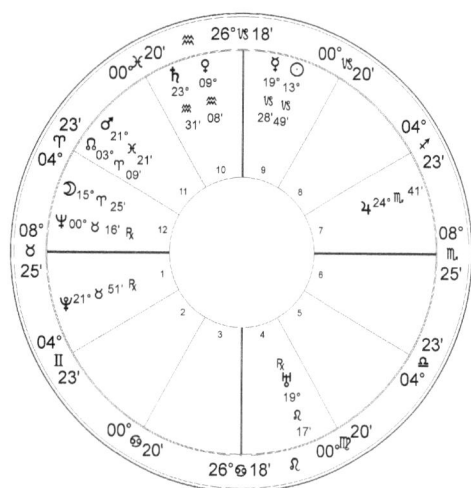

**January 4, 1876
82W39, 27N46
1:29 PM EST**

First settled in 1843, the city was conceived in 1876 and land was purchased the following March. Peter Demends asked the railroad to go there in 1887 and took the privilege of naming the city after his birthplace in Russia.

Known as the "Sunshine City," the newspaper will give away a free copy on any day the Sun fails to shine by 3:00 p.m. Fortunately, this happens only five times a year. Once known as a city of retired people, because of its healthful climate, it boasted park benches along its main avenues and ramps were placed over curbs to facilitate movement for the handicapped. All that has changed in recent years as more young people have found the joys of living there. St. Petersburg is a major aerospace center and is the major exporter of tropical fish in our country.

Incorporated: June 6, 1903
Elevation: 20 feet
Area: 56 square miles
Source: St. Petersburg City Hall

Tallahassee

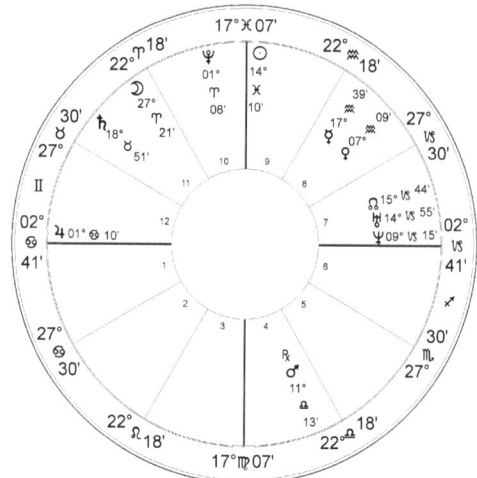

**March 4, 1824
84W17, 30N27
1:00 PM EST**

Chosen by the Florida Legislature to be the capital of the territory in March 1824, it was first settled exactly thirty-five days later. The legislature moved there later in November. During the Civil War, Tallahassee was the only state capital east of the Mississippi that was not captured by Union forces.

Incorporated: December 9, 1825
Elevation: 150 feet
Source: Tallahassee Public Library

Tampa

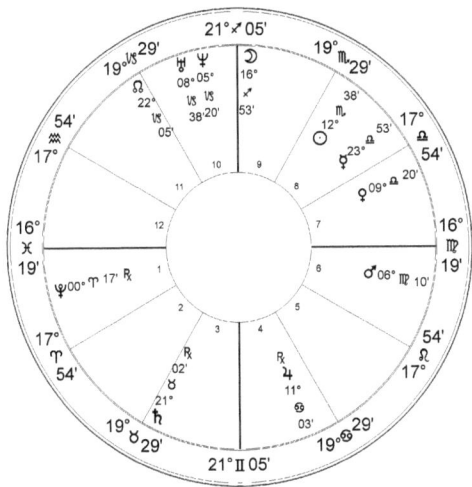

November 5, 1823
82W27, 27N58
2:54 PM EST

Founded by the military as Fort Brooks in November 1823, the first buildings were completed the following January. Blockaded during the Civil War, it survived almost intact. In 1886, Tampa became the chief cigar manufacturer in the country due to Cuban political instability. Tampa was the chief port of embarkation during the Spanish-American War (Midheaven opposition Mars). During World War II, three air force bases were built and the city became a major shipbuilding center.

Despite being a large industrial city, it still has quite a bit of charm. Stroll through the Latin quarter, called Ybor City, and see why this city takes pride in its ethnic variety. Tampa is also the largest port on Florida's west coast.

Incorporated: December 15, 1855
Elevation: 15 feet
Area: 85 square miles
Source: Tampa City Hall

West Palm Beach

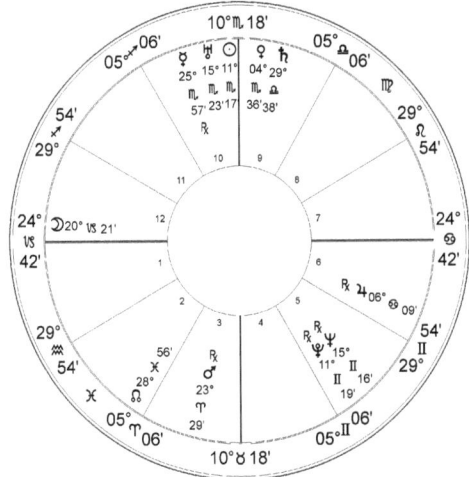

November 3, 1894
80W03, 26N43
Noon EST

First settled in 1872, the present town was founded four years later. Flagler built the Royal Poinciana Hotel in 1893 during the building of the railroad down the east coast of Florida. The hurricane of September 1926 caused $10 million damage and caused the land boom to collapse.

West Palm Beach is the commercial hub for the posh and glamorous resort city of Palm Beach, which lies east across Lake Worth. That community was a millionaires' playground, and the Newport of the South. The Kennedys made this town their home, as did Marjorie Meriwether Post, who built the fabulous Mar el Lago, the largest home in the region, now owned by Donald Trump.

Incorporated: 1894
Elevation: 10 feet
Source: Florida Historical Society

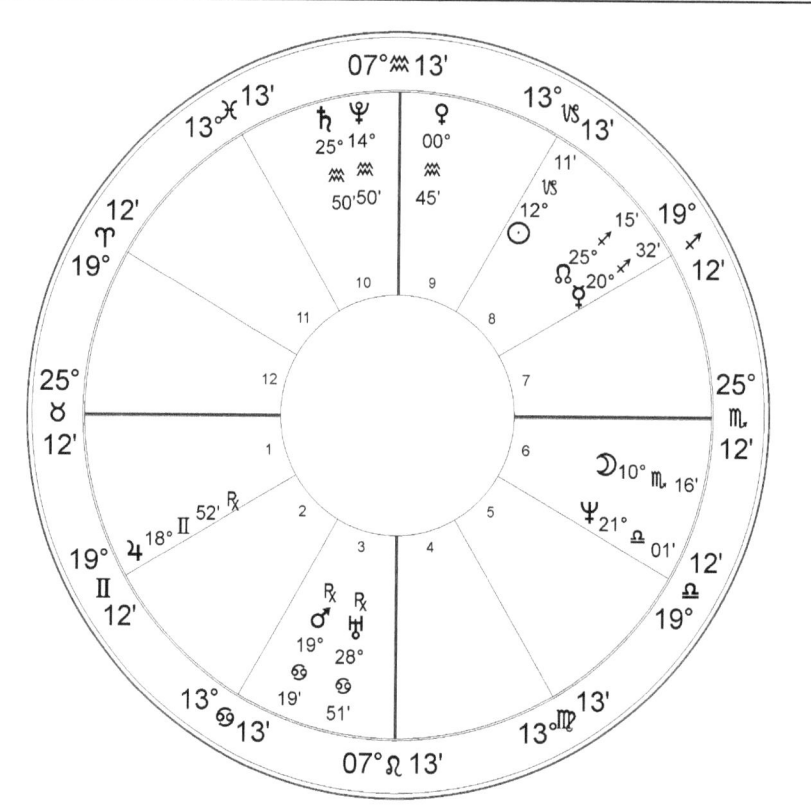

Georgia

January 2, 1788
Augusta
81W58, 33N28
2:18 PM EST
Source: Rectified

Georgia was the last of the original thirteen colonies to be settled, when on June 9, 1732 James Oglethorpe was granted a royal charter. He founded the City of Savannah the following year and Augusta shortly afterwards. Oglethorpe defeated the Spanish in 1742 at Saint Simons Island, and in 1753 Georgia became a royal colony. The colony was founded as an asylum for debtors. With the invention of the cotton gin by Eli Whitney in 1793, Georgia became one of the biggest agricultural states in the South. In 1838 the Cherokee Indians were moved to Oklahoma and the interior became safe for European settlement. Atlanta was founded and soon became the transportation hub of the South. On January 19, 1861, Georgia seceded from the Union, not to reenter until July 15, 1870. In 1864 General Sherman cut a swath through the heart of the state on his march to the sea. In his wake he left scores of towns in ruins. Recovery dragged on during the remainder of the 19th century. Georgia was the first state to give eighteen-year-olds the vote in 1943, and from this state Jimmy Carter became the first president to be elected from the South in many years.

The largest state east of the Mississippi ranks number one in peanuts and second in chickens and eggs. Georgia is also famous for its peaches and its marble. Manufacturing is the leading employer in the state, including textiles and paper products.

Area: 58,876 square miles

Athens

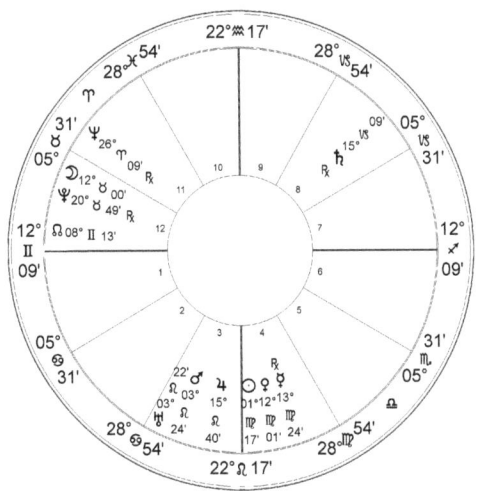

August 24, 1872
83W23, 33N57
12:01 AM EST

Founded in the fall of 1801 when the first sale of lots was held, the first building was completed four years later. The University of Georgia, which moved there in 1805, was closed briefly during the Civil War.

Incorporated: 1872
Elevation: 771 feet
Source: Athens Public Library

Atlanta

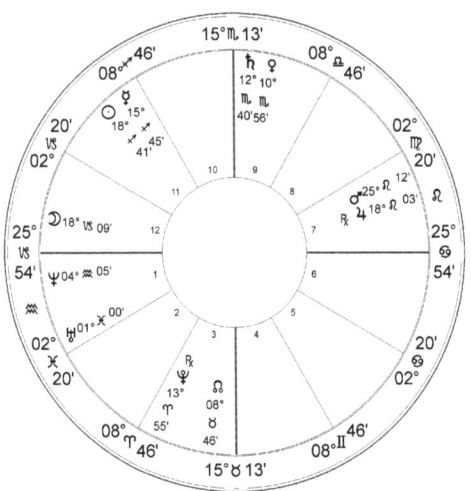

December 10, 1836
84W23, 33N45
9:11 AM CST

Founded by the legislature which chartered the Western Georgia and Atlantic Railroad in December 1836, a stake was driven the following year to mark the spot of the future city. Known simply as Terminus, then Marthasville, it took the feminine form of Atlantic as its name in 1847. It was placed under martial law in 1862. When Lincoln ordered Sherman to crush the south, he had Atlanta in mind for it was the chief rail center of the Confederacy. When the shelling began in September 1864, citizens panicked and cowered in fear until the cannon booms stopped. Then the city was set ablaze on November 15, 1864 and burned to the ground. More than ninety percent of the city was in ruins (Midheaven trine Pluto, Ascendant conjunct Uranus, transiting Pluto opposition Midheaven). Three years later it was made capital of the state (Midheaven conjunct Mercury). During the 1880s two trade fairs put Atlanta on the map. A large fire in May 1917 burned much of the downtown area (Ascendant square Mars) and a hotel fire in December 1946 killed 119 people (Ascendant sesquare Venus).

In recent years Atlanta has been undergoing a massive construction boom. Sleek, modern skyscraper complexes like the Peachtree and Omni Centers have transformed this gracious southern city into the financial and business heart of the South. Atlanta now has the second busiest airport in the U.S. In 1979, Atlanta completed its subway, the first in a southern city outside Washington. In 1996, this dynamic metropolis played host to the Olympics (Midheaven trine Mars).

Anyone who has ever read Gone with the Wind knows the true spirit of Atlanta. The symbol of this city is the Phoenix, and like that mythical bird, this city rose from Sherman's ashes to become what many deem to be a supercity.

Atlanta is a city of contradictions, however. Friendly and gracious, it's also smart and cunning (Capricorn rising). Sophisticated and ladylike in social affairs, it's pushy and full of vitality where it counts in the boardroom (Scorpio Midheaven). Atlanta is a dynamic and prosperous community that hasn't forgotten the fact that it was once the heart of the plantation country. Atlanta is a white collar town whose citizens love to dress up. But Atlantans detest pomposity of any kind (Sun in Sagittarius) and much of their entertaining is done at home. Atlanta is still a young town with enough brashness to appeal to outsiders (Mars in Leo conjunct Jupiter). This town has no ghosts and tradition is respected but not allowed to interfere with progress.

In the summer of 1996, Atlanta was host city for the Olympics, during which time a car bomb exploded, putting the city on edge (Midheaven trine Mars, Ascendant opposition Neptune).

Incorporated: December 29, 1847
Elevation: 1,050 feet
Area: 132 square miles
Source: Georgia State Archives; *American Guide Series* says December 21, 1836

Augusta

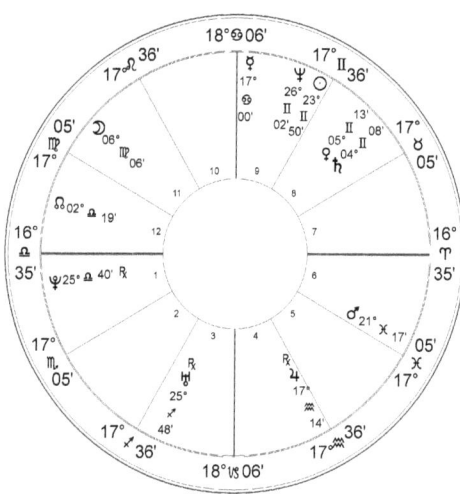

June 14, 1736
81W 58, 33N28
2:13 PM EST

Founded as a trading post by James Oglethorpe in 1736, Augusta was the capital of Georgia from 1785 until 1796 (Midheaven conjunct Moon). In 1793, Eli Whitney invented the cotton gin here, but took his invention north to have it manufactured. Between 1840 and 1854, many epidemics of yellow fever ravaged the city. During 1861 Union troops occupied the arsenal, which was the ordnance center for the south (Midheaven inconjunct Mars). During the early 20th century two floods caused severe damage: 1908 (Midheaven opposition Neptune) and 1912. In 1916 a fire burned much of the downtown. Today Augusta calls itself the winter golf capital of America.

Incorporated: January 31, 1798
Elevation: 109 feet
Source: Augusta City Hall

Columbus

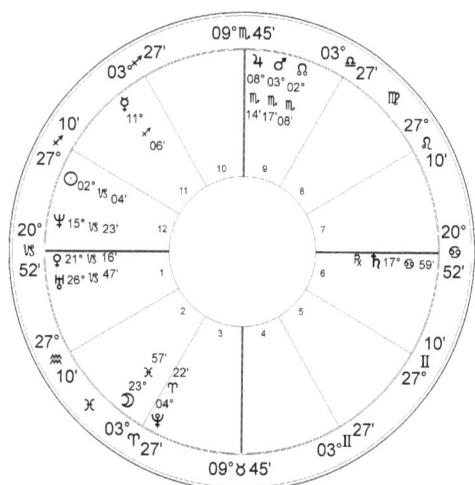

December 24, 1827
84W59, 32N28
8:00 AM CST

Founded on Christmas Eve 1827, it became a large cotton port by 1840 (Ascendant sextile Pluto). The last battle of the Civil War was fought here on April 16, 1865 (Midheaven square Mercury). Columbus is the second largest textile center in the nation and nearby Fort Benning is one of the largest military posts in the South.

Incorporated: December 23, 1835
Elevation: 445 feet
Area: 220 square miles
Source: *Columbus, Georgia* by John Martin

Macon

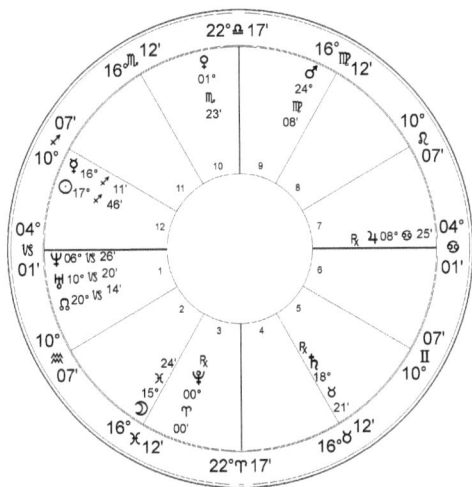

**December 10, 1823
83W38, 32N50
8:43 AM EST**

Founded as Newtowne in 1806, the city was formally laid out in 1823. Newtowne was annexed six years later. Macon surrendered to the Union Army in April 1865. Macon is a center for a vast agricultural region and is the third largest city in the state.

Incorporated: January 7, 1833
Elevation: 434 feet
Area: 50 square miles
Source: Macon Public Library

Savannah

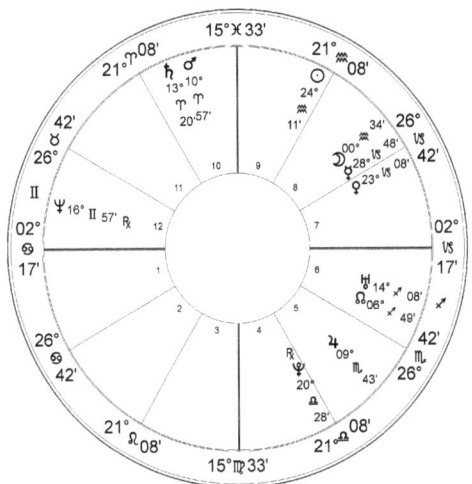

**February 12, 1733
81W06, 32N05
2:00 PM EST**

Founded by Oglethorpe in 1733, it was one of the first planned cities in the country. The city was besieged by the British in 1778 (Midheaven square Moon) and the following year by the French (Midheaven semisquare Neptune). Fires in 1796 and 1804 caused considerable damage to many colonial mansions, and during the War of 1812 the economy was crippled due to constant bombardments. In 1820 a fire burned 463 buildings (Ascendant square Uranus). Being the site of a Confederate navy yard and a major supply port for the South, it fell to Union forces in April 1862 after the capture of Fort Pulaski. Sherman occupied the city in December 1864, but its citizens had been evacuated to prevent the city's total destruction (Midheaven opposition Venus).

The downtown area of Savannah is a pleasure to walk through. Its many parks and squares offer a pleasant respite from the usual commercial hubbub of city life. Savannah is the quintessential southern city, replete with oak trees heavily laden with moss. Flowers abound everywhere and the ambience is slow and easy. Savannah preserves its past (Cancer rising) and unlike many other cities, these colonial homes are lived in throughout the year. More than two and a half miles of this city is a national landmark.

Incorporated: December 23, 1789
Elevation: 20 feet
Area: 61 square miles
Source: *The Savannah* by Thomas Stokes

Hawaii

August 21, 1959
Honolulu
157W52, 21N19
10:10 AM HST
Source: *The New York Times* says 4:10 p.m. in Washington

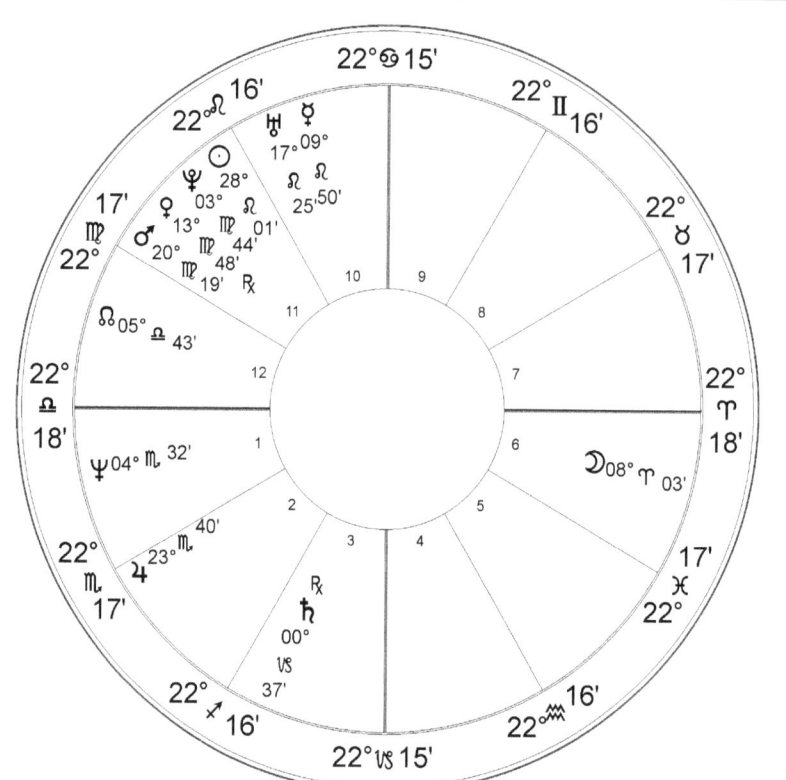

First settled hundreds of years ago by the Polynesians, the first white man to discover the islands was Captain James Cook in 1778. He was killed by the natives the following year on the island of Hawaii, near Kona. Unified by King Kamehameha I in 1795, Protestant missionaries arrived at Kailua in 1819 and forever changed the pleasant, peaceful existence. The transformation is quite well chronicled in Michener's book *Hawaii*. The monarchy was abolished in 1893 when Queen Liluokalani was deposed, and the following year the Republic of Hawaii was proclaimed with Sanford Dole (the pineapple king) as president. The U.S. annexed Hawaii in 1898, and two years later, on April 30, 1900, it became a territory. Four decades later, on December 7, 1941, a day that will live in infamy, the Japanese bombed Pearl Harbor and America entered World War II. Hawaii became the youngest state in 1959 and, with statehood, tourists by the planeload began to arrive to relax in this tropical paradise.

Actually a chain of islands that stretch almost 2,000 miles across the north Pacific, only the largest are inhabited: Niihau, Kauai, Oahu, Maui, Molokai, Lanai and Hawaii. The island of Kahoolawe is a military test site. The islands lie 2,400 miles from San Francisco in the path of the tradewinds, which causes the eastern part of each island to be wetter than the more inhabitable and dry western part. The wettest spot in the U.S. is on Kauai, but Hawaii also has deserts (on Hawaii) and many big volcanoes like Mauna Loa, Mauna Kea, Kilauea, and the now dormant Haleakala.

The major source of income is the military, then tourism and finally sugar and pineapples. Most of the foodstuffs must be imported—thus the high price of goods. Honolulu is the "Crossroads of the Pacific" and its airport a pleasant stopover on your way to the Orient.

Area: 6,450 square miles

Hilo

January 31, 1824
155W05, 19N44
6:03 PM HST

Founded by missionaries at sunset at a new Moon (Hilo means "new Moon"), it is governed by Hawaii County, and is not an incorporated community. Because of its location on the windward side of the big island, Hilo has suffered considerably over the years when tsunamis (tidal waves) have struck with virulent intensity. In 1946, more than 170 were drowned (Midheaven trine Neptune) when a wave swept over the city, and on May 22, 1960, a tidal wave killed sixty-one (Midheaven inconjunct Moon, Ascendant sesquare Pluto) and almost wiped Hilo off the map.

Hilo gets more rainfall than Honolulu (annual total: 140 inches) as it's on the windward shore. It is the jumping-off point for Mauna Kea and Mauna Loa, the two volcanoes which dominate the big island of Hawaii.

Source: Hilo Public Library

Honolulu

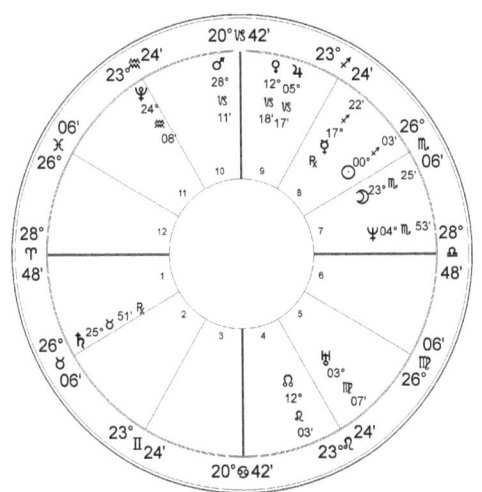

November 21, 1794
157W52, 21N19
3:56 PM HST

Discovered in 1794, the community remained relatively peaceful and undisturbed until the arrival of the missionaries in 1819 (Midheaven opposition Sun). Kamehameha made Honolulu his capital in 1845 (Midheaven sextile Venus, Ascendant trine Pluto) and five years later declared it a royal city. Americans took possession of the islands on August 12, 1898 (Midheaven opposition Neptune trine Jupiter). Nine years later Honolulu merged with Oahu to form one single metropolitan government.

On December 7, 1941, a day that will live in infamy, the Japanese bombed Pearl Harbor (Midheaven sesquare Neptune, progressed Sun conjunct Ascendant, Ascendant square Mercury). Several battleships were sunk, among them the Arizona which lies in the harbor to remind us all of those who lost their lives on the first day of World War II. After the war, tourists flocked in by the thousands due to cheap airfares and reasonable hotel rates. Honolulu lost much of its tropical charm and became, to many, a Pacific version of Miami Beach.

Honolulu holds the distinction of being the only American city ever to be a royal capital. Waikiki is the center of the tourist industry on Oahu and is the most densely populated region in the Pacific. With the number of Orientals (Chinese and Japanese) plus Polynesians (Hawaiians, Tahitians, Samoans), you feel you're in a foreign land. Even the street names are difficult to pronounce. Remember, there are only thirteen letters in the Hawaiian alphabet, and all vowels are pronounced.

Incorporated: August 30, 1850
Elevation: 21 feet
Area: 84 square miles
Source: *History of the Hawaiians* by W.O. Alexander

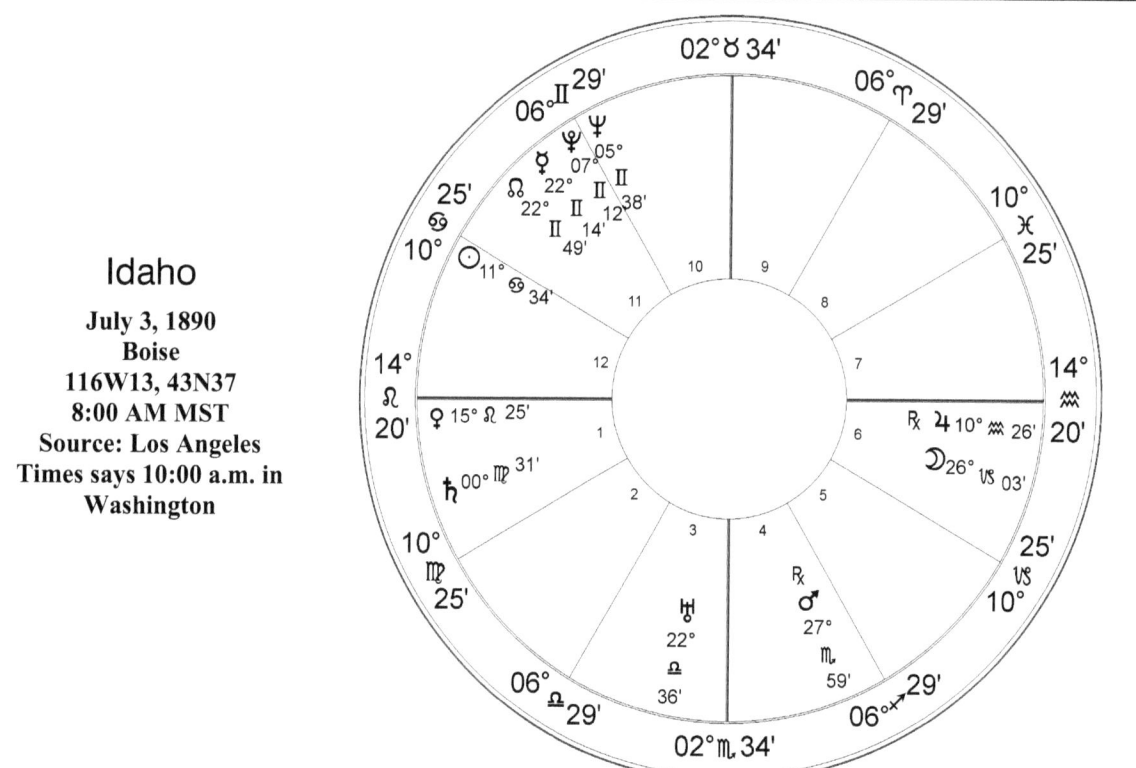

Idaho

July 3, 1890
Boise
116W13, 43N37
8:00 AM MST
Source: Los Angeles Times says 10:00 a.m. in Washington

Idaho was first explored by Lewis and Clark in 1805. Britain ceded the Oregon Territory to the U.S. in 1846 and the first American settlement took place in 1860 near Franklin. On March 3, 1863, the Territory of Idaho was formed. From 1877 to 1879, battles between U.S. troops and the Nez Perce Indians took place. Idaho became a state in 1890. The Snake River Project was completed in 1975, thus opening up that river to navigation from Lewiston, Idaho to Astoria on the Pacific coast. In 1976 the Teton Dam collapsed, causing more than $1 billion in damage. Much of southeastern Idaho was under water.

Idaho ranks number one in potatoes and ninth in sheep. It produces much of the world's pine and is a leading producer of silver (fifty percent of the U.S. total).

Area: 83,557 square miles

Boise

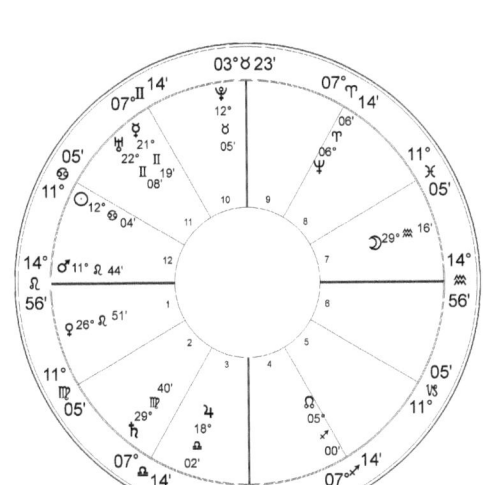

July 4, 1863
116W13, 43N37
8:01 AM MST

Founded on Independence Day 1863, it was made capital of Idaho the following year. In 1864 the legislature decided to incorporate the city, but the citizens protested and put off the final vote until 1867. During the past two decades, annexation has tripled the population.

If you detest paying hot water bills, then move to Boise. Mineral springs heat the water to 170 degrees due to underground volcanic activity. Boise is a peaceful and tranquil place (Venus rising), sedate and level headed (Taurus Midheaven). Being a government center, however, makes it somewhat dull. Natives prefer the outdoors to nightlife (Leo rising) and they have the typical western friendliness and informal attitude. Boise is clean, neat, and not pretentious or caste conscious. It has a large Mormon population, which means the laws are strict and are to be obeyed.

Incorporated: December 12, 1864
Elevation: 2,704 feet
Area: 39 square miles
Source: *Forts of the West* by Robert Frazier; Boise by Merle Wells says July 7, 1863

Idaho Falls

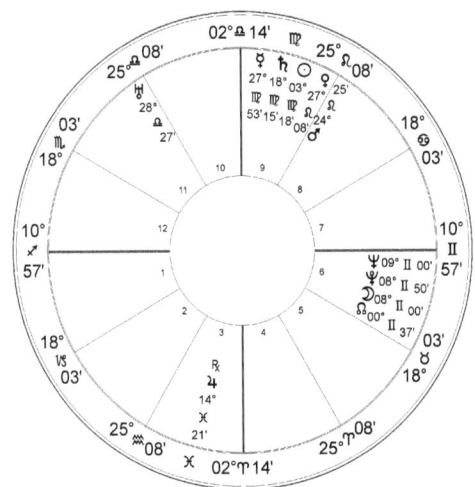

August 26, 1891
112W02, 43N30
2:17 PM MST

Founded as Hell Gate in the fall of 1864, it was renamed in 1891. In 1976 it suffered extensive damage after the collapse of the Teton Dam, which left much of the city and surrounding farmland inundated.

Incorporated: January 5, 1900
Elevation: 4,709 feet
Source: Idaho Falls City Hall

Lewiston

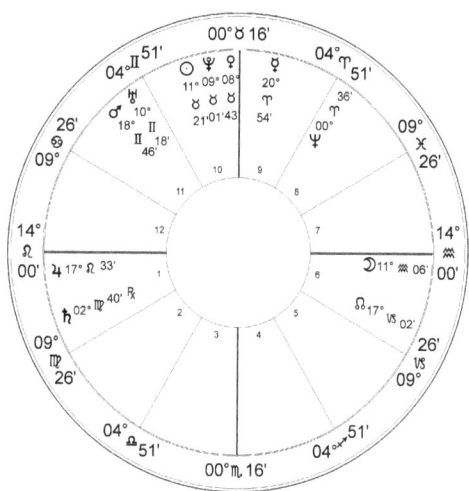

May 1, 1861
117W01, 46N25
11:02 AM PST

Founded in 1861, it became the first territorial capital of Idaho two years later. With the completion of the Snake River Project, seagoing vessels can now navigate up the river all the way from the Pacific.

Incorporated: December 27, 1866
Elevation: 741 feet
Source: Idaho Historical Society

Pocatello

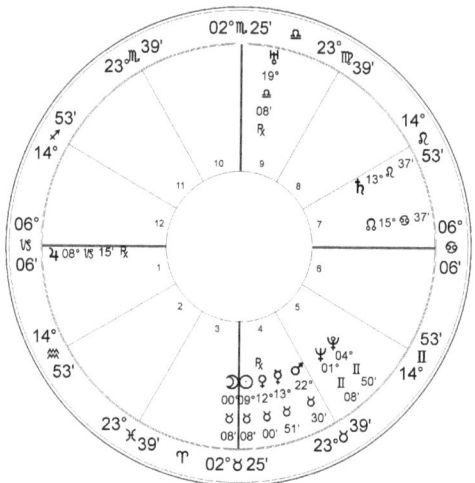

April 29, 1889
112W27, 42N52
12:01 AM MST

Founded as a railroad tent town in 1881, it was named for a friendly Indian chief. Idaho State University opened its doors in 1901, and the following year Fort Hall Indian Reservation opened for settlement. Pocatello is a large railroad center and has many repair shops.

Incorporated: 1889
Elevation: 4,464 feet
Source: Pocatello Public Library

Illinois

**December 3, 1818
Kaskaskia
89W55, 37N55
9:08 AM CST
Source: Rectified from sources which stated "morning."**

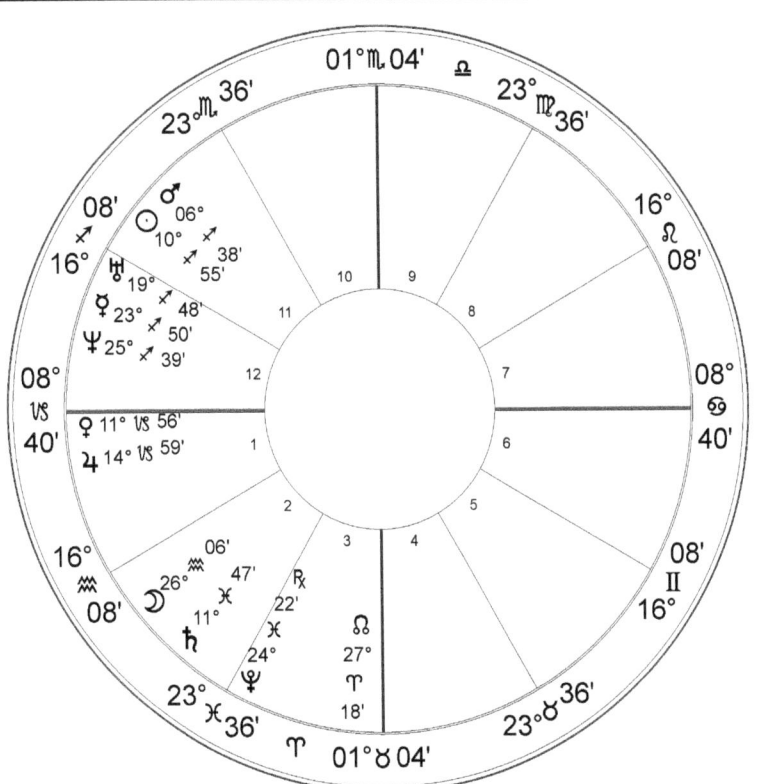

Illinois was first explored by Marquette and Joliet for France in 1673. Two years later a Catholic mission was founded at Kaskaskia, but the first permanent European settlement occurred at Cahokia in 1699. George Rogers Clark captured both Kaskaskia and Cahokia during the Revolution, and in 1787 the region became part of the Northwest Territory. Created as a separate territory on February 3, 1809, it entered the Union nine years later. The Black Hawk War was fought against the Indians in 1832, and in 1844, a mob killed the founder of the Mormon faith, Joseph Smith, at Carthage. The Illinois and Michigan Canal was completed in 1848, linking the Mississippi to Lake Michigan; shortly after, Chicago became the transportation hub of the nation with the arrival of the railroads. In 1871 a fire destroyed most of Chicago and before the turn of the century it had become the second largest city in the U.S. and the leading industrial center. In 1942, the Atomic Age began in Chicago, which also became home to the world's tallest building with the completion of the Sears Tower in 1973.

Illinois is the fourth largest manufacturing state and ranks fourth in coal. It's the second largest agricultural state and harvests twenty-five percent of the nation's corn. It ranks number one in soybeans, second in hogs, and seventh in livestock.

Area: 56,400 square miles

Chicago

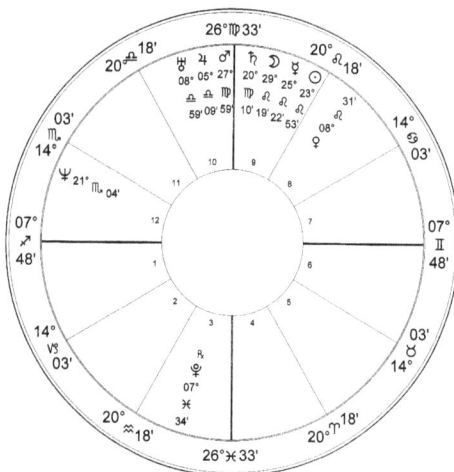

August 17, 1803
87W39, 41N51
1:57 PM CST

Founded by the military as Fort Dearborn, the original settlement was abandoned in the summer of 1812 and most of its settlers massacred by the Indians (progressed Midheaven opposition Jupiter semisquare Neptune, progressed Ascendant square Saturn/Pluto). The fort was rebuilt in 1816 and a town was platted in August 1830 and incorporated as a city in March 1837 (Midheaven sextile Moon, Ascendant square Jupiter). A canal connecting the Chicago River to the Illinois River was completed in 1848 (Ascendant square Moon), the same year the railroad arrived from the east. Because Chicago lies in a swamp, its streets were raised in 1855 (Ascendant sextile Neptune) and five years later, this city hosted the first Republican convention, which nominated Abraham Lincoln for president.

Known as the "Hog Butcher of the World" after the first stockyards were erected in 1864 (Midheaven square Mercury), the entire downtown section was reduced to ashes after the great fire of October 1871 (Midheaven trine Jupiter, Ascendant sesquare natal Mars square progressed Mars, progressed Saturn conjunct natal Mars). More than 17,500 buildings were burned in a four square mile area, more than 250 were killed and 250,000 were homeless. But like the phoenix, Chicago rose from the ashes at breakneck speed and by 1884 gave birth to the world's first skyscraper. In May 1886, the Haymarket Riot occurred, which gave birth to better working conditions for the masses (Ascendant conjunct Pluto inconjunct Jupiter). Ever since then, Chicago has been a strong union town.

The crowning achievement of the Gay '90s was the Columbian Exposition of 1893. Known as the "White City," its classical buildings were designed by the architect Daniel Burnham (Midheaven trine Sun, Ascendant opposition Saturn). In 1900, the Chicago River was reversed to prevent sewage from polluting Lake Michigan—locks were built at the mouth of the river. In December 1903, the Iroquois Theater fire killed 602 people and the terrible loss of life prompted more stringent safety measures for indoor auditoriums (Midheaven square Jupiter, Ascendant opposition Uranus). In July 1915, the lake steamer Eastland capsized in the river, sending 812 people to a watery grave.

In the summer of 1919, a race riot broke out on the city's south side and the following year, with the advent of Prohibition, the name Chicago became synonymous with gangsters who vied for control of the liquor industry (Midheaven sextile Neptune semisquare Pluto, Ascendant square Venus inconjunct Uranus). The most famous mobster of all, Al Capone, literally ran the city during the Roaring '20s. Warfare between rival gangs culminated in the 1929 St. Valentine's Day Massacre, which sent shockwaves throughout the city (Ascendant square Sun). To honor its 100th anniversary, the Century of Progress was held in 1933 (Midheaven trine Jupiter, Ascendant square Moon) during the middle of the Depression. During the early days of World War II, the Atomic Age was born at the University of Chicago when Enrico Fermi split the atom in December 1942 (Ascendant trine Uranus).

During the 1950s, Chicago experienced new vitality when Richard J. Daley became mayor. Numerous skyscrapers were constructed, expressways were built, housing projects were erected and a massive program of urban renewal changed a large portion of the city. Chicago became known as "the city that works." Daley ran the city with an iron hand and won cooperation from both business and labor. He was the last of the old time big city bosses. The major blot of his administration came during the Democratic convention of August 1968 when troops were called in to quell demonstrators trying to disrupt the convention. Chicago had already gone through hell earlier that year when in April 1968 a sizeable portion of the Black community on the west and south sides of the city went up in flames after the assassination of Martin Luther King (Ascendant square Jupiter sesquare Neptune). Much of downtown Chicago was flooded in April 1992 when a break in a river embankment sent millions of gallons of river water cascading into numerous tunnels running beneath the streets of the central business district, known as the Loop (Midheaven opposition Jupiter, Ascendant sesquare Pluto).

Chicago is home to the world's tallest building, the Sears Tower, which rises 1,452 feet over the prairie. Despite Chicago no longer being the "Second City," it's still a city of superlatives. It has the world's largest commercial building (Merchandise Mart), the world's tallest apartment building (Lake Point Tower), the world's largest fountain (Buckingham in Grant Park), the world's busiest airport (O'Hare), the busiest grain exchange (Chicago Board of Trade) and is the hub of America's rail system with sixty-five trunk lines. Chicago has certainly lived up to its name, Checagou, which means great. Chicago ranks number one in steel production, televisions and radios, railroad equipment and machine tools. It's also the world's largest mail order center.

Chicago is imbued with the pioneer spirit that made America great (Sagittarius rising). An urbane and exciting city, it's known to be tough, proud and blunt (Sun in Leo, Sagittarius rising and Mars at the Midheaven). It's also been known to be corrupt (Neptune in the twelfth house) audacious, dynamic and full of considerable vigor and vitality (Pluto square the Ascendant). It's a place that makes its own rules and is highly individualistic regardless of the consequences. Often violent and brutal, Chicagoans have lusty spirits and love a good time (Leo stellium). It also passionately defends its detractors and manages somehow to ignore negative publicity. Chicago is also a highly segregated town (Midheaven in Virgo) and racial balance, especially in its schools, is often out of kilter. Chicagoans are loyal to the nth degree, especially to its Cubs baseball team, which despite not having won a pennant in years, still manages to attract loyal fans during the summer.

Chicago has always been a place where strong leaders prevail (Mars and Saturn at the Midheaven), for its political machine was indomitable and results were always forthcoming due to the patronizing efforts of its aldermen. Daley once ruled this city like a benevolent dictator, and despite Chicago being a rather cynical place, it's still possibly the most friendly and frisky large urban area in America. Maybe it's the weather that charges up its citizens with passionate intensity, for its natives seem to do nothing in half measures. The successes of Chicago are as great as its failures, and Chicagoans relish them both.

Incorporated: March 4, 1837
Elevation: 598 feet
Area: 223 square miles
Source: *Checagou* by Milo M. Quaife says 2:00 p.m.

Decatur

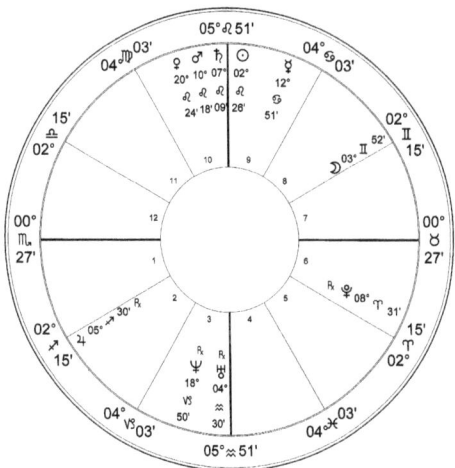

**July 25, 1829
88W57, 39N51
12:16 PM CST**

First settled in 1822, the city was laid out in July 1829. The first post of the Grand Army of the Republic was founded there in 1866. Coal veins were discovered eight years later (Ascendant conjunct Jupiter).

Incorporated: January 7, 1856
Elevation: 682 feet
Source: Rectified; exact date unknown

Evanston

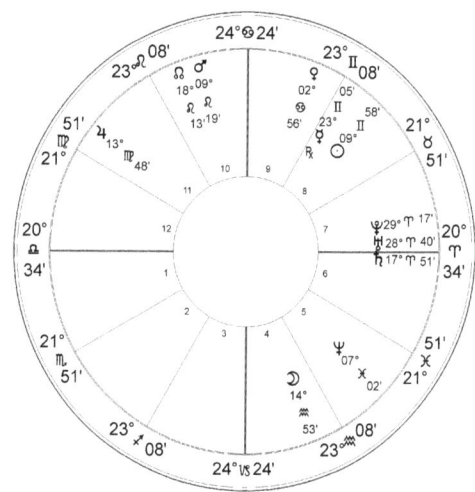

**May 31, 1850
87W41, 42N03
3:00 PM CST**

Founded at a board meeting in 1850, Northwestern University was established three years later and the community grew up around it (Ascendant trine Mercury in the ninth house). A leading educational and religious center (ruler of the Ascendant in the ninth house), it was quite a straightlaced community for many years due to the Women's Christian Temperance Union (WCTU) being located there.

Incorporated: 1892
Elevation: 601 feet
Source: *Evanston* by Viola Reeling

Peoria

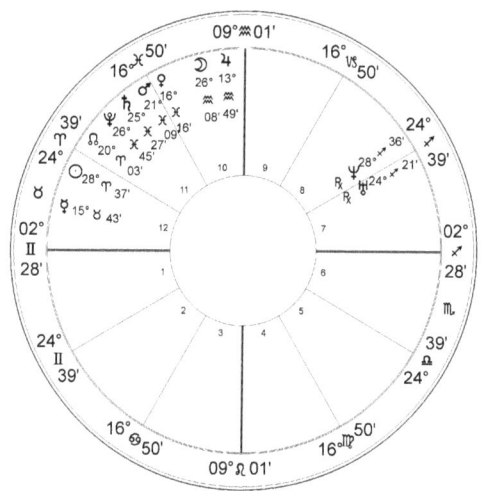

**April 19, 1819
89W35, 40N42
6:57 AM CST**

Peoria has a long history of military forts (Sun in Aries) prior to the arrival of the first civilians in 1819. LaSalle founded Fort Creve Coeur in 1680, Fort Saint Louis was completed eleven years later, and in 1730 Fort Peoria. The entire community was moved downriver in 1788 and during the War of 1812 the fort was burned and its residents arrested.

Peoria ia a large manufacturing center (tractors), a major distilling center, and a large railroad transfer point. It was the scene of a major debate between Lincoln and Douglas in 1854 where slavery was first publicly denounced.

Incorporated: April 21, 1845
Elevation: 608 feet
Area: 38 square miles
Source: Peoria City Hall

Rockford

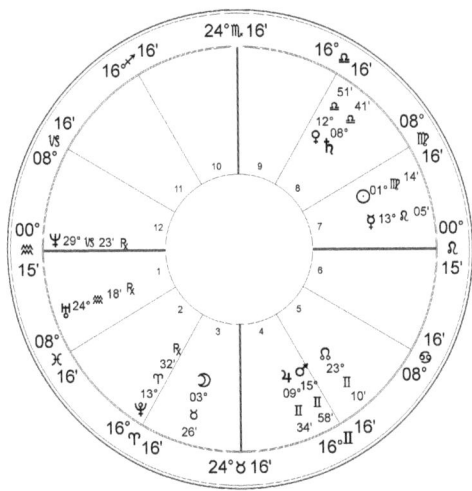

August 24, 1834
89W06, 42N16
5:13 PM CST

Founded in 1834 by New Englanders from Galena, Illinois, it was called Midway. Settled largely by Scandinavians and Germans, it grew to become the second largest machine tool center in the nation.

Incorporated: 1853
Elevation: 715 feet
Area: 36 square miles
Source: Public library states "just before sundown."

Springfield

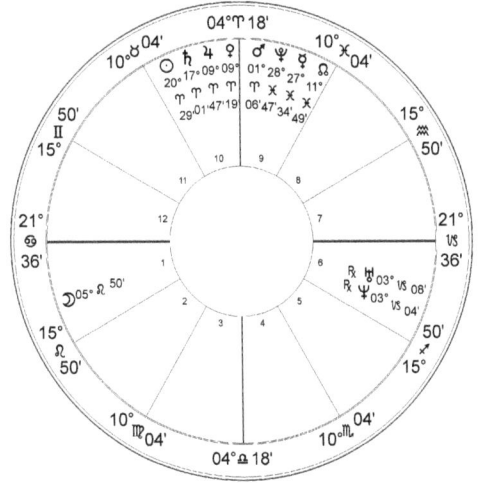

April 10, 1821
89W39, 39N48
11:00 AM CST

First settled in 1818, it was formally founded three years later. Springfield became the state capital in 1837, the same year its most famous and illustrious citizen arrived: Abraham Lincoln. Probably no other city in the nation owes so much of its reputation to a person long since departed. Here is the only home Lincoln ever owned, the building where he practiced law, and his tomb. He's revered beyond belief, for his "ghost" lies waiting at every turn.

Springfield is a pleasant, small prairie town that has simply failed to grow up (Cancer rising). It still lives in the glory years of Lincoln. It wants industry, but only on a limited basis (Neptune/Uranus square Midheaven) and it relies heavily on tourism and the state government for support. Once apathetic to corruption outside its limits, it's known as a liberal, tolerant and open-minded community, often indifferent and disinterested.

Incorporated: February 3, 1840
Elevation: 610 feet
Area: 40 square miles
Source: *Historical Encyclopedia of Illinois* by Newton Bateman

Urbana

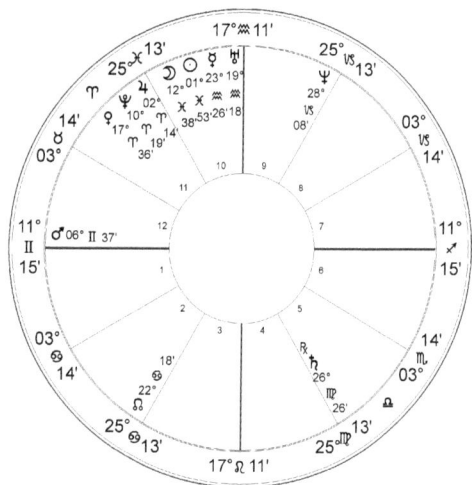

**February 20, 1833
88W15, 40N07
11:10 AM CST**

First settled in 1822, it was named county seat eleven years later and platted later that June. Champaign was founded by the Illinois Central Railroad in 1853 and incorporated as West Urbana in 1857. The University of Illinois was founded in 1868 (Ascendant trine Moon) and remains the lifeblood of the city.

Incorporated: September 8, 1851
Elevation: 743 feet
Source: Urbana Public Library

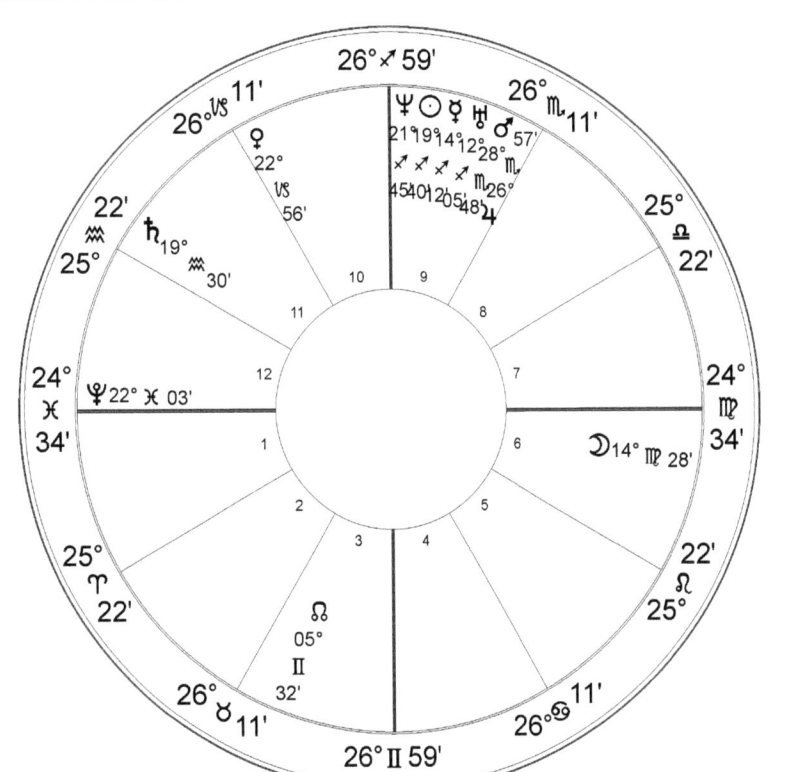

Indiana

December 11, 1816
Corydon
86W07, 38N12
12:10 PM CST
Source: Rectified

Indiana was first explored by LaSalle in 1679 for France; in 1731, the first settlement was made at Vincennes. The region passed into British hands in 1763 and into American territory twenty years later. Created as part of the vast Northwest Territory in 1787, it became separate on May 7, 1800. In November 1811, the Shawnees were defeated at the Battle of Tippecanoe by General William Henry Harrison, later president of the U.S. In 1816, Indiana became a state. Siding with the Union during the Civil War even though much of the southern part of the state wanted Dixie to win, it sent 200,000 soldiers into the war. In 1906, Gary was founded and quickly became the chief steel producer in the country. Five years later the first "500" was held in Indianapolis. The floods of 1913 caused extensive damage along the Wabash and Ohio Rivers and killed 732 people.

The Calumet region around Gary and Hammond is the chief industrial center of the state; the remainder is largely agricultural. Indiana ranks third in corn and hogs, seventh in chickens and is a large producer of soybeans. Coal is the chief mineral resource and the limestone from the southern part of the state has sheathed thousands of buildings.

Area: 36,291 square miles

Bloomington

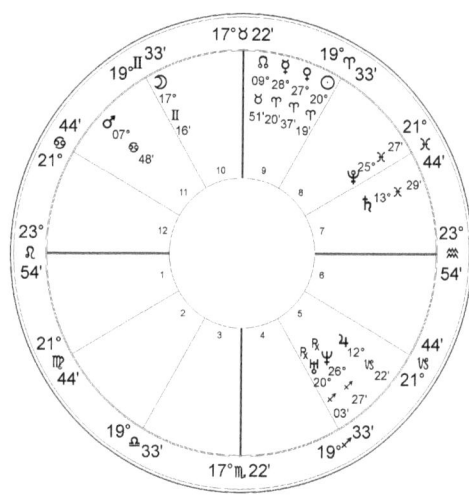

April 10, 1818
86W32, 39N10
1:32 PM CST

First settled in 1815, Bloomington was formally founded during a picnic three years later. Indiana University, around which the community thrives, was established in 1820.

Incorporated: 1877
Elevation: 752 feet
Source: Bloomington Public Library

Evansville

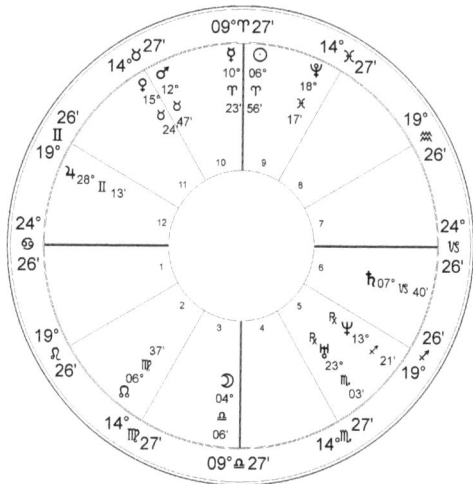

March 27, 1812
87W35, 37N58
12:05 PM CST

Founded in 1812, it was platted six years later. During the 1820s it experienced disastrous financial woes (Ascendant sesquare Pluto). During the winter of 1831-32, the Ohio River froze over, causing a flood (Ascendant inconjunct Saturn), and in the fall a cholera epidemic added further distress. In 1853 a canal was completed to Lake Erie (Ascendant square Uranus). During the 20th century, two major floods have made headlines: in 1913 and 1937 (Ascendant sesquare Pluto) when half the city was under water. Today, Evansville is a leading coal and oil center.

Incorporated: January 27, 1847
Elevation: 383 feet
Area: 37 square miles
Source: *The Evansville Story* by James Morlock

Fort Wayne

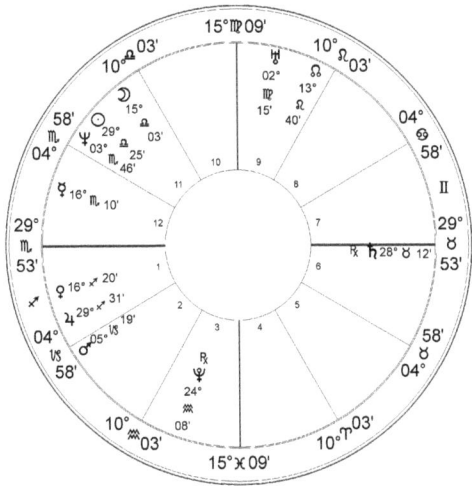

October 22, 1794
85W09, 41N04
8:41 AM CST

Founded by General "Mad" Anthony Wayne as a frontier outpost in 1794, the fort was evacuated in 1819 (Midheaven sesquare Pluto) and the present city platted five years later (Midheaven conjunct Moon). With the completion of a canal to Lake Erie in 1843 (Midheaven sextile Mars), Fort Wayne grew to become the commercial and industrial center of northern Indiana. Flooding has always been a problem there and the inundation of March 1913 killed seven people (Midheaven square Moon), but the floods of March 1982 were considerably less damaging (Ascendant square Moon).

Incorporated: February 22, 1840
Elevation: 790 feet
Area: 55 square miles
Source: *American Guide Series*

Gary

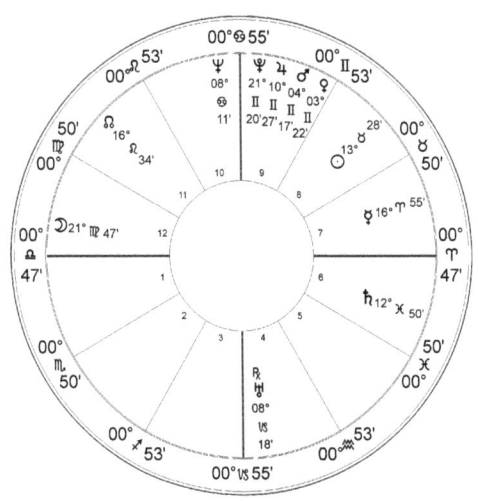

May 4, 1906
87W20, 41N36
3:06 PM CST

Surveyed in March 1906, it was founded two months later and named for the chairman of US Steel Corporation, Judge Elbert H. Gary. The first blast furnace was fired in December 1908 and with the exception of the 116 day strike in 1959, the skies over Gary have been ablaze ever since. Gary and the surrounding cities of the Calumet district are the greatest steel producers in the world.

Incorporated: 1909
Elevation: 613 feet
Area: 43 square miles
Source: Gary Public Library

Indianapolis

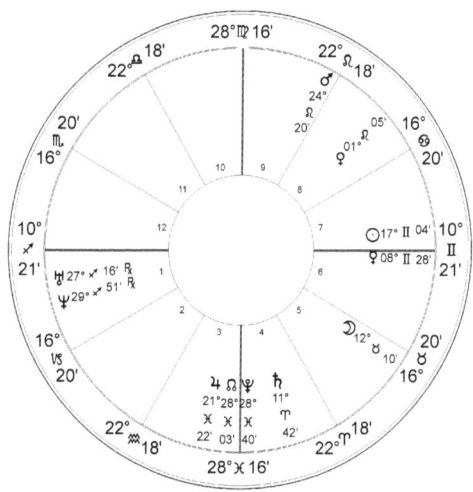

June 7, 1820
86W09, 39N46
6:33 PM CST

First settled on February 26, 1820, it was chosen by the state legislature to be the capital of Indiana, due to its central location, in June the same year. The legislature moved there the following January and on October 9, 1821 the first public sale of lots was held. For many years Indianapolis has been associated with automobiles. The first one was built in 1891 (Ascendant trine Sun) and the city remained a top car manufacturer well into the 1920s. The last car built rolled off the assembly line in 1937.

Indianapolis is famous every Memorial Day weekend when the famed "Indy 500" takes place at the track in nearby Speedway. The first race was in 1911 (Midheaven conjunct Uranus, Ascendant conjunct Jupiter). With the consolidation of Marion County and Indianapolis into one government in 1970, the population increased considerably.

Designed after Washington with four avenues radiating from a central point (Monument Circle), it's a clean city filled with big homes and large yards (Moon in Taurus). Much of the city is being renovated as parts are quite plain and ugly. Political life occupies much of the time, for it is the capital city. Indianapolis is crossed by more interstate highways than any city in the U.S. and is a large trucking and transportation center (Sagittarius rising). The city is home to Eli Lilly, one of the largest chemical companies in the world.

Incorporated: March 30, 1847
Elevation: 710 feet
Area: 379 square miles
Source: *The Hoosier City* by Jeanette Nolan says "twilight."

South Bend

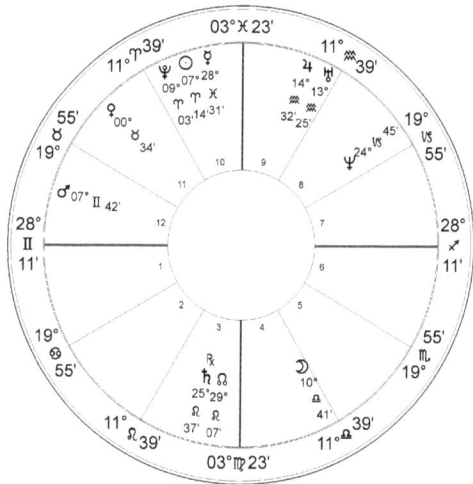

March 28, 1831
86W15, 41N41
9:45 AM CST

First settled in 1823, it was named St. Joseph's four years later. Southold was founded in 1829, and to end the identity crisis, the name was changed to South Bend in 1831. Notre Dame University was founded in 1843 (Ascendant square Pluto) and in 1852 the Studebaker brothers founded their carriage factory (Midheaven sextile Neptune). In 1883 a massive fire burned seven manufacturing plants during a blizzard (Ascendant opposition Neptune).

Even though Studebaker stopped making autos decades ago, South Bend is an industrial center which produces many products, including airplanes. Notre Dame is the most football conscious school in the country and owes much of its initial success on the gridiron to Knute Rockne. On weekends when the "Fighting Irish" are playing a home game, you can't get a hotel room for miles around (Moon in the fifth house, Sun conjunct Pluto sextile Mars).

Incorporated: May 22, 1865
Elevation: 724 feet
Area: 30 square miles
Source: *History of St. Joseph County* by T.E. Howard

Terre Haute

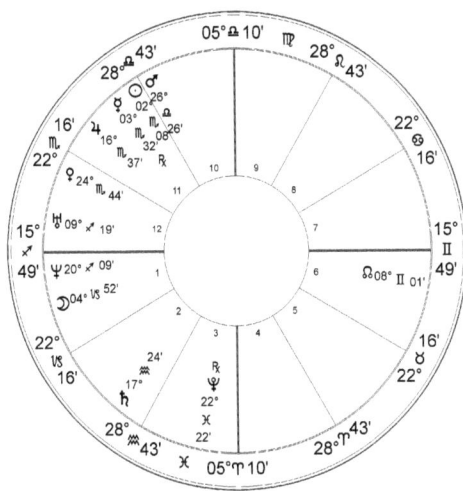

October 25, 1816
87W25, 39N28
9:53 AM CST

Fort Harrison was built here in 1811 and the present city founded five years later. A canal was completed to Lake Erie in 1843 (Midheaven conjunct Sun) and in 1852 the railroad arrived. Coal fields were opened in 1875 (Ascendant conjunct Saturn). Because of a general strike in July 1935, martial law was declared (Midheaven semisquare Pluto).

Incorporated: 1853
Elevation: 495 feet
Source: *History of Terre Haute* by Blackford Condit

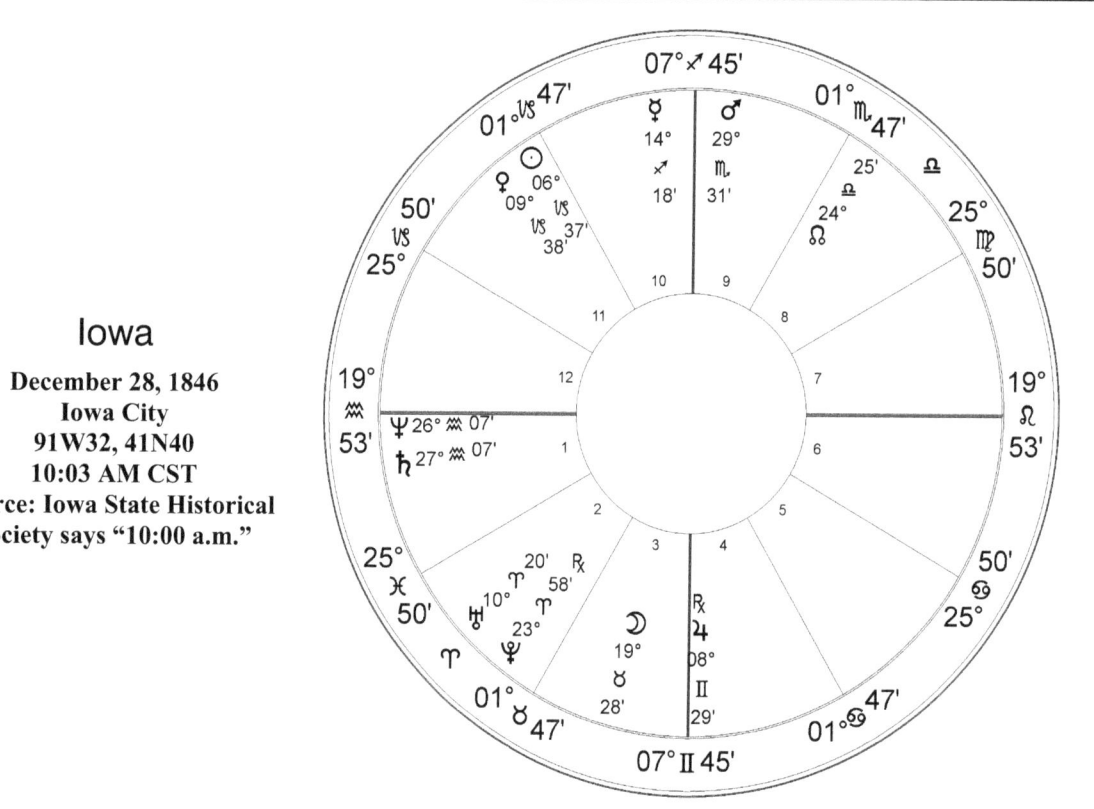

Iowa

December 28, 1846
Iowa City
91W32, 41N40
10:03 AM CST
Source: Iowa State Historical Society says "10:00 a.m."

Originally a part of France, the region was ceded to Spain in 1762. The first European settlement occurred at Dubuque in 1788; fifteen years later the area passed into American hands with the Louisiana Purchase. The Territory of Iowa was organized on June 12, 1838 and in 1846 it became a state. Strongly traditional and Republican in outlook, it fully supported the Union during the Civil War. During the Depression of the 1930s, many farmers lost their land due to mortgage foreclosures.

Iowa is one of the richest agricultural states in the nation and sits in the middle of the vast farm belt. Its broad, rolling plains contain some of the richest soil on earth and the state has the nation's richest livestock industry. It ranks number one in hogs, second in cattle and is a large producer of chickens and turkeys, but surprisingly it comes second in corn, soybeans and oats. It's the third largest agricultural state in the union and the chief manufacturer of farm products and implements.

Area: 56,290 square miles

Cedar Rapids

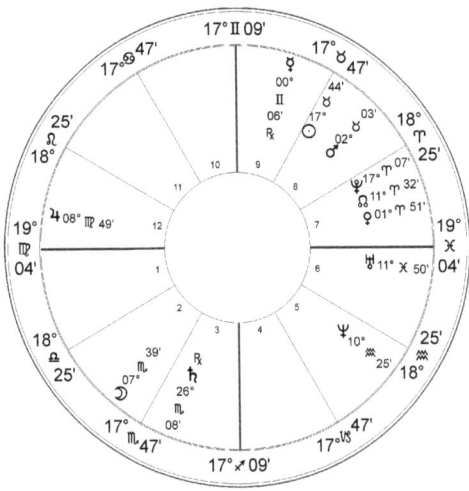

May 8, 1838
91W40, 41N59
2:06 PM CST

Founded in 1838, Cedar Rapids is one of the most civic minded communities in the nation. A clean and prosperous city, its economy has withstood depressions better than most due to the nation's necessity for its chief product: food. Its citizens are homebodies, well mannered and hospitable, for they are healthy and self-satisfied (Jupiter rising in the twelfth house). They're a self-reliant lot, but cooperative. Cedar Rapids is a picturesque city, practically free of slums and poor people. It's the type of place that all America aspires to be, for its citizens seem to be making the most of the American dream.

Once known primarily for Quaker Oats, it's also the largest producer of popcorn in the world. South of the city are the interesting Amana colonies, a group of seven villages populated by Amish-Mennonite people.

Incorporated: 1856
Elevation: 733 feet
Area: 54 square miles
Source: Public library

Davenport

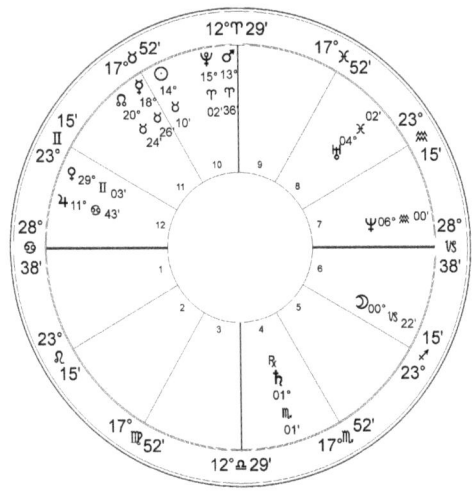

May 4, 1836
90W35, 41N31
9:58 AM CST

The future site of Davenport was acquired by Antoine LeClaire in 1832 and the present city founded in May 1836. The first bridge across the Mississippi was completed there in 1856 (Midheaven trine Moon) and the first chiropractic school in America opened in 1895.

Situated on high bluffs above the river, it has experienced few floods in its history. Davenport is the largest of the Quad Cities which include Moline, East Moline and Rock Island across the river in Illinois.

Incorporated: 1851
Elevation: 559 feet
Area: 63 square miles
Source: Public library says founded in May 1836; exact date unknown; rectified

Des Moines

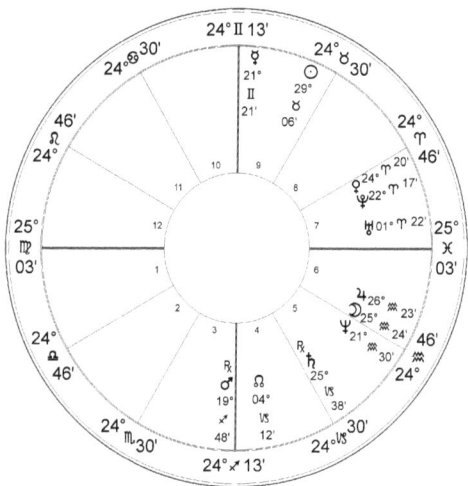

May 20, 1843
93W37, 41N35
1:58 PM CST

Founded as a fort in 1843, real settlement began two years later during a land rush (Ascendant trine Saturn). In 1858 it was made the capital of Iowa and nine years later the insurance industry was founded there. Des Moines was the first city in the U.S. to adopt a commission form of government in 1907 (Midheaven opposition Jupiter).

Des Moines is a conservative and prosperous city, capital of the most productive farming state in the nation. It's typically middle class with little disparity between rich and poor (Virgo rising). Comfortable tree shaded streets and homes with big lawns typify this city which has much open land within its corporate limits. The pace is easygoing (Sun in Taurus trine Saturn). The city is a large publishing center, as well as home to many insurance companies and the state government.

Incorporated: January 28, 1857
Elevation: 805 feet
Area: 64 square miles
Source: Public library

Iowa City

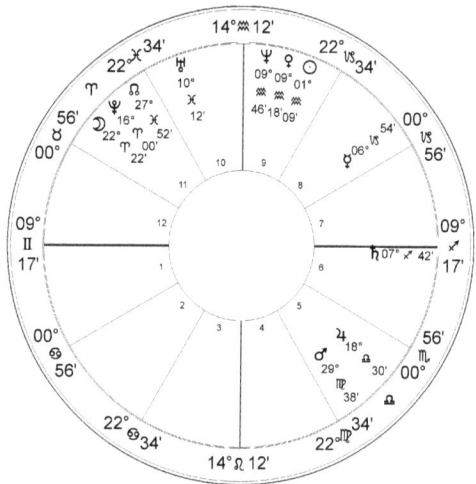

January 21, 1839
91W32, 41N40
1:11 PM CST

Founded and settled by the Amish in 1839, it was the first capital of the state. The University of Iowa was founded in 1847 (Midheaven sextile Moon, Ascendant trine Jupiter) and remains the chief attraction in this city. The legislature moved to Des Moines in 1857.

Incorporated: 1853
Elevation: 698 feet
Source: Iowa City Public Library

Sioux City

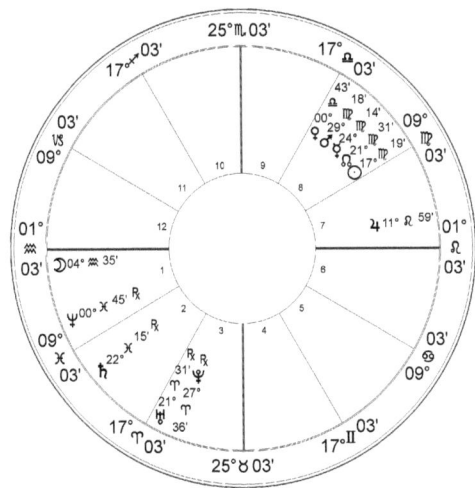

**September 9, 1848
96W24, 42N30
4:40 PM CST**

Founded as Thompsonville in September 1848, the following May, Brugier settled there with his Indian wives and Chief War Eagle. Platted in 1854, the railroad came in 1868. Four years later the packing industry began and Sioux City remains one of the largest meat packing centers in the country.

The most famous structure in the city is dedicated to Iowa's chief product. Its name, the Corn Palace, of course, which was completed in 1887.

Incorporated: July 25, 1857
Elevation: 1,135 feet
Source: Public library says September 1848, exact date unknown; chart rectified

Waterloo

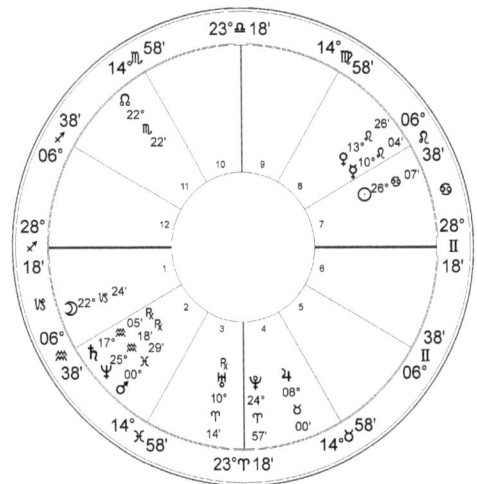

**July 18, 1845
92W20, 42N30
5:49 PM CST**

Founded during a picnic in 1845, it was known as Prairie Rapids until 1851 when it was renamed by a guy who was reading a book on Napoleon. In 1858 a flood almost wiped out the tiny settlement (Uranus conjunct the fourth house cusp). Waterloo is the largest industrial city in northeastern Iowa and hosts the National Dairy Cattle Congress.

Incorporated: June 23, 1868
Elevation: 856 feet
Source: Centennial Prairiedrama

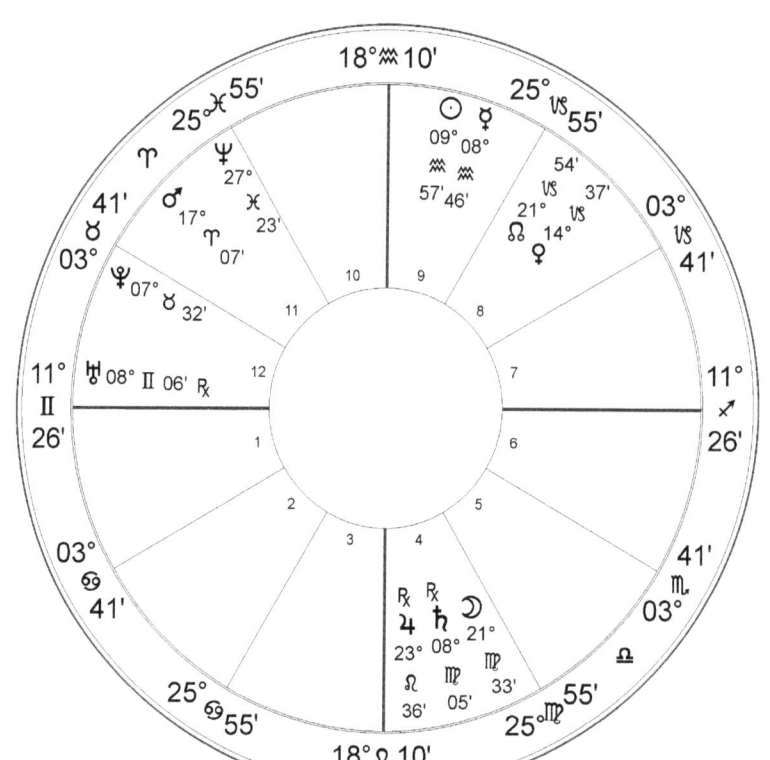

Kansas

January 29, 1861
Lecompton
95W24, 39N01
1:08 PM CST
Source: Kansas Historical Society says "2:00 p.m. in Washington"

The region was explored by Coronado in 1541 for Spain and in 1682 the area passed into French hands. In 1803 the U.S. acquired the territory in the Louisiana Purchase. The opening of the Santa Fe Trail in 1821 brought American settlers by droves and in 1827 the first settlement was made at Fort Leavenworth. On May 30, 1854, the Territory of Kansas was created, which set off guerrilla warfare between pro-slavery and anti-slavery factions; thus, "Bleeding Kansas" was born and abolitionists like John Brown fought against slavery. Shortly after becoming a state in 1861, the Civil War began and Kansas, like Missouri, became a battleground between Union and Confederate forces. Quantrill burned Lawrence in 1863 and many small skirmishes took place before the war was over. After the 1870s, the many miles of railroads made towns like Abilene and Dodge City prime cattle markets. That decade also saw the introduction of wheat by Mennonite farmers. Oil was discovered in 1892 and in 1919 the first airplane factory opened in Wichita. Many farmers were driven from the state during the mid-1930s when the Dust Bowl plagued the state.

Kansas ranks first in wheat, second in sorghum and fourth in cattle. Wichita produces more airplanes than any other city in the nation, and Kansas leads the nation in the production of helium. Oil and natural gas also are big contributors to the economy.

Area: 82,264 square miles

Dodge City

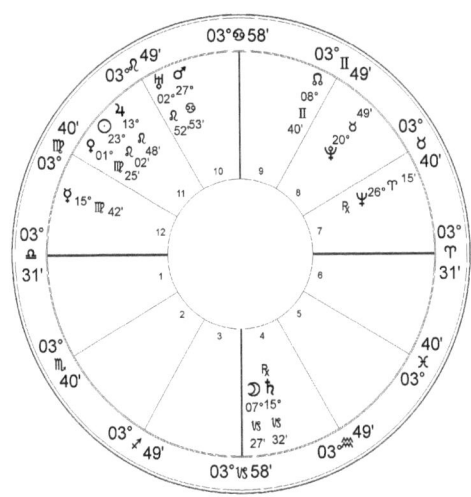

August 15, 1872
100W01, 37N45
9:20 AM CST

Fort Dodge was founded in 1864 and eight years later the present city was laid out. During the first three years of its existence, Dodge City had no formal government and, consequently, lawlessness reigned. During the 1870s it was the buffalo hide center of the world and in the 1880s it was the cowboy capital as it was on several cattle trails. In 1884, America's first bullfight was held (Ascendant sextile Jupiter).

Once known as the roughest and wildest town in the West, its streets saw the likes of Bat Masterson, Wyatt Earp and Doc Holliday. In recent years Dodge City has regained some of its former eminence as a cattle center.

Incorporated: November 2, 1875
Elevation: 2,845 feet
Source: Dodge City Public Library

Kansas City

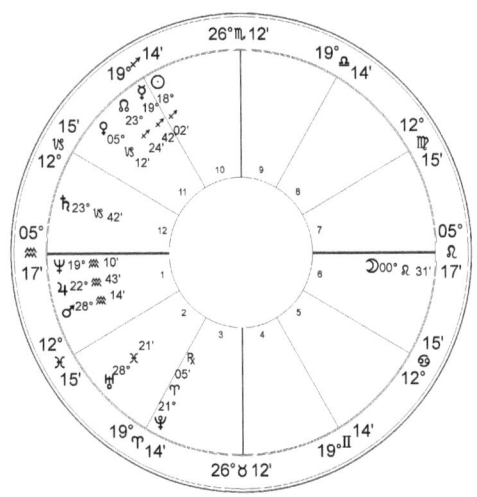

December 10, 1843
94W38, 39N07
10:39 AM CST

Land was purchased from the Indians in 1843 and later that December the first building was completed. Twelve years later the entire region passed into the hands of Americans. The first packing house opened in 1871 (Ascendant square Mercury) and three years later the city was platted. In 1886 it changed its name from Kansas to Kansas City (Midheaven sextile Mars).

Incorporated: 1859
Elevation: 773 feet
Area: 111 square miles
Source: *American Guide Series*

Topeka

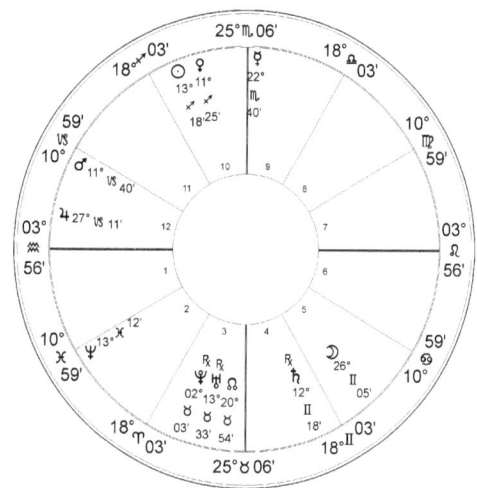

December 5, 1854
95W40, 39N03
10:57 AM CST

Founded by an association of nine men (Aquarius rising) in 1854, it became the capital of Kansas in 1861 (Ascendant sextile Sun trine Saturn). The Santa Fe railroad shops were built during the 1870s and are some of the largest in the world. In 1903 a flood caused considerable havoc (Ascendant square Jupiter).

Topeka is the home of the world famous Menninger Clinic where scientific research into mental illness is conducted.

Incorporated: February 14, 1857
Elevation: 930 feet
Area: 59 square miles
Source: *Kansas* by Frank Blackmar

Wichita

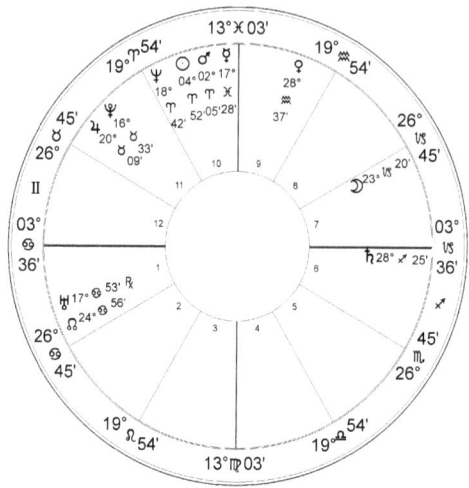

March 25, 1870
97W20, 37N42
11:15 AM CST

First settled in July 1868, the first plat was recorded two years later. With the arrival of the railroad in 1872 (Midheaven conjunct Mercury), prosperity came in leaps and bounds. The land boom collapsed, however, in 1886 (Midheaven conjunct Mars, Ascendant conjunct Uranus). Since 1920 Wichita has been one of the nation's chief centers of aviation. Four aircraft plants are located there, including Cessna, the world's largest producer of small planes.

Wichita is a city of contrasts. A neat and busy city, it's also pushy and determined (Sun in Aries). It thrives on misfortunes, most of them revolving around the weather, which is a hot topic in this city (Moon opposition Uranus). A people of extremes, Wichitans know little moderation, especially where religion is concerned. This is natural as Wichita is at the northern end of the Bible Belt.

Incorporated: April 3, 1871

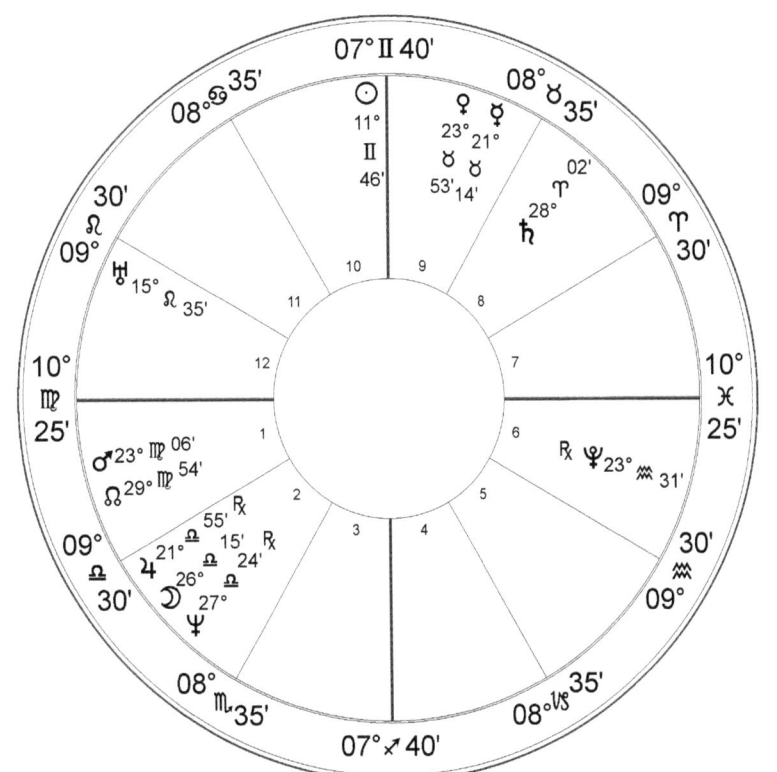

Kentucky

June 1, 1792
Lexington
84W30, 38N03
12:18 PM EST
Source: Rectified

Originally part of the state of Virginia, Daniel Boone explored the eastern part of the state in 1767 and six years later led a band of settlers into Kentucky through the Cumberland Gap. The first permanent settlement was established in 1774 at Harrodsburg. In 1792, Kentucky was the first state admitted into the Union west of the Alleghenies. In 1815 the first steamboat reached Louisville from New Orleans. The state was caught between divided loyalties during the Civil War. It vowed to stay neutral, but often families saw one son fight for the Union while another fought for the Confederacy. This happened even in Mary Todd Lincoln's family. Nevertheless, Kentucky remained with the Union and refused to secede. In 1875 the first Kentucky Derby was held. Probably the most famous family feud in the nation took place between the Hatfields and McCoys; the mountain regions of eastern Kentucky are alien territory to outsiders, who are viewed with disdain and suspicion.

More than forty percent of the state stands forested and timber is a leading contributor to the economy. Tobacco is the principal crop and Kentucky ranks second only to North Carolina. It mines more coal than any other state, but less in value than neighboring West Virginia. Since 1966 a law has required strip miners to restore the earth that has been torn up through mining. Kentucky is a leading distiller of bourbon and whiskey and is known for its fine horse farms in the Bluegrass country.

Kentucky has many tourist attractions and among them is Mammoth Cave, which has 150 miles of passageways and 200-foot ceilings some 360 feet below the ground. Kentucky also is home to Fort Knox, repository of our nation's gold reserves.

Area: 40,395 square miles

Frankfort

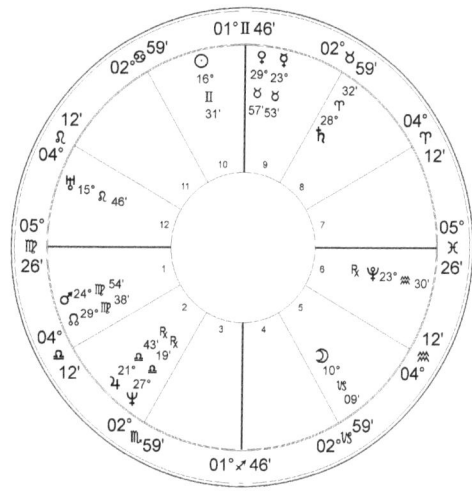

June 6, 1792
84W52, 38N12
10:35 AM CST

First settled in 1786, it was chosen by the state legislature to be the new state capital exactly five days after Kentucky's admission into the Union. The capitol building has burned twice: 1815 and 1824. Occupied by Union forces during the Civil War, it survived unscathed. A flood in 1937 crippled the economy (Ascendant sesquare Uranus).

Incorporated 1839
Elevation: 504 feet
Source: Frankfort Public Library

Lexington

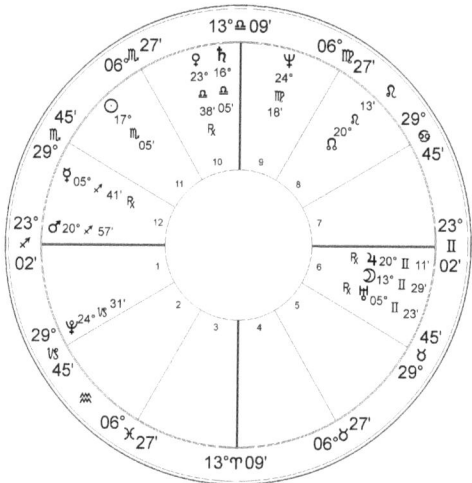

November 9, 1775
84W30, 38N03
9:12 AM CST

Founded by Robert Patterson in 1775, actual settlement began four years later. Chartered by the Virginia legislature in 1782, the nationwide financial panic of 1837 crippled the economy (Ascendant square Mercury and Uranus). The tobacco industry began there in 1825.

Lexington is a quaint blend of yesterday and today, nestled in the beautiful Bluegrass country. A serene city (Libra Midheaven), it's largely satisfied with the status quo, conservative and content, placid and calm. Its natives are typically southern: friendly, cordial and courtly (Sagittarius rising). It's an agrarian community, famous for both its horses (Sagittarius rising) and its large loose leaf tobacco (Neptune square Ascendant). Lexington also is home to the University of Kentucky, which was founded in 1865 (Ascendant square Pluto opposite Venus). Lexington merged with Fayette County in 1974.

Incorporated: 1832
Elevation: 957 feet
Area: 73 square miles
Source: *Builders in New Fields* by Charlotte Conover

Louisville

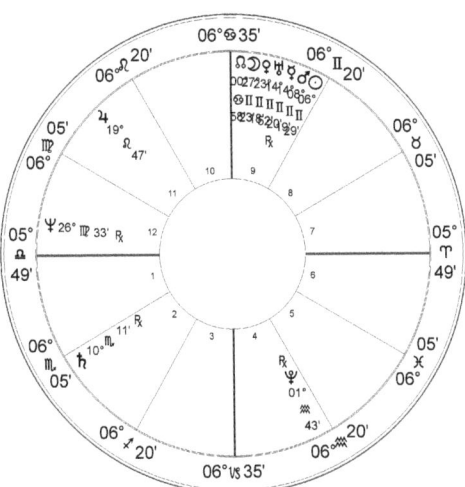

May 27, 1778
85W56, 38N15
1:50 PM CST

Founded by George Rogers Clark at the falls of the Ohio River in 1778, its location made it an important embarkation point for settlers moving west. Earthquakes began to rattle the city in December 1811 and continued for many months (Midheaven sextile Mars). A canal was completed around the falls in 1830. Ten years later a fire broke out and burned most of the downtown (Midheaven square Sun). The first Kentucky Derby was held in 1875 (Midheaven trine Mars, Ascendant trine Jupiter). Louisville has suffered through two horrendous disasters: An 1890 tornado wrecked the west side (Midheaven square Pluto) and in January 1937 the Ohio inundated a good portion of the city (Midheaven opposition Mars). Since that time, a flood wall has been built around the city. In January 2003, Louisville merged with Jefferson County to become the country's 16th largest city (Midheaven trine Mercury/Uranus, Ascendant conjunct Sun/Mars).

Louisville is on the map each year with the running of the most famous horse race in the world—the Kentucky Derby. The city literally lives for this event and the economy is boosted considerably. A rich and proud city (Sun trine Ascendant conjunct Mars), Louisville loves to eat and is quite fussy about the cuisine (Cancer Midheaven). A conflict exists between traditionalism and progressiveness (Sun in Gemini, Cancer Midheaven). Despite its apparent urbanity, Louisville is not a night city. There are few restaurants or cabarets and most entertaining is done at home. And whenever possible, the famous Kentucky drink, the mint julep, is served.

Louisville produces half of all bourbon distilled in the U.S. and a good portion of the whiskey. It's also a large tobacco manufacturing center and a large port. The Ohio River handles more tonnage than the Panama Canal.

Incorporated: February 13, 1828
Elevation: 463 feet
Area: 385 square miles
Source: *Louisville Panorama* by R.C. Riebel

Owensboro

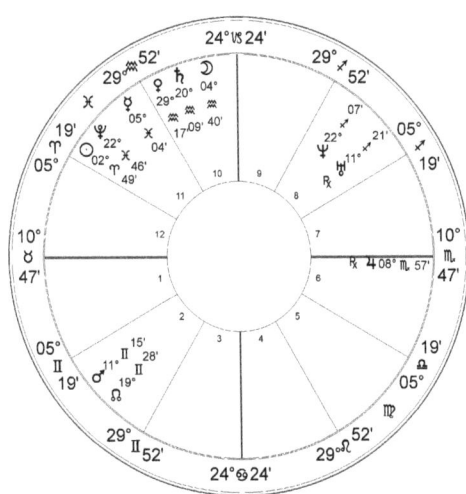

March 23, 1816
87W06, 37N46
7:30 AM CST

First settled as Yellow Banks in 1798, it was renamed Rossborough in 1816 and Owensboro upon incorporation the following year. During the Civil War a battle took place near here in September 1862 (Midheaven trine Jupiter); two years later the city was burned to the ground (Midheaven square Mars). During February 1937 the city was inundated as the Ohio spilled over its banks in the worst flood in history, but the damage was slight.

Incorporated: February 16, 1866
Elevation: 401 feet
Source: Owensboro City Hall

Paducah

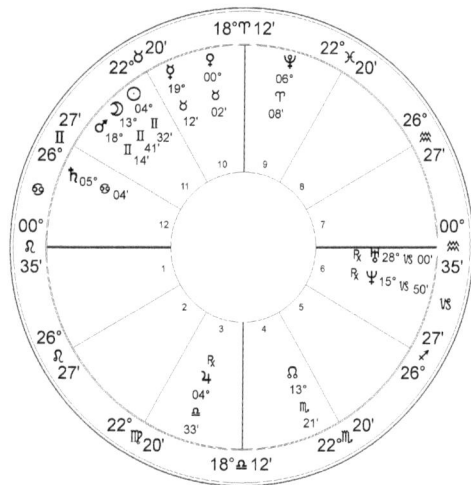

May 26, 1827
88W37, 37N05
8:48 AM CST

First settled in 1817, one year later the Jackson Purchase evacuated the Chickasaw Indians and made the area safe for European settlement. Formally founded in April 1821, it was platted six years later. Grant occupied the town in September 1861 (Ascendant inconjunct Uranus) and in 1864 the Battle of Paducah took place. In January 1937 the Ohio caused $30 million damage as floodwater raced through the city (Midheaven opposite Venus).

Incorporated: March 10, 1856
Elevation: 326 feet
Source: *Story of Paducah* by Fred Neuman

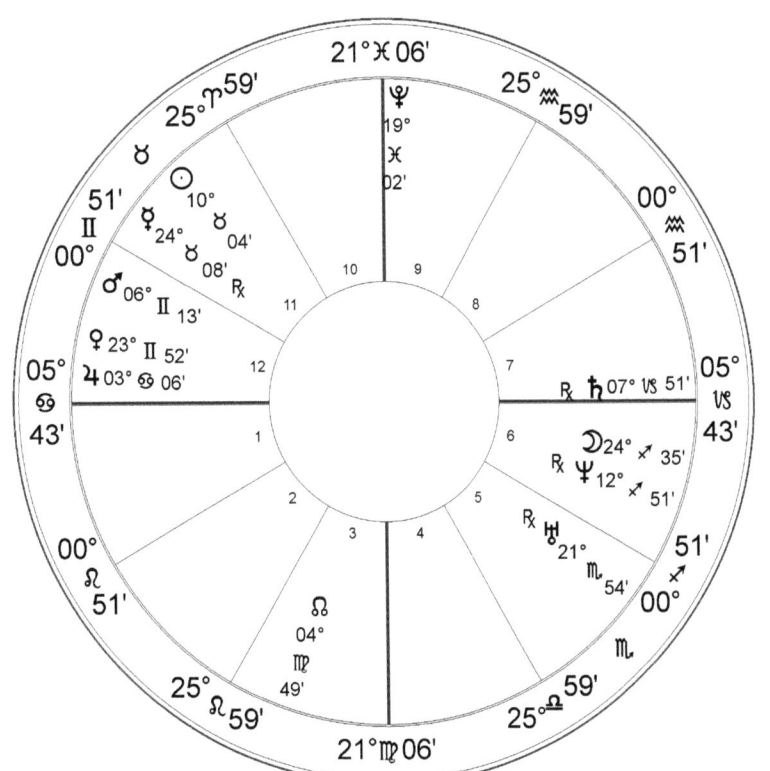

Louisiana

April 30, 1812
New Orleans
90W04, 29N58
8:54 AM CST
Source: Rectified

In 1541 Hernando de Soto explored the region and claimed it for Spain. In 1682, however, LaSalle claimed the entire Mississippi watershed for France and in 1714 the first settlement was made at Natchitoches. New Orleans was founded four years later and quickly became the capital of Louisiana. Spain acquired the region in 1762 from France, which regained the territory in 1800. On December 20, 1803, the U.S. took formal possession of this vast region called Louisiana, the largest acquisition in the nation's history. The U.S. annexed the region east of the Mississippi in 1810, six years after creating the Territory of Louisiana on March 26, 1804. Shortly after becoming a state in 1812, it saw the birth of the Steamboat Age. In January 1815, Andrew Jackson defeated the British at the Battle of New Orleans. By 1840, New Orleans had become the second largest port in the country thanks to the steamboat traffic. On January 16, 1861, Louisiana seceded from the Union and one year later New Orleans surrendered to Admiral Farragut. Readmitted on June 25, 1868, the Civil War ruined the plantation system and sharecropping was instituted in its place. Reconstruction ended with the withdrawal of federal troops in 1877 and two years later New Orleans became an ocean port after the lower Mississippi was dredged. Oil was discovered in 1901 and soon the lower part of the state was filled with oil rigs and chemical plants. The floods of 1927 caused huge property losses and more than 300,000 were driven from their homes. The governor of Louisiana, Huey P. Long, was assassinated in 1935 on the steps of the new state capitol building in Baton Rouge.

Louisiana ranks first in salt and second in oil, natural gas, and sulphur. It's third in sugarcane, fourth in rice, and is a large grower of sweet potatoes. Much of the gulf region is swamp land, home of countless species of wildlife. This is Cajun Country, where descendants of the Acadians (who were driven out of Canada in 1755) reside—the land of bayous and one of the most virgin territories in the U.S.

Area: 48,532 square miles

Baton Rouge

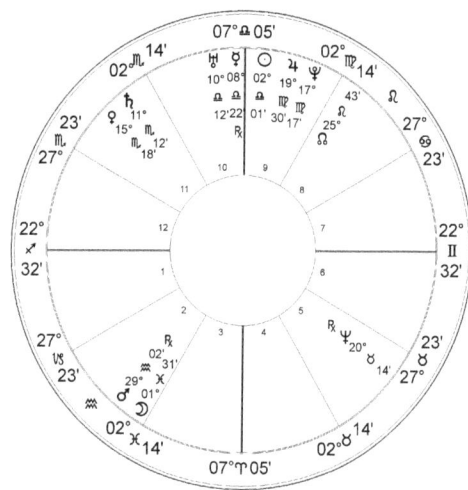

September 25, 1719
91W11, 30N27
12:15 PM CST

Founded at the junction of two tribal lands marked by a red stick (Baton Rouge in French), the fort was completed in 1719 or early 1720. The settlement was moved by the British in 1763 (Midheaven opposition Neptune). During its history Baton Rouge has been the scene of three major battles. The first took place in 1779 during the Revolution (Midheaven sextile Mercury), the second during the War of 1812 (Midheaven square Mercury) and the third in 1862 during the Civil War (Ascendant square Pluto). The city was made capital of Louisiana in 1849 (Ascendant trine Sun) and the new capitol building, which is the tallest in our country, was completed in 1932 (Midheaven opposition Saturn). On the steps of this building, Governor Huey Long was assassinated on September 8, 1935.

Standard Oil built a refinery there in 1909 and the city is now the second largest refining center in the land. It's at the northern end of the stretch of the Mississippi River known as the "Chemical Strip," due to the profusion of petrochemical plants.

Incorporated: January 16, 1817
Elevation: 57 feet
Area: 59 square miles
Source: *Louisiana Historical Quarterly*, Volume XII, states the fort was completed some time between May 1719 and September 1720; chart rectified

Lake Charles

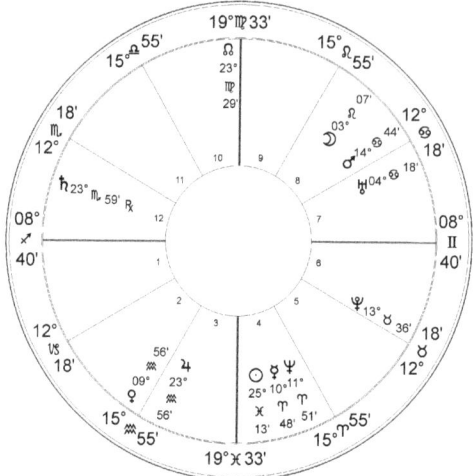

March 16, 1867
93W13, 30N14
12:01 AM CST

The region around Lake Charles was first settled in 1771 by Messrs. Salia from New Orleans and Le Bleu from France. In 1803 the first dwelling was completed and in 1852 the site was laid out as the town of Charleston. In 1880 the railroad connected the city to New Orleans and Houston, which made shipments of salt (discovered in 1905) considerably easier. In 1933 Lake Charles started its vast chemical industry due to the abundance of sulphur, oil and natural gas in the region.

Incorporated: 1867
Elevation: 20 feet
Source: Louisiana Historical Society

Monroe

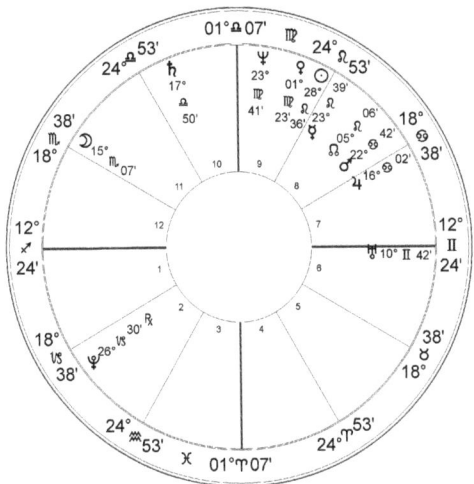

September 8, 1790
92W07, 32N30
11:50 AM CST

First settled by Don Juan Filhiol in 1785, Fort Miro was erected five years later; thus the city was born. When the steamboat Monroe arrived there in May 1819, citizens were so overjoyed they decided to rename the community after the ship. Federal troops burned the courthouse after a battle in 1863, and gas fields were discovered nearby in 1916.

Incorporated: May 4, 1871
Elevation: 77 feet
Source: *Don Juan Filhiol and the Founding of Ft. Miro* by J.F. Hardin states "before noon."

New Orleans

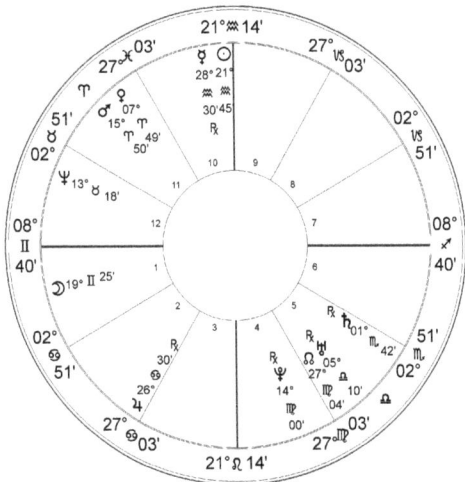

February 10, 1718
90W04, 29N58
12:13 PM CST

Founded by Lord Bienville in 1718, a flood almost wiped out the tiny settlement the following year (Midheaven semisquare Venus). A hurricane in 1722 also made settlers wonder if life there was really worth living (Ascendant square Pluto). That same year New Orleans was named capital of Louisiana, a title it held until 1849 when the legislature moved to Baton Rouge. In 1788 a fire seriously destroyed most of the French colonial buildings and eighty-five percent of the city was in ruins (Midheaven opposition Saturn). The architecture that remains in the Vieux Carre (French Quarter) is largely of Spanish design. During the War of 1812 New Orleans was crucial to the American victory over the British. Whoever controlled the Mississippi Valley controlled the interior of the continent. Andrew Jackson routed the British on the plains of Chalmette on January 8, 1815 two weeks after the treaty ending the war was signed (Midheaven sextile Jupiter). By 1850 New Orleans was the fourth largest city in the country and the epitome of southern grace, elegance and chivalry. Its position as a port caused it to be blockaded by Farragut in 1862 and for twelve years after the Civil War, New Orleans was placed under martial law (Ascendant sesquare Mercury). Home rule returned in 1877 (Midheaven conjunct Jupiter). Since then, New Orleans has declined somewhat in importance as a position of power, but it remains the third largest port in our nation. Some might say it's the "city that care forgot," but its cultural attractions and culinary delights make it one of the most unique cities in North America.

In 1994, a scandal in the police department threatened to turn this crime ravaged city upside down (Midheaven inconjunct Moon, Ascendant square Saturn). Rumors of officers moonlighting to supplant their meager salaries and whispers of collusion with drug lords caused several to resign as the federal government began looking into the system.

Located just a few feet above the mighty Mississippi, New Orleans is a delight to visitors from around the world. Famous for its food (Moon rising) and music (Aquarius Midheaven, Uranus trine Ascendant), it gave birth to the blues and to that brand of jazz known as Dixieland. Seldom taking itself seriously (Gemini rising), it pulls out all the stops during the early part of the year when Mardi Gras is in season. Long noted as the only real center of culture west of the colonies, it's actually two cities in one. Canal Street roughly divides the city into French and English sectors—the east side being French and the west side, including the Garden District, being British. Even the street names bear this out (Gemini rising).

It's a city where all deceased persons are interred above ground due to the problem of water seepage a few feet below the earth, and where funerals look and sound more like a triumphal parade than a march to the graveyard. Bourbon Street beckons those looking for fun and games, and in this noisy area almost anything can happen. There's always room for the unexpected (Sun in Aquarius) and the city can tell many a spicy tale with not a flick of the eyebrow. The city tempts you not only with flesh, but with food and music. New Orleans, like San Francisco, appeals to your senses. A gay and charming, sophisticated and elegant city, it manages to blend the cultures of the Cajuns and Creoles (descendants of the original French and Spanish settlers) equally well with that of the American Negro. It has survived hurricanes, floods and fires to become the most popular spot in the South for foreigners. New Orleans looks a bit down on its luck, but it doesn't care about appearances. It's too busy having a good time.

Incorporated: February 17, 1805
Elevation: 4 feet
Area: 199 square miles
Source: *The French Quarter* by Herbert Asbury says between February 9 and 11, 1718; chart rectified

Shreveport

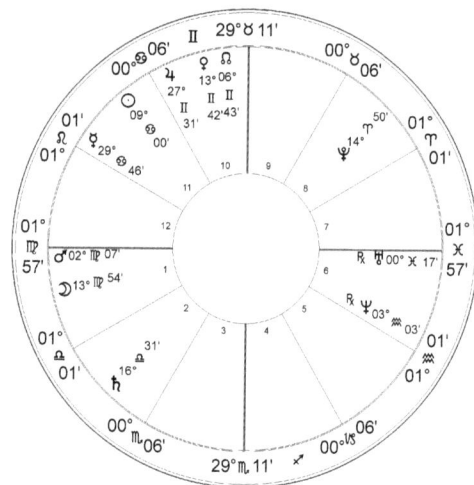

July 1, 1835
93W45, 32N31
9:27 AM CST

Founded in 1835 by Henry Shreve, who broke a logjam that blocked the Red River to navigation, one year later a town company was formed. During the Civil War, Shreveport was briefly the state capital (Midheaven conjunct Jupiter). With the discovery of oil in 1906 (Ascendant sextile Mars square Neptune), the city became a large oil refining and natural gas center.

Incorporated: March 20, 1839
Elevation: 204 feet
Area: 90 square miles
Source: Shreveport Public Library

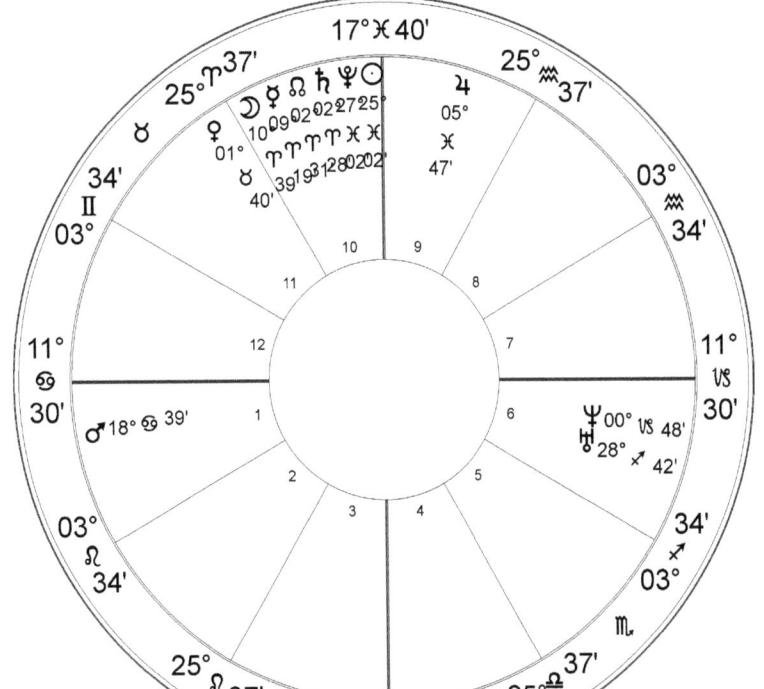

Maine

**March 15, 1820
Portland
70W16, 43N39
11:23 AM EST
Source: Maine State Historical
Society says 11:00 a.m. to noon**

Maine was first explored by John Cabot in 1498 and settled on St. Croix Island by the French in 1604. The first English colony was founded in 1607 on the Kennebec River but abandoned one year later. Maine and New Hampshire were granted to Sir Ferdinando Gorges and John Mason on August 10, 1622 and the following year permanent settlement was begun. Gorges ended up keeping Maine by himself after 1629, but in 1677 Massachusetts gained title to the region known as Somersetshire. The British burned Falmouth (now Portland) in 1775 and during the War of 1812 Eastport was captured by the British. With the Missouri Compromise of 1820, Maine was allowed to enter the Union as a free state. A boundary war between Maine and New Brunswick erupted in 1838 and four years later a treaty was signed settling the border with Canada. The first state prohibition law was enacted in 1851. Elections were often held before the rest of the country, which prompted the statement, "As Maine goes, so goes the nation."

The largest of the New England states, it's bigger than all the other five combined. It is the northernmost state on the East Coast and borders only one other state, New Hampshire. Its rugged coastline measures 3,500 miles and tides are unusually high and treacherous. Maine produces seventy-five percent of the nation's lobsters and half of its soft shelled clams. It grows ninety percent of our blueberries and twelve percent of our potatoes. More than eighty percent of the state is forested, so Maine ranks as the top lumber producer in the East.

Area: 33,215 square miles

Augusta

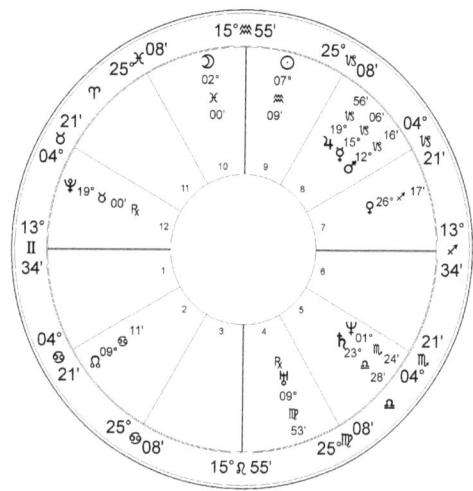

January 26, 1629
69W47, 44N19
12:28 PM EST

The Kennebec Patent was granted in 1629, which gave impetus to settle the region. Fort Augusta was completed in 1754 (Ascendant trine Pluto) and the name changed in 1797 (Midheaven square Neptune). Augusta became the capital of Maine in 1832 (Ascendant sextile Jupiter) and in 1865 a massive fire burned much of the city (Ascendant semisquare Neptune).

Incorporated: December 31, 1849
Elevation: 45 feet
Source: *History of Augusta* by Charles E. Nash

Bangor

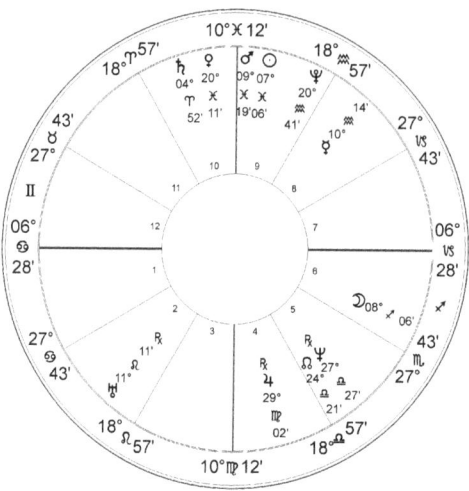

February 25, 1791
68W46, 44N48
Noon EST

It first was settled in 1769 as Kenduskeag Plantation. When the community spokesperson was presenting the papers to incorporate the town, due to a clerical error it took the name of Bangor after the hymn the spokesman was singing, instead of the intended name. It surrendered to the British in September 1814. The University of Maine was founded at Orono, nine miles north, in 1865.

Once the logging capital of the world, Bangor was the typical rowdy lumber town during the first half of the 19th century. Now a very practical and prim city, it has strong civic pride and a very lived-in look. There is a civility that comes with age and a surprising kindness towards outsiders, which is rare among New Englanders.

Incorporated: February 12, 1834
Elevation: 61 feet
Source: Bangor Public Library

Lewiston

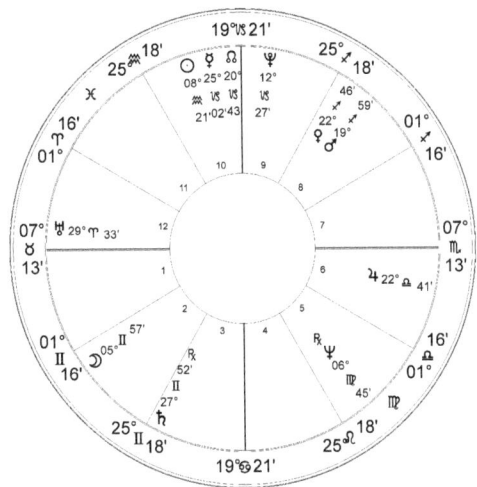

January 28, 1768
70W13, 44N06
10:35 AM EST

When the land grant was given in 1768, it was with the stipulation that the region be settled within six years. The first cabin was completed in 1770. In 1819 the first textile mill opened and that industry became the lifeblood of the city until recent years.

Incorporated: March 15, 1861
Elevation: 196 feet
Source: Lewiston Public Library

Portland

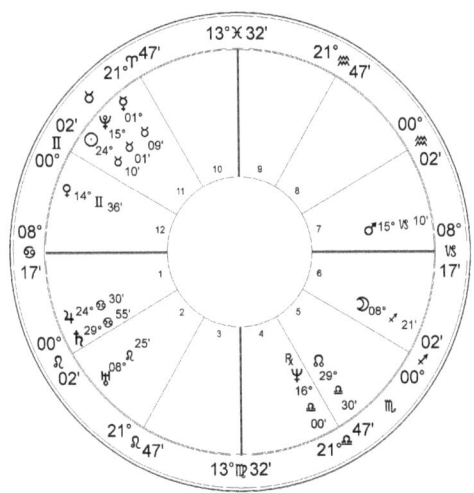

May 15, 1623
70W16, 43N40
7:09 AM EST

The land grant of 1623 gave the region to Ferdinando Gorges, but actual settlement didn't begin until nine years later. Indians attacked the town, then called Famouth, in 1676 (Ascendant square Pluto inconjunct Mars) and fourteen years later the entire community was abandoned until 1716 (Midheaven conjunct Pluto, Ascendant square Sun). Burned by the British in 1775 (Midheaven conjunct Uranus), it suffered considerably from 1807 to 1809 due to the Embargo Act (Midheaven semisquare Saturn). Upon Maine's admission into the Union in 1820, Portland became its first capital (Midheaven trine Sun). A fire on July 4, 1866 burned much of the city and gutted more than 1,500 buildings (Ascendant conjunct Mars trine Pluto).

Situated on a peninsula, Portland is one of the largest oil refining centers on the East Coast and it's also the closest American port to the European continent. In its harbor, called Casco Bay, are the 365 Calendar Islands.

Incorporated: March 26, 1832
Elevation: 25 feet
Area: 22 square miles
Source: *Portland by the Sea* by Augustus Moulton; *Forerunners of the Pilgrims* by Fred Noble says June 26, 1623

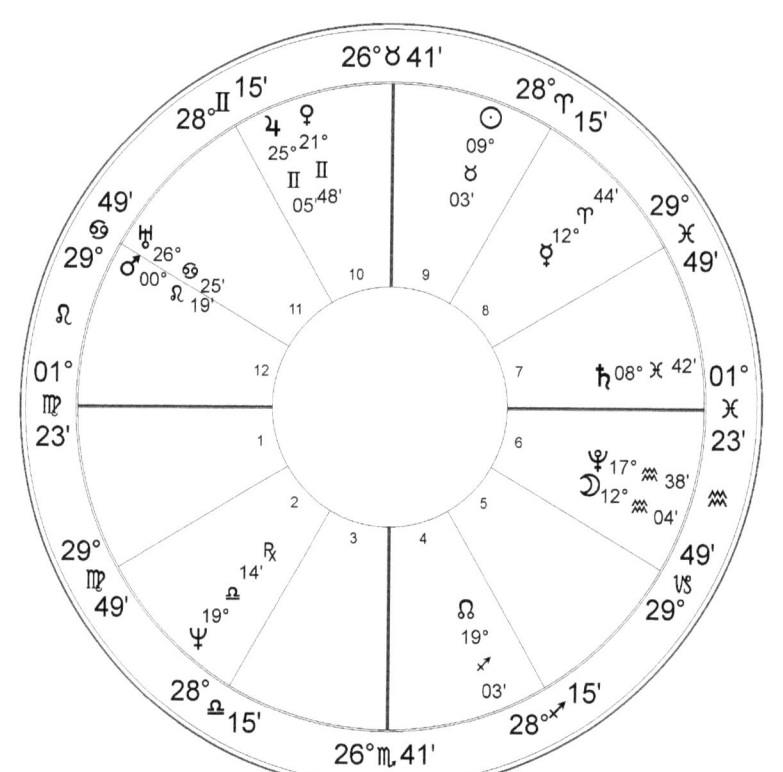

Maryland

April 28, 1788
Annapolis
76W30, 38N59
1:14 PM EST
Source: Maryland State Historical Society says "early afternoon"; chart recitified

Chesapeake Bay was first explored by John Smith in 1608 and the first settlement was made in 1631 on Kent Island. Lord Calvert, the second Lord Baltimore, was granted a charter on June 30, 1632 by King Charles I; two years later the first English Catholics landed at St. Mary's. Religious freedom was granted to all settlers by the legislature in 1649, the same year Annapolis was founded; but a revolt by Puritans in 1658 ended that religious tolerance. The Church of England was abolished in 1692 and Catholics were forbidden to vote or hold office. The Calvert family regained control of the colony in 1715, and in 1767 the boundary dispute between Maryland and Pennsylvania was finally settled thanks to Mason and Dixon. Maryland became a state in 1788 and during the War of 1812 saw action at Bladensburg and Baltimore. Maryland saw the completion of several canals during the 1830s and the nation's first railroad, the Baltimore and Ohio.

During the Civil War Maryland was divided in its sympathies. Technically a slave state (as it was below the Mason-Dixon line), it chose to remain with the Union. The battles of Antietam and Monocacy took place here. In 1938 the first state income tax in the nation was adopted and in 1952 the Chesapeake Bay Bridge was completed, linking the mainland to the eastern shore.

Divided by the Chesapeake Bay, Maryland leads the nation in oysters, clams, and striped bass. The bay is a treasure house for seafood and the restaurants of Baltimore and Annapolis attest to this fact. But basically Maryland is an industrial state and the region around Baltimore its major producer. The District of Columbia also contributes heavily to its economy as many workers in the capital live in neighboring Maryland.

Area: 10,577 square miles

Annapolis

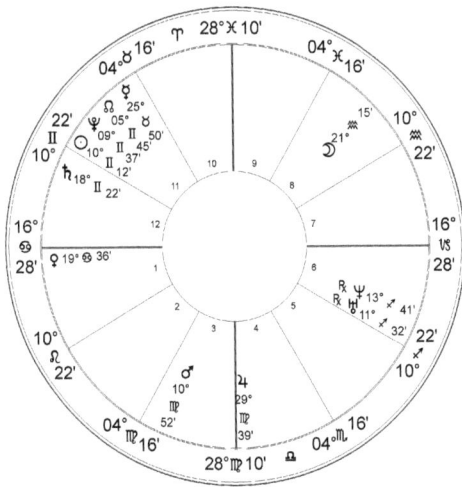

**May 31, 1649
76W30, 38N59
7:22 AM EST**

Founded as New Providence in 1649, it became the capital of Maryland in 1694 (Midheaven trine Mars, Ascendant sextile Saturn). It changed its name in 1708 from Anne Arundel Town to honor the Queen of England. From 1783 to 1784, it was the capital of the United States and in 1845 the U.S. Naval Academy was established (Midheaven trine Pluto).

Annapolis is the most historic city in the state and contains the original waterfront it had during the Revolution. Its capitol building is the only one in the country to have a wooden dome and it also is the oldest continuously operated seat of government in the land (1772).

Incorporated: December 3, 1708
Elevation: 40 feet
Source: American Federation of Astrologers

Baltimore

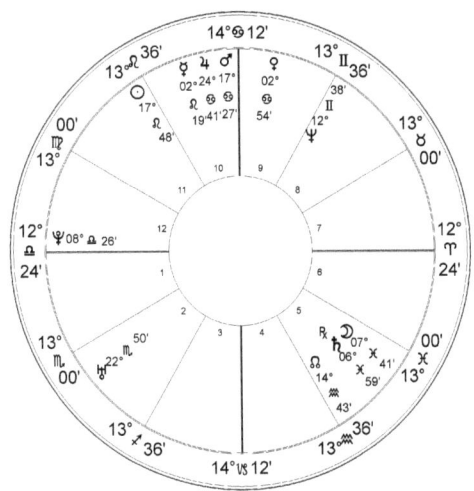

**August 10, 1729
76W37, 39N17
9:52 AM EST**

First settled in 1661, Baltimore Town was founded by the state legislature in 1729. During the Revolution it was the headquarters of the Continental Navy. It witnessed the shelling of Fort McHenry on September 13, 1814, which prompted Francis Scott Key to write our national anthem, "The Star Spangled Banner" (Midheaven conjunct Pluto). Our nation's first railroad, the B&O, was born there in 1827, and in 1852 Baltimore became an independent city after separating from the county (Midheaven square Sun, Ascendant sextile Uranus). During the early days of the Civil War the city was placed under martial law due to wavering sympathies between North and South (Ascendant opposition Mercury). Downtown Baltimore has few old buildings due to the fire which swept through the area on February 7, 1904 (Midheaven semisquare Uranus square Pluto, Ascendant trine Sun). Fortunately no lives were lost. In 1913 a ship was dynamited in the harbor, killing fifty-five persons (Midheaven opposition Mars).

Baltimore is one of the largest ports on the eastern seaboard, a major steel center and a leader in educational and medical research. It is a working class town full of busty women and lusty men (Venus in Cancer and Sun in Leo, perhaps). It is a city known for its numerous row houses, each with its polished white marble steps, and its cuisine of clams, crabs, and oysters (Cancer Midheaven). Being midway between the North and the South (Libra rising), it's a blend of Boston and New Orleans, but with a more sluggish tempo. Its ethnic neighborhoods are strong and the city is home to many Ukrainians and Slavs. Baltimoreans can be quite snobby (Sun in Leo) and indifferent to outside criticism (Moon in Pisces). It's a city that you must walk through in order to really know it, for by rail much of the city is obscured by tunnels, and by auto most people bypass this city. Its downtown area has undergone quite a renovation in recent years, especially around the inner harbor where rests the USS Constellation, the flagship of the Continental Navy.

Even though Baltimore might not appear to be an exciting town, some find it much more livable and human than the capital city of Washington, which is a scant forty miles to the south.

Incorporated: June 2, 1797
Elevation: 20 feet
Area: 78 square miles
Source: *American Guide Series* says August 10, 1729 (NS)

Cumberland

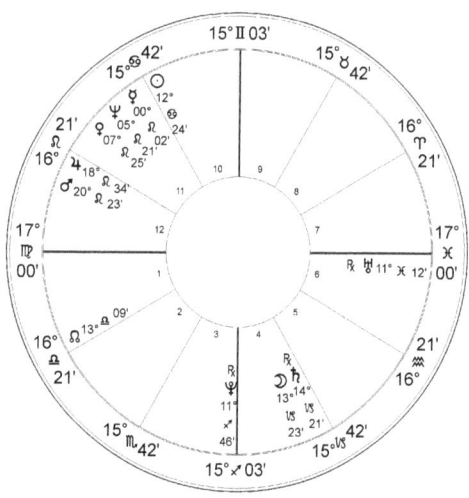

July 4, 1754
78W46, 39N39
10:20 AM EST

The Ohio Company established a trading post in 1750 and four years later George Washington helped establish Fort Pleasant, as Cumberland was first known. Laid out in 1763 as Washington Town, it became Cumberland in 1787. With the completion of the National Road in 1811, the Baltimore and Ohio Railroad in 1842 (Midheaven opposition Uranus) and the Chesapeake and Ohio Canal in 1850, Cumberland became a prime transportation hub in the movement west. A fire in 1833 burned seventy-five buildings (Ascendant square Mars) and three major floods have caused extensive damage over the years: 1889 (Ascendant inconjunct Neptune), 1936, and 1937 (Ascendant inconjunct Neptune). Occupied by federal troops between 1861 and 1865 (Ascendant conjunct Pluto square Uranus), it is the largest city in western Maryland.

Incorporated: 1856
Elevation: 641 feet
Source: *American Guide Series*

Hagerstown

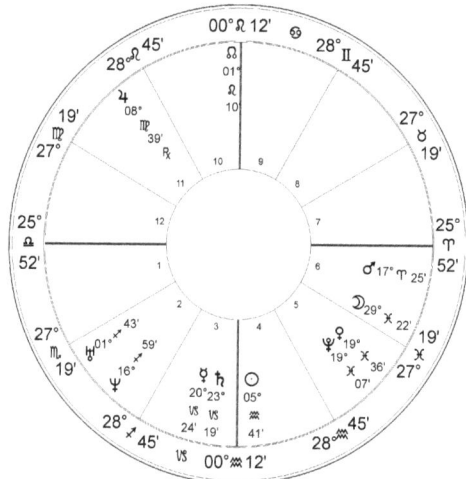

January 26, 1814
77W43, 39N39
12:01 AM EST

First settled in the 1730s by Scotch-Irish and Germans, it was laid out in 1762 by Jonathan Hager as Elizabeth Town to honor his wife. It was renamed Hagerstown upon incorporation in 1814. During the 1820s it became a major stopping point on the road west and later a major rail center. During the Civil War it changed hands many times.

Incorporated: 1814
Elevation: 552 feet
Source: *History of Western Maryland* by J.T. Scharf

Massachusetts

February 6, 1788
Boston
71W04, 42N22
2:06 PM EST

Source: Massachusetts Historical Society relates "mid-afternoon after a heated debate;" rectified

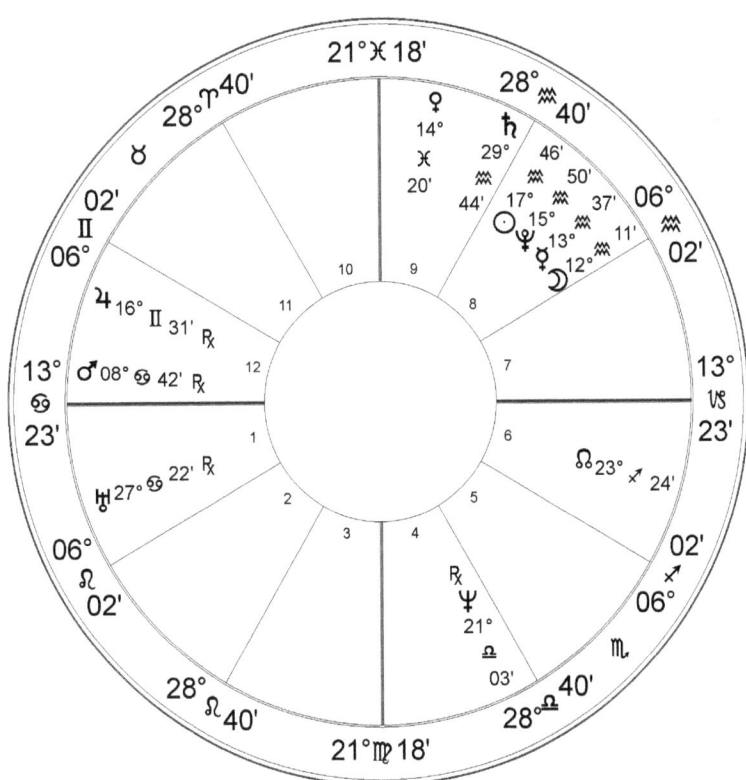

The first European settlement in New England occurred at Plymouth on December 21, 1620. The Massachusetts Bay Colony was granted a royal charter on March 4, 1629 and Boston was founded the following year. Many settlers were killed during King Philip's War of 1675-78, and in 1684 the royal charter was revoked. Five years later a revolt in Boston overthrew the English governor. In 1692 the infamous witch trials took place in Salem. During the latter 18th century, Bostonians became increasingly irritated at what they considered unfair treatment by the British. Taxation was too high; thus, the Boston Tea Party was staged in 1773. Two years later, on April 19, 1775, the Revolution began at Concord and Lexington; two months later the British defeated the militia at Bunker Hill. After a nine month siege, the British finally evacuated Boston in March 1776. Massachusetts ratified the Constitution in 1788 and its role in colonial politics began to wane.

The state became increasingly industrial during the 19th century and led in textile production. Thousands of Irish and Italian immigrants changed the face of this Puritan stronghold forever. It became the wealthiest in new England and played an important role in the early intellectual, political and economic development of the nation. Its tourist attractions are too numerous to mention.

During the 19th century, shipping and foreign trade, along with whaling, were the main industries. Massachusetts leads in the production of shoes, medical instruments and personal computers. The Bay State leads in cranberries, the traditional fruit to serve at Thanksgiving, which was first celebrated in Massachusetts by the Pilgrims in 1621.

Area: 8,257 square miles

Boston

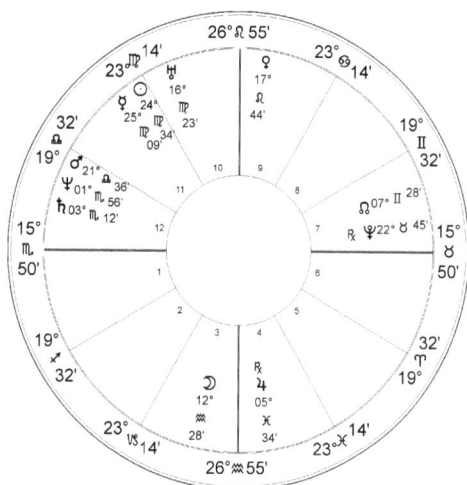

September 17, 1630
71W04, 42N22
9:55 AM EST

Founded on a peninsula in 1630, it became capital of the Massachusetts Bay Colony two years later. In 1692, a witch hunt took place and 100 were jailed (Ascendant sextile Jupiter). The Stamp Act of 1765 caused a riot and was a prelude to the grisly Boston Massacre of March 1770 (Ascendant opposition Saturn). Three years later, natives dressed as Indians threw tea into Boston Harbor (Midheaven square Mars). Boston was clearly a city in foment, and the British were determined to show them a lesson. On the night of April 18-19, 1775, a lantern shone in the Old North Church signaling Paul Revere that the Redcoats were coming by land. The following morning the Minutemen fought the first Battle of the Revolution on the greens of Lexington and Concord (Midheaven trine Sun, Ascendant square Moon). America's fight for freedom had begun. During the Embargo Act (1807-09) the city's economy suffered immensely. Then came the War of 1812, and when Boston had just about recovered, the Erie Canal opened and took much of its shipping business to the west.

In 1863, draft riots took place (Midheaven opposition Mars, Ascendant square Saturn) but thousands went to the fray in spite of their outrage and the city's Abolitionist sympathies. On November 9, 1872, a fire in the North End burned countless buildings (Ascendant semisquare Sun), but Boston rebuilt anew and gave birth to America's first subway twenty-five years later. The suburb of Chelsea burned in 1908: 3,500 structures were torched, an event that was to repeat itself in the mid-1970s. During the 1970s Boston was the scene of much dissension due to school integration. The old-line Irish families of Dorchester fought valiantly against the issue, and much ill feeling was created.

Boston has undergone a massive transformation in the past two decades. No longer a low-rise city, structures like the John Hancock Center and Prudential Tower have given impetus to massive renovations in the Back Bay region, the poshest sector of the city. Old Scollay Square was torn down and the new Government Center instituted in its place.

Boston is a complex and fascinating city, the most English metropolis in the land. An insular city, wary of change and mistrustful of outsiders (Scorpio rising), it's proud and conservative, venerable and stately, It's probably the most civilized large city in the country due to its strong British heritage. Formerly known as a bigoted community where certain materials were banned due to questionable community standards (Sun in Virgo), it's also the largest university and college town in the country. In the region are fifty-six colleges and universities and thousands of students. For this reason Boston was known as the "Athens of America," but its natives call it the "Hub of the Universe." Largely inhabited by Irish and Italians, its neighborhoods are some of the strongest in the nation. Having the most expensive municipal government in the country causes living costs to be unusually high. Boston is still a very personal city, full of considerable charm and beauty, but in order to appreciate it, you must get out and walk those narrow streets that pass by structures like the Old North Church, Paul Revere's house and the Old Granary Burying Ground along the "Freedom Trail." Boston has the oldest public park in the country, called the Common, and to the west are the Public Gardens and the Fenway. Back Bay is the bastion of the nouveau-riche, while Beacon Hill was once home to the Boston Brahmins like the Cabots, Lowells and Lodges. Boston is also a leader in medical research, and Massachusetts General Hospital is one of the finest in the world. The city is also the scene of the most famous foot race in the world, the Boston Marathon. Its citizens love to keep fit and trim.

Bostonians are a fascinating lot, being interested in innovation (Uranus in the tenth house sextile the Ascendant) and freedom, which caused this country to be separated from Britain. The foment that was roused then can still be roused today (Mars in the twelfth house) for Bostonians like to be left alone and are somewhat anti-social (Moon opposition Venus) and detest being controlled by outside forces (Pluto in the seventh house). Despite its rich heritage and immense contributions to American history Boston is shrinking in size today and houses many poor people of various minorities who have not been allowed to come into the mainstream of Boston society (Jupiter in the fourth house trine Saturn/Neptune in the twelfth house).

Incorporated: May 1, 1822
Elevation: 21 feet
Area: 49 square miles
Source: *Crooked and Narrow Streets of Boston* by Annie Thwing for date; American Federation of Astrologers for the time.

Cambridge

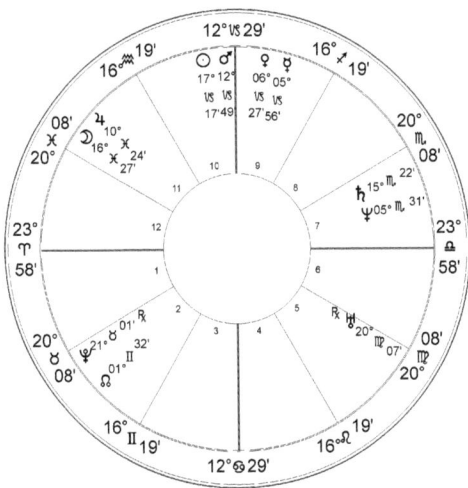

January 7, 1631
71W06, 42N22
11:31 AM EST

Founded as Newtowne in 1631, the most prestigious university in the country, Harvard, was founded five years later (Midheaven conjunct Sun). During the 1640s the Cambridge Platform gave almost total power to the church, a system not unlike many other New England towns. Massachusetts Institute of Technology was founded in 1861 (Ascendant conjunct Saturn, Sun trine Moon) and eighteen years later Radcliffe was established (Midheaven sextile Saturn trine Sun).

Today, Cambridge is a prosperous university center populated by thousands of young people on their way to becoming leaders of business and politics. A few blocks from Harvard Square, the heart of the city, is the home of America's most beloved poet, Henry Wadsworth Longfellow.

Incorporated: March 17, 1846
Elevation: 20 feet
Area: 6 square miles
Source: *History of Middlesex County* by D.H. Hurd

Concord

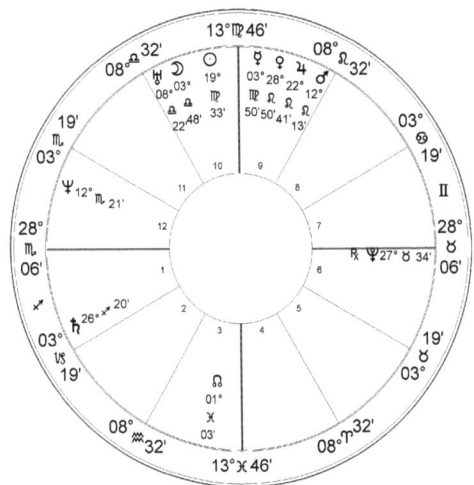

September 12, 1635
71W21, 42N28
11:20 AM EST

Founded as Musketaquid in 1635, it held the first provincial congress of the Bay State in 1774. The following year, on April 19, 1775, the second battle of the Revolution took place at the Old North Bridge (Ascendant conjunct Pluto). During the 19th century, Concord was the home of such notables as Emerson, Thoreau, Hawthorne, Alcott, Elizabeth Peabody, and Daniel Chester French. It was the intellectual heart of this young nation. The town also gave birth to the concord grape in 1853.

Elevation: 130 feet
Source: *Story of Concord* by Josephine Swayne

Fall River

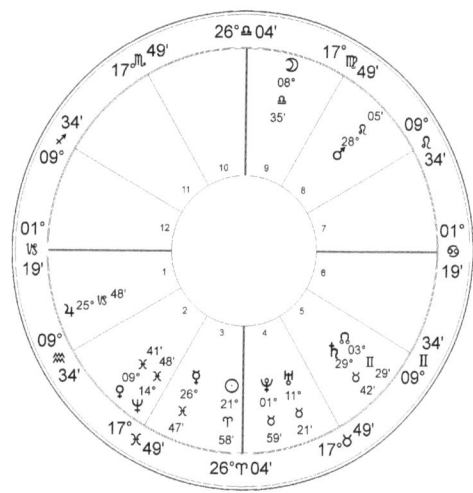

April 12, 1854
71W09, 41N42
12:01 AM EST

In 1656 the land around New Bedford was acquired as Freeman's Purchase and settled nearly thirty years later as Quequechan. Incorporated in 1803 as a village, it was known as Troy until 1834. The United Textile Workers' Union was formed here in 1901 and Fall River was one of the largest milling centers in the land until the Depression, when many mills moved to the South due to cheap labor.

Incorporated: 1854
Elevation: 140 feet
Area: 33 square miles
Source: Fall River Public Library

Lawrence

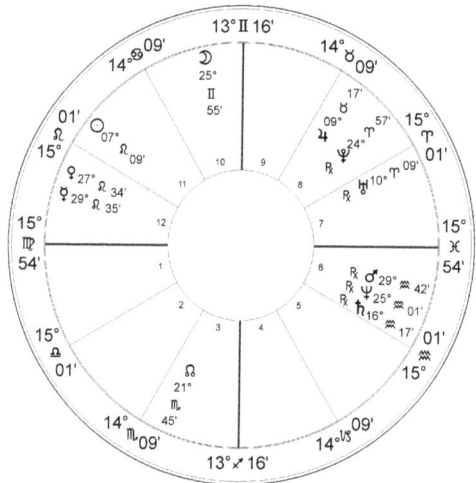

July 30, 1845
71W10, 42N43
8:00 AM EST

Originally settled in 1655, the Essex Company purchased the region in 1845 from the Merrimack Valley Association. On the site was built a model factory town for textile workers. In 1860 a factory roof caved in, causing 525 casualties, and in 1912 a labor strike idled the economy. With the depression of the 1930s, many of the mills closed forever, and the plants moved south where labor was cheaper and unions not as powerful.

Incorporated: March 21, 1853
Elevation: 50 feet
Source: The Essex Company Archives

Lowell

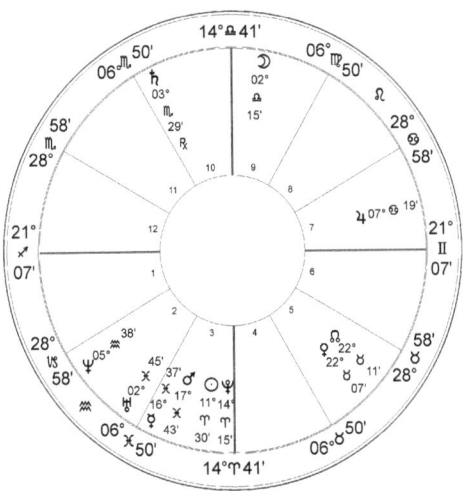

April 1, 1836
71W19, 42N38
12:01 AM EST

Settled in 1653, it was founded as a company town in 1822 and advertised as the factory town of the future. Like many other New England mill towns, most of the mills closed during the Depression.

Incorporated: 1836
Elevation: 100 feet
Source: Lowell Public Library

Nantucket

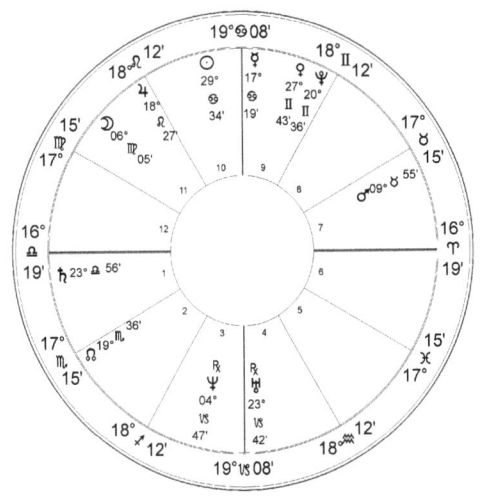

July 22, 1659
70W06, 41N17
11:02 AM EST

Purchased by Mayhew in 1641, it was sold in 1659 and settled two years later. Because of legal problems it remained part of New York until 1692. The whaling industry, which put Nantucket on the map, began in 1768 (Midheaven sextile Moon) and for the next century it was the dominant industry of the island. During the Revolution the British raided the town (Midheaven square Jupiter, Ascendant conjunct Uranus) and from 1812 to 1814 the entire island was blockaded (Midheaven opposition Pluto). During the late 19th century Nantucket became a summer resort: a perfect place to get away from the frenetic life of the city and to enjoy nature at its most unspoiled. The town has never been incorporated and is run by a council.

Source: *Nantucket* by William Stevens

New Bedford

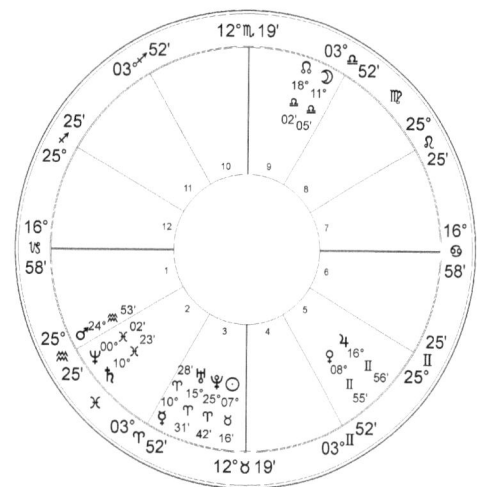

**April 28, 1847
70W56, 41N38
12:01 AM EST**

Founded as Dartmouth by Miles Standish and William Bradford in 1652, the whaling industry began here in 1765. Two years later the first ship sailed from this port and before long New Bedford was the largest whaling port in the world. The British burned the entire city in 1775 as it was a haven for privateers. By the middle of the 19th century, New Bedford was the world's fourth largest port and the richest city per capita on the globe. With the coming of the textile industry in the 1880s, whaling dropped in importance. In 1928 a depression closed the mills for six months and before long, many of those mills moved south. This city has one of the largest Portuguese colonies in the country.

Incorporated: 1847
Elevation: 50 feet
Area: 19 square miles
Source: New Bedford Public Library

Pittsfield

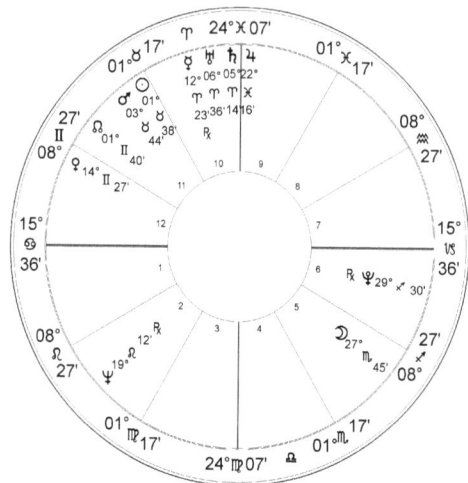

**April 21, 1761
73W15, 42N27
9:32 AM EST**

First settled in 1752 as Pontoosuck Plantation, it was chartered as a town in 1761. In its early years the economy was mostly agricultural. Ten miles away is the famed outdoor music center of Tanglewood, located in the picturesque Berkshire Mountains. In recent years Pittsfield has become a paper making center, and much of its produce is used to make U.S. bank notes.

Incorporated: 1890
Elevation: 1,020 feet
Source: Carolyn Dodson for date; time rectified

Plymouth

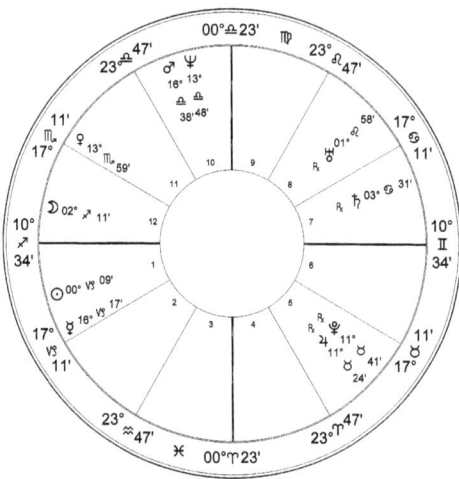

**December 21, 1620
70W40, 41N57
6:00 AM LMT**

The Pilgrims arrived in Massachusetts Bay in November 1620, after a two-month voyage across the Atlantic Ocean from southern England. Soon after, they signed the Mayflower Compact on November 21 (NS), whereby the will of the colonists rather than the will of the British Crown formed the first concept of democracy in the colonies.

Four days before Christmas, the Pilgrims came ashore at Plymouth Rock and began the first British settlement in New England. The first winter was extremely harsh and half of the settlers perished (Ascendant inconjunct Jupiter). The first Thanksgiving feast was held sometime after the harvest in 1621, with help from the native inhabitants. By 1642, the Church had assumed control of the new colony (Ascendant sesquare Jupiter), as it had done in other New England colonies.

In 1957, the Plimouth Foundation was established to protect and preserve as much as possible of this important site. A reconstruction of the original settlement, called Plimouth Plantation, was build (Midheaven square Moon trine Sun, Ascendant opposition Pluto sesquare Saturn).

Source: American Federation of Astrologers

Provincetown

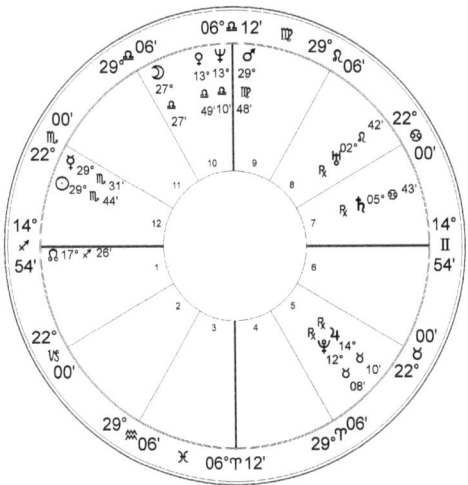

**November 21, 1620
70W11, 42N03
8:00 AM EST**

On the morning of November 21, 1620, the Pilgrims made their landfall in the New World. Later that afternoon (about 3:00 p.m.), the Mayflower Compact was signed. The area remained largely unsettled until 1700, when fishermen arrived (Midheaven sextile Moon). In 1714, the town separated from Truro (Ascendant square Venus/Neptune trine Jupiter) and between 1760 and 1780, it was abandoned several times due to Indian attacks and British raids during the Revolution. At the turn of the 20th century, Provincetown started to become famous as an art colony and summer resort (Ascendant conjunct Venus/Neptune). The community has a large Portuguese colony and the Pilgrim Monument (253 feet high) is the highest point on Cape Cod.

Incorporated as town: 1727
Elevation: 13 feet
Source: Provincetown Public Library

Salem

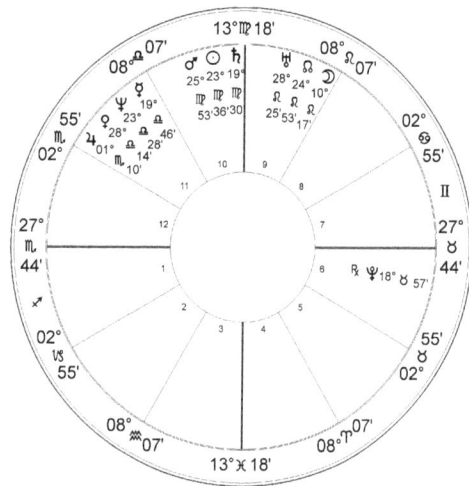

September 16, 1626
70W53, 42N31
11:00 AM EST

Founded in 1626, four years before Boston, its most famous, or infamous, event occurred in 1692 when nineteen were hanged and two died in prison during the witch trials (Midheaven progressed to 19 Scorpio sextile Saturn, Ascendant trine Sun and Pluto). Trade with China began in 1785 (Midheaven trine Neptune, Ascendant trine Mercury) and Salem became one of the richest ports in the country. In 1914 a fire burned 1,600 buildings (Midheaven sextile Uranus).

Besides being famous for the witch hunt (Scorpio rising), Salem was also the home of Nathaniel Hawthorne, who wrote The Scarlet Letter (Sun in Virgo advocates purity). On its tree shaded streets are many fine examples of colonial and federalist architecture, a permanent symbol of this city's once powerful position.

Incorporated: February 15, 1836
Elevation: 13 feet
Source: *History of Essex County*

Springfield

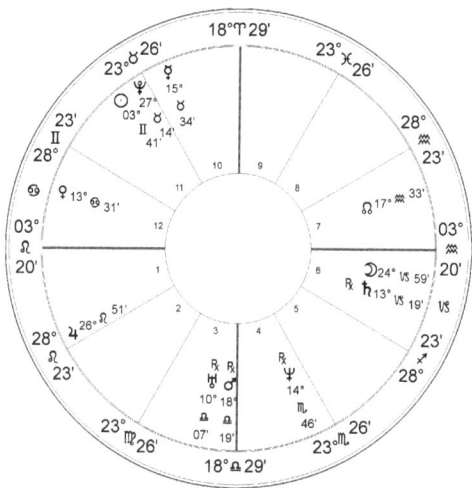

May 24, 1636
72W35, 42N06
8:48 AM EST

Founded in 1636, Springfield experienced a witch hunt as early as 1651 (Ascendant square Neptune). In 1675 during King Philip's War, most of the town was burned (Midheaven conjunct Pluto). The federal government built an arsenal here in 1794, and for many years Springfield was the ammunition center of the nation. In 1927 (Ascendant conjunct Sun/Pluto) and 1936 (Midheaven square Neptune), much of the city was under water as the banks of the Connecticut overflowed with fierce intensity.

Incorporated: May 25, 1852
Elevation: 85 feet
Area: 32 square miles
Source: *History of Springfield* by Henry M. Burt

Worcester

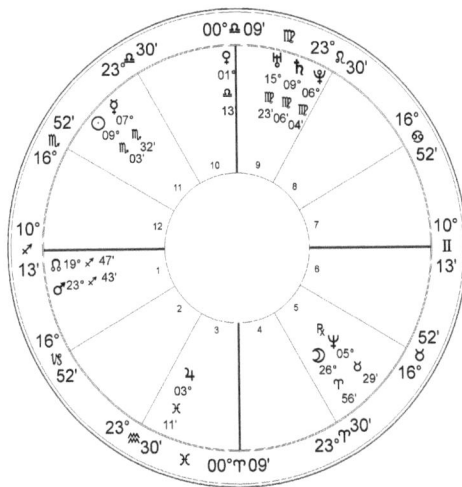

November 1, 1713
71W48, 42N16
9:05 AM EST

First settled in 1674, the community was abandoned the following year during King Philip's War. A second settlement was attempted in 1684 but abandoned in 1702 during Queen Anne's War. The third, and final, settlement attempt was successful in 1713. The textile industry was founded in 1789 (Ascendant trine Mercury) and in 1828 a canal was completed to Providence. Previously, Worcester was the largest city in the country not on navigable water. The Free Soil Party was founded here in 1848, and in 1938 a hurricane caused extensive damage.

Incorporated: February 29, 1848
Elevation: 475 feet
Area: 38 square miles
Source: Jottings from *Worcester's History* by Waldo Cutler

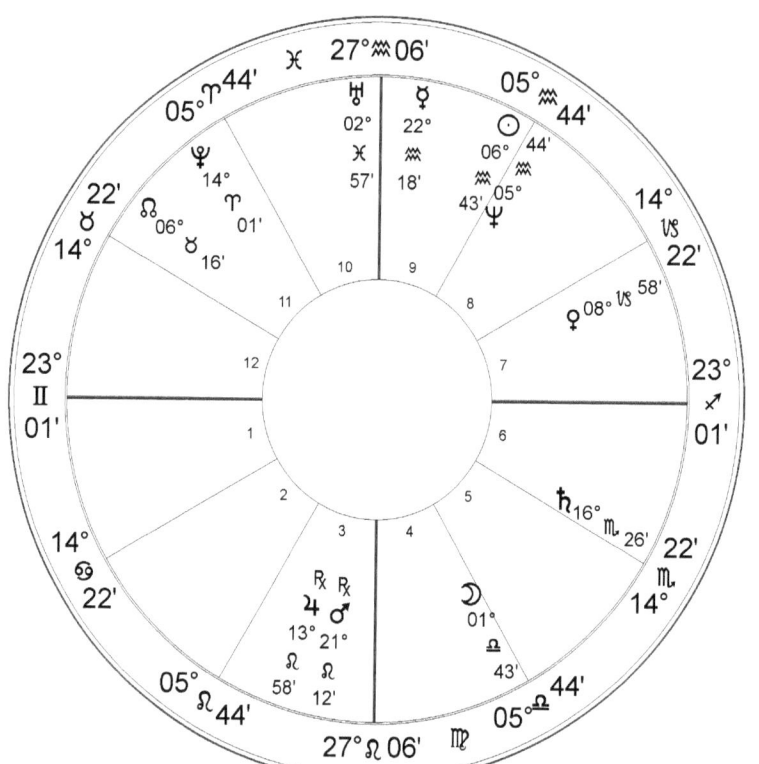

Michigan

January 26, 1837
Detroit
83W03, 42N20
2:06 PM EST
Source: Rectified

The first permanent French settlement was established in 1668 at Sault Ste. Marie by Father Marquette. Three years later, Mackinac was built. In 1763 Britain acquired the region from France and twenty years later it passed into American hands, except for the region around Detroit. Becoming part of the Northwest Territory in 1787, it was made part of the Indiana Territory in 1800. A separate territory on January 11, 1805, Detroit surrendered to the British in 1812. The border with Ohio was finally settled in 1835, and two years later Michigan became a state. The newly created Republican Party was given its name in 1854 at Jackson, and the following year the first Soo Canal was completed, linking Lakes Superior and Huron. The first automobile factory opened at Detroit in 1896, and with the genius of Henry Ford, autos were soon being produced by the thousands due to his invention of the assembly line. The Straits of Mackinac Bridge was opened in 1957, linking the Upper and Lower Peninsulas.

Michigan is the only state that borders on four of the five Great Lakes, and the only one which contains two peninsulas. The state is the leading maker of automobiles, ranks sixth in dairy cows, and ranks high in apples, pears and grapes, and number one in cherries. Michigan ranks second in iron ore production, all of it centered in the Upper Peninsula. The state is also a large food processor, especially cereals. And Grand Rapids, the city that furniture made famous, must be mentioned.

Area: 58,216 square miles

Ann Arbor

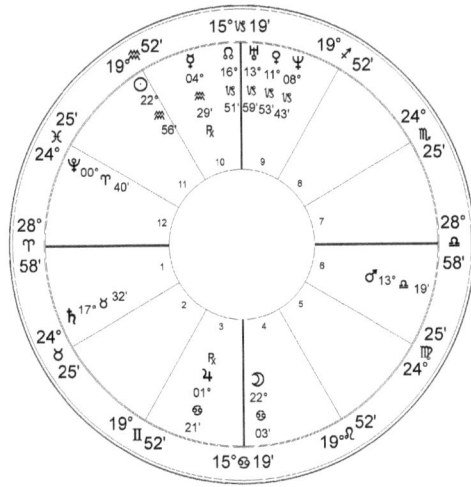

February 12, 1824
83W45, 42N17
10:15 AM EST

Settled by John and Ann Allen and Elisha and Ann Rumsey in 1824, it was called Ann's Arbor to honor the wives of the first settlers. The University of Michigan was founded in 1837 and moved here in 1841 (Midheaven conjunct Mercury). Ann Arbor is also a leader in electronics, research and science (Sun in Aquarius, Uranus conjunct Midheaven).

Incorporated: 1851
Elevation: 802 feet
Are: 24 square miles
Source: *History of Wahtenaw County*

Detroit

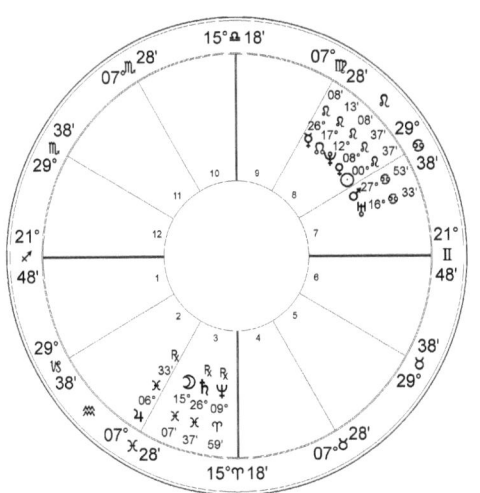

July 23, 1701
83W03, 42N20
5:23 PM EST

First sighted by Antoine de la Mothe Cadillac on the afternoon of July 23, 1701, he went ashore the following morning about sunrise. In 1760 the British occupied the city, and in 1796 the Americans took possession. A fire in 1805 burned most of the downtown (Midheaven opposition Mars) and a new city arose designed after Washington, D.C., with radial avenues and plazas. During most of the 19th century, Detroit was a small, sleepy town; then Henry Ford built the first auto in 1896 (Midheaven sextile Sun and Uranus, Ascendant conjunct Pluto trine Neptune). American industry hasn't been the same since due to Ford's invention of the assembly line. During the 20th century, Detroit has experienced much racial strife. A riot in 1943 (Midheaven square Moon) caused considerable damage, and the July 1967 riot erupted into a full scale conflagration when much of the Black district was set ablaze (Midheaven semisquare Mercury).

During the 20th century, Detroit has become an industrial giant. It produces twenty-three percent of all U.S. autos, twenty-three percent of all machine tools and twelve percent of the hardware. The city is the fourth largest financial center in the country and its port ranks third in customs collections. Known as the "Motor City," its chief industry has transformed the American way of life. A raw and brassy city (Sun in Leo, Sagittarius rising), it's typically blue collar and team oriented. It's a strong union town where machines come first and people are manipulated along with the materials that are devoured in the production of the automobile. Detroit has the highest per capita income of any U.S. metropolitan area, even though the region is suffering due to America's desire for more fuel efficient means of transportation.

Much of the downtown area is being renovated, and

the fulcrum of this renewal is the Renaissance Center: five cylindrical towers that front the Detroit River, through which passes twice the annual tonnage of the Panama Canal. From these towers you can look south into Canada, the only place in the U.S. that you can do so.

Incorporated: October 24, 1815
Elevation: 585 feet
Area: 140 square miles
Source: Detroit Public Library; *American Guide Series* and American Federation of Astrologers say July 24, 1701

Flint

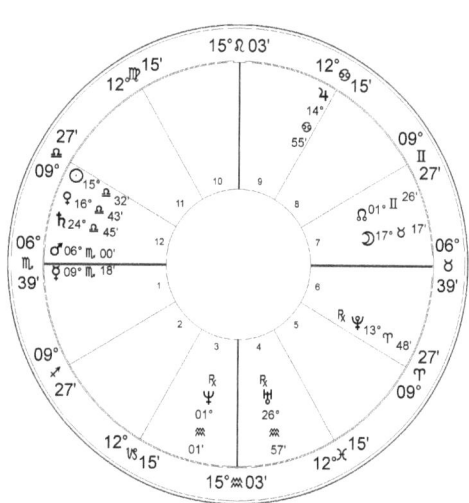

**October 9, 1835
83W41, 43N01
8:35 AM EST**

Settled in October 1819 by Louis Campau, it was laid out sixteen years later. The Durant Carriage Company was established in 1886 (Ascendant trine Pluto) and the first auto plant opened in 1904 (Midheaven trine Uranus). After Detroit, Flint is the largest automobile center in the country and is home to both General Motors and Fisher Body.

Incorporated: February 13, 1855
Elevation: 780 feet
Area: 33 square miles
Source: Flint Public Library

Grand Rapids

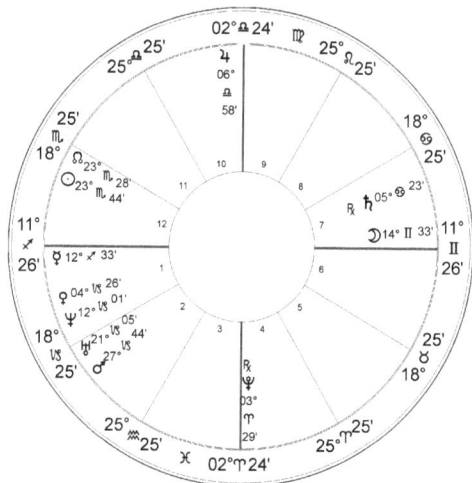

**November 16, 1826
85W40, 42N58
8:11 AM CST**

Founded by Louis Campau in November 1826, it became famous after 1838 when the first furniture plant opened (Midheaven sextile Mercury trine Moon). Over the years, the city has suffered floods with those of 1852 (Midheaven square Mars) and 1904 (Ascendant square Moon) being particularly severe.

Incorporated: April 2, 1850
Elevation: 610 feet
Area: 45 square miles
Source: Grand Rapids Public Library and City Hall agree on November 1826; exact date uncertain; chart rectified

Kalamazoo

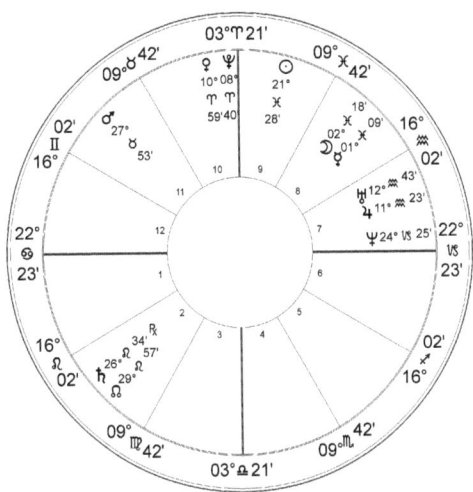

March 12, 1831
85W35, 42N17
12:36 PM CST

Settled on June 21, 1829, it was platted two years later as Bronsonville. Renamed in 1836, it became a village in 1843 and was the largest town in the nation when it became a city in 1884. Largely populated by the Dutch in its early years, it became a paper manufacturing center in 1867. In June 1980 a tornado swept through the city and destroyed much of the downtown (Midheaven conjunct Saturn).

Incorporated: April 15, 1884
Elevation: 775 feet
Source: *Kalamazoo Gazette*

Lansing

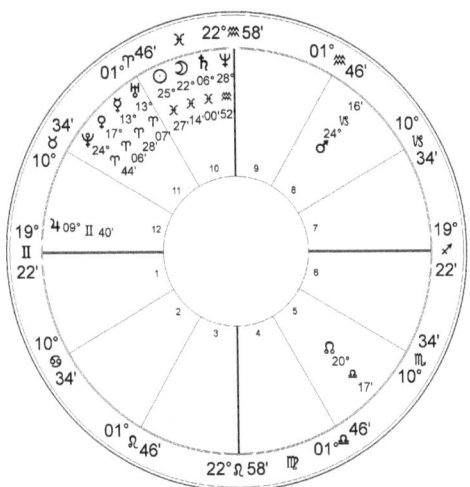

March 16, 1847
84W33, 42N44
10:45 AM EST

Chosen to be the capital of Michigan in 1847 the legislature moved here one year later. Getting there was difficult until a plank road was built in 1852 from Detroit. In 1903 the Reo Motor company was founded and Lansing was on its way to becoming a major automotive center. Lansing is also home to Michigan State University, located in East Lansing, and is the home of the Oldsmobile Division of General Motors.

Incorporated: February 15, 1859
Elevation: 830 feet
Area: 34 square miles
Source: *American Guide Series*

Muskegon

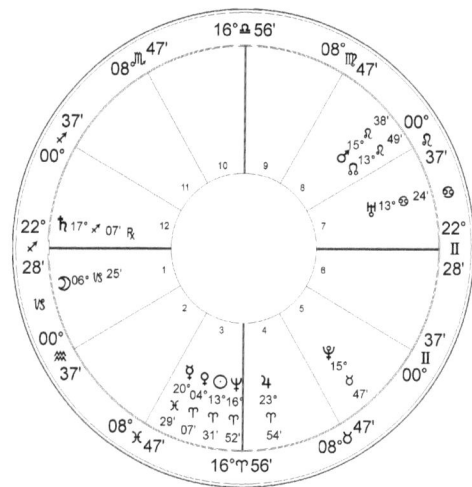

April 3, 1869
86W15, 43N14
12:01 AM CST

Founded as a trading post in 1812, it was formally settled in 1834. From 1873 until 1888, it was the lumber capital of the world. The nationwide financial panic of 1893 closed down most of the mills. Muskegon is the largest port on Lake Michigan in the state.

Incorporated: 1869
Elevation: 625 feet
Source: Muskegon Public Library

Saginaw

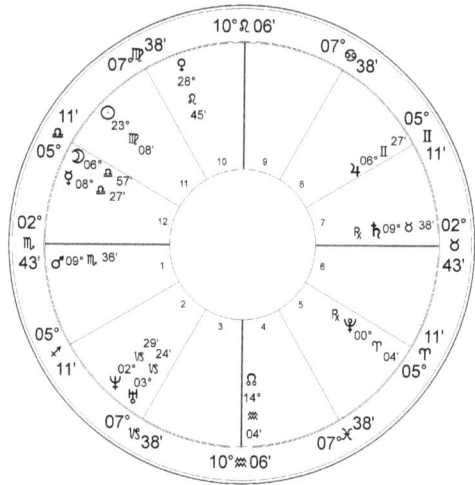

September 16, 1822
83W56, 43N26
9:46 AM EST

A trading post was founded by Louis Campau in 1816, but real settlement didn't begin until six years later when a fort was completed. Almost abandoned the following year because of flood and disease (Midheaven square Saturn and Mars), it became the sawmill center of the country between 1834 and 1900. Saginaw is now a leading industrial city and close to Saginaw Bay, an arm of Lake Huron.

Incorporated: February 17, 1857
Elevation: 593 feet
Source: Saginaw Public Library

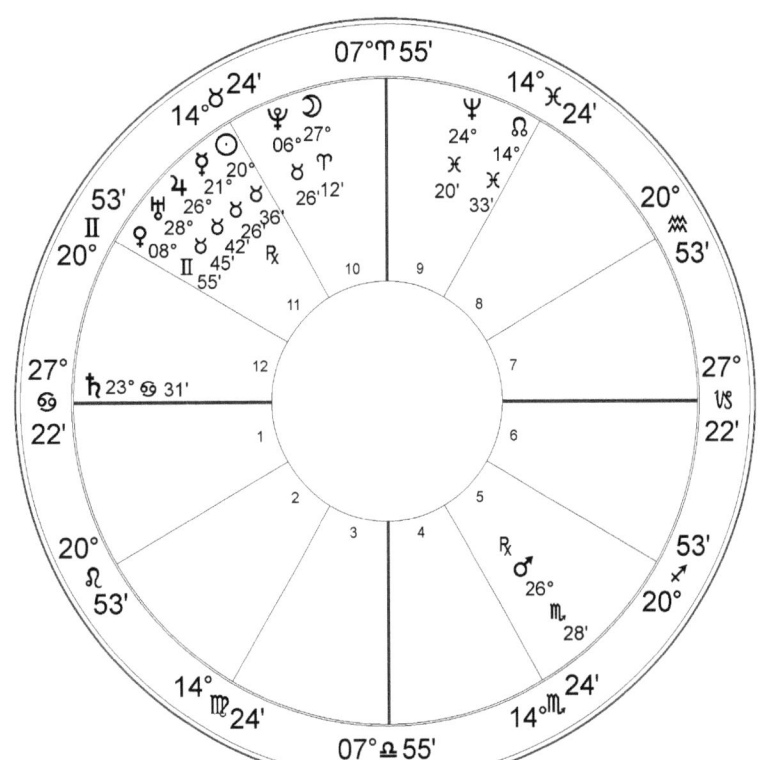

Minnesota

May 11, 1858
Saint Paul
93W06, 44N57
9:25 AM CST
Source: Rectified

In 1679 the region was claimed for France by Duluth, and the following year Hennepin named the Falls of St. Anthony. Spain acquired western Minnesota from France in 1762, while Britain got the eastern half a year later. America got the eastern portion in 1783 from Britain and the western part from France in the Louisiana Purchase of 1803. Northern Minnesota, near the Canadian border, was ceded to the U.S. in 1818 by Britain, and two years later Fort Snelling near Minneapolis was built. The first steamboat reached the fort in 1823, and in 1832 the source of the mighty Mississippi, Lake Itasca, was discovered. On March 3, 1849, the Territory of Minnesota was created, and in 1858 it became a state. A Sioux Indian uprising in 1862 killed hundreds of settlers. The rich iron ore deposits near Hibbing were discovered in 1890, and in the next thirty years two massive forest fires would wipe out many thousands of acres (1894 and 1918).

Minnesota is the leader in iron ore production (sixty percent of the U.S. total), and its forests produce tons of pulp for paper. It leads the nation in butter, turkeys and non-fat milk, and ranks third in milk cows. It grows the most oats and is a leader in wheat, corn, alfalfa and sugar beets. It's also fifth in hogs.

Area: 84,068 square miles

Duluth

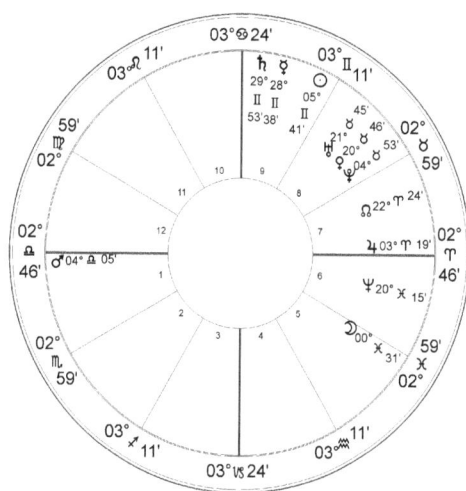

May 26, 1856
92W07, 46N47
2:05 PM CST

A trading post was established here on September 24, 1793, but any attempt at settling the region didn't come until 1856 when the city was platted. Two years later Duluth suffered a double calamity: a nationwide financial panic crippled the economy (Midheaven square Mars Ascendant opposition Jupiter) and a yellow fever epidemic struck (Ascendant conjunct Mars, Midheaven semisquare Uranus). Iron ore was discovered in 1865, eight years before another financial panic ruined the economy (Ascendant sesquare Moon). The resulting problems were so great that Duluth lost its charter until 1887 when it was reincorporated.

Duluth is the world's largest shipper of iron ore due to the vast fields in the nearby Mesabi Range. Hugging the shoreline below the bluffs, the city overlooks Lake Superior, the largest and northernmost of the Great Lakes.

Incorporated: March 3, 1870
Elevation: 610 feet
Area: 67 square miles
Source: *American Guide Series*

Minneapolis

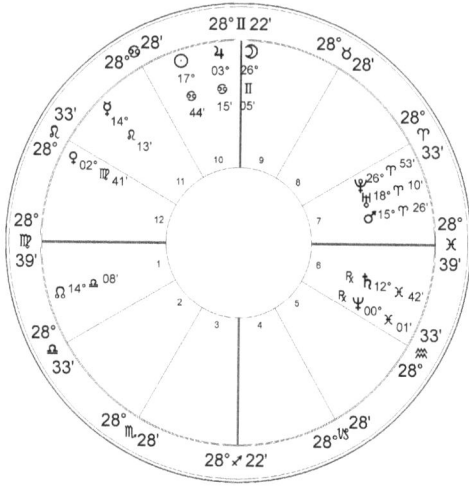

July 10, 1847
93W16, 44N59
10:54 AM CST

The first settlement in the region was at Fort Snelling, near the airport, which was founded September 20, 1820. Three years later a sawmill was erected at Saint Anthony. Minneapolis was founded in 1847 and annexed Saint Anthony in 1872. In 1869, erosion threatened to undermine the falls (Midheaven square Uranus, Ascendant opposition Mars). Minneapolis used to be known as the largest milling center in the world, but now prefers clean industries such as electronics or those with high technology.

Being the larger of the Twin Cities, it's also the more liberal. It's an aggressive and well-muscled city that pursues money, pleasure and bigness in an extrovertive and enthusiastic manner (Jupiter in the tenth house). Because of its Siberian climate, it has managed to make life more bearable for its shoppers downtown with the construction of skyways which connect many office buildings and stores. Minneapolis is a city with clean government which has managed to get cooperation between labor and business (Mercury, ruler of the tenth house, trine Mars and Uranus). A city of few slums, it has practically no graffiti and little pollution or crime. It's a progressive and receptive city (Moon conjunct Midheaven), full of beautiful parks and numerous lakes. Settled largely by Protestants and Scandinavians, the natives are nice and polite, brimming with self-assurance (Mercury in Leo, ruler of Ascendant and Midheaven). Minneapolis is the largest city between Chicago and Seattle and is home to the University of Minnesota, one of the largest institutions of higher learning in the U.S.

Incorporated: February 6, 1867
Elevation: 812 feet
Area: 59 square miles
Source: *History of Minnesota Valley* by Edward Neill

Rochester

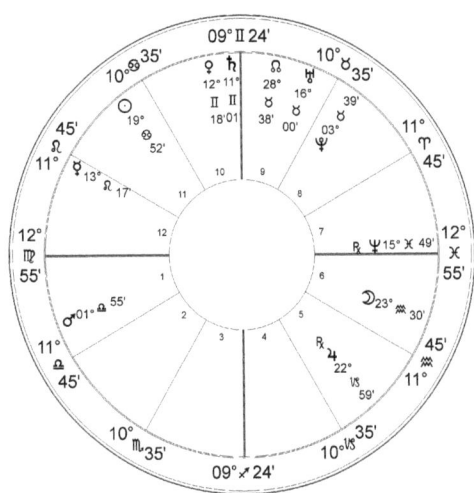

**July 12, 1854
92W28, 44N01
9:20 AM CST**

Founded in 1854, it was platted the following year in October. Dr. William Mayo (father of the famous brothers) arrived in 1863 and set up his practice. His sons set up the famous Mayo Clinic in 1889. It's probably the best known hospital in the world.

Incorporated: August 5, 1858
Elevation: 990 feet
Source: *The Rochester Story* by M.W. Raygor

Saint Cloud

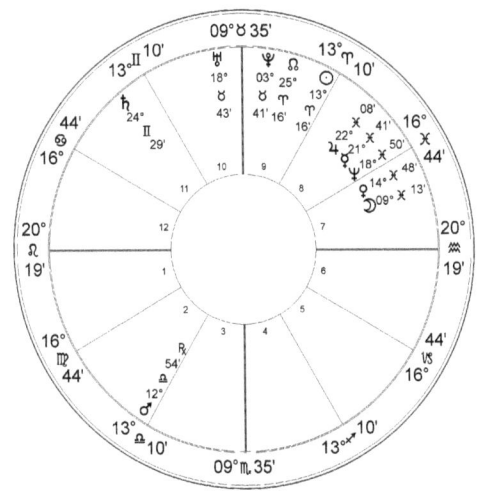

**April 2, 1856
94W10, 45N34
2:00 PM CST**

Originally settled as three villages in 1853, one town was platted the following year. United in 1856, it witnessed the last battle of the Civil War on May 13, 1865. Center for a large dairy and grain empire, it's also a large producer of granite.

Incorporated: 1868
Elevation: 1,032 feet
Source: *History of Saint Cloud*

Saint Paul

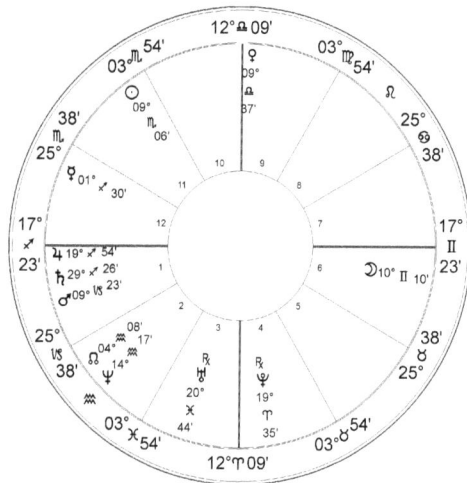

November 1, 1841
93W06, 44N57
10:14 AM CST

Founded in 1838 by a motley character nicknamed Pig's Eye, it changed its name in 1841 when Father Gaultier built a chapel to Saint Paul on the site. In 1849 it became the capital of Minnesota (Midheaven sextile Jupiter). It turned to the river trade for its chief source of income, unlike Minneapolis which seems to ignore the fact that the longest river in the land went right through its borders. Saint Paul became a packing center in 1882 when the stockyards were founded, and later became the railroad hub of the Northwest.

Saint Paul is conservative and sedate (Sun in Scorpio, Sagittarius rising), a rather parochial city which is slightly on the defensive. Seldom entertaining a new idea or proposition, it has remained slow and poky through the years and looks rather middle aged compared to its more illustrious cousin next door. Careful and deliberate, it is the Boston of the Midwest. Largely peopled by Irish and German Catholics, its downtown streets are narrow and crowded and its neighborhoods are more varied than its twin sister. It's a surprisingly casual city despite its corporate mien (Libra Midheaven), but compared to Minneapolis it's refined and dignified (Jupiter and Saturn rising). Saint Paul is a lovely terraced city full of big mansions and huge trees. It lets down its hair once a year during the Winter Carnival, a northern version of the Mardi Gras.

Incorporated: March 4, 1854
Elevation: 780 feet
Area: 55 square miles
Source: *Minnesota* by William Falwell; *History of Saint Paul* by J.F. Williams says July 13, 1838

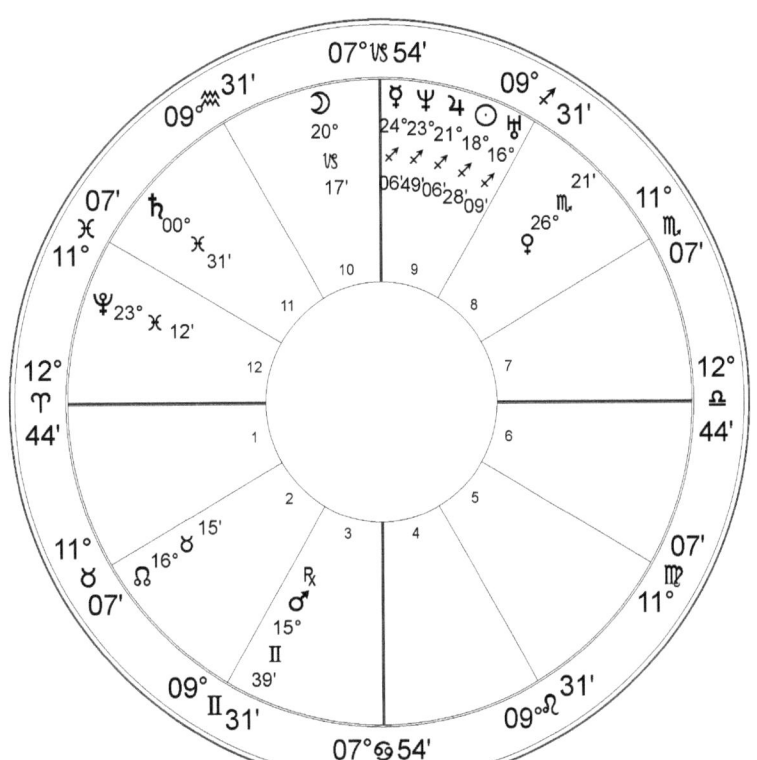

Mississippi

December 10, 1817
Washington
91W18, 31N35
1:23 PM CST
Source: Rectified

In 1541 the region was explored for Spain by De Soto and in 1682 the region was claimed for France, which founded the first settlement at Biloxi in 1699. The French were prevented from conquering the Mississippi Valley due to repeated attacks by the Chickasaws. Britain acquired the region in 1763, and the U.S. got part of the region from Spain in 1795. Mississippi was organized as a territory on April 7, 1798, and in 1810 the U.S. annexed West Florida—what is now southern Mississippi. In 1817 it became a state. At the beginning of the Civil War, Mississippi was one of the wealthiest states in the South, but after seceding from the Union on January 9, 1861, it lost its preeminence forever. Not readmitted until February 17, 1870, it suffered greatly during the war. It's almost as if the North tried to wipe this state off the map in extreme acts of cruelty and vengeance. Vicksburg was the scene of one of the bloodiest conflicts of the War Between the States. Mississippi suffered more than any other southern state with the exception of Virginia. Never fully regaining its former glory, it is now a ghost of its former self. Recovery didn't come until the 1920s and then in small doses. The massive Mississippi River floods of 1927 caused vast property damage and 100,000 were driven from their homes. It is the poorest in the nation, as it has the lowest per capita income of any state.

Soybeans now rank as the chief crop and cotton (once king in this region) is now third in U.S. total production. The Gulf region has a large shrimp industry and Mississippi produces more hardwood wood pulp than any other state due to its vast forests, which cover fifty percent of the state. Oil and natural gas are also coming into importance, and tourism is increasing.

Area: 47,716 square miles

Biloxi

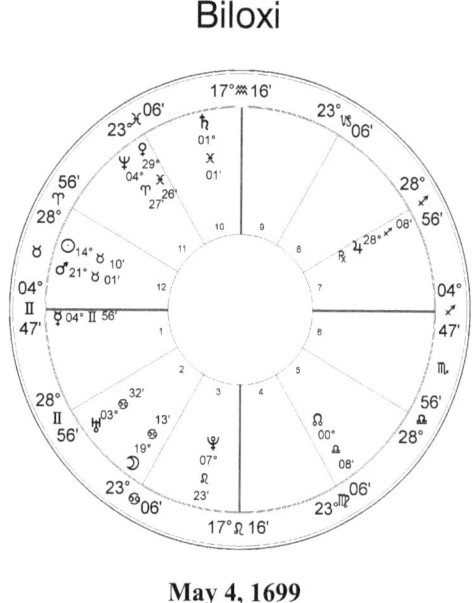

May 4, 1699
88W53, 30N24
6:24 AM CST

Founded by Bienville in 1699, a fire in 1702 caused the capital to move to Mobile (Midheaven square Mars). The present city was founded in 1719 (Ascendant semisquare Pluto) and until 1722 it was the capital of French Louisiana. Britain controlled the region from 1763 until the Spanish ousted them seventeen years later. Yellow fever epidemics in 1853 (Midheaven sesquare Saturn), 1878 (Midheaven sesquare Jupiter) and 1897 (Midheaven opposition Saturn) kept the population down. Biloxi suffered extensive damage in August 1969 when Hurricane Camille tore through the town with winds in excess of 200 m.p.h. (Midheaven opposition Sun). Many old colonial buildings were lost forever. Today Biloxi is not only famous for its shrimp and oysters, but is also a large shipbuilding center.

Incorporated: 1896
Elevation: 22 feet
Source: *History of Mississippi* by Richard McLemore; *History of Mississippi* by Rowland Dunbar says August 8, 1699

Gulfport

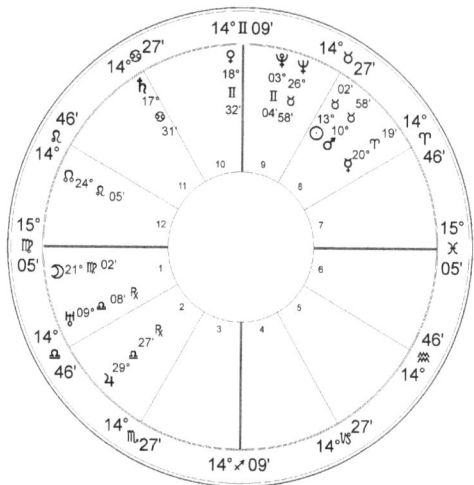

May 3, 1887
89W06, 30N22
2:02 PM CST

Selected as a harbor for the railroad in 1887, it suffered until 1890 when yellow fever was finally controlled. A hurricane in 1906 caused severe financial panic, and Hurricane Camille in 1969 wrecked much of the city (Ascendant opposition Neptune). Gulfport is located on "The Silver Strip," a twenty-eight mile man-made beach which has become a popular resort area.

Incorporated: 1904
Elevation: 19 feet
Source: *American Guide Series*

Jackson

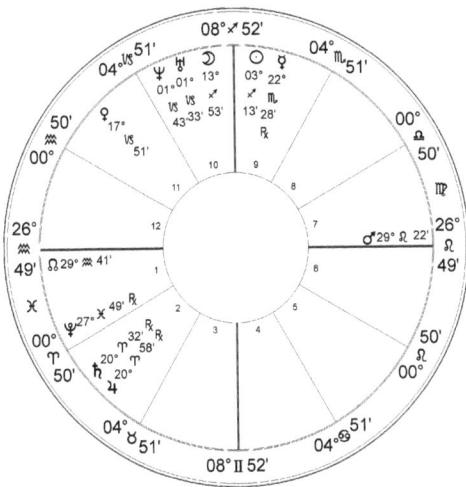

**November 25, 1821
90W12, 32N18
12:12 PM CST**

Chosen to be the state capital in 1821, it was platted the following year and named for the famous general. Jackson was burned by Sherman on July 16, 1863 (Midheaven square Jupiter and Saturn) and after the Civil War, its recovery was slow and arduous. With the discovery of natural gas during the 1930s, Jackson began to take on the appearance of a city more in keeping with its political importance. In 1966 a tornado claimed 57 lives (Midheaven quincunx Sun) and in 1979 a flood inundated much of the city (Midheaven sesquare Uranus and Neptune).

Once known as a pious, provincial and unpromising community, Jackson has grown to become a spacious and clean city in recent years. Located on unstable terrain (it rests on a former seabed), its landscape is dotted with oil derricks. Energy is plentiful and cheap due to the abundance of natural gas in the region.

Incorporated: January 21, 1833
Elevation: 298 feet
Area: 105 square miles
Source: *American Guide Series* says three days after Thanksgiving 1821; ironically, this was a Sunday

Meridian

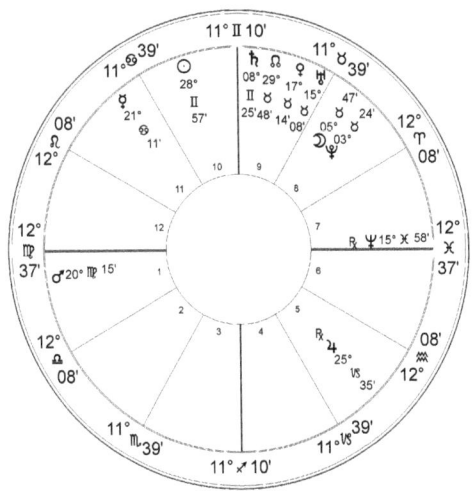

**June 20, 1854
88W42, 32N22
10:39 AM CST**

First settled in 1831 by Richard McLemore, a post office was established in 1854, the same year the site was chosen to be a railroad juncture. The first train pulled into town seven years later. In February 1864 Sherman burned the town (Ascendant conjunct Mars) and seven years later a riot took place and thirty Blacks were killed (Midheaven quincunx Jupiter). The riot did have one positive outcome, however, for it got rid of the carpetbaggers. In 1878 Meridian endured an epidemic of yellow fever, and four years later a fire burned much of the town. Two tornadoes have caused much damage over the years: 1906 and 1930 (Midheaven square Uranus). Today Meridian is a leading railroad center for the south (Gemini Midheaven).

Incorporated: January 10, 1860
Elevation: 341 feet
Source: Mississippi Department of Archives

Natchez

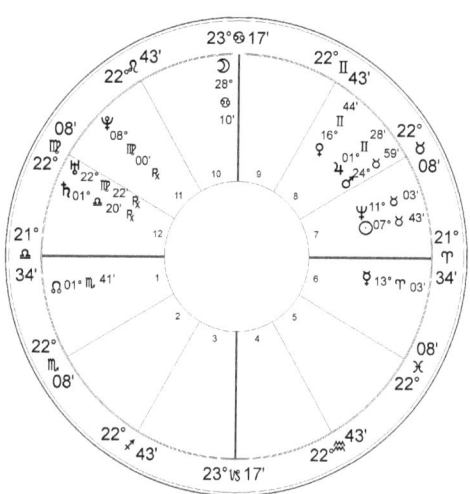

April 27, 1716
91W24, 31N34
5:22 PM CST

Founded as Fort Rosalie in 1716, Indians massacred the settlers thirteen years later and drove them from the area (Midheaven semisquare Uranus). From 1763 until 1779 the British occupied the city; then came the Spanish until 1798 when the Americans took over. Steamboats began plying their trade along the Mississippi in 1812 and Natchez became one of the leading cotton ports of the South. Occupied by Union forces from 1863 to 1865 (Ascendant opposition Pluto), many of its antebellum homes were ruined forever. In 1940 a dance hall fire left 198 dead (Midheaven square Jupiter quincunx Saturn).

Like Charleston and Savannah, Natchez is a treasure house of Southern architecture. One of the main industries today is tourism, and this city has more mansions of the antebellum period than any other city in the South. Many are state or national historical sites.

Incorporated: March 10, 1803
Elevation: 210 feet
Source: *History of Mississippi* by Rowland Dunbar

Oxford

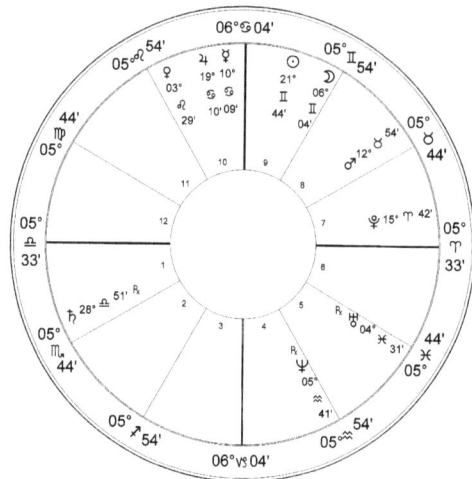

June 12, 1836
89W31, 34N21
1:00 PM CST

Oxford was founded in 1836 and named for the famous British university city. Its founders had aspirations for this new settlement to become home base for the future University of Mississippi. Classes began in 1848 at Ole Miss (Midheaven conjunct Jupiter, Ascendant opposition Pluto). Oxford was occupied by the Union Army in 1862, during the Civil War (Ascendant conjunct Saturn) and survived the conflict with little real damage except to the egos of the townspeople.

Oxford today is home to numerous bookstores, art galleries and other cultural venues. Sports become a mania during autumn football season and local hostelries are swamped with hordes of sports enthusiasts. Oxford was also the former home of novelists William Faulkner and John Grisham. A local friend once boasted to me that "Oxford is an island of civility in a sea of relative barbarity," remarking on the number of cultural sites in this small and pleasant community.

Incorporated: May 11, 1837
Elevation: 416 feet
Source: Public library

Vicksburg

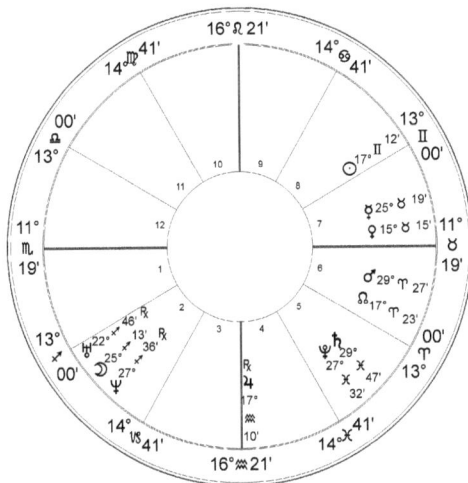

**June 8, 1819
90W53, 32N21
4:13 PM CST**

Founded as a Spanish outpost in 1790, a mission was erected in 1814. Five years later the city was platted. Vicksburg was the typical river town full of steamboats, gamblers and saloons. When the gamblers rebelled in 1835, the local authorities ran them out of town (Ascendant opposition Mercury). In June 1862, Admiral Farragut bombarded the city, and one year later, from May 18 until July 4, the city endured General Grant's siege (Midheaven opposition Saturn/Pluto square Neptune, Ascendant sesquare Mars). After the battle most of the town was laid waste. In 1875, home rule returned (Ascendant conjunct Moon). In 1876, the Mississippi changed course and left the town high and dry. To correct this situation, the Yazoo Canal was completed in 1902. A flood in 1927 caused extensive destruction (Ascendant semisquare Saturn).

Incorporated: August 14, 1912
Elevation: 206 feet
Source: Vicksburg Public Library

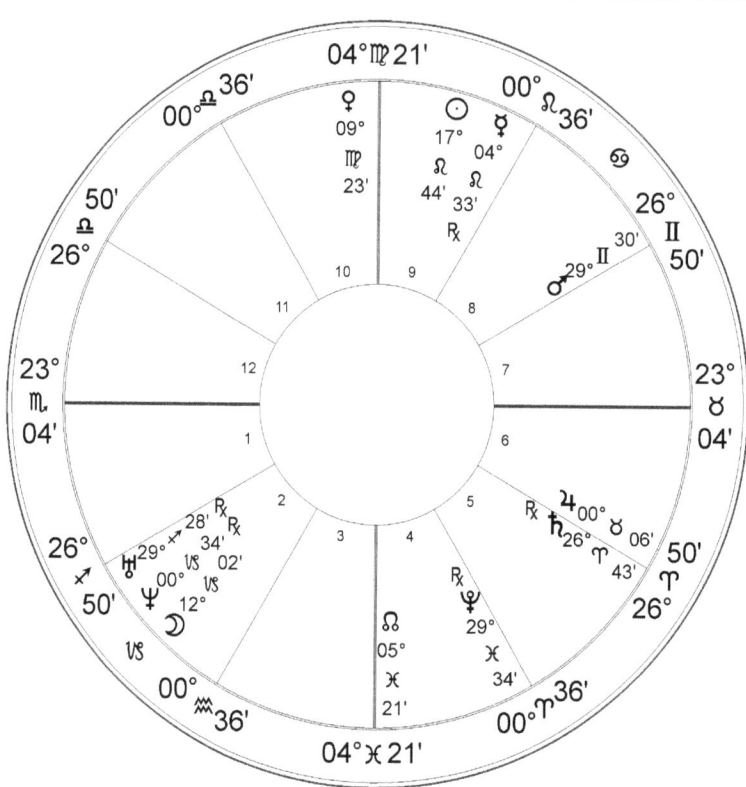

Missouri

**August 10, 1821
Saint Louis
90W12, 38N38
1:10 PM CST
Source: Missouri State Historical Society and various newspapers imply an afternoon birth;**

In 1673 the mouth of the Missouri was discovered by Marquette and Joliet and nine years later the region was claimed for France by LaSalle. The first permanent settlement was made at Saint Genevieve in 1736, and in 1762 Spain acquired the entire state from France. St. Louis was founded two years later and soon became the largest port on the upper Mississippi. Spain ceded the territory to France in 1800, which ceded it to the U.S. in 1803 as part of the Louisiana Purchase. The Territory of Missouri was organized on June 4, 1812, and five years later the first steamboat reached Saint Louis from New Orleans. The Missouri Compromise allowed the state to enter the Union as a slave state, which it did in 1821. Border warfare with Kansas occurred between 1854 and the end of the Civil War, but Missouri chose to stay with the Union in February 1861. Nevertheless, many guerrilla attacks took place in the state during the following four years. In 1874 the first bridge across the Mississippi was completed and the end of the James gang occurred in 1882 when Jesse was shot in Saint Joseph. Saint Louis hosted both a World's Fair and the Olympics in 1904. It was from Missouri that Lewis and Clark left on their journey to the Pacific in 1805, and both the Santa Fe and Oregon Trails originated in Independence, near Kansas City. Missouri was also the eastern terminus of the Pony Express, and the state rightly deserves the title of "Gateway to the West."

Missouri is the number one producer of lead, fourth in hogs, fifth in cattle, and sixth in turkeys. Industrially, Missouri is a giant and the aerospace industry and the manufacture of transportation equipment are the top employers.

Area: 69,686 square miles

Columbia

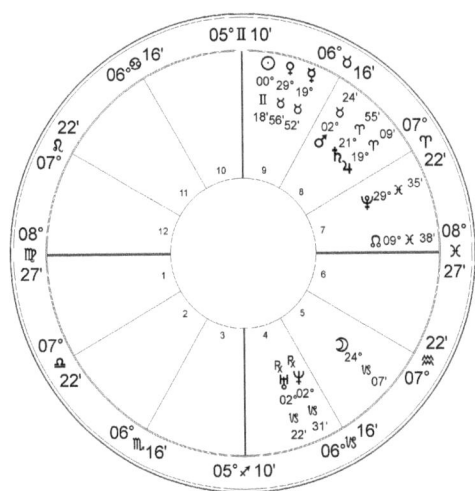

May 21, 1821
92W20, 38N57
12:26 PM CST

Founded as Smithtown in 1819, the site was chosen two years later. Columbia is home of the University of Missouri, which was founded on July 4, 1840 (Ascendant trine Moon).

Incorporated: March 15, 1892
Elevation: 748 feet
Source: *History of Columbia* by J.C. Crighton

Jefferson City

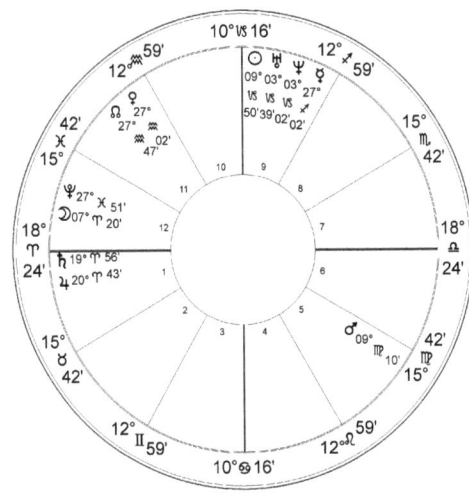

December 31, 1821
92W10, 38N34
12:14 PM CST

Founded by the legislature in 1821 to be the state capital, the first capitol building burned in 1842. When the railroad arrived in 1855, the bridge over the Missouri collapsed, killing twenty-eight people (Ascendant square Mars). The present capitol building was completed in 1911.

Incorporated: 1839
Elevation: 557 feet
Source: *American Guide Series*

Joplin

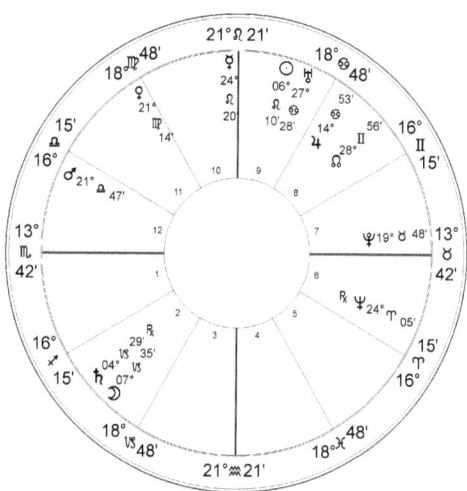

**July 29, 1871
94W31, 37N06
1:25 PM CST**

Settled as Turkey Creek in 1838, lead was discovered eleven years later. In 1871 Joplin was platted and for the first two years a reign of terror ensued. Lawlessness reigned until the city was united with Murphysburg, its sister city, the source of most of the dissension.

Joplin is situated in the greatest zinc producing region in the world, and neighboring mines also produce much of the country's supply of lead.

Incorporated: March 23, 1873
Elevation: 1,009 feet
Source: *Story of Joplin* by Dolph Shaner

Kansas City

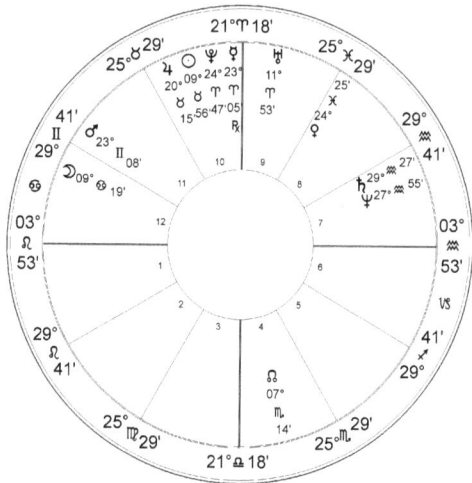

**April 30, 1846
94W35, 39N06
11:04 AM CST**

In 1821 Auguste Chouteau founded a trading post on the banks of the Missouri River, but permanent settlement didn't come until 1834 when nearby Westport was founded. Because of the rivalry of neighboring Independence (which was the eastern terminus for the Santa Fe and Oregon Trails), it was decided a more central location was needed. Thus was the town of Kansas formed in 1846. Three years later a massive cholera epidemic swept through the new community (Midheaven conjunct Pluto). During the Civil War the city was occupied by Federal troops, and in 1864 a battle was fought in nearby Westport and Independence (Midheaven semisquare Mars). With the arrival of the first railroad in 1865 (Midheaven conjunct Sun), Kansas City soon developed into the crossroads of America. Cattle coming north from Texas prompted the erection of the first stockyards in 1870 (Ascendant square Jupiter) and the completion of the country's first Union Station eight years later (Midheaven conjunct Jupiter). In 1910 the massive parkway system for which the city is so famous was begun (Midheaven conjunct Mars, Ascendant opposition Venus). During Prohibition the city was wide open due to the leniency of the Pendergast machine. Gangsters like Bonnie and Clyde and Pretty Boy Floyd found they could operate with impunity in the early days of the Depression. In July 1951 a torrential flood wiped out much of the lowlands along the river (Ascendant opposition Pluto), but the biggest disaster ever to befall this city came on July 17, 1981 when two skyways in the lobby of the Hyatt Regency Hotel collapsed, killing 111 and injuring 188 (Midheaven opposition Saturn).

Known as the "Crossroads of America" due to its geographical setting, Kansas City sits in the middle of the nation, at the junction of the Southwest, the Midwest and the South. This blending has given Kansas City a surprising amount of culture and sophistication, not to mention a great deal of vitality and dynamism (Mars rules Midheaven). It's a typically middle class community, but one which still contains many old mansions and much old wealth. The founder of the city's largest newspaper, William Rockhill Nelson, donated his art collection to the city. It is housed in the largest art museum in the U.S. west of Chicago. Kansas City also boasts several other superlatives: It has the nation's largest stockyards, its second largest grain elevator, the largest waiting room in the world in its Union Station, and the country's first shopping center, the Country Club Plaza.

Being less interested in ideas than in things (Sun in Taurus), Kansas City is a pragmatic and sensible place, full of friendly and unpretentious people (Aquarius on the Descendant). It's a city of gracious living (Leo rising) with more parkland per capita than any city in the country (10,000 acres), more miles of boulevards than Paris (140 miles), and more fountains (fifty-eight) than any city in the world except Rome. It is undoubtedly the most typically American city in the land, and the home of Hallmark Cards.

Incorporated: February 22, 1853
Elevation: 750 feet
Area: 316 square miles
Sources: Kansas City Public Library gives the 1846 date; Juliann Ryan of Kansas City says Westport's first lots were sold July 7, 1838; Darrell Garwood's book, *Crossroads of America*, gives the date as "a Saturday in November 1838."

Saint Joseph

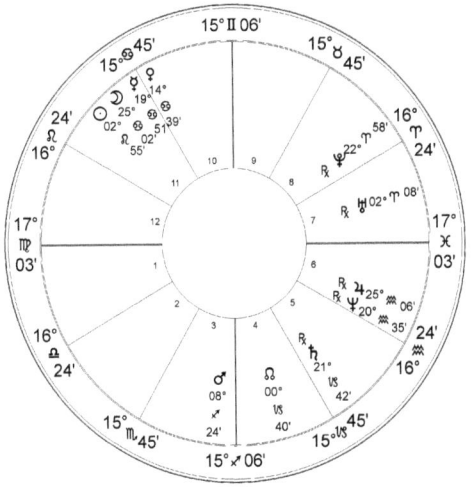

July 26, 1843
94W50, 39N46
9:00 AM CST

Founded as a trading post by Rubidoux in 1826, he platted the city in 1843 and named it for his patron saint. With the gold rush in California, Saint Joseph became a major wagon train center and supply depot (Midheaven trine Neptune). Nine years later the gold rush in Colorado saw thousands trek west from this city. Saint Joseph was the eastern terminus of the Pony Express, which first left the city on April 3, 1860 (Midheaven square Uranus, Ascendant sextile Sun). Confederate guerrilla bands terrorized the region in 1862, and twenty years later Bob Ford shot Jesse James. In 1890 Saint Joseph was the wealthiest city per capita in the nation (Ascendant trine Jupiter) and by 1940 it became the world's fifth largest livestock market and the tenth largest producer of flour.

Incorporated: 1851
Elevation: 814 feet
Source: Carolyn Dodson for the date; chart rectified

Saint Louis

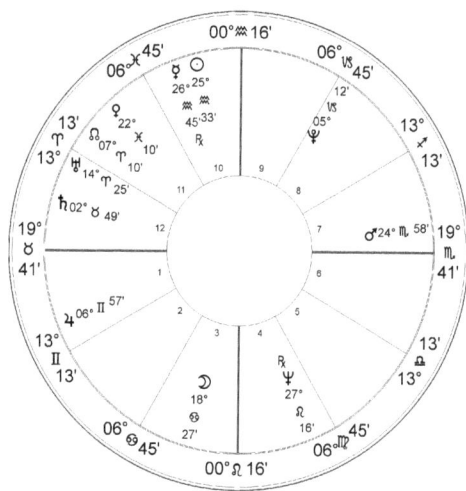

February 14, 1764
90W12, 38N37
10:34 AM CST

Founded in 1764 by thirteen year old Auguste Chouteau, Indians attacked the settlement thirteen years later. Saint Louis was made capital of Missouri in 1805, the same year Lewis and Clark left on their journey to the Pacific. The Astor Fur Company was founded in 1822 and soon the city became the largest fur market in the world. In 1832 a cholera epidemic killed thousands. In 1849 Saint Louis suffered a double calamity: A cholera epidemic killed ten percent of the population and a fire burned more than 400 buildings (Midheaven quincunx Mars, Ascendant quincunx Pluto). In May 1861 the city was placed under martial law for the duration of the war (Midheaven trine Pluto, Ascendant trine Uranus). When the Eads Bridge was completed across the Mississippi in 1874, Saint Louis soon became a major transportation hub, currently the second in the U.S. Separated from Saint Louis County in 1876, its boundaries have remained the same for more than a century (Taurus rising) with no room for expansion (progressed Ascendant square Mars opposite Sun). The Louisiana Purchase Exposition of 1904 introduced the world to ice cream cones, hot dogs and iced tea, plus giving the city its art museum, the Jefferson Memorial and Jewel Box (Ascendant sextile Moon). In 1940 a smoke abatement law was enacted as its air was almost as filthy as Pittsburgh's. Tornadoes are always a fact of life in the Midwest and those of 1927 (Ascendant trine Jupiter) and 1959 (Ascendant opposition Saturn) were particularly severe.

After decades of decline, during the 1960s the spirit of the city began to change with the completion in 1965 of the Gateway Arch. Blocks around the arch were torn down to make way for hotels and office buildings. The skyline also changed and Saint Louis finally began to acquire skyscrapers (Taurus is built close to the ground).

Residents of the city hold firm opinions and tastes (Sun and Ascendant in fixed signs) and they hate to take a chance. It's a conservative city which has had limited objectives in the past, but in the end, it's always practical and solid (Taurus rising). Natives are hospitable but suspicious (Mars in Scorpio in the seventh house). They possess a stuffy pride and are impervious to outside cultural events. Liberal and tolerant (Sun in Aquarius), Saint Louisians really get off on music (Venus equals MC/ASC). Saint Louis is slow paced and well behaved; its citizens are imperturbable and not easily excited. Sounds very much like the salt of the earth, doesn't it?

Saint Louis produces much of our country's beer (Anheuser-Busch), and is a large transportation center (Sun conjunct Mercury). It's the largest market for wool, furs, and lumber, and has one of the largest aircraft plants in the nation (McDonnell-Douglas). Somewhat like Baltimore, it's caught between wanting the slow and refined pace of the South and the industrious and efficient tempo of the North. In this oldest city west of the Mississippi, you'll find them both.

Incorporated: March 3, 1823
Elevation: 455 feet
Area: 61 square miles
Source: Saint Louis Public Library says February 14, 1764; some source books give February 15; time from American Federation of Astrologers

Springfield

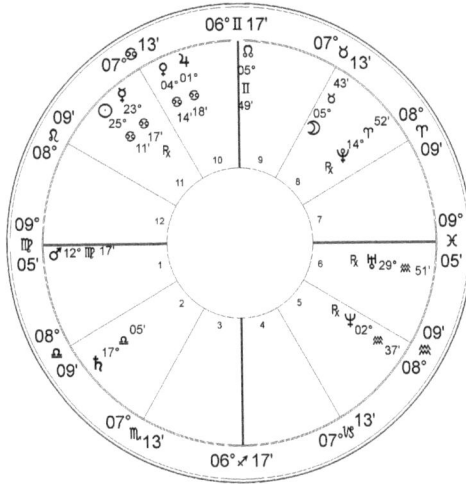

**July 18, 1835
93W17, 37N13
8:48 AM CST**

Settled by the Campbells in February 1830, the community was formally platted in 1835. Confederates took the city in August 1861 (Midheaven conjunct Jupiter) until the following February when they were driven out (Ascendant trine Neptune). Springfield has one of the lowest cost-of-living indexes in the nation and is the commercial and industrial center of southwestern Missouri.

Incorporated: March 1847
Elevation: 1,345 feet
Area: 63 square miles
Source: *History of Greene County* by Fairbanks and Tuck

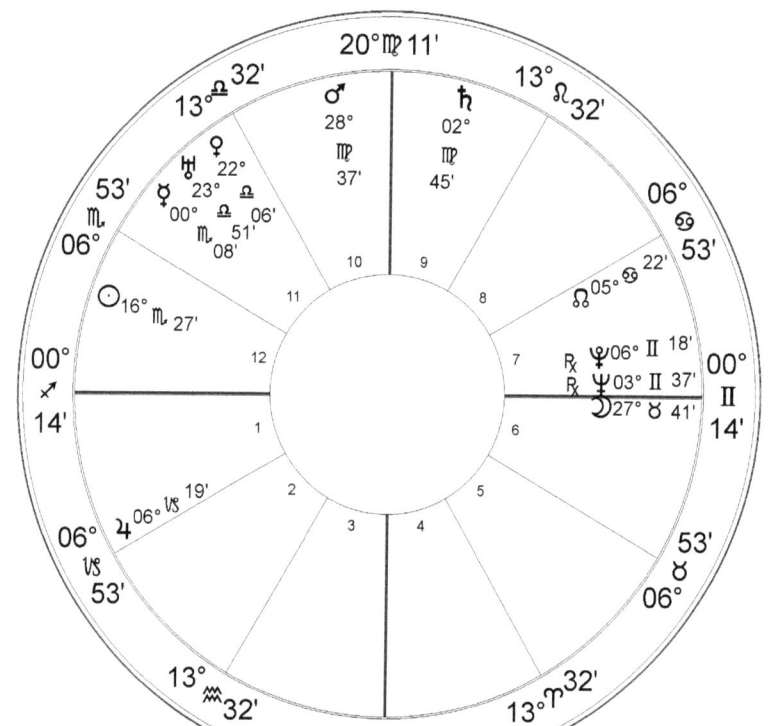

Montana

November 8, 1889
Helena
112W02, 46N36
8:40 AM MST
Source: *Los Angeles Times* says 10:40 AM in Washington

First explored for France in 1742, it was acquired in the Louisiana Purchase of 1803. Lewis and Clark journeyed through the region in 1805, and in 1818 the northern boundary with Canada was finally established. The first permanent settlement occurred at Fort Benton in 1846, the same year the western part of Montana was acquired in the Oregon Cession. Gold was discovered in 1852 and settlers came in droves seeking their fortunes. Organized as a territory on May 26, 1864, it witnessed Custer's Last Stand on June 25, 1876 at the Battle of the Little Bighorn. The next year Chief Joseph of the Nez Perce surrendered, thus ending the long and bitter Indian wars. Copper was discovered at Anaconda in 1882, and in 1889 Montana became a state. Fort Peck Dam was completed across the Missouri in 1940 and oil wells began producing in 1975.

Montana ranks sixth in sheep and twelfth in cattle. Copper is the principal mineral resource, and Montana is a large supplier of Christmas trees due to its abundant forests, which cover about forty percent of the state.

Area: 147,138 square miles

Billings

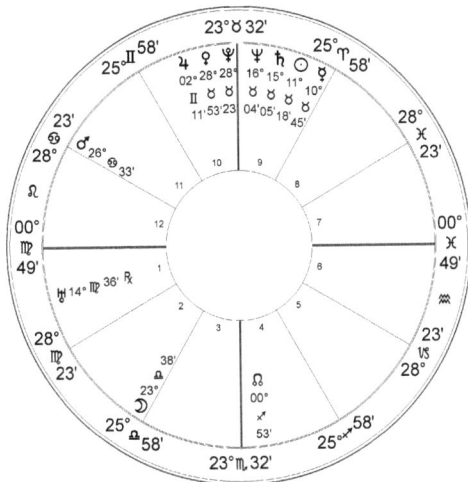

May 1, 1882
108W30, 45N47
1:00 PM MST

Founded by railroad crews in April 1882, the first building was completed on the first of the following month. Three fires burned the new town in 1883 (Ascendant square Jupiter) and the winter of 1886-87 caused the economy to freeze up. By 1890 only half of the settlers remained because of the negative economic conditions.

Billings is a large industrial center and heart of the vast agricultural region of southern Montana.

Incorporated: March 10, 1885
Elevation: 3,177 feet
Source: Public library and Montana by Tom Stout

Butte

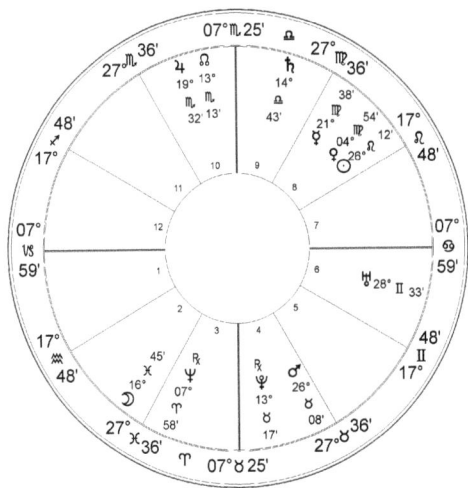

August 18, 1864
112W32, 46N00
5:00 PM MST

Gold was discovered here in May 1864 and three months later the town was founded. A town site was platted in 1867, and silver was discovered in 1875. Butte was the largest silver town in the country until 1893 when the U.S. Congress repealed the Silver Purchase Act, creating a massive depression (Midheaven square Venus, Ascendant square Pluto). Copper mines started operating in 1881.

Butte was known as the "Richest Hill on Earth" due to the fact it has produced ten percent of the country's copper, thirteen percent of the zinc, four percent of the lead and ninety-five percent of the manganese. Once the biggest mining town on earth, the town has an ugly countenance and looks like the wrong side of the tracks. Weather beaten houses line its steep streets. Once famous for gold and silver, Butte now produces mostly copper. Its chief employer is Anaconda. Butte has endured depressions before, like the one that lasted from 1940 to 1960. Note that the ruler of the Midheaven is in the fourth house and that Capricorn, which rules mines, ascends.

Incorporated: 1879
Elevation: 5,765 feet
Source: Butte Public Library

Great Falls

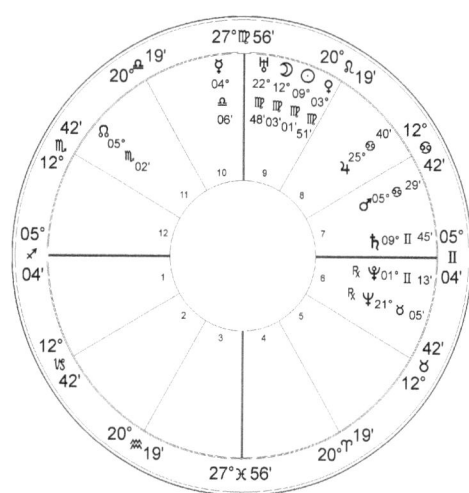

September 1, 1883
111W18, 47N30
1:35 PM MST

Through this region passed Lewis and Clark, who named the region in 1805. Founded by Paris Gibson in 1883, it was surveyed shortly after. It became a meat packing center in 1890, and today Great Falls is the financial, commercial and industrial center of the state. Many copper and zinc smelters are located nearby.

Incorporated: November 28, 1888
Elevation: 3,330 feet
Source: Public library says September 1883, exact date uncertain; chart rectified

Helena

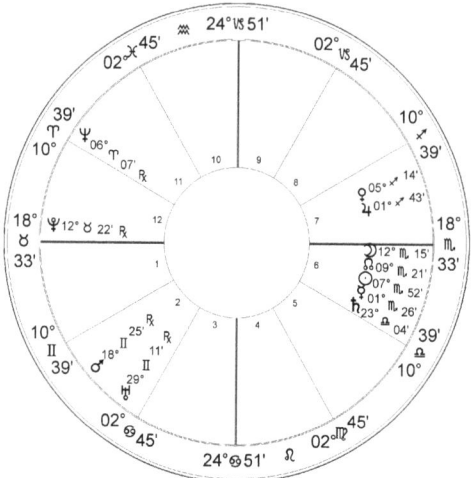

October 30, 1864
112W02, 46N36
5:37 PM MST

Gold was discovered here on July 10, 1864 at Last Chance Gulch, today the name of the main street of this city. Formally founded at a town meeting in October 1864, it became the capital of the state almost from its inception. The gold boom ended in 1893 during a nationwide financial panic. In October 1935 a series of earthquakes began to rattle the city for more than three years. In all, more than 1,200 shocks were felt (Midheaven conjunct Neptune inconjunct Sun), but little damage was done.

Incorporated: February 23, 1881
Elevation: 4,155 feet
Source: Helena Public Library; *American Guide Series* says July 14, 1864

Missoula

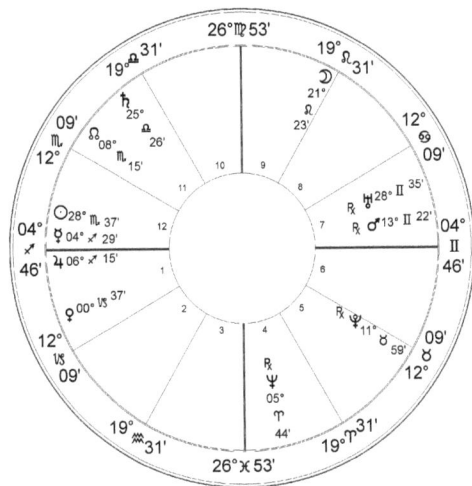

**November 20, 1864
114W00, 46N52
8:25 AM MST**

Founded as Hell Gate in the winter of 1860, it was formally founded in November 1864 by Worden and Higgins. A sawmill was completed the following year, and in 1893 the University of Montana was established (Midheaven conjunct Saturn).

Incorporated: March 12, 1885
Elevation: 3,223 feet
Source: Public library says November 1864, exact date unknown; chart rectified

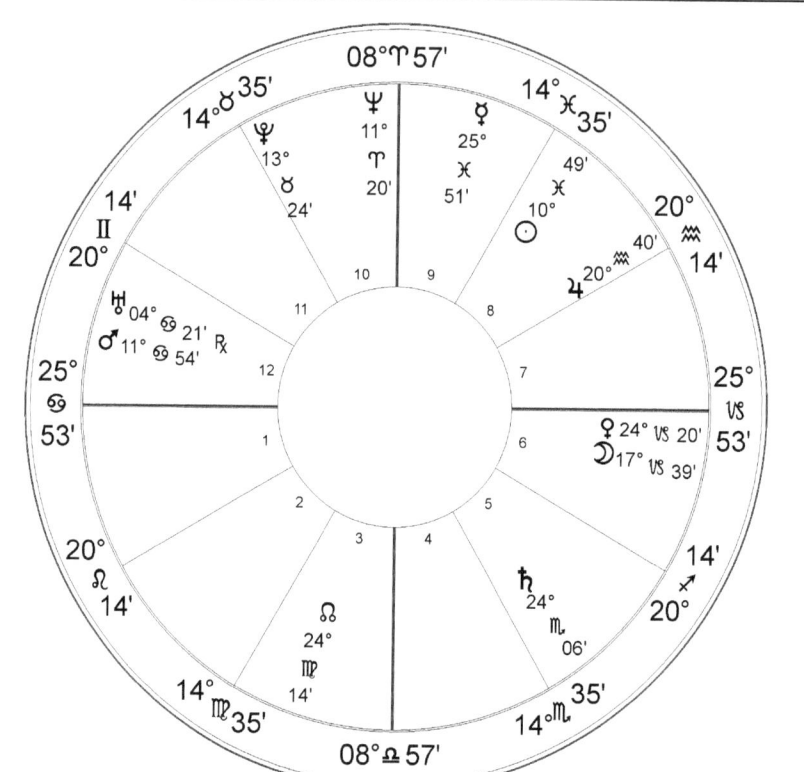

Nebraska

March 1, 1867
Omaha
95W57, 41N15
2:20 PM CST
Source: Rectified

America acquired Nebraska in the Louisiana Purchase of 1803, and twenty years later the first permanent settlement took place at Bellevue. Western Nebraska was acquired in the Mexican Cession of 1848, and on May 30, 1854, it was created a territory. Construction of the Union Pacific Railroad began in Omaha during 1865; two years later Nebraska became a state. Because of its central location, this state has been affected by the climate more than any other in the country. A plague of grasshoppers from 1874 to 1877 drove farmers away, and the blizzards and droughts over the years, like the Dust Bowl of the 1930s, hit this state very hard. Nebraska adopted a unicameral legislature (only one house) in 1934, the only state in the U.S. to do so. Oil was discovered in the southeast in 1939.

Nebraska ranks fifth in cattle and sixth in hogs, and Omaha is one of the main food processors in the U.S. Manufacturing of farm equipment also is important.

Area: 77,227 square miles

Grand Island

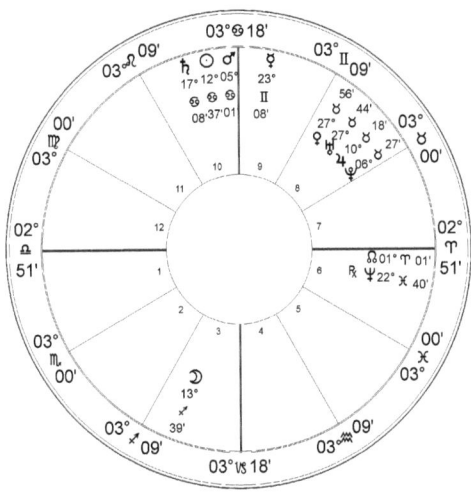

July 4, 1857
98W21, 40N55
11:57 AM CST

Settled by Germans in 1857, it was burned two years later (Midheaven conjunct Mars). Founded again by railroad crews in June 1866, Grand Island was the first city in the country to install mercury vapor lamps in 1936. On June 3, 1980, a massive tornado tore through the town, destroying more than 700 buildings.

Incorporated: December 10, 1872
Elevation: 1,861 feet
Source: Grand Island Public Library

Lincoln

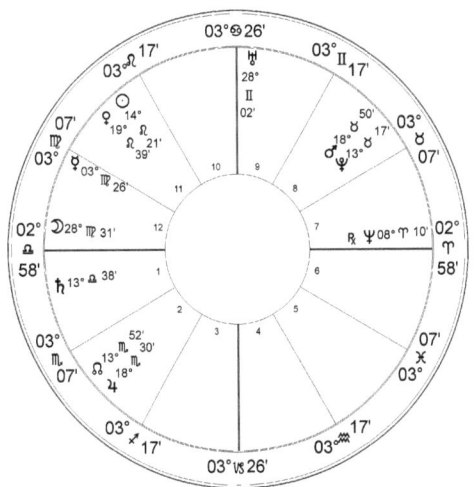

August 6, 1864
96W41, 40N49
9:40 AM CST

A female seminary was established here in the summer of 1863, and the following year a plat was filed for the town of Lancaster. Chosen to be the new state capital on July 29, 1867, it was renamed after the recently assassinated president. William Jennings Bryan made his home in Lincoln from 1888 to 1916. The University of Nebraska was founded in 1869 (Midheaven square Neptune).

Lincoln is known as the "City of Churches" as it once had a place of worship for each 100 residents. Located on the edge of the Bible Belt, it hosts many religious conventions during the year. The most impressive sight in the city is the State Capitol building, designed in Byzantine and Romanesque style by Bertram Goodhue. It was begun in 1922 and completed ten years later. Towering 400 feet over the surrounding plains, it can be seen for miles, this Skyscraper of the Plains.

Incorporated: Mach 18, 1871
Elevation: 1,148 feet
Area: 59 square miles
Source: *History of Lincoln* by A.B. Hayes

North Platte

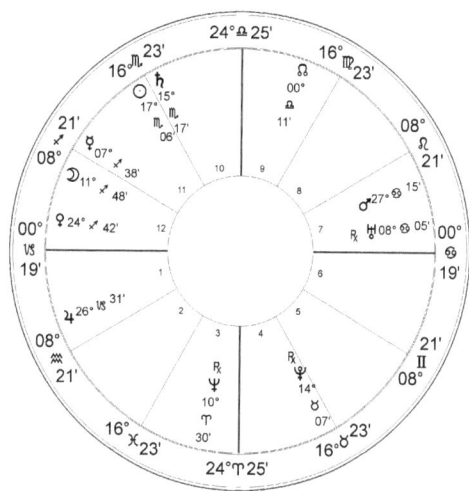

November 9, 1866
100W46, 41N08
9:59 AM MST

Founded by the Union Pacific in 1866, the following June the railroad moved on and the town shrunk to almost nothing. A fire from the prairie swept through town in April 1893 and destroyed thirty-five houses (Ascendant opposition Mars). In 1884 William F. "Buffalo" Bill Cody established his Wild West Show here, and to this day remains the town's most famous citizen.

Incorporated: 1873
Elevation: 2,821 feet
Source: *American Guide Series*

Omaha

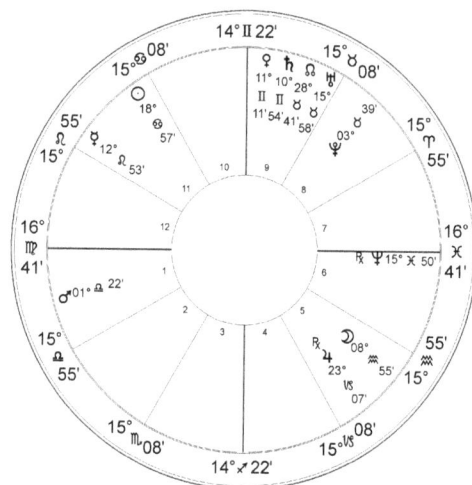

July 11, 1854
95W57, 41N45
9:59 AM CST

During the winter of 1846-47, Mormons camped north of the city on their way to the promised land. Land was thrown open for settlement in June 1854, and Omaha was founded the following month. Capital of Nebraska until 1867, President Lincoln designated it as the eastern terminus of the Transcontinental Railroad in 1863 (Ascendant trine Jupiter). The nationwide financial panics of 1873 (Ascendant conjunct Mars) and 1893 (Ascendant square Sun) severely crippled the economy, as did the one in 1907 (Midheaven square Pluto). Father Flanagan founded Boys' Town west of Omaha in 1917 (Midheaven conjunct Mercury), and the Strategic Air Command (SAC) was established at Offutt AFB in 1946. Due to its geographic location in the heartland of America, Omaha has borne the brunt of erratic climactic changes. A tornado in 1913 killed ninety-five (Ascendant opposition Pluto) and another in May 1975 (Ascendant sesquare Sun) tore up the northwest side.

Omaha is a butter-and-egg town (Virgo rising, Cancer Sun) and is the largest producer of butter in the land. It's heavily dependent on farm products and favorable weather conditions for its economic survival. Omaha has the largest stockyards in the nation, which were founded in 1884 (Ascendant trine Saturn). It also depends on grain, for Omaha is one of the leading food processors in the U.S. Omaha is also the fourth largest rail center in America.

Omaha is a city that conforms to habits (Sun in Cancer), and is typically Midwestern in appearance with big homes, large lawns, and an abundance of trees. Someone once said Omaha was as friendly as a wet dog (Venus in Gemini at Midheaven), had an unspectacular reputation, and wasn't very up to date (Saturn also at Midheaven). More than just an overgrown cow town, which once had a reputation for being wild and woolly, Omaha does have clean air and a very low crime rate, but not much nightlife (Saturn rules the fifth house).

Incorporated: February 2, 1857
Elevation: 1,040 feet
Area: 83 square miles
Source: *Early History of Omaha* by Alfred Sorensen; *History of Nebraska* by James Olson says July 4, 1854

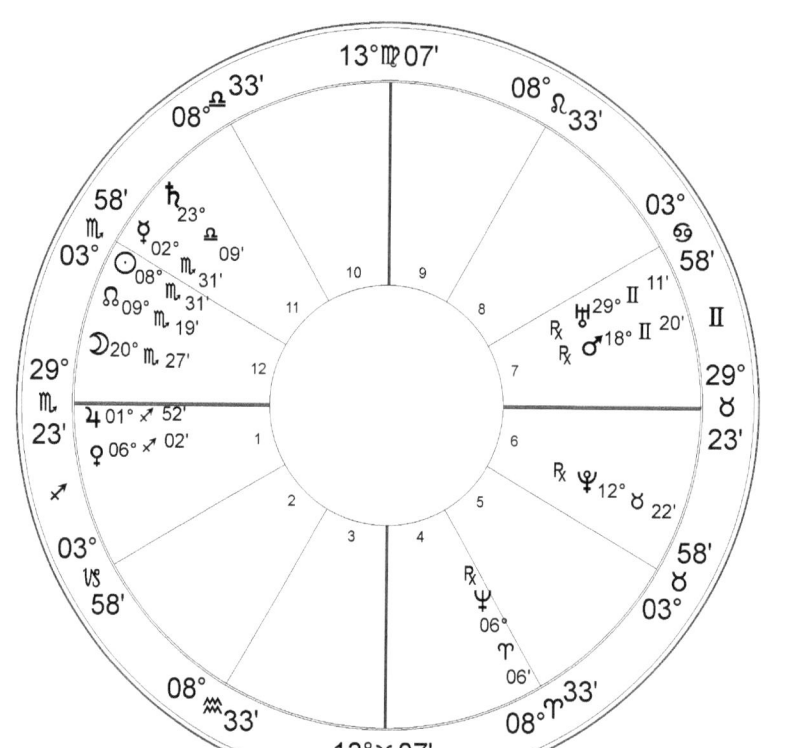

Nevada

**October 31, 1864
Carson City
119W46, 39N10
8:16 AM PST
Source: Rectified from various newspaper reports which imply a morning birthtime**

In 1830 the Old Spanish Trail crossed the state from Santa Fe to Los Angeles; three years later the California Trail, from Utah to the Pacific, was founded. The U.S. acquired the state in the Mexican Cession, and in 1849 the first settlement was established at Genoa. The richest silver strike in history occurred on June 11, 1859 when the Comstock Lode put this state on the map. On March 2, 1861, Nevada was organized as a territory, and without the usual population requirements it became a state in order that the Union would have enough silver for its bullets. The state remained sparsely populated until the early 20th century when liberal divorce laws brought thousands to Reno in search of happiness. Gambling was legalized in 1931, and within two decades Las Vegas became the gambling mecca of the world and the flashiest city on earth. The U.S. government began testing atomic weapons in the Nevada desert in 1951 near Las Vegas.

Having the lowest average rainfall of any state, Nevada has turned to grazing instead of agriculture. Outside of tourism, mining is the biggest industry, and this state produces twenty-five percent of the gold supply and a good portion of copper and silver. Nevada makes more gambling devices, naturally, than any other state. Warehousing recently has become quite popular due to the fact that there is no inventory tax on goods not sold in Nevada.

Area: 110,540 square miles

Carson City

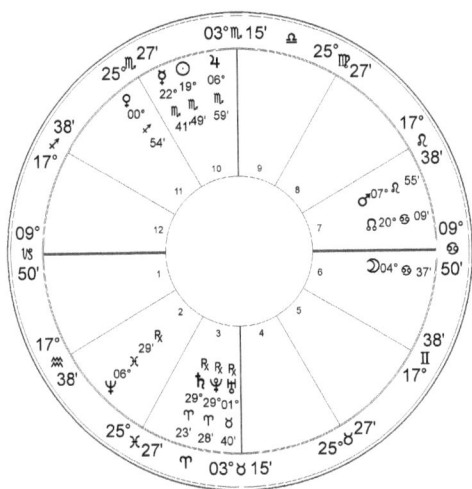

November 12, 1851
119W46, 39N10
10:38 AM PST

Founded in 1851, Carson City was platted seven years later. Capital of Nevada since 1861 (Ascendant sextile Sun), it also housed a U.S. Mint from 1870 until 1893 when the Silver Purchase Act was repealed. Prior to 1969 when Carson City merged with Ormsby County, this was the smallest state capital in the nation.

Incorporated: March 1, 1875
Elevation: 4,680 feet
Source: *American Guide Series*

Las Vegas

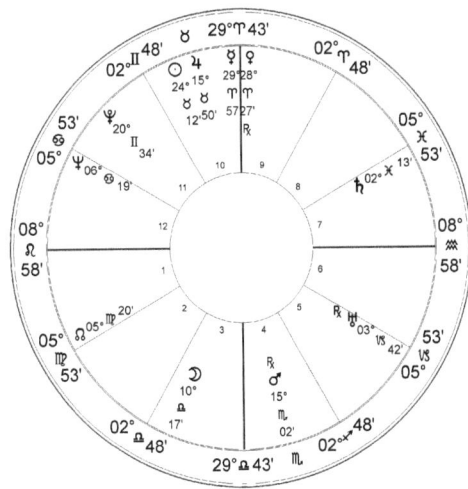

May 15, 1905
115W09, 36N10
10:00 AM PST

During the 1850s, Mormons camped north of the city on their journey to California. If they had stayed and founded this city, what a different place it would be today! With the arrival of the railroad in 1905, lots were put up for sale in May, and the entertainment capital of the world was born. Growth was slow due to lack of water until the Hoover Dam was begun in 1928. Three years later Nevada legalized gambling (Midheaven conjunct Sun) and Las Vegas was on its way to fame and glory. After World War II, massive hotels along the Strip began to be built. Many were constructed by underworld figures like Bugsy Siegel, who built the Flamingo in 1946. As years went by, newer and gaudier hotels were opened and to lure tourists, big name entertainment stars were given outlandish salaries to appear in the showrooms. Food was a bargain and hotel rooms were kept relatively low so the gambler had more money to spend at the tables. On November 22, 1980, the biggest disaster ever to hit the city occurred when a fire in the MGM Grand Hotel caused eighty-five people to perish (Midheaven conjunct Moon). The following February 10, another mysterious fire in the Hilton Hotel killed another eight people. Many said the New Jersey mob set the fires to keep eastern gamblers closer to Atlantic City. In late 1994, several mega-hotels opened up on the Strip as Las Vegas was trying to turn its image around and become a more family oriented vacation resort (Ascendant trine Pluto). With more and more states entering the field of gambling, this city is feeling pressure to come up with more and more lures for the American vacationer.

Las Vegas is both hostile and beautiful, forbidding and alluring, glamorous or gaudy. Depending on whether you're winning or not, this is the best place in the world to make a fast buck. It's a twenty-four hour nonstop nightmare of neon lights that bombard you to take a chance and hit the big time. Money is the only god in this town (Sun in Taurus conjunct Jupiter) and much of the city is a tasteless, gaudy, and extravagant display of energy. Downtown Fremont Street is the most brightly lighted avenue in the world, and midnight never really comes in this fairy tale fantasy city.

Las Vegas is the convention center of the world for it has more than 45,000 hotel rooms at its disposal. The city is a memorial to tinseled affluence and places like Caesar's Palace are paeans to extravagance and wealth. The lure of easy money draws ten million visitors annually to this desert oasis of fun and excitement (Leo rising). Everything in this city is big time and, who knows, you might just hit that million dollar jackpot. Needless to say, Las Vegas has scores of pawnshops for those who don't, and some who come in limousines end up taking the bus back home.

Incorporated: March 16, 1911
Elevation: 2,033 feet
Area: 54 square miles
Source: *Las Vegas* by Stanley Paher and Nevada Bell Telephone both say 10:00 a.m.

Calling itself "The Biggest Little City in the World," it's a conservative city (Sun in Taurus)—informal, hospitable, and friendly (Libra rising, Moon in Sagittarius). Its people are straightforward and can't stand either hypocrisy or pretense. Besides being famous for its quickie divorces, let's not forget that one could get married here far easier than in other states (Libra rising); there are about four marriages to every divorce granted. Reno is a far prettier, more pleasant, and more human city than its gaudier cousin to the south, and its neighborhoods remind one that Reno is a city where people live and work, not just play like they do in Las Vegas. Living in Nevada is quite profitable even if you don't gamble, for there are no inheritance, gift, or income taxes to contend with.

Incorporated: April 8, 1879
Elevation: 4,492 feet
Area: 36 square miles
Source: Reno Public Library says 3:00 p.m.; *American Guide Series* says May 4, 1868, in error

Virginia City

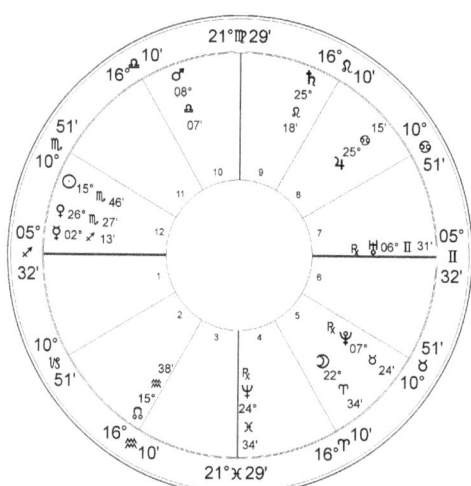

**November 8, 1859
119W39, 39N19
8:10 AM PST**

Reno

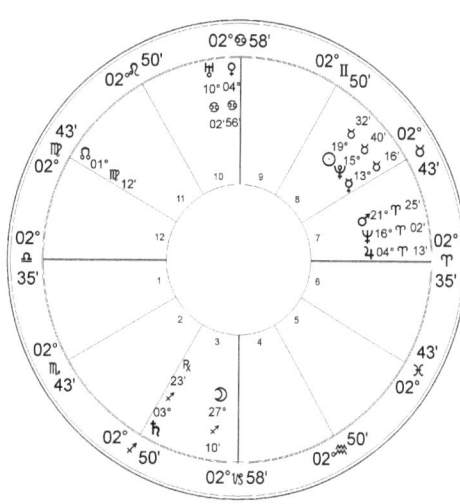

**May 9, 1868
119W48, 39N31
3:00 PM PST**

Founded by the railroad in 1868 during a sale of lots, a fire burned most of the city eleven years later (Ascendant square Uranus). Due to increased laxity in divorce laws, the population increased greatly after the turn of the century. With the legalization of gambling in 1931 (Midheaven square Saturn sextile Venus), Reno became the place to dump one's spouse and possibly dump the settlement at the crap tables. It was the gambling center of the nation until it was eclipsed by Las Vegas. Reno also is home of the University of Nevada, which was moved here in 1886 (Midheaven sextile Sun).

Even though Virginia City is technically a ghost town, its contribution to American history, and the wealth it produced, merit special attention.

Settled as a mining camp on June 12, 1859, it was formally founded the following November. The discovery of the largest silver strike in history, the Comstock Lode, turned this town into a booming metropolis overnight. Due to the importance of silver, Nevada was admitted into the Union even though it had not yet achieved the required minimum population. The "Big Bonanza," discovered in 1873, preceded the disastrous fire of 1876 which caused $12 million in damages and led to Virginia City losing its charter. Despite its 100 saloons, this city did have some culture, largely revolving around the Opera House at which Broadway hits were performed. During the 1880s the silver ran out and many of the buildings were dismantled and moved to Oakland or Los Angeles. By 1885 it was a ghost town with only 1,000 residents, a far cry from the 25,000 who had walked its streets only a decade before. Today, Virginia City is visited by 40,000 tourists a week during the summer season.

Incorporated: 1864
Source: Nevada State Historical Society

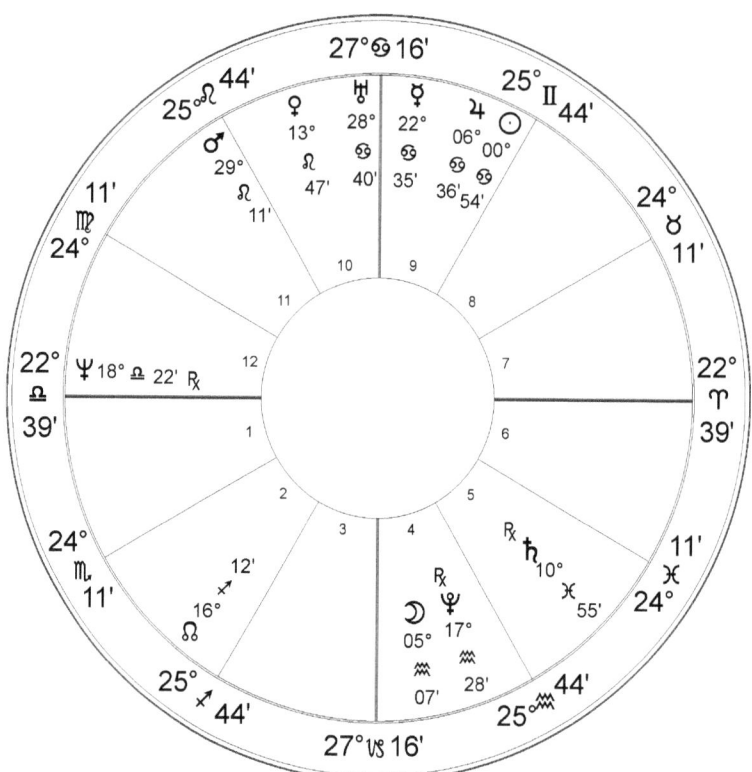

New Hampshire

June 21, 1788
Concord
71W32, 43N12
1:41 PM EST
Source: New Hampshire State Historical Society says 2:00 p.m.; rectified

In 1622 the region was granted jointly to both Gorges and Mason. The following year the first permanent settlement was made at Portsmouth. Divided again in 1629, Mason received New Hampshire in its entirety. During King Philip's War (1675-76), many settlers were killed in the Indian raids. In 1679 it became a royal colony. For the next eighty years, more Indian raids made life miserable for the inhabitants and the colony remained sparsely settled. New Hampshire holds the honor of being the first state to vote for independence in 1776, and the state that made the U.S. Constitution legal when it became the ninth state to ratify it in 1788. In 1803 the first of many t extile mills opened, and before long, this state was one of the biggest millers in the East. In 1963 New Hampshire became the first state to adopt a lottery in order to support public education.

Shoes and textiles are the main industries, with tourism ranking second. More than half its farm income is garnered from dairy products. And don't forget that New Hampshire is the Granite State and mines huge quantities of this stone, the hardest one known to man.

Area: 9,304 square miles

Concord

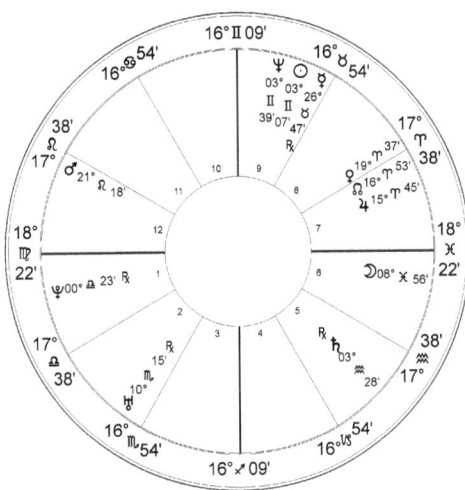

May 24, 1726
71W32, 43N12
12:38 PM EST

Founded in 1726, it became the capital of New Hampshire in 1808 (Midheaven sextile Sun and Pluto). It's a gray and granite city that somehow manages to remain detached from state politics, which it considers a nuisance (Mercury, ruler of the Midheaven, is retrograde square Mars). However, it once paid the legislature to keep the capital here instead of moving it elsewhere. Slightly schizophrenic, don't you think (Sun in Gemini)? Concord was inundated heavily during the floods of 1927 and 1936.

Incorporated: April 6, 1853
Elevation: 288 feet
Source: Concord Public Library; *American Guide Series* says the first lots were sold on June 17, 1725

Manchester

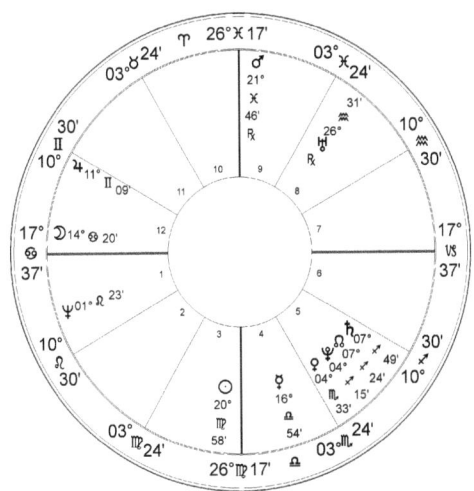

September 14, 1751
71W28, 43N00
12:01 AM EST

Settled as Amoskeag in 1722, it became known as Tyngstown in 1735, and Derryfield in 1751 when Manchester was chartered as a borough. The first textile mill was completed in 1805, and five years later its name was changed to Manchester. Traffic up the Merrimac River was made easier with the completion of a canal around the falls in 1807. During 1935 most of the mills closed down, and many moved south where labor was cheaper.

Incorporated: June 1, 1846
Elevation: 220 feet
Area: 35 square miles
Source: *New Hampshire* by Edwin Charlton; *Manchester* by John Clarke says September 9, 1751

Nashua

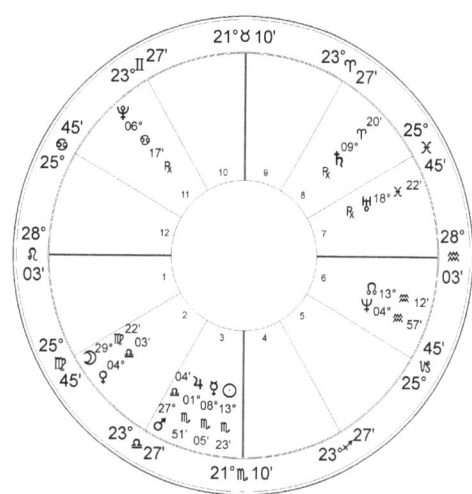

November 5, 1673
71W28, 42N45
12:01 AM EST

First settled in 1655, it became the Town of Dunstable in 1673. Indians attacked the community in 1724 and drove many settlers away. A canal was completed around the falls in 1826, and eleven years later Nashua merged with Indian Head. Five years later, in 1853, Nashville seceded and became the city we know today. In 1930 a fire destroyed twenty-five percent of the city.

Incorporated: June 27, 1853
Elevation: 152 feet
Source: Nashua Public Library

Portsmouth

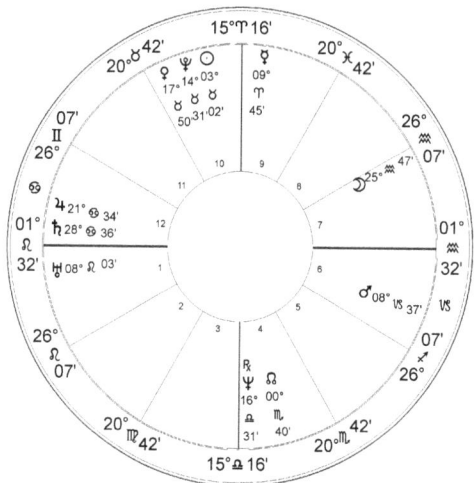

April 23, 1623
70W45, 43N04
10:34 AM EST

Founded as Strawberry Banks in 1623, it's the oldest European settlement in the state and the only port in New Hampshire. The first Tea Party occurred here in 1773 (Midheaven trine Mars) and two years later a patriotic woman saved the city from being burned by the British. From 1776 until 1812, privateering increased the economy greatly, and in 1790 a Navy Yard was founded across the river in Kittery, Maine. In 1905 the treaty that ended the Russo-Japanese War was signed here.

Incorporated: July 6, 1849
Elevation: 20 feet
Source: Rectified, exact date unknown; most sources simply state April 1623

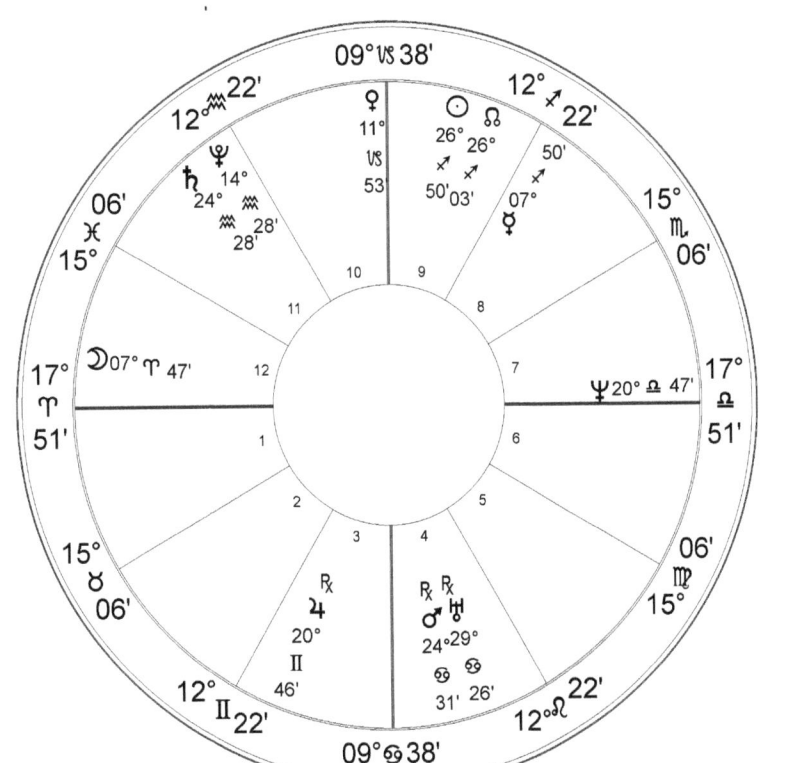

New Jersey

December 18, 1787
Trenton
74W46, 40N14
12:52 PM EST

Source: New Jersey Historical Society says "afternoon," rectified

In 1524 Verrazzano explored the region for France, and in 1609 came Henry Hudson for the Netherlands. The Dutch established a fort near Gloucester in 1623, but the first permanent settlement was made at Bergen in 1660. The Dutch surrendered the region to the British in 1664, and on June 20, 1664 it was granted the status of a colony to Lord Carteret. Twelve years later the colony was divided: East Jersey went to Carteret and West Jersey to William Penn and the Quakers. The two colonies were again united in 1702, even though it was administered from New York until 1738. During the Revolution, many battles were fought in this state, including Trenton, Princeton and Monmouth. It ratified the U.S. Constitution in 1787 and became the third state. New Jersey's proximity to both New York and Philadelphia has made it extremely dense and the corridor between those cities is the most heavily traveled in the nation. The New Jersey Turnpike opened in 1952 to alleviate the traffic and in 1976 the state voted to legalize gambling.

Even though it's a powerful industrial state, almost two-thirds of the region is farms and forests. Known as the Garden State because of the variety of vegetables grown there, one of the biggest industries is the New York Port Authority, which is shared by New Jersey. Much of the tonnage is unloaded in this state, especially in the Port of Newark. New Jersey ranks first in chemical products, and is a leader in petroleum and electrical products.

Area: 7,836 square miles

Atlantic City

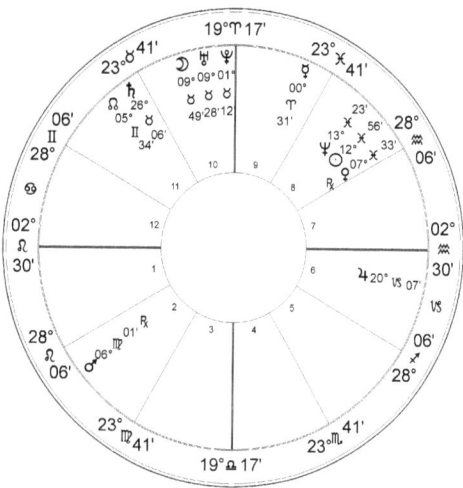

March 3, 1854
74W27, 39N21
2:24 PM EST

First settled as Absecon in 1783, the railroad gave the real impetus for settlement in 1852 when it decided to build a line from Philadelphia. Chartered in 1854, the railroad arrived later that summer. The famous boardwalk was completed in 1870 (Midheaven sextile Mars). In this city the world's first salt water taffy was made in 1883, the first rolling chair in 1884, and the first picture postcard in 1895. In order to keep tourists a bit longer in the summer, the Miss America Pageant was founded in 1921 (Ascendant trine Saturn). In 1976 New Jersey legalized gambling (Ascendant opposition Moon/Uranus) and before long hotels were being refurbished and casinos were being erected.

Once the premier seaside resort in America (Leo rising), Atlantic city had fallen on hard times prior to the arrival of the casinos. But the legislature controls the industry so greatly that many operators find it difficult to make a profit. Las Vegas it isn't, but within a day's drive are millions of Americans who could come here and find lady luck.

Incorporated: May 1, 1855
Elevation: 10 feet
Source: Atlantic City Public Library

Camden

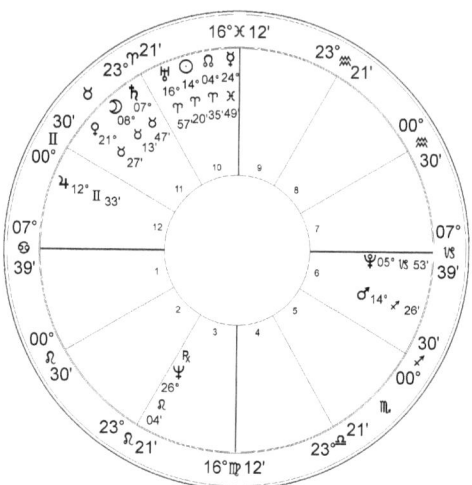

April 3, 1764
75W07, 39N52
10:20 AM EST

Settled by the Swedes in 1638, it was founded in 1764 and platted nine years later. A ferry was completed to Philadelphia in 1809 and the Benjamin Franklin Bridge was opened in 1926.

Largely a suburb of the City of Brotherly Love across the Delaware River, Camden is a large industrial city where the first steel pen was invented. It is now home to Campbell Soup and the Victor Talking Machine Company (Victrola). Shipbuilding began in 1899.

Incorporated: 1828
Elevation: 25 feet
Source: *History of New Jersey*

Elizabeth

October 8, 1664
74W13, 40N39
7:43 AM EST

In 1664, land was purchased from the Delaware Indians; four years later the first colonial assembly began to meet. In 1746, the College of New Jersey was founded (Ascendant conjunct Jupiter); it later became Princeton University. In 1928, Elizabeth was connected to Staten Island with the completion of the Goethals Bridge.

Elizabeth is a highly industrial city, a major railroad and shipping port under the jurisdiction of the New York Port Authority.

Incorporated: 1855
Elevation: 38 feet
Area: 12 square miles
Source: *Encyclopedia of American Cities*

Jersey City

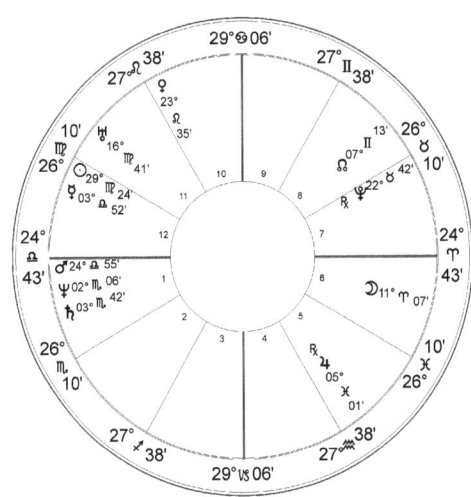

September 22, 1630
74W04, 40N44
7:56 AM EST

In 1630, Michael Pauw purchased the site from the Indians, who later drove out the settlers in 1654 (Midheaven square Pluto). In 1779, General Henry Lee stormed the town (Midheaven square Sun) and in 1812 a ferry was established across the Hudson to Manhattan (Ascendant conjunct Pluto). Chartered as the City of Jersey in 1820, it finally settled the boundary dispute with New York in 1834 (Midheaven square Pluto opposition Venus). In 1910 the Hudson Tubes were completed under the river and in 1927 the Holland tunnel was finished (Ascendant sextile Saturn/Neptune).

Jersey City is a major port and is part of the New York Port Authority. Its railroad yards are immense and handle much of the freight traffic into the nation's largest city.

Incorporated: 1820
Elevation: 60 feet
Area: 17 square miles
Source: Jersey City Public Library; American Federation of Astrologers says November 22, 1630, in error

Newark

May 28, 1666
74W10, 40N44
5:34 AM EST

Founded as a theocracy by William Treat in 1666, it became the home of the College of New Jersey (later Princeton) in 1748 (Ascendant opposition Uranus inconjunct Jupiter). Newark's first industry was iron making; then tanning shoes and leather; and now chemicals. In 1915 the Port of Newark was founded (Ascendant semisquare Jupiter). During the Depression many of its factories closed, and with the influx of poor Blacks from the South, the character of the city was changed forever. In July 1967 a race riot broke out (Midheaven opposition Pluto, Ascendant opposition Mars conjunct Jupiter) which caused so much damage that many of the burned out buildings remain in ruins after many years.

During the 1970s, Newark was a place to avoid. It had one of the highest crime rates in the nation: murder, rape, and robbery were part of its daily existence. Newark's infant mortality rate was appallingly high and the number of hospital beds and doctors shockingly low. Its housing was in sad shape and almost twenty percent lived in abject poverty. Fortunately, with the election of its first Black mayor, things have slowly begun to change for the better. In Newark, up was the only way it could go.

Incorporated: February 29, 1836
Elevation: 55 feet
Area: 24 square miles
Sources: Newark Public Library; The History of New Jersey by Gordon Thomas says May 21, 1666

Paterson

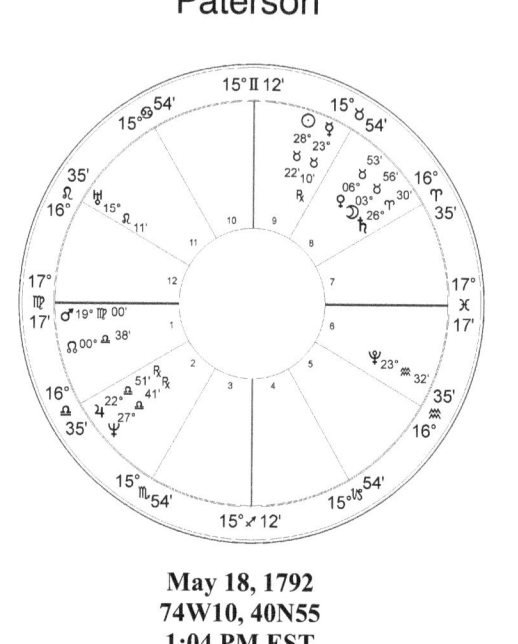

May 18, 1792
74W10, 40N55
1:04 PM EST

In 1791, Alexander Hamilton founded the Society for Establishing Useful Manufacturers. The following year Paterson was selected as a site for his model industrial city. Cotton milling was one of the first industries, and in 1837 the cotton industry was replaced by silk. Locomotive engines began rolling out of the factories that same year (Midheaven trine Pluto), and linen manufacture began in 1864. Starting in 1907, Paterson elected to form a commission form of government which elected a mayor every three years with the mayor appointing all department heads, instead of them being elected (Midheaven trine Uranus). A financial panic in 1912 caused many strikes the following year (Ascendant square Mars).

Incorporated: 1851
Elevation: 101 feet
Area: 8 square miles
Sources: *Encyclopedia Britannica*; *Encyclopedia of American Cities*

Trenton

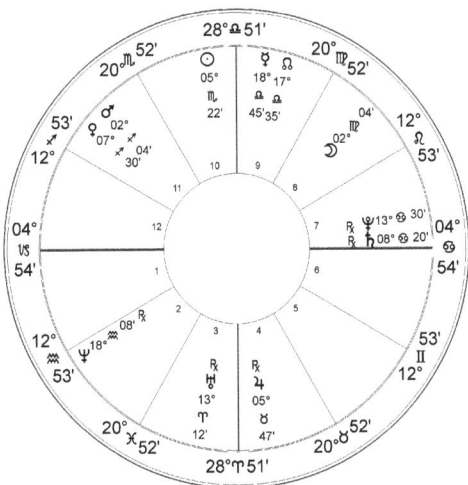

**October 28, 1679
74W46, 40N14
11:18 AM EST**

Settled in 1679, it was known simply as The Falls until William Trent bought the site in 1714 (Midheaven conjunct Mars sextile Moon). It was at Trenton that Washington crossed the Delaware on December 26, 1776, surprising the British and their Hessian mercenaries (Midheaven square Jupiter, Ascendant semisquare Uranus). Briefly the capital of the United States in 1784 (Midheaven trine Mercury), it became the capital of New Jersey in 1790 (Ascendant trine Mercury and Neptune). It's the only state capital without a governor's mansion, and government is the chief employer.

A highly industrial city, Trenton is rather pleased with itself. It's had serious growing pains (Capricorn rising) and wants to control future growth (Sun in Scorpio). Complacent, yet ready for innovation, it makes everything from soup to nuts in its more than 300 manufacturing plants.

Incorporated: November 13, 1792
Elevation: 35 feet
Area: 8 square miles
Source: American Federation of Astrologers

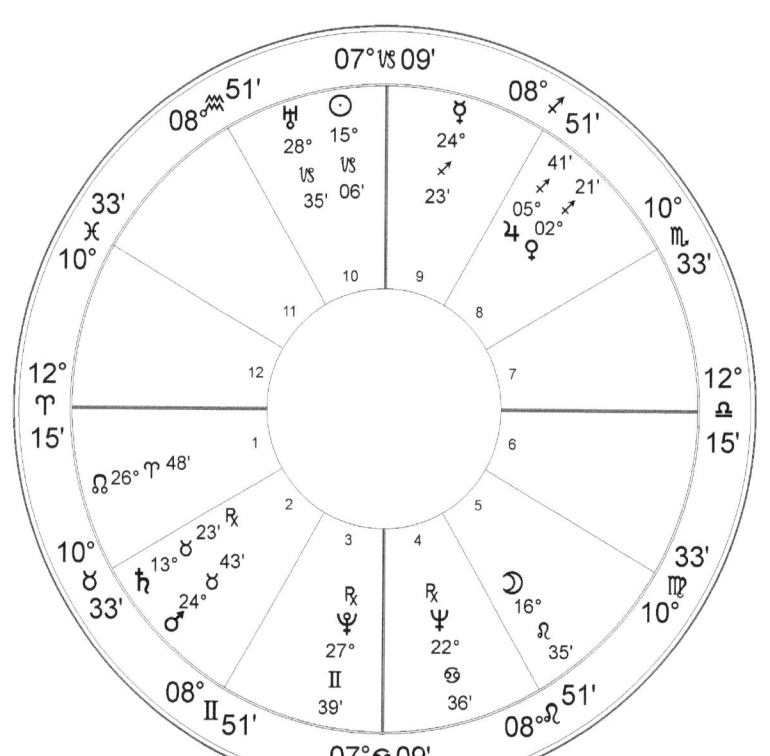

New Mexico

January 6, 1912
Santa Fe
105W57, 35N41
11:35 AM MST
Source: *Los Angeles Times* says 1:35 p.m. in Washington

In the 1530s this land was explored by Cabeza de Vaca for Spain; ten years later Coronado conquered the Indian pueblos. The first Spanish settlement was made in 1598 along the Rio Grande, and in 1610 the oldest seat of government in America was founded—Santa Fe. A revolt by the Indians in 1680 drove the settlers into Texas, but in 1692, Spanish rule was again restored. In 1821 the Santa Fe Trail was begun, and in 1848 the U.S. acquired the region in the Mexican Cession. On September 9, 1850, it was organized as a territory. During the Civil War, Confederate troops from Texas captured much of the state, but were driven out shortly after. Kit Carson subdued the Navajo and Apache nations during this period as well. Martial law was declared in Lincoln County during 1876 when cattlemen fought one another over range rights. Until the capture of Geronimo in 1886, the Apaches were a continual threat to new settlements. In 1912, New Mexico finally became state, and four years later the Mexican bandit Pancho Villa raided Columbus, New Mexico, killing seventeen persons. The first atomic bomb was detonated at Alamogordo on July 16, 1945, three weeks before being dropped on Hiroshima and Nagasaki. Los Alamos remains a major center for atomic research in this country.

New Mexico leads the nation in the production of uranium and potassium. It ranks high in the manufacture of carbon dioxide, and the petroleum, natural gas, and copper industries are enormous. The state ranks eighth in sheep.

Area: 121,666 square miles

Albuquerque

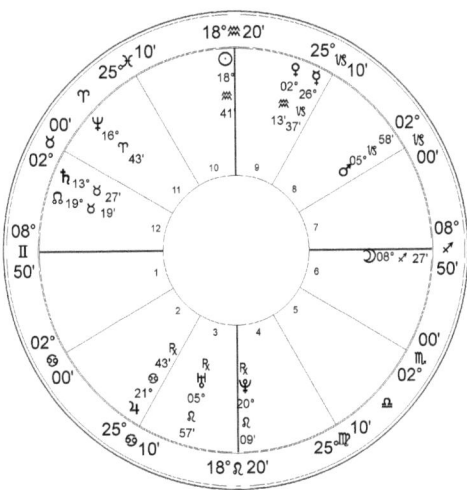

February 7, 1706
106W39, 35N05
12:20 PM MST

Founded in 1706 and named for the Duke of Alburquerque, the first "r" was inadvertently dropped by settlers who couldn't pronounce its name. Americans established a garrison here in 1846 (Midheaven opposition Mars) and in 1862 it was occupied by Confederate troops (Midheaven conjunct Jupiter). With the arrival of the railroad in 1880, a new town was formed (Midheaven trine Moon, Ascendant square Venus). Albuquerque is the home of the University of New Mexico, which was founded in 1889.

Home to many "clean" industries like electronics and research, the city has practically no smoke or smog of any kind. Its clean, pure air makes it the ballooning capital of the country (Gemini rising) and the altitude can give you a real "Rocky Mountain high." Friendly and neighborly, Albuquerque is really two cities: one Spanish and one American (Ascendant and Moon in mutable signs). It has managed to retain much of its Indian heritage along with the innovations of the 20th century. A nice blend.

Incorporated: April 15, 1891
Elevation: 4,943 feet
Area: 88 square miles
Source: Albuquerque Public Library; *Great River* by Paul Horgan says April 23, 1706

Las Cruces

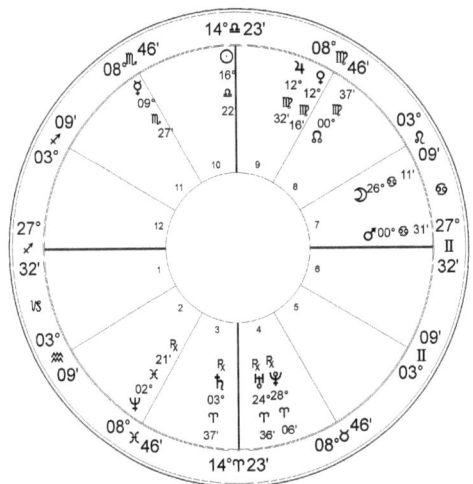

October 9, 1849
106W47, 32N19
11:47 AM MST

Founded in 1849, Las Cruces is situated on the Rio Grande river a few miles above El Paso. Nearby is the Alamogordo test range where the first atomic bomb was dropped in July 1945. Las Cruces is also home to New Mexico State University.

Incorporated: 1946
Elevation: 3,895 feet
Source: Las Cruces Public Library

Roswell

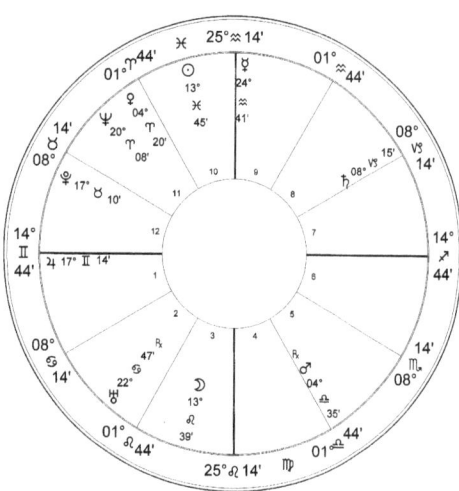

**March 4, 1871
104W32, 33N24
11:00 AM MST**

Settled by a gambler from Omaha in 1869, two years later the first claim was filed by Van Smith, who named it for his father. In July 1947, reports of a UFO having crashed outside of town caused quite a stir. The government tried to pass it off as a weather balloon landing, especially after reputed photos of a alien autopsy began to surface (Midheaven trine Saturn, Ascendant square Pluto). Because of this incident, Roswell has been a tourist stop for UFO enthusiasiasts ever since. Oil was discovered nearby during the 1950s.

Incorporated: 1891
Elevation: 3,573 feet
Source: American Guide Series

Santa Fe

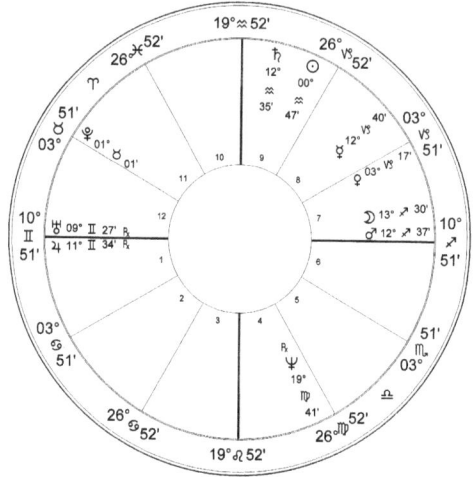

**January 20, 1610
105W57, 35N41
1:33 PM MST**

Founded by the Spanish in the early months of 1610, Santa Fe is the oldest continuous seat of government in the U.S. and the highest capital city in America. In 1680, the Indians revolted against their Spanish overlords and drove them from the city (Midheaven conjunct Pluto). In 1692, the Spanish retook the city (Midheaven square Saturn). With the arrival of the Santa Fe Trail in 1821 (Midheaven sesquare Pluto and Sun), Santa Fe was connected to the rest of the continent. A riot in the state prison in February 1980 killed thirty-three inmates (Ascendant semisquare Pluto sesquare Sun).

Isolated in the mountains, Santa Fe was passed by the very railroad that bears its name. A unique city (Sun in Aquarius) possessing inimitable charm and variety (Gemini rising), Santa Fe is actually two cities: one Spanish/Indian and one Anglo/American. It is the religious and political capital of the state and is famous as an art colony.

Incorporated: July 4, 1851
Elevation: 6,950 feet
Source: Rectified as the exact date is unknown; *Soldiers of the Cross* by J.B. Salpointe says about January 28, 1605; *History of New Mexico* by L.P. Prince says about April 26, 1605; the year 1610 seems reasonable in light of recent discoveries

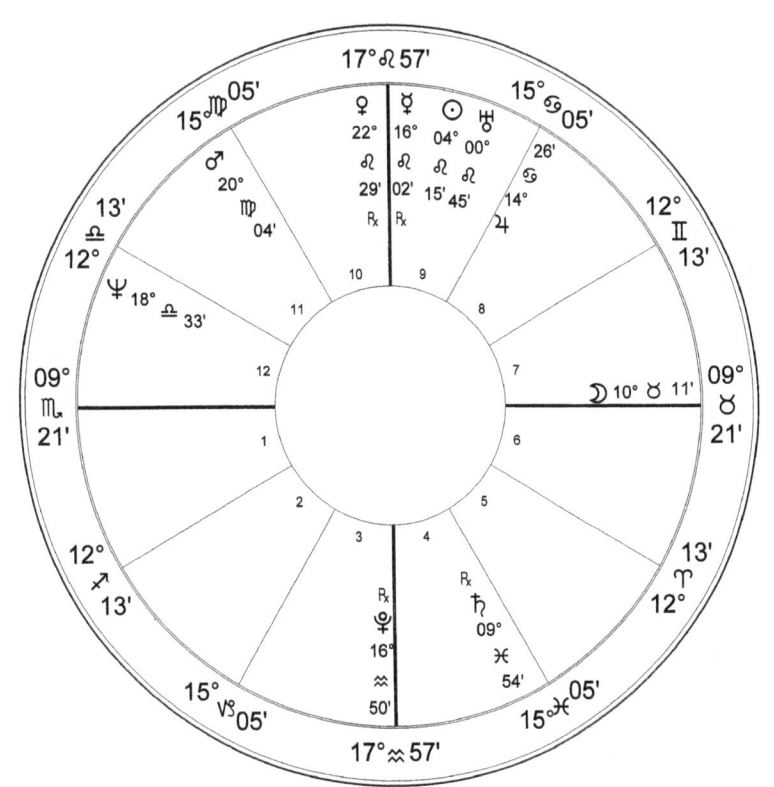

New York

July 26, 1788
Poughkeepsie
73W56, 41N42
12:57 PM EST
Source: New York State Historical Society says "early afternoon;" rectified

In 1524, Verrazzano explored New York Bay and in 1609 Henry Hudson traversed the river that bears his name all the way to Albany. In 1614, the first trading post was founded at Albany, and nine years later the first permanent settlement was made by Walloons from Belgium at Nieuw Amsterdam, now New York City. Three years later Peter Minuit bought the island of Manhattan for a mere $24 in trinkets. The English captured New Amsterdam in 1664 and renamed it after the king's brother. In 1673, the Dutch again occupied the region, but vacated after only one year. In 1683, the Charter of Liberties was adopted, guaranteeing freedom of religion and taxation only at the consent of the voters. From 1690 until 1763, upper New York was the scene of many battles between European settlers and the Iroquois nation. Freedom of the press was firmly established after the trial of Peter Zenger in 1735. During the American Revolution, the British occupied New York City and major battles included Ticonderoga, Long Island, White Plains and Saratoga. In 1788, New York ratified the Constitution after a long and bitter battle. The first capital of the country in 1789, it saw the inauguration of Washington as the first president. In 1825, the Erie Canal was opened and transport between the Hudson and the Great Lakes was made considerably easier. During the Civil War, riots took place in New York City protesting the draft and 2,000 were killed in the melee. During the latter part of the 19th century, New York became the symbol of freedom as the Statue of Liberty was unveiled. Unfortunately, too many believed that the streets were paved with gold and soon ended up on the Lower East Side in the worst slums in the nation. The newcomers made a mighty contribution to the country's wealth and culture, but New York was still a city of foreigners at the turn of the century. With the completion of the St. Lawrence Seaway in 1959, Buffalo became an international port. New York in recent years has been losing population to more healthful climates. Its power base has eroded somewhat and its finances drained by the multitudes that come in search of the good life and simply end up on welfare. New York has the largest budget of any state and doles out huge quantities to those who either refuse or cannot work. One-seventh of the nation's largest city lives on the dole. New York gives Albany more than it receives and the fiscal crisis of 1975 almost brought this great city to a grinding halt.

Nevertheless, New York is the nation's top manufacturing state. It ranks number one in apparel, publishing, paper products, jewelry, silverware, toys and sporting goods. It makes seventy percent of the photo equipment, forty percent of the books, fifty-two percent of the magazines and thirty percent of the garments. New York handles twenty-five percent of the foreign trade and Kennedy International Airport handles fifty percent of the overseas air traffic. Next to California, it has the largest wine industry in the nation, ranks third in diary cows and produces thirty-four percent of the instruments. It is first in maple syrup and cottage cheese, and second in apples. Its chief mineral resources are zinc, titanium, salt and garnets.

New York State is almost as varied as California in the number of regions that occupy this eastern state. Long Island stretches out into the Atlantic, offering weekenders a chance to get away from it all, especially at the far end near Montauk. The Hudson river Valley has been compared to the Rhine Valley where castles and sumptuous mansions overlook this majestic river. The Catskills and the Adirondacks offer countless respites from the turmoils of the city, while the Finger Lake region abounds in beauty and simplicity. The Mohawk Valley is heavily industrialized with cities like Rome and Utica, and the Southern tier reminds one of neighboring Pennsylvania in its serenity. The Lake Erie and Ontario shorelines abound in recreational facilities, while the St. Lawrence River Valley is dotted with a thousand islands.

Area: 47,831 square miles

Albany

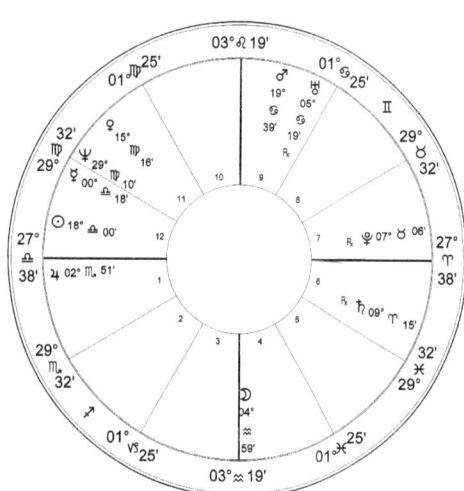

October 11, 1614
73W45, 42N39
6:58 AM EST

Founded as Fort Nassau in 1614 by the Dutch, the Walloons arrived in 1623 shortly before Fort Orange was completed (Ascendant square Moon trine Uranus). Albany surrendered to the British in 1664 (Ascendant sextile Moon inconjunct Uranus), and in 1686 it became the first incorporated city in the nation (Ascendant sesquare Pluto). The Albany Congress of 1754 was the forerunner of the Continental Congress and laid out a plan to unite the colonies (Ascendant trine Mars). Capital of the state since 1797 (Midheaven square Pluto), it saw the arrival of Robert Fulton's steamboat "Clermont" ten years later. With the completion of the Erie Canal in 1825, Albany became a major jumping-off point in the movement west (Ascendant square Neptune). A fire in August 1848 burned more than 600 downtown buildings.

Albany is the third oldest city in the U.S. after St. Augustine and Santa Fe. Situated at the head of the Hudson tidewater, it's the hub of a once powerful political machine. A city of red brick buildings and numerous trees, its main attraction is the massive capitol building which was completed in 1898 at the staggering cost of $25 million. The skyline has changed appreciably in recent years with the completion of the Empire State Plaza south of the downtown area. Albany also is home of the University of New York, which was founded in 1844 (Midheaven semisquare Pluto).

Incorporated: August 1, 1686
Elevation: 18 feet
Area: 22 square miles
Source: *Hollanders Who Built America* by H.M. Van Vlekke

Binghamton

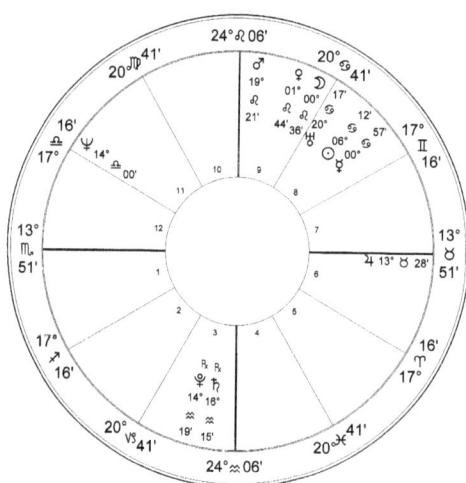

June 27, 1786
75W55, 42N06
3:25 PM EST

The land around this city was ceded by the Indians in 1786 and sold to William Bingham the following year. Laid out as Chenango in 1799, its name was changed in 1816. The Chenango Canal was completed in 1837 (Ascendant opposition Mercury) and from 1870 to 1890 Binghamton was the second largest cigar manufacturer in the U.S.

Incorporated: April 9, 1867
Elevation: 845 feet
Source: *Binghamton and Broome County* by William F. Seward

Buffalo

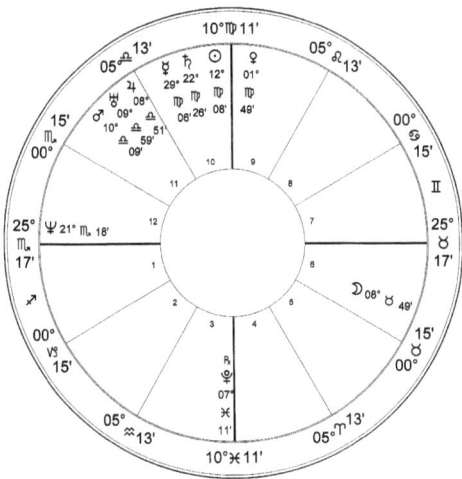

September 5, 1803
78W53, 42N53
12:07 PM EST

Founded by the Holland Land Company in 1803, Ellicott named it after a corruption of the French words for beautiful river (beau fleuve). Burned by the British in 1813 (Midheaven conjunct Saturn), the first steamboat on the Great Lakes sailed from here in 1819. When the Erie Canal was completed in 1825 (Ascendant square Sun sextile Mars and Uranus), Buffalo became a large port. The first coal shipment from Pennsylvania arrived in 1873, which gave birth to Buffalo's steel industry. In September 1901 President McKinley was shot here. The St. Lawrence Seaway was completed in 1959 (Ascendant square Sun trine Uranus) and Buffalo became a seagoing port. The blizzard of January 1977 buried Buffalo under tons of snow and when it melted the following spring, more than 200 inches had accumulated (Midheaven conjunct Pluto). Because of the snow, among other things, Buffalo has lost much of its population in recent decades. In the 1970s Buffalo had more than 1,100 inches of snow, the highest of any major city in the U.S.

Buffalo grew slowly (Moon in Taurus) and managed to integrate its many ethnic groups with relative ease. Its natives are sociable and stable, conservative and peaceful, a trait which has led to favorable labor relations (Sun in Virgo trine Moon). Buffalo is America's jack-of-all-trades city, and even though it is the largest grain miller, it's also an important transportation hub and the third largest railroad center in the country. Iron and steel are also big contributors to the economy of this city which is practically ringed by parks. Don't sell Buffalo short! It might have oodles of snow, but it's a pleasant place to visit.

Incorporated: April 20, 1832
Elevation: 585 feet
Area: 41 square miles
Source: *Cradle of the Queen City* by Robert W. Bingham

Elmira

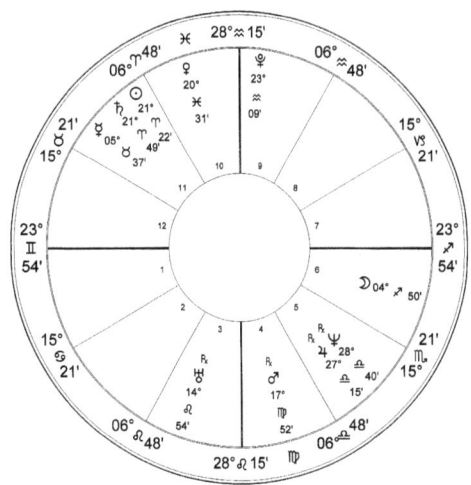

April 10, 1792
76W48, 42N06
8:51 AM EST

First settled as Newtown in 1788, a famine the following year caused untold starvation and grief. In 1792 the present city was formed from Chemung and sixteen years later changed its name to Elmira. With the completion of the Chemung Canal in 1832 and the arrival of the Erie Railroad in 1849 (Midheaven sextile Pluto), Elmira was no longer isolated from the outside. A flood caused by Hurricane Agnes in June 1972 caused millions of dollars in damage (Midheaven opposition Pluto, Ascendant square Uranus).

Incorporated: 1864
Elevation: 860 feet
Source: *Gazeteer of New York* by J.A. French

New York

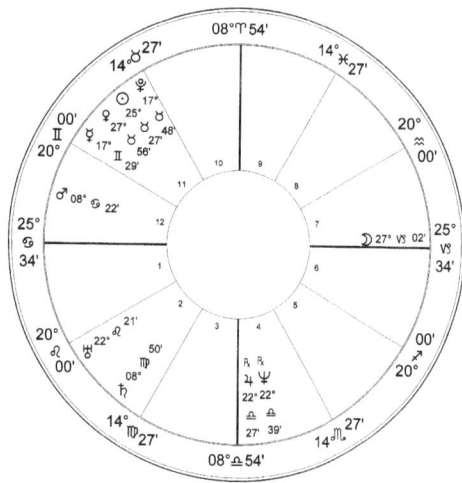

May 16, 1626
74W00, 40N43
8:52 AM EST

Manhattan was first settled in the spring of 1623 by Walloons from Belgium. The biggest real estate swindle of all time occurred three years later when Peter Minuit bought the island from the Canarsie Indians for a paltry sum of $24 in trinkets. The Indians gladly accepted the gift, for they didn't even own the land. Today the island is worth more than a billion times that amount. In 1653 it was chartered under Dutch law as the City of Nieuw Amsterdam; twelve years later, after the British captured the city, it was chartered under British law (Ascendant conjunct Uranus sextile Jupiter/Neptune). Negroes revolted in 1712 and 1741; the second time some thirty-two were hanged. During the early days of the Revolution in 1776, New York was occupied by the British (Ascendant opposition Sun/Pluto) and later that autumn a fire burned 943 buildings. New York was the capital of the United States when Washington was inaugurated as the first president in 1789 (Midheaven square Mercury), and in 1797 the state capital was moved to Albany. During the early 19th century, yellow fever epidemics were a constant threat: Those of 1819, 1822, and 1823 were particularly severe. Much of lower Manhattan was burned on December 16, 1835 when the Great Fire raged out of control, consuming 654 structures (Ascendant opposition Mars trine Saturn). The first World's Fair opened at the Crystal Palace in Central Park in 1853, then the northern limits of the city. In July 1863, draft riots took place in Union Square: 2,000 were killed and federal troops were called out to keep the peace. In 1883 the most famous suspension bridge in history opened—the Brooklyn Bridge—making access to neighboring Brooklyn much easier (Midheaven trine Uranus sextile Jupiter/Neptune). The blizzard of March 1888 killed 200 and buried the city for days. In 1898 New York City was formed by the merger of five counties: New York (Manhattan), Kings (Brooklyn), Queens, Bronx, and Richmond (Staten Island). It was the first metropolitan government in the country (Midheaven opposition Mars trine Saturn).

In 1904, the first leg of New York's 230 mile subway opened; the same year, the Gen. Slocum sank in the Hudson with the loss of 1,021 lives (Ascendant square Moon). New York hosted two World's Fairs during this century: 1939 and 1964. On November 9, 1965, lights went out all over the city, as well as most of the northeastern U.S., when a power station at Niagara Falls failed (Midheaven semisquare Moon). There was a feeling of camaraderie and little, if any, crime that night, which is more than can be said about a recurrence on July 13, 1977. Then, hoodlums roamed the streets breaking windows and stealing everything in sight. But by then, New York was in the throes of a massive fiscal crisis that threatened to bankrupt the city. New York has always been a city where minorities were the rule rather than the exception, and today is no different. Many find the suburbs not only safer but more appealing due to the lower tax base. Muslim terrorists bombed the World Trade Center in the financial district at the end of February 1993 (Midheaven inconjunct Saturn, Ascendant opposition Moon). In September 2001, militant Islamic terrorists hijacked two airplanes and crashed them into the World Trade Center, killing nearly 3,000 people. The two towers fell to the ground in less than two hours, creating a massive dust cloud which shrouded lower Manhattan for days afterward. The NYSE was closed down, several subway tunnels were closed and the world's largest financial center was in a state of shock for weeks. New York City has been in a state of high alert ever since (Ascendant semisquare Mercury).

What can be said about New York that hasn't been said a thousand times before in magazines, movies, or the media? Everyone knows it's America's largest city and the chief port of entry. It's the financial, theatrical, garment, advertising, publishing, and corporate capital of the land. It's alternately rich and poor, glamorous and sleazy, noisy, exciting, and very expensive. It's the largest Irish city in the world, has half as many Puerto Ricans as live on that West Indian island, and more Jews than any other place outside Israel. It's home to the United Nations, the Statue of Liberty, the Empire State Building, Wall Street, and Times Square. Each year some seventeen million tourists visit this city which could be truly called the "Capital of the Western World." Each day about six and a half million people enter Manhattan to work, creating some of the most horrendous traffic jams on earth as they crowd the subways and trains, and try to get across the bridges and through the tunnels.

New York is a city of countless neighborhoods, each of them distinct in its own way. Often you can tell which area a resident comes from just by the accent (Mercury in Gemini sextile Uranus). New Yorkers are tolerant of all eccentrics (Mercury/Uranus=Ascendant) but hate pretense. If you've got the talent, you'll soon find out for they have no patience with anyone who's second best.

Most outsiders think New Yorkers are rude and pushy (Cancer rising, Moon in Capricorn), but it's just that they must insulate themselves from the hordes who descend on the city. They find refuge and solace in the ability to crawl into their shells and are thus shock resistant to traumas that would make other Americans cringe with fear. New York is a city that's interested in power and money (Sun conjunct Pluto in Taurus) as well as business and commerce. Natives are earthy, practical and often materialistic (Sun and Moon in earth signs). They may seem cold and indifferent to your plight (Moon in Capricorn square Neptune) until they get to know you better. An undercurrent of aggression and hostility that is felt (Mars in the twelfth house) is often due to crowded living conditions. This city is the most densely populated region in the country and in parts of Manhattan it approaches 100,000 per square mile.

Uranus in the second house points to one of the causes of the recent fiscal crisis: The city simply doled out too much in welfare to those less fortunate, and the poor just kept going there to collect. Saturn in the second house points to the eventual results of belt tightening and lowering people's expectations.

Despite all its problems and hazards, New York is still the most exciting and stimulating city in the U.S. Sam Johnson once said that whomever became bored with London was bored with life. The same could be said of New York, for it you can't find it there, it probably doesn't exist.

New York handles forty percent of all foreign trade in the country and each year it sees 26,000 vessels pass under the Verrazzano Bridge that connects Brooklyn with Staten Island. In its massive harbor, one of the finest in the world, is located the symbol of hope to all foreigners, the Statue of Liberty, and the symbol of hate, Ellis Island, where millions were often detained due to questionable background or disease. The city has the busiest international airport in the world (Kennedy) and is home to the corporate headquarters of such media as CBS, NBC and ABC. Almost seventy-five percent of the U.S. books and magazines are published there, and most of the advertising firms are located around Madison Avenue. It's also the largest garment center in the nation and home to six of the seven largest banks in the country.

Incorporated: February 12, 1653 (Dutch); June 22, 1665 (English); January 1, 1898 (consolidated)
Elevation: from 17 feet at the Battery to 242 feet at the Cloisters
Area: Manhattan, 23 square miles; Brooklyn, 70 square miles; Queens, 108 square miles; Bronx, 41 square miles; Richmond, 58 square miles; total, 300 square miles
Sources: *Manhattan Stories from Early New York History* by Sherman Williams states May 6, 1626; the question of Old Style or New Style was cleared up during a visit with researchers in Holland some years ago; *Brooklyn Long Island's Story* by Jacqueline Overton; Bronx New York Public Library

Bronx

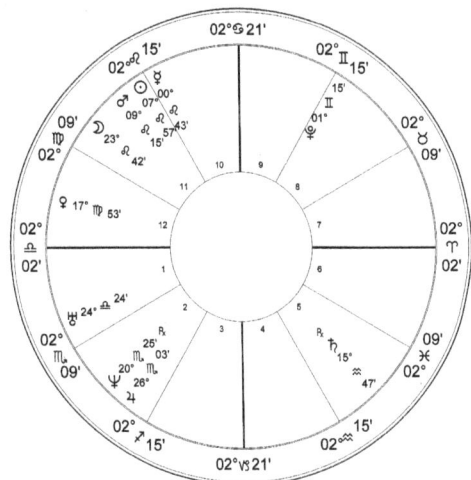

**July 31, 1639
73W54, 40N51
9:30 AM EST**

Founded by Jonas Bronck in 1639, it was part of Westchester County until 1874. Famous for the Bronx Zoo and Yankee Stadium, it has some of the worst slums in the world, and much of the southern part of this borough is a devastated ruin. Many buildings have fallen victim to the arsonist.

Brooklyn

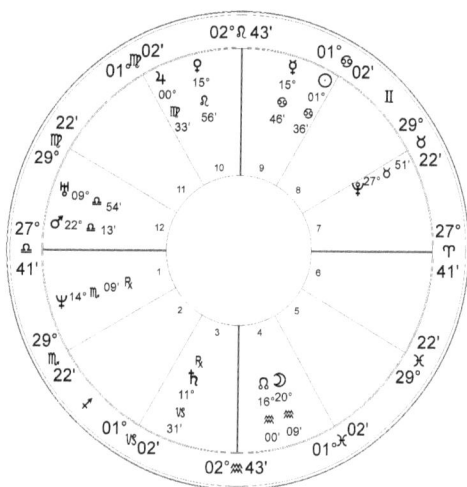

June 22, 1636
73W56, 40N38
2:10 PM EST

Founded in 1636, it was an independent city until 1898. Known as the City of Churches (ASC/MC=Jupiter), it's largely a bedroom community that housed the huddled masses entering this country. It's an independent acting city (Uranus rising) and rather boisterous (Mars just above the Ascendant). It has the largest downtown area in New York outside Manhattan and many diverse and intensely proud neighborhoods (Sun in Cancer).

Queens

Founded in 1642, it's a borough of garden apartments. It contains both of New York's airports (La Guardia and Kennedy) and Shea Stadium. Flushing Meadow Park housed both World's Fairs in past years.

Richmond

First settled in 1661, it was once the most isolated of all the boroughs until the Verrazzano Bridge was completed. Most commuters reach Manhattan via the ferry. Some of its area is still rural countryside, but the island is becoming increasingly industrialized with petrochemical plants.

Niagara Falls

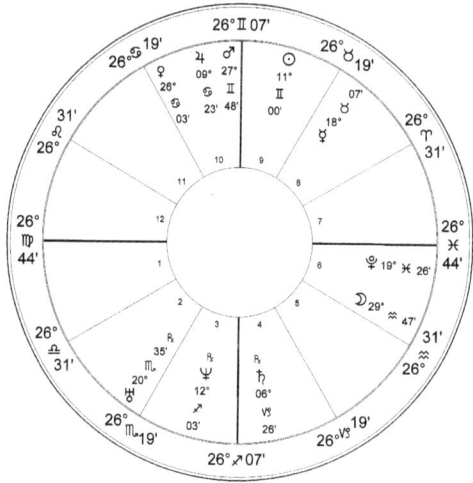

June 1, 1812
79W03, 43N06
1:19 PM EST

Long before the arrival of the white man, Indians marveled at what was to become the most famous falls in the world. Between 1745 and 1750, the French erected two forts in the region. Both were burned in 1795 after the Battle of Niagara. Settled as Manchester in 1806, it was formally founded in 1812 and burned by the British one year later (Midheaven conjunct Mars). A canal was constructed from 1852 to 1862 that connected the upper and lower parts of the Niagara River (Midheaven trine Neptune) and in 1879, the falls were illuminated for the first time. The View Falls Bridge collapsed in 1938 to be replaced by the Rainbow Bridge three years later (Midheaven trine Moon, Ascendant conjunct Saturn). Over the years, millions of honeymooners from around the world have gone there to marvel at the most spectacular display of water on the continent.

Incorporated: March 17, 1892
Elevation: 575 feet
Source: *Gazeteer of New York* by J.A. French

Rochester

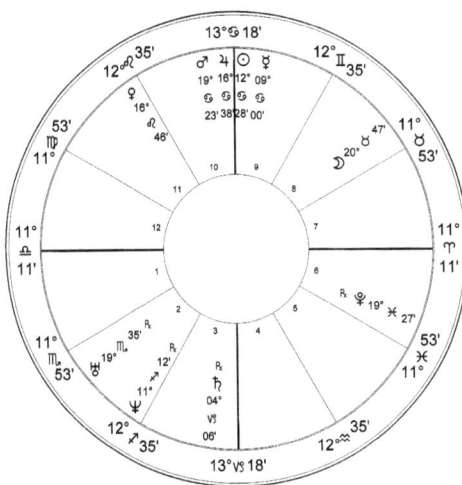

July 4, 1812
77W37, 43N10
12:18 PM EST

Founded during an Independence Day picnic in 1812, it was the nation's first boom town after the completion of the Erie Canal in 1825 (Ascendant trine Mars). Eastman established his Kodak factory there in 1888 and really put the city on the map. An ocean port since the completion of the St. Lawrence Seaway in 1959, it is the third largest city in the state.

The next time you take a photo or copy a document, think of Rochester, home of Eastman Kodak and Xerox. Also located there is the nation's largest optical company, Bausch and Lomb. Known as the Flour City in the 1840s, it was subsequently titled the Flower City due to its many gardens. A complacent and comfortable city (Libra rising), it possesses much self-confidence and quiet assurance (Sun conjunct Jupiter at Midheaven). A strong moral code pervades Rochester, making it somewhat dull and unexciting (Moon in Taurus square Venus). Well kept lawns show off the spacious homes of these people, who are reserved but neighborly.

Incorporated: June 9, 1834
Elevation: 515 feet
Area: 37 square miles
Source: *Rochester American Guide Series*; *New York American Guide Series* says May 5, 1812

Schenectady

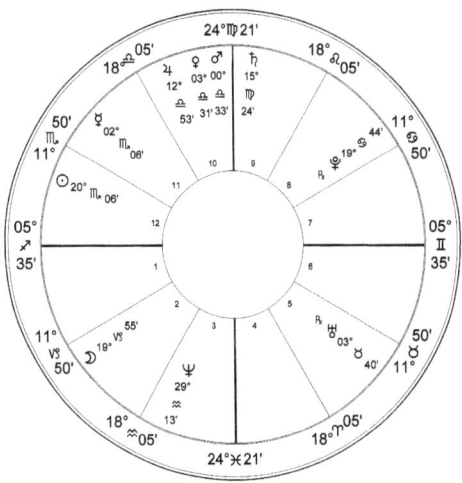

November 11, 1684
73W57, 42N49
8:09 AM EST

Purchased by the Dutch from the Indians in 1661, a patent was issued by Governor Dongan in 1664 which became the foundation of this city with a difficult name to spell or pronounce. In 1690 the French and Indians massacred the settlers and burned the community to the ground (Midheaven conjunct Mars). Queen's Fort was erected in 1705 and twenty-two years later free trade began with the Indians. The Erie Canal was finished in 1825 (Ascendant trine Jupiter) and in 1848 the first locomotive factory was opened. Thomas Edison moved his electric pant there in 1886 (Ascendant square Mercury).

Incorporated: March 26, 1798
Elevation: 220 feet
Source: Carolyn Dodson for the date; chart rectified

Syracuse

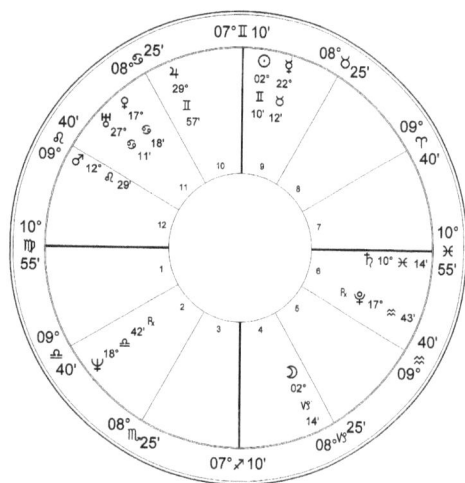

May 22, 1788
76W09, 43N03
12:22 PM EST

Founded in 1788, the first salt mine opened in 1796 and the first saltwork eight years later. The Erie Canal gave impetus to its economy after 1825 (Midheaven trine Saturn). During the late 19th century, salt mining declined but flour milling began to take its place. Syracuse today is a heavily industrialized community and manufactures an abundance of electrical products, as well as being the china center for the country.

Incorporated: December 14, 1847
Elevation: 400 feet
Area: 26 square miles
Source: *American Guide Series*

Troy

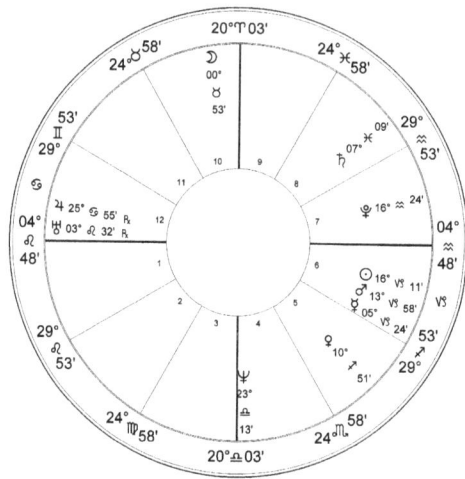

January 5, 1789
73W41, 42N44
6:05 PM EST

A town site was founded in 1786 and known as Vanderheyden's Ferry until 1789 when its name was changed. In 1823 Troy became a beef center and Sam Wilson, also known as Uncle Sam, gave his nickname to the product which became synonymous with the United States. Rensellear Polytechnic Institute was founded in 1824 (Midheaven sextile Jupiter) and between 1864 and 1873, Troy was a major steel producer.

Incorporated: 1816
Elevation: 34 feet
Source: Troy Public Library

Utica

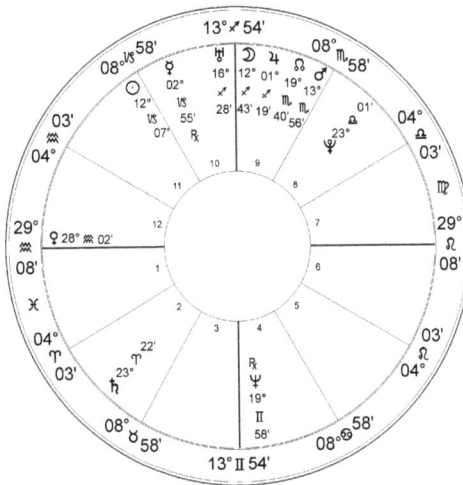

January 2, 1734
75W13, 43N06
10:03 AM EST

Land around Utica was granted to Cosby in 1734 and famous Fort Schuyler was erected in 1758 to stem the tide of Iroquois uprisings (Ascendant trine Uranus). On July 4, 1772, a public sale of the tract was held, but the first real settlement didn't occur until the winter of 1788 (Midheaven square Pluto). When it was deemed necessary to name the newfound community, the name Utica was drawn from a hat (Midheaven trine Neptune, Ascendant opposite Uranus). In 1825 the Erie Canal was completed and the city's economy soared overnight (Midheaven square Uranus). Woolen and cotton mills opened in 1847 and in 1879 F.W. Woolworth opened his first five and dime store in Utica.

Incorporated: February 13, 1832
Elevation: 500 feet
Source: *History of Utica* by L.C. Childs says winter 1788, while the Utica Public Library gave the date for the land deeds

North Carolina

**November 21, 1789
Fayetteville
78W53, 35N03
3:14 PM EST
Source: Rectified to give it Sun in Sagittarius, which I feel fits better than Scorpio**

In 1585, Sir Walter Raleigh established the ill-fated colony on Roanoke Island. After attempting to settle twice, he accepted defeat and went back to England. The first permanent European settlers came in 1653, and ten years later on March 24, 1683, the region was granted a charter—it was called Albemarle County. In 1677, colonists overthrew the governor and in 1691 the entire region began to be ruled from Charleston, South Carolina. Hundreds of settlers were slain during the Tuscarora War of 1711-13, and the following year North Carolina separated from South Carolina. The pirate Bluebeard was killed here in 1718, and in 1729 it became a royal colony. On May 20, 1775, patriots adopted the Mecklenburg Declaration of Independence, the first in the nation. Several battles took place in the state during the Revolution, and in 1789 North Carolina ratified the constitution. With the removal of the Cherokee Indians to more western lands, the interior was made safe for settlement. Gold was discovered in 1801, and until the gold rush of 1849, North Carolina led the nation in production of this valuable mineral. On May 20, 1861, this state seceded from the Union and wasn't readmitted until July 11, 1868. After 1890, tobacco became the chief industry, and in 1903 the Wright brothers made the first successful airplane flight at Kitty Hawk. North Carolina is the chief industrial state of the South and has come a long way since the turn of the century.

North Carolina leads the nation in the production of textiles, furniture, and cigarettes. It's first in sweet potatoes, second in turkeys, fourth in peanuts and fifth in chickens. Minerals include mica, feldspar, and lithium.

Area: 52, 586 square miles

Asheville

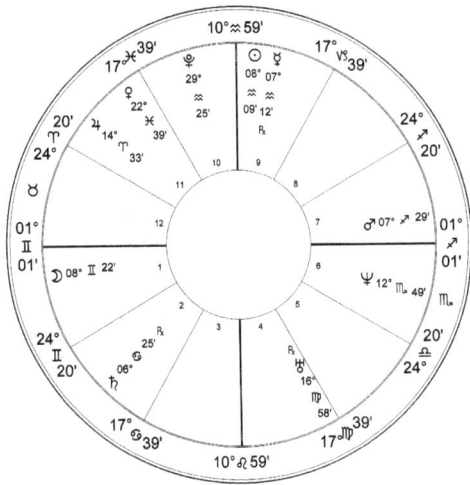

**January 27, 1798
82W33, 35N36
12:55 PM EST**

First settled in 1794, Asheville was formally founded during a town meeting four years later. A turnpike linked it to other southern towns in 1824. In 1913 the city's most famous structure, Biltmore, was completed; it is the largest private house in the world open to the public. During the Depression, the tobacco industry started its decline and Asheville turned to tourism to fill the gap. Just west of the city is the Great Smokies National Park

Incorporated: March 8, 1883
Elevation: 1,985 feet
Source: Asheville in the Sky by Martha Allen; time from American Federation of Astrologers and Mercury Hour

Chapel Hill

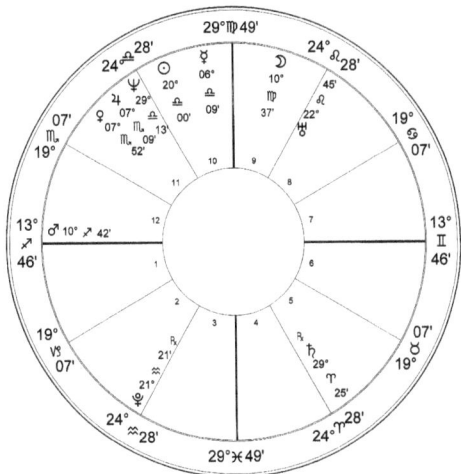

**October 12, 1792
79W04, 35N55
10:48 AM EST**

Chosen to be the site of the University of North Carolina in 1792, the cornerstone was laid exactly one year later. The university opened in 1795 and from 1868 to 1875 it was closed during the rule of the carpetbaggers (Ascendant opposite Moon).

Incorporated: Unknown
Elevation: 501 feet
Source: North Carolina State Library and Archives

Charlotte

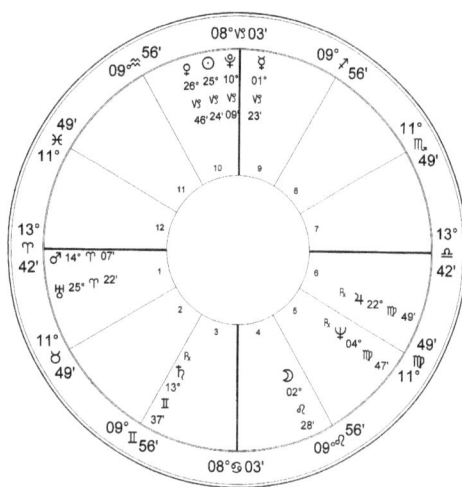

January 15, 1767
80W51, 35N13
11:19 AM EST

First settled by Moravians from Pennsylvania in 1750, a town site was platted in 1767 and incorporated the following year (Midheaven conjunct Pluto). The nation's first cry for freedom, the Mecklenburg Declaration of Independence, was issued on May 20, 1775 (Ascendant conjunct Uranus), a full year before Congress in Philadelphia decided to make its intentions known. During 1780 the city was occupied by the British (Ascendant trine Neptune). Gold was discovered near Charlotte in 1800 and the nation's first gold rush was underway. A mint was established there in 1837 to coin the valuable mineral. In 1865 the last meeting of the Confederate cabinet took place in this largest city of the Carolinas.

Charlotte is the crossroads of the Carolinas, a youngish boom town (Aries rising), aggressive and plucky. A cheerful and buoyant community, it is known as the greatest church going city in the world after Edinburgh (Sun trine Jupiter). Charlotte is a center for Calvinist Presbyterian philosophy, and the city is thought of as being rather pious. Tolerant of gambling and liquor (Neptunian the fifth house), it is the textile center of America and the largest industrial center between Baltimore and Atlanta.

Incorporated: November 7, 1768
Elevation: 720 feet
Area: 76 square miles
Source: Charlotte City Hall

Durham

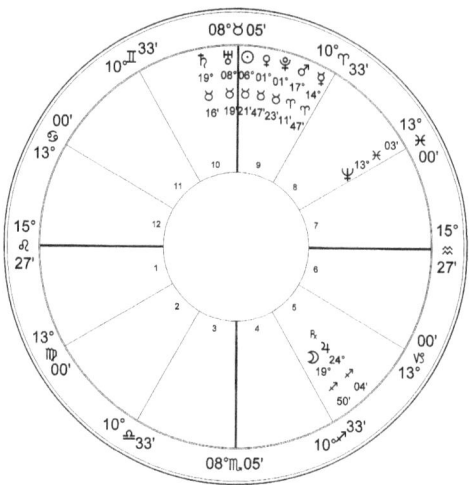

April 26, 1853
78W54, 36N00
12:20 PM EST

Settled in 1750, the villages of Durhamville and Prattsburg weren't really founded until 1850. When the railroad arrived in 1853, Durham got the edge and the present city was born. Robert Morris opened his tobacco plant in 1858 (Midheaven sextile Neptune) and the American Tobacco Company was established in 1881 (Ascendant trine Sun). On April 26, 1865, General Johnston surrendered to General Sherman shortly before both sides raided a nearby tobacco warehouse.

Durham manufactures twenty-five percent of the nation's cigarettes and has the highest per capita concentration of scientists and engineers in the country. The surrounding region is known as "The Research Triangle."

Incorporated: April 10, 1869
Elevation: 405 feet
Area: 41 square miles
Source: *Durham* by F.A. and J.A. Kostyn

Greensboro

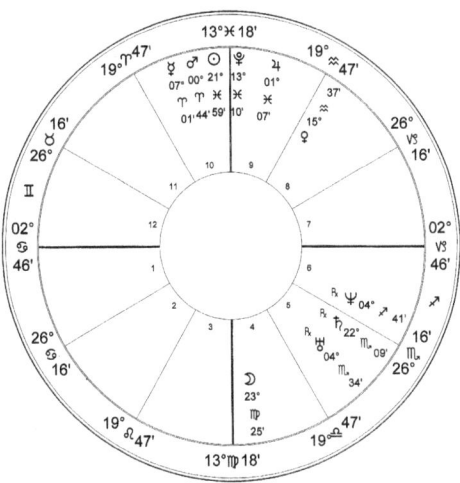

March 12, 1808
79W48, 36N04
11:57 AM EST

Designated as the county seat in 1808, it was the temporary capital of the state during the latter days of the Civil War. Greensboro witnessed the first lunch counter sit-in on February 1, 1960 (Ascendant conjunct Uranus), and shortly after, the civil rights movement was born. During 1980 Greensboro experienced some racial tension as the Ku Klux Klan demonstrated, causing much concern among the citizens of this peaceful community. Greensboro is a large insurance center and textile manufacturer.

Incorporated: March 28, 1870
Elevation: 838 feet
Area: 61 square miles
Source: Greensboro Public Library

Raleigh

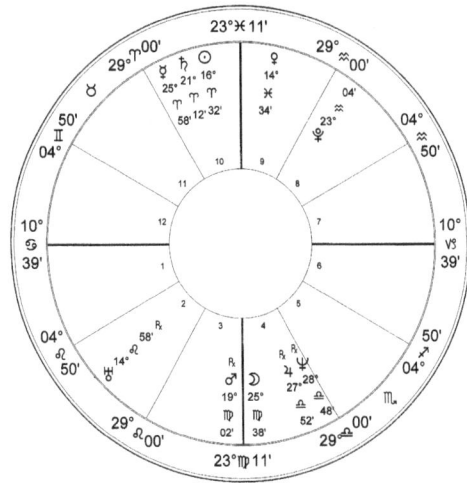

April 5, 1792
78W38, 35N46
10:51 AM EST

First settled in 1741, it was chosen by the legislature to be their new headquarters in 1792. Fires in 1818 (Ascendant square Neptune), 1821 (Midheaven conjunct Saturn), and 1831 erased many of the colonial structures downtown. Occupied by Union forces in April 1865 (Ascendant sesquare Saturn), it managed to escape Sherman's destruction even though part of the city lay in ruins.

Raleigh is a happy and fun loving town, which is unusual as political centers are not usually known for their gaiety. Democratic and unpretentious (Pisces Midheaven), politicians are still treated as people and not as gods. There's also little worship of the old line families (Cancer rising sesquare Pluto). A trifle boring and bland, Raleigh is affable and informally friendly. Today, the city is a center for scientific and industrial research (Moon in Virgo).

Incorporated: February 7, 1795
Elevation: 363 feet
Area: 49 square miles
Source: Raleigh Public Library

Winston-Salem

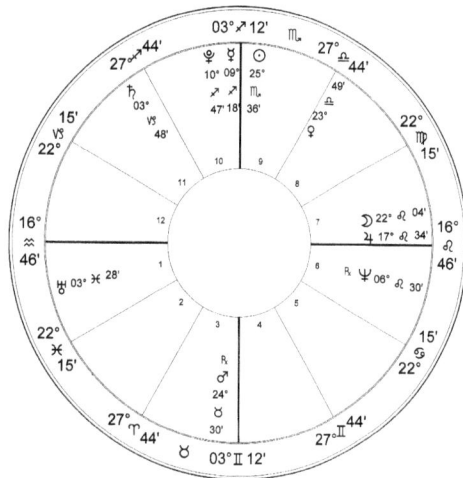

November 17, 1753
80W15, 36N06
12:38 PM EST

In 1752, a group of Moravians purchased land in what later became known as the Wachovia Tract. Arriving from Pennsylvania the following year, they founded the city of Salem on January 6, 1766 and Winston on May 12, 1849. Because both communities had the same destiny, they merged in 1913. The first tobacco plant opened in 1773 (Midheaven sextile Venus trine Moon) and cotton mills were founded in 1836 (Ascendant sextile Jupiter). R.J. Reynolds opened his tobacco plant in 1872 (Midheaven square Saturn) and is now the largest employer in the city.

Incorporated: January 27, 1913
Elevation: 860 feet
Area: 58 square miles
Source: *Forsyth* by Adelaide L. Fries

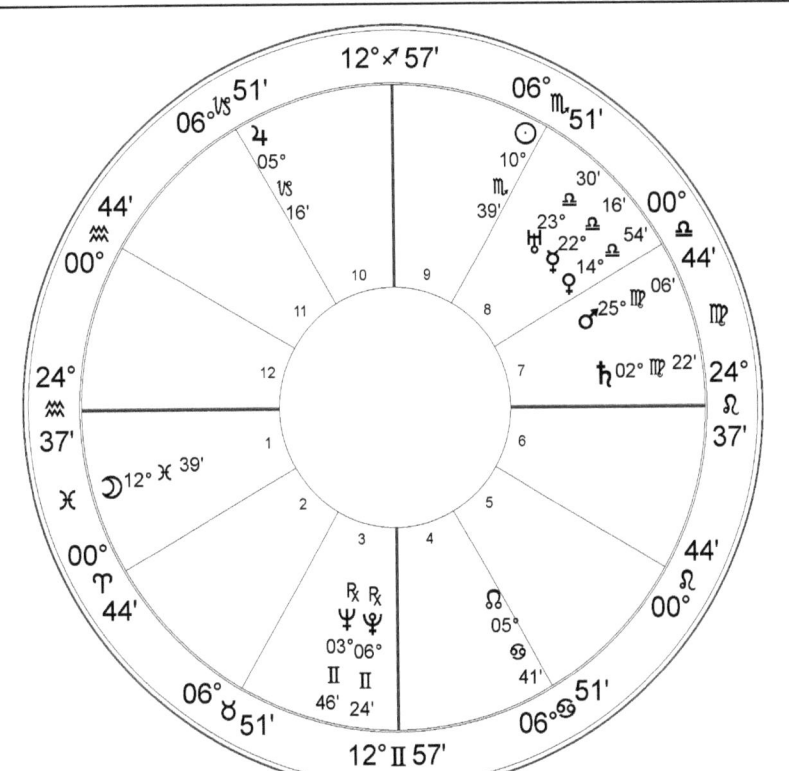

North Dakota

November 2, 1889
Bismarck
100W47, 46N48
2:40 PM CST
Source: *New York Times* says 3:40 p.m. in Washington

In 1803 the U.S. acquired most of this state in the Louisiana Purchase, and nine years later the first settlement sprang up at Pembina, populated by Scottish and Irish families from Canada. On March 2, 1861 the Dakota Territory was created and in the years before statehood many battles were fought with the Sioux. On November 1, 1889, the Dakota Territory was separated and North Dakota entered as either the thirty-ninth or fortieth state—no one knows for sure. It was the first state to adopt a presidential primary (in 1912), the first referendum (in 1914) and the first recall procedure (in 1920). Oil was discovered in 1951, and nine years later the massive Garrison Dam was finished across the Missouri.

Almost ninety percent of the land is farmed and North Dakota leads the nation in spring wheat, barley and flaxseed. It ranks second in total wheat production after Kansas. It's the most rural of all states in the country.

Area: 70,665 square miles

Bismarck

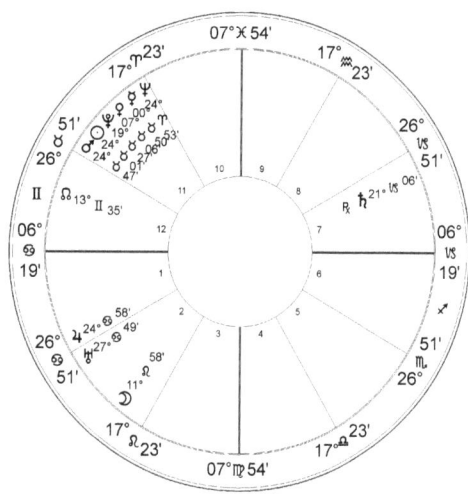

May 14, 1872
100W47, 46N48
7:51 AM CST

Founded as Edwinton in 1872, its name was changed three years later to honor the chancellor of Germany, from where so many of its early settlers had come. In 1881 and again in 1951 (Midheaven conjunct Sun/Mars), the Missouri overflowed its banks and almost submerged the city. Bismarck was made capital of the state in 1883 (Midheaven sextile Pluto). Two years after the old capitol building burned (1932), the new and radical skyscraper capitol building was completed. Looking more like an office building than the seat of the legislature, it towers over the plains and can be seen for miles

Incorporated: January 14, 1875
Elevation: 1,674 feet
Source: *North Dakota of Today* by Zena Trinka

Fargo

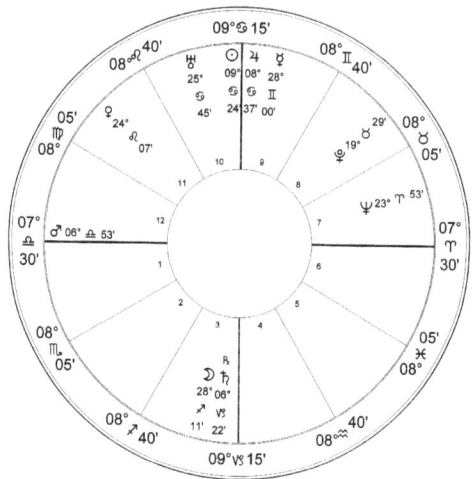

July 1, 1871
96W48, 46N53
12:30 PM CST

Founded by the railroad in 1871, citizens of this new town were arrested the following year for selling liquor to the Indians (Ascendant conjunct Mars). A fire in 1893 burned most of the downtown (Ascendant opposition Neptune) and four years later an ice jam on the Red river completely wrecked the waterfront (Ascendant trine Mercury). Along with Sioux Falls, Fargo was the divorce capital of the nation around the turn of the 20th century. Fargo holds the record for being the coldest overall city in the country, even though its snowfall is not as great as cities further south. It is the largest city between Minneapolis and the Rockies.

Incorporated: January 15, 1875
Elevation: 907 feet
Source: North Dakota Historical Society

Grand Forks

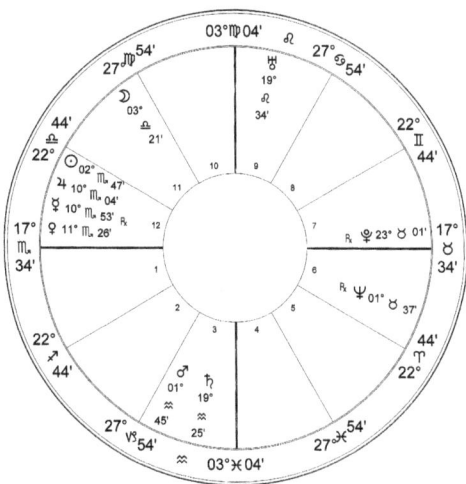

October 26, 1875
97W03, 47N55
8:30 AM CST

First settled in 1871, a plat filed in 1875 gave birth to the present city. The cornerstone of the University of North Dakota was laid in 1883 (Midheaven sextile Jupiter) and a tornado four years later caused extensive damage (Midheaven semisquare Jupiter/Mercury).

Incorporated: 1881
Elevation: 830 feet
Source: *American Guide Series*

Minot

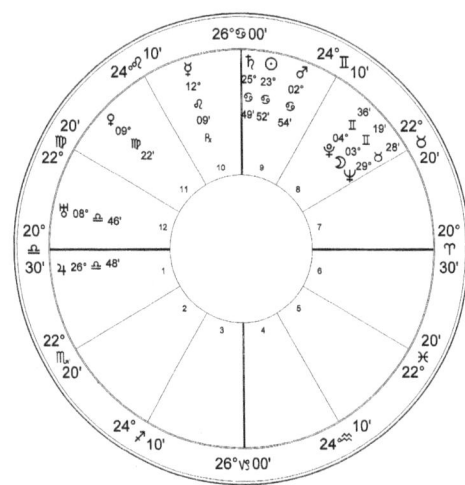

July 16, 1887
101W18, 48N14
Noon MST

Settled in May 1885, a tent town sprang up two years later with the arrival of the railroad. On July 16, 1887, the town was formally founded, incorporated and named for a friend of Theodore Roosevelt, who came to this region to rid himself of asthma. Minot has endured many floods during its short history. Those of 1904 (Midheaven conjunct Mercury), 1916 (Ascendant square Mercury), 1923 (Ascendant sesquare Mars) and 1927 were quite damaging.

Incorporated: 1887
Elevation: 1,557 feet
Source: *American Guide Series*

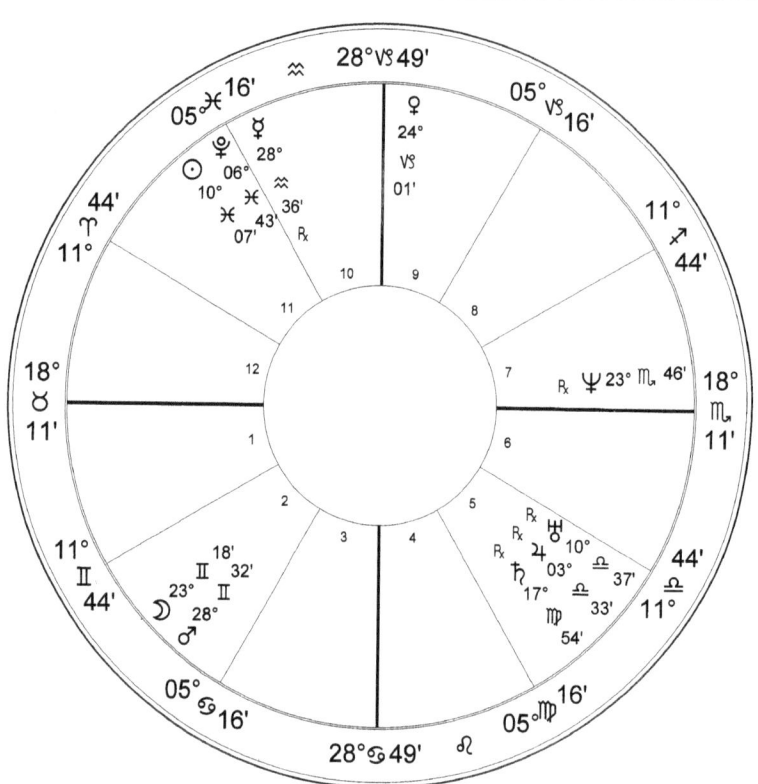

Ohio

**March 1, 1803
Chillicothe
82W59, 39N20
9:30 AM LMT
Source:** Ohio State Historical Society says the legislature first met on March 1, 1803 at 9:30 a.m. in Chillicothe

After the French and Indian War in 1763, Britain won the region from the French. Early settlements at New Philadelphia in 1772 and Chillicothe and Piqua in 1780 were destroyed by the Indians, who conducted raids during the 1780s. In 1783, the U.S. acquired the region, and on July 13, 1787, it became part of the Northwest Territory. In 1788 the first permanent settlement was made at Marietta. More severe fighting with the Indians resulted in General Anthony Wayne defeating the Indians at Fallen Timbers in 1794. Without the president ever signing a formal bill of admission, Ohio's first legislature met in 1803 after the Enabling Act and its constitution had been approved. Ohio is the only state to enter the Union like this. During the War of 1812, Admiral Perry defeated the British on Lake Erie in 1813, and during the 1840s many canals were completed throughout the state. The border with Michigan was settled in 1835 without one drop of bloodshed, placing Toledo in Ohio. The abolitionist movement began in Ohio and during the Civil War, Confederates almost captured the town of New Lisbon. Floods in 1913 caused extensive damage along the Ohio and Miami Rivers in the southwestern part of the state.

Ohio is the nation's third largest industrial state and it leads the U.S. in production of rubber tires, playing cards, business machines, glassware, and cutlery. The chief mineral resource is coal. It's first in lime, second in pig iron, and fifth in coal.

Area: 41,222 square miles

Akron

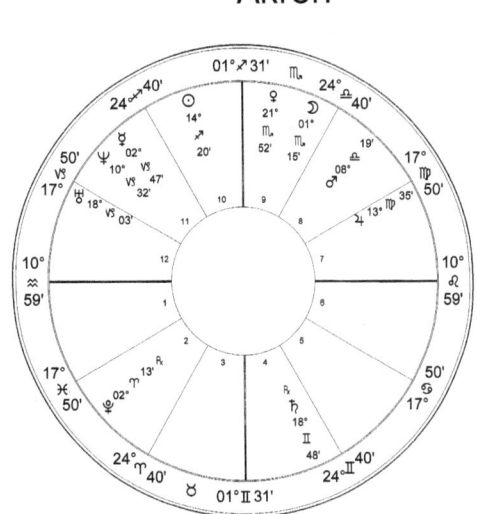

**December 6, 1825
81W31, 41N05
11:23 AM EST**

First settled on February 12, 1812, the town site was laid out thirteen years later. In 1827 a canal linked Akron to Lake Erie and nine years later to Pittsburgh. The first rubber factory opened in 1870 (Midheaven conjunct Uranus, Ascendant trine Mercury) and Akron was on its way to becoming the "Rubber Capital of the World." Firms like Goodyear, Goodrich, Firestone, General Tire and Mohawk helped America enter the automobile age, and today this city is also the center of the trucking industry.

Incorporated: January 21, 1865
Elevation: 950 feet
Area: 58 square miles
Source: *Akron* by Karl Grismer

Canton

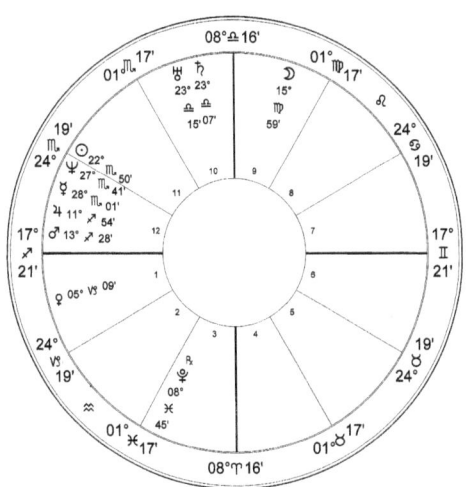

**November 15, 1805
81W23, 40N48
9:19 AM EST**

First settled in 1805, Canton gave birth to professional football and houses the Football Hall of Fame. Jim Thorpe was elected its first president in 1920. Canton is a pleasant city with unusually wide streets.

Incorporated: 1854
Elevation: 1,050 feet
Area: 19 square miles
Source: *The Stark County Story* by Edward Heald

Cincinnati

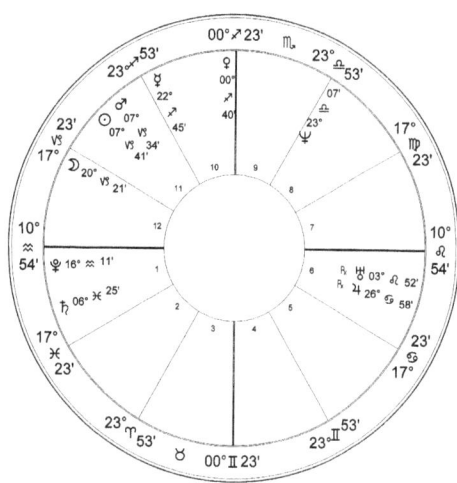

December 28, 1788
84W31, 39N06
10:00 AM EST

Founded in 1788 by Robert Patterson, three months after he chose the site and named it Losantiville, two years later it was changed to honor the Society of the Cincinnati (Aquarius rising). In 1811 the first steamboat chugged up the Ohio on its way to New Orleans. During 1830 (Ascendant opposition Neptune) and again in 1849 (Midheaven opposition Uranus), the city was stricken by cholera. During 1862, Cincinnati was placed under martial law because of wavering sympathies (Midheaven conjunct Pluto). Incline railways were finally completed in 1870, which alleviated overcrowding along the waterfront (Midheaven sextile Uranus, Ascendant sextile Pluto). In 1884 the last of two summers of riots ceased, but the corruption which caused the riots continued to flourish (Midheaven conjunct Saturn). Cincinnati became the scene of a battle regarding community standards in 1990 when the erotically graphic photos of Robert Mapplethorpe were displayed in a local gallery (Midheaven opposition Mercury). Before long, the city's gay rights protection law was overturned. In April 2001, several nights of rioting and civil disturbance convulsed Cincinnati because of over-zealous police action after shooting a black teenager (Midheaven inconjunct Sun/Mars, Ascendant semisquare Jupiter).

Once the largest city west of the Alleghenies, it was called Porkopolis during the 1840s because of its huge packing industry. Longfellow had a better description of the place: he called it the "Queen City of the West." During the mid-19th century, Cincinnati was the most densely populated city in the country, inhabited largely by Germans as the region reminded them of the Rhine Valley. A highly cultured city (Venus conjunct Midheaven), Cincinnati is known for its fine orchestra and university. It has remembered to be elegant and graceful like the old South, yet establishing itself as a major industrial city. Cincinnati has a very mature outlook on life, calm and poised, serene and complacent. A conservative and moral city (both lights in Capricorn), its natives are friendly but reserved (Aquarius Ascendant) and rather laconic. Being sedately satisfied with their lives, Cincinnatians live in a city with much class but little glamour. However, the city is situated in a beautiful setting and the view from Mt. Adams or Eden Park of the Ohio River Valley is a breathtaking sight to behold.

Cincinnati is the world's largest producer of machine tools, the leader in soap products (Proctor and Gamble) and playing cards, and the largest inland coal port in the country.

Incorporated: March 1, 1819
Elevation: 550 feet
Area: 78 square miles
Source: *The Life of Col. Israel Ludlow* by Henry Teetor; many other sources state the city was founded between December 27 and 29, 1788; *Builders in New Fields* by Charlotte Conover says September 22, 1788, the date the site was chosen

Cleveland

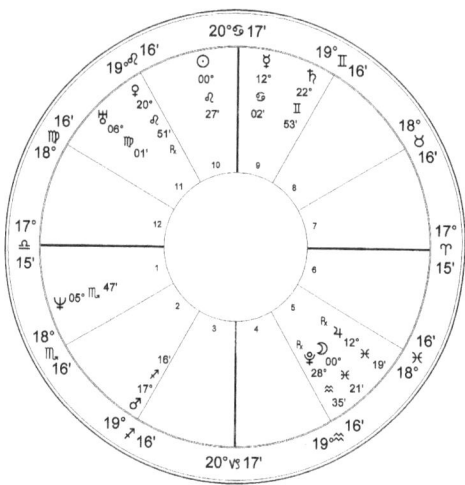

July 22, 1796
81W42, 41N30
11:50 AM EST

Founded by Moses Cleaveland in 1796, it was part of the Western Reserve which belonged to Connecticut. It was laid out like a New England town with a public square, now the heart of the city. In 1825 a canal was completed to the Ohio River and in 1832 the city's name was changed to accommodate a newspaper masthead by shortening one letter. Rockefeller arrived in 1860, one year after oil was discovered in nearby Pennsylvania. Ten years later he founded what was to become the Standard Oil Company (Midheaven sextile Sun, Ascendant square Jupiter). In 1944 a liquid gas tank exploded in the industrial district, sending 135 to their death (Midheaven conjunct Mars). In 1966 a race riot erupted which caused the election shortly afterward of Cleveland's first Black mayor, Carl Stokes (Ascendant semisquare Moon and Saturn).

Cleveland is a working class city known for its muscle and toil. Composed of many varied ethnic communities, it was once known as an economic bellwether due to the fact that it had one percent of everything in the country. One of the great corporate centers of the U.S., Cleveland defaulted due to the failure of the business community to cooperate with the politicians. Cleveland also has transformed its formerly polluted shoreline and river, which once caught fire due to the number of chemicals dumped into it. Cleveland has the longest shoreline of any American city and its eastern suburbs are some of the finest in the nation.

Cleveland is headquarters to many companies and is one of the great steel centers of the U.S. It's also the largest iron ore port in the country.

Incorporated: March 5, 1836
Elevation: 660 feet
Area: 77 square miles
Source: *The Western Reserve* by Harland Hatcher

center for the Union armies and held the largest prisoner of war camp in the country. During March 1913 a flood killed more than 100 people (Ascendant square Jupiter) and in 1930 a fire broke out in the state penitentiary that took the lives of 320 inmates (Ascendant square Mars).

Columbus is a clean and open town (Sun in Aquarius) with a sleepy ambience. Neat, smug and provincial (Cancer rising), some consider it dull and overly conservative. Natives are deliberate and in no big hurry to do anything, but during business hours Columbus is busy, thriving and bustling. Life tends to center around politics, as this is the state capital and the home of The Ohio State University. But Columbus is a home oriented town and after dark the downtown area is deserted. Home of many insurance companies, as well as the largest nonprofit laboratory in the world (the Batelle Institute), Columbus has been called the quintessential American city. Market researchers often try out their products here before you see them on the shelves. Columbus seems to know what consumers desire (Cancer rising, Moon at Midheaven).

Incorporated: March 3, 1834
Elevation: 780 feet
Area: 173 square miles
Source: *American Guide Series*

Columbus

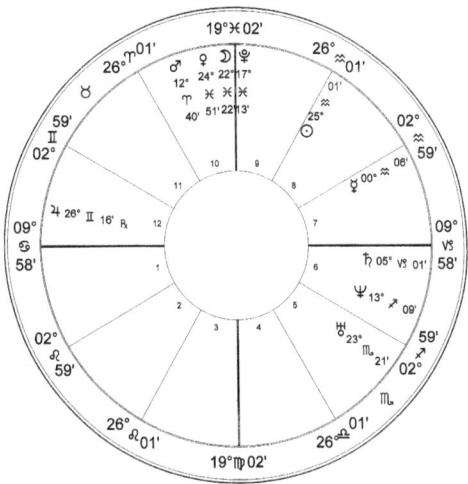

February 14, 1812
83W00, 39N58
2:17 PM EST

Franklintown was settled in 1797 across the Scioto River from present day Columbus, which was chosen to be the new state capital in 1812. The first sale of lots took place the following June and in 1816 the legislature moved here from Chillicothe (Midheaven conjunct Venus). By 1833, canals were completed to both Lake Erie and the Ohio River, the same year the National Road (now US 40) made Columbus the crossroads of Ohio. During the Civil War the city was a major military supply

Dayton

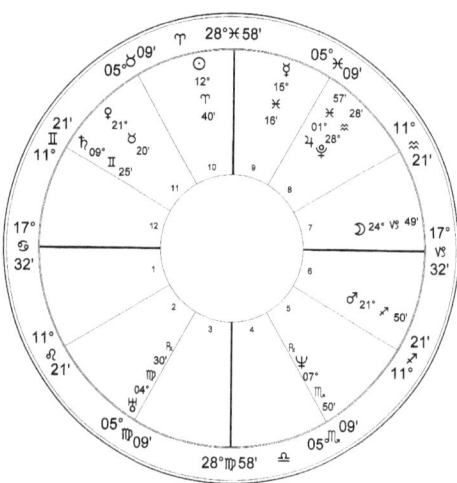

April 1, 1796
84W12, 39N45
11:50 AM EST

Founded by Robert Patterson (who also founded Cincinnati and Lexington) in 1796, it was connected to the Ohio River via canal in 1829. Dayton was a center of Copperhead activity during the Civil War (Midheaven square Uranus). The first glass office building in the world was erected here in 1886. Throughout the years, Dayton has suffered extensively from floods as the Miami River inundated a good portion of the city. Those of 1805 (Ascendant semisquare Saturn), 1883 and March 1913 (Midheaven opposition Moon) were particularly bad. The last one caused 361 deaths and shortly afterward a flood control system was completed, much to the relief of Daytonians.

Dayton is known as the "Birthplace of Aviation" as the Wright brothers lived there for many years. It has many aircraft plants within its limits (Uranus in the second house) and is the home of NCR, the cash register people.

Incorporated: March 8, 1841
Elevation: 574 feet
Area: 49 square miles
Source: *American Guide Series*

Springfield

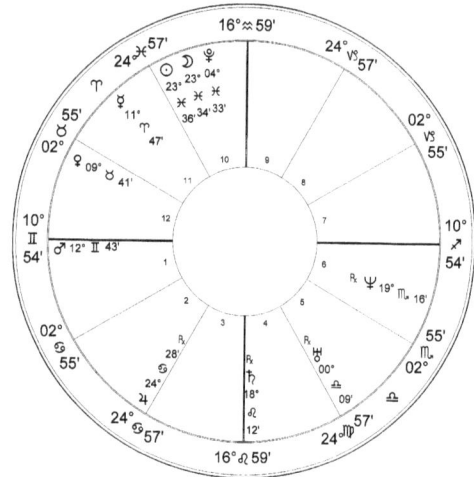

March 14, 1801
83W49, 39N55
10:26 AM EST

Founded in 1799, it was platted two years later. With the arrival of the National Road (now US 40) in 1838 (Midheaven conjunct Sun) and the railroad in 1846 (Midheaven opposition Uranus), Springfield became the leading industrial and commercial center of western Ohio.

Incorporated: March 21, 1850
Elevation: 980 feet
Source: Ohio State Historical Society

Toledo

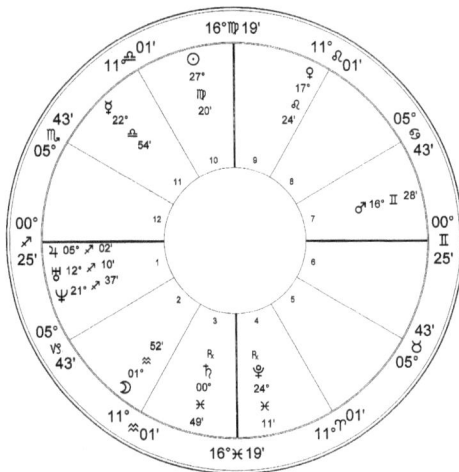

September 20, 1817
83W33, 41N39
11:47 AM EST

Port Lawrence was founded in 1817 and Vistula on December 19, 1833. Upon merging in 1837 to form Toledo, they renamed the communities after a city in one of Washington Irving's novels, as he was popular with one of the council members. In 1835 Toledo was caught in the middle of a brief war between Michigan and Ohio over who controlled the region. Ohio won without shedding a drop of blood (Midheaven sextile Jupiter, Ascendant conjunct Uranus). A canal linked Toledo to the Ohio River in 1845 (Ascendant sextile Mercury). Libby Glass Company opened for business in 1888 (Ascendant sextile Jupiter) and before long, Toledo was the leading producer of that product in the world. Those famous scales are also made there, along with auto parts. Toledo is the nation's fifth largest rail center, the largest oil and gas refining center between Chicago and New York and the biggest coal shipping port in the U.S.

Toledo is a typical blue collar industrial town, filled with neighborhoods that contain many big houses with well kept laws Its natives are tolerant about the law (Venus in the ninth house, Jupiter rising) and really like being a small city (Sun in Virgo). It has no desire to rank as number one in anything.

Incorporated: January 7, 1837
Elevation: 587 feet
Area: 86 square miles
Source: Ohio State Historical Society; *Early History of the Maumee Valley* by John Gunckel says August 23, 1794 when Fort Industry was founded

Youngstown

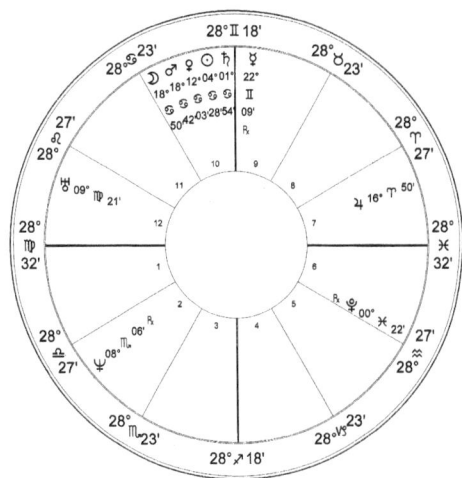

June 25, 1797
80W39, 41N06
11:58 AM EST

Founded in 1797, Ohio's first blast furnace was completed here in 1802 (Midheaven conjunct Sun) using charcoal and limestone. During the canal building era of the 19th century, Youngstown was connected to both Pennsylvania and Lake Erie. In 1892 the first steel plant opened (Ascendant square Uranus) and this city today ranks as the fourth largest producer of steel in the U.S.

Incorporated: 1868
Elevation: 960 feet
Area: 34 square miles
Source: *History of Youngstown* by Joseph Butler

Oklahoma

November 16, 1907
Guthrie
97W25, 35N53
9:16 AM CST
Source: *Los Angeles Times* says 10:16 a.m. in Washington

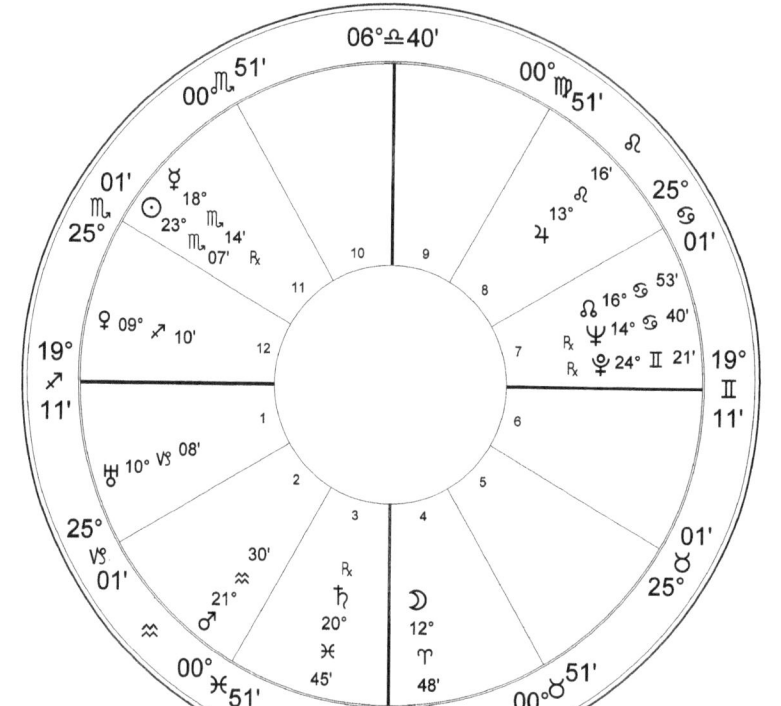

America acquired most of Oklahoma in the Louisiana Purchase and in 1821, the Santa Fe Trail began crossing the region. Between 1823 and 1842, many eastern Indian tribes were forced to move to this area, known as Indian Territory until 1889 when it was thrown open for settlement. During the first day, more than 50,000 settlers poured in and founded many communities before nightfall. On May 2, 1890 the Oklahoma Territory was created; three years later, the Cherokee Strip was thrown open for settlement. Oil was discovered in 1897 and ten years later Oklahoma became a state. During the Dust Bowl years of the Depression, Oklahoma was hard hit and thousands migrated to California and other points west. In 1970, the Arkansas River was finally made navigable, opening up Tulsa and Muskogee as river ports.

Oklahoma is a leader in petroleum production, and oil wells even dot the front yard of the capitol building in Oklahoma City. Natural gas is the second largest industry, and Oklahoma ranks second in winter wheat and sixth in cattle. The federal government had the last laugh during the early part of the 20th century when it found that the supposed worthless land on which the Indian tribes were settled contained some of the biggest reserves of oil in the world. Many of the Indians are millionaires today.

Area: 69,919 square miles

Lawton

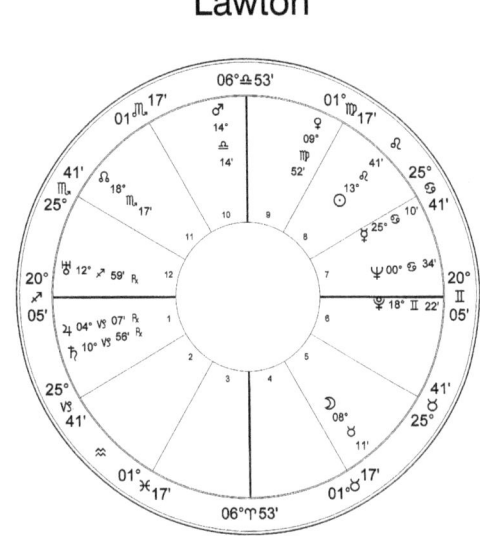

August 6, 1901
98W25, 34N37
4:00 PM CST

In 1901, a lottery was held to promote development in this area. Five days later, the U.S. Land Office was opened and Lawton became a county seat. Nearby Fort Sill, established in 1869, is the chief employer in the region.

Incorporated: Unknown
Elevation: 1,116 feet
Source: *American Guide Series*

Muskogee

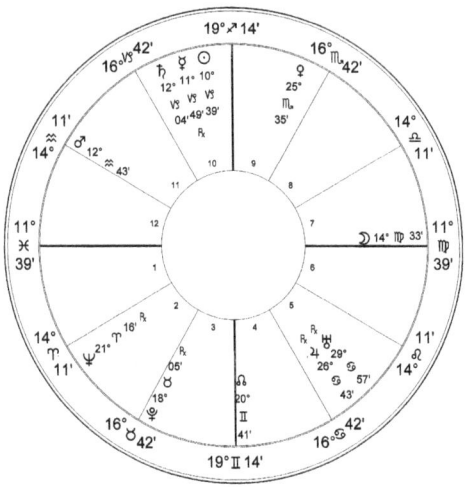

January 1, 1872
95W22, 35N45
10:52 AM CST

Founded by the railroad on New Year's Day 1872, its importance grew with the discovery of natural gas and petroleum in 1904 (Midheaven conjunct Mercury/Saturn). The U.S. Indian Agency for the Five Civilized Tribes is located in this city, which was formative in bringing statehood to Oklahoma.

Incorporated: March 19, 1898
Elevation: 617 feet
Source: Muskogee Public Library

Oklahoma City

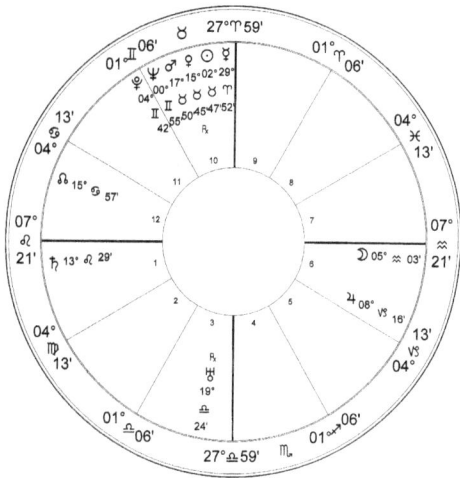

April 22, 1889
97W30, 35N30
12:10 PM CST

At high noon on April 22, 1889, a gun went off announcing the beginning of the great Oklahoma land rush. Before nightfall, more than 10,000 had settled in this region. In nearby Norman, also founded on the same day, is the University of Oklahoma which was founded in 1892. Oil was discovered in 1928 (Ascendant trine Jupiter) one year after Oklahoma City became the first community in the U.S. to install parking meters (Midheaven conjunct Pluto). Capital of the state since 1910 (Midheaven conjunct Mars), oil wells dot the front lawn of the state's capitol building. In mid-April 1995, the Murrah Federal Building was destroyed when a car bomb went off, killing 168 people, including many infants; the nine floors of the structure pancaked (Midheaven square Sun/Mars, Ascendant square Pluto). It was the most devastating act of terrorism to date on American soil.

After Jacksonville, Oklahoma City is the largest city in area in the country. Plenty of cheap land and plenty of room on which to grow has created a very prosperous community. Its natives are solid, businesslike, and rather materialistic (Sun in Taurus). They have a distaste for glitter and show (Saturn rising in Leo) and prefer to center their interests on sports and religion (Leo rising). Oklahoma City is the third largest cattle market in the country and has a large meat packing industry.

Incorporated: August 12, 1890
Elevation: 1,194 feet
Area: 621 square miles
Source: *Story of Oklahoma* by Muriel Wright; *American Guide Series*

Tulsa

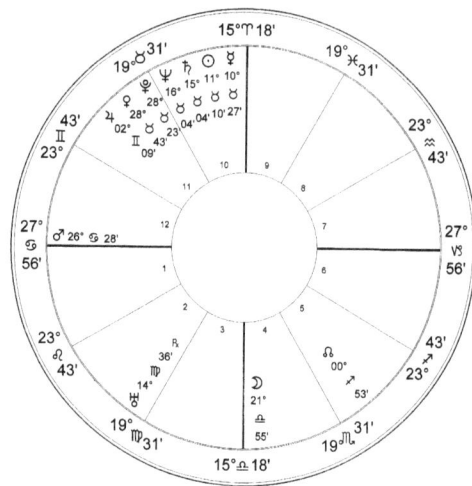

May 1, 1882
95W55, 36N10
10:42 AM CST

Even though a post office was established at Tulsey Town in 1879, formal settlement didn't begin until the railroad arrived three years later. Once known as a peaceful and orderly community, the discovery of oil across the river in 1901 changed Tulsa into a rip-roaring boom town (Ascendant square Jupiter). Soon it was calling itself the "Oil Capital of the World." Due to the arrival of cheap Negro labor, a race riot occurred in 1921 that killed thirty-six people (Ascendant square Pluto).

Located in the heart of the Bible Belt, Tulsa is a city of churches. The Boston Avenue Methodist church is one of the most beautiful places of worship in the country. Its most famous campus, Oral Roberts University, is probably the most attractive and distinctive looking architecturally in the U.S. Tulsa is a down to earth city which takes pride in its architecture (Cancer Ascendant) and does most of its entertaining at home.

Incorporated: January 18, 1898
Elevation: 804 feet
Area: 181 square miles
Source: *Tulsa* by Angie Debo

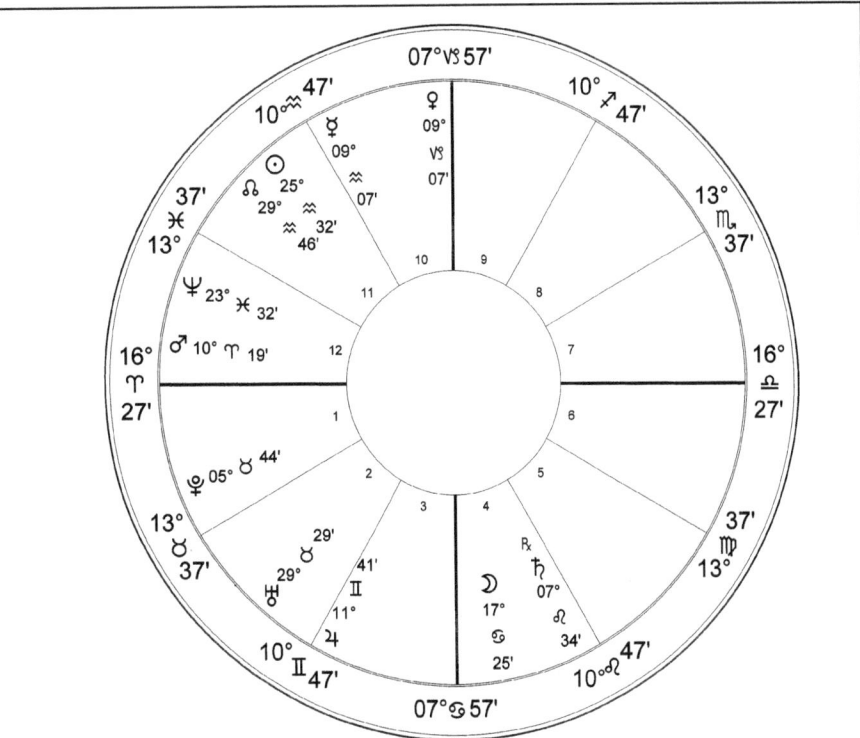

Oregon

February 14, 1859
Salem
123W02, 44N56
9:10 AM PST
Source: Rectified

On May 7, 1792, the Columbia River was discovered; thirteen years later Lewis and Clark built a fort at the mouth of that river and in 1811 John Jacob Astor founded Astoria. In 1818, the U.S. and Britain agreed to jointly administer the region, but due to the massive immigration of the 1840s, Britain ceded its rights to America in 1846. Oregon became a territory on August 14, 1848 and nine years later it entered the Union. In 1877 fighting with the Nez Perce, Paiute, and Bannock Indians finally ceased as Chief Joseph signed a treaty. In 1937 the Bonneville Dam was completed, enabling Oregon to produce cheap hydroelectric power. Oregon was the first state to legalize marijuana and to adopt a bottle law requiring deposits on all non-returnable beverage containers. It also made early strides in the movement to grant homosexuals their rights and over the years has been a pioneer in humanitarian projects.

Oregon is the number one producer of forest products, as almost one-third of the state is forested. It ranks first in berries, cherries, and pears.

Area: 96,981 square miles

Eugene

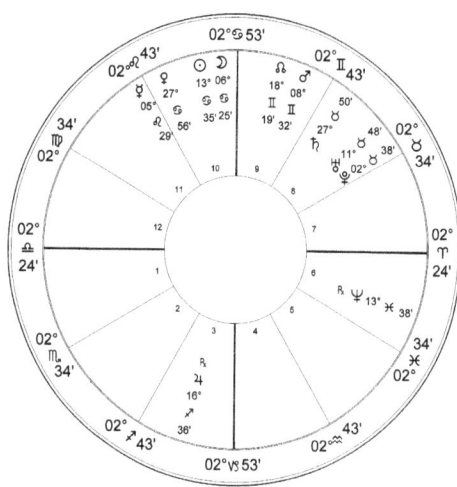

July 5, 1853
123W04, 44N05
11:30 AM PST

Founded by Eugene Skinner in 1846, it was named for him in 1853 when the present town was founded. Home of the University of Oregon, which was founded in 1872 (Ascendant sextile Jupiter), Eugene is often cited as one of the most desirable places in the country in which to reside. It's a clean, pleasant, intellectual community on the banks of the Willamette.

Incorporated: 1905
Elevation: 423 feet
Source: *Story of Eugene* by Lucia Moore

Medford

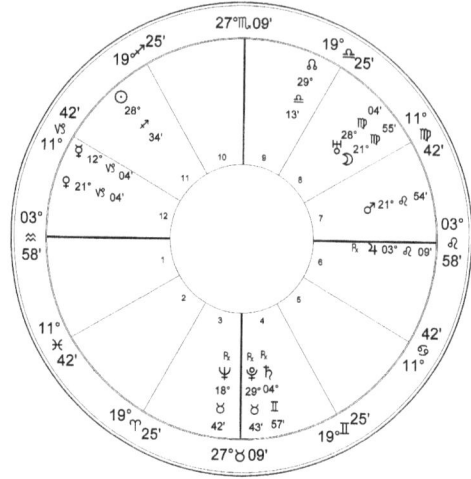

December 20, 1883
122W52, 42N19
9:55 AM PST

Founded as a rail depot in 1883, it's the largest city in southern Oregon. From 1921 until 1934 it witnessed considerable violence due to the Ku Klux Klan, which terrorized the city (transiting Neptune in the seventh house).

Incorporated: February 7, 1905
Elevation: 1,380 feet
Source: *Story of Medford* by Jane Snedicor

Portland

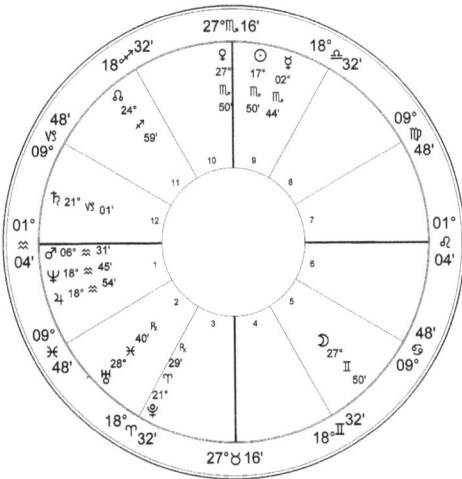

November 10, 1843
122W37, 45N32
12:33 PM PST

During the 1840s many communities sprang up along the Willamette Valley but the future site of Portland was passed up until November 1843 when Overton visioned the area as a future deep water port. Because he couldn't afford the filing fee to record his claim, he sold half to Lovejoy for the paltry sum of twenty-five cents. Soon Overton wanted to move on, so he sold half his interest to Pettygrove for $50, but the site had no name. Lovejoy proposed Boston and Pettygrove chose Portland. With the toss of a coin, its patronym was decided. With the discovery of gold in California, the town emptied of all but three adult men. Another gold rush in Idaho during 1865 boosted the city's coffers, but the following year Portland somehow went broke (Midheaven sextile Neptune trine Pluto). Fires were always a constant threat to western towns and Portland was no exception. Two conflagrations, one in 1872 and one in 1873, leveled the business district (Midheaven opposition Moon, Ascendant semisquare Mars). The Klondike Gold Rush in 1897 caused more pioneers to appear on the scene and Portland became one of the chief outfitting depots of the trek northward (Midheaven square Pluto conjunct Saturn). To celebrate the 100th anniversary of Lewis and Clark's discovery of the Northwest, an exposition was held in 1905. Two years later, the first Rose Festival was held (Ascendant opposition Venus).

Portland is a city with a split personality (Moon in Gemini). On one hand it wants the conveniences of being a metropolis, but on the other it wants to retain its rustic environment. Through diligent foresight, Portland has managed to conserve much of what nature gave the region: More than 6,000 acres of parkland line the western edges of the city and Portland has more evergreen trees than any other city in the U.S.

Known as the "Rose City," its natives tend their gardens with such loving care it would make an Englishman green with envy.

When several magazines voted Portland as one of the most liveable cities in the country, its natives worried about the favorable attention it would cause. Portland has always prided itself on a stable growth pattern and rather tight economic controls that could weather depressions much easier than other cities in the Northwest because of its diversified industry. Portlanders wanted to keep the status quo (Sun in Scorpio) and didn't want outsiders coming in and wrecking the place. It was a place that seemed resistant to both change and expansion (Sun sextile Saturn square Jupiter).

Known for its tolerance of divergent lifestyles (Aquarius rising), Portland is a place where you can do your thing and be neither condemned or condoned for your actions. The pace is slow and easygoing, but natives are cautious about outside interference. They want to keep this city beautiful (Venus at Midheaven) for Portland has neither graffiti, slums or racial problems. Harmony reigns supreme and natives and tourists can feel free to walk the streets alone at night without fear of being attacked. They love the single family homes and have resisted high rises pretty well so far. Portlanders don't want to obscure the views of Mt. Hood, which lies fifty miles east of their Edenlike city. On a clear and rain free day (about half the time), you can also see two volcanoes: Mt. Adams and Mt. St. Helen's, which spewed tons of ash upon the city in June 1980 during its second violent explosion.

Like Oregon, Portland leads the nation in environmental, social and health reforms (ruler of the Ascendant in Aries).

Incorporated: April 7, 1851
Elevation: 77 feet
Area: 94 square miles
Source: *Early Portland* by Eugene Snyder says Overton and Lovejoy stopped for their noon rest during November 1843 on their journey to Oregon City; exact date unknown; chart rectified

Salem

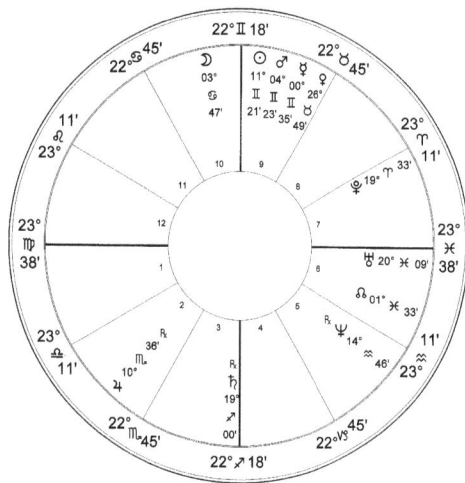

June 1, 1840
123W02, 44N56
12:57 PM PST

First settled in 1834, a mission was founded here in 1840 and a town site platted fourteen years later. Salem has been the capital of Oregon since 1864 and in 1935 the old capitol building burned. Soon after, it was replaced by one of the most beautiful legislative headquarters in the country. Strongly New England in its outlook, Salem ranks as one of the more pleasant communities in this country due to its low crime rate and absence of pollution.

Incorporated: 1860
Elevation: 155 feet

Pennsylvania

December 12, 1787
Philadelphia
75W11, 39N57
2:03 PM EST
Source: Pennsylvania
State Historical Society
says "mid-afternoon";
chart rectified

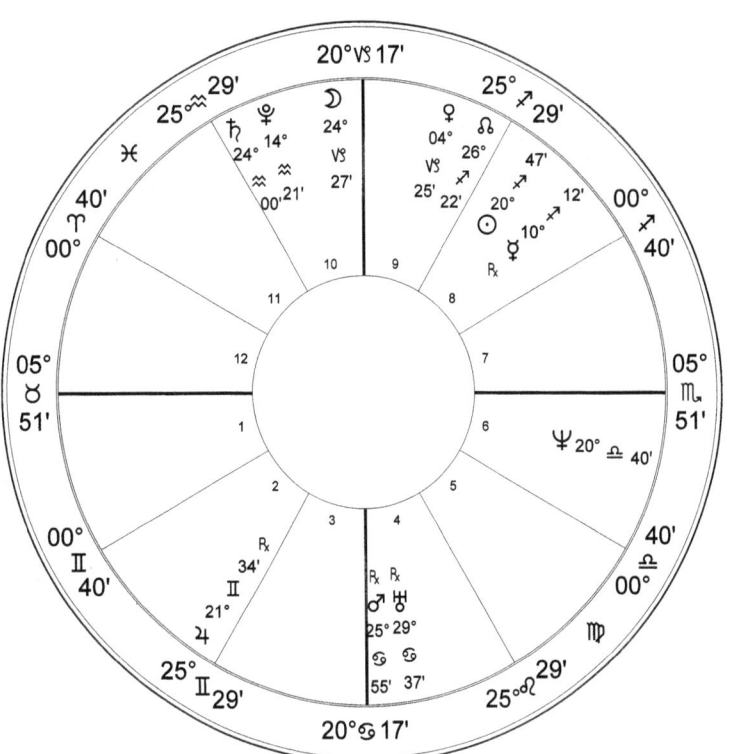

In 1609 Henry Hudson explored Delaware Bay and in 1643 the first settlements were made by the Swedes near Philadelphia. The Dutch captured the region in 1655, but nine years later lost it to the English. On March 4, 1681, the region was granted to William Penn; the next summer the city of Philadelphia was laid out.

During the French and Indian War (1754-1763), many battles were fought in the state. Washington surrendered Fort Necessity in 1754 and Braddock routed the French from Fort Duquesne, now Pittsburgh, in 1758. In 1775 Congress met and decided that independence was no longer just an idle threat and the following year, on July 4, delegates signed the famous document that became a beacon of freedom to the colonists. In the winter of 1777-78, Washington camped at Valley Forge. The U.S. Constitution was adopted in 1787 and later that year Pennsylvania became the second state to ratify it. From 1790 to 1800, Philadelphia was the capital of the U.S. In 1792 the legislature purchased the region around Erie so Pennsylvania could have a lake port. In 1794 the Whiskey Rebellion occurred in the western part of the state and in the first test of the U.S. law, it was quickly put down by the militia. The nation's first paved road, the Lancaster Pike, was completed in 1795 and the first railroad began operating in 1829. Oil was discovered at Titusville in 1859 and four years later the most famous battle of the Civil War occurred near the town of Gettysburg. The Confederacy was defeated and Lincoln later dedicated the cemetery. In 1889 a massive flood killed 2,200 people in Johnstown and in 1937 the Ohio overflowed its banks and left Pittsburgh under water. Hurricane Agnes in 1972 caused the Susquehanna to inundate the eastern part of the state.

Most of the largest steel plants are located in this state. Pittsburgh was once the most industrialized community in the country and the foulest smelling due to its dirty air. Pennsylvania leads the nation in the production of anthracite (hard coal) and is ranked third in bituminous coal (soft coal). It also ranks first in pig iron, sausages and pretzels, and is a leading producer of ice cream and chocolate.

Area: 45,333 square miles

Allentown

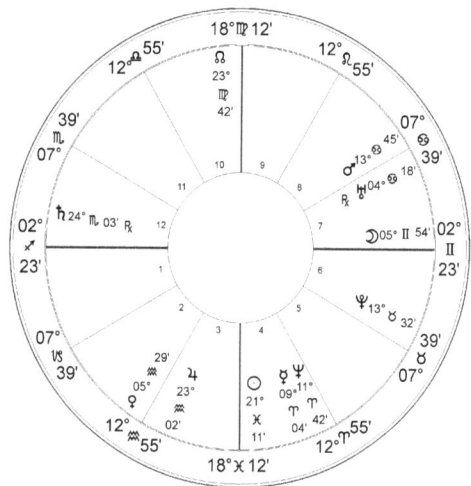

March 12, 1867
75W29, 40n36
12:01 AM EST

Founded by William Allen in 1735, it was laid out in 1762. Known as the nation's armory during the Revolution, it was renamed in 1838 to honor its founder. Later that year, several catastrophes hit: fire, flood and business failures. The first iron mill opened in 1847 and today Allentown is Pennsylvania's third largest manufacturing city and the "Trucking Capital of the World."

Incorporated: 1867
Elevation: 364 feet
Area: 18 square miles
Source: Allentown Public Library

Altoona

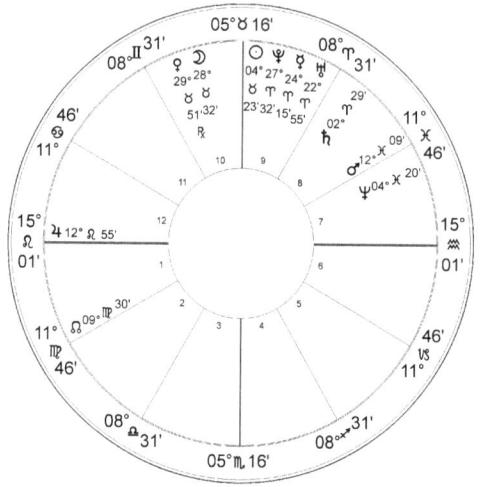

April 24, 1849
78W24, 40N31
12:15 PM EST

Founded by the Pennsylvania Railroad in 1849, it was named for the city in Germany. Its massive rail yards make it a large transportation hub and the old Pennsylvania Railroad is the largest employer in the city.

Incorporated: February 8, 1868
Elevation: 1,206 feet
Source: Altoona Public Library

Bethlehem

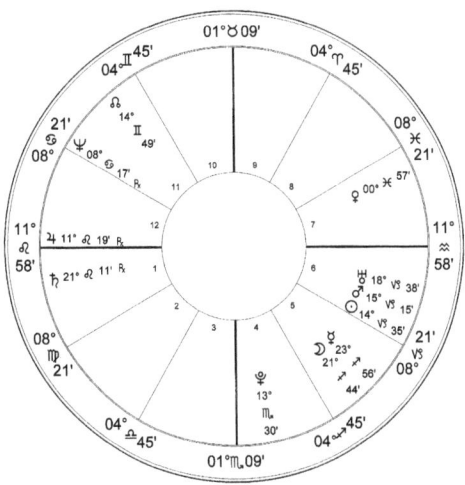

January 4, 1742
75W23, 40N37
7:00 PM EST

First settled by the Moravians in March 1741, it decided on a name during the singing of "O Little Town of Bethlehem" the following Christmas Eve during services. In 1829 the Lehigh Canal was completed (Ascendant sextile Moratur) and the first steel mill opened in 1857 (Ascendant sextile Mars). Lehigh University was founded eight years later.

Incorporated: 1865
Elevation: 340 feet
Source: *Northampton County Guide*; *American Guide Series*; old church records state the service began shortly after sundown; chart rectified

Erie

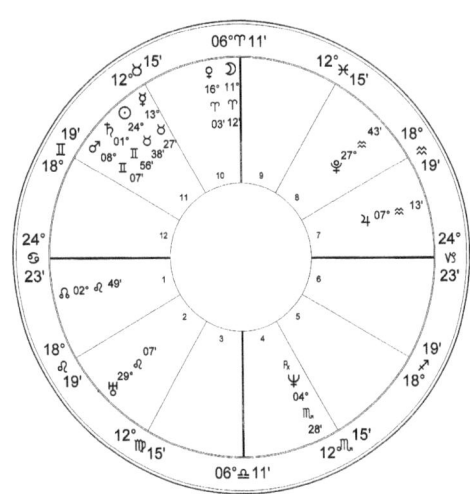

May 15, 1795
80W05, 42N08
9:10 AM EST

Fort Presque Isle was erected on this spot in 1753, but the present city wasn't founded until 1795, three years after the region was purchased from the State of New York so that Pennsylvania could have a lake port. Shipbuilding was the first industry arriving in 1798 (Midheaven semisquare Sun). In September 1813, Admiral Perry forced the British to surrender during the Battle of Lake Erie (Ascendant opposition Jupiter). The first iron foundry opened in 1833 (Midheaven conjunct Mercury) and eleven years later the Erie Extension Canal was completed (Ascendant opposition Moon).

Incorporated: 1851
Elevation: 709 feet
Area: 19 square miles
Source: *Erie County* by Herbert Spencer

Harrisburg

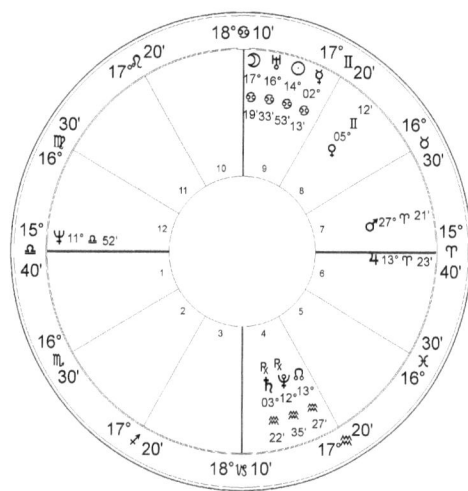

**July 6, 1785
76W53, 40N16
12:26 PM EST**

First settled in 1712 by John Harris, the town site was platted in 1785. Harrisburg became the capital of Pennsylvania in 1812 (Midheaven trine Jupiter). After the old capitol building burned in 1897, the new one was completed. Its dome is modeled after St. Peter's in Rome and is one of the most beautiful legislative structures in the nation. In March 1979, the nuclear power plant at nearby Three Mile Island melted down, causing the evacuation of thousands from the region (transiting Pluto over the Ascendant). It caused many Americans and environmentalists to question the safety of nuclear energy.

Incorporated: April 16, 1838
Elevation: 365 feet
Source: *Annals of Harrisburg* by George Morgan

Johnstown

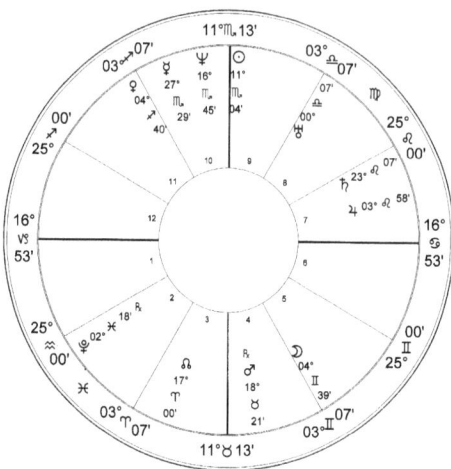

**November 3, 1800
78W55, 40N20
Noon EST**

Laid out as Conemaugh in 1800 by Joseph Johns, its name was changed in 1834 to honor its founder (Ascendant square Mercury). This town has been the scene of three of the worst floods ever to hit an American community. The inundation of May 31, 1889 was caused when a dam burst upstream and swept a wall of water forty feet high through the narrow river gorge. After the debris was cleared, more than 2,200 had lost their lives. At the time, it was the worst single disaster ever to befall the country (Ascendant square Pluto). During the 20th century, the floods of March 1936 and July 1977 (Ascendant square Neptune) have left their high water marks on the downtown buildings.

Johnstown seems to be extremely sensitive to economic downturns, as was witnessed during the Depression when the steel mills closed. The city ranks at the bottom of the list in crime statistics, and its thrifty Slavic citizens save more per capita than any other metropolitan area in the U.S. Capricorn rising might also point to the fact that almost thirty percent of its residents are over age sixty.

Incorporated: December 18, 1889
Elevation: 1,180 feet
Source: Pennsylvania State Archives

Lancaster

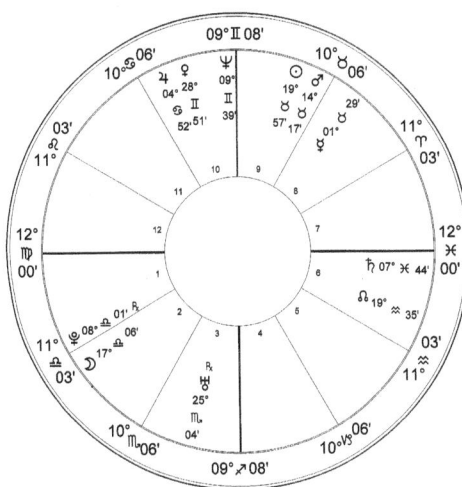

May 10, 1729
76W19, 40N02
1:21 PM EST

In 1729, Lancaster County was formed and the present city laid out the following year. For one brief day on September 27, 1777, Lancaster was the capital of the U.S. (Midheaven trine Uranus). Capital of Pennsylvania from 1799 until the legislature was moved to Harrisburg in 1812, the city produced both the Conestoga wagon and the Pennsylvania rifle during the early days of the 19th century. In 1794 the nation's first highway, the Lancaster Pike, connected the city to Philadelphia (Ascendant trine Jupiter).

Lancaster is located in the heart of the Pennsylvania Dutch country, land of the Amish and the Mennonites. Horse drawn wagons are seen on the roads being driven by bearded men in black garments. These people shun most modern conveniences, preferring to retain the simple life of days gone by.

Incorporated: March 20, 1818
Elevation: 380 feet
Source: Lancaster City Hall

Philadelphia

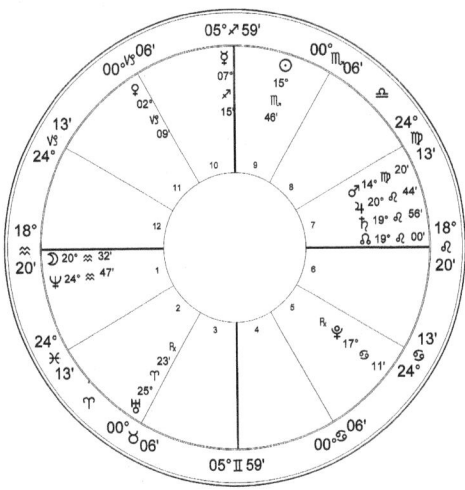

November 7, 1682
75W11, 39N57
1:08 PM EST

First settled in the summer of 1681, it was dedicated by William Penn the following year as the "City of Brotherly Love." Most of its early settlers were Quakers, like Penn, and religious freedom was the rule rather than the exception (Aquarius Ascendant, Sagittarius Midheaven). Benjamin Franklin arrived from Boston in 1723, contributing much to the city's stature by giving it the first circulating library in the country (1731) and its first lighted and paved streets (1751). Philadelphia was the first designed city in America, laid out geometrically around five squares. During the 18th century, Philly was the social, cultural, educational and political center of the colonies; artists, writers, men of science, educators, politicians and merchants made this the second largest English speaking city in the world. The first Continental Congress opened in 1774, and from 1775 until 1789, it was the capital of the United States. The most memorable event in the city's history, the one that gave birth to our country, occurred on July 4, 1776 when the Declaration of Independence was signed at the Statehouse. With the British occupying the city during the winter of 1777-78, Washington had to camp in nearby Valley Forge (Midheaven opposition Jupiter/Saturn conjunct Moon, Ascendant square Mars). After the Revolution ended, the Articles of Confederation were drawn up, but proved short lived due to bickering between the colonies. The Constitution of the United States, signed in 1787, changed all that and gave the country its first code of laws. Shortly thereafter, the Bill of Rights was written into the Constitution. From 1790 until 1800, Philadelphia was again the capital of the new nation until the legislature moved to that swampy village on the Potomac. During the last decade of the 18th century, the city experienced two bouts with yellow fever: 1793 (Ascendant sesquare Sun) and 1798 (Ascendant sesquare Moon). In

1801, the Navy Yard was constructed (Midheaven trine Sun), the first one in the infant country.

In July 1850, a fire burned 400 buildings and killed thirty-nine people (Midheaven square Neptune). Due to overcrowding, Philadelphia decided to merge with Philadelphia County in 1854, thus greatly increasing its area and population. To celebrate the nation's first centennial, a fair was held in Fairmount Park. Exhibits showed the world what the country had produced during its first 100 years. A second exhibit, in 1926, also took place in this park. On New Years' Day, Philadelphia turns out en masse for the Mummer's Parade, as it has done each year since 1901. In May 1985, the police department bombed the headquarters of MOVE, a radical political action group, setting fire to sixty-two homes on the west side of the city (Midheaven semisquare Jupiter and Saturn).

Philadelphia had the country's first hospital, library, university, law school, medical school, paper mill, theater, bank, insurance company, stock exchange, street lighting, navy yard, fire company, and U.S. Mint. Due to its diversified economy, it is far less vulnerable to economic fluctuations than many other cities in the U.S. Printing and publishing are two of the main industries, along with petrochemicals, pharmaceuticals and banking.

If William Penn could come alive from his statue atop city hall and see what the past 300 years have wrought, he would most likely recognize much of his "greene country towne," for Philly has managed to preserve many of its colonial buildings which line narrow streets and alleys. A city like London in spirit, it's low key with an aura of elegance and grace (Moon in Aquarius conjunct Ascendant). A city of parks and squares, it has a regal, stately and manorial manner that gives it an aura of quiet sophistication. They might call Philly provincial or backward but it follows its own drummer and refuses to follow the crowd (Aquarius rising, Sagittarius Midheaven). Some detractors see this city as unprogressive and lethargic (both lights in fixed signs along with the Ascendant and Descendant), but it does have a strong social conscience. For its size, Philly has the fewest major crimes of any city. Beautiful suburbs stretch westward along the Main Line, which has become synonymous with wealth, prestige and snobbery. Philly may not be New York, but its civility is remarkable in this day and age where cities deteriorate before your very eyes. Downtown Philadelphia has undergone massive transformations and the center city remains a place where people live as well as work. Society Hill is now a restored area of late 18th century homes and east Market Street was cleaned up. The sights in this city are too numerous to mention, but like Boston, the best way to see them is to walk through the neighborhoods and see where so much of our country's history took place. You will agree that Philadelphia is the most charming and gracious large city in the nation.

Incorporated: November 8, 1701
Elevation: 100 feet
Area: 128 square miles
Source: *Pennsylvania* by S.C. Fisher says October 28 or 29, 1682 O.S.; *Pennsylvania* by Paul Wallace says October 27 O.S.; *My Pennsylvania* by Amy Oakley says October 29; the median date between all sources has been chosen

Pittsburgh

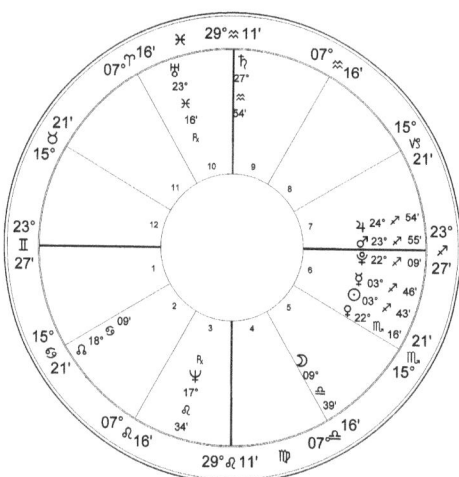

**November 25, 1758
80W00, 40N27
6:06 PM EST**

First settled on February 17, 1754, the foundation of Pittsburgh took place when the British took Fort Duquesne from the French four years later. They burned the stockade and renamed it in honor of British Prime Minister William Pitt. Six years later, the town site was laid out. During the Revolution, it was occupied by the British (Ascendant square Moon). Pittsburgh saw its first blast furnace completed in 1792 (Ascendant trine Uranus) and in 1811 the first steamboat left on its journey down the Ohio. In April 1845, a major fire burned 982 buildings downtown (Midheaven square Saturn), but even that didn't dampen the city's spirit. By the time the Civil War began, Pittsburgh was the most important manufacturing center in the land. In 1907, Pittsburgh annexed the neighboring city of Allegheny across the river where Gertrude Stein was born.

Over the years, due to its location in a narrow gorge between the Allegheny and Monongahela Rivers, Pittsburgh has been prone to both smoke and floods. Many times, the Golden Triangle (where the two rivers meet to form the Ohio) has been under water. On St. Patrick's Day 1936, the worst inundation ever swept through the city and water was up to the second story of many stores and offices (Midheaven opposition Saturn, Ascendant square Neptune). With the completion of several dams and controls. Pittsburgh has been spared serious flooding since. After World War II, Richard King Mellon and many other powerful businessmen decided that Pittsburgh needed to "clean up its act." The air was so foul and dirty that streetlights had to be kept on during the entire day. In 1947, an ordinance was adopted by businessmen and city hall which paved the way for the massive transformation that was about to take place (Ascendant trine Uranus). If you haven't seen Pittsburgh in years, you wouldn't know the place. Old and decaying steel mills along the river were torn down, parks were built and skyscrapers erected that can be seen from the heights across the river. Dickens once called Pittsburgh "Hell with the lid off" as it reminded him of Dante's inferno. Today, the city has the cleanest air of any city its size in the country and with the closing of the mills, Pittsburgh will try to keep it that way.

Once called "Steel City," Pittsburgh was the industrial giant that made men like Mellon, Carnegie and Frick wealthy. Once home to thirty-five steel mills, 100 chemical plants, 350 coal mines and sixty glass factories, the city has attracted new industries like electronics and research. A strong union town, Pittsburgh was often strike prone; but without this city, Detroit would have withered on the vine long ago. Home of twenty-three major corporations like U.S. Steel, Alcoa, Gulf Oil and Westinghouse, its importance is considerably greater than many cities twice its size. A city of strong ethnic neighborhoods, its residents are some of the hardest working people on earth (stellium in the sixth house). As recently as 1940, however, many of their homes were substandard, with half of them without proper plumbing or electricity.

Pittsburgh is also a cultural giant and institutes like the University of Pittsburgh and Carnegie Institute of Technology are famous around the globe. It has a fine orchestra and a civic opera company that packs them in night after night. And let's not forget that the city is the home of the Pirates baseball team. Pittsburgh's philosophy could well be that statement by Teddy Roosevelt: "Work hard and play hard." It may have had a grimy past, but its future is bright and sunny.

Incorporated: March 18, 1816
Elevation: 744 feet
Area: 55 square miles
Source: Pittsburgh Public Library says the city was captured about 6:00 p.m. on November 25, 1758; *Historic Towns of the Middle States* by Lyman Powell says February 17, 1754

Reading

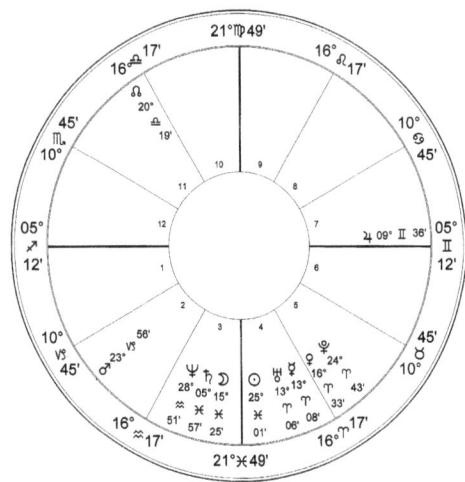

March 16, 1847
75W56, 40N20
12:01 AM EST

Settled in 1733 by relatives of William Penn, the town site was laid out fifteen years later. The first coal blast furnace was completed in 1790, and during the 1820s, two canals linked the city to Philadelphia and the Susquehanna. Between 1900 and 1912, Reading was a major automobile center.

Incorporated: 1847
Elevation: 264 feet
Source: Reading Public Library

Scranton

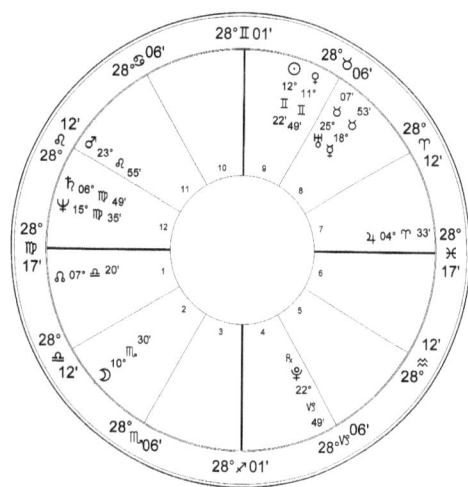

June 2, 1773
75W40, 41N25
1:08 PM EST

In 1773, an ordinance was adopted to establish a town; thirteen years later the first gristmill was founded (Midheaven trine Moon). The first coal company was formed in 1840 (Ascendant sextile Saturn and Pluto) and Scranton Steel was born in 1880 (Midheaven trine Sun/Venus). During the 1920s, the coal industry started to wane, but Scranton is still the "Anthracite Capital of the World." This region produces more coal than anywhere else in the nation. During its history, Scranton has been known by many names: Uniontown from 1800 until 1845, when it was renamed Harrison, until 1851, when it finally chose its present name.

Incorporated: April 23, 1866
Elevation: 741 feet
Source: Carolyn Dodson for the date; chart rectified

Wilkes Barre

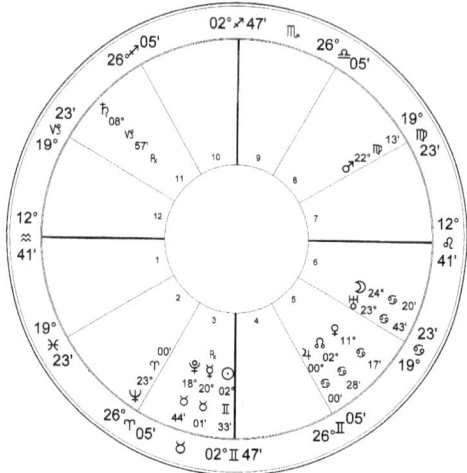

May 24, 1871
75W53, 41N15
12:01 AM EST

Originally founded in 1769 and named for John Wilkes and Isaac Barre, it was laid out the following year. During its first fifteen years of existence, Wilkes Barre witnessed many differing land claims. In July 1778, the Wyoming Massacre took place. In June 1972, Hurricane Agnes caused the evacuation of more than 100,000 people from the valley when the Susquehanna River rose to unprecedented heights due to the enormous amount of rainfall.

Incorporated: 1871
Elevation: 550 feet
Source: Wilkes Barre Public Library

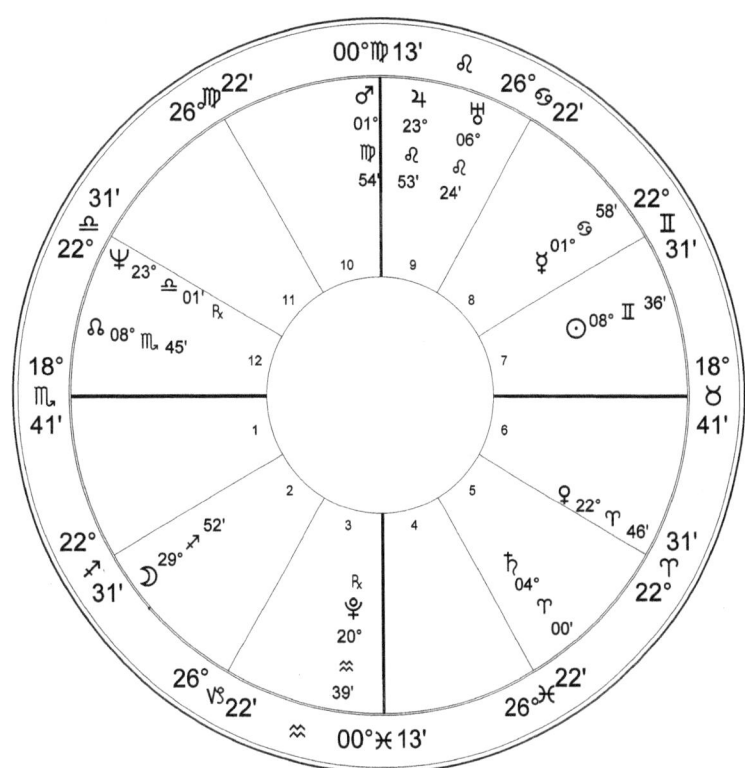

Rhode Island

May 29, 1790
Newport
71W19, 41N29
5:24 PM EST
Source: Rhode Island Historical Society says 5:00 p.m.

Adriaen Block explored the region for Holland in 1614, lending his name to the large island just off the southern coast. In 1636 Roger Williams left Massachusetts and founded Providence. England granted a patent on March 14, 1644 and called the region Rhode Island and the Providence Plantations—quite a name, but the legal one for the smallest state in the country. During King Philip's War (1675-76), many settlers were killed battling the Indians. On May 4, 1776, Rhode Island declared its own independence from Britain and in 1787 it refused to send delegates to the Constitutional Convention in Philadelphia. Known for extreme independence and iconoclasm, Rhode Island narrowly agreed to enter the Union in 1790, the last of the original thirteen colonies to do so. Its citizens balked at the Embargo Act of 1807 and allowed its militia to serve outside its borders during the War of 1812. In 1842 Dorr's Rebellion occurred when Thomas Dorr set up his own government protesting the property requirement necessary for voting. In 1901 Rhode Island finally consolidated its legislative functions and decided to allow Providence to become the sole state capital.

The textile industry is the chief employer, but jewelry and silverware also rank high on the list. It is the U.S. leader in those industries.

Area: 1,214 square miles

Newport

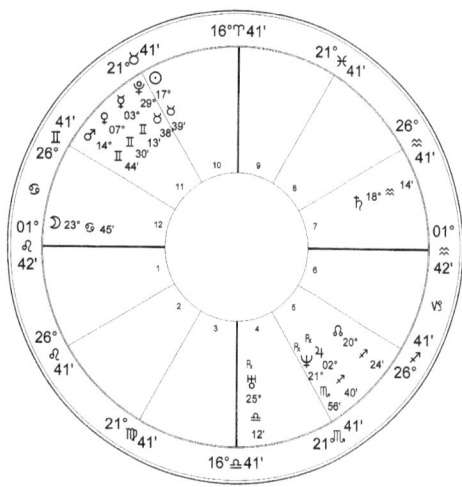

May 8, 1639
71W19, 41N29
9:42 AM EST

Founded in 1639, it was known for its shipbuilding after 1646. Newport was home to the first Jews in America when they arrived from Spain in 1658, and in 1763, the first synagogue in America was erected. From 1776 until 1779, the British occupied the city (Ascendant opposition Sun square Saturn). In 1836 Newport became a fashionable resort for the wealthy and before the end of the century, mansions like the Breakers and the Marble House lined the south shore overlooking the ocean. In 1865 Mrs. Astor founded the "400" as that was all her ballroom could accommodate. In 1901 Newport lost its title as co-capital to Providence. Newport also was the place where Jacqueline Bouvier was reared and the site of her marriage to John F. Kennedy.

Incorporated: June 1, 1784 and again on May 20, 1853
Elevation: 25 feet
Source: *American Guide Series*; other sources list May 16 or July 11 as alternate dates

Providence

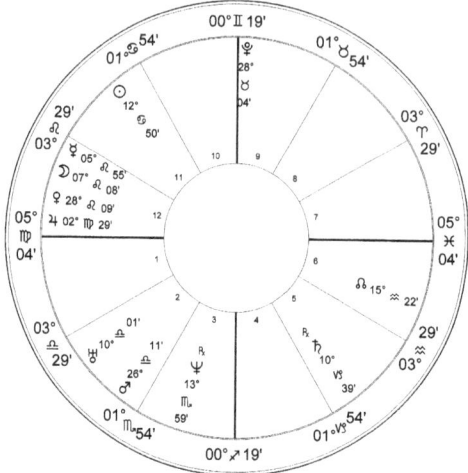

July 4, 1636
71W24, 41N49
8:46 AM EST

Founded and named in 1636 by Roger Williams, who was escaping the religious constriction in Massachusetts, Providence was burned by the Indians in 1676 (Midheaven opposition Saturn square Uranus). It became quite prosperous due to trade with the West Indies during the following century. In 1776 Rhode Island issued its own Declaration of Independence two months before it was done in Philadelphia. But Rhode Island almost lost out on becoming a state in 1790 when it failed to ratify the Constitution. Delays caused the Congress in Philadelphia to issue an ultimatum: sign or forget it!

Until 1901 Providence alternated with Newport as capital of this tiny state. Hurricanes have always been a threat to life on the east coast and those of 1815 and 1938 (Midheaven opposition Mars/Uranus) caused considerable damage.

Providence is a city of paradoxes, alternately explosive and charming, prosperous yet unpredictable (Pluto conjunct Midheaven). Its residents possess a reserved friendliness, are self-reliant and nonconforming. Red hot politically, it clings tenaciously to the past (Sun in Cancer) and is inhabited by many elderly people. The downtown area is crowded, and the street numbering system is the screwiest in the country to outsiders because of repeated attempts to renumber its structures. Providence is a lovely city of old colonial homes with large flower gardens and is the center of the country's jewelry trade (Moon in Leo conjunct Mercury, ruler of the Ascendant and Midheaven).

Incorporated: June 4, 1832
Elevation: 80 feet
Area: 20 square miles
Source: *Roger Williams* by Arthur Strickland and the Rhode Island State Archives both give the same date

South Carolina

May 23, 1788
Charleston
79W56, 32N46
5:08 PM EST
Source: South Carolina Historical Society says 5:00 p.m.

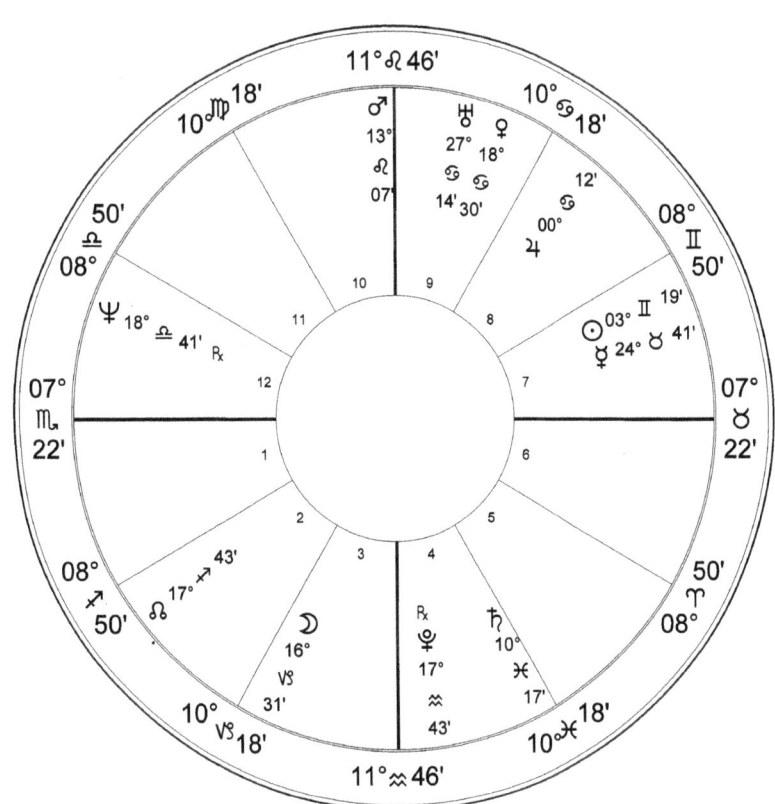

In 1527 the Spanish tried unsuccessfully to establish a colony near Georgetown; in 1564, the French Huguenots tried to do the same near Parris Island. On March 24, 1663, Britain granted a charter to eight proprietors and seven years later Charleston was founded. From 1711 until 1713, the Tuscarora War was fought between the settlers and the Indians. The following year, South Carolina became a separate province. However, the boundaries weren't clear until 1815. During the Revolution, Charleston was attacked three times by the British, who succeeded on the third try. Upon ratification of the Constitution in 1788, it became a state. In 1832, the Ordinance of Nullification was adopted, which forbade the collection of federal tariffs. Twenty-eight years later, on December 20, 1860, South Carolina became the first state to secede from the United States. Four months later, federal troops fired on Fort Sumter and the Civil War began. During the war, Charleston withstood a siege for more than two years and in 1865, Sherman marched across the state burning everything in sight. Readmitted to the Union on June 25, 1868, federal occupation finally ended in 1877.

Textiles are the main industry of this state. Agriculturally, it ranks second in peaches and fourth in tobacco. It also produces more vermiculite (used in insulation) and kaolin (an ingredient used in ceramics) than any other state.

Area: 31,055 square miles

Charleston

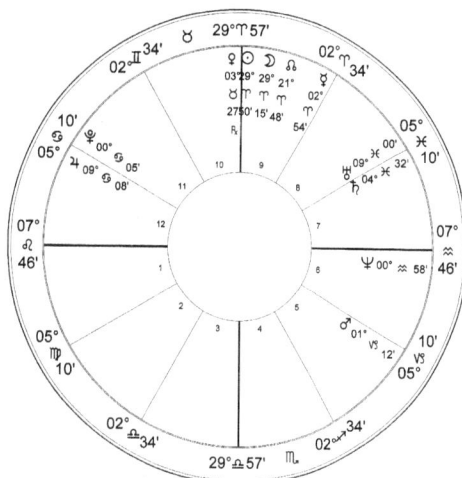

**April 19, 1670
79W56, 32N46
12:19 PM EST**

Founded as Charles Towne in 1670, it was moved to its present site ten years later (Ascendant semisquare Pluto). Pirates attacked the city in 1718 (Midheaven semisquare Sun/Moon) and the British invaded in 1776 and 1779. Patriots held out until the following year when it finally surrendered after a siege of forty-five days (Ascendant trine Jupiter and Uranus). Capital of the state until 1790, the Ordinance of Secession was passed here on December 20, 1860; it led to the formation of the Confederacy. On April 12, 1861, Federal troops fired on Fort Sumter and the Civil War began (Midheaven trine Saturn, transiting Pluto square natal Ascendant). During the war, Charleston was constantly bombarded and blockaded until February 1865, when it was evacuated and then set fire (Ascendant semisquare Saturn). Lying on an active earthquake fault, the city was shaken tremendously on August 31, 1886 (Ascendant sesquare Pluto), destroying more than ninety percent of this historic colonial city. A tornado in 1938 took the lives of thirty-two persons. In September 1989, Hurricane Hugo ravaged the city with the loss of forty-nine lives (Midheaven square Saturn, inconjunct Venus).

Situated on a peninsula between the Ashley and Cooper Rivers, Charleston has had a violent and turbulent history (both luminaries in Aries). Known as Dixie's most fightin' town, it's an aggressive city that was once the Athens of the South before Nashville usurped the title. Possessing an extraordinary amount of energy for a southern city, it has restored most of the historic buildings that line its dignified streets. Composed of an elegant social set (Leo rising), it still reeks of southern charm and grace. Many of the old mansions are open to the public, but until recent years, Charleston didn't want tourism at all. Recent events like the Spoleto Festival have again put this beautiful city on the agenda for tourists who desire to see how the South once lived.

Incorporated: August 13, 1783
Elevation: 9 feet
Area: 16 square miles
Source: *Landmarks of Charleston* by Thomas Lesesne says the city was founded in mid-April 1670; *Charleston* by Robert Rhett says March 15, 1670; chart rectified

Columbia

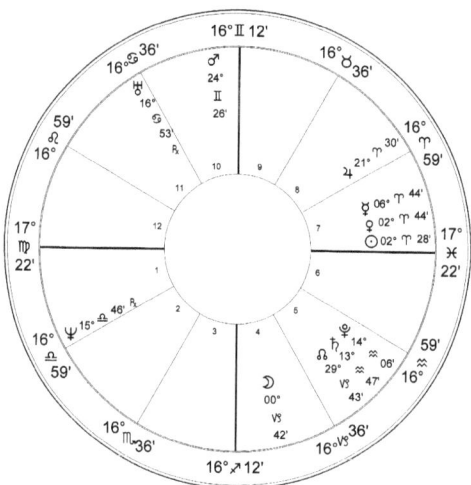

**March 22, 1786
81W03, 34N00
5:22 PM EST**

The first settlement in the region was Fort Congaree, which was founded in 1718. Chosen to be the state capital in 1786, the legislature moved here four years later (Midheaven sextile Jupiter). On December 17, 1860, a momentous decision took place: The South Carolina legislature decided to secede from the United States. But before the motion could be passed, a smallpox scare caused the lawmakers to adjourn to Charleston where it was passed three days later (Ascendant sesquare Mercury). General Sherman reached the city in February 1865 and burned sixty-five percent of the town (Midheaven sesquare Sun, Ascendant quincunx Mars). During the following decade, much strife and tension were caused by Carpetbaggers and the Ku Klux Klan.

Columbia is considerably more modern in appearance than Charleston and was one of the first planned cities in the country.

Incorporated: December 21, 1854
Elevation: 190 feet
Area: 109 square miles
Source: *Origin and Development of Columbia* by A S. Salley

Greenville

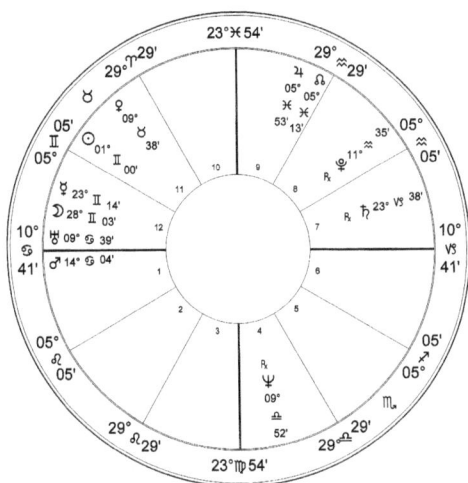

May 21, 1784
82W24, 34N51
8:08 AM EST

First settled in 1768, the land around Greenville was thrown open for settlement in 1784. Pleasantburg, the first real community, was founded thirteen years later (Midheaven opposition Saturn) and changed its name to Greenville in 1831 (Midheaven semisquare Neptune). The city's textile industry began in 1875 and remains one of the biggest employers in the region.

Incorporated: 1868
Elevation: 966 feet
Source: *Bridging the Gap* by Laura Ebaugh

Spartanburg

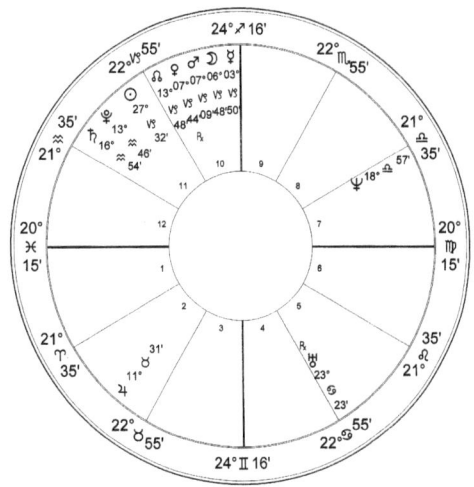

January 17, 1787
81W57, 34N56
10:15 AM EST

Chosen to become the new county seat in March 1785, it was formally founded two years later. It was named for the Spartan Regiment that fought during the Revolution from this state. By 1900 this city had many cotton mills (Midheaven sextile Saturn), the leading industry to this day. Spartanburg is also a leading center of education.

Incorporated: December 17, 1831
Elevation: 875 feet
Source: Spartanburg City Hall

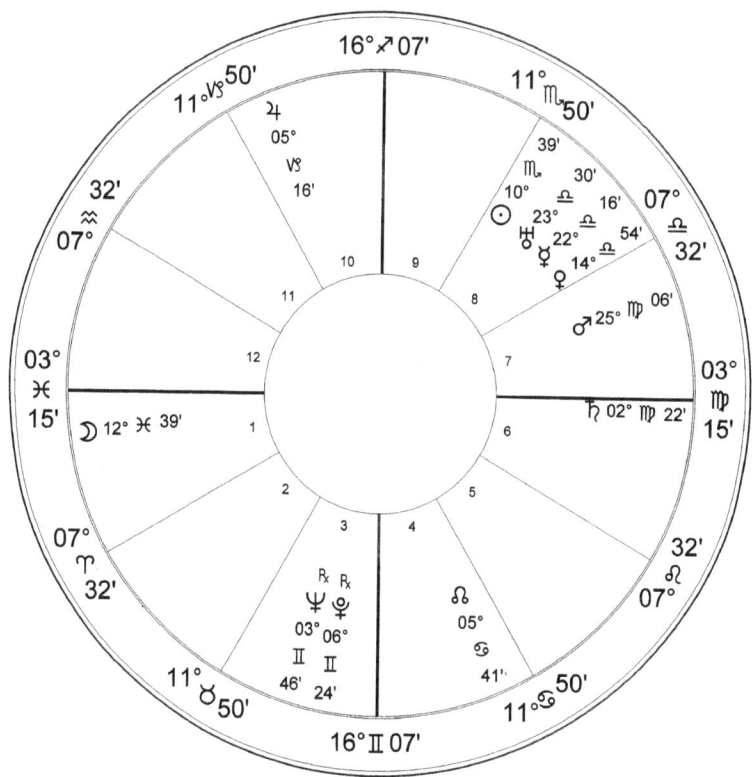

South Dakota

November 2, 1889
Yankton
97W23, 42N53
2:40 PM CST
Source: *New York Times* says 3:40 p.m. in Washington.

In 1743 the region was claimed for France, which sold it to the U.S. in 1803 along with the rest of Louisiana. Fort Pierre was the first trading post in the state, and in 1831, the steamboat reached the fort. On March 2, 1861, the Dakota Territory was created. Gold was discovered in the Black Hills in 1874, and colorful characters like Calamity Jane and Wild Bill Hickok soon populated the mining towns. The state really remained in the hands of the Sioux nation until 1889 when it became a separate state. On December 29, 1890, a massacre at Wounded Knee occurred and 300 Indians were killed by federal troops. It was the last Indian war in the west. About 50,000 farmers left the state during the Dust Bowl of the 1930s. In 1963 the Oahe Dam was completed across the Missouri and a flood in Rapid City in 1972 killed 242 people. In 1973 Indians occupied the village of Wounded Knee, protesting federal Indian policies.

South Dakota ranks first in rye, fifth in sheep and tenth in cattle and hogs. It leads the nation in gold and beryllium.

Depending on whether President Harrison signed the Bill of Admission first for North Dakota, or South Dakota, this is either the thirty-ninth or fortieth state; it's hard to tell. Because they entered the Union together, their horoscopes in Washington are identical. But are the states identical? Are the people the same? Certainly not! For one thing, South Dakota has the Black Hills, the highest mountains between the Appalachians and the Rockies; North Dakota is almost entirely flat.

North Dakota is populated largely by people from northern Europe and Scandinavia, while South Dakota has a more varied ethnic composition. Both states have a treacherous piece of real estate called the Badlands and both capital cities are located on the Missouri River. But Bismark is considerably more modern in appearance than Pierre, which still retains some of its frontier image.

North Dakota has Aquarius rising when you relocate the chart to the state capital at the time of admission, while South Dakota has Pisces ascending. One is progressive and unburdened by past tradition (North Dakota), while the other is representative of more mainline politics (South Dakota). North Dakota is a farming state, while South Dakota is mountainous and has many mines in the Black Hills. South Dakota is the more urban of the two states, while North Dakota still retains its preference for small towns and hamlets. If you left the charts alone and attempted to ascertain the basic character of each state from the horoscope as drawn up in Washington, you would probably think that the residents of these two prairie states were identical. One has an air sign on the Ascendant, while the other has a water sign rising. True, the planetary positions are the same, but right there, the similarity stops.

Area: 77,047 square miles

Aberdeen

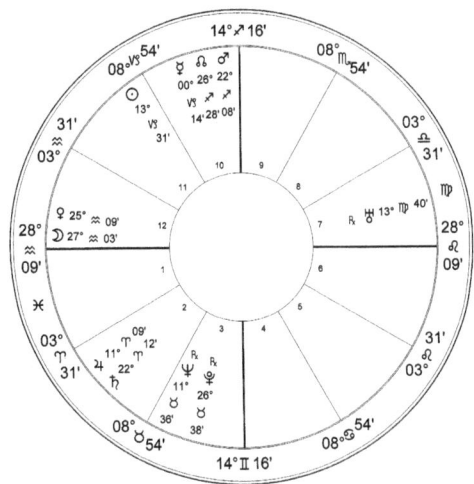

January 3, 1881
98W30, 45N28
10:32 AM CST

Settled in the spring of 1880, it was platted later that summer, but not formally founded until January 1881. Settled largely by Germans, Russians and Scandinavians, it is a wholesale center of a vast region.

Incorporated: March 15, 1883
Elevation: 1,229 feet
Source: Aberdeen Public Library

Pierre

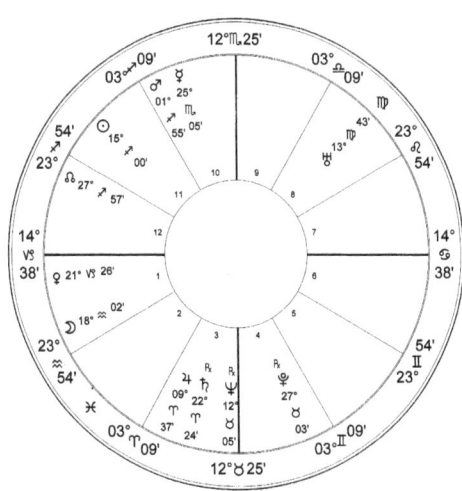

December 6, 1880
100W21, 44N22
10:18 AM CST

Founded in June 1880, it was platted the following December. In 1889, it became capital of South Dakota even though it wasn't confirmed until 1908 (Midheaven sextile Venus). Pierre is situated high above the Missouri River and is the second smallest capital city in the nation.

Incorporated: March 9, 1883
Elevation: 1,480 feet
Source: Pierre Public Library

Rapid City

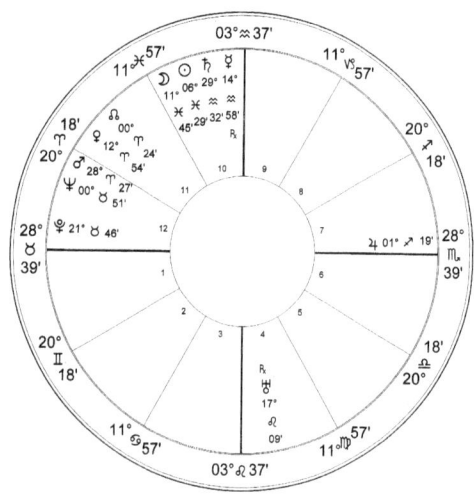

February 25, 1876
103W14, 44N05
9:57 AM MST

Founded during the Gold Rush of 1876, almost all the settlers left that summer because of Indian troubles. In 1886, the railroad arrived and the first train was held up by bandits (Ascendant square Moon). In 1927 Gutzon Borglum began his work sculpting the heads of Washington, Jefferson, Lincoln and Roosevelt on the side of Mt. Rushmore. In June 1972 a swift moving torrent of water swept 236 people to their deaths (Ascendant conjunct Uranus) during a freak thunderstorm.

Rapid City is the gateway to the Black Hills where Mt. Rushmore is located. Sometime in the future, the statue of Crazy Horse, the largest ever attempted by man, will hopefully be completed.

Incorporated: 1883
Elevation: 3,231 feet
Source: The Black Hills by Robert Casey

Sioux Falls

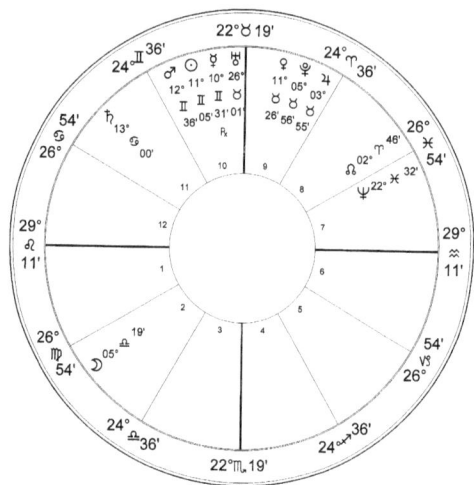

June 1, 1857
96W44, 43N33
11:06 AM CST

Founded in 1857 by settlers from neighboring Minnesota, it was burned five years later by the Indians (Midheaven conjunct Uranus). Fort Dakota was completed in 1865 to quell further uprisings among the Sioux Indians (Ascendant trine Jupiter). In 1890 because of lax laws, Sioux Falls became, along with Fargo, the divorce capital of the country until 1908 (Midheaven sextile Venus).

Incorporated: March 3, 1883
Elevation: 1,395 feet
Area: 26 square miles
Source: *History of South Dakota* by Doane Robinson; *History of South Dakota Territory* by George M Smith says August 27, 1857

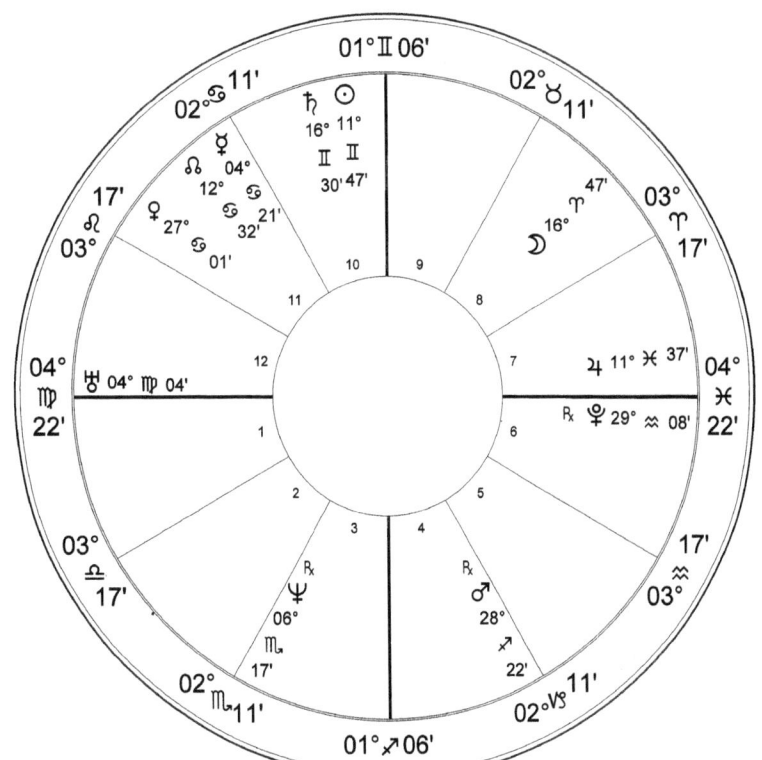

Tennessee

June 1, 1796
Knoxville
83W55, 35N58
11:48 AM EST
Source: Rectified

In 1673 the eastern part was explored for Virginia, while the western part was explored by the French. In 1682 the entire region was claimed by France, and a fort was built near Memphis. In 1763 Britain acquired title to the area after the French and Indian Wars, and in 1784, the State of Franklin was formed by settlers. In 1788 they were allowed to elect representatives in the North Carolina legislature. On May 26, 1790, the Territory South of the Ohio was organized, and in 1796, Tennessee became a state. In 1818 western Tennessee was purchased from the Chickasaw Indians by Andrew Jackson, who founded Memphis the following year. On June 24, 1861, Tennessee voters agreed to join the Confederacy even though eastern Tennessee supported the Union. It was the last state to secede and the first to be readmitted on July 24, 1866. During the Civil War, many battles were fought on this land: Shiloh, Fort Henry, Fort Donelson, Chickamauga, Lookout Mountain and Franklin. During the reconstruction period, the Ku Klux Klan was founded and Tennessee experienced many bouts with cholera and yellow fever. More than twenty-five percent of the population of Memphis perished in 1878. In 1933 the TVA was formed, which boosted the state's economy and supply of cheap electricity, and in 1942, the atomic plant at Oak Ridge was built. On April 4, 1968, Martin Luther King was gunned down in Memphis, touching off riots all across the nation.

Tennessee ranks first in zinc and pyrites, and fifth in tobacco. Hardwood flooring is also important, and the U.S. is the leader in this. Music is also one of the chief industries, especially in Nashville, home of the Grand Ole Opry.

Area: 42,244 square miles

Chattanooga

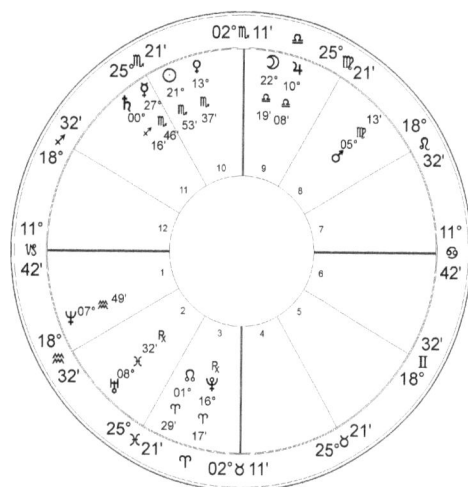

November 14, 1838
85W19, 35N02
11:08 AM EST

Settled as Ross' Landing in 1815, the town site was laid out in 1838. During the Civil War in 1863, federal troops occupied the city and the Battle of Chickamauga took place (Ascendant conjunct Neptune). From this city, Sherman marched on to Georgia burning and pillaging everything in sight. One year after the war was over, a smallpox epidemic struck (Midheaven conjunct Saturn), and in 1867, a flood nearly wiped the town off the map. The cholera epidemic of 1873 (Midheaven square Uranus) and yellow fever scare of 1878 (Ascendant square Saturn) caused untold loss of life. Another flood in 1883 (Ascendant conjunct Uranus) necessitated the construction of dams and levees to harness the mighty Tennessee River.

For a southern city, Chattanooga is surprisingly energetic and dynamic (Capricorn rising). The leading industrial and commercial center of southeastern Tennessee, it's a completely unostentatious community, with few old families to tie things down. Chattanooga is headquarters for the largest reclamation project ever in this country, the TVA, which was formed during the Depression.

Incorporated: December 5, 1851
Elevation: 674 feet
Area: 127 square miles
Source: *History of Hamilton County and Chattanooga*

Knoxville

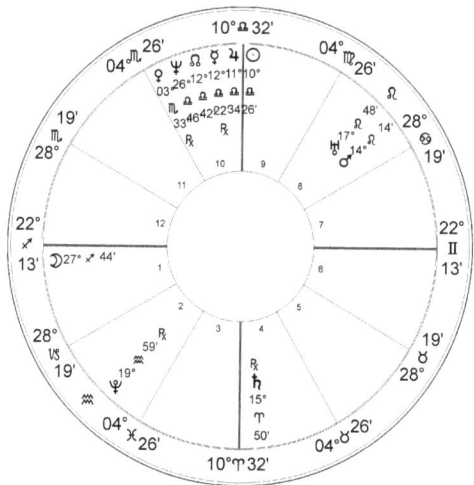

October 3, 1791
83W55, 35N58
12:25 PM EST

First settled in 1786, it was laid out five years later. After Tennessee's admission into the Union, it was the first state capital until 1812 (Ascendant conjunct Moon, Midheaven sextile Mars). Burned during a siege in 1863 (Ascendant quincunx Uranus), it boomed during Reconstruction. With the establishment of the TVA during the 1930s and the Oak Ridge Atomic Research Center the following decade, its economy greatly improved. During 1982 Knoxville hosted a World's Fair (Ascendant square Venus).

Located at the foothills of the Smokies, Knoxville is a large industrial city and home of the University of Tennessee which was founded in 1807 (Midheaven sextile Moon conjunct Neptune).

Incorporated: October 27, 1815
Elevation: 890 feet
Area: 77 square miles
Source: *Knoxville* by Betsey Creekmore

Memphis

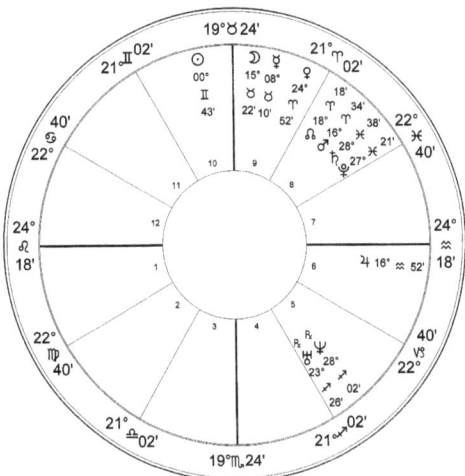

**May 22, 1819
90W03, 35N08
11:10 AM CST**

Fort Adams was completed here in 1797, but the foundation of the present city didn't take place until 1819 when Andrew Jackson broke the first ground, and the first sale of lots was held. During the second half of the 19th century, Memphis endured more than its share of misfortune. In 1855, 1867 and 1873, yellow fever epidemics broke out. Seized by federal troops in 1862 (Midheaven sesquare Jupiter), it survived the war practically intact compared to many other southern cities. During the summer of 1878, the greatest calamity ever to befall Memphis took place when 5,000 died during the yellow fever plague. Half the population fled the city and the remaining residents were quarantined. So great was the cost, that Memphis went broke and lost its charter (Midheaven quincunx Jupiter semisquare Sun square Mars). During the 1920s, Memphis was the vice capital of the nation and Beale Street became like Bourbon Street in New Orleans, a place where every taste could be satisfied. On April 4, 1968, Martin Luther King was assassinated in his motel (Ascendant square Uranus), an event which touched off riots all across this country.

Memphis today is known as a medical and research center and one of the quietest and cleanest cities in the U.S. Through its port passes one-third of the cotton crop. A rather sedate and elegant city (Leo rising, Moon in Taurus), it has some of the most sumptuous homes in the nation, such as Graceland, former home of Elvis Presley. There's a fixity to Memphis which resists change and sticks to the traditional. Memphis is also the second largest soybean processor and the third largest meat packer in the nation. It is also the home of Holiday Inns of America, the largest hotel chain in the world.

Incorporated: December 1849
Elevation: 331 feet
Area: 281 square miles
Source: *The Founding of Memphis* by J. Roper

Nashville

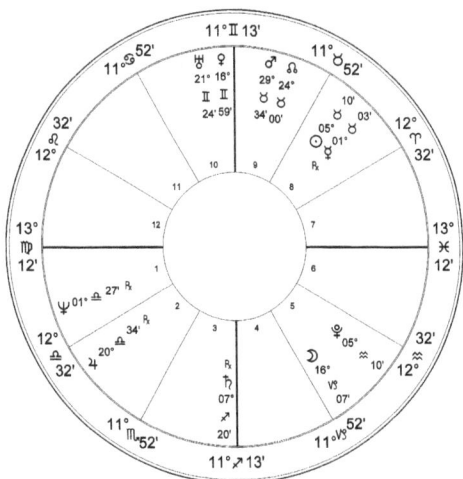

**April 24, 1780
86W47, 36N10
2:12 PM CST**

The first group of settlers arrived here on Christmas Day 1779, but with the arrival of the second group the following April, Nashborough was founded. Four years later, the name was changed. Nashville became capital of the state in 1843 (Ascendant square Pluto opposition Sun) and surrendered to federal troops in 1862 after which the city was left in ruins (Midheaven square Mars). The two cholera epidemics of 1866 and 1873 didn't help efforts to rebuild what was left. In 1916 a fire burned 648 buildings in the downtown area (Midheaven conjunct Jupiter trine Uranus, Ascendant square Neptune). After its merger with Davidson County in 1963, its population increased substantially.

Nashville is the "Music Capital of the World," home to more than sixty recording studios, 240 music publishers and thirty-four talent agencies. Clearly, if you want to make it in country music, you've got to make it big in Nashville (Sun in Taurus). Also known as the "Athens of the South" due to its thirteen colleges and universities, it has an exact replica of the Parthenon within its city limits. To the southeast is the home of Andrew Jackson, the Hermitage. Nashville natives are possessed with an unabashed good sense of humor, are unpretentious, gracious, genteel and very friendly (Venus conjunct Midheaven). But like most mountain folks, they view outsiders with some suspicion and cling to traditional ways. Nashville is one of the most church going cities in the land and a place where the old-fashioned, staid and conservative reigns supreme (Sun in Taurus, Virgo rising). Unless you're frantically trying to hit the big time, it's a rather lackadaisical place, and the pace is rather slow.

Incorporated: September 11, 1806
Elevation: 450 feet
Area 532 square miles
Source: *Historic Towns of the Southern States* by Lyman Powell

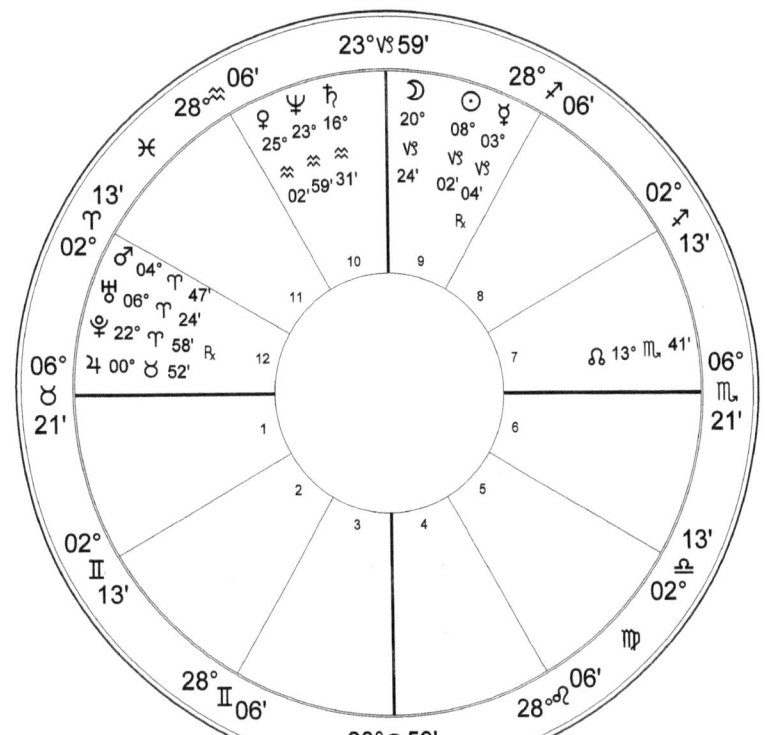

Texas

December 29, 1845
Austin
97W45, 30N17
1:42 PM CST
Source: Rectified from sources in newspapers which implied the president signed the bill during the afternoon

The first Spanish settlement was made at El Paso in 1680 and five years later, the French built a fort on Matagorda Bay. Stephen Austin settled along the Brazos River in 1821, the same year Texas became independent of Spain and a province of Mexico. The Texas Revolution began on March 2, 1836 when Sam Houston was elected as the first president of The Republic of Texas. The siege of the Alamo took place in San Antonio during this time, and 187 lost their lives to the Mexicans. The Battle of San Jacinto occurred east of Houston in October 1836 and General Santa Anna was captured. In 1845 Texas became part of the U.S.; the following June, the Mexican War began because of the state's admission. The Mexicans failed to realize that the Texans had asked for annexation—nobody forced it on them. On February 23, 1861, Texas seceded from the United States and was readmitted on March 30, 1870. In 1866 the Chisholm Trail opened to Kansas and the massive cattle drives began.

The hurricane and tidal wave of 1900 killed 6,000 in Galveston, and the following year, oil was discovered near Beaumont. NASA was established in Houston in 1962, and Texas became one of the leaders in space exploration. President Kennedy was assassinated in Dallas on November 22, 1963.

As would be expected, Texas leads the nation in oil (thirty-five percent of the U.S. total) and natural gas, but also in cattle, sheep, and cotton. It's also the top producer of asphalt, sulphur, and graphite. It ranks second in salt and helium, and third in cement. It ranks fifth in turkeys and ninth in chickens. It grows more pecans and sorghum, and ranks second in rice, third in peanuts and fifth in sweet potatoes. Chemicals are the largest industry, and it ranks third in fishing.

Area: 267,338 square miles

Abilene

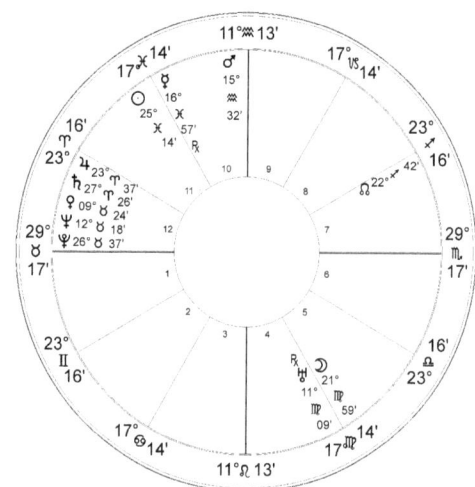

March 15, 1881
99W43, 32N28
10:00 AM CST

Founded in March 1881, it was named after the famous cowtown in Kansas. Serious flooding in October 1981 caused extensive damage after the city received fifteen inches of rainfall in a few days.

Incorporated: January 2, 1883
Elevation: 1,738 ft.
Source: Abilene Public Library

Amarillo

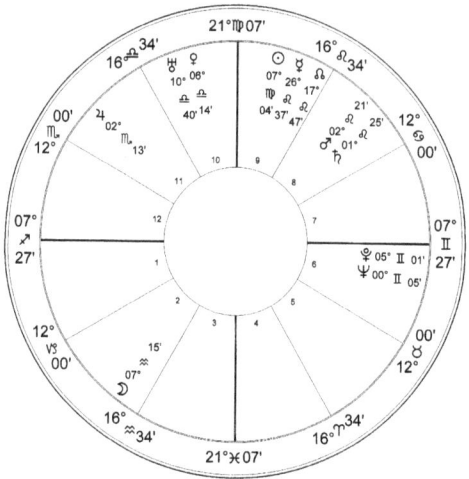

August 30, 1887
101W50, 35N13
1:40 PM CST

Founded in 1887 by railroad crews who called it Ragtown, it was policed by the Texas Rangers until 1899. Devastated during the Dust Bowl years of the 1930s, it has since become the world's largest producer of helium. Natural gas was discovered in the region in 1918, and oil came three years later.

Incorporated: 1892
Elevation: 3676 feet
Area: 80 square miles
Source: *Amarillo* by Clara Hammond

Austin

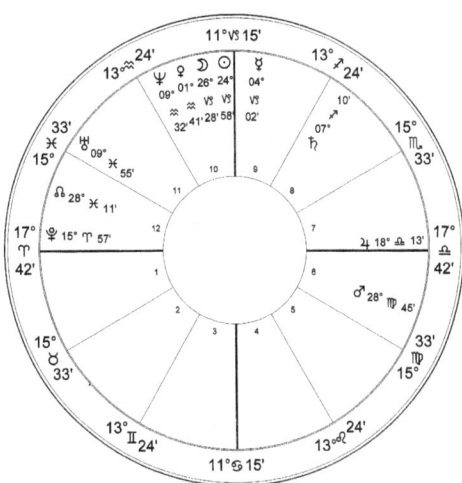

January 15, 1839
97W45, 30N17
11:42 AM CST

Founded in January 1839, the first sale of lots took place the following August 1. Originally named Waterloo, it later changed its name to honor the "Father of Texas." Mexican troops moved into the city in 1842 (Midheaven square Pluto) and the capital was temporarily moved to Houston. In 1881, the University of Texas was founded; seven years later, the Chicago syndicate helped to build the state capitol building in exchange for some valuable Texas real estate. In 1900 a flood inundated much of the city.

Being the state capital, much of the populace works for the government (Sun and Moon in Capricorn in the tenth house). Social life tends to surround the university, one of the largest in the nation. Austin is a pleasant looking city in the heart of the Texas hill country.

Incorporated: December 27, 1839
Elevation: 505 feet
Area: 106 square miles
Source: Austin Public Library; *Austin and Commodore Perry* by A.G. Adair says August 1, 1839 in the morning

Beaumont

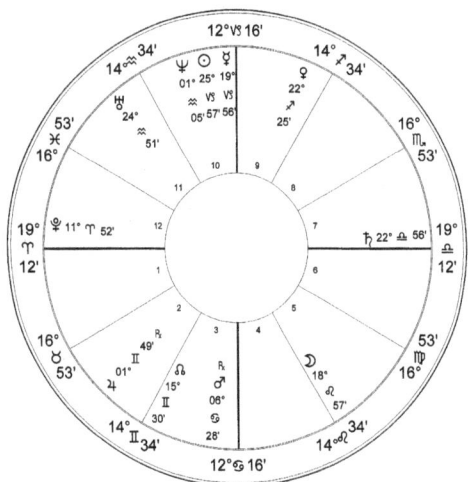

January 16, 1835
94W06, 30N05
11:28 AM CST

Settled as Tevis Bluff in 1825, a land grant was issued in 1835; two years later, the town was platted. Lumber was the main industry after 1876 (Midheaven trine Saturn) until the first gusher erupted on the morning of January 10, 1901. It was called Spindletop and Texas hasn't been the same since (Midheaven semisquare Neptune). A channel was completed in 1908 to facilitate ship movements, and a new one constructed twenty years later.

Beaumont is the oil center of Texas, and along with Port Arthur and Orange, the largest refining and petrochemical center in the nation.

Incorporated: July 12, 1881
Elevation: 21 feet
Area: 72 square miles
Source: *Women in Early Texas* by Evelyn Carrington

Corpus Christi

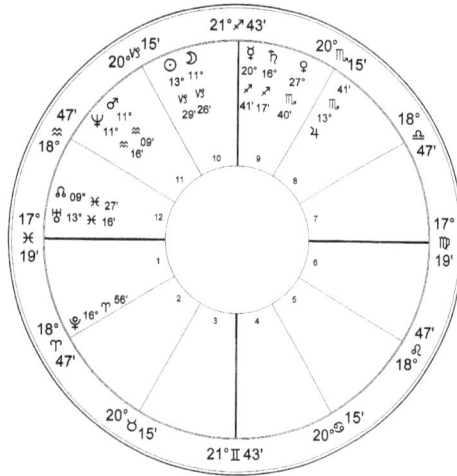

January 4, 1840
97W24, 27N47
11:00 AM CST

Settled in 1838, it was formally founded two years later and named Corpus Christi as that was the feast day on which Pineda discovered the site in 1519. During the Mexican War, it was a base for General Zachary Taylor. Blockaded during August 1862, it was captured two years later. In 1923 a natural gas well was successfully drilled (Midheaven square Saturn) and in 1926, Corpus Christi became a deep water port. Petroleum was discovered in 1939 (Ascendant trine Uranus). Today, this city is the ninth largest port in the U.S. and a major oil refining and fishing center.

Incorporated: 1852
Elevation: 40 feet
Area: 105 square miles
Source: *Saga of a Frontier Seaport* by G. McCampbell

Dallas

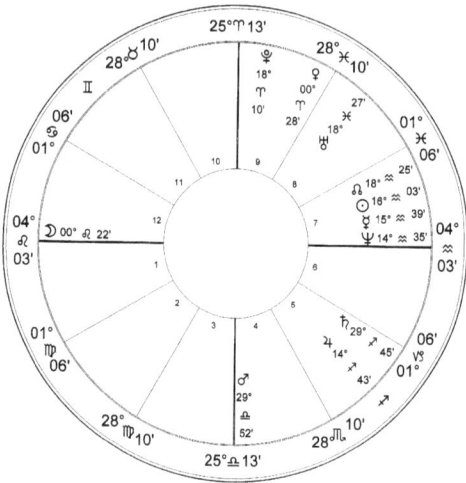

February 4, 1841
96W49, 32N47
5:01 PM CST

Founded by John Neely Bryan to whom a land grant was given in February 1841, he settled on the banks of the Trinity River that following November. He platted the new city the next spring. In July 1860 a fire burned most of the city (Midheaven square Sun/Neptune, Ascendant trine Pluto), but Dallas was spared most of the ravages other cities suffered during the Civil War. A flood in 1908 inundated much of the southwest part of Dallas (Ascendant sesquare Neptune) and flood control became a priority issue. During the early 1930s oil was discovered in east Texas (progressed Sun square Neptune), and in 1936 Dallas hosted the Texas Centennial Exposition. The first aircraft plant opened in 1948 and Dallas became a leader in that field shortly afterward. On November 22, 1963, the one event Dallas would prefer to forget occurred when President Kennedy was assassinated in Dealey Plaza (Ascendant quincunx Pluto trine Uranus). In the years that followed, this site would become almost as famous as Arlington National Cemetery where he lies buried under the "Eternal Flame."

Residents of "Big D" like to consider themselves as living in the New York of the Southwest, in a cultured, sophisticated city which is the commercial and business center of the state. Stores like Neiman-Marcus illustrate the opulence of this city (Ascendant in Leo), and the skyline keeps soaring ever upwards year after year. Dallas is high pressure and preoccupied with bigness and wealth (Leo Ascendant). It's a vain city that pursues the good life with utter abandon; Dallas boasts more Cadillacs per capita than any city in the U.S. An extremely proud city, Dallas is very competitive and showy. But appearances aside, Dallas does have quite a bit going for it. Sitting in the middle of seventy percent of the nation's oil fields, Dallas is headquarters to more petroleum companies than any city in the land with the exception of Houston. It's also the banking and fashion center of the Southwest, and recently it usurped Hartford and Des Moines as the insurance capital of the nation. Dallas is also the largest inland cotton market in the world and one of the leading transportation centers of the U.S. The Dallas-Fort Worth Airport is one of the busiest in the country, and occupies more acreage than Manhattan island.

Incorporated: 1871
Elevation: 512 feet
Area: 378 square miles
Source: Dallas Public Library

El Paso

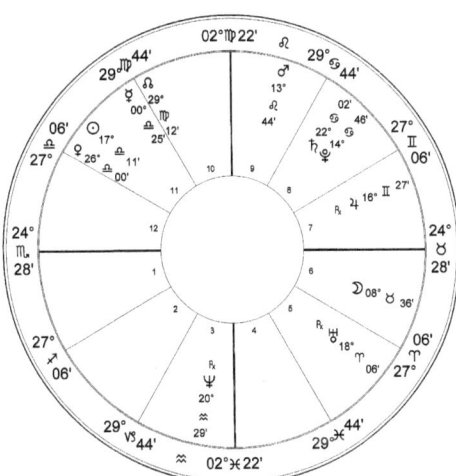

October 9, 1680
106W29, 31N45
9:07 AM MST

Refugees fleeing the Indian uprising in Santa Fe during 1680 established two communities on opposite banks of the Rio Grande. Over the years, the northern side of the river became American, while the south side remained Mexican. Today, it's called Juarez. By 1827 the division was made clear (Ascendant sesquare Pluto); the treaty of Guadelupe Hidalgo in 1848 separated the cities legally (Midheaven trine Mercury). In 1859 a town site was platted; three years later, federal troops captured the town (Ascendant square Neptune). With the arrival of the railroad in 1881, El Paso became the most lawless city in the land (Midheaven inconjunct Venus). Due to the favorable exchange rate, El Paso is a major employer for those citizens south of the border in neighboring Mexico.

El Paso is the only city in the United States where two cultures constantly intermingle; more than sixty percent of the population is Mexican. It also has the most sunshine of any large city and has become a retirement haven for the military. Its natives are self-reliant, rugged and straightforward (Scorpio rising) but less vain and taciturn than would be expected (Moon in Taurus).

Incorporated: August 15, 1873
Elevation: 3,695 feet
Area: 239 square miles
Source: *Great River* by Paul Horgan

Fort Worth

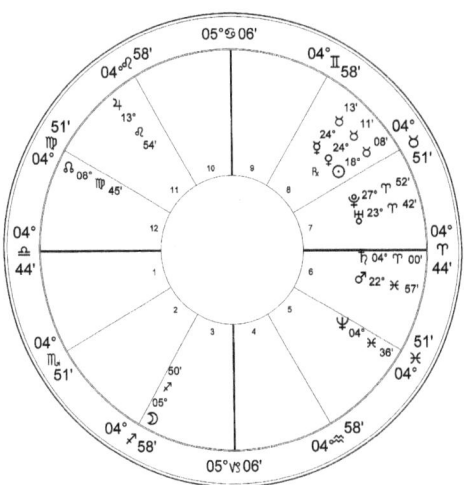

May 8, 1849
97W18, 32N45
3:45 PM CST

Founded by the army in 1849, it was never a fort at all. Four years later, the military settlement was abandoned (Midheaven semisquare Mercury/Venus) and became a trading post. During the 1860s, Fort Worth was a cowtown but in 1873, because of a nationwide financial panic, eighty percent of its people got up and left (Midheaven square Pluto). Meat packing houses opened in 1902 (Midheaven square Venus/Mercury) and in 1909, a fire burned most of the business district (Ascendant opposition Mercury/Venus). Oil was discovered in 1912 (Midheaven opposition Neptune) and by 1949, the first of many aircraft plants opened for business (Ascendant trine Uranus).

Fort Worth is the most Texan of all cities—the land of cattle barons, oil kings, cowboys, dudes and wranglers, gamblers and gunmen. Many consider it an overgrown cowtown (Sun in Taurus sextile Mars) for it's often loud mouthed and big hearted (Moon in Sagittarius). Famous not only for its airplanes and stock yards, the spirit of this city makes it famous, for Fort Worth is a hustler at heart and hasn't lost its pioneer ways. Truly, this city is "where the west begins" and is as different from its neighbor to the east, Big D, as New York is from Miami.

Incorporated: March 1, 1873

Elevation: 670 feet
Area: 244 square miles
Source: Fort Worth Public Library; Encyclopedia Britannica says June 6, 1849

Galveston

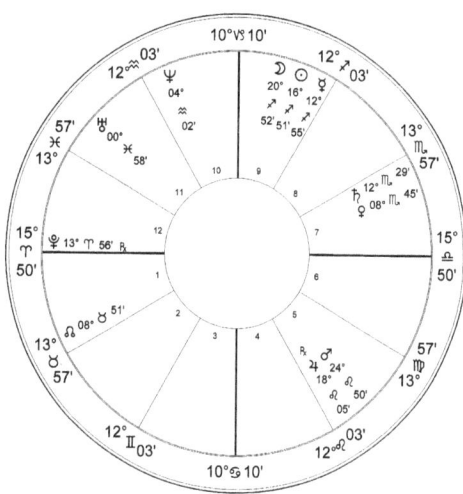

December 8, 1836
94W47, 29N18
1:53 PM CST

First settled in 1777, it was claimed by Mexico in 1816. Until 1821 it was the headquarters of the pirate Jean Lafitte. The present city was founded in 1836, but was isolated from the mainland until the railroad came in 1853. Blockaded for three months during the Civil War in 1862 (Midheaven square Saturn), its port was deepened in 1896. On September 8, 1900, a tidal wave killed more than 6,000 people (Midheaven square Sun, Ascendant trine Uranus); it was the most terrible hurricane ever to hit the U.S. mainland. The following year, Galveston adopted the first commission form of government in the country. Another hurricane in August 1915 (Ascendant trine Saturn) caused much less damage and loss of life as the city had erected a sea wall to protect itself, plus it had raised the entire city eight feet. Hurricane Carla in September 1961 also proved the seawall could withstand the strongest winds ever recorded in a tropical storm (MC square Jupiter, Ascendant conjunct Jupiter trine Moon).

Galveston is the second largest cotton port in the U.S. and an important grain and sulphur center. Its location on an island fronting the Gulf of Mexico has made it a popular resort over the years.

Incorporated: January 28, 1839
Elevation: 15 feet
Source: *Galveston* by Charles Hayes

Houston

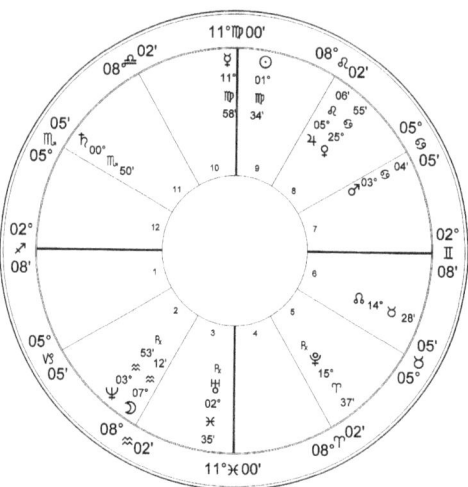

August 24, 1836
95W22, 29N46
12:59 PM CST

Founded in 1836, it became the capital of Texas from 1837 until 1839 (Ascendant square Sun), when a yellow fever epidemic caused the legislature to adjourn to Austin (Ascendant sesquare Mars). In 1859 three fires broke out and burned most of the city (Midheaven square Mars). From 1865 until 1874, Houston was occupied by federal troops under martial law (Midheaven trine Moon). With the discovery of oil at Spindletop in 1901 (Midheaven quincunx Pluto), Houston found it necessary to dig a channel to the Gulf. Completed in 1914 (Ascendant sextile Pluto), Houston thus became a world seaport. During July 1979, a double tragedy hit the city: rainfall totaling more than thirty inches inundated much of the east side, and an apartment building fire burned 325 units (Midheaven conjunct Neptune quincunx Mars). Due to the removal of much ground water, parts of the city are sinking into the earth at an alarming rate. In June 2001, tropical storm Allison dropped 38 inches of rain, inundating downtown Houston, which was underwater; tunnels were submerged, commerce ground to a halt and damage was more than $5 billion (Midheaven inconjunct Venus, Ascendant square Mercury sesquare Saturn sextile Neptune).

Even though Houston is fifty miles from the Gulf, it is the second largest port in the nation. Its weather is one of the worst imaginable: Heat and humidity in the summer are oppressive and nights are seldom cool. Massive in area as well as population, Houston sprawls due to unrestricted zoning laws. People are drawn by the bravado, newness and prosperity of the region, and Houston also has an extremely low unemployment rate combined with a low cost of living. The "Energy Capital" of the U.S., it is one of the top ten manufacturing centers and the largest oil port in the country. Houstonians are materialistic (Sun in Virgo) with a gusty and vital behavior (Sagittarius rising) but possess few close family ties (Moon conjunct Neptune opposition Jupiter square Saturn). They work hard for only one thing: money and business, for class isn't all that important at first. It's a raw, turbulent place with what many consider bad government, which, because of its desire to remain independent of Washington, provides few city services. Pockets of poverty are within eye view of the towering downtown skyscrapers, and the lack of parks and open spaces is appalling. Some consider the cops a bit too trigger happy, for the murder rate is quite high in proportion to the type of crimes committed. A virile city, Houston is decidedly a man's town, both in action and in attitude. Houstonians are friendly, warm and hospitable, but extremely sensitive to outside criticism (Sun in Virgo opposition Uranus). Because of their love of sports, plus the lack of comfort in watching them during the summer, they built the Astrodome, the world's first indoor baseball arena. Yet, with all its corporate power and glamour, Houston still looks disordered and incomplete. A crazy quilt city with little apparent cohesion, it fortunately has the energy to correct its faults, which are many. It's still possessed with the frontier spirit whose only credo is bigness. Houston will continue to thrive, becoming a pleasant and attractive city; until then, one can only hope the oil doesn't dry up and the air conditioning doesn't go off. Either one could spell disaster.

Incorporated: June 5, 1837
Elevation: 55 feet
Area: 556 square miles
Source: *American Guide Series*

Laredo

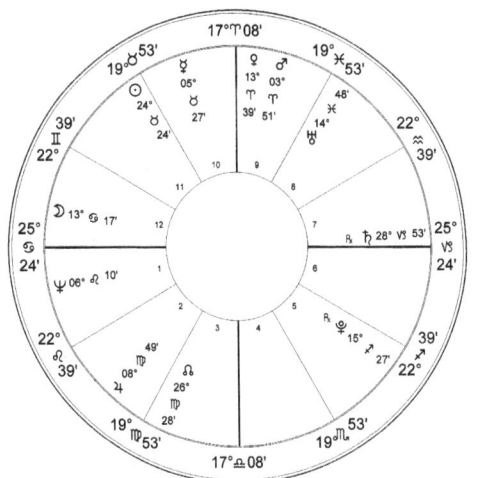

May 15, 1755
99W30, 27N30
10:09 AM CST

Settled in 1755, it was one of the first towns in Texas not founded by either the clergy or the military. In 1846 it was occupied by the Texas Rangers and during the following year by General Lamar (Midheaven conjunct Moon, Ascendant inconjunct Uranus). Camp Crawford was completed in 1849 to deter smugglers. In 1862, during the Civil War, Laredo was occupied by Confederates. (Midheaven opposition Saturn). Like many other towns in the state, it was a cowtown during the last days of the 19th century.

More than just another border town, Laredo is also a major railroad center and terminus for the Pan American Highway. Half the overland imports from Mexico pass through this city.

Incorporated: 1852
Elevation: 440 feet
Source: *American Guide Series*

Lubbock

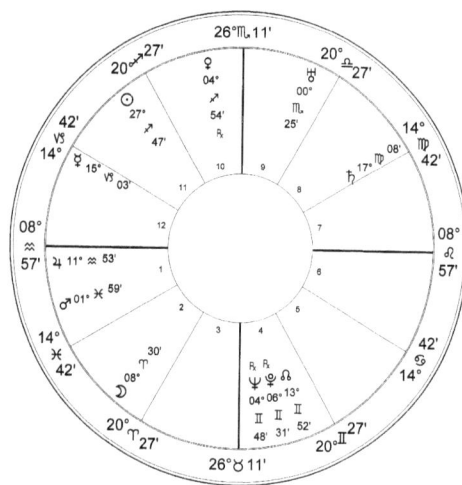

December 19, 1890
101W51, 33N35
10:30 AM CST

Founded in 1890 as an agreement between old Lubbock and Monterey, the first cotton was planted ten years later and made it the world's largest inland cotton market. With the discovery of ground water, Lubbock became an important agricultural center and produces twenty percent of the nation's sorghum. It's also a large meat packing center for this cattle country. In May 1970 a tornado caused extensive damage throughout the region (Ascendant conjunct Neptune/Pluto).

Incorporated: March 24, 1909
Elevation: 3,251 feet
Area: 84 square miles
Source: *History of Lubbock* by Lawrence Graves

San Antonio

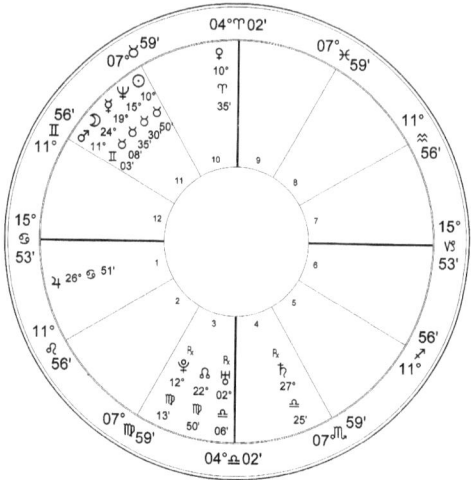

May 1, 1718
98W30, 29N25
10:12 AM CST

Founded as San Antonio de Bexar in 1718, five missions were founded in the region shortly afterward. With the cessation of mission activity in 1794, the community became deserted by 1813 (Ascendant sesquare Mercury). During the early days of Texas' fight for independence, the Alamo became a focal point in the fight for liberty. On March 6, 1836, a battle was fought that killed 155 Texans (including Davy Crockett and Jim Bowie) and more than 1,500 Mexican soldiers. A battle cry went up all over Texas: "Remember the Alamo." In 1879 Fort Sam Houston opened (Midheaven trine Sun) and in 1917 Kelly AFB was completed (Ascendant square Uranus). San Antonio hosted the Hemisfair in 1968 (Midheaven trine Venus).

Six flags have flown over this most historic of Texas cities: French, Spanish, Mexican, Texas, the Confederacy and the United States. A gay and beautiful city, it has a large Mexican population which gives this city charm and fine cuisine (Cancer rising). A walk along the Paseo del Rio is a treat for visitors and natives alike. Within the region are many military establishments (Midheaven in Aries)—Fort Sam Houston, and Kelly, Brooks, Lackland and Randolph Air Force Bases—which make San Antonio the mother of the Air Force. Despite the residents' distaste for the military, they somehow manage to tolerate the 100,000 servicemen that pass through here each year. More than 30,000 military personnel are on active duty at all times and many retired generals live in the surrounding area.

San Antonio's largest employer, needless to say, is the government, but it's also the chief manufacturing, wholesale and retail center for Mexico.

Incorporated: June 5, 1837
Elevation: 656 feet

Area: 264 square miles
Source: *San Antonio* by Green Peyton

Waco

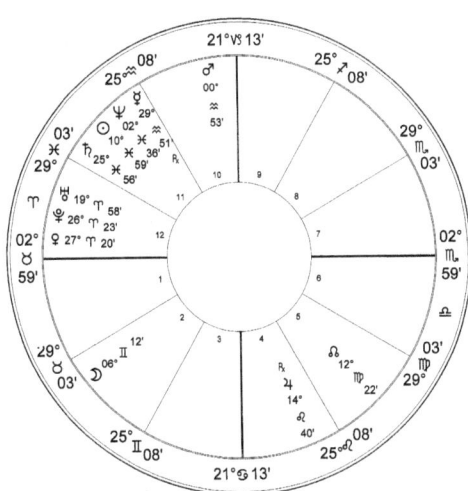

**March 1, 1849
97W08, 31N33
9:23 AM CST**

Waco was settled in 1848 and platted the following year. The first suspension bridge across the Brazos was completed in 1870 and in 1886, Baylor University moved here (Midheaven conjunct Mercury). In May 1953 a tornado caused over $40 million in damage and killed 114 people (Midheaven square Mars). The Branch Davidian Cult outside of town was attacked and fire bombed by agents of the federal government in April 1993. It was believed the cult was stockpiling weapons for a future conflict with the government. More than eighty-five people died in the inferno, including the leader, David Koresh (Midheaven square Sun semisquare Pluto).

Incorporated: 1856
Elevation: 427 feet
Source: *Pictorial History* by Roger Conger

Wichita Falls

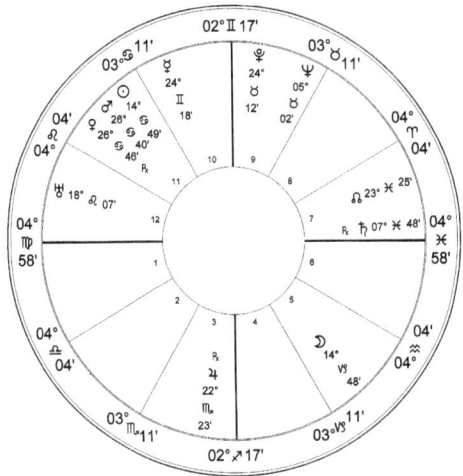

**July 6, 1876
98W30, 33N54
9:35 AM CST**

In 1837 John Scott won this land during a poker game, and in 1876, he filed a plat claiming his right to the region. With the arrival of the railroad in September 1882, the first sale of lots was held. Oil drilling began in 1910 (Midheaven trine Saturn) and in April 1964, a tornado devastated a good portion of this city (Ascendant square Uranus).

Incorporated: 1889
Elevation: 946 feet
Source: *American Guide Series*

Utah

January 4, 1896
Salt Lake City
111W53, 40N45
8:03 AM MST
Source: Los Angeles
Times says 10:03 a.m.
in Washington.

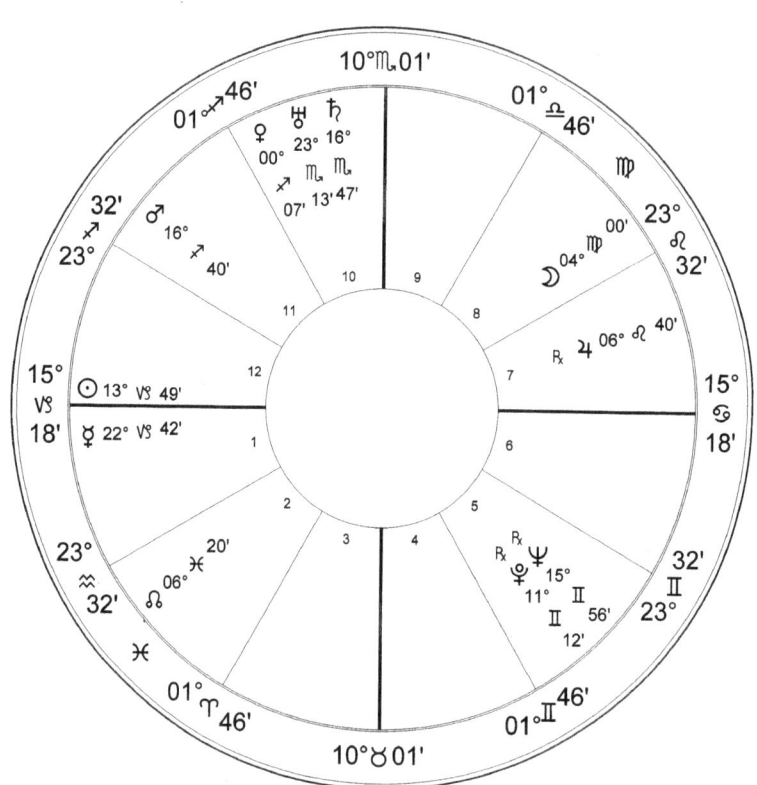

In 1824 the Great Salt Lake was discovered by James Bridger, and in 1847 Brigham Young led his band of Mormons to this region in search of the land he had seen in a dream. In 1848 the U.S. acquired the region in the Mexican Cession, and the following year, the State of Deseret was organized. On September 9, 1850, the Territory of Utah was organized which created much dissension between the Mormons and the federal government. Federal troops were sent in during 1857, after President Buchanan removed Brigham Young as governor. The Transcontinental Railroad was completed at Promontory Point in 1869, linking the U.S. from the Atlantic to the Pacific. Polygamy was made a federal crime in 1862 and in 1890, the Mormon church outlawed multiple marriages. Statehood came six years later. In 1916 the first non-Mormon was elected governor, and in 1952, uranium was discovered near Moab. Probably because of their "peculiar" ways, at least to non-Mormons, natives of Utah have been a society unto themselves. Indian troubles were few during the formative years due to Young's belief that it was cheaper to feed the Indians than to fight them. A strict people who have large and close-bonded families, Utah has one of the lowest crime rates in the country, and the highest level of education.

Utah ranks second in copper, and third in gold and silver. It shares with Colorado and Wyoming the largest oil shale deposits in the nation. It ranks seventh in sheep.

Area: 84,916 square miles

Logan

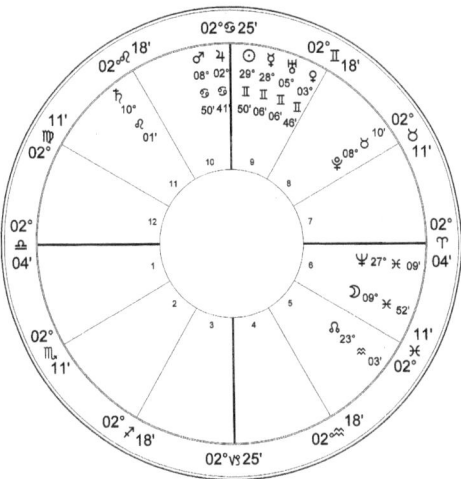

June 21, 1859
111W50, 41N44
12:40 PM MST

Because the Mormons believed the region to be too cold for agriculture, it wasn't settled until 1856. Formally founded three years later, Utah State University was dedicated in 1888.

Incorporated: 1866
Elevation: 4,535 feet
Source: Logan Public Library

Ogden

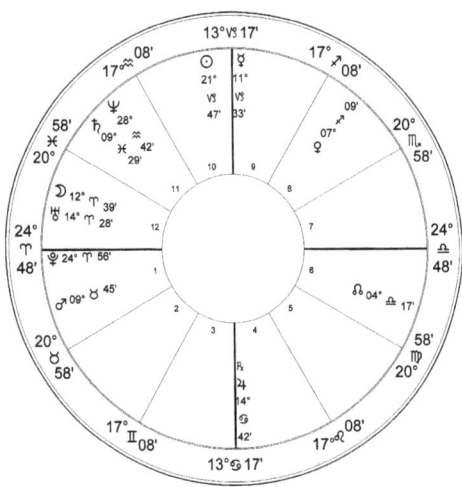

January 12, 1848
111W58, 41N13
12:00 Noon MST

Fort Buenaventura was founded here in 1846, and settled by the Mormons two years later as Brownsville. Platted in 1850, the Union Pacific Railroad arrived in 1869, and remains the city's biggest employer.

Ogden is the chief railroad center of the west and a major military supply center.

Incorporated: 1851
Elevation: 4,310 feet
Source: *Beneath Ben Lomond's Peak* by Milton Hunter

Provo

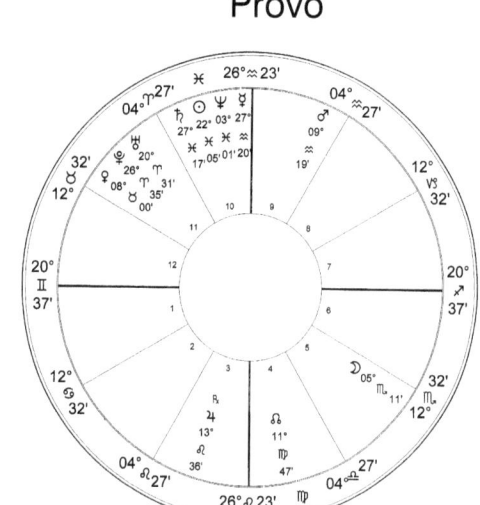

March 12, 1849
111W39, 40N14
11:00 AM MST

Settled as Fort Utah in 1849, its name comes from an early explorer of the region, Etienne Provost. Provo is home to Brigham Young University, founded in 1875 (Midheaven conjunct Sun) along with Utah's first steel mill. It's a pleasant town with a strong religious background.

Incorporated: 1851
Elevation: 4,549 feet
Source: *History of Provo* by J.M. Jensen

Salt Lake City

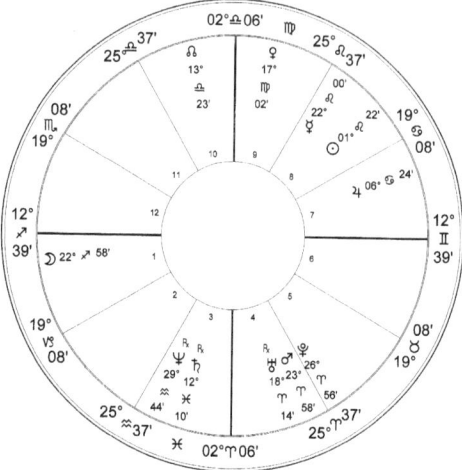

July 24, 1847
111W53, 40N45
4:27 PM MST

Many years before Brigham Young actually saw this valley, he viewed it in a dream. Upon first sighting the region on July 22, 1847, he said, "This is the Place." Two days later, he entered the valley himself and laid the cornerstone for the Mormon Temple. During the following summer, a plague of grasshoppers almost destroyed the crops until a swarm of seagulls swooped down and devoured the insects (Ascendant square Saturn). During 1858 the U.S. Army moved in because of the Mormon's unusual religious practices, and the city became deserted (Midheaven quincunx Saturn). Congress passed the anti-polygamy laws in 1862 (Midheaven opposition Uranus) which made most of the residents criminals in the eyes of U.S. law. When polygamy was formally outlawed in 1890 (Midheaven trine Saturn), it paved the way for statehood six years later. A series of earthquakes during 1934 rumbled through the city for months but caused little apparent damage (Midheaven trine Pluto). Salt Lake City hosted the 2002 Winter Olympics (Midheaven trine Jupiter, Ascendant trine Neptune).

Despite its size, Salt Lake City is a highly sophisticated, literate and cultured community. Laid out in blocks of ten acres each, and separated by streets that are 132 feet wide, it has an aura of being isolated and lonely. Early residents were taught to be self sufficient economically as well as socially; many theatrical groups were formed and the Mormons kept pretty much to themselves (all higher octave planets below the horizon). Despite the fact the church forbade coffee, tobacco and alcohol, they managed to amuse themselves in less dangerous ways. Natives of this holy city are members of the good neighbor society, for the church takes care of its own and poverty or slums are seldom seen in this attractive and well designed metropolis (Libra Midheaven).

But the chief attraction of this city is that it's the headquarters for the Mormon church. Like Mecca and Rome, it's an ecclesiastical community (Sagittarius rising) where the church pervades much of daily life. The focal point for the city is Temple Square where the Mormon Temple and the Tabernacle are located. Nearby is the famous genealogical library where anyone, who has the patience, can trace their family tree. North of the city is the copper domed capitol building which overlooks this smog-free city and the towering snow-capped Wasatch range. In those mountains are the popular ski slopes of Park City, Alta, and Sundance. This makes Salt Lake City the closest large city to three major winter resorts in the country. Salt Lake City is also home of the University of Utah located near Emigration Canyon, where the settlers first arrived many years ago.

Incorporated: January 9, 1851
Elevation: 4,290 feet
Area: 70 square miles
Source: *Utah* by Milton Hunger says July 24, 1847 at 2 p.m.; in fact, it should have been 2 p.m. on July 22 when the region was first sighted. About 11 a.m. the next morning, crops were planted, and on July 24, Young entered the valley for the first time. Later that afternoon, he laid the cornerstone for the Temple. Chart rectified.

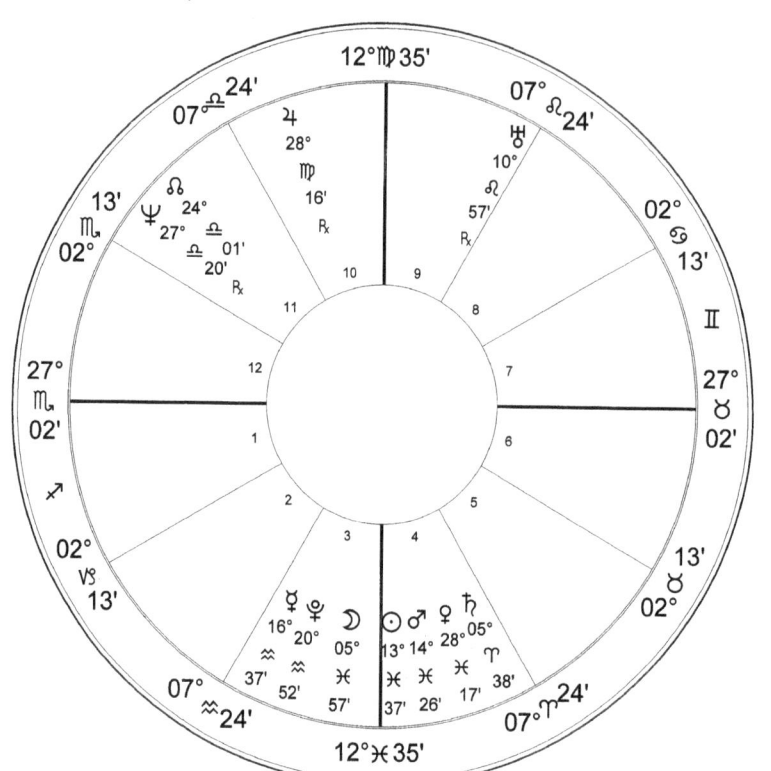

Vermont

**March 4, 1791
Bennington
73W12, 42N53
12:01 AM EST
Source: United States
Government Papers**

In 1666 the first permanent settlement was established on Lake Champlain by the French; the first English settlers arrived in 1724 at Brattleboro. The region was claimed by New Hampshire in 1749, but New York ruled the region after 1764. Resenting interference, the settlers declared their independence on January 15, 1777, calling the region New Connecticut. During the Revolution, Ethan Allen and his Green Mountain Boys captured Fort Ticonderoga in 1775, and in 1777, the British were defeated at Bennington. In 1790, New York gave up her claims to the region. Vermont was the first state to outlaw slavery and provide universal suffrage without property qualifications. Washington signed the Bill of Admission in February 1791, to become effective March 4, 1791. Thus, Vermont is the only state in the Union to have been born in this manner, except Ohio and West Virginia, which is another story. In 1823 a canal linked Lake Champlain with the Hudson River. During the Civil War, Confederate troops robbed banks in St. Albans of $200,000 and fled into Canada. Strongly Republican and self reliant, Vermonters resent the intrusion of the federal government into their lives. They wish to keep their state rural and unspoiled, which gives them an air of insularity.

Vermont is famous for its marble, and has the largest mines in the country. Maple syrup and dairy products are the chief agricultural products.

Scorpio rising illustrates the necessity to remain self reliant against all odds, and Uranus in the ninth house points to the refusal to follow, or receive, federal jurisdictions without a good fight. The three planets in Pisces in the fourth house point to the insularity and privacy these people crave.

Area: 9,609 square miles

Bennington

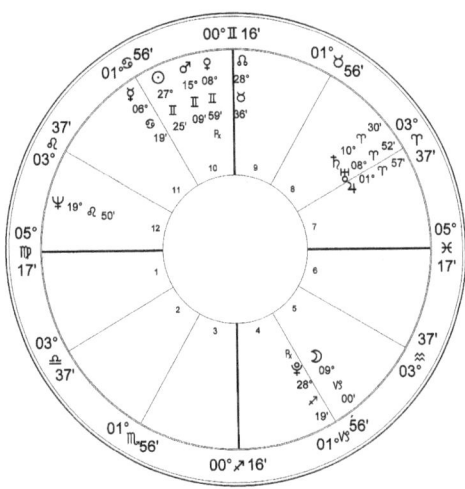

June 18, 1761
73W12, 42N53
9:57 AM EST

Chartered in 1749, Bennington was formally founded in 1761. Nearby Fort Ticonderoga was the scene of Ethan's Allen's victory over the British on August 16, 1777 (Midheaven conjunct Mars). Bennington was briefly the capital of Vermont in 1791 when it entered the Union.

Incorporated: Unknown
Elevation: 672 feet
Source: Bennington Public Library

Burlington

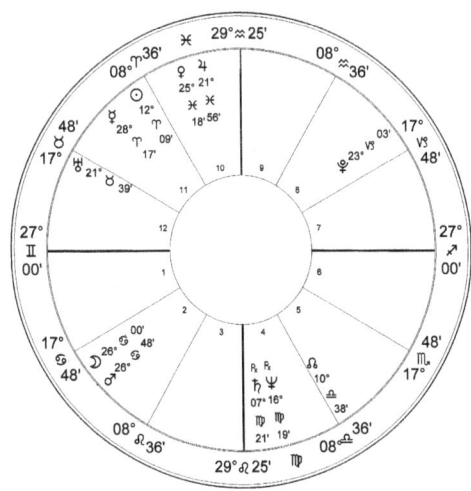

April 1, 1773
73W12, 44N29
9:18 AM EST

Ira Allen was granted this land in 1773 on which to build a town. Ten years later, soldiers returning from the revolution were the first settlers. A canal was competed in 1823 connecting Lake Champlain to the Hudson River.

An overgrown little village, Burlington is nevertheless the largest city in Vermont. A thrifty and conservative community (Moon in Cancer), it's cautious and puritanical in outlook. Its natives are like most Vermonters; secretive and taciturn, minding their own business and wishing you'd do the same. The city has many elms and maples which offer a spectacular display of color during the fall, and above those trees are the many church spires that dot this town. Burlington is largely Catholic due to its French Canadian, Irish, and Italian population.

Incorporated: February 21, 1865
Elevation: 110 feet
Source: *Ira Allen* by James B. Wilbur

Montpelier

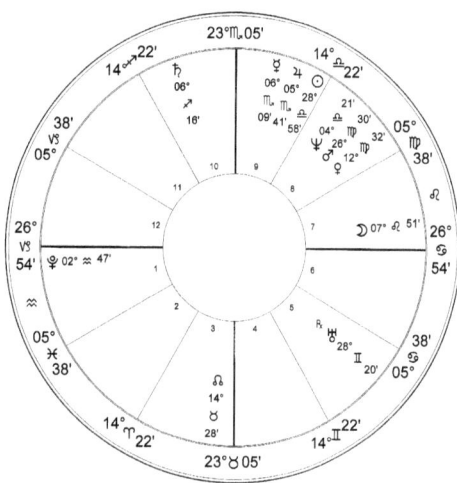

**October 21, 1780
72W35, 44N16
1:10 PM EST**

Founded during a land grant in 1780, it was settled seven years later. Montpelier became the state capital in 1805 (Ascendant trine Mercury and Jupiter). A flood in November 1927 caused serious damage due to this town's location in a narrow valley (Midheaven sesquare Saturn). Nearby is the city of Barre, famous for producing some of the world's most beautiful marble.

Incorporated: 1895
Elevation: 485 feet
Source: *History of the Town of Montpelier*

Rutland

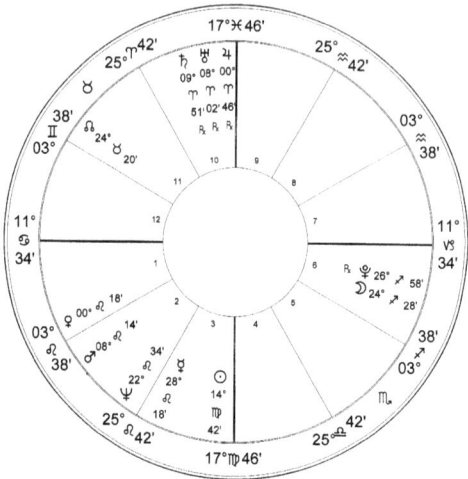

**September 7, 1761
72W58, 43N37
12:01 AM EST**

Chartered in 1761, Rutland was settled nine years later. The Republic of Vermont was established here in 1784 (Midheaven conjunct Saturn and Uranus), and until 1804, it was the capital of Vermont. Rutland is slightly smaller than it was a century ago because three communities seceded and went their way.

Incorporated: 1892
Elevation: 550 feet
Source: Carolyn Dodson for the date; chart rectified as this was an incorporation date and not a founding date

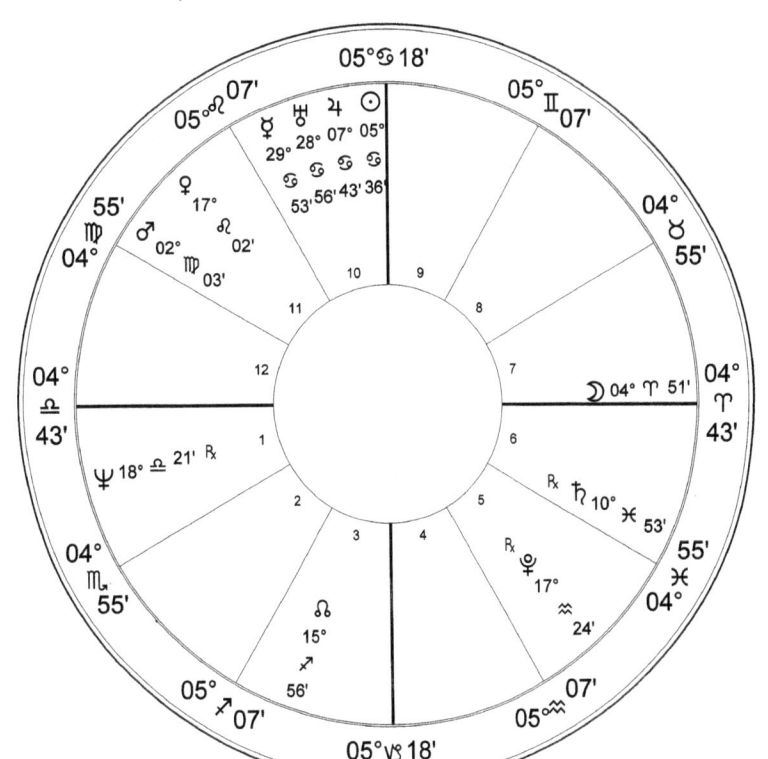

Virginia

June 26, 1788
Richmond
77W27, 37N32
12:11 PM EST
Source: Virginia Historical Society says "noon"

On April 10, 1606 a charter was granted to Virginia; the following year on May 23, 1607, the first English settlement in the New World was made at Jamestown. Black slaves first arrived in 1619, the same year the House of Burgesses was founded. Virginia was made a royal colony in 1624, and during the remainder of the 17th century, it suffered numerous Indian raids. Jamestown was burned in 1676 during Bacon's Rebellion. During the French and Indian Wars (1754-1763), Virginia was the focal point for control between the North and the South. During the Revolution, the state endured repeated British attacks until Cornwallis finally surrendered to Washington at Yorktown in 1781. Seven years later, Virginia ratified the Constitution, and became the largest state in the nation, stretching all the way to the Mississippi and the Great Lakes. Virginia is known as the "Mother of Presidents" for within its borders were born Washington, Jefferson, Madison, Monroe, William Harrison, Tyler, Taylor and Wilson. Her native sons are too numerous to mention, but without them, America probably couldn't have been born. A slave rebellion in 1831, led by Nat Turner, killed 100 Negroes. Thirty years later, Virginia joined the Confederacy on April 17, 1861. Richmond was made capital of the Confederate States later that year. During the Civil War, battles such as Manassas, Spotsylvania, Chancellorsville, Fredericksburg, and the Wilderness were fought on the soil of Old Dominion. General Lee surrendered to Grant at Appomattox on April 9, 1865, thus ending the bloodiest conflict in the nation's history. Readmitted into the Union on January 16, 1870, Virginia was stripped of her former glory and never regained the stature she once possessed.

Textiles and chemicals rank as the number one industries, with tobacco and ship building coming in second. Hampton Roads is the largest port in the south Atlantic and is home to more naval facilities than any other area in the country. Coal is the principal mineral resource.

Area: 40,817 square miles

Alexandria

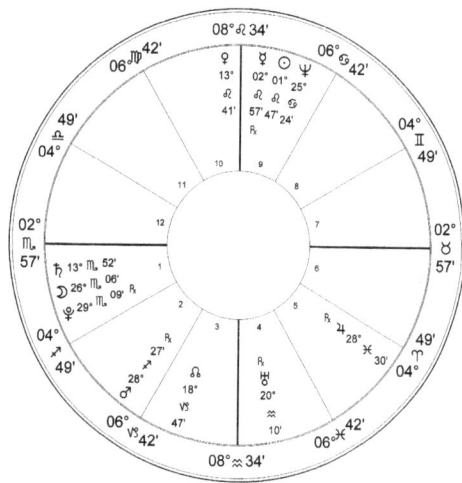

July 24, 1749
77W03, 38N48
12:42 PM EST

Founded by the Virginia legislature in 1749, the first sale of lots was held April 3, 1752. Washington was one of the surveyors of the new town. On April 15, 1791, Alexandria became part of the newly created Federal City when Washington laid the cornerstone at Jones Point (Midheaven semisquare Mercury, Ascendant trine Sun). A fire in 1824 burned much of the community (Ascendant conjunct Mars square Moon), and in 1846, Alexandria was returned to the State of Virginia (Midheaven square Venus) It then became an independent city of Fairfax County. Occupied by Union forces in 1861 (Midheaven conjunct Pluto), it was the temporary capital of Virginia during 1863 and was burned the following year.

A good portion of its residents work in Washington, but the largest employer in Alexandria is the railroad. Just south of the city is the home of Washington, Mount Vernon, and within the city limits of Alexandria are many spots he frequented during his lifetime.

Incorporated: May 7, 1852
Elevation: 52 feet
Area: 16 square miles
Source: Alexandria Public Library

Arlington

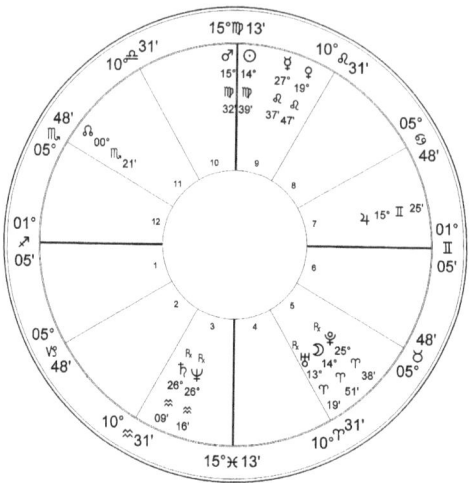

September 7, 1846
77W07, 38N53
12:00 PM EST

When the District of Columbia was envisioned in 1790, this region of northern Virginia became part of the new Federal City, later called Washington, D.C. Due to lack of settlement in this area, however, it was ceded back to the state of Virginia in 1846. Arlington National Cemetery was founded in 1864 on land once owned by Robert E. Lee (Ascendant trine Moon and Uranus square Sun and Mars opposition Jupiter).

In 1942, the Pentagon was begun during the early days of World War II. It's still the world's largest office building, nearly a mile in circumference, and completely surrounded by freeways just across the Potomac from the nation's capital (Ascendant trine Venus semisquare Pluto). In September 2001, militant Islamic terrorists crashed a plane into the side of this massive building, killing nearly 200 people (Midheaven opposition Venus, Ascendant conjunct Jupiter square Sun and Mars sextile Moon and Jupiter). Crystal City, just south of Reagan National Airport, is home to many government agencies.

Elevation: 40 feet
Area: 31 square miles
Source: Library of Congress

Charlottesville

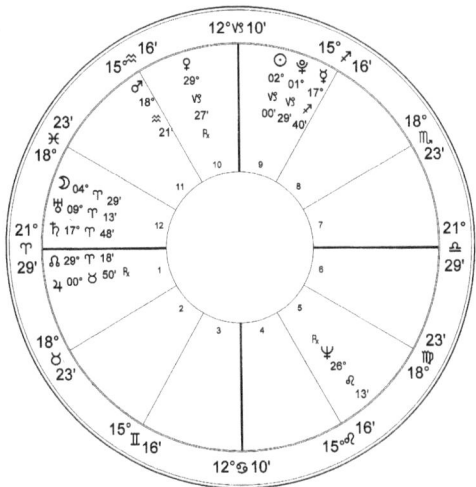

**December 23, 1762
78W30, 38N02
12:58 PM EST**

Albemarle County laid out fifty acres upon which to establish a town in 1761, which was authorized by the state legislature the following year. Largely associated with Thomas Jefferson who founded the University of Virginia in 1819 (Ascendant sextile Jupiter), it is an intellectual community with pleasant neighborhoods. Nearby are the homes of Jefferson (Monticello) and James Monroe (Ash Lawn).

Incorporated: 1888
Elevation: 480 feet
Source: *Albemarle* by John H Moore

Hampton

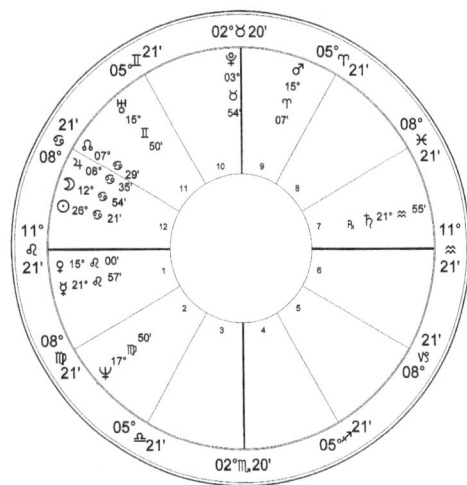

**July 19, 1610
76W23, 37N02
6:18 AM EST**

Founded in 1610, Hampton is the oldest continuously settled English-speaking city in the country. It was known as Kecoughtan until 1680. British troops pillaged the city in 1775 (Midheaven square Moon opposition Mars) and it was burned by the British in 1813 (Ascendant sesquare Neptune). In order to protect the city, Fort Monroe was erected between 1819 and 1834. Despite its impregnable walls, the Confederates burned the town in August 1861 (Ascendant conjunct Mars). After the Civil War, Jefferson Davis was imprisoned within its walls. Fort Langley was completed in 1917 (Midheaven trine Jupiter) and is today one of the leading research centers in the U.S. Over seventy-five percent of Hamptonians are employed in the transportation field, many of them at the Newport News shipyards. Hampton merged with Elizabeth County in 1952.

Incorporated: 1980
Elevation: 12 feet
Area: 55 square miles
Source: *Encyclopedia of American Cities*

Lynchburg

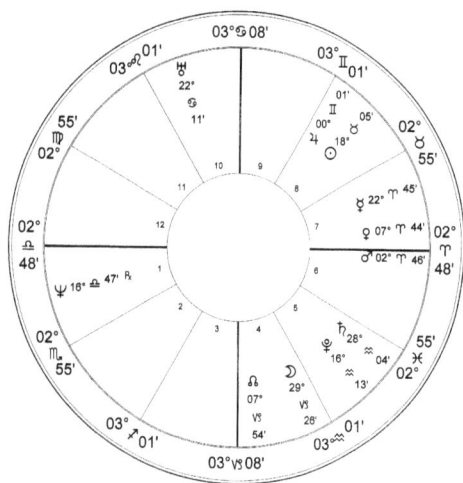

May 8, 1787
79W09, 37N25
3:24 PM EST

In 1757 a ferry was established by John Lynch: thirty years later the town was formally founded, one year after it was authorized by the Virginia legislature. In 1791 the first tobacco warehouse was completed, and in 1840 a canal was completed to Richmond. It's the largest dark tobacco market in the South.

Lynchburg is famous for being the home of Jerry Falwell, self-appointed leader of the so called Moral Majority, and Edith Custer who founded The Mercury Hour, the finest astrological magazine in the country. If you don't subscribe to it, you'd better send her a letter and get with it.

Incorporated: 1852
Elevation: 800 feet
Source: *Lynchburg and its People* by W.A. Christian

Newport News

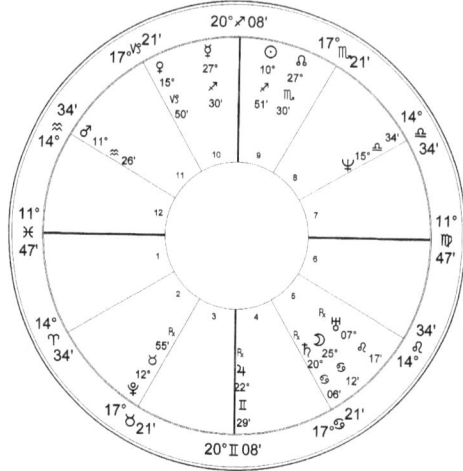

December 2, 1621
76W25, 39N59
12:36 PM EST

Founded in 1621 as Newport Newes, most of the ships in its harbor were burned in 1667 by Dutch invaders (Midheaven opposition Uranus). In this harbor, called Hampton Roads, took place the first battle between two ironclad ships, the Monitor and the Merrimack, in March 1862 (Midheaven sextile Jupiter). Newport News was chosen as a railroad terminus in March 1880, and the town was platted the following October. Ship building began in 1886 (Ascendant trine Moon); in its yards have been born ships like the United States, the America and the Independence. Independent of Warwick County in 1952, it merged with Warwick City six years later (Midheaven trine Moon).

Incorporated: 1896
Elevation: 25 feet
Area: 69 square miles
Source: *Newport News* by Annie Jester

Norfolk

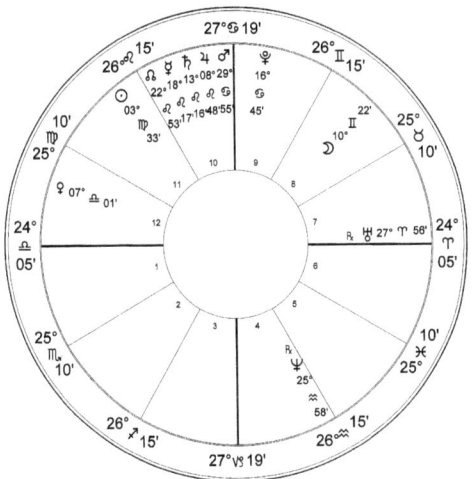

August 26, 1682
76W17, 36N51
9:42 AM EST

First settled in 1636, land was purchased for settlement in 1680 and Norfolk was formally founded two years later. A fire burned the city on New Year's Day 1776 (Midheaven square Mars) to prevent the British from capturing the port, but the Redcoats blockaded it anyway. Due to the Embargo Act, 1807 to 1815 were difficult years (Midheaven sesquisquare Pluto, Ascendant opposition Saturn) and the economy suffered considerably. A yellow fever epidemic in 1855 killed more than 1,500 and half the city evacuated (Ascendant trine Sun). During the Civil War, the first battle between ironclad ships, the Monitor and the Merrimack, took place in 1862 (Midheaven square Uranus). After the war, recovery was slow, but by 1882, Norfolk was the largest coal port in the South due to the arrival of the railroads (Ascendant sextile Jupiter).

Norfolk is the world's number one navy town (Midheaven in Cancer conjunct Mars). Half the city's income goes to sailors. Situated at the mouth of Hampton Roads, it is the outlet for Chesapeake Bay and the largest natural port in the nation, crisscrossed by many bridges and tunnels. It is a city which has put up with the numerous servicemen who pass through whether in war or peace. Even though most natives dislike the military, they blandly tolerate them. But to other outsiders, Norfolk exhibits the typical hospitality and graciousness of other southern cities. Norfolk is headquarters for sixty-four naval commands and is home to both the Atlantic and Mediterranean fleets.

Incorporated: February 11, 1845
Elevation: 12 feet
Area: 64 square miles
Source: *Through the Years with Norfolk* by W.H. Squires

Portsmouth

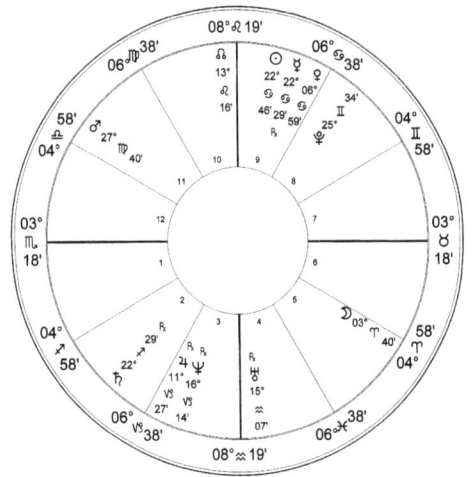

July 14, 1664
76W18, 36N50
1:15 PM EST

Settled in 1664 by William Carver shortly after receiving a land grant, it was laid out in February 1752 (Ascendant conjunct Jupiter). Shipbuilding started in 1763 (Ascendant opposition Sun) and is today the largest industry in the city. During 1776 the British took this city after burning Norfolk (Midheaven sextile Mars, Ascendant quincunx Venus); three years later, both the Navy Yard and Fort Nelson were put to the torch (Ascendant sesquisquare Mars). A fire in 1821 burned much of Portsmouth and a yellow fever epidemic during 1855 killed hundreds. Confederate solders burned the Navy Yard during the Civil War in 1862.

Incorporated: March 1, 1858
Elevation: 12 feet
Area: 46 square miles
Source: *Cavaliers and Pioneers* by N.M. Nugent

Richmond

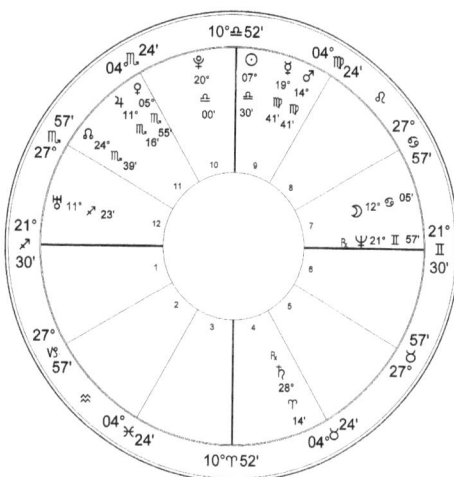

**September 30, 1733
77W27, 37N33
12:12 PM EST**

First settled in 1609 by Captain John Smith who bought the land from Powhatan, it was formally founded by William Byrd in 1733. He laid out the city four years later. Capital of Virginia since 1779 (Midheaven sesquisquare Moon, Ascendant trine Sun), it was captured by the British in 1781 under the leadership of Benedict Arnold (MC inconjunct Neptune). It was freed by Lafayette the following year. Richmond started America's tobacco industry and mined the first coal, made the first bricks and forged the first iron. Three decades prior to the Civil War, it became the leading slave market of the South. In July 1861 it became capital of the Confederacy (Midheaven trine Pluto, Ascendant opposition Uranus). During the next four years, many battles and skirmishes took place around the city, and on April 3, 1865, its citizens burned the city rather than having it fall into the hands of General Grant (Ascendant square Uranus/Neptune square Mars). During the last few decades, Richmond has experienced less racial strife than other southern cities.

Richmond is a romantic symbol of a long forgotten age when chivalry reigned. Much of the city is a museum containing some of the finest colonial and antebellum architecture to be around anywhere (Moon in Cancer). Many of its former residents were founders of this great nation who walked the streets of this trim and gracious city. Richmond is polite but strict (Libra MC), especially in its drinking laws. Very family-oriented, it has few really good restaurants. Known as the "Tobacco Capital of the World," Richmond produces twenty-five percent of the cigarettes and a large supply of snuff, cigars, and chewing tobacco (Neptune opposition Ascendant). Chemicals are also a large source of income. The most historic building in the city is the impressive capitol building, designed by Thomas Jefferson after a Roman temple in southern France. It was completed in 1788, the same year Virginia ratified the Constitution. Here in Richmond is also the church where Patrick Henry uttered his "Give me liberty or give me death" speech back in 1755.

Incorporated: May 19, 1782
Elevation: 160 feet
Area: 63 miles
Source: *Journey to the Land of Eden* by William Byrd says "noon"

Roanoke

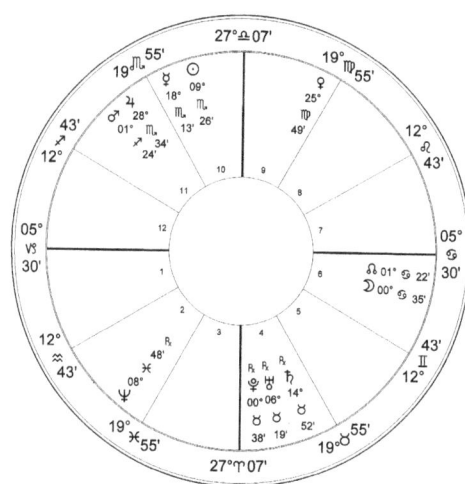

**November 1, 1852
79W56, 37N16
11:16 AM EST**

Founded as the town of Big Lick in 1852, upon the arrival of the railroad, a new city, called Roanoke, was begun in 1882 (Midheaven conjunct Jupiter, Ascendant square Uranus). Rayon factories were founded in 1917, and until 1957, Roanoke was one of the leading manufacturers of that fabric. Today, Roanoke is a large transportation center for western Virginia.

Incorporated: February 28, 1874
Elevation: 905 feet
Area: 43 square miles
Source: Roanoke Public Library

Virginia Beach

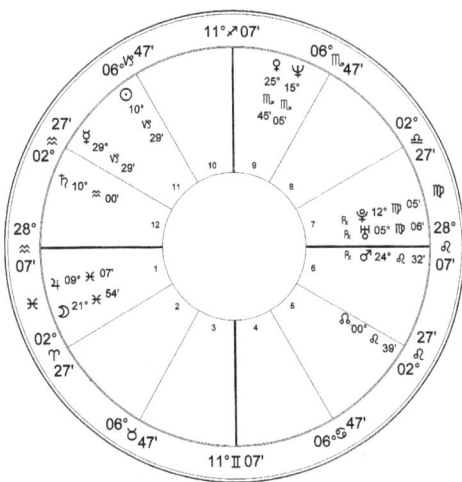

January 1, 1963
75W59, 36N51
10:00 AM EST

During the past three decades, Virginia Beach has grown immensely due to its merger with Princess Anne County in 1963. Known as the first landing spot of the English colonists in 1607, it was established as a seaside resort one century ago. Tourism is the leading contributor to its economy as it has thirty-eight miles of beaches.

Incorporated: 1963
Elevation: 16 feet
Area: 310 square miles
Source: Virginia Beach Public Library

Williamsburg

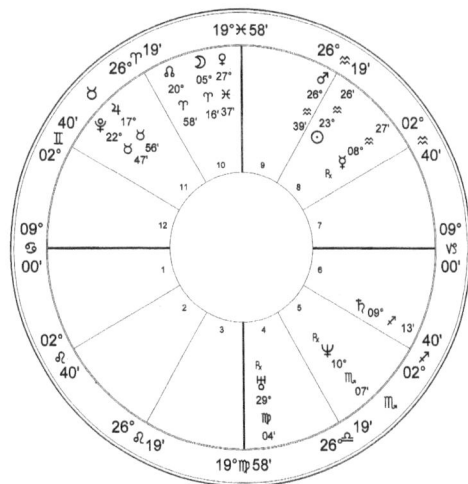

February 11, 1633
76W43, 37N16
1:55 PM LMT

What is today the most perfectly preserved colonial settlement in the United States was founded in 1633 as the Middle Plantation. In 1676, Nathaniel Bacon led a revolt against the British governor, Sir William Berkeley. Rebels burned neighboring Jamestown, but the revolt collapsed with Bacon's death and the execution of most of his followers (Ascendant square Neptune). The capital of Virginia was moved here from Jamestown in 1689 (Ascendant sesquare Moon), and four years later in 1693, the College of William and Mary was founded. It is America's second-oldest institution of higher learning, after Harvard (Midheaven conjunct Jupiter, Ascendant opposition Sun).

During the American Revolution, Lord Dunsmore had to flee the city in 1775 (Midheaven opposition Mercury trine Moon), and the capital was moved to Richmond four years later (Midheaven square Neptune, Ascendant trine Moon). During the Battle of Yorktown in 1781, Williamsburg and its surroundings became headquarters for both the Americans and the British. In October 1781, Lord Cornwallis surrendered to George Washington and America had won her freedom (Ascendant opposition Mercury).

In 1926, the Rockefeller Foundation began restoration of this colonial gem. All structures built after 1800 were torn down, 500 buildings were restored and Williamsburg soon after became a major tourist attraction (Ascendant conjunct Moon). Even tour guides must wear period costumes.

Incorporated: 1722
Source: *A Brief Report Concerning Williamsburg* by R. Goodwin

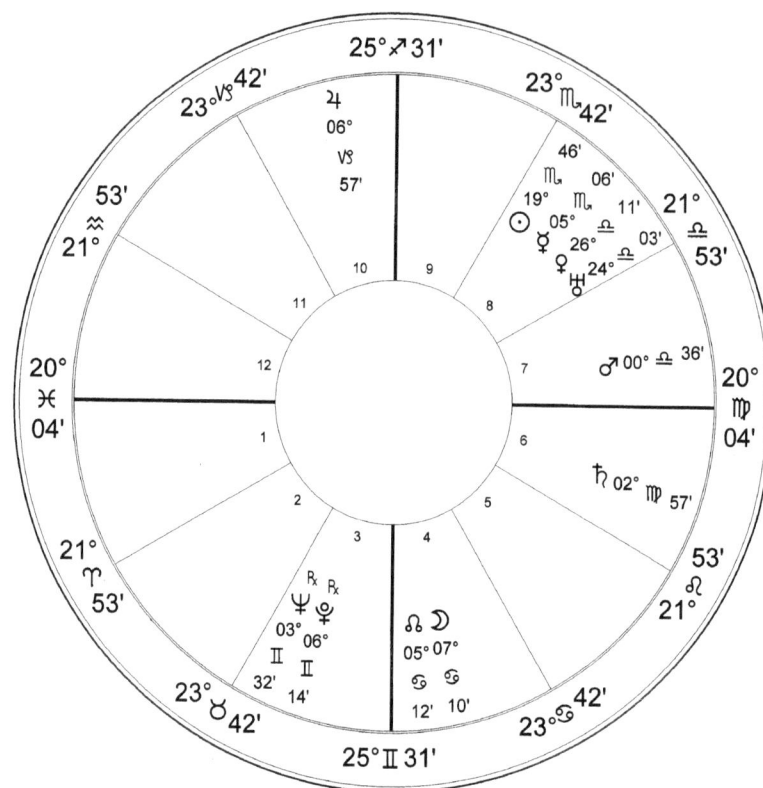

Washington

**November 11, 1889
Olympia
122W53, 47N03
2:27 PM PST
Source:** *Los Angeles Times* **says 5:27 PM in Washington**

In 1792 the mouth of the Columbia River was discovered and surveyed by Vancouver during the next two years. Lewis and Clark arrived in 1805, and in 1810, a trading post was built near Spokane. The first American settlement was made the following year at Okanogan. In 1818 the U.S. and Britain agreed to jointly administer the region, which Britain ceded in 1846. The Cayuse Indians massacred Marcus Whitman and his followers in 1847 near Walla Walla, touching off a war. Seattle was founded in 1851, and during the 1850s, the Yakima Indians fought with settlers to protect their land. On March 2, 1853, Washington was organized as a territory, and it entered the Union in 1889. In 1941 the Grand Coulee Dam began its operation, the largest hydroelectric plant in the world. Washington has been in the forefront environmentally for many years, and continues to fight against encroachment of its forests and streams. Mt. St. Helens blew her stack on May 18, 1980 sending tons of ash eastward causing much damage to crops and cities. It was the largest volcanic explosion during modern times in this country.

Washington ranks first in apples, blueberries and raspberries, and third in wheat. The state produces twenty-five percent of the country's aluminum, much of the world's aircraft (Boeing) and, has a vast fishing fleet. Washington has the second largest timber reserves in the nation.

Washington is the only state in the nation named for an American citizen.

Area: 68,192 square miles

Olympia

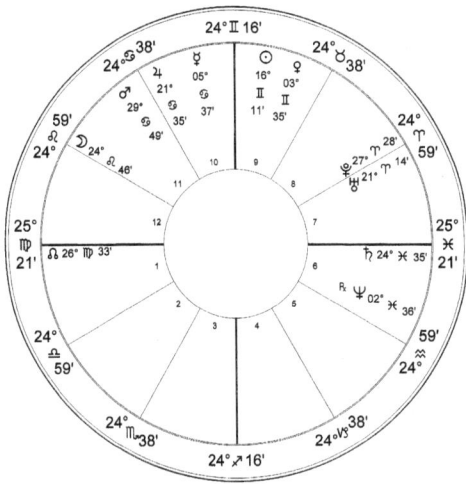

June 6, 1848
122W53, 47N03
12:45 PM PST

Founded as a mission in 1848, three years later Olympia became the first port of entry on Puget Sound with the establishment of a customs house (Ascendant sextile Pluto). Capital of Washington since 1854, it's known for its sparkling water (Olympia Beer) and for being one of the most desirable small communities in the nation.

Incorporated: September 4, 1859
Elevation: 71 feet
Source: Olympia Public Library says early June 1848; chart rectified

Seattle

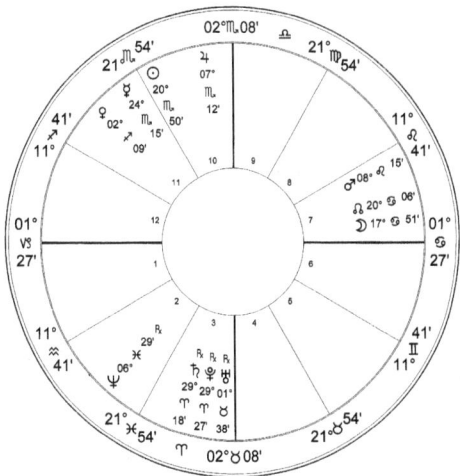

November 13, 1851
122W20, 47N36
10:40 AM PST

The first settlers arrived on September 28, 1851 at Elliot Bay and the following November 13, a colony was established at Alki Point southwest of the current downtown area. Five years later, the Indians massacred many of these settlers (Midheaven square Mars). In 1858 a gold rush on the Fraser River in British Columbia brought many new immigrants to this outpost of North America. Many of those newcomers were men, and in 1862, Asa Mercer was hired to go back east and bring back a wagon load of women for the bachelors. After several ventures like that, the population evened out. In June 1889 a fire leveled thirty-one blocks downtown (Ascendant square Sun) but no lives were lost. In 1897 the Klondike gold rush brought newfound prosperity to Seattle, which became the chief outfitting center for the sourdoughs.

In 1909 Seattle hosted the Alaska-Yukon Expo and in 1916, a canal connecting Puget Sound with Lake Washington was completed (Midheaven sextile Jupiter). America's only general strike occurred in Seattle in 1919 (Ascendant inconjunct Mercury). America's first woman mayor was elected here in Seattle back in 1926 (Midheaven semisquare Venus), and in 1940, the first floating bridge across Lake Washington was completed (Midheaven Square Uranus). The symbol of Seattle is the Space Needle, the focal point for the Century 21 Exposition which opened in 1962 (Midheaven square Mercury, Ascendant semisquare Mars). A ride to the top gives you a breathtaking view of the city and the Olympic Mountains to the west across Puget Sound, and the Cascades to the east. Southeast of the city is majestic Mr. Rainier, the highest volcano in the nation. In recent years, Seattle has become quite the cultural mecca, especially for young people who flock to its numerous coffee houses or nightclubs which feature its unique brand of music called Grunge rock. In August 1992, a series of arson fires erupted throughout the city before the culprit was caught (Midheaven sesquare Mars, Ascendant conjunct Moon).

Like most parts of California, the Puget Sound area is prone to violent earthquakes due to its proximity to several fault lines which traverse the region. Quakes in 1949 (Midheaven square Uranus) and 1965 caused minor damage (Midheaven sextile Saturn and Pluto, Ascendant sextile Saturn and Pluto) due to the fact the tremors were situated many miles below Earth's surface. Another quake measuring 6.8 in late February 2001 destroyed several buildings in the Pioneer Square district of Seattle, but the loss of life was minimal (Sun inconjunct Sun).

Surrounded by water on two sides, and ringed by two majestic mountain ranges, Seattle is an urban community in the midst of a forest. Within its corporate limits are many lakes, and sometimes it appears there are more boats than cars. Seattle has managed to transform much of its downtown area by tearing down some of its hills and filling in the bay to facilitate an easier traffic flow (Sun in Scorpio). Seattle also gave the world the term "Skid Road" when a plank was constructed to move logs down to the harbor. An isolated yet cosmopolitan city, it has one of the screwiest street numbering systems in the country—one needs a map to survive. Because of its seemingly endless drizzle for moments on end, Seattle has some of the lushest gardens in the world (Cancer Moon). Most Seattleites are touchy about outside criticism, especially about the weather. It's a conservative community (Capricorn rising) that has an inferiority complex of sorts, probably because of its isolation. It felt left out by the rest of the nation; thus it turned its eyes to Alaska and the Orient for its inspiration. Concerned with its past heritage (Cancer Moon), it's also a very sport oriented town, and weekends are anxiously anticipated as the natives want to experience the wonders of nature (Venus in Sagittarius). Seattle is very conscious of its environment and has taken pains to preserve its natural beauty. In recent years, the economy has been diversified so that the massive layoffs which occurred some years ago at Boeing don't completely stifle the economy.

Incorporated: December 1, 1869
Elevation: 25 feet
Area: 92 square miles
Source: *Four Wagons West* by Robert Watt say 8:00 a.m. at low tide; Dorothy Hughes prefers this time, which gives Sagittarius rising; chart rectified to a slightly later time

Spokane

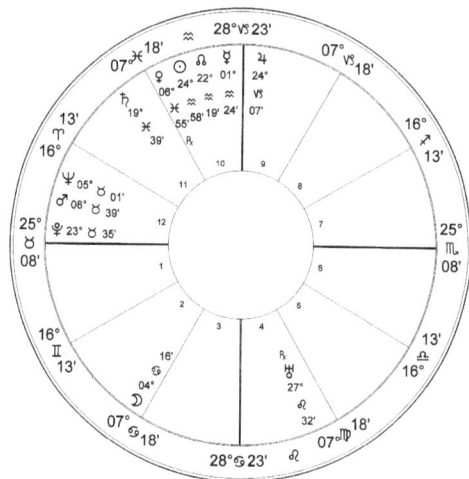

February 13, 1878
117W24, 47N40
10:17 AM PST

First settled in May 1873, the first sale of lots was held five years later. In 1883 a gold rush in Idaho boosted business and in August 1889, a fire swept through town (Midheaven square Mars). Cheap rail fares in 1902 brought a flood tide of immigration and Spokane became the largest rail center west of Omaha. In 1974 Spokane hosted a World's Fair (Midheaven sextile Moon).

Known as the "Heart of the Inland Empire," Spokane is a city of beautiful homes, spacious lawns, and verdant gardens (Moon in Cancer). It's an urban city that manages to be down to earth and informal at the same time (Taurus rising and Sun in Aquarius). Abhorring dullness has caused its citizens to develop a screwy sense of humor (Mercury in Aquarius); they're all fond of a good belly laugh or gag. A healthy and wealthy city, slot machines once funded the local schools and charities.

Incorporated: November 29, 1890
Elevation: 1,890 feet
Area: 52 square miles
Source: *American Guide Series*; *Spokane Story* by Lucil Fargo says May 11, 1873

Tacoma

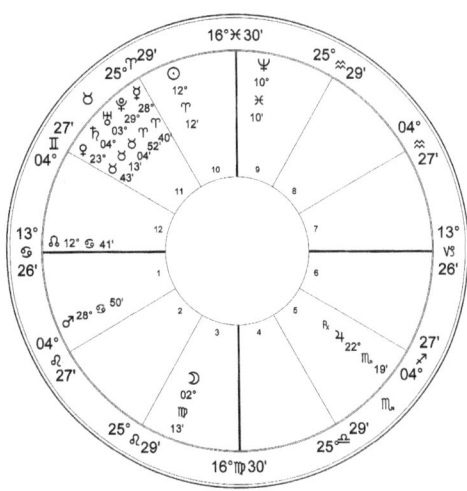

**April 1, 1852
122W26, 47N14
10:39 AM PST**

Founded in 1852, a town site was platted sixteen years later. Lumber became the dominant industry in 1869, making Tacoma the "Lumber Capital of the World" shortly afterwards. Originally called Commencement City, then Old Tacoma, it became the western terminus of the Northern Pacific Railroad in 1873 and changed its name to New Tacoma. The two cities merged in 1884. In November 1950 the suspension bridge across the Narrows collapsed during a high wind storm (Midheaven square Neptune). In the vicinity are many military installations (Sun in Aries).

Incorporated: November 12, 1875
Elevation: 110 feet
Area: 48 square miles
Source: *American Guide Series*

Yakima

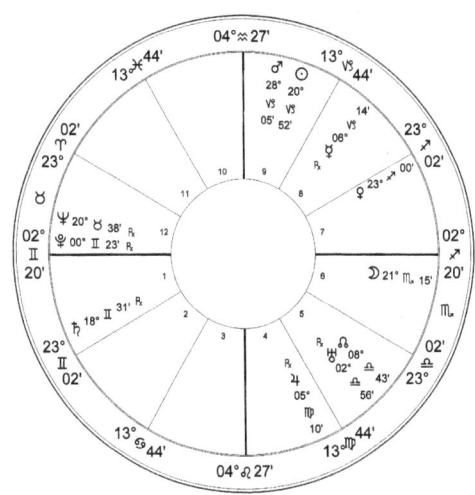

**January 10, 1885
120W31, 46N36
1:07 PM PST**

Yakima City was founded in December 1883 and the railroad arrived one year later. New Yakima was founded in January 1885 and a plat filed shortly after. It became simply Yakima in 1918. Irrigation was introduced into this valley in 1891 making it one of richest agricultural regions in the northwest. On May 18, 1980, nearby Mt. St. Helens erupted violently, sending tons of ash down onto this city (Ascendant square Moon). Streets turned gray with soot, and it was many months before the damage was cleaned up.

Incorporated: January 27, 1886
Elevation: 1,666 feet
Source: Yakima Public Library

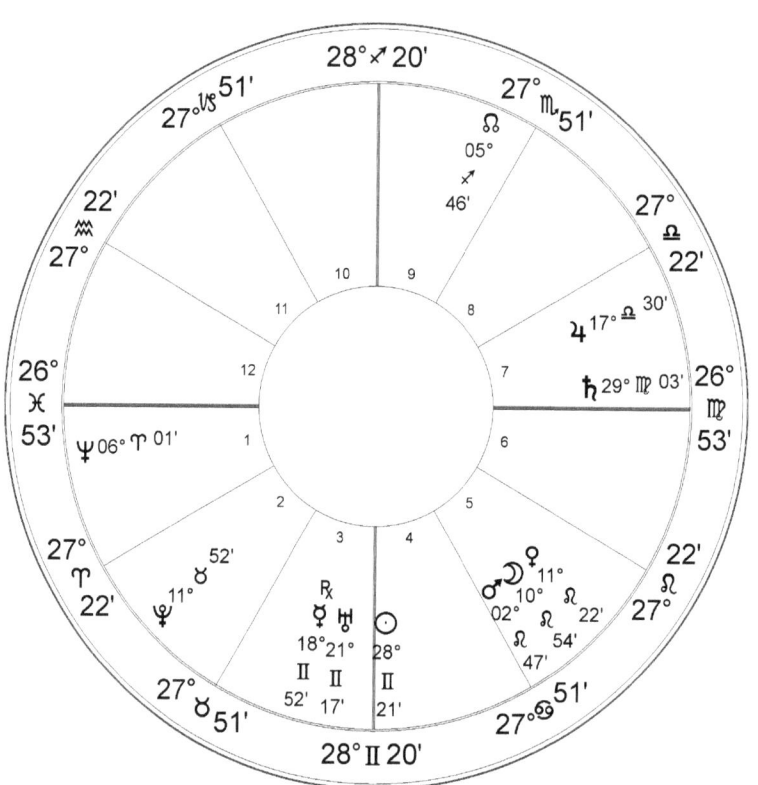

West Virginia

June 20, 1863
Wheeling
80W43, 40N04
12:01 AM LMT

Source: Jeanne Mozier cites the papers of Abraham Lincoln, who signed the proclamation granting statehood to West Virginia on April 20, 1863 to become effective at 12:01 a.m. on June 20, 1863

Until 1863 the history of this state is identical to that of Virginia. Coal was first discovered in 1742 and remains the lifeblood of this state's economy. In 1859, John Brown seized the arsenal at Harper's Ferry which resulted in this region's opposition to secession which came in 1861. The western counties of Virginia, which now comprise this state, decided to separate from the mother state in 1863 and remain with the Union. In 1915 the U.S. Supreme Court ruled that West Virginia owed Virginia more then $12 million in debt because of that decision. During the 1950s the population declined thirteen percent; poverty and unemployment were widespread. West Virginia has experienced many mine disasters over the years, one of the worst occurring in 1972 when a flood, caused by the collapse of a waste dam, killed 118 people. This state was instrumental in the formation of the United Mine Workers union.

West Virginia produces seventeen percent of the coal supply, ranking second in the U.S. It also produces more natural gas than any state east of the Mississippi, and the chemical industry is growing. Needless to say, this state has the highest concentration of union workers in the nation: forty-three percent of all those employed.

Area: 24,181 square miles

Charleston

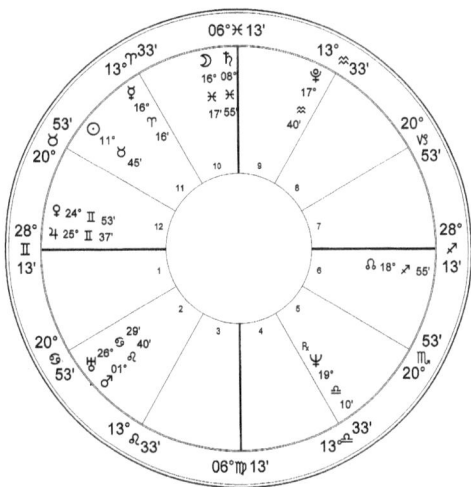

**May 1, 1788
81W38, 38N21
8:18 AM EST**

Founded as Fort Clendenin in 1788, the town site was platted six years later. Charleston was capital of West Virginia from 1870 to 1875, and made the permanent seat of state government in 1885 (Midheaven square Saturn, Ascendant opposition Saturn).

Nestled in a narrow valley along the Kanawha River, the surrounding region contains many chemical plants, the city's second largest industry after the government. Its capitol building is one of the handsomest in the nation.

Incorporated: January 19, 1818
Elevation: 601 feet
Area 29 square miles
Source: Charleston Public Library

Huntington

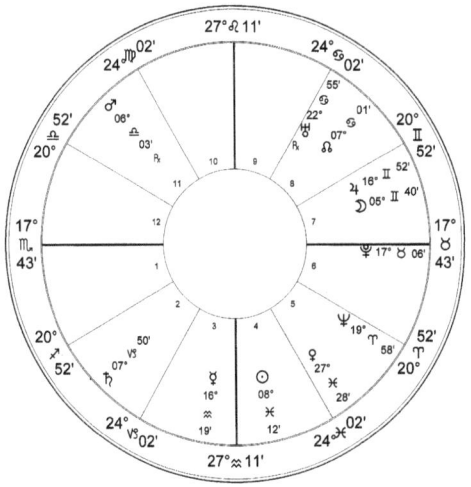

**February 27, 1871
82W27, 38N25
12:01 AM EST**

Founded by railroad magnate Collis P. Huntington, and modestly named after himself in 1870, it was chartered the following year. It quickly became the major coal port for the entire state. Situated in the banks of the Ohio, it's been plagued by floods many times over the years. Those of 1913 and 1937 completely inundated the business district, and seventy-five percent of the city was under water. Since that time, an eleven mile flood wall has been constructed to prevent future flooding.

Incorporated: 1871
Elevation: 564 feet
Source: Huntington Public Library

Parkersburg

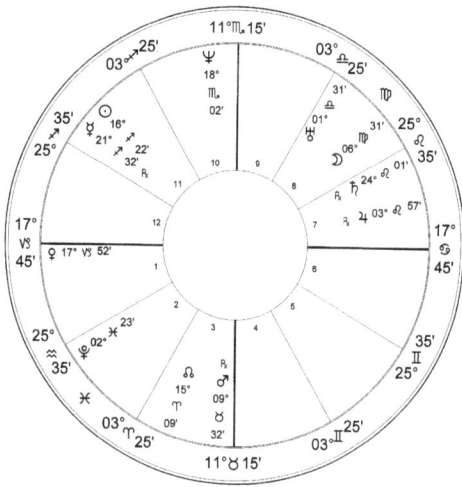

December 8, 1800
81W33, 39N16
9:53 AM EST

First settled in 1785 by John Neal, the region was granted to him two years later. Platted as Newport in 1800, a new town was formed ten years later and called Parkersburg. Over the years floods have been a major source of concern: Those of 1832 (Ascendant conjunct Pluto) and 1852 (Midheaven inconjunct Jupiter) were particularly severe. Oil drilling began here in 1859 but petroleum wasn't really discovered until the 1890s and Parkersburg became the chief oil port for the state.

Incorporated: November 5, 1863
Elevation: 625 feet
Source: Parkersburg Public Library

Wheeling

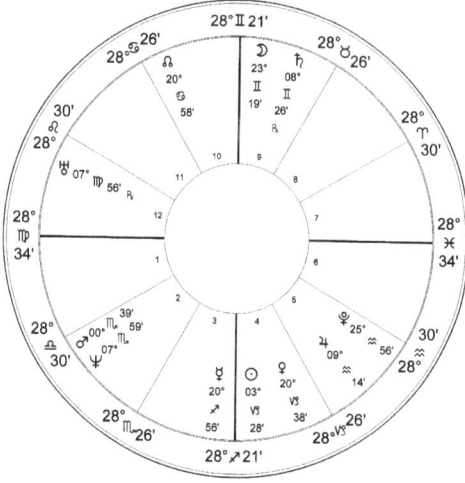

December 25, 1795
80W43, 40N04
12:01 AM EST

Settled in the summer of 1769 by the Zane brothers, Fort Fincastle was erected five years later. Platted in 1793 it was renamed in 1806. Wheeling was made a port of entry in 1831 and soon became the chief city in the region. For this reason, the convention which decided to remain with the Union met here, two years after the opening of the Civil War. Wheeling became the first capital of West Virginia until 1885, when the legislature finally moved to Charleston. A flood in 1936 almost wiped Wheeling off the map as the Ohio reached its highest level in recorded history. Wheeling is the iron and steel center for the state and contains many chemical planets and coal processing factories.

Incorporated: 1795
Elevation: 687 feet
Source: Wheeling Public Library

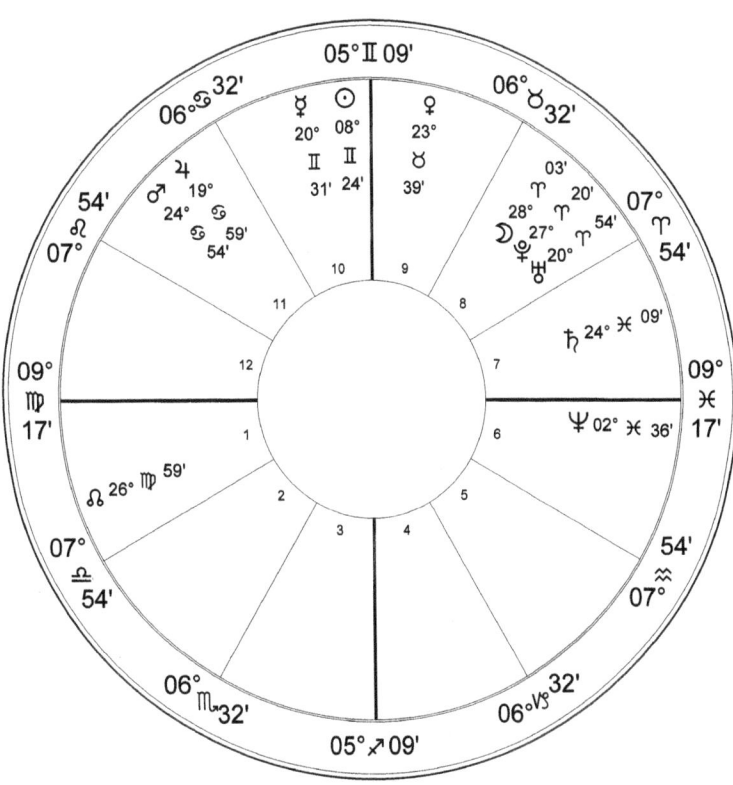

Wisconsin

May 29, 1848
Madison
89W24, 43N04
11:41 AM CST
Source: All newspapers consulted state the bill was signed "around noon;" chart rectified.

The region was first explored by Nicollet in 1634, and in 1660 a trading post and mission were founded near Ashland. A war between the French and the Fox Indians occurred between 1712 and 1740. Britain acquired the area in 1763 but lost it to America twenty years later. Until 1836 Wisconsin was governed as part of either the Indiana, Illinois or Michigan Territories. It became a separate territory on April 20, 1836, and entered the Union twelve years later. The Republican party was founded at Ripon in 1854 and in October 1871 a massive fire near Peshtigo killed more than 800 people. Ringling Brothers began their circus at Baraboo in 1884, just north of Madison. During the 19th century, thousands of Germans and Scandinavians migrated to this region.

Known as "America's Dairyland," Wisconsin produces more milk and cheese than any other state, and also ranks first in hay and alfalfa. It ranks third in oats and seventh in corn. Due to the many acres of forests, Wisconsin has a large paper industry.

Area: 56,164 square miles

Appleton

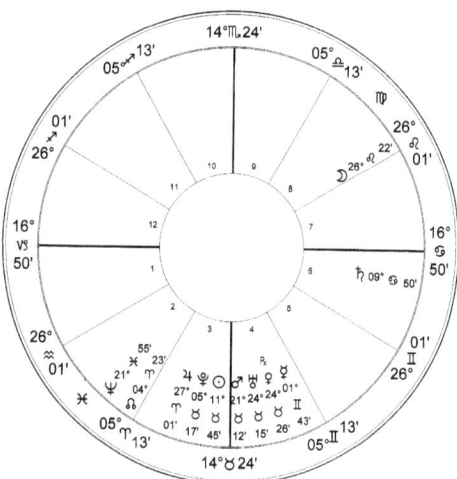

May 2, 1857
88W25, 44N16
12:01 AM CST

One year after the founding of Lawrence University in 1847, the region around the campus was laid out as Appleton. In 1853 it merged with Grand Chute and Lewesburg. In 1882 the first commercial hydroelectric plant in America opened in this pleasant lakeside community.

Incorporated: 1857
Elevation: 780 feet
Source: Appleton Public Library

Green Bay

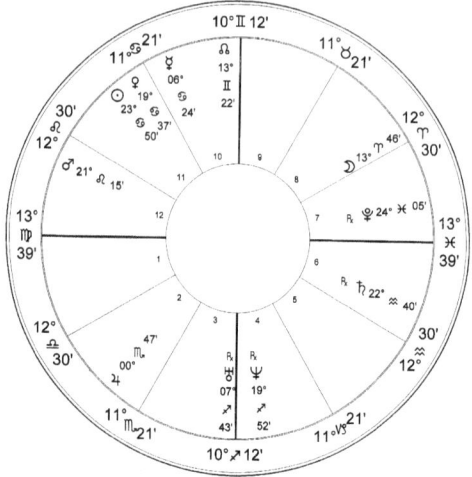

July 16, 1816
88W00, 44N31
8:49 AM CST

A trading post was established here in 1634 by Jean Nicollet, and Fort St. Francis was completed in 1717. The British took the fort in 1763; the Americans renamed it Fort Howard in 1816. Platted as Navarino in 1830 (Midheaven square Pluto, Ascendant sextile Sun), it merged with the town of Fort Howard in 1895. The city's most famous citizens are members of the Green Bay Packers football team, founded in 1919, and their former coach, the late Vince Lombardi.

Incorporated: 1854
Elevation: 590 feet
Source: *History of Wisconsin* by Charles Tuttle

Kenosha

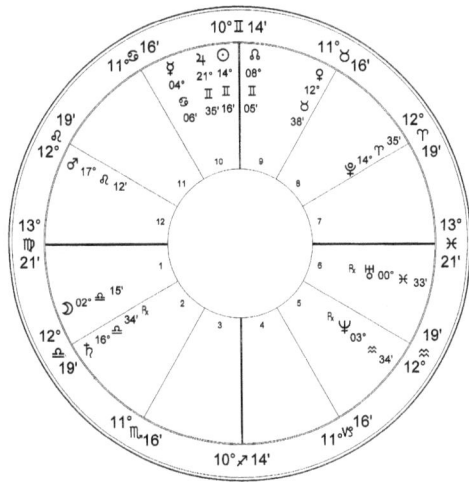

June 5, 1835
87W49, 42N35
11:32 AM CST

Kenosha was founded as Pike Creek in 1835. During the next decade, it pioneered in free education for the masses due to its number of New Englanders and New Yorkers who initially inhabited the city. Kenosha is a large manufacturing center, and home to America's smallest auto maker, American Motors.

Incorporated: February 8, 1850
Elevation: 601 feet
Source: Kenosha Public Library

La Crosse

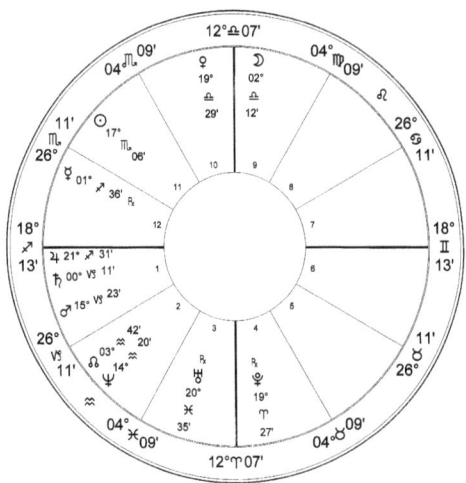

November 9, 1841
91W15, 43N48
9:35 AM CST

Founded in 1841, a nationwide financial panic sixteen years later caused untold havoc (Ascendant conjunct Saturn). In 1876 a bridge was built across the Mississippi (Midheaven conjunct Sun), linking the city to western markets. La Crosse, which means "cross" in French, has a very large German population.

Incorporated: 1856
Elevation: 649 feet
Source: La Crosse Public Library

Madison

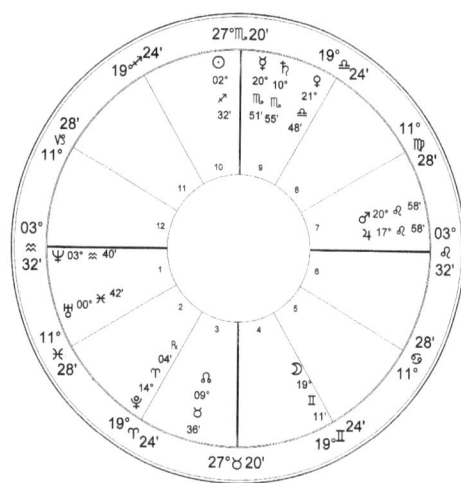

November 24, 1836
89W24, 43N04
11:23 AM CST

Selected to be the state capital in 1836, the University of Wisconsin was founded twelve years later (Ascendant trine Venus and Moon square Mercury). A meat packing plant was founded here in 1919 (Midheaven opposition Mars), but state government and the university remain the chief employers.

Situated on an isthmus between Lakes Mendota and Monona, Madison is one of the most beautiful capitals in the country. The focal point for the entire city is the state capitol building which has the second highest dome in our nation, only two feet shorter than the capitol in Washington. Madison has a strong political and intellectual life (Aquarius rising) and the natives are independent but friendly (Sun in Sagittarius). Surrounded by quiet beauty, Madison is a city of graceful and stately old elms and maples. Athletic and arty, its natives enjoy a stable economy, which probably explains why so many "retired" hippies have chosen to live here. This "Athens of the Midwest" lets people live their own life and seldom makes judgments (Aquarius rising).

Incorporated: March 4, 1856
Elevation: 859 feet
Area 54 square miles
Source: Madison Public Library

Milwaukee

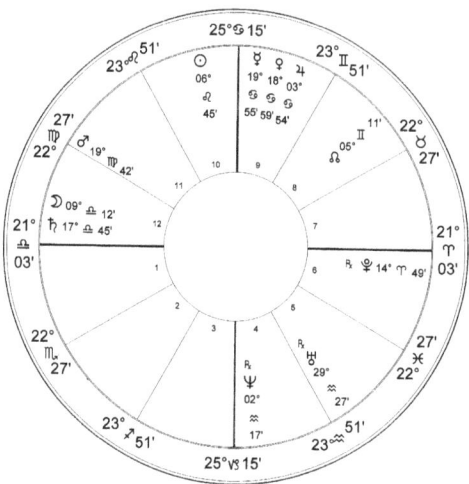

July 30, 1835
87W55, 43N02
11:10 AM CST

A trading post was founded on August 18, 1795 by Jacques Vieau, but during the following forty years, settlement was sparse. When the rival towns of Kilbourntown and Juneautown were founded in 1835, the city known as Milwaukee was born. Soon after, two other villages began, and the street patterns started to cause considerable confusion, especially when bridges were constructed to link the various communities. The first brewery was built in 1840 (Midheaven opposition Neptune) and eight years later, the mass influx of German immigrants began to arrive (Midheaven sextile Moon, Ascendant square Neptune). A fire in October 1892 burned most of the downtown area (Midheaven conjunct Mars, Ascendant sextile Neptune). During World War I, anti-Teutonic sentiment surfaced and many Germans were forced to change their names. Several streets were renamed and German was forbidden to be spoken in public (Midheaven opposition Pluto). In 1920 the worst calamity that could ever befall a city dependent on liquor occurred when Prohibition became the law of the land (Midheaven conjunct Saturn). Suddenly, its chief product was illegal, and Milwaukee suddenly realized it had to diversify in order to survive. During the '20s Milwaukee also experienced considerable labor strife due to the election of a Socialist majority some years before. When Prohibition ended in 1933, Milwaukee was well on its way to becoming the industrial giant it is today. In 1959, with the completion of the St. Lawrence Seaway, Milwaukee became a world seaport for the first time.

Once known as the city that beer made famous, Milwaukee has in recent years seen many of its breweries shut down. But "beertown" needn't worry because now it manufactures everything from A to Z: It's America's jack-of-all-trades city and the largest machine tool maker in the nation.

Known as a city that worships all things judicial (Saturn rising in Libra), Milwaukee strictly enforces the law: Tourists have found out they can get a ticket for jaywalking. Big time criminals from other cities have been told politely to stay out of town. The large German and Slavic population simply won't tolerate their antics. A city with a high degree of community involvement, Milwaukee also has a very low crime rate. Practically free from corruption in high places, this beautiful lake city is consistently rated as having the best government in the nation. It's clean and orderly, if not a trifle dull.

But basically, Milwaukee is an overgrown small town at heart. Men still go down to the corner tavern and drink with their buddies, and their kids drive up and down the main drag (Wisconsin Avenue), showing off on weekends. Milwaukee is "American Graffiti" personified. A city populated by modest unassuming people who prefer the slow, reassured life, Milwaukee has managed to preserve a lifestyle that is unhurried, yet progressive. Also known for its fine restaurants (Venus in Cancer), it also sells more sauerkraut and bratwurst during sporting events than it does hot dogs. A highly cultural community, Milwaukee has one of the finest zoos in the nation and a uniquely designed conservatory for tropical plants. Like other cities populated by Germans (St. Louis and Cincinnati), it also loves classical music and its orchestra ranks up there with the best. Everywhere you venture, the spirit of "Gemutchlekeit" pervades. Just the kind of place you'd love to raise a family, providing you can stand the winter weather.

Incorporated: January 31, 1845
Elevation: 635 feet
Area: 95 square miles
Source: *Milwaukee* by Bayrd Still

Oshkosh

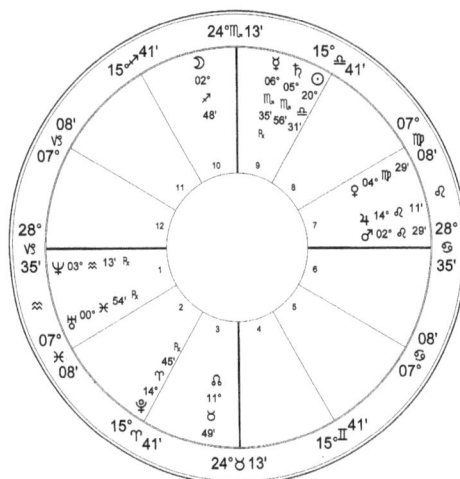

October 13, 1836
88W33, 44N01
1:52 PM CST

Algoma, the forerunner of Oshkosh, was founded in 1833; three years later, the community of Athens was formed. Renamed Oshkosh in 1840, it annexed Algoma in 1856 (Ascendant conjunct Neptune). The first sawmill was built in 1839 and was the major employer in the city for many years. Oshkosh has had three major fires during its short history: 1859, 1866 and 1875.

Incorporated: April 5, 1853
Elevation: 761 feet
Source: Oshkosh Public Library says October 1836; exact date uncertain; chart rectified

Racine

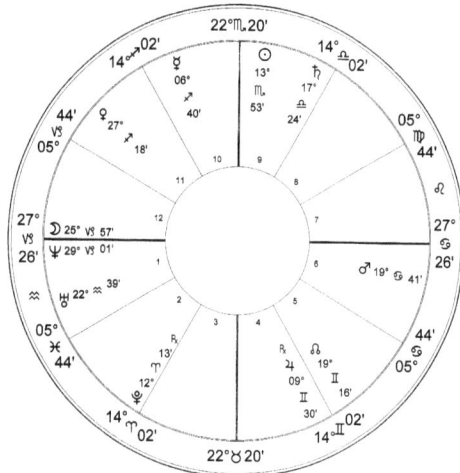

November 6, 1834
87W48, 42N44
12:09 PM CST

Founded as Port Gilbert in 1834, it changed its name three years later (Midheaven sextile Moon, Ascendant conjunct Neptune), not to honor the French writer, as most think, but for an Indian word which means "root." Racine is a large industrial center and home to Johnson and Johnson, makers of all those paper products.

Incorporated: August 8, 1848
Elevation: 600 feet
Source: *Racine* by Fanny Stone says November 1834; exact date uncertain; chart rectified

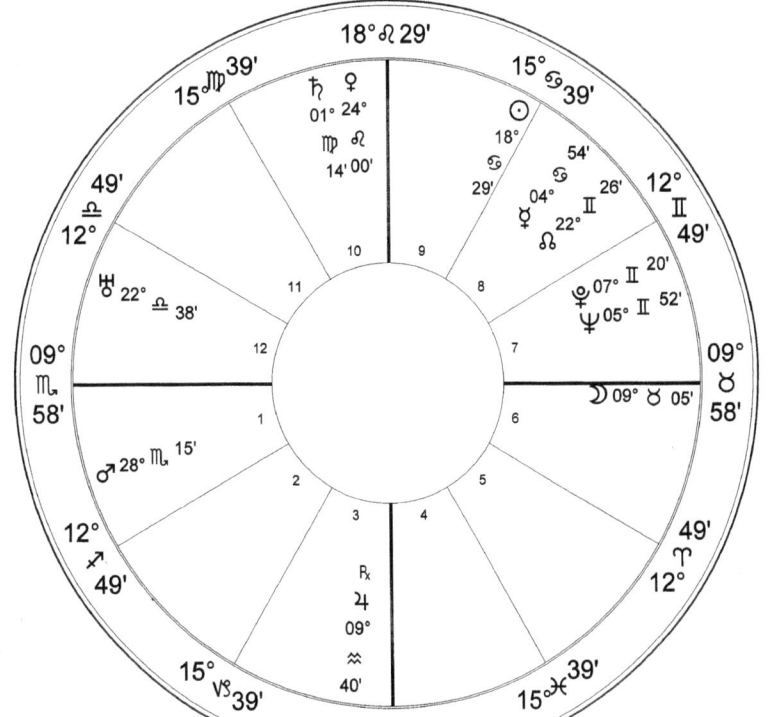

Wyoming

**July 10, 1890
Cheyenne
104W49, 41N08
2:08 PM MST
Source:** *Los Angeles Times* **says around 4:00 p.m. in Washington; no definite time given; chart rectified**

In 1803 this region was acquired in the Louisiana Purchase, and ten years later the Oregon Trail began running through the territory. Oil was first discovered in 1833, and the following year Fort Laramie was founded. Western Wyoming was obtained with the Oregon Cession of 1846 and the railroad came in 1867. Wyoming was created a territory on July 25, 1868.

During the following year, it was the first state to allow women to vote and hold public office. Yellowstone became the nation's first national park in 1872, eighteen years before Wyoming entered the Union. Conflict between cattlemen and rustlers erupted into the Johnson County War in 1892. In 1924 the first woman ever elected governor, Nellie Ross, took office. Uranium was found in 1951, but with the discovery of oil shale deposits, Wyoming is currently experiencing a fantastic boom.

Wyoming ranks second in sheep as much of the land is good only for grazing. Petroleum is the principal mineral resource and the state ranks second in uranium. Wyoming is the source of three great rivers: Missouri, Colorado and Columbia. Tourism is also important to its economy and during the summer months, the Yellowstone and Grand Teton National Parks bring them in by the thousands.

Area: 97,914 square miles

Casper

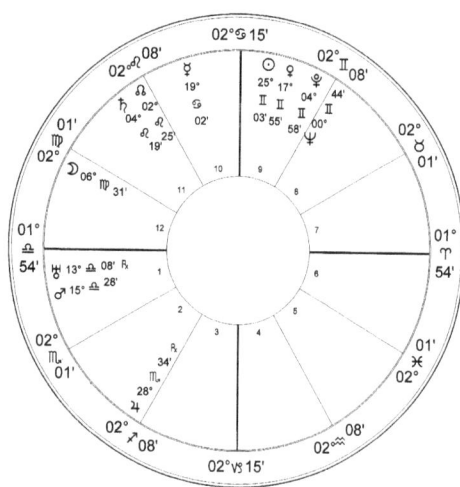

June 15, 1888
106W19, 42N51
12:37 PM MST

Founded in 1888 by the railroad, oil was discovered near here two years later at Teapot Dome. Fraudulent speculation with this oil field during the early 1920s led to a scandal which tarnished the administration of President Harding. With discovery of vast oil fields, Casper experienced a surge in population, surpassing Cheyenne as the largest city in the state. With the increase in population, came a surge in crime and marital discord. Casper is also located near several coal fields which might turn this city into a miniature "energy capital" sometime in the future.

Incorporated: 1917
Elevation: 5,123 feet
Source: *American Guide Series*

Cheyenne

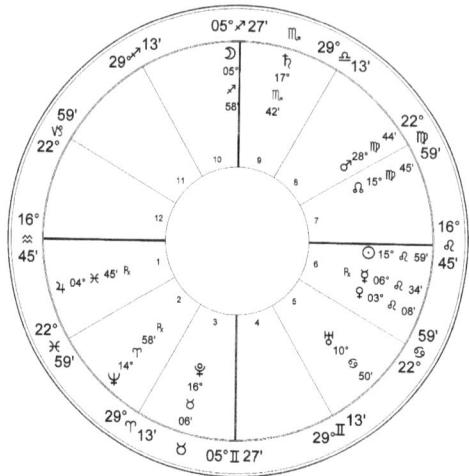

August 8, 1867
104W49, 41N08
7:05 PM MST

First settled in July 1867, it was called Hell by its first residents because of rampant lawlessness. During a town meeting the following month, Cheyenne was formally founded. The railroad crews moved on the next year, but a few of the unsavory characters remained. In 1869 Cheyenne became the capital of Wyoming. In July 1979 a tornado damaged more than 200 homes in the city (Ascendant square Neptune).

Cheyenne's business is government, but during the closing days of July it hosts the world's largest rodeo, Frontier Days. The first one was held in 1897 and it's a big money maker for this city.

Incorporated: December 15, 1869
Elevation: 6,101 feet
Source: *American Guide Series*; *Wyoming* by Velma Linford says July 4, 1867; *History of Wyoming* by T.A. Larson says July 9, 1867

Laramie

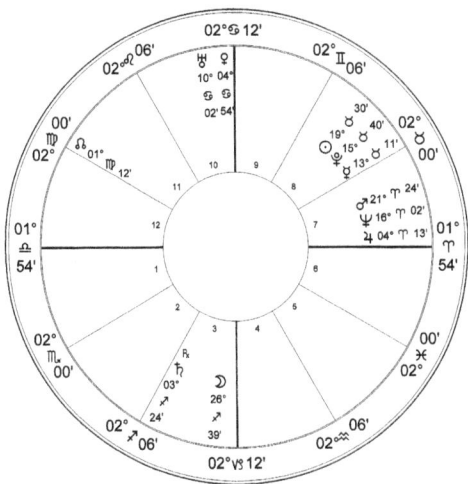

**May 9, 1868
105W35, 41N19
3:00 PM MST**

Founded by railroad crews in 1868, the University of Wyoming was founded eighteen years later (Midheaven sextile Sun) and remains the lifeblood of the city to this day.

Incorporated: 1874
Elevation: 7,165 feet
Source: *American Guide Series*

Rock Springs

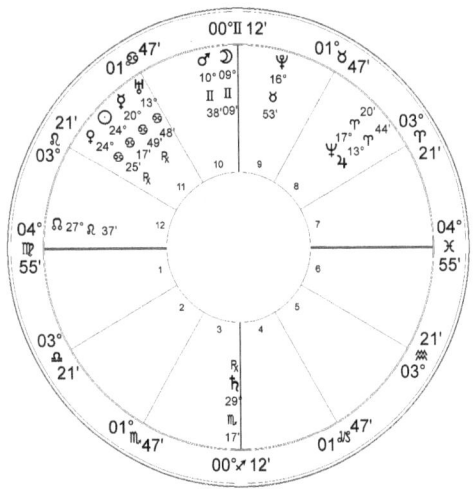

**July 16, 1868
109W13, 41N35
8:30 AM MST**

First settled in 1866 as a trading post, the present city was founded two years later when the first coal mine opened for business. Chinese were imported to work the mines in 1875. Ten years later a riot ensued and thirty Orientals were killed (Midheaven conjunct Mars, Ascendant inconjunct Jupiter). During the 1970s with the discovery of oil shale deposits in the region, Rock Springs lost its small town image. As the population increased, so did prostitution and gambling. Because there's so little to do for amusement, fights and brawls are common, especially on weekends when the miners come into town. Just like the days of the Old West, isn't it?

Incorporated: 1919
Elevation: 6,271 feet
Source: Wyoming State Historical Society

Sheridan

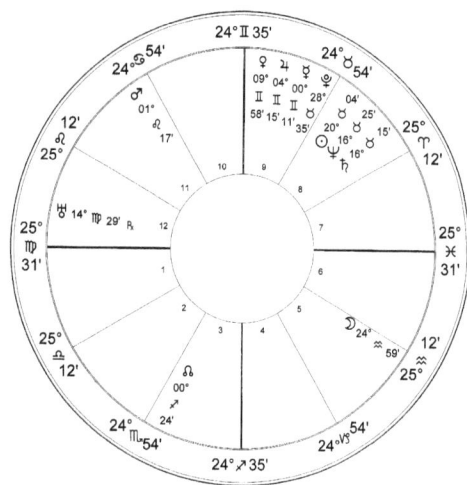

**May 10, 1882
106W58, 44N48
2:30 PM MST**

Founded in 1882, it remained isolated until the arrival of the railroad ten years later. Nearby is the Big Horn National Forest and the Fort Kearny State historical site.

Incorporated: 1907
Elevation: 4,500 feet
Source: *American Guide Series*

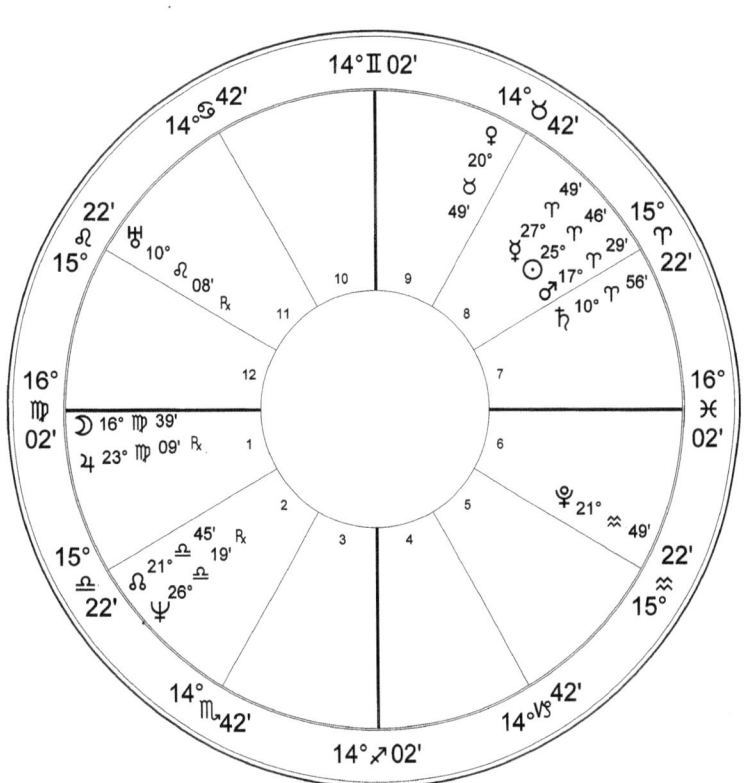

Washington DC

April 15, 1791
77W00, 38N53
3:23 PM EST
Source: *Washington Post* verifies the date and the time of "shortly after 3pm" comes from the *Alexandria Gazette*

When Washington was inaugurated as our first president in New York City, that was only a temporary capital as our government had no permanent base. The following spring (1790), Congress moved back to Philadelphia and on July 12 a Residency Bill was passed authorizing a region no more than ten miles square along the Potomac to be the capital city. It was to be established no later than 1800. Four days later, Washington signed the bill. For some time, Washington had his eye on an area a few miles north of his home at Mount Vernon and on October 16, he selected a site which encompassed the already thriving port cities of Georgetown, Maryland and Alexandria, Virginia. He made his decision known on January 24, 1791, some two days after he had hired surveyors to begin surveying the site. Pierre L'Enfant, a French architect and student of design who served under Washington during the Revolution, was chosen to design the new city. The region was toured by L'Enfant in mid-March and a preliminary plan was ready by June 22, 1791. L'Enfant's design was quite radical at the time for an American city. Fifteen wide boulevards (160 feet wide) named for the states then in the Union were to radiate from the two principal structures, the executive mansion and the capitol building. At the junction of those avenues were to be situated parks or traffic circles, which have been the bane of drivers ever since. The city was divided into four sectors: NE, NW, SE and SW, with the center being the capitol. Numbered streets were to run north and south and streets alphabetically east and west. No building could be more than thirty-five feet high along the boulevards, as the capitol was to be the highest structure in town. That standard remains to this day even though the height limit is currently 160 feet. Only the Washington Monument exceeds this limit.

Before work could begin, however, an agreement had to be made with the current landowners and this was accomplished on March 30, 1791. Two weeks later, on April 15 shortly after 3:00 p.m., the first boundary stone was dedicated at Jones Point in Alexandria. On September 8, the region was named the Territory of Columbia and its chief city Washington. After a dispute with a local property owner, L'Enfant was fired from his post in late February 1792 and Andrew Ellicott took over his position. During the summer of 1792, a contest was held for the best design for the executive mansion and capitol building. James Hoban won for the "White House" and William Thornton for the capitol, even though his entry was after the deadline. Both men won $500 for their efforts. The cornerstone for the executive mansion was laid about noon on October 13, 1792 and nearly a year later, on September 18, 1793, Washington officiated at a Masonic ceremony when the cornerstone for the capitol building was laid.

To finance construction, Washington thought a sale of lots would be the most desirable as it would keep real estate speculators out of reach. But the first sale which took place on October 17, 1791 brought disappointment. Two subsequent sales in 1792 and 1793 also saw meager sales so that by 1800 only ten percent of the lots had been sold. A lottery was begun in the summer of 1793 and a second one the following year also collapsed. As a result, it was time for big time speculators like Robert Morris to get their feet wet, but their scheme collapsed as well. Funds were somehow obtained from Congress and the states of Maryland and Virginia, so much of the important work was completed by the time Washington died on December 14, 1799, just six months before the government moved to the city named after him.

President John Adams arrived in the new city in June 1800 and Congress met for the first time on November 17, 1800 (Midheaven square Jupiter, Ascendant sextile Jupiter). Only one wing of the U.S. Capitol was finished and several rooms in the White House were as yet unfinished. Abigail Adams hung her laundry in the East Room. As the capital had been built on low lying land near the river, the region was plagued by mosquitoes, snakes and other unsavory elements. A canal along what is now Constitution Avenue was little more than an open sewer and the river lapped up to the hill on which the Washington Monument now stands. But despite the aforementioned difficulties and perils, our country had a permanent home for its legislators. In August 1812, the British attacked the city, which was relatively defenseless, and burned the U.S. Capitol and White House (Midheaven sesquare Pluto, Ascendant sesquare Venus). After the flames died down, some thought it wise to move the capital to a safer locale, but Madison prevailed and simply moved his quarters into the Octagon House for the remainder of his term.

It was hoped from the beginning that Washington would become a port city, but as Washington, D.C. lay at the head of navigable water, the only method of transport to the interior would have to be a canal. In July 1828, ground was broken for the Chesapeake & Ohio Canal, which was to run to Cumberland, Maryland. Unfortunately, on the same day ground was also laid for a new and much more efficient method of transportation, the Baltimore & Ohio Railroad (Midheaven sextile Moon/Jupiter, Ascendant opposition Mars). Washington never did become the port city its founding fathers envisioned. Due to its muggy climate and slack sanitation, cholera took many lives in the summer of 1832 (Ascendant opposition Sun/Mars). Fires were also a constant threat: The Treasury Building burned in 1833 and a few years later the post office went up in flames. Due to sparse settlement on the west side of the Potomac, that portion of the District of Columbia was returned to Virginia in September 1846 (Midheaven semisquare Jupiter, Ascendent semisquare Moon).

When the Civil War began in April 1861, Washington became a city under siege. Situated as it was across the river from Confederate territory, the District was protected by sixty-eight forts and twenty-two batteries, and became the most heavily fortified city in the world (Midheaven opposition Pluto). Before long, the city was swarming with 150,000 soldiers and after the Battle of Bull Run at Manassas, only twenty-five miles west of the capital in neighboring Virginia, public buildings in the city were soon housing the wounded as hospitals were filled to capacity. Rebel troops, under Jubal Early, attacked near Silver Spring on the northern outskirts of the city in August 1864, but were repelled. When news of Lee's surrender to Grant surfaced on Palm Sunday 1865, the city went wild with jubilation. But festivities were short lived, for on Good Friday President Lincoln was shot at Ford's Theatre and died the following morning. The city was in mourning, draped in black, and citizens who might have had anything to do with the assassination plot were rounded up in haste (Midheaven trine Sun sesquare Saturn).

Over the years, Washington has tried many experiments in self-government. When the original city charter was granted in May 1802, the mayor was appointed by the president (Midheaven sextile Sun semisquare Uranus). Ten years later, the city council appointed the mayor and by 1820, Washingtonians were electing their chief officials. In February 1871, Congress placed the District of Columbia under a territorial government (Midheaven sesquare Mars, Ascendant opposition Venus). A governor was appointed to run the city but during the first three years expenditures for numerous public improvements so bankrupted the city that Congress appointed three commissioners to run matters (Ascendant square Pluto). Their position became permanent in July 1878 (Ascendant inconjunct Sun sesquare Saturn). Home rule didn't return to Washington until January 1975 (Midheaven trine Saturn and Uranus, Ascendant sextile Sun trine Neptune). Citizens of Washington have been able to vote in national elections ever since the Twenty-third Amendment to the Constitution was passed, but attempts to make Washington, D.C. our nation's fifty-first state have so far failed.

In 1901, the McMillan Plan was adopted to enlarge upon L'Enfant's original plan as the city had expanded beyond its original boundaries (Ascendant trine Saturn and Uranus). New parks and public spaces were constructed and railroad tracks were finally removed from the Mall after Union Station was completed in 1907 north of the capitol. During World War I, the city's population grew thirty-two percent and numerous temporary buildings were thrown up around town, some of which remained through World War II. The Depression of the 1930s didn't hurt Washington all that much at first, but when the Bonus Army marched on the city in the summer of 1932, reality of life in the rest of America hit hard. Hoover refused to bend to the demands of the 20,000 veterans from the Great War who wanted their bonus pay a bit early; it wasn't due until 1945. Troops under Douglas MacArthur were sent in to destroy their encampments in nearby Anacostia in the SE part of the city. With the election of FDR in 1932, major changes began to emerge (Midheaven semisquare Moon, Ascendant semisquare Pluto). The Supreme Court was finished and the Federal Triangle between the Mall and Pennsylvania Avenue was constructed. During World War II, thousands of office seekers poured in, creating a severe housing shortage and an oversupply of women.

During the 1960s, Washington witnessed some of the largest demonstrations and protests in American history. Martin Luther King spoke before the Lincoln Memorial of his dream of a color blind society and young people protested U.S. involvement in southeast Asia. After King's assassination in April 1968, numerous fires broke out (Midheaven sesquare Sun/Saturn, Ascendant sextile Mars inconjunct Moon), which laid groundwork for massive urban renewal projects which took place during the next decade. Most of the old and dilapidated structures in the SW sector of the city were torn down and replaced with townhouses, marinas and playgrounds. In 1976, the first leg of the Metro, the subway, was completed and when finally finished the system will connect suburbs in Maryland and Virginia to the central city.

Washington is a feast for the tourist and historian. Besides the usual tours of the White House and U.S. Capitol, visitors flock to the city's numerous monuments and memorials, especially those honoring Presidents Washington, Lincoln and Jefferson. The Vietnam Memorial and the newly completed Korean War Memorial also have become quite popular. Washington is also a city of numerous museums, most of them affiliated with the Smithsonian Institution. The Air and Space Museum near the Mall is one of the "must sees," as is the Kennedy Center for the Performing Arts on the Potomac near the Watergate Building, site of that infamous break-in which led to Nixon's resignation. Washington also is home to the Bureau of Engraving and Printing, where paper money is printed, as well as the Government Printing Office, the largest publishing house in the world. Fronting the U.S. Capitol on the east side is the Supreme Court Building and the Library of Congress, the largest repository of reading material on this planet. Across the river in Virginia sits the Pentagon, the world's largest office building, the Iwo Jima Memorial and Arlington National Cemetery, burial sites for the Unknown Soldier and President Kennedy and his brother Robert. Further south along the Potomac lies Mount Vernon, home of the man who gave his name to this great world capital.

Unless you're a tourist, Washington can be a maddening and frustrating place due to that rising Moon inconjunct Mars and Pluto, the planets of aggression and anger. Life here is high pressured, which explains the reason there are more psychiatrists per capita than any other city in the world. Washington also has a very high rate of alcoholism and drug addiction. With Uranus in the eleventh house, Washington is a city of organizations, trade councils and associations which require numerous attorneys and lobbyists to promote their interests. Uranus trine Saturn indicates they are the backbone of industry in this town whose chief business is government.

Many Americans feel that those living inside the Beltway (I-495) have lost touch with reality and have been protected for entirely too long inside their ivory tower. With the Sun opposing Neptune from the second to the eighth houses, the question of financial and fiscal responsibility often comes up, as Washington (especially Congress) has the reputation for wasting millions of dollars on programs that are totally ridiculous. That opposition, along with Mercury, also indicates the mild form of paranoia and anxiety which pervades the region; with such a highly transient population, which often is replaced every other year, there is often little job stability for those who are not elected year after year.

As would be expected with the Sun in Aries, Washington is a highly competitive place with legislators and other officials jockeying for position. With Mercury opposite Neptune, lies and "governmentese gobbledegook" take the place of direct, forward communication, and secrets seem to appear around every corner. Social functions are often nothing more than one group trying to influence the other, shown by Venus square Pluto yet trine the Moon. Despite the apparent small talk, important decisions are being made which will in one way or another affect us all. Most feel the bureaucracy is overwhelming and intimidating, and is indifferent to those who don't have the right connections (Mercury sextile Pluto). Washingtonians are highly protective of their prerogatives and privileges due to that rising Moon and they have the reputation for being overly smug and self-satisfied. Concerned more with security and comfort (Moon trine Venus) than in getting the job done right or in record time, this place is often agonizing, frustrating or irritating, depending on your point of view. Washington seems to have a split personality, as shown by its four mutable angles. There is a love-hate relationship with the rest of America. For those who play by the rules, the rewards are high. Those who try to upset the status quo are quickly given the shaft. It's a ruthless and power hungry place (Pluto inconjunct Ascendant) and is seldom ever sentimental, ingratiating, or mildly relaxing due to that Moon squaring the Midheaven. With Saturn in the seventh house, it's a beautiful and inspiring place to visit, but one which can be hard on outsiders who try to break into its inner circle.

Incorporated: May 3, 1802
Elevation: 25 feet
Area: 69 square miles

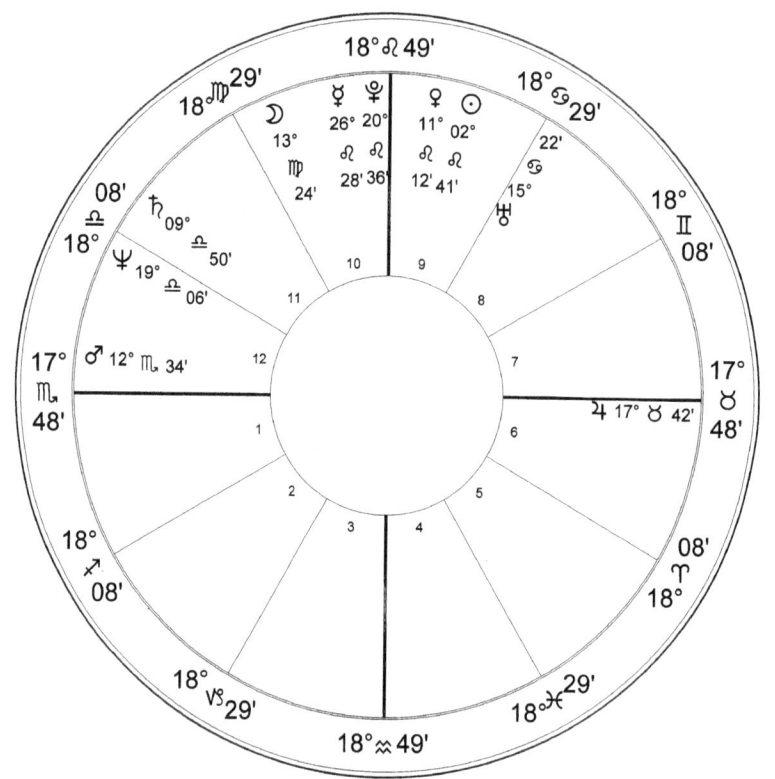

Puerto Rico

**July 25, 1952
San Juan
66W07, 18N28
1:36 PM AST
Source: Congressional Record**

Puerto Rico, called Borinquen by the native Taino Indians, was discovered by Columbus on his second voyage to the New World on Novmeber 19, 1493. Ponce de Leon founded the first Euopean settlement at Caparra on August 12, 1508. Ironically, the capital city was called Puerto Rico and the island was named San Juan, but an Italian mapmaker confused the two. Sugar cane was first planted in 1515, and slaves arrived from Africa three years later. Pirate raids began in the late 16th century and continued for the next two centuries. The English and the Dutch briefly alleviated strict trade regulations imposed by Spain and it wasn't until 1815 that Spain opened up Puerto Rico to free trade. Slavery was abolished in 1873.

Puerto Rico became a U.S. possession after the Spanish-American War. Spain ceded the island to the U.S. on December 10, 1898. The island was granted commonwealth status in 1952, shortly after "Operation Bootstrap" was instituted to alleviate poverty and increase self-sufficiency. Puerto Ricans are equally divided as to whether they wish to remain a Commonwealth or become a state. At present, they enjoy exemption from income tax and cannot vote for president. If Puerto Rico were to become a state, residents would qualify for more federal aid (food stamps and welfare) but would lose their special tax exemption.

Area: 3,435 square miles in the Caribbean, 1,700 miles southeast of Miami; 75 percent mountainous, 16 percent forested, only four percent arable.

Economy: Tourism ranks high. main industries are pharmaceuticals, apparel, electronic equipment and industrial machinery. Chief crops are coffee, sugar, pineapples and bananas.

Ponce

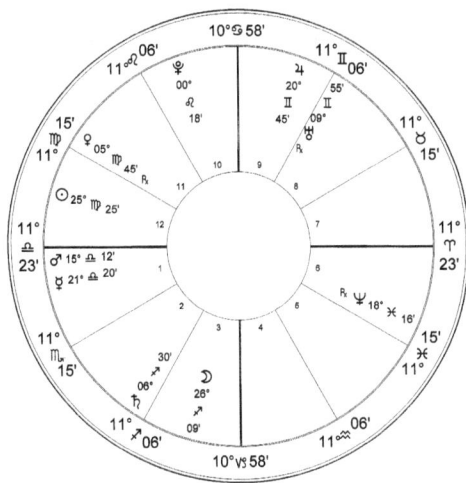

**September 17, 1692
66W37, 18N01
7:25 AM AST**

Ponce was founded in 1692, and named for the explorer Ponce de Leon, the first governor of Puerto Rico. Unlike San Juan, Ponce is an industrial working-class city whose largest industry is petroleum refining. The most famous sight in the second-largest city in Puerto Rico is the fire station which sits in front of the cathedral. Called the Parque de Bombas, its red and black striped walls are the most photographed site in the city.

Incorporated: 1877
Elevation: 15 feet
Source: Biblioteca de Ponce

San Juan

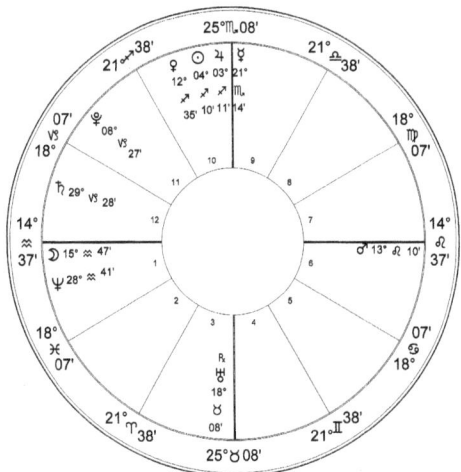

**November 16, 1520
66W07, 18N28
11:35 AM AST**

The original settlement of Caparra was founded on August 12, 1508 by Ponce de Leon. That community moved to the present site of Old San Juan in mid-November 1520, and was called Puerto Rico. But due to an Italian mapmaker's error, it would henceforth be known as San Juan.

San Juan was attacked numerous times by pirates over the next two centuries. The only time the city was forced by surrender was in 1598 (Midheaven opposition Mars trine Venus, Midheaven sextile Pluto). It was burned by the Dutch in 1625 (Midheaven sextile Pluto), and the British tried, but failed, to take the city in 1797. San Juan has also witnessed two great fires in its history: The Mayaguez Theater fire of June 1919 killed 150 people (Midheaven sextile Neptune sesquare Mars) and the Dupont Hotel fire of December 1986 killed 96 individuals (Midheaven square Sun, Ascendant trine Moon sesquare Saturn).

San Juan is the third-largest city in the West Indies, a city famous for both its Old Town, which has preserved its colonial ambience and Spanish architecture, and its fabulous beaches farther east in the Condado district, which are lined with luxury hotels. The most famous site in San Juan is the El Morro fortress, which was begun in 1539 (Midheaven conjunct Venus trine Mars, Ascendant sextile Pluto). It shares the entrance to the harbor with San Cristobal, which was begun in 1631. The residence of the governor, La Fortaleza, overlooks the harbor, and nearby is the Hotel El Convento, a former religious building.

Incorporated: January 22, 1537
Area: 47 square miles
Elevation: 35 feet
Source: *History of Puerto Rico* by R.A. van Middledyk

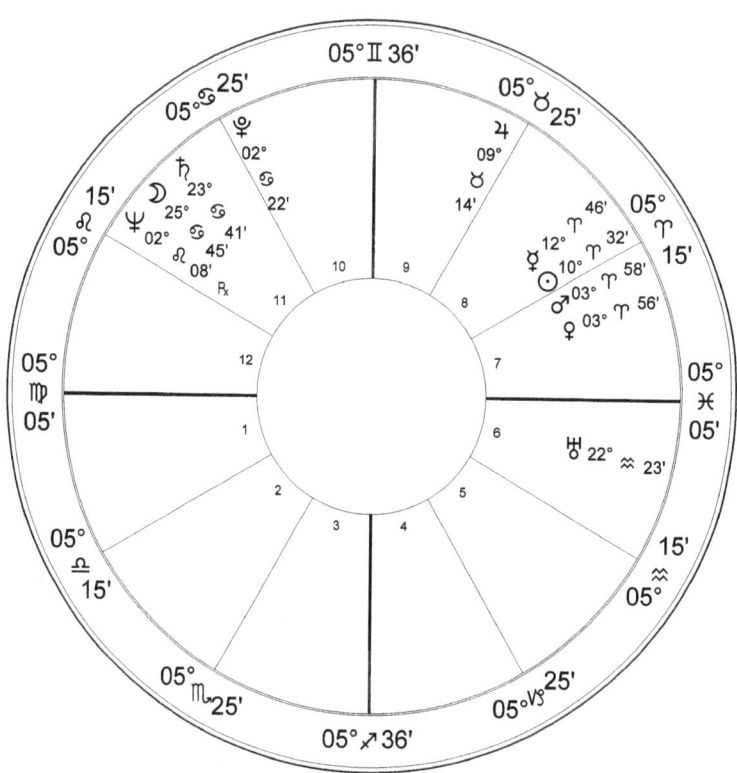

Virgin Islands

March 31, 1917
Charlotte Amalie
64W56, 18N21
4:00 PM AST
Source: U.S. State Department

The Virgin Islands were discovered by Columbus on his second voyage to the New World in 1493. The Spanish arrived in 1555, and within forty years the native Caribs were decimated. The Danes purchased St. Thomas in 1672, and took over St. John in 1683. St. Croix was purchased from the French in 1773. The U.S. bought the Virgin Islands from Denmark for $25 million on January 25, 1917, and two months later the U.S. took control. Residents became U.S. citizens in 1927, and elected their first governor in 1970. Originally under control of the Navy Department, the Interior Department now has jurisdiction.

Area: 136 square miles in the Caribbean, 40 miles east of Puerto Rico. Twenty-six percent of the islands are pastureland, 15 percent are arable and six percent are forested.

Economy: Tourism provides 70 percent of the island's income. Rum and perfume are also important.
Source: U.S. State Department

Charlotte Amalie

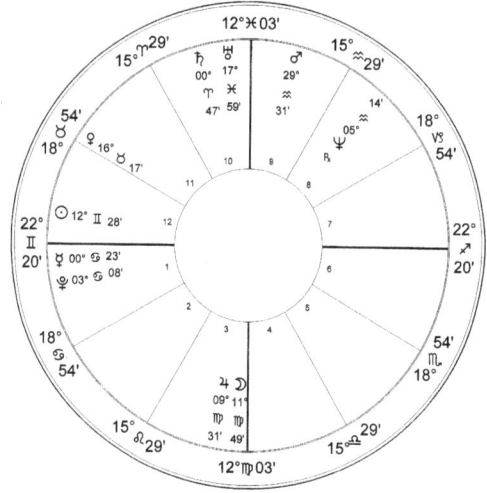

June 2, 1672
6:30 a.m. AST
64W56, 18N21

Source: Virgin Islands Tourist Board

Canada

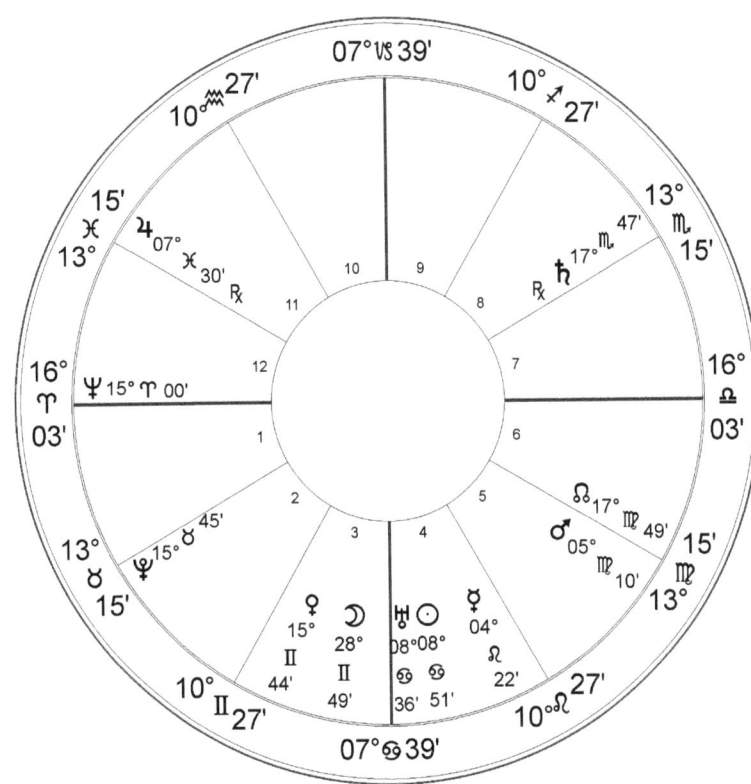

July 1, 1867
Ottawa
75W42, 45N25
Effective at 12:01 AM EST
Source: Canadian National Library

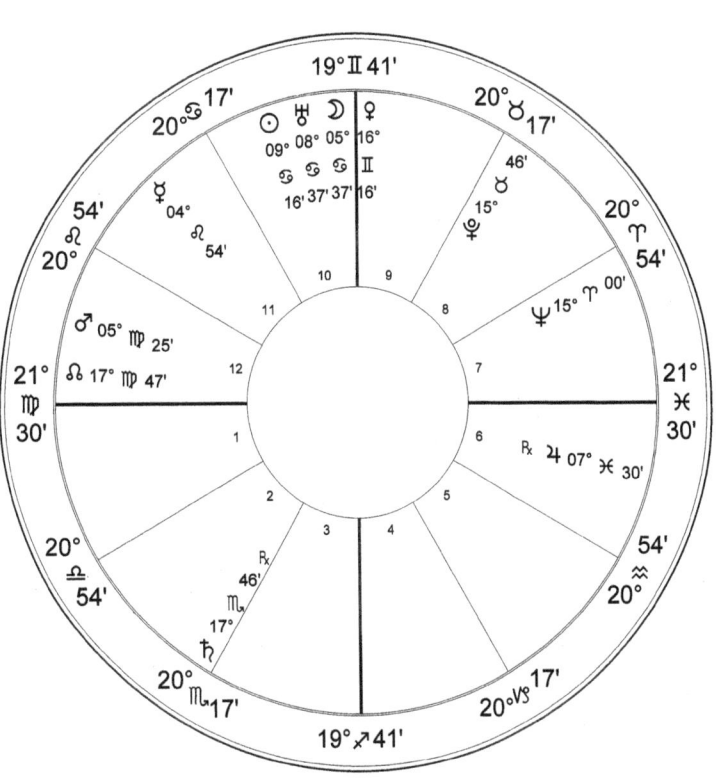

July 1, 1867
Ottawa
75W42, 45N25
Proclaimed at 10:41 AM EST
Source: Canadian National Library

Canada was first discovered by Europeans in 1497 when John Cabot sailed into St. John's on the island of Newfoundland. Thirty-seven years later Cartier came and claimed the mainland for France. The first permanent settlement took place in the summer of 1605 on the banks of the St. Croix River, which divides Maine and New Brunswick. The settlement was moved the next year to Port Royal, now Annapolis Royal, Nova Scotia. Quebec was founded by Champlain in 1608 and became the most strategic site in New France. During the 17th century, the Iroquois Indians were a constant threat to survival and in 1666, an attempt was made to end this harassment when regiments were sent to hound the Indians for the next twenty-three years. A treaty was finally signed in 1701, ending future attacks with the Iroquois. In 1713 a treaty gave Britain control of Hudson Bay, Newfoundland, Nova Scotia and New Brunswick. Louisbourg was built in the 1740s and became the most impregnable fortress in Canada. Twice it surrendered to the British: 1745 and 1758. The Acadians, French settlers in Nova Scotia, were ordered deported in 1755 by the British, and four years later, the final decisive battle for control of the region took place on the Plains of Abraham outside the city of Quebec. On the morning of September 13, 1759, General Wolf scaled the heights and fought the French, under the leadership of Montcalm. Britain won and France lost, but both generals died. Britain formally won the territory after the Treaty of Paris in 1763, thus ending France's aspirations for a New World Empire. In order to protect the rights, customs and religion, not to mention the language, of the French in Quebec, an act was passed guaranteeing them protection in 1774. In 1791 the provinces of Upper and Lower Canada were formed, which were to be united in 1841. Americans captured Fort York (Toronto) in 1813, but a treaty forced them to surrender their conquests one year later. The first settlement in the rich Red River Valley was at Winnipeg in 1812. The region was inhabited by the Metis (half-breeds of French and Indian extraction) who disliked outsiders immensely. In 1816 their leader, Riel, massacred many settlers near Winnipeg. In 1869 Louis Riel, his grandson, started a rebellion when his followers occupied Fort Garry. The rights of the Metis were finally assured with the admission of Manitoba into the Canadian Confederation in 1870.

During the 1840s many important events took place in Canada. In 1846 a treaty fixed the 49th parallel as the boundary between the United States and Canada, and the Oregon Territory was lost to America. Riots broke out in Montreal in 1849, and the Parliament buildings were burned to protest the Governor's plan to compensate those who lost severely during the earlier rebellion of 1837.

Plans to form a Confederation were begun at Charlottetown in 1864. When Parliament passed the British North American Act in the spring of 1867, the inception date was chosen to be July 1. Like all countries granted their independence by Britain, the "birthtime" is always one minute past midnight. This is the Aries rising chart most often used throughout the world. More recent research found some old newspapers which reported in great detail the Proclamation Ceremony which began at 10:00 a.m. on July 1, 1867 in Ottawa with the usual processional, a fifty gun salute and then some nominal hymn singing. Finally, the governor general read the Proclamation which that day gave Canada her independence. The time of 10:41 a.m. was derived through rectification giving Virgo on the Ascendant.

Canada's Chart Delineation

I feel this chart describes well the people of Canada, and thanks to Lois Rodden (a native of Saskatchewan) here is the delineation of this chart.

Canadians are modest, reserved, thrifty, and hard-working individuals, but not as priggish as Virgo rising would suggest, due to the Ascendant ruler in Leo. A quiet dignity pervades the essence of Canada as well as an aura of permanence and stolidity (the Ascendant is in the Taurus decan). The absence of squares points to Canada's lack of assertiveness in world arena, for it is rather shy and timid about demanding a front row seat. Both luminaries in Cancer plus Virgo rising account for this tendency.

Venus rules the second house and is posited in the ninth house in the sign of neighbors, Gemini. More than seventy percent of Canada's trade is with the United States and the sextile of Venus to Neptune facilitates this relationship. Saturn in the second indicates the vast agricultural resources which make Canada, like America, a world granary or breadbasket. But Saturn conserves its assets wisely, so Canada won't rape the land of its precious resources if at all possible.

Scorpio ruling the third house, and Pluto placed in the eighth, accounts for the dominance and control that Canada's only neighbor (the U.S.) has exerted over its internal affairs. As Scorpio and Taurus are both money signs, the current fluctuation of the world money market is a source of worry and concern to all Canadians. In recent years, the value of the Canadian dollar has depreciated at an alarming rate, and inflation is considerably higher than the government has anticipated.

Canadians love their freedom and detest being cramped. Sagittarius ruling the fourth has made this an expansive-thinking land, though the majority live within fifty miles of the American border. Canada is the second-largest nation on earth, exceeded only by Russia. This desire for space accounts for the lack of crowding in the cities, not to mention the relative absence of ghettoes. Being a young country, there is still room to homestead and pioneer, even if much of the land is frozen tundra. Jupiter in Pisces makes the natives spiritually tied to the earth. The desire is to preserve the land for future generations relatively unspoiled by the industrial pollution found in many American landscapes.

Saturn ruling the fifth house does not make Canadians possessed of unabandoned hilarity. They take their amusements very seriously, especially sports like hockey. As Saturn is a cold and wintry sign, all recreational activates relating to snow and ice are accentuated.

Another winter sign, Aquarius, rules the sixth house, so the climate in Canada is truly arctic, except on the coasts. Uranus in Cancer plus Jupiter in Pisces accounts for the vast fishing industry, not to mention the abundance of wealth beneath the surface. As the sixth house also governs labor relations, it should come as no surprise that with Uranus ruling this house, the unions are quite strong, as they are in most socialist countries. This house also rules the armed forces and the national police force, called the Mounties, known the world over for their determination and persistence (Aquarius is fixed and Uranus is stubborn).

Neptune not only rules the seventh house, but is posited therein. With this configuration, Canada has probably felt like its desires were often overlooked, ignored or mistaken as Neptune tends to make the outside world visualize Canada through faulty lenses. Canada must assertively fight to retain its own unique and distinct identity as she has a great deal to offer in the way of compassion and understanding where the underdog is concerned. But with Neptune, none of this will be easy: Neptune prefers to be a follower rather than a leader.

With Venus ruling the ninth house of law, and placed in the ninth as well, it does not come as any surprise that until 1982 (when the progressed Ascendant opposed Venus) the Constitution of Canada was in British hands. All acts passed by the Canadian Parliament had to be approved in a foreign country before they could become law in the land that passed them. Slightly anachronistic, but then the inconjunct of Saturn might have accounted for this anomaly. A Bill of Rights was incorporated into the new Constitution, the first in Canadian history. Until now there wasn't even a habeas-corpus law in Canada.

With Gemini on the Midheaven, we find that Canada is actually two nations: one Anglo-Protestant and one French-Catholic. Venus close to the Midheaven proposes that relations between these two remain peaceful and harmonious, but the history of Canada has often been fraught with bitter internal dispute (e.g. the Metis and the Quebecois). The recent separatist movement in Quebec began when transiting Neptune started to oppose Venus at the same time Uranus was in the process of squaring Mercury. Canada is a Federation, so the ten provinces retain more autonomy than do their counterparts (the states) in America. Many provinces have tried to over-ride decisions made in Ottawa that might adversely affect their own welfare, many with success. Gemini demands freedom as much as Sagittarius, so the unified central government of the U.S. (which has Leo on the Midheaven) is conspicuously absent in Canada.

Both luminaries conjunct Uranus in Cancer points to the necessity for complete freedom and independence not often shown in Cancer. The usual keywords for the sign of the crab (patriotism and clannishness) are strangely missing from the Canadian temperament. This vast land, until a few years ago, didn't have an official national anthem, not to mention a distinct national flag. Canadians aren't impressed by heroics or bravado, so it comes as no surprise that when members of the Canadian embassy in Teheran freed several American hostages being held by Iranian terrorists, the nation's reaction was "so what. It's no big deal really. Any decent person would have done the same thing." Uranus is always perverse and its actions are always contrary to what is expected. Being a Cancer nation, Canadians would prefer to go their own quiet way, making a few waves as possible, hoping to be left alone in peace and quiet.

Mercury sits at the midpoint of the ASC/MC, and is ruler of both those angles. Being unaspected, except for a wide inconjunct to Jupiter, Mercury stands alone, regal and steadfast, seemingly indifferent to outside interference. Mercury is also at the Moon/Mars midpoint, which explains the logical and rational thinking that is imbued into daily life. Mercury in the eleventh house illustrates Canada's desire to be a true and lasting friend, loyal and trustworthy to the bitter end. Being that the ruler of both angles is in Leo, Canada will not stoop to the level of other nations in its race for military supremacy. It would be beneath her dignity to do so.

Mars in the twelfth house accounts for the lack of inherent violence found in Canadian society. Compared to the U.S., crime is almost nil, and natives and tourists are free to walk the streets at night without fear of assault. Mars in this house points to the tendency to subdue most negative instincts (Mars in Virgo is rather weak and non-violent to begin with) and all impulses are kept in check as much as possible. It's true that Canada has not had the history that America has had with respect to imported minorities (like the Blacks in the South): her problems were internal.

Possibly the opposition to Jupiter has given Canadians a natural respect for authority. After all, in this cold and beautiful land life is often a struggle to survive. Why waste energy on non-essentials like fighting with one's neighbor? Mars in Virgo wastes not, wants not.

The Sun and Moon conjunct Uranus, plus the Midheaven in the Aquarian decan of Gemini point to the hospitality that Canada will show in the future to all mankind. Her spirit is abundant, her ambitions noble, and her people possessed with good old fashioned virtues. Canadians have learned to work with both their land and their countrymen in relative harmony. It's a lesson we could all partake of, if we are to survive the coming decades.

The History of Canada Continued

Four provinces were charter members: Ontario, Quebec, New Brunswick, and Nova Scotia. Others joined through the years until 1949, when Newfoundland became its youngest member.

In 1885 the Transcontinental Railroad was completed, and Canada was linked coast to coast. Two years later, Riel proclaimed an illegal government in Saskatchewan and another Meti rebellion began. Canada entered the Great War on the side of Great Britain in 1915, but after the passage of the Treaty of Westminster in 1931, Canada's parliament was on equal footing with that of Great Britain. Thus, Canada elected to join Wold War II instead of automatically entering the fracas on the side of Britain, as she had done before.

In recent years there has been much discussion in Quebec about separatism. Rene Levesque won office a few years back on the promise to secede from Canada and become an independent nation. Terrorist acts, riots, and bombings took place in the ensuing years, and businesses moved out. In a referendum in 1981, Quebeckers defeated the separatist measure, but dissension still exists in the ranks. Quebec passed a law that makes it mandatory to conduct all business affairs in French, and outsiders must register their children in French speaking schools. Businesses have had to change their names, often with reluctance. There is another battle going on right now in Canada, and that is the formation of the Canadian Constitution. You see, Canada is technically governed by the governor general, who is appointed by the English monarch, and who sits in residence at Ottawa as its spokesman. The head of state of course is the English monarch, but the people elect the prime minister, who has been Pierre Elliott Trudeau since 1968, with the exception of one year. The Parliament is bicameral with the House of Commons and a Senate. Senate members are appointed and serve until 75 years of age on the advice of the prime minister. The House of Commons and its representatives are elected for five years. The ten provinces are governed by a premier, and the two territories are governed by a commission. Canada wants the right to make its own Constitution and have it rest in Canada instead of Britain where it remains due to the fact that, even though Canada is an independent country, Britain still has the final say-so on Constitutional matters. A slight case of the parent not letting go of its child.

On December 8, 1981 an agreement was reached by an overwhelming majority: only Quebec abstained from the victory celebration. Canada became at long last, a fully independent country during the early part of 1982. To insure the rights of its citizens, a Bill of Rights will be inserted as well as a revenue sharing provision to help the poorer provinces.

Being the second largest nation on earth (only Russia is larger), Canada is sparsely populated, and most of the people live within fifty miles of the American border. French and English are the official languages; sixty-seven percent speak only English, eighteen percent only French, and thirteen percent are bilingual. Roman Catholics make up forty-six percent of the population, and the Protestants are largely members of the Anglican church. Those of the Eastern Orthodox religion live mainly in the prairie provinces, where many of the settlers are from the Ukraine. Nearly half of the people are British or Scottish extraction and thirty percent of French origin. Canada is seventy-six percent urban and has a mere six persons per square mile. Much of the country is uninhabited due to the severe climate.

Highlights of Canadian History

1497, June 24 John Cabot discovers Newfoundland for England

1534, July 24 Jacques Cartier lands on the Gaspe Peninsula and claims the region for France

1605, August First settlement founded at Port Royal, Nova Scotia

1629, July 3 Quebec City founded by Champlain

1629, July 20 Champlains surrenders Quebec to the British

1632, March 29 Quebec returned to France

1642, May 17 Montreal founded as Ville-Marie

1666, September 14 Regiment leaves Quebec to raid Iroquois settlements that will end Indian harassment 23 years later

1670, May 2 Hudson's Bay Company chartered

1669, July 4 Frontenac leaves on an expedition that will permanently end the Iroquois uprisings

1701, August 3 Treaty signed with the Iroquois nation

1713, April 11 Treaty gives Hudson Bay, Newfoundland, Nova Scotia and New Brunswick to England

1745, June 15 Louisbourg surrenders to the English

1755, July 28 Acadians ordered deported

<%-2>1758, July 26 Louisbourg surrenders again to the British.

1759, September 13 Wolf defeats Montcalm at Quebec and the French Empire in North America ends; both generals are killed

1774, June 22 Quebec Act formed giving French citizens protection

1783, September 3 Americans gain Canadian land and fishing rights

1791, June 19 Provinces of Upper and Lower Canada established

1793, July 23 Mackinzie lands in British Columbia after crossing the continent

1808, July 2 Fraser reaches the mouth of the river that will bear his name

1813, April 27 Americans capture Fort York (now Toronto)

1814, December 24 Treaty returned captured land

to the Canadians

1816, June 19 The Metis massacre settlers near Winnipeg

1832, June 7 Cholera epidemic begins in Quebec.

1841, February 10 Upper and Lower Canada united

1846, June 15 49th parallel settled as boundary between the US and Canada

1849, April 25 Tory mob burns the Parliament Buildings in Montreal

1864, September 1 Conference opens in Charlottetown to discuss the question of Canadian Confederation

1867, March 8 British Parliament passes the North American Act

1867, July 1 Canadian Confederation becomes a reality. The Dominion of Canada is born

1869, November 2 Louis Riel and the Metis occupy Fort Garry

1870, May American hunters massacre the Assiniboine Indians; the RCMP formed shortly afterwards

1885, November 7 Transcontinental railroad completed, last spike driven

1885, March 18 Riel proclaims a rebellion in Saskatchewan

1906, August 31 Amundsen becomes the first person to sail the NW passage

1914, August 4 Canada enters the Great War along with Britain

1918, March 29 Draft riots begin in Quebec

1919, June 21 General strike smashed in Winnipeg by the Mounties

1931, December 11 Britain finally gives Canada complete independence

1939, September 10 Canadian Parliament approves the Declaration of War

1981, May Quebeckers defeat referendum asking for separation and end four years of riots and terrorist acts

Alberta

September 1, 1905
Edmonton
113W38, 53N33
12:01 AM MST
Source: Canadian
National Library

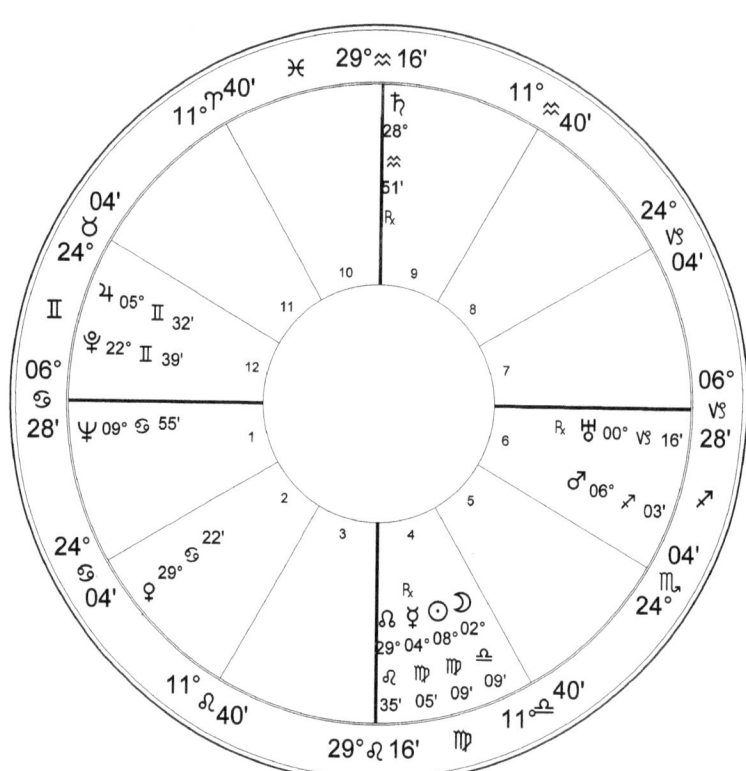

First settled at Edmonton in 1795, both the Hudson's Bay Company and the Northwest Company established trading posts in the region. Hudson's Bay Company was granted the monopoly in 1869, but settlement was delayed until the arrival of the railroad in the 1880s. Alberta became part of the Canadian Confederation in 1905, along with Saskatchewan.

The mainstay of its economy is oil. Ever since 1947 it has led Canada in petroleum production, and is the third wealthiest province. The province also has many cattle ranches and ranks near the top in wheat production.

Area: 255,285 square miles

Calgary

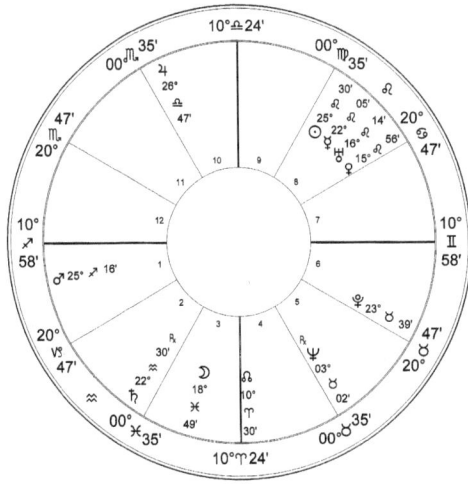

**August 18, 1875
114W04, 51N03
3:27 PM MST**

Founded by the Royal Canadian Mounted Police in 1875, oil was discovered nearby in 1914 (Midheaven trine Moon) and near Leduc in 1947 (Midheaven trine Mercury).

Calgary today is Canada's boom town due to Alberta's vast oil fields. Slightly uncultured (Mars rising in Sagittarius), it is venturing into the 21st century with gusto and vigor unmatched by other century cities. Home of the Calgary Stampede, the largest rodeo in Canada, it's the "Energy Capital of Canada" and its skyline is beginning to look like Houston.

Incorporated: September 16, 1893
Elevation: 3,557 feet
Area: 157 square miles
Source: Calgary Public Library; *The Silent Force* by T.N. Longstreth says September 4, 1875

Edmonton

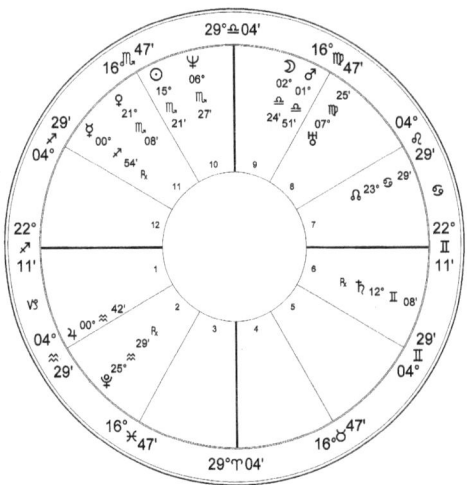

**November 7, 1795
113W38, 53N33
11:15 AM MST**

Fort Edmonton was founded in 1795 by fur trappers, and made capital of Alberta in 1905 when Alberta became part of the Canadian Confederation. The University of Alberta was founded the next year. When oil was found near Leduc in 1947 (Midheaven opposition Moon, Ascendant opposition Jupiter), Edmonton became a boom town.

The most northerly metropolis on the North American continent, Edmonton is the mother of the Arctic. Remote and isolated, the city is rather prim and sedate (Sun in Scorpio) and extremely conservative. It once had no nightclubs, cocktail bars, or burlesque shows due to its puritan heritage. A polyglot community, Edmonton is the supply point for explorations north and one of the major oil centers of Canada; 7,000 wells in the vicinity produce more than eighty percent of all Canadian oil.

Incorporated: October 8, 1904
Elevation: 2,373 feet
Area: 121 square miles
Source: Edmonton Public Library

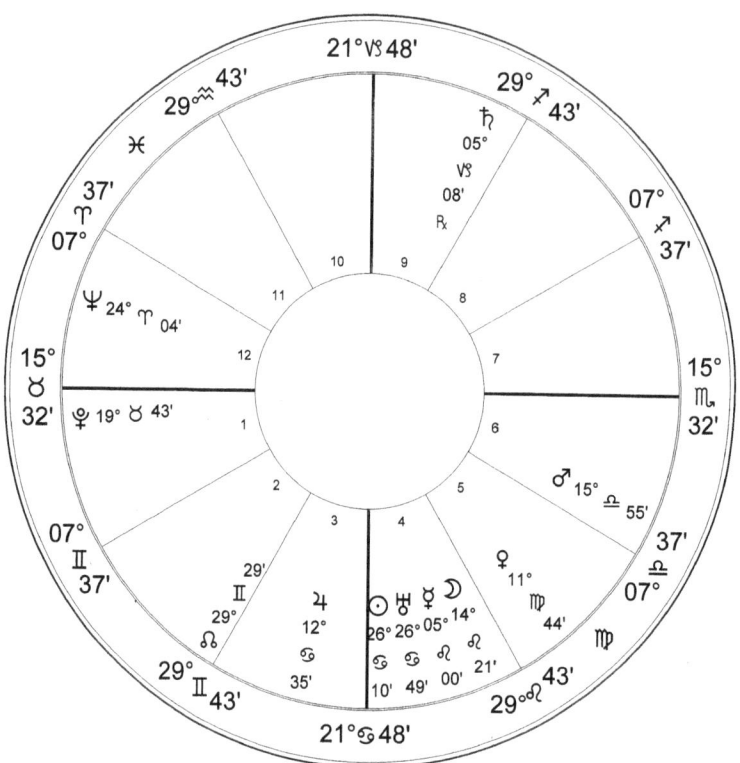

British Columbia

July 19, 1871
Victoria
123W22, 48N25
12:01 AM PST
Source: Canadian National Library

British Columbia is Canada's third largest province in both area and population. Fur trading was the impetus in the early days. In 1849 Vancouver Island was made an English colony, and nine years later the mainland was annexed. It agreed to become part of Canada on the condition that a railroad be built to connect it with the eastern provinces. The railroad was completed in 1885. With the completion of the Panama Canal in 1914, Vancouver became Canada's largest port of the Pacific.

Lumber is the chief resource of this province, and British Columbia has an exceptionally large fishing fleet. Tourism is also important.

Area: 365,945 square miles

Vancouver

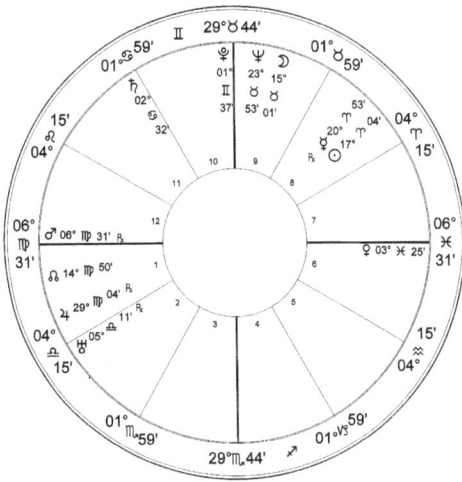

April 6, 1886
123W07, 49N14
3:02 PM PST

First settled in October, 1862, the town's most famous departed citizen, "Gassy" Jack Deighton, opened his first saloon on September 30, 1867, the same year the first sawmill was completed. Incorporated in 1886, Vancouver burned to the ground on June 13th that same year (Ascendant conjunct Mars). The University of British Columbia was founded in 1908 (Midheaven sextile Mercury).

Located a mere fifteen miles from the U.S. border, Vancouver is possibly the most beautiful city in Canada. Situated on a peninsula, the snow covered mountains <%-2>north of the city are within easy reach for morning or afternoon skiing. A happy town, full of healthy looking people, Vancouverites are vibrant and energetic (Sun in Aries) with zest for the outdoor life. A city that usually gets what it wants, Vancouver has become the financial, industrial, shipping and cultural center of western Canada. It also has a large ethnic population, and is home to the second largest Chinese community in the Western Hemisphere after San Francisco. It also has a large Scottish population. Young thinking and often brash in spirit (Mars rising), Vancouver has become Canada's most expensive and densely populated city. The West End is the most crowded parcel of real estate in North America after Manhattan Island. This scenic city also contains some of the most beautiful gardens in the hemisphere, due to Vancouver's temperate, and wet, climate. Unlike most other Canadian cities, Vancouver is not snowbound during the winter months.

Incorporated: 1886
Elevation: 38 feet
Area: 45 square miles
Source: Vancouver Public Library says 3:00 p.m.

Victoria

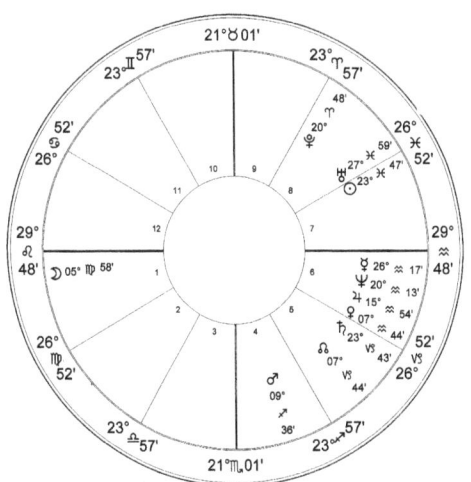

March 14, 1843
123W22, 48N25
4:00 PM PST

Founded as a military post in 1843, Victoria became capital of the province in 1868. This city gives visitors the impression of being the most British city on this continent. Double decker busses wend their way through the city's streets, and afternoon tea is a ritual not to be missed. Many retired people live here due to its equable climate, probably the best overall in Canada. Situated on an island, it's connected to the mainland by ferries to both Vancouver and Seattle.

Incorporated: August 2, 1862
Elevation: 56 feet
Source: Victoria Public Library says 4:00 p.m.

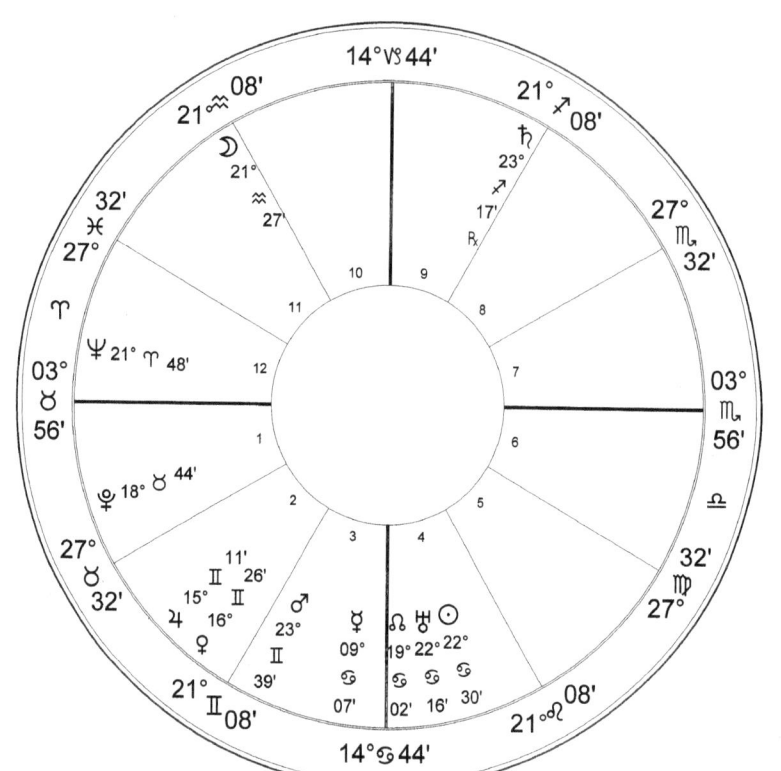

Manitoba

**July 15, 1870
Winnipeg
97W09, 49N53
12:01 AM CST
Source: Canadian
National Library**

First settled at Churchill in 1650, the Hudson's Bay Company and the French Northwest Company were rivals until 1821 when the two were united. Access to the province was limited until the arrival of the steamboat, and the first real settlement was on the Red River at Winnipeg in 1812. Manitoba became a province in 1870, and was linked to the U.S. by railroad in 1878 and to the rest of Canada in 1881.

More than twenty-five percent of Manitoba's income comes from wheat, for this is the heart of prairie country. Copper, nickel, and zinc are the prime minerals.

Area: 250,950 square miles

Brandon

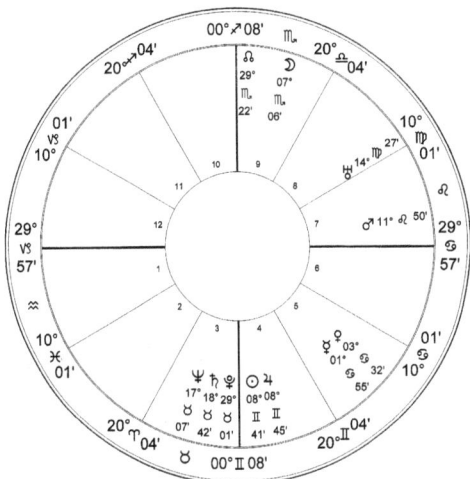

**May 30, 1882
99W57, 49N51
12:01 AM CST**

Founded in May 1881, it was incorporated the following year. Brandon is the second largest city in Manitoba and a large regional center for the many agricultural products that are produced in the region.

Incorporated: 1882
Elevation: 1,265 ft.
Source: Brandon Public Library

Winnipeg

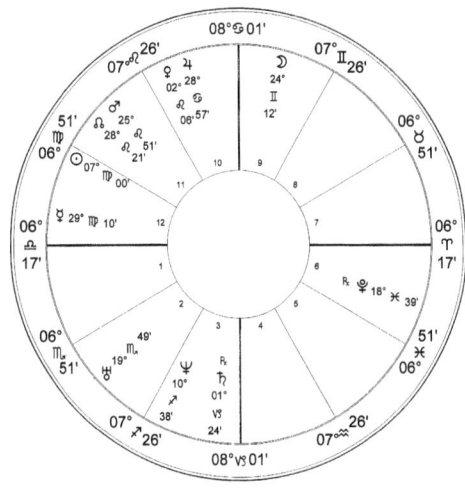

**August 30, 1812
97W09, 49N53
8:29 AM CST**

Founded by Selkirk as the Red River Colony in 1812, Winnipeg became the capital of Manitoba in 1870. In 1877 the University of Manitoba was founded. To enlarge its tax base, Winnipeg formed a metropolitan form of government in 1972.

Winnipeg is the heart of the prairie provinces; consequently agriculture has played a major role in its history. Known for its many church spires and extremely wide streets, Winnipeg is headquarters of Canada's two largest railroads: the Canadian National and Canadian Pacific.

Incorporated: November 8, 1873
Elevation: 765 feet
Area 218 square miles
Source: *The Red River Colony* by Louis A Wood

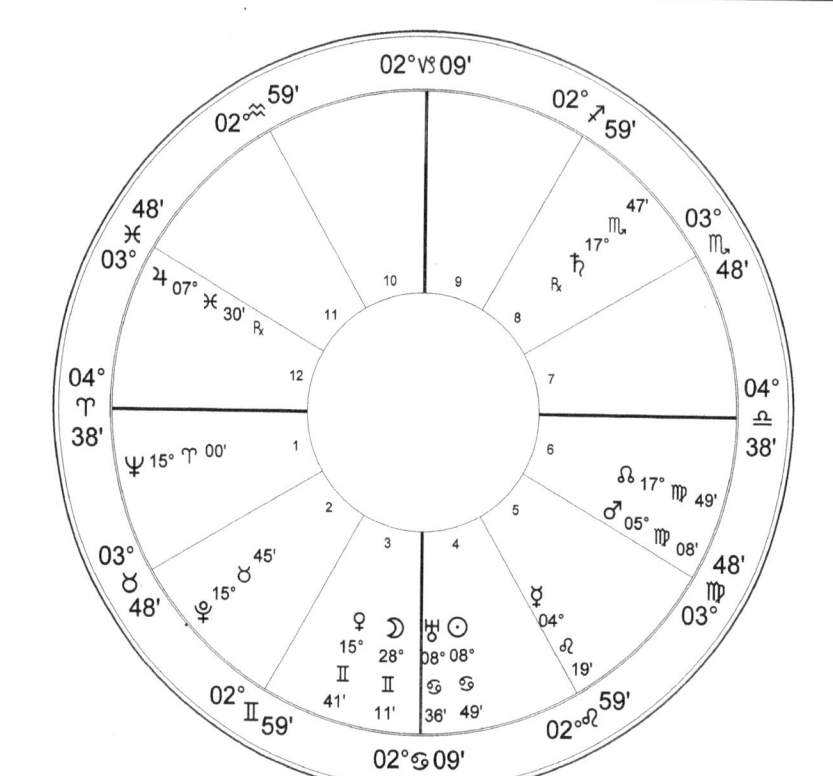

New Brunswick

**July 1, 1867
66W39, 45N58
12:01 AM AST
Source: National
Canadian Library**

First settled by Tories from the U.S. escaping the Revolution, the province was governed as part of Nova Scotia until 1784. After the Napoleonic wars, hordes of Scottish immigrants landed and made this province quite wealthy. Prior to becoming one of the four original provinces in the Confederation, its fortunes had declined so badly that New Brunswick was admitted with reluctance. With the arrival of the railroad and the steamboat, its economic importance was gone and many industries left the province.

Lumber is the main industry, followed by fishing. New Brunswick has the third lowest income in Canada and the unemployment rate is unusually high.

Area: 28,354 square miles

Fredericton

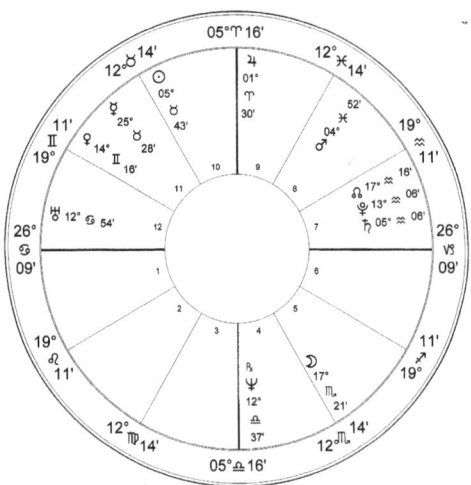

April 25, 1785
66W39, 45N58
10:30 AM AST

Founded by Americans in 1785, it became the capital of the province later the following year. Built in the site of the French village of St. Anne's, Fredericton is the least known of all Canadian capitals, and is seldom visited by tourists.

Incorporated: March 30, 1848
Elevation: 36 feet
Source: New Brunswick Archives

Saint John

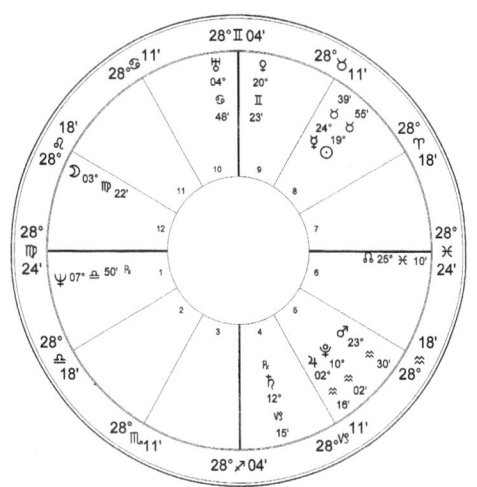

May 10, 1783
66W03, 45N16
3:02 PM AST

Founded in 1783 by Tories escaping from New England, it became Canada's first chartered city two years later. A fire in June 1877 caused 100 deaths (Ascendant sextile Neptune). Today, Saint John is the largest city in the province and its chief port of entry.

Incorporated: May 17, 1785
Elevation: 42 feet
Source: *The Canadians* by George Wrong

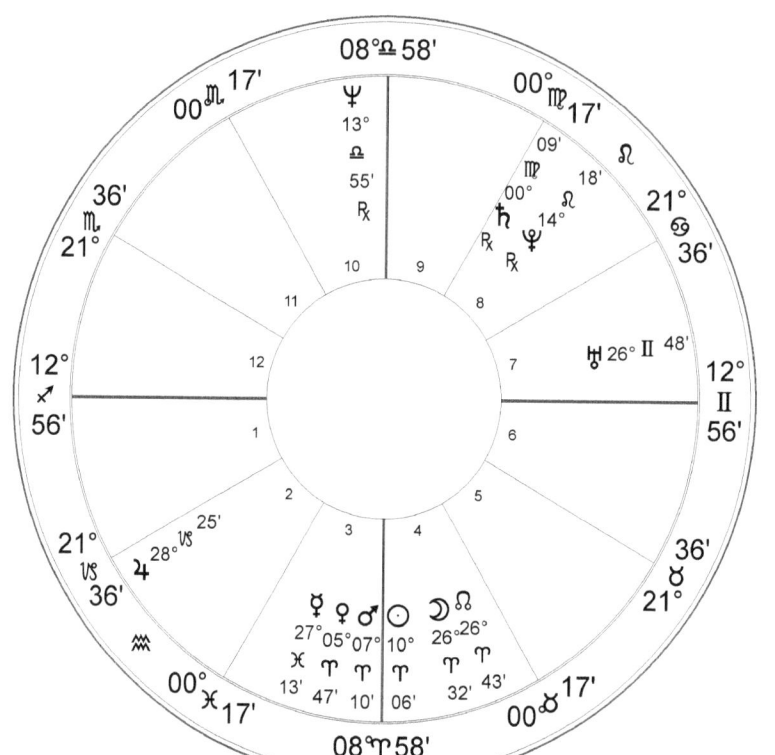

Newfoundland

**March 31, 1949
52W42, 47N34
12:01 AM NFT
Source: Canadian
National Library and
*New York Times***

Newfoundland is Canada's oldest settled area, and its youngest province. The Grand Banks were known as a lucrative fishing area even before the arrival of John Cabot in 1497. Sir Humphrey Gilbert claimed the region for England in 1583, but permanent settlement was discouraged until the early 19th century. From 1885 until 1934 Newfoundland was a self-governing territory of Great Britain, separate and distinct of Canada. The Depression of 1933 forced an end to home rule, and sixteen years later, the Canadian Parliament finally agreed to annex the region.

The province has the largest fishing fleet in Canada, but its income is the second lowest in Canada. Agriculture is limited due to its rocky terrain, but lumber is abundant due to its many forests. Newfoundland consists of two divisions: Labrador on the mainland and the island of Newfoundland.

Area: 156,656 square miles

Saint John's

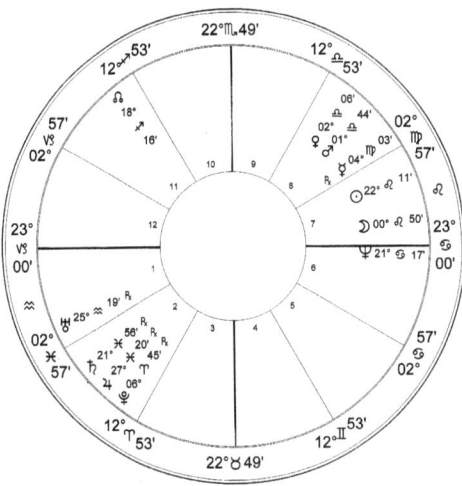

**August 15, 1583 (N.S.)
52W42, 47N34
5:48 PM ST**

John Cabot discovered the region in June 1497 but formal settlement didn't begin until August 1583. Known as the oldest city in Canada, and the second oldest in North America (after St. Augustine), its fame came from its proximity to the Grand Banks, one of the world's most lucrative fishing areas. A fire in July 1892 burned a good portion of the city and killed 600 people (Midheaven conjunct Mars). When Newfoundland became the youngest member of the Canadian Confederation in 1949, St. John's, as its largest city became its capital (Midheaven square Sun). This city is the closest North American city to the European continent, and its airport, Gander, is a major refueling stop.

Incorporated: January 1, 1902
Elevation: 110 feet
Source: Meredith Newspapers, July 30, 1986

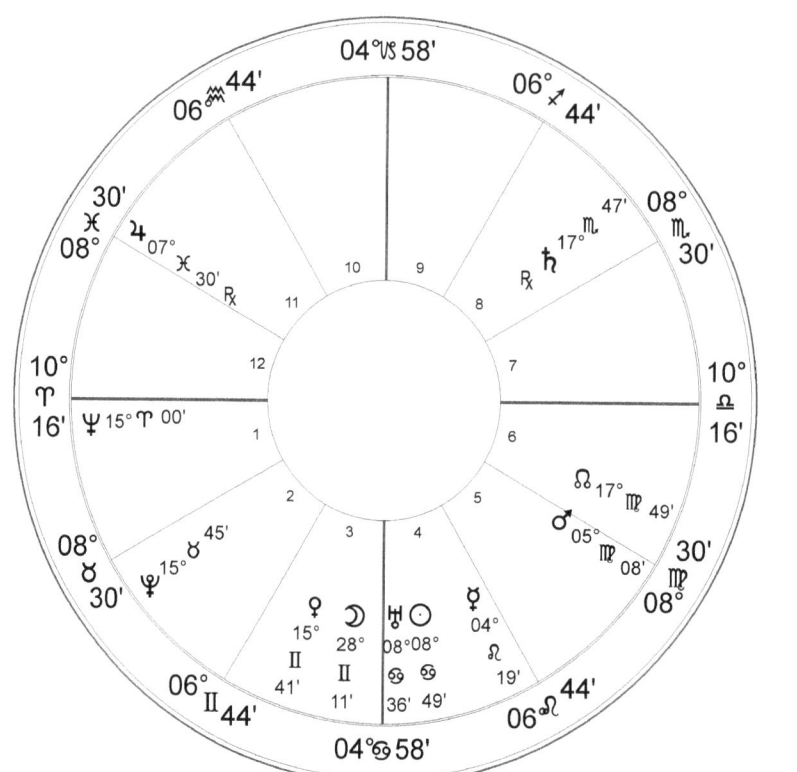

Nova Scotia

July 1, 1867
Halifax
63W35, 44N38
12:01 AM AST
Source: Canadian National Library

Nova Scotia (meaning New Scotland in Latin) was a highly contested region. For years both the French and the English fought for possession; in 1749, Lord Cornwallis landed and founded the fortress city of Halifax. The Acadians were expelled six years later and fled to Louisiana. After the American Revolution, many Tories settled here. Upon becoming part of the Confederation of Canada in 1867, many of its citizens disliked the idea intensely and it's been a sore spot in this province ever since.

Nova Scotia has the largest fishing fleet in Canada, and many manufacturing establishments. But the unemployment rate ranks very high.

Area: 21,425 square miles

Halifax

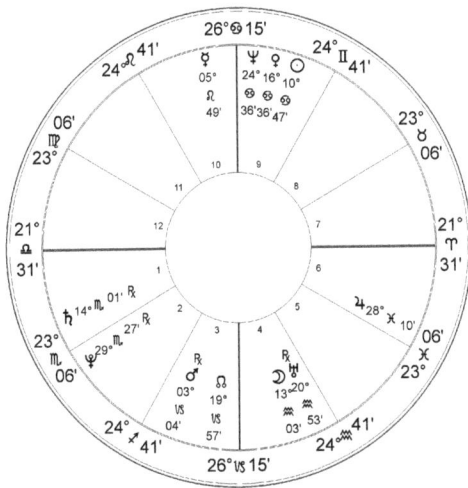

**July 2, 1749
63W35, 44N38
1:24 PM AST**

Founded by Lord Cornwallis in 1749, who later surrendered to Washington at Yorktown, it was established as a fortress. It's nickname was the "Gibraltar of the West" due to its many fortifications. The first legislative assembly in Canada met here in 1758 (Midheaven conjunct Mercury). In December 1917 the steamer Mt. Blanc exploded in the harbor causing untold damage to the waterfront and killing more than 200 people (Midheaven opposition Sun, Ascendant sextile Uranus). In 1945 a munitions depot blew up.

Halifax is situated in a strategic position, and due to its large harbor, it became Canada's principal naval base. The older part of the city was once the most crowded on the continent, as it lay on a peninsula.

Incorporated: April 19, 1841
Elevation: 56 feet
Area: 24 sq. miles
Source: *Halifax* by Thomas Raddall

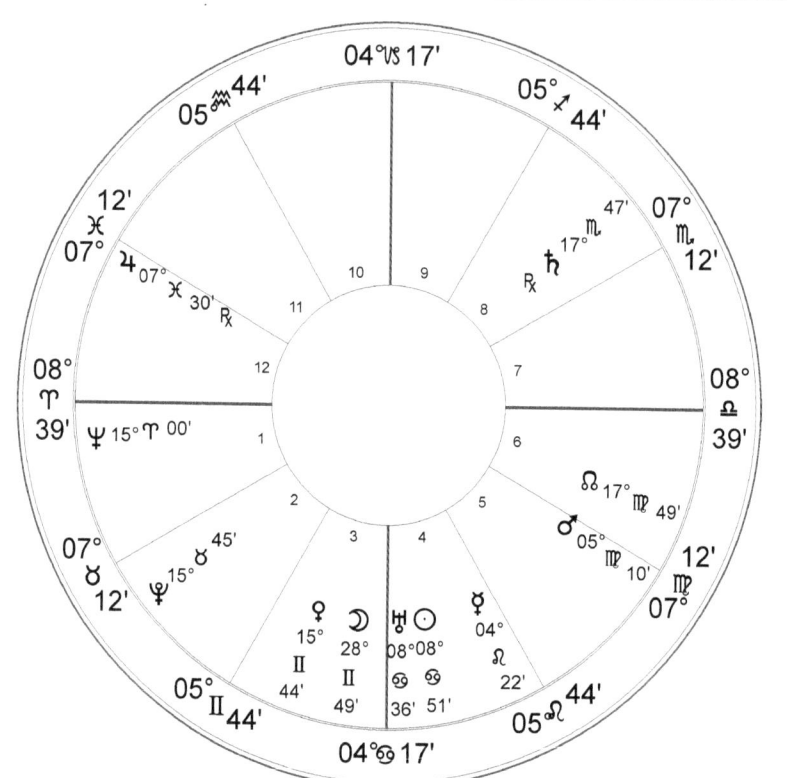

Ontario

**July 1, 1867
Toronto
79W22, 43N39
12:01 AM EST
Source: Canadian
National Library**

First settled in 1639, permanent settlement was delayed until passage of the Quebec Act of 1774. During the War of 1812, Americans burned the town of York (now Toronto). With the establishment of the Canadian Confederation in 1867, it became the wealthiest province in Canada, and today contains one-third of the nation's population.

Ontario accounts for eighty percent of all manufactured goods exported, and forty percent of the national income. It produces ninety-eight percent of the nation's autos, ninety-three percent of its heavy equipment,4 and ninety-two percent of its agricultural machinery. Ontario has the most farms of any province in Canada. The world's largest supply of nickel surrounds Sudbury.

Area: 412,575 square miles

Hamilton

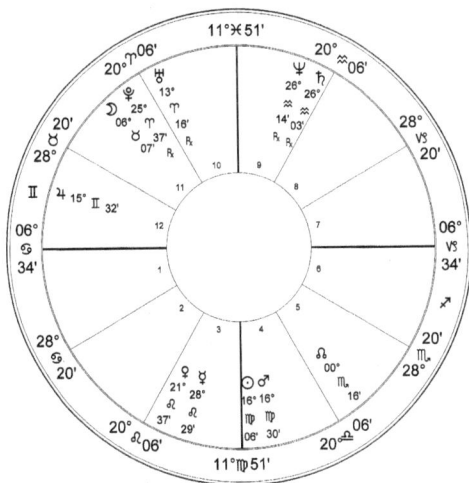

**September 9, 1846
79W51, 43N15
12:01 AM EST**

First settled in 1778, a sale of lots was held in 1813 and the city was named after its chief realtor, George Hamilton. In 1830 the Burlington Canal was completed, and in 1893, the first steel mill opened.

Hamilton is Canada's third largest industrial center and home to two of Canada's largest steel foundries.

Incorporated: 1845
Elevation: 306 feet
Source: *A Mountain and a City* by M.F. Campbell

London

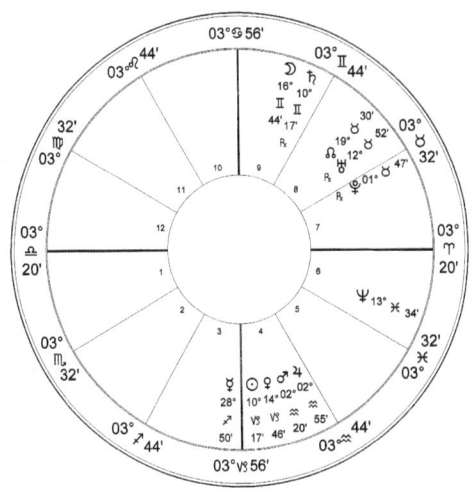

**January 1, 1855
81W15, 42N59
12:01 AM EST**

In 1793 John Simcoe planned this city to be the future capital of Upper Canada, as Ontario was then known. Formally settled in 1826, it became a garrison town from 1838 until 1853. London is a large manufacturing center with a very diversified economy.

Incorporated: 1855
Elevation: 804 feet
Source: London Public Library

Ottawa

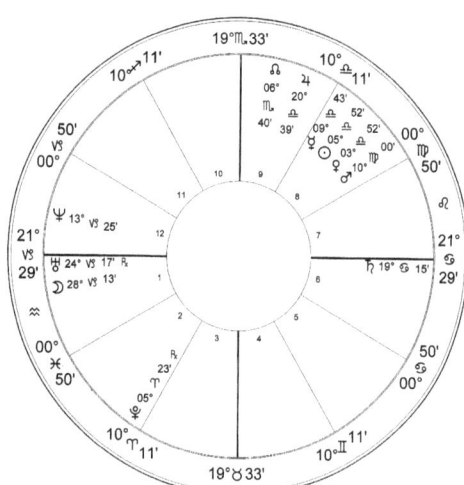

**September 29, 1827
75W42, 45N25
2:40 PM EST**

The region around Ottawa was first settled in 1800 when the neighboring city of Hull, Quebec was founded. Settlement in the south side of the river didn't begin until after the Napoleonic wars when veterans were given large parcels of land in the region. Originally called Bytown, it was a rip-roaring lumber town in its early days. Construction of the Rideau Canal to link the Ottawa and St. Lawerence rivers began in 1827 and was completed six years later. Because Ottawa was located midway between the French stronghold of Quebec and the English settlements in Ontario, Queen Victoria chose this community to become the capital of Canada in 1858 (Midheaven sextile Jupiter, Ascendant opposition Mars semisquare Uranus). Two years later, construction of the Gothic Parliament Buildings was begun. A massive fire in 1916 burned these buildings, with the exception of the library (Midheaven quincunx Saturn semisquare the Sun trine Jupiter). Ottawa is also home to a fine university, founded in 1848 (Ascendant trine Jupiter).

Situated at the confluence of the Ottawa and Gatineau rivers, the capital city of Canada is a planned city (Capricorn rising) with many beautiful parks and handsome structures. During the winter months, skaters glide for five miles down the frozen Rideau canal which is flanked by beautiful drives. Even though Ottawa is not as far north as Helsinki or Moscow, it is the world's coldest capital city. But in springtime, the city comes alive and tulips are to be found everywhere. They were a gift from Queen Wilhemina of Holland who was given refuge here during World War II. Needless to say, Ottawa is, like Washington, a company town, and the chief business is government.

Incorporated: January 1, 1855

Elevation: 276 feet
Area: 47 square miles
Source: *Ottawa* by Shirley Wood says the cornerstone for the Rideau Canal was laid at 3:00 p.m.

Sudbury

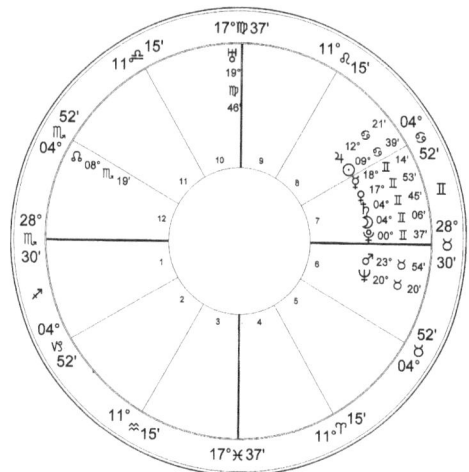

**July 1, 1883
81W00, 46N30
5:00 PM EST**

Founded in 1883 by a couple during the building of the Canadian Pacific, the first sale of lots was held four years later. Sudbury is located in a region of vast mineral wealth which produces seventy-five percent of the world's supply of nickel.

Incorporated: 1930
Source: *Sudbury Basin* by D.M. Liberties says late in the afternoon

Toronto

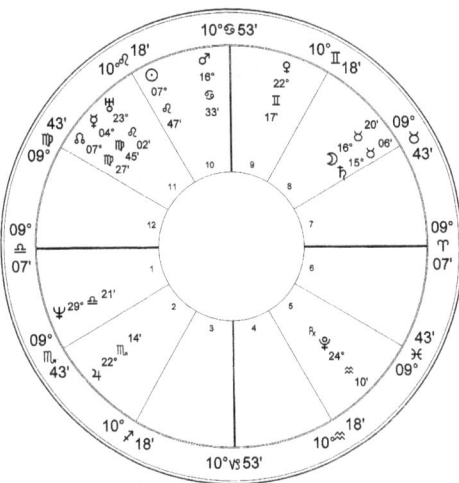

**July 30, 1793
79W22, 43N39
10:30 AM EST**

Founded by John Graves Simcoe in 1793, it became the capital of Upper Canada (Ontario) four years later (Midheaven conjunct Mars sextile Saturn). In 1813 Americans captured the city, then known as York, and burned the town (Midheaven square Neptune). The University of Toronto was founded in 1850, and in 1867, it became the capital of the province of Ontario. A fire in April 1904 burned much of the downtown area (Midheaven conjunct Neptune) an event which was repeated in 1977 when several buildings in the financial district were torched (Ascendant opposition Neptune). Greater Toronto was established in 1954 and is the largest civic government in Canada: it comprises five boroughs. The tallest structure in the world, the Canadian National Tower, standing at 1815 ft. above Lake Ontario, was completed in 1976.

Once known as a prim and proper community with largely British and Scottish ties, Toronto has become the most cosmopolitan and international city in Canada in recent years, due to Quebec's desire for separatism. Scores of businesses have moved here from Montreal, and the city is now the financial heart of Canada. Once known for its fear of change (Sun and Moon in fixed signs), Toronto has become the largest city in Canada, and the skyline is the most impressive in the country. Possessed with great drive and civic pride (Mars conjunct Midheaven trine Jupiter), it has a sharp eye for the dollar (Sun in Leo), loves bigness and being unique. But it still has that missionary spirit and boosterism so typical of all boom towns.

Toronto has the most unique City Hall on the continent: two hemispherical towers which overlook one of the largest shopping complexes in the world, Eaton Center. Toronto built Canada's first subway back in 1952 and hosts the world's largest annual fair, the Canadian National Exposition. It's the Chicago of Canada, a large industrial, financial and cultural center that is also big on publishing. Neighborhoods like Yorkville have been renovated in recent years to attract the many young people in the surrounding area. Toronto has many other ethnic areas populated by people from around the world. Once known as the town where Sunday was the dullest day of the week, Toronto offers a multitude of diversions that would have been unheard of two decades ago.

Incorporated: March 6, 1834
Elevation: 356 feet
Area: 43 square miles
Source: Diary of Mrs. John Graves Simcoe says her husband went ashore about 8:00 a.m.; chart rectified

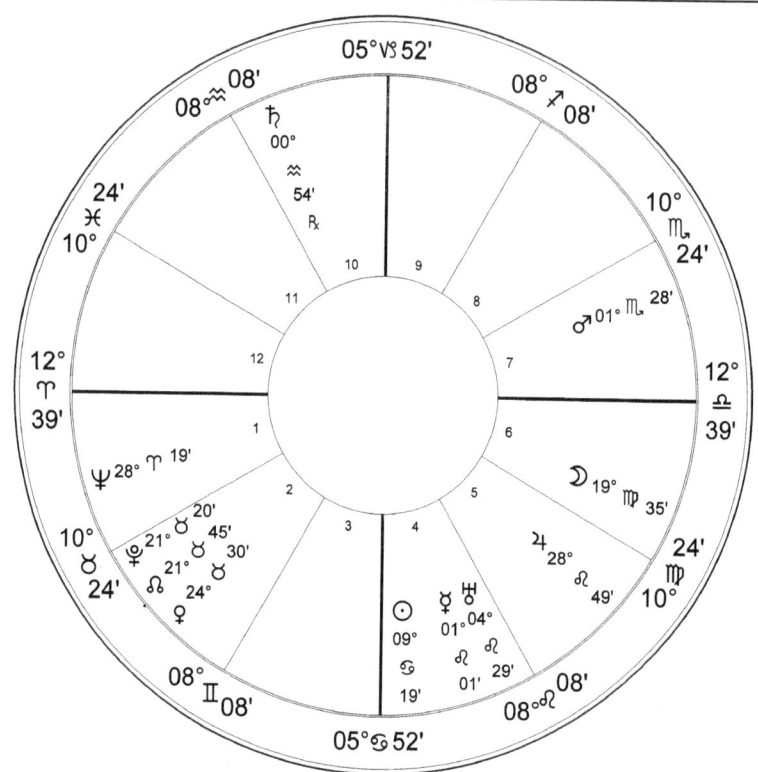

Prince Edward Island

July 1, 1873
Charlottetown
63W08, 46N14
12:01 AM AST
Source: Canadian National Library

The French called it Ile St. Jean when they settled it in the early 18th century. The British took over in 1758, and most of the Acadians were deported. New settlers, mostly Scots, arrived and land feuds lasted nearly a century afterward. The dream of Canadian Confederation was born in Charlottetown in 1864, but the island didn't enter for another nine years. Today, this province is the poorest in Canada, and the only one not connected with the mainland.

Agriculture is the mainstay of the economy, and potatoes, beef, bacon and dairy products its chief produce.

Area: 2,180 square miles

Charlottetown

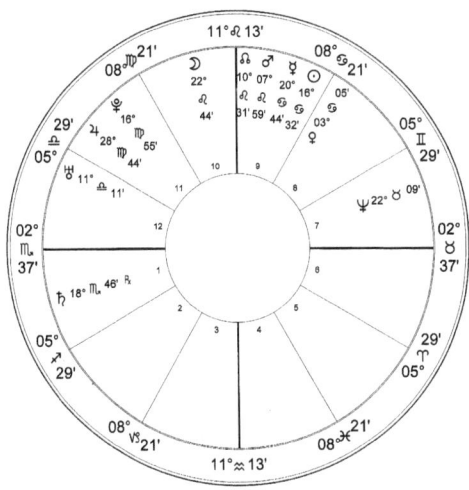

July 8, 1720
63W08, 46N14
2:00 PM AST

Founded as Fort LaJoye by the French in 1720, the settlement moved to its present site in 1763 (Midheaven conjunct Moon). Charlottetown can rightly be called the "Birthplace of Canada," as the council which set the rules for the future confederation took place here in the summer of 1864 (Ascendant opposition Mars). Upon the island's entry into the Confederation in 1873, it became the capital of the province.

Incorporated: April 17, 1855
Elevation: 18 feet
Source: *The French Regime in Prince Edward Island* by D.C. Harvey says between July 7 and November 11, 1720; chart rectified

Quebec

July 1, 1867
Quebec
71W13, 46N48
12:01 AM EST
Source: Canadian National Library

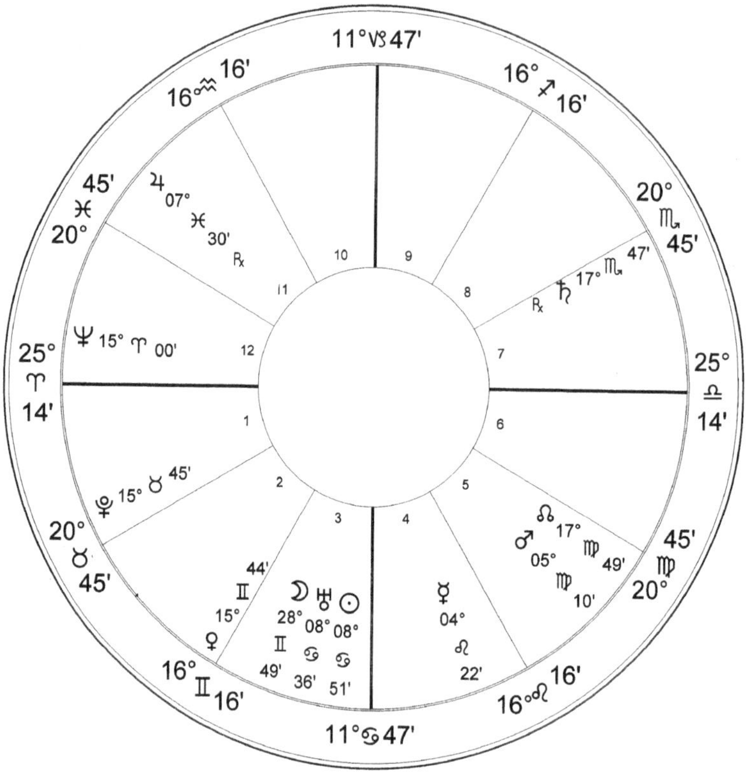

Discovered by Cartier in 1534, the region was first settled at Quebec in 1608 by Champlain. With the fall of the French Empire in America in 1759, the province was ceded to Britain in 1763. Firmly entrenched in French customs and language, this dichotomy was erased slightly in 1774 with the passage of the Quebec Act which insured that local traditions would endure. Quebec was one of the four charter members of the Canadian Confederation in 1867, but recently a movement was begun to separate from the rest of the nation due to what Quebeckers consider unfair treatment and relegation to being second-class citizens. Many terrorist attacks have taken place, and property losses were so severe that many businesses moved to Ontario. Quebec is nevertheless the most interesting province in Canada, for to visit it is like going back in time to a picturesque village in France when life was simpler and less frenetic. More than eighty percent of its citizens are French and eighty-eight percent are Catholic. Montreal is the second largest French-speaking city in the world, and Quebec is the only walled town in North America. It's Canada's largest province in area, and the second in population.

Quebec's vast forests produce huge quantities of lumber and wood pulp, and its hydroelectric plants provide cheap and efficient waterpower. Tourism ranks high in the economy, but manufacturing is the principal industry.

Area: 594,860 square miles

Montreal

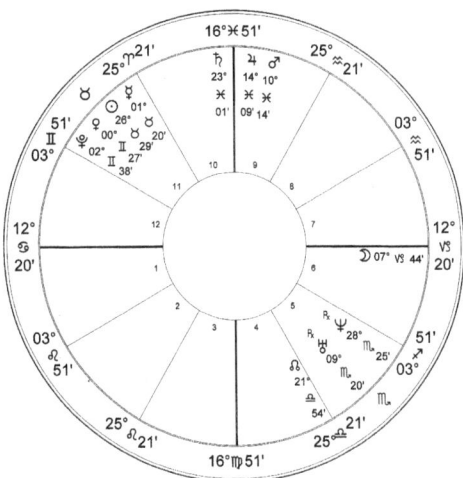

May 17, 1642
73W34, 45N32
7:25 AM EST

Founded as Ville Marie in 1642, the settlement was constantly plagued by the Iroquois Indians. The Lachine massacre of 1689 scared citizens half to death (Ascendant quincunx Jupiter). In September 1760 Montreal surrendered to the British (Midheaven square Moon, Ascendant trine Uranus) and Quebec passed into English hands, but only on paper. Captured by the Americans in 1775 (Midheaven trine Saturn), it suffered little during the remainder of the U.S. Revolution. The old city walls were finally torn down in 1803 (Midheaven quincunx Saturn), thus creating room for expansion. During 1837 and 1838 political riots caused a series of rebellions which climaxed in 1849 with the burning of the houses of Parliament (Midheaven square Moon, Ascendant square Jupiter). It was time to find another capital for Canada, and in 1858, the legislature moved to Ottawa (Midheaven sesquisquare Pluto). Three years prior in 1855, a smallpox epidemic caused many deaths (Midheaven quincunx Jupiter).

Recently, Montreal has hosted a world's fair (Expo 67) (Ascendant conjunct Pluto) and the 1976 Olympics (Ascendant square Jupiter). During the 1970s however, Montreal lost much of its pre-eminence in business and finance due to the separatist policies of Quebec. Businessmen were forced to conduct their affairs only in French and the end result was that many of them simply moved to neighboring Ontario, where the climate was more relaxed.

Montreal is a classy, sophisticated, elegant, and stately city, an urban jewel in the midst if a vast country. It is the only large city in the North American continent (except New Orleans) that never possessed the Puritan work ethic, and thus, it knows how to have fun. Seemingly at all hours of the night, the cafes and bistros are full of people, drinking and talking. It reminds one of Paris.

Being Canada's second largest city, it's also the second-largest French speaking city in the world, after Paris. Fully two-thirds speak French, and the remainder either English or some other foreign tongue. Because of this contest between language groups, there's a vitality present in Montreal that's been absent in cities twice her size (Mars trine Ascendant). Due to the abhorrently cold winters (Moon in Capricorn), Montreal had constructed many underground cities like Place Bonaventure, Place Canada, and Place Ville Marie. All are connected to the city's famous subway, the Metro, patterned after the one in Paris. All it's stations are different and the noise level is low due to the rubber tires on each train. In the middle of the city lies Mount Royal, after which the city is named; an oasis of greenery and relaxation, just like Central Park in New York, but much hillier. In the wintertime, it's popular with skiers and sledders. Known for its fine restaurants and shops (Cancer rising), it has the feeling of a European city and the rest of Canada is far off in the distance. Only the skyline reminds you that Montreal is still a large commercial and industrial metropolis, and the chief port of Canada, even though it's 1,000 miles from the Atlantic. Montreal to some may be past her prime, but with age comes the grace and maturity which this city has in abundance. The old quarter of the city near the waterfront contains many historic buildings which are popular with tourists.

Incorporated: June 5, 1832
Elevation: 117 feet
Area: 68 square miles
Source: *Montreal* by Stephen Leacock

Quebec City

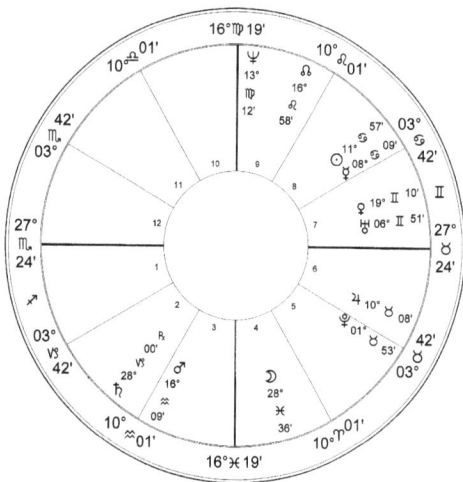

**July 3, 1608
71W13, 46N48
4:06 PM EST**

Founded by Champlain in 1608, it was the first permanent settlement in Canada. Strategically placed, and thus politically vulnerable, Quebec was attacked many times during its first two centuries. The British seized it in 1629 and held it for three years (Midheaven trine Uranus, Ascendant square Venus) but on September 13, 1759, a battle on the Plains of Abraham forever changed the course of Canadian history. On that day, New France passed into British hands, and both leaders, Montcalm and Wolfe, were killed in the battle (Midheaven semisquare Moon, Midheaven quincunx Neptune, Ascendant square Neptune). Having been the capital of New France since 1663 Quebec suffered the ultimate humiliation and retreated into the past, which has remained her strength to this day. The final assault on Quebec came in December 1775 when Benedict Arnold raided the city (Ascendant square Moon sesquisquare Mars). During World War II, Quebec hosted two major conferences—1943 and 1944.

Quebec is unquestionably the most impressive city in Canada, especially from the St. Lawrence River. Situated high above the river on a bluff, the city's most famous landmark, the Chateau Frontenac, dominates the skyline. It beckons you to explore the only remaining walled city in North America. Actually, Quebec is composed of two towns, one along the river, and the other atop the bluff. The narrow streets remind one of France and with today's political climate, English is heard only from tourists, so brush up on your high-school French and feel the pulse of the city.

Stroll along the Dufferin Terrace and watch the natives if you want to get the real feeling of this city. Quebeckers are polite, yet distant, like their French counterparts in Europe (Scorpio rising). Rather intellectual in attitude, they'll argue over a cup of coffee for hours on the virtues of their way of life, which to an American is as foreign as you get. Strongly attached to the past (Sun in Cancer) they mystify their heritage (Moon in Pisces) almost to the point of reverence. A difficult people to know, Quebec is a city cloaked in drama and passion (Neptune at Midheaven) where the past is just around the corner and the future is somewhere off yonder. Like most French, they don't really like outsiders (Uranus in the seventh house) and would prefer to be left alone. But they need the almighty tourist dollar as their economy would suffer considerable pains if the Americans stayed home (Saturn in the second house). Quick to point out the errors of your ways (Mars in Aquarius square Jupiter), this city comes the closest to giving the feeling of being in a foreign country of any city in the country, and a must-see for any student of history.

Incorporated: May 1, 1833
Elevation: 239 feet
Area: 30 square miles.
Source: *The Lure of Quebec* by W.P. Percival

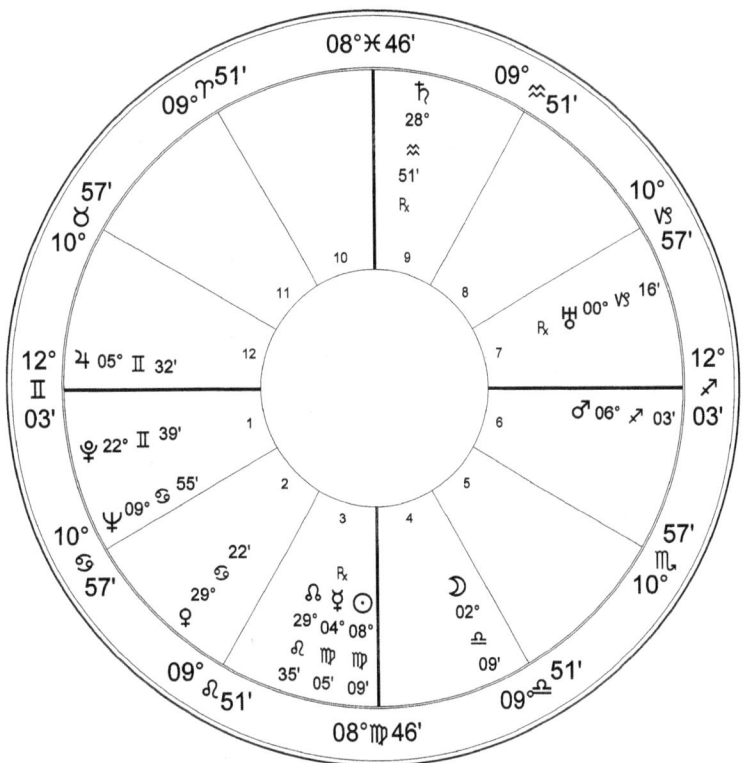

Saskatchewan

**September 1, 1905
Regina
104W9, 0N25
12:01 AM MST
Source: Canadian
National Library**

With the arrival of the railroad in 1870, this region was first settled. In 1873 the Northwest Mounted Police was established. Entering the Confederation 1905., it had the first socialist government in Canada from 1944 until 1964.

Almost half of this province's income comes from agriculture, mostly from wheat. It grows two-thirds of Canada's supply, and has large reserves of oil.

Area: 251,870 square miles

Regina

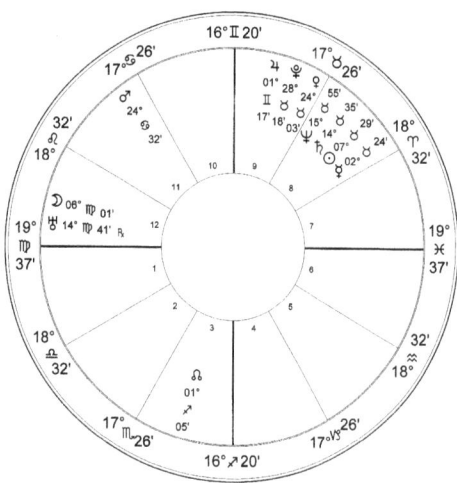

April 27, 1882
103w36, 52N08
2:32 PM MST

Founded in 1882 it was known simply as Pile O'Bones. Later that year, it became the headquarters for the Royal Canadian Mounted Police. In 1883 Regina became the capital of the Northwest Territories until 1905, when Saskatchewan separated and became a separate province. A massive cyclone hit the city in 1912 (Midheaven semisquare Jupiter). An oil pipeline was completed from neighboring Alberta in 1950 (Ascendant sextile Moon). Named after the reigning Queen of England, Victoria Regina, the city maintains the grace and elegance that would make that monarch proud.

Incorporated: June 19, 1903
Elevation: 1,894 feet
Area 31 square miles
Source: Regina Public Library

Saskatoon

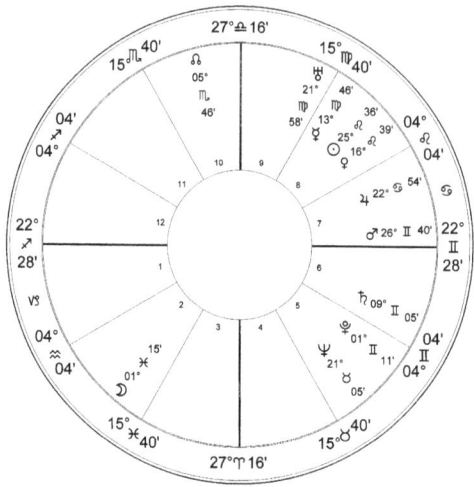

August 18, 1883
106W39, 52N08
4:00 PM MST

Founded in 1883, the railroad arrived seven years later to connect this remote community to the outside world. A flood in 1904 lasted for 45 days and almost wiped Saskatoon off the map (Ascendant quincunx Saturn).

Incorporated: July 1, 1906
Elevation: 1,596 feet
Population (1976) 133,750
Source: *The Saskatoon Story* by Bruce Peel

Northwest Territories

July 15, 1870
75W42, 45N25
12:01 AM EST
Source: Canadian National Library

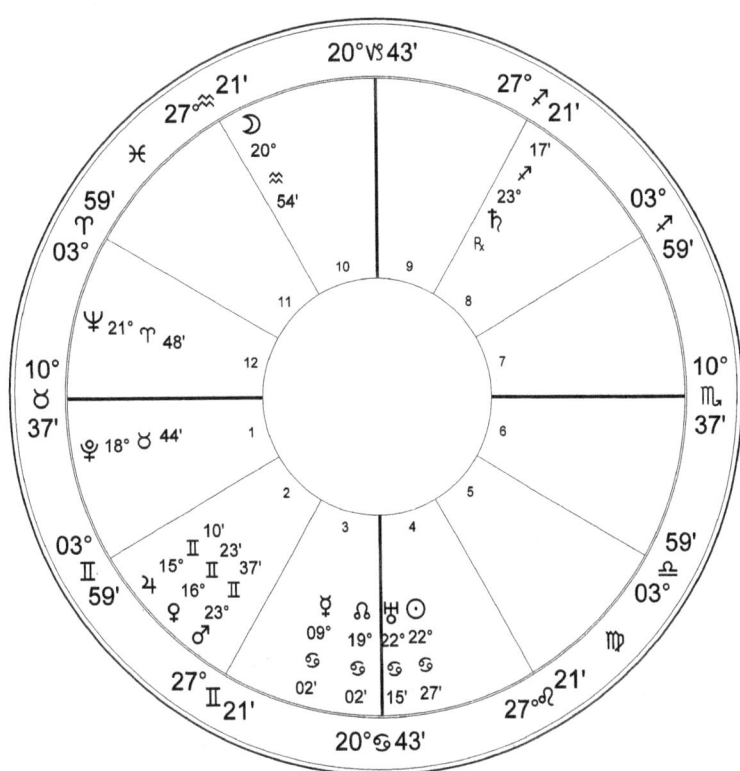

In 1576 Martin Frobisher explored the region around Baffin Island in search of the Northwest Passage. In 1670 the Hudson Bay Company was granted a charter and began to establish trading posts around Hudson Bay, and in 1788, the Mackenzie River was mapped and a trading post founded on the Great Slave Lake. In April 1999, the eastern part of this vast region became the newly-formed territory of Nunavut.

During the 19th century, most of the islands were mapped, and recently, there has been renewed interest in the Arctic and its possible future portents of wealth.

Area: 572,000 square miles

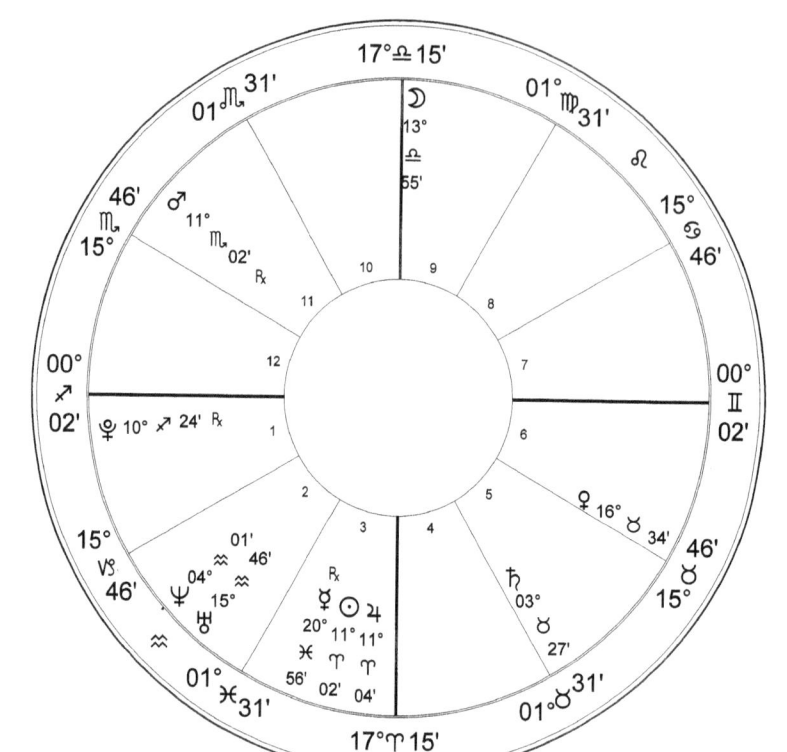

Nunavut

April 1, 1999
Iqaluit
68W28, 63N44
12:01 AM EST
Source: The New York Times and Los Angeles Times

Formerly part of the Northwest Territories, legislation was first introduced in 1963 to form a separate territory for the Inuit, or Eskimo, people. Land claims by the Inuit begun in 1971 led to a settlement five years later which would eventually grant complete autonomy to the native people. The Canadian Parliament gave the green light in 1982 to the division of the Northwest Territories and, in April 1999, this dream became a reality for 27,000 people (85 percent Inuit).

Area: 750,000 square miles

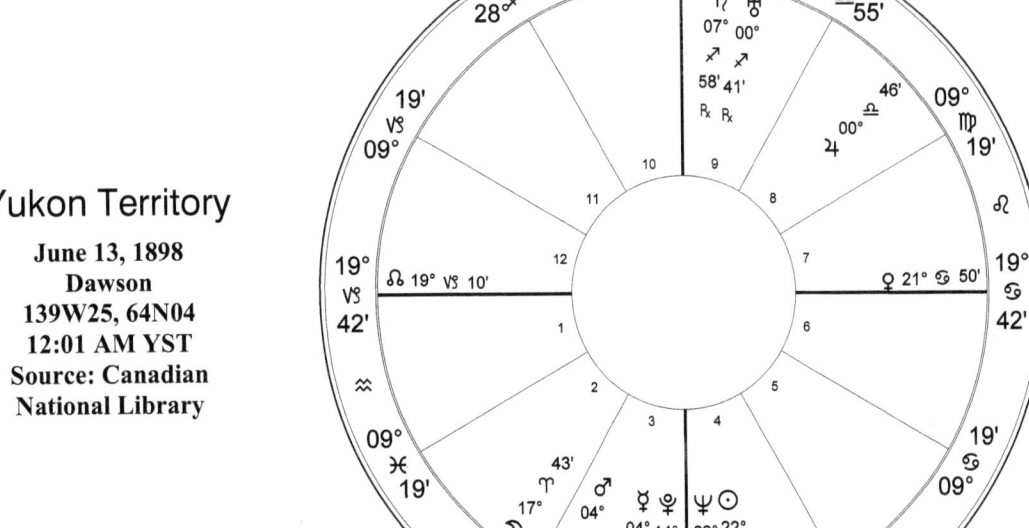

Yukon Territory

**June 13, 1898
Dawson
139W25, 64N04
12:01 AM YST
Source: Canadian
National Library**

During the 1840s the Yukon River was explored, and fur trading posts were established. After the gold rushes in British Columbia during the 1860s, prospectors moved northward during the following decade. Steamers brought miners from Alaska during the 1880's but the real rush began with the discovery of gold on the Klondike in 1896. During the next eight years, over $100 million was obtained in the region. Prior to the discovery of gold, the Yukon was administered as part of the Northwest Territories but it separated in 1898 with its capital at Dawson, the largest city in the Northwest. Entry into the region was facilitated with the completion of the railroad in 1900: Prior to that, the prospectors had to cross the treacherous White and Chilcott Passes. During the first decade of the 20th century, half the population left as gold deposits declined. By 1941 it was only twenty percent as large as in 1901. With the construction of airports, transportation around this vast territory has been improved. In 1951 the capital was moved to Whitehorse.

Area: 186,660 square miles

Dawson

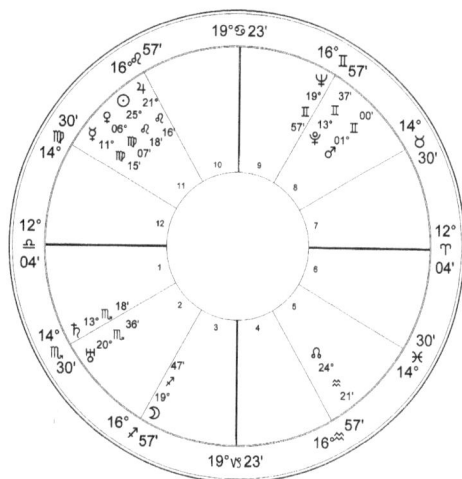

August 17, 1896
139W25, 64N04
9:55 AM YST

When gold was discovered in 1896 on the Klondike, Dawson became the boom town of the century. Prospectors trekked over dangerous passes to get the ore; by the turn of the century, the city had over 10,000 inhabitants. But with the luck of most mining towns, the gold was harder and harder to find. Twenty years after the rush began, only 1,000 settlers remained. Dawson was the largest city in the Northwest a long time ago, but its fortunes declined so badly that the legislature decided to move its offices to Whitehorse in 1951 (Midheaven square Pluto). Today, Dawson is largely a tourist haven during the summer months and is only a remnant of her former glory as the biggest metropolis west of the Rockies.

Source: Canadian National Library

Whitehorse

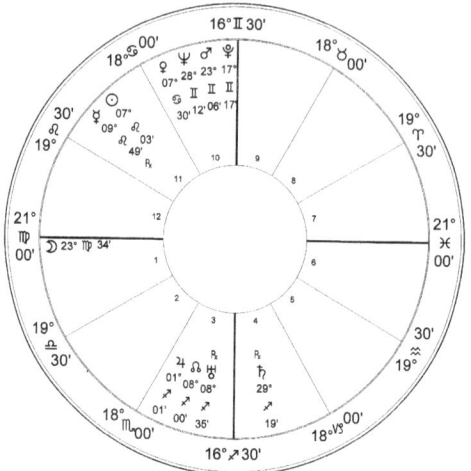

July 30, 1900
135W03, 60N43
8:30 AM YST

Founded in 1900, it remained an isolated outpost until the completion of the Alcan Highway. Whitehorse became capital of the Yukon in 1951 when the legislature moved here from Dawson (Midheaven conjunct Sun).

Incorporated: June 16, 1950
Source: *History of Whitehorse* by Douglas Sack